Mastering C++

Mastering C++

K R VENUGOPAL
University Visvesvaraya College of Engineering
Bangalore University, Bangalore

RAJKUMAR BUYYA
School of Computer Science & Software Engineering
Monash University
Melbourne, Australia

T RAVISHANKAR
University Visvesvaraya College of Engineering
Bangalore University, Bangalore

Tata McGraw-Hill Publishing Company Limited
NEW DELHI

McGraw-Hill Offices

New Delhi New York St Louis San Francisco Auckland Bogotá Caracas
Kuala Lumpur Lisbon London Madrid Mexico City Milan Montreal
San Juan Santiago Singapore Sydney Tokyo Toronto

Tata McGraw-Hill

*A Division of The **McGraw-Hill** Companies*

Ninth reprint 2001
RQLLCRBLRABBY

This edition can be exported from India only by the publishers, Tata McGraw-Hill Publishing Company Limited

ISBN 0-07-463454-2

Published by Tata McGraw-Hill Publishing Company Limited, 7 West Patel Nagar, New Delhi 110 008, typeset at Computer Science Laboratory, University Visvesvaraya College of Engineering, Bangalore University, Bangalore and printed at Saurabh Print-O-Pack, A-16, Sector IV, NOIDA.

Dedicated
to
Tejaswi Venugopal

Foreword

Object-oriented programming languages are playing an increasingly important role in computing science and its applications. With the declining hardware costs, the cost of computing systems is largely dominated by software. The software industry is facing a large-scale software development crisis currently due to the usage of conventional technologies, which are turning obsolete by the end of the day. It has resulted in considerable increase in development cost plus time overrun and poor quality products. *Object-oriented analysis and design is an upcoming technology* that software professionals have employed successfully in the development of large software projects.

Programming as every practitioner knows is a delicate art, where the main problem is not so much to obtain a *working* program (which is mandatory of course), but to have a program designed in such a way that it is not fragile, i.e., it can be modified/updated/debugged easily. In order to attain these goals programmers need tools.

Among the tools that allow a programmer to express ideas are of course the programming languages. One such programming language used popularly these days is the C++ language. This book by Venugopal K R, Rajkumar and T Ravishankar is a timely and relevant publication.

This book is unique in many ways. The concepts such as programming paradigms, the need for OOPs technology, extending C, C++ at a glance, fundamental constructs of the C++ language, classes and objects, inheritance, polymorphism, generic programming, streams computations, fault tolerant programming with exceptions are covered prominently. Every aspect is prominently illustrated with figures and examples which are well tested, illustrative and impressive in the manner the solutions are designed. The authors, with their rich industrial and academic experience in Computer Science have made their best effort to bring out this book for the benefit of students, teachers, and software professionals.

This book besides being illustrative includes a wide array of typical programs, which help OOP aspirants to grasp the fundamentals of the subject without external assistance. The earlier works of the authors *Microprocessor x86 Programming* has been very well received by the students of Science and Engineering. I am confident that this book will serve the needs of all those who are serious about object-oriented technology.

In this book, the approach followed by the authors make the exploration of the OOPs territory as easy and interesting as possible, starting slowly and working up gradually to more challenging concepts. I am confident that the reader will find the book an appealing vehicle for embarking into the challenging world of *Object Oriented Programming with C++*. Good Luck !

S Sasi Kumar

Director
Centre for Development of Advanced Computing
(A Scientific Society of Government of India)
Brunton Road, Bangalore 560 025
Karnataka, India

Preface

In the real-world everything (including you and me!) exist in the form of objects. These objects are identified by the system analyst upon request of a customer (who actually uses services of objects) and handed-over to the designer. The designer in turn creates classes which group all those objects exhibiting similar characteristics and behaviors into a single unit. These units are then passed to programmers, who implement object's framework given by the designer. Thus, objects move from the customer to the programmer.

Programmers create objects using its framework. These objects work in a collaborative and cooperative manner to produce the required output. These software objects now start moving from programmers to test-engineers, and finally to the customer, who is the actual user of these objects, to solve real-world problems. To realize this effective migration of objects from one person to another, there must be an effective means of communication among all those involved in the development of a software project. They need to communicate their ideas in terms of objects. That is, system analyst delivers requirement specification in terms of objects, software designer delivers design specification in terms of classes (object groups). And even programmers need to express their ideas or write code in terms of objects. Hence, the demand for an *object oriented requirement specification (OORS), object oriented analysis (OOA), object oriented design (OOD), and object oriented programming (OOP)* has grown tremendously.

Currently there is no standard method of OORS, OOA, and OOD available. But, there are many standard programming languages supporting OOP available and one of the most popular OOP language is C++.

C++ is an object-oriented language that a C programmer can appreciate, especially who is an early-age assembly language programmer. C++, was first oriented towards execution performance and then towards flexibility. Most of the features which C++ adds to C involve no runtime overhead; few that do can be avoided by the efficiency conscious programmers.

Yet, C being a structured programming language offered the ease of software development but failed to support maintenance of large code. This has motivated the search for a new language which is as efficient as C but simplifies the maintenance of large code. It is not enough to offer a language that is just as good as C. If people are to switch, the replacement language must not only equal C in terms of efficiency and code reuse, but it must also be a lot better in terms of productivity, maintenance, and power. C++ meets these criteria, making it the first serious contender to challenge Fortran's supremacy.

The last couple of years have seen a growing wave of enthusiasm for object-oriented approaches to requirements analysis, application design, and programming. The same period has been marked by the increasing popularity of the C++ language and its acceptance as a logical successor to C. Since C++ is designed to support object-oriented development, it seems only natural to see a strong link between C++ and OOP. Programmers who move to C++ will apparently adopt an object-oriented style of programming.

With C++, it is much easier to build and maintain a really big code. This is made possible with C++'s enhancements to C and more importantly its object-oriented support. Some of the most prominent concepts of object-oriented programming are encapsulation, data abstraction, inheritance, delegation, polymorphism, and streams. All these features are covered in this book with illustrative programs.

A few other reasons for the success of C++ (unlike other OOP languages) are:

- A strong backing from world class software organizations (such as AT&T, Borland, Microsoft, Sun Microsystems Inc, etc.)
- It is a mature language
- Availability of programming environment (language sensitive editors, compilers, tools, profilers, code analyzers, etc.)
- It is available on machines from microcomputers to supercomputers

Organization of the Book

This book spreads discussion on C++ language and object-oriented concepts over twenty chapters. Each chapter explains C++ constructs needed for object-oriented programming with numerous programming solutions. The book is organized as follows:

Chapter 1 (*Object Oriented Paradigm*) discusses the need for new programming paradigms and various aspects of object-oriented programming. It covers the evolution of programming paradigms, elements of OOPs, popular OOP languages, OO learning curve, software reuse, and demonstrates how objects hold the key in driving the future technologies.

Chapter 2 (*Moving from C to C++*) starts with the *Hello World* program demonstrating various elements of a C++ program. It also presents new features added to C++ (apart from OOP) such as streams based I/O, scope resolution operator, inline functions, function overloading, enhancements to C structures, function templates, new and delete operators for runtime memory management. Chapter 3 (*C++ at a Glance*) illustrates the various features supported by C++ for object-oriented programming. Both chapters include illustrative examples of complete programs, rather than isolated fragments. It discusses classes, objects, derived classes, operator overloading, virtual functions, class templates, exceptions handling, and streams.

Chapters 4 through 9, discuss various fundamental elements of C and C++. These chapters are devised keeping in mind the readers who are not familiar to C language. The readers with C background will also benefit from these chapters, since emphasis is placed on their (data types, functions, pointers, etc.) availability in C++ in a powerful form. Chapter 4 deals with basic *data types, operators, and expressions*. Chapter 5 explains *control flow*: if, if-else, switch, for, while, break, etc. Chapter 6 covers *Arrays and Strings*. Chapter 7 describes *modular programming* with functions. It presents techniques of managing large software system development by breaking it into multiple functions and modules. Chapter 8 emphasizes on *structures and unions*. Chapter 9 deals with *runtime memory management* using Pointers, emphasizing new features of C++ for dynamic memory management.

Chapter 10 (*Classes and Objects*) describes how data and functions can be combined into a single unit. Such a unit (class) can be instantiated to create objects, and they can be manipulated. This chapter covers class declaration, object creation, accessing class members, passing objects as arguments, difference between structures and classes, and memory resource requirement for classes and objects.

Chapter 11 (*Object Initialization and Cleanup*) mainly focuses on two special functions called constructors and destructors. These are invoked automatically during the creation of objects and destruction of objects respectively. Chapter 12 (*Dynamic Objects*) covers the creation and manipulation of objects at runtime.

Chapter 13 (*Operators Overloading*) illustrates overloading of C++ operators to operate on user defined data types. It includes overloading of both unary and binary operators such as +, -, *, [], etc. It also covers overloading of new and delete operator for tracing memory leaks.

Chapter 14 (*Inheritance*) illustrates the creation of a new class called derived class from existing classes. It covers various forms of inheritance with complete example programs. It also describes object composition for delegation.

Chapter 15 (*Virtual Functions*) illustrates the dynamic binding of functions to realize runtime polymorphism. Chapter 16 (*Generic Programming with Templates*) discusses the creation of function and class templates for those functions and classes having the same body but operating on different data types.

Chapter 17 (*Streams Computation with Console*) discusses the unformatted and formatted I/O operations with keyboard and screen using streams. Chapter 18 (*Streams Computation with Files*) deals with I/O operations on files used for storing data on secondary storage devices using file streams. Chapter 19 (*Exception Handling*) covers error handling model of C++ and concludes with guidelines on better handling of exceptions.

Chapter 20 (*OO Analysis, Design, and Development*) covers software life cycle, object-oriented analysis, object-oriented design, and class design. It also provides some guidelines on how to build a reliable code, OO software performance tuning, software project management, and a plan for OO battle.

The topics of *Appendices* include: C++ Keywords and Operators, C++ Library Functions, Glossary, ASCII Character Set, Bibliography and Index.

Suggestions for further improvement of this book can be forwarded to *vkrajuk@bronto.iitm.ernet.in*, *raj@cdacb.ernet.in* or *rthammai@in.oracle.com*.

Road Map to Readers

This book is designed keeping in mind the following three categories of users:

1. Well-versed in C and wants to learn C++ thoroughly
2. Well-versed with C and wants to learn C++ quickly
3. Not familiar with C and has good knowledge of programming

The *first category* of users can read first three chapters: Object-Oriented Paradigm, Moving from C to C++, and C++ at a Glance. The remaining seven chapters can be skipped without the loss of continuity. However, it is advisable to study these chapters so that strong foundation on C++'s new features can be built. The *second category* of users can read the first three chapters to learn C++ quickly. The *third category* of users are advised to study the entire book. They can skip the second and third chapters in the first reading and read them later after gaining some foundations of C++ programming.

Venugopal K R
Rajkumar
T Ravishankar

Acknowledgements

We owe a debt of gratitude to Prof. K. Venkatagiri Gowda, Prof. P. Sreenivasa Kumar, Prof. S. Lakshmana Reddy, Prof. N.R. Shetty, Prof. P. Narayana Reddy, Prof. N. S. Somasekhar, Prof. K. Mallikarjuna Chetty, Prof. H.N. Shivashankar, Prof. C. Sivarama Murthy, Prof. A. R. Virupaksha, Prof. T. Basavaraju, Prof. M. Chenna Reddy, Prof. B. Narayanappa, Prof. N. Srinivasan, Prof. K. N. Krishnamurthy, Prof. F. A. Mecci, Prof. G. R. Venkateshaiah, Prof. V. Sathyanagakumar for their encouragement. Our sincere thanks to Sri. K.P. Jayarama Reddy, T.G. Girikumar, P. Palani, M. G. Muniyappa, and C. Keshavamurthy for their support.

We thank Mr. S. Sasi Kumar, Director, Centre for Development of Advanced Computing, Bangalore for his foreword to this book and Prof. M. Venkatachalappa, Department of Mathematics, Bangalore University, Bangalore for providing us the necessary infrastructure in the preparation of this book.

We thank Ms. Mangala, Ms. Savithri S, Ms. Deepa, Mr. Ravi Kiran N, and Mr.Bijo Thomas for their constant support during the preparation of this book.

Dr. Bjarne Stroustrup, the designer of C++ language was kind enough to answer many of our queries by electronic mail and allowed us to use his comments on C++ competency gap directly in this book without any mutation. We thank him for his support to our work.

We thank Prof. G. Krishna, Prof. M.A.L. Thathachar, Prof. N. Viswanadham, Prof. V.V.S. Sharma, Prof. D. K. Subramanian, Prof. U. R. Prasad, Prof. C. E. Veni Madhavan, Prof. Y. N. Srikanth, Prof. Y. Narahari, Prof. T. Jacob Matthew, Prof. K. Gopinath, Prof. R. C. Hansdah, all from IISc, Bangalore for their suggestions. We thank Prof. C R Muthukrishnan, Deputy Director, Chairman Department of Computer Science, Prof. Kamala Krithivasan, Prof. T A Gonsalves, Prof. C Pandu Rangan, Prof. D Janaki Ram all from IIT Madras, for their encouragement.

We thank Anand K N, A. Prashanth Kumar, Sudeep R Prasad, Maya C. M, Bala Kishore B, Krishna Mohan, and Sasikiran N for proof reading. We are thankful to N Mohan Ram, Mallikarjuna Gumma and Gopi Chand T for their comments.

We thank Tejaswi, Prakash, and Prasad for their help.

Our special thanks to Sri.Eshwarappa Buyya, Smt. Parvathi Eshwarappa, Smt. Smrithi Rajkumar, Ashokumar, Chinnama, Dullappa, Kalpana, Shivakumar, Sri.Vishwanath Dharni, Shankerayya Swamy, Rajkumar Shelke, and Sangashetty Gadge our well wishers for their moral support and inspiration.

We express our gratitude to Sri.M.C. Jayadeva, Sri.V. Nagaraj, Sri.V. Manjunath, Sri.K. Thyagaraj, Sri.T. S. Ravichander, Sri. M. Thammaiah, Smt. Chandramma T, Smt. Savithri Venkatagiri Gowda, Smt. P SaiPrabha, Smt. Karthyayini Venugopal, and Smt. Rukmini Thyagaraj, our well wishers for inspiring us.

We thank Mr. Anand P. for his neat Desk Top Composing of the book. We thank Dr. N Subrahmanyam, Mr. Roystan Laporte, Ms. Vibha Mahajan, Ms. Mini Narayanan, and the management, editorial, and production staff of Tata McGraw Hill Publications, New Delhi for bringing out this book in record time.

Venugopal K R
Rajkumar
T Ravishankar

Contents

1

Object-Oriented Paradigm

Object-Oriented Programming popularly called *OOPs* is one of the buzzwords in the software industry. On one hand, OOP is a programming paradigm in its own right and on the other, it is a set of software engineering tools which can be used to build more reliable and reusable systems. Another kind of programming methodology which has already revealed its power in the software field, is structured programming. At present, Object-Oriented Programming is emerging from research laboratories and invading the field of industrial applications. The software industry has always been in pursuit of a methodology or philosophy, which would eliminate the problems endemic to software in one shot. The latest candidate for this role is Object Oriented methodology.

Structured programming and object-oriented programming are equally popular today although structured programming has a longer history. The current popularity of OOP and its connection to structured programming is pointed out by Tim Rentsch—*What is object oriented programming ? My guess is that object oriented programming will be in the 1980's what structured programming was in the 1970's. Everyone will be in favor of it. Every manufacturer will promote his products as supporting it. Every manager will pay lip-service to it. Every programmer will practice it (differently). And no one will know just what it is.* Rentsch's predictions still hold true in the 90's.

Structured programming and Object-Oriented Programming fundamentally differ in the following way: Structured programming views the two core elements of any program—*data and functions* as *two separate entities* whereas, OOP views them as a single entity. The benefits of uniting both data and functions into a single unit, will be discussed in later sections.

Object-oriented programming as a paradigm is playing an increasingly significant role in the analysis, design, and implementation of software systems. Object-oriented analysis, design, and programming appear to be the *structured programming* of the 1990's. Proponents assert that OOP is the solution to the *software problem.* Software developed using object-oriented techniques are proclaimed as more reliable, easier to maintain, easier to reuse and enhance, and so on. The Object-Oriented Paradigm is effective in solving many of the outstanding problems in software engineering.

1.1 Why New Programming Paradigms ?

With the continuous decline of hardware cost, high speed computing systems are becoming economically feasible. Innovations in the field of computer architecture supporting complex instructions is in turn leading to the development of better programming environments, which suit the hardware architecture. More powerful tools, operating systems, and programming languages are evolving to keep up with the pace of hardware development. Software for different applications need to be developed under these environments, which is a complex process. As a result, the relative cost of software is increasing substantially when compared to the cost of the hardware of a computing system. Rate of increase in the cost of software development and maintenance and declining hardware cost over several years is depicted in Figure 1.1. Software maintenance is the process of modifying or extending the capabilities of the existing software. It requires mastery over the understanding and modifying the existing software, and finally revalidating the modified software.

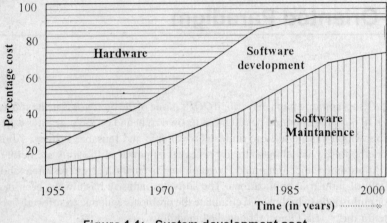

Figure 1.1:   System development cost

The cost effectiveness of hardware has been growing by about three orders of magnitude every decade and simultaneously the market for computers is also expanding. This multiplies the number of applications of computers and in turn places greater demands on software. While demand for software has been growing rapidly to keep pace with the growth of hardware, the actual software development has been progressing slowly. Unfortunately, even with all the innovations in the area of languages, programming environments, software engineering concepts, etc., there has been no significant improvement in the productivity of software development, leading to *software crises*. The term "software crises" refers to the overrun of the cost of software development in terms of both budget and time-target.

The software crisis, right from the beginning, is providing an impetus for the development of software engineering principles, tools, and better programming paradigms to build more reliable and reusable systems. The state-of-the-art solution to overcome software crisis is the Object-Oriented Paradigm.

1.2 OOPs ! a New Paradigm

Object-Oriented Programming is a new way of solving problems with computers; instead of trying to mould the problem into something familiar to the computer, the computer is adapted to the problem. Object-Oriented Programming is designed around the data being operated upon as opposed to the operations themselves. Instead of making certain types of data fit to specific and rigid computer operations, these operations are designed to fit to the data. This is as it should be, because the sole purpose of a computer program is to manipulate data.

OOP languages provide the programmer the ability to create class hierarchies, instantiate co-operative objects collectively working on a problem to produce the solution and send messages between objects to process themselves. The power of object-oriented languages is that the programmer can create modular, reusable code and as a result, formulate a program by composition and modification of

Structured Programming

Structured programming has evolved as a mechanism to address the growing issues of programming-in-the-large. Larger programming projects consist of large development teams, developing different parts of the same project independently. The usage of separately compiled modules (algorithmic decomposition) was the answer for managing large development teams (see Figure 1.5). Programs consist of multiple modules and in turn, each module has a set of functions of related types.

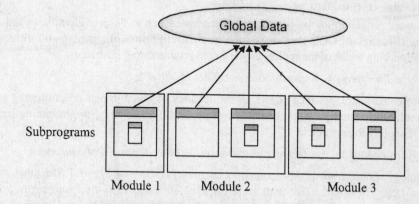

Figure 1.5:   Structured programming

The following are the important features of structured programming:

- Emphasis on algorithm rather than data
- Programs are divided into individual procedures that perform discrete tasks
- Procedures are independent of each other as far as possible
- Procedures have their own local data and processing logic
- Parameter passing facility between the procedures for information communication
- Controlled scope of data
- Introduction of the concepts of user defined data types
- Support for modular programming
- Projects can be broken up into modules and programmed independently
- Scope of data items is further controlled across modules
- A rich set of control structures are available to further abstract the procedures
- Co-ordination among multiple programmers is required for handling the changes made to mutually shared data items
- Maintenance of a large software system is tedious and costly

Examples: Pascal and C

Object Oriented Programming

The easy way to master the management of complexity in the development of a software system is through the use of data abstraction. Procedure abstraction is suitable for the description of abstract operations, but it is not suitable for the description of abstract objects. This is a serious drawback in many applications since, the complexity of the data objects to be manipulated contribute substantially to the overall complexity of the problem.

The emergence of data-driven methods provides a disciplined approach to the problems of data abstractions in algorithmic oriented languages. It has resulted in the development of object-based language supporting only data abstraction. Object-based languages do not support features such as inheritance and polymorphism which will be discussed later. Depending on the object features supported, the languages are classified into two categories:

1. Object-Based Programming Languages
2. Object-Oriented Programming Languages

Object-based programming languages support encapsulation and object identity without supporting important features of OOP languages such as polymorphism, inheritance, and message based communication. Ada is one of the typical object-based programming languages.

Object-based language = Encapsulation + Object Identity

Object-oriented languages incorporate all the features of object-based programming languages along with inheritance and polymorphism. Therefore, an object-oriented programming language is defined by the following statement:

Object-oriented language = Object based features + Inheritance + Polymorphism

The topology of object-oriented programming languages is shown in Figure 1.6 for small, moderate, and large projects. The *modules* represent the physical building blocks of these languages; a module is a logical collection of classes and objects, instead of subprograms as in the earlier languages. Thus making classes and objects as the fundamental building blocks of OOPs.

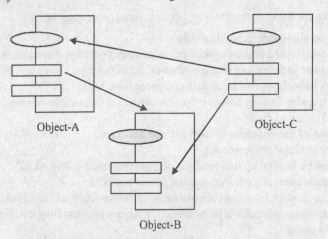

Figure 1.6: Object oriented programming

Object-oriented programming is a methodology that allows the association of data structures with operations similar to the way it is perceived in the human mind. They associate a specific set of actions with a given type of object and actions are based on these associations.

The following are the important features of object-oriented programming:

• Improvement over the structured programming paradigm
• Emphasis on data rather than algorithm
• Data abstraction is introduced in addition to procedural abstraction

- Data and associated operations are unified into a single unit,thus the objects are grouped with common attributes,operations and semantics
- Programs are designed around the data being operated, rather than operations themselves (data decomposition·rather than algorithmic decomposition)
- Relationships can be created between similar, yet distinct data types

Examples: C++, Smalltalk, Eiffel, Java, etc.

1.4 Structured Versus Object-Oriented Development

Program and data are two basic elements of any computation. Among these, data plays an important role and it can exist without a program, but a program has no relevance without data. The conventional high level languages stress on the algorithms used to solve a problem. Complex procedures have been simplified by structured programming which is well established to date. Software designers and programmers have faced difficulty in the design, maintenance, and enhancement of software developed using traditional languages, and their search for a better methodology has resulted in the development of the object-oriented approach. In the conventional method, the data are defined as global and accessible to all the functions of a program without any restriction. It has reduced data security and integrity, since the entire data is available to all the functions and any function can change any data without impunity. (See Figure 1.7.)

Unlike the traditional methodology (Function-Oriented Programming -FOP), Object-Oriented Programming emphasizes on the data rather than the algorithm. In OOPs, data is compartmentalized or encapsulated with the associated functions (that operate on it) and this compartment or *capsule* is called an *object*. In the OO approach, the problem is divided into objects, whereas in FOP the problem is divided into functions. Although, both approaches adopt the same philosophy of *divide and conquer,* OOP conquers a bigger region, while FOP is content with conquering a smaller region. OOP contains FOP and so OOP can be referred to as the super set of FOP (like C++, which is a superset of C) and hence, it can be concluded that OOP has an edge over FOP.

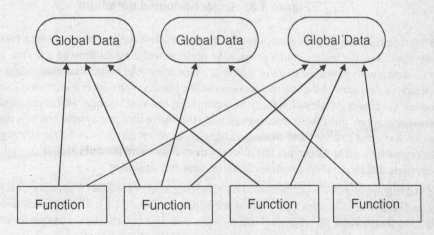

Figure 1.7:   Function oriented paradigm

Unlike traditional languages, OO languages allow localization of data and code and restrict other objects from referring to its local region. OOP is centered around the concepts of objects, encapsulations, abstract data types, inheritance, polymorphism, message based communication, etc. An OO language views the data and its associated set of functions as an object and treats this combination as a single entity. Thus, an object is visualized as a combination of data and functions which manipulate them.

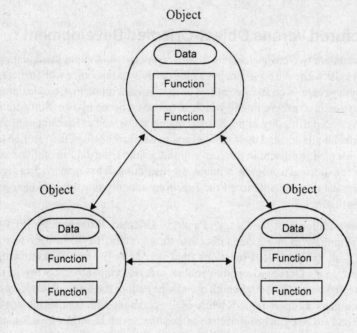

Figure 1.8: Object-oriented paradigm

During the execution of a program, the objects interact with each other by sending messages and receiving responses. For instance, in a program to perform withdrawals from an account, a *customer* object can send a withdrawal message to a *bank account* object. An object communicating with other objects need not be aware of the internal working of the objects with which it interacts. This situation is analogous to operating a television receiver, a computer, or an automobile, where one need not know the internal operations since these machines provide the user with some system controls that hide the complexity of internal structure and working. Likewise, an object can be manipulated through an interface that responds to a few messages. The object's internal structure is totally hidden from the user and this property is called *data/information hiding* or *data encapsulation*.

The external interfaces are implemented by providing a set of methods (functions), each of which accepts and responds to a particular kind of message (see Figure 1.8). The methods defined in an object's class are the same for all objects belonging to that class but, the data is unique for each object.

1.5 Elements of Object-Oriented Programming

Object-Oriented Programming is centered around new concepts such as objects, classes, polymorphism, inheritance, etc. It is a well-suited paradigm for the following:

- Modeling the real-world problem as close as possible to the user's perspective.
- Interacting easily with computational environment using familiar metaphors.
- Constructing reusable software components and easily extendable libraries.
- Easily modifying and extending implementations of components without having to recode every thing from scratch.

A language's quality (and its elements) is judged by twelve important criteria. They are a well defined *syntactic and semantic structure*, *reliability*, *fast translation*, *efficient object code*, *orthogonality* (language should have only a few basic features, each of which is separately understandable), *machine independence*, *provability*, *generality*, *consistency with commonly used notations*, *subsets*, *uniformity*, and *extensibility*. The various constructs of OOP languages (such as C++) are designed to achieve these with ease.

Definition of OOP

In the 70s, the concept of the *object* became popular among researchers of programming languages. An object is a combination or collection of data and code designed to emulate a physical or abstract entity. Each object has its own identity and is distinguishable from other objects. *Programming with objects* is as efficient as programming with basic data items such as integers, floats, or arrays. Thus, it provides a direct abstraction of commonly used items and hides most of the complexity of implementation from the users.

Object-Oriented Programming is a programming methodology that associates data structures with a set of operators which act upon it. In OOPs terminology, an instance of such an entity is known as an object. It gives importance to relationships between objects rather than implementation details. Hiding the implementation details within an object results in the user being more concerned with an object's relationship to the rest of the system, than the implementation of the object's behavior. This distinction is a fundamental departure from earlier imperative languages (such as Pascal and C), in which functions and function calls are the centre of activity.

C++ Style of OOP Definition

Grady Booch, a renowned contributor to the development of object-oriented technology defines OOPs as follows: *OOP is a method of implementation in which programs are organized as co-operative collections of objects, each of which represents an instance of some class and whose classes are all members of a hierarchy of classes united through the property called inheritance.*

Three important concepts to be noted in the above definition are: *objects, classes, and inheritance.* OOP uses objects and not algorithms as its fundamental building blocks. Each object is an instance of some class. *Classes* allow the mechanism of data abstraction for creating *new* data types. Inheritance allows building of new classes from the existing classes. Hence, if any of these elements are missing in a program, then, it is not object-oriented. In particular, a program *without inheritance* is definitely not an object oriented one; it resembles the program with abstract data types.

1.6 Objects

Initially, different parts (entities) of a problem are examined independently. These entities are chosen because they have some physical or conceptual boundaries that separate them from the rest of the problem. The entities are then represented as objects in the program. The goal is to have a clear correspondence between physical entities in the problem domain and objects in the program. A well designed object oriented program is organized according to the objects being manipulated.

Figure 1.9 shows few entities and each of them can be treated as an object. In other words, an object can be a person, a place, or a thing with which the computer must deal. Some objects may correspond to real-world entities such as students, employees, bank accounts, inventory items, etc., whereas, others may correspond to computer hardware and software components. Hardware components include a keyboard, port, video display, mouse, etc., and software components include stacks, queues, trees, etc. In an application simulating a parking lot, car, parking spaces, traffic signals, or even the persons manning the parking lot can be conceptualized as objects. Objects can be concrete such as a file system, or conceptual such as a scheduling policy in a multiprocessor operating system. Objects mainly serve the following purposes:

- Understanding of the real world and a practical base for designers.
- Decomposition of a problem into objects depends on judgement and nature of the problem.

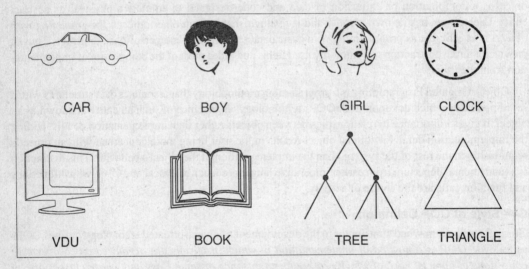

Figure 1.9: Examples of objects

Every object will have data structures called attributes and behavior called operations. The different notations of an object uniting both the data and operations, are shown in Figure 1.10.

Consider the object *account* having the attributes: *AccountNumber*, *AccountType*, *Name*, and *Balance* and operations:*Deposit*, *Withdraw*, and *Enquire*. Its pictorial notation is shown in Figure 1.11. Each object will have its own identity though its attributes and operations are same; the objects will never become equal. In case of *person* object for instance, two persons have the same attributes like *name*, *age*, and *sex*, but they are not equal (technically). Objects are the basic run-time entities in an object-oriented system.

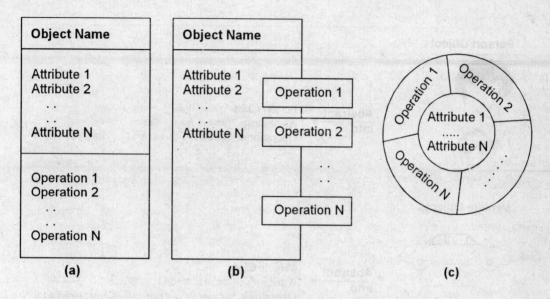

Figure 1.10: Different styles of representing an object

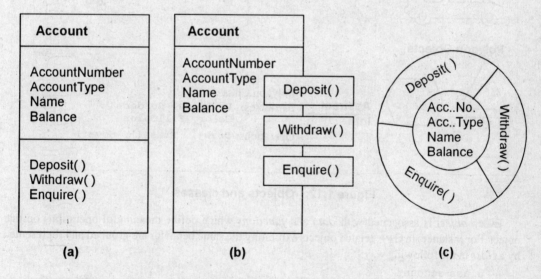

Figure 1.11: Different styles of representing the account object

1.7 Classes

The objects with the same data structure (attributes) and behavior (operations) are grouped into a *class*. All those objects possessing similar properties are grouped into the same unit. The concept of *class*-ing the real world objects is demonstrated in Figure 1.12. It consists of the *Person* class, *Vehicle* class, and *Polygon* class. In the case of *Person* class, all objects have similar attributes like *Name*, *Age*, *Sex* and similar operations like *Speak*, *Listen*, *Walk*. So *boy* and *girl* objects are grouped into the *Person* class. Similarly, other related objects such as triangle, hexagon, and so on, are grouped into the *Polygon* class.

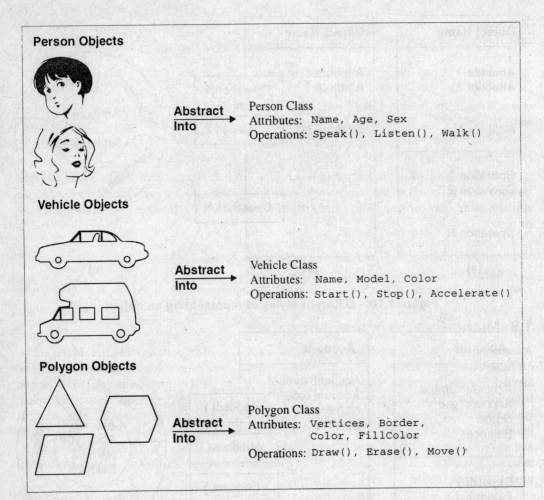

Person Objects

Person Class
Attributes: Name, Age, Sex
Operations: Speak(), Listen(), Walk()

Vehicle Objects

Vehicle Class
Attributes: Name, Model, Color
Operations: Start(), Stop(), Accelerate()

Polygon Objects

Polygon Class
Attributes: Vertices, Border,
                     Color, FillColor
Operations: Draw(), Erase(), Move()

Figure 1.12: Objects and classes

Every *object* is associated with *data* and *functions* which define meaningful operations on that object. For instance, in C++, related objects exhibiting the same behavior are grouped and represented by a *class* in the following way:

```
class account
{
    private:
        char Name[20];              // data members
        int AccountType;
        int AccountNumber;
        float Balance;
    public:
        Deposit();                  // member functions
        Withdraw();
        Enquire();
};
```

This declaration is similar to the structure declaration in C. It enables the creation of the *class* variables called *objects*. For example, the following statements,

```
account   savings_account;
account   current_account;
account   FD_account;
```

create instances of the class `account`. They define `savings_account`, `current_account`, and `FD_account` as the objects of the class `account`. From this, it can be inferred that, the account class groups objects such as saving account, current account, etc. Thus, objects having the same structural and behavioral properties are grouped together to form a class.

Each class describes a possibly infinite set of individual objects; each object is said to be an instance of its class and each instance of the class has its own value for each attribute but shares the attribute name and operations with other instances of the class. The following points on classes can be noted:

- A class is a template that unites data and operations.
- A class is an abstraction of the real world entities with similar properties.
- A class identifies a set of similar objects.
- Ideally, the class is an implementation of abstract data type.

1.8 Multiple Views of the Same Object

A commonly accepted notion about objects is illustrated through the definition of a tree. In this classical model, a tree is defined as a class, in terms of internal state information and methods that can be applied. The designer of such an object-oriented tree, ideally works with the intrinsic properties and behavior of the tree. In the real world, properties of a tree like its height, cell-count, density, leaf-mass, etc., are intrinsic properties. Intrinsic behavior includes like growth, photosynthesis, etc., that affect the intrinsic properties. This idea of a classical model is inadequate to deal with the construction of large and growing suites of applications that manipulate the objects. Every observer (for instance, a tax-assessor, a woods man and a bird) of the tree, with different backgrounds, has his own view on the ideal model of a tree as shown in Figure 1.13.

A *tax-assessor* has his own view of the features and behavior associated with a tree. The characteristics include its contribution to the assessed value of the property on which it grows. The behavior includes the methods, by which this contribution is derived. These methods vary from *tree-type* to *tree-type*. In fact, such methods may form a part of a tax assessor's view of all objects, tree and non-tree alike. These characteristics and behaviors are extrinsic to the tree. They form the part of a tax-assessor's subjective view of the object-oriented tree.

Figure 1.13 reminds that the *tax-assessor* is merely one of a suite (type) of applications, each having its own subjective view, its own extrinsic state and behavior for the tree. The views of a woodsman and a bird on the same object, are also different compared to the tax-assessor's view. A *woodsman's* view of the tree, is in terms of sales price and time required to cut the tree with capital profit as a method. A *bird's* view of the same tree is different and its view characteristics include `FoodValue` and `ComputeFlight()`. Thus, a woodsman views the tree in terms of the amount of time required to cut the tree and the price it would fetch. The bird views it in terms of the food value and the amount of energy required to carry the food from the tree to its nest.

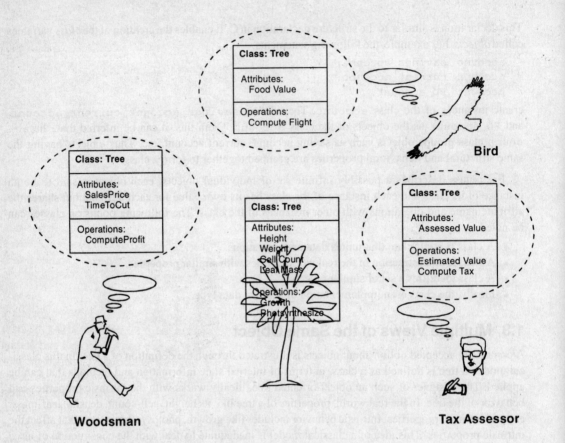

Figure 1.13: Multiple views of an object-oriented tree

1.9 Encapsulation and Data Abstraction

Encapsulation is a mechanism that associates the code and the data it manipulates and keeps them safe from external interference and misuse. Creating new data types using encapsulated-items, that are well suited to an application to be programmed, is known as *data abstraction*. The data types created by the data abstraction process are known as Abstract Data Types (ADTs). Data abstraction is a powerful technique, and its proper usage will result in optimal, more readable, and flexible programs.

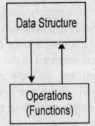

Figure 1.14: An abstract data type

Data abstraction is supported by several other modern programming languages such as Smalltalk, Ada, etc. In these languages, and in C++ as well, a programmer can define a new abstract data type by specifying a data structure, together with the operations permissible on that data structure as shown in Figure 1.14. The important feature of C++, the *class* declaration, allows encapsulation and creation of abstract data types.

The use of encapsulation in protecting the members (data and code) of a class from unauthorized access is a good programming practice; it enforces the separation between the specification and implementation of abstract data types, and it enables the debugging of programs easily.

1.10 Inheritance

Inheritance is the process, by which one object can acquire the properties of another. It allows the declaration and implementation of one class to be based on an existing class. Inheritance is the most promising concept of OOP, which helps realize the goal of constructing software systems from reusable parts, rather than hand coding every system from scratch. Inheritance not only supports reuse across systems, but also directly facilitates extensibility within a given system. Inheritance coupled with polymorphism and dynamic binding, minimizes the amount of existing code to be modified while enhancing a system.

To understand inheritance, consider the simple example shown in Figure 1.15. When the class *Child,* inherits the class *Parent*, the class *Child* is referred to as derived class (sub-class), and the class *Parent* as a base class (super-class). In this case, the class *Child* has two parts: a derived part and an incremental part. The derived part is inherited from the class *Parent*. The incremental part is the new code written specifically for the class *Child*. In general, a feature of *Parent* may be renamed, re-implemented, duplicated, voided (nullified), have its visibility status changed or subjected to almost any other kind of transformation when it is mapped from *Parent* to *Child*. The inheritance relation is often called the *is-a* relation. This is because when the class *Child* inherits the base class *Parent*, it acquires all the properties of the *Parent* class. It can also have its own properties, in addition to those acquired from its *Parent*. This is an example of single inheritance; the child class has inherited properties from only one base class.

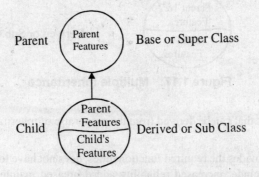

Figure 1.15: Single inheritance

The inheritance relation is often used to reflect the elements present in an application domain. For example, consider a rectangle which is a special kind of polygon as shown in Figure 1.16. This relationship is easily captured by the inheritance relation. When the *rectangle* is inherited from the *polygon*, it gets all the features of the *polygon*. Further, the *polygon* is a *closed* figure and so, the *rectangle* inherits all the features of the *closed* figure.

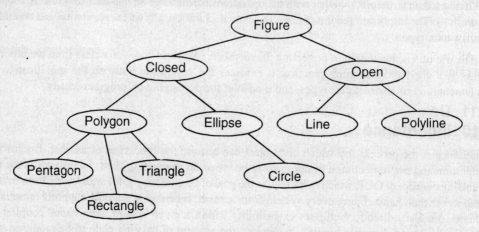

Figure 1.16:   Inheritance graph (class hierarchy)

Multiple Inheritance

In the case of multiple inheritance, the derived class inherits the features of more than one base class. Consider Figure 1.17, in which the class *Child* is inherited from the base classes *Parent1* and *Parent2*. Here, the class *Child* possesses all the properties of parents classes in addition to its own.

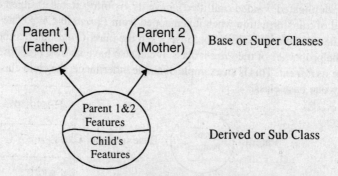

Figure 1.17:   Multiple inheritance

Benefits of Inheritance

There are numerous benefits that can be derived from the proper use of inheritance, which include the following:

- The inherited code that provides the required functionalities, does not have to be rewritten. Benefits of such reusable code include, increased reliability and decreased maintenance cost because of sharing by all the users.

- Code sharing can occur at several levels. For example, at a higher level, individual or group users can use the same classes. These are referred to as software components. At a lower level, code can be shared by two or more classes within a project.

- Inheritance will permit the construction of reusable software components. Already, several such libraries are commercially available and many more are expected to come.

- When a software system can be constructed largely out of reusable components, development time can be concentrated for understanding that portion of the system which is new and unusual. Thus, software systems can be generated more quickly, and easily, by rapid prototyping.

All the above benefits of inheritance emphasize code reuse, ease of code maintenance, extension, and reduction in development time.

1.11 Delegation - Object Composition

Most people can understand concepts such as objects, interfaces, classes, and inheritance. The challenge lies in applying them to build flexible and reusable software. The two most common techniques for reusing functionality in object-oriented systems are class inheritance and object composition. As explained, inheritance is a mechanism of building a new class by deriving certain properties from other classes. In inheritance, if the class D is derived from the class B, it is said that *D is a kind of B*. The new approach to object composition, takes a view that an object can be a collection of many other objects, and the relationship is called a *has-a* (D has-a B) relationship or containership.

Delegation is a way of making object composition as powerful as inheritance for reuse. In delegation, two objects are involved in handling a request: a receiving object delegates operations to its *delegate*. This is analogous to subclasses sending requests to parent classes. In certain situations, inheritance and containership relationships can serve the same purpose. For example, instead of creating a class `Window` as a derived class of `Rectangle` (because, the window happens to be rectangular), the class `Window` can reuse the behavior of Rectangle by having a `Rectangle` instance variable and delegating the `Rectangle` specific behavior to it. In other words, instead of the class Window being a Rectangle, it would have a Rectangle composed into it. Window must now forward all requests to its Rectangle instance explicitly. In inheritance, it would have inherited the same operation from the class Rectangle. The Window class delegating its Area operation to a Rectangle instance is depicted in Figure 1.18.

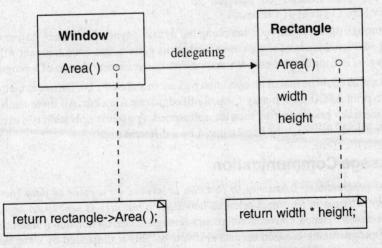

Figure 1.18: Delegation-object composition

Delegation makes it easy to compose behavior at runtime and to change the manner, they are composed. The window can become circular at runtime, simply by replacing its Rectangle instance with a Circle instance, assuming Rectangle and Circle have the same type. Thus, delegation shows that inheritance can be replaced with object composition as a mechanism for code reuse.

1.12 Polymorphism

In the real world, the meaning of an operation varies with context and the same operation may behave differently, in different situations. The *move* operation, for example, behaves differently on the class *person*, and on the class *polygon* on the screen. A specific implementation of an operation by a certain class is called a *method*. An object oriented operation, being polymorphic, may have more than one method of implementing it. The word *polymorphism* is derived from the Greek meaning *many forms*. It allows a single name to be used for more than one related purpose, which are technically different. The following are the different ways of achieving polymorphism in a C++ program:

- Function Name Overloading
- Operator Overloading
- Dynamic Binding

Polymorphism permits the programmer to generate high level reusable components that can be tailored to fit different applications, by changing their low level parts.

Dynamic Binding

Binding refers to the tie-up of a procedure call to the address code to be executed in response to the call. Dynamic binding (also called *late binding*) means that the code associated with a given procedure call is not known until its call at run-time. For example, consider a graphics application (see Figure 1.17), in which the class *Figure*, contains a procedure draw(). By inheritance, every graphics primitive in this diagram has a procedure draw(). The draw() algorithm is, however, unique to each graphical shape, and so the draw() procedure will be redefined in each class that defines a graphic primitive. To redraw the entire graphics window, the following code will suffice:

```
for i = 1 to number_of_shapes do
    ptr_to_figure[i]->draw();
```

At each pass through the loop, the code matching the dynamic type of ptr_to_figure[i] will be called. Even if additional kinds of shapes are added to the system, this code segment will still remain unchanged. This is, in contrast to the traditional *case/switch* statement design of a program.

Another example could be that of an operation print in a class File. Different methods could be implemented to print ASCII files, binary files, digitized picture files, etc. All these methods logically perform the same task - printing a file; thus the corresponding generic operation is print. However, the individual methods may each be implemented by a different code.

1.13 Message Communication

In conventional programming languages, *a function is invoked on a piece of data (function-driven communication)*, whereas in an object-oriented language, *a message is sent to an object (message-driven communication)*. Hence, conventional programming is based on functional abstraction whereas, object oriented programming is based on data abstraction. This is illustrated by a simple example of evaluating the square root of a number. In conventional functional programming, the function sqrt(x) for different data types (x's type), will be defined with different names, which takes a number as an input and returns its square root. For each data type of x, there will be a different version of the function *sqrt*. In contrast, in an OOPL (Object-Oriented Programming language), the expression for evaluating the square root of x takes the form `x.sqrt()`, implying that the object x has sent a message to perform the square root operation on itself. Different data types of x, invoke a different function code for `sqrt`, but the expression (code) for evaluating the square root will remain the same. By its very nature, OO (Object-Oriented) computation resembles the client-server computing model.

In object-oriented programming, the process of programming involves the following steps:
- Create classes for defining objects and their behaviors.
- Define the required objects.
- Establish communication among objects through message passing.

Communication among the objects occur in the same way as people exchange messages among themselves. The concept of programming, with the message passing model, is an easy way of modeling real-world problems on computers. A message for an object is interpreted as a request for the execution of a function. A suitable function is invoked soon after receiving the message and the desired results are generated within an object. A message comprises the name of the object, name of the function and the information to be sent to the object as shown in Figure 1.19.

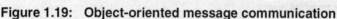
```
Student.Marks( RollNo )
```

Figure 1.19:   Object-oriented message communication

Like in the real world, *objects* also have a life cycle! They can be created and destroyed automatically, whenever necessary. *Communication between the objects can take place as long as they are alive!* In Figure 1.19, `Student` is treated as an object sending the message `Marks` to find the marks secured by the student with the specified `RollNo`. In this case, a function call `Marks()` is treated as a *message* and a parameter `RollNo` is treated as *information* passed to the object.

In OOPs, the correct method to execute an operation based on the name of the operation and the class of the object being operated, is automatically selected depending on the type of message received. The user of an operation need not be aware of the alternative methods available to implement a given polymorphic operation. New classes can be added without changing the existing code, but methods have to be provided for each applicable operation on the new class.

1.14 Popular OOP Languages

Every programming methodology emphasizes on some new concepts in programming. In OO programming, the attention is focused on objects. In this, data do not flow around a system; it is the messages that move around the system. By sending messages, the clients (user/application program) request objects to perform operations. The kinds of services the objects can provide are known to the clients. This, basically, represents the client-server model, where the client calls on a server, which performs some service and sends the result back to the client. The client must know the interface of the server, but the server need not know the interfaces of the clients, because all the interactions are initiated by clients using the server's interface.

Feature	C++	Smalltalk 80	Objective C	Simula	Ada	Charm ++	Eiffel	Java
Encapsulation (Data hiding)	√	Poor	√	√	√	√	√	√
Single inheritance	√	√	√	√	✗	√	√	√
Multiple inheritance	√	✗	√	✗	✗	√	√	✗
Polymorphism	√	√	√	√	√	√	√	√
Binding (early or late)	Both	Late	Both	Both	Early	Both	Early	Late
Concurrency	Poor	Poor	Poor	√	Difficult	√	Promised	√
Garbage collection	✗	√	√	√	✗	✗	√	√
Persistent objects	✗	Promised	✗	✗	Like 3GL	✗	Limited	✗
Genericity	√	✗	✗	✗	√	√	√	✗
Class libraries	√	√	√	√	Limited	√	√	√

* Pure object-oriented languages
** Object-based languages
   Others are extended conventional languages

Table 1.2: Comparing object-oriented language features

Every OO language implements the basic OO concepts in a different way. They vary in their support of some of the advanced OO concepts such as multiple inheritance, class library, memory management, templates, exceptions, etc. Some of the popular OO languages namely C++, Smalltalk, Eiffel and CLOS are discussed. The *genealogy* of different languages is shown in Table 1.2 indicating various features supported by them.

One great divide in programming exists between *exploratory programming* languages that aim at dynamism and run-time flexibility, and *software engineering* languages which have static typing and other features that aid verifiability and/or efficiency. While both languages have their applications, the latter group to which C++ belongs, is of interest for further discussion. Smalltalk is the best-known representative of the former group.

C++

Bjarne Stroustrup developed C++ at AT & T Bell laboratories as an extension of C in the year 1980. (in fact, C was also invented at the same place by Dennis Ritchie in the early 1970's). C++ was first installed outside the designer's research group in July, 1983; however, quite a few current C++ features had not been invented. Suggested advantages of C++ are the "...*previous C users can quite well upgrade gradually to programming in C++, in the first step just feeding their existing C code through the C++ translator and checking if some small modifications would be necessary*". However, some consider this as a disadvantage. They claim that an abrupt change of paradigm is necessary to make programmers think in an object-oriented fashion.

C++ is evolved from a dialect of C known as *C with Classes* as a language for writing effective event-driven simulations. Several key ideas were borrowed from the Simula67 and ALGOL68 programming languages. The heritage of C++ is shown in Figure 1.20. Earlier version of the language, collectively known as "C with Classes" has been in use since 1980. It lacked operator overloading, references, virtual functions, and all these are overcome in C++. The name C++ (pronounced as C plus plus) was coined by Rick Mascitti in the summer of 1983. The name signifies the evolutionary nature of the changes from C. "++" is the C increment operator. The slightly short name C+ is a syntax error; it has also been used as the name of an unrelated language. Connoisseurs of C semantics find C++ inferior to ++C. The language is not called D, because it is an extension of C, and does not attempt to remedy the problems by removing features.

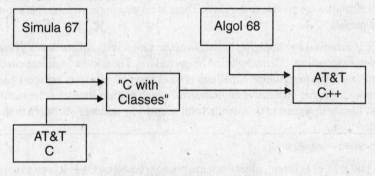

Figure 1.20: Heritage of C++

The C++ language corrects most of the deficiencies of C by offering improved compile-time type checking and support for modular and object-oriented programming. Some of the most prominent features of C++ are *classes, operator and function overloading, free store management, constant types, references, inline functions, inheritance, virtual functions, streams for console and file manipulation, templates, and exception handling.*

In C++, both attributes (data) and methods (functions) are members of a class. The members must be declared either as *private* or *public*. Public members can be accessed by any function; private members can only be accessed by methods of the same class. C++ has a special *constructor function* to initialize new instances and a *destructor function* to perform necessary cleanup when an object is to be destroyed. C++ provides three kinds of memory allocation for objects: *static* (preallocated by the compiler in fixed global memory); *automatic* (allocated on the stack) and *dynamic* (allocated from a heap). Static storage is obtained by defining a variable outside any function using the `static` keyword . Local variables within functions normally use automatic storage. Dynamic storage is allocated from a heap on an explicit request from the programmer and it must be explicitly released since, standard implementations of C++ do not have a garbage collector.

The superclass of a class is specified as a part of class declarations. A superclass is known as *base class* and a subclass is known as *derived class*. Attributes once declared in the superclass, which are inherited by its subclasses, need not be repeated. They can be accessed from any subclass unless they are declared *private*. Only the methods of a class can access its private attributes: Attributes declared *protected*, are accessible to subclasses, but not to a direct client object like private members. Methods declared in a superclass are also inherited. If a method can be overridden by the subclass, then it must be declared virtual in its first appearance in a superclass. Thus, the need to override the method must be anticipated and written into the base class itself. C++ does not support the concept of dynamic binding in a thorough sense and hence it is (some times) considered as a poor OOP language.

Smalltalk

Smalltalk is the first popular OO language developed at Xerox's Palo Alto Research Center (PARC). Apart from being a language, it has a development environment. Smalltalk programs are normally entered using the Smalltalk browser. Objects are called instance variables. All Smalltalk objects are dynamic, and are allocated from a heap. Smalltalk offers fully automatic garbage collection and deallocation is performed by a built-in garbage collector. All variables are untyped and can hold objects of any class. New objects are created using the same message passing mechanism used for operations on objects. All attributes are private to the class. There is no way to restrict the operations of a class. All operations are public.

Inheritance is achieved by supplying the name of the superclass. All attributes of the superclass are available to all its descendants. All methods can be overridden. The standard implementation of Smalltalk does not support multiple inheritance. Smalltalk is weakly typed, so errors are more likely to appear at runtime. It provides a highly interactive environment, which permits rapid development of programs. It has a rich class library designed to be extended and adapted by adding subclasses to meet the needs of a specific application.

Charm ++

Charm++ is a portable, concurrent, object-oriented system based on C++. It is an extension of C++ and provides a clear separation between sequential and parallel objects. The execution model of Charm++ is message driven, which helps the programmer to write programs that are latency-tolerant. The language supports multiple inheritance, dynamic binding, overloading, strong typing, and reuse of parallel objects. Charm++ provides specific modes for sharing information between parallel objects. It is based on the Charm parallel processing system and its runtime system implementation reuses most of the runtime system of Charm. Extensive dynamic load balancing strategies are provided. Charm++ has been implemented to run on different parallel systems, including shared memory machines (e.g., Sequent Symmetry), non-shared machines (e.g., nCUBE/2), uniprocessor, and network of workstations.

Java

The Java programming language is the result of several years of research and development at SUN (Stanford University Net) Microsystems, Inc., USA. SUN defines Java as follows: Java is a *new, simple, object-oriented, distributed, portable, architecture neutral, robust, secure, multi-threaded, interpreted*, and *high-performance programming language*. Java is mainly intended for the development of object-oriented network based software for *Internet* applications. Its syntax is similar to C and C++, but it omits semantic features that make C and C++ complex, confusing, and insecure. It does not support some of the more difficult to use features of C++ such as pointers. It also features built-in safety mechanisms (like absence of pointers) which provide some level of security on network. Hence, Java as a logical successor to C++ can also be called as C++--++ (C-plus-plus-minus-minus-plus-plus i.e., remove some difficult to use features of C++ and add some good features).

Java is the first language to provide a comprehensive, robust, platform-independent solution to the challenges of programming for the Internet and other complex networks. Java features portability, security and advanced networking without compromising on performance. Sun Microsystems' traditional family of SPARC processors, as well as processors of other architectures, will run Java software. By optimizing the new Java processor family for Java-only applications, an unprecedented level of price versus performance will be reached. Java was initially designed to address the problems of building software for small distributed systems to embed in consumer devices. As such it is designed for heterogeneous networks, multiple host architectures, and secure delivery. To meet these requirements, compiled Java code had to survive transport across networks, operate on any client, and assure the client that it is safe to run.

Java's future is promising. It is robust, object-oriented, and portable (source and byte code-executable) i.e., Java's application byte code runs on any platform without any modification or re-compilation; Java byte codes are interpreted by Java Virtual Machine (JVM) running on a local machine. Java integrates the flexibility of interpreted languages and power of compiler languages. Java comes bundled with a suite of classes for GUI (Graphical User Interface), multithreading, networking, file I/O, and the like. To add to this, APIs (Application Program Interface) for database access (Java Database Connectivity), more robust multimedia processing, and remote object access are in the development.

1.15 Merits and Demerits of OO Methodology

OOP systems are sold on the promise of improved productivity through object reuse and high level of code modularity. These aspects precisely lead to their greatest benefit, namely improved software quality, considering the objective of OO design is to *mirror the real world objects* in the software systems. OO languages have many advantages over traditional procedure-oriented languages.

Advantages

We perceive the world around us as being made up of objects and the brain arranges this information into chunks (groups). OO design uses objects in a programming language, which aids in trapping an existing pattern of human thought into programming.

Since the objects are autonomous entities and share their responsibilities only by executing methods relevant to the received messages, each object lends itself to greater modularity. Cooperation among different objects to achieve the system operation is done through exchange of messages. The independence of each object eases development and maintenance of the program.

Information hiding and data abstraction increase reliability and help decouple the procedural and representational specification from its implementation. Dynamic binding increases flexibility by permitting the addition of a new class of objects without having to modify the existing code. Inheritance coupled with dynamic binding enhances the reusability of a code, thus increasing the productivity of a programmer.

Many OO languages provide a standard class library that can be extended by the users, thus saving a lot of coding and debugging effort. Reducing the amount of code simplifies understanding and thus allows to build reliable programs. Code reuse is possible in conventional languages as well, but OO languages greatly enhance the possibility of reuse.

Object-oriented design involves the identification and implementation of different classes of objects and their behavior. The objects of the system closely correspond and relate in a one-to-one manner to the objects in the real world. Thus, it is easier to design and implement the system consisting of objects, as observed and understood by the brain.

Object orientation provides many other advantages in the production and maintenance of software; shorter development times, high degree of code sharing and malleability (can be moulded to any shape). These advantages make OOPs an important technology for building complex software systems.

Disadvantages

The runtime cost of dynamic binding mechanism is the major disadvantage of object oriented languages. The following were the demerits of adopting object-orientation in software developments in the early days of computing (some remain forever):

- Compiler overhead
- Runtime overhead
- Re-orientation of software developer to object-oriented thinking
- Requires the mastery over the following areas:
  - Software Engineering
  - Programming Methodologies
- Benefits only in long run while managing large software projects, atleast moderately large ones.

Object oriented concepts are becoming important in many areas of computer science, including programming, graphics, CAD systems, databases, user interfaces, application integration platforms, distributed systems and network management architectures. OO technology is more than just a way of programming. It is a way of thinking abstractly about a problem using real world concepts rather than computer concepts.

Although object orientation has been around for many years, it is only recently that it has received major attention from vendors and methodologists. OO programming is gradually picking up as an important technology for building complex software systems. For any programming language to succeed, it must be easy to learn i.e., programmers must be able to master language constructs easily; they must be able to reuse code written by them earlier without much modifications in a new software project; and above all, the programming language should be received well by application and system software developers. The following sections (OO Learning Curve, Software Reuse, and Objects Hold the Key) discuss these issues by taking object-oriented methodologies into consideration.

1.16 OO Learning Curve

The transition from an early linear programming language, BASIC, to the latest structured programming language, C, is easy as long as an `if` statement is an `if` statement, and a *function* is a *function* regardless of the language. While using function oriented methodology, the programmers need not think in terms of a specific language, because the individual syntax and capabilities are generally equivalent.

Programming in an object oriented paradigm, is different from programming in function oriented paradigm. Object-oriented programs should be structurally different from function oriented programs. Whereas a function-oriented program is organized around the actions being performed, a well designed object-oriented program is organized according to the objects being manipulated. This shift in perspective causes trouble for function-oriented programmers stepping into an object-oriented programming environment. Obviously, they have to *unlearn* known concepts while switching to object-oriented programming. (The communication between subroutines takes place through an explicit call to a required subroutine in the functional languages; whereas in OO languages, it takes place through message communication.)

Object-oriented techniques have promised to produce faster, smaller, and easier-to-maintain programs. The difference between function-oriented and object-oriented programming is that the programmer must switch from designing programs based on actions to designing programs around data types and their interactions.

The designer of C++, Bjarne Stroustrup, recommends that the shift from C to C++ should be a gradual one, with programmers learning the improvements a small step at a time. With C++, quite often, people, as a first exercise, write a string class and as a second exercise, try to implement a graphics system. That is very challenging and might be good for a professional programmer, but it's not the best way of teaching an average student programmer. What we need is an environment that has a very good string class that you can take apart and look at one which has a very nice graphics system, so that you never care about MS-windows or X-windows again, unless you absolutely want to. So, the two components needed to start OO programming are an *environment* and a *library* supporting resuability.

1.17 Software Reuse

Programmers have to write code from scratch, when a new software is being developed, using traditional languages, because there is hardly any reuse of the existing components. Software systems have become so complex that even *coding is considered as a liability today*. Reusing existing software components is treated as a key element in improving software development productivity. It facilitates the use of existing well tested and proven software code as a base module and then develop on it, instead of developing from scratch. The simplest approach in this direction involves the development and use of libraries of software components.

Once a class has been developed, implemented, and tested, it can be distributed to other programmers for use in their programs (called reusability). It is similar to the way library functions are used in different programs. However, in OOP, the concept of inheritance provides an important extension to the idea of reusability. A programmer can use an existing class without modifying it and add new additional features and capabilities to build a new class. A newly created derived class has all the inherited features of the old one with additional features of its own. The ease with which the existing software can be reused is a major benefit of OOP.

Reuse is becoming one of the key areas in dealing with the cost and quality of the software systems. The basis for reuse is the reliability of the components intended for reuse and gains achieved through its application. The components developed for reuse must have a quality stamp, for example, concerned with reliability and performance. Object-Oriented techniques make it possible to develop components in general, and to develop reusable components in particular.

One of the important problems of the software component reuse consists of their localization and retrieval from a large collection. In fact, reuse implies the following three actions: (i) Retrieve needed component, (ii) Understand them, and (iii) Use them.

A method to reduce the effort of reusable components' search, comprehension, and adaptation consists of developing a reuse, strategy which defines a component classification, a component structure, and search-and-use mechanism. The OO concepts such as classes and inheritance provide a better mechanism for grouping related entities and simplifying the identification of reusable components.

Reuse through Inheritance and its Quantification

Inheritance is considered as an excellent way to organize abstraction, and as a tool to support reuse. The use of inheritance does have some trade-offs (costs) - inheritance increases the complexity of the system and the coupling between classes. Booch recommends that inheritance hierarchies be built as balanced lattices and that the maximum number of levels and their width be limited to 7 ± 2 classes.

A study of inheritance was conducted on nineteen C++ software systems ranging from language tools, Graphical User Interfaces and toolkits, applications, thread packages from public domain to proprietary systems implemented using C++. It revealed that, only 37% of the systems have a median class inheritance depth greater than 1. However, an individual inheritance tree can be deep.

The inheritance depth varies from system to system depending on the application domain. Software systems that have been designed as applications also differ notably from the reuse libraries. The Graphical User Interface (GUI) applications tend to have greater reuse through inheritance. GUI software are more suitable for design with inheritance. The reuse of classes in a reusable software library is more than in an application system. Developers put more effort into the design of reusable libraries than application software. Therefore, the reuse software library developer can take greater advantage of inheritance. Experiments have revealed that, a lot of code and standard structures are common in many applications and a great improvement in programmers' productivity can be achieved by code reusability. Before the use of software components become an established methodology (code reuse), major efforts are needed in the area of reusable data, reusable architecture, and reusable design.

Reusable Data: The concept of reusable data implies a standard data interchange format. However there is no universal format to allow easy transport of data from one system to another.

Reusable Architecture: The architecture of reusable components should have the following attributes:
- all data descriptions should be external to the programs or modules intended for reuse
- all literals and constants should be external to the programs or modules intended for reuse
- all input/output controls should be external to the programs or modules intended for reuse
- the programs or modules intended for reuse should consist primarily of application logic

Reusable Design: A factor affecting the software reusability is the non-availability of good design principles for major application types. OO software components can be designed in a consistent way and can become a defacto standard for further development.

Reuse and Porting

Software reuse refers to the usage of existing software knowledge or artifacts to build new software artifacts. It is sometimes confused with porting. Reuse and porting are distinguished as follows: *Reuse* refers to using an asset in different systems; *Porting* is moving a system across different environments (moving software from DOS to UNIX operating system) or platforms (moving software from x86 to SUN's UltraSPARC processor). For example, in Figure 1.21, a component in System A is used again in System B, which is an example of reuse. System A, developed for Environment 1, is moved into Environment 2, which is an example of porting.

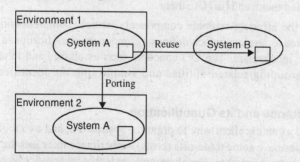

Figure 1.21: Reuse versus porting

Factors Influencing Reuse

An organization trying to improve systematic reuse, should concentrate on educating developers about reuse so as to improve their understanding of the economic feasibility of reuse, instituting a common development process, and making high-quality assets available to developers (see Figure 1.22a). The other factors (see Figure 1.22b), do not seem to be important, inspite of conventional wisdom. It should be understood, however, that these conclusions are based on data gathered from the industries; the salient factors of a particular organization may be different. The best course is to investigate the factors affecting reuse in the target organization (through surveys, case studies, or other techniques), and take action based on those results.

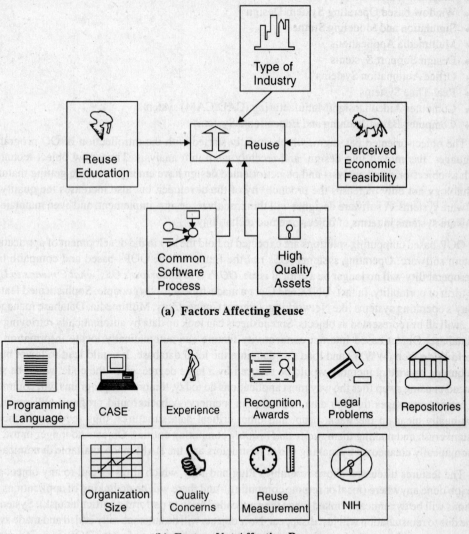

(a) **Factors Affecting Reuse**

(b) **Factors Not Affecting Reuse**

Figure 1.22:   Effects on systematic reuse of the factors

1.18 Objects Hold the Key

Popularity of OOPs in the development of most software systems with ease, has created a great deal of excitement and interest among software communities. OOP finds its application from design of database systems to the future generation operating systems, which have *computing, communication,* and *imaging* capabilities built into it. Today, OOP is used extensively in the design of Graphics User Interfaces on systems such as Windows. Some promising applications of OOP include the following:

- Object-Oriented Database Systems
- Object-Oriented Operating Systems
- Graphical User Interfaces
- Window based Operating System Design
- Simulation and Modeling Studies
- Multimedia Applications
- Design Support Systems
- Office Automation Systems
- Real-Time Systems
- Computer Aided Design/Manufacturing (CAD/CAM) systems
- Computer-Based Training and Educational Systems

The object-oriented paradigm, which initially started with the introduction of OO programming languages, has moved into design, and recently even into analysis. Thus, new object technologies such as object-oriented analysis and object-oriented design have emerged and are getting mature. OO technology not only increases the productivity of the developer, but also increases the quality of the software systems. A software designer will think, analyze, design, implement, and even maintain future software systems in terms of object-oriented technology.

OOP-based computing solutions are expected to hold the key in the development of application and system software. Operating systems (OSs') of the future will be OOPs-based and compatibility and interoperability will no longer be a critical issue. *OOPs is to tomorrow's OSs' what C means to UNIX* in the form of portability. In fact, UNIX and C are a made-for-each-other couple. Sophisticated features of today's operating systems like Networking, Internet Connectivity, Multimedia, Database management, etc., will all be represented as objects. Spreadsheets can look up data by automatically retrieving it from a database. Object-based Internet connectivity feature can automatically locate information on the World Wide Web (WWW) and load this data into the local database. It would lead to fewer bugs and the burden on virtual memory would be reduced by a large degree, since the code would be smaller. Instead of using swap files the way most applications do today, tomorrow's programs will communicate by passing messages through data structures in memory. A background program will monitor and continually clear up the stack, heap, and other critical data structures, thus reducing chances of a system crash and making them *stable and reliable* computing entities. Objects no longer in use will be automatically cleaned up by making use of destructors and the RAM made available dynamically.

The features discussed above resembles Plug-and-Play, which allows a call to any object and get the job done anywhere (local or remote computing); and there will be no linking of applications (applications will be dynamically linked when they are called upon to perform a particular task). System down time due to reinstallation will just disappear. New objects will be automatically added and made available to any program that needs them, thereby eliminating the redundancy of code. OOPs is an indispensable part of the future, and it calls for an unconditional restructuring of today's methodologies. These features will automatically migrate to tomorrow's operating systems.

The usage of OO concepts in the development of futuristic operating systems sounds impossible yet fascinating. An OO-based operating system, Oberon, has already been implemented by Nicklaus Wirth, the chief proponent of Pascal and Modula-2. Another implementation of Object-Oriented OS is *Cronus*. Cronus is a distributed operating system developed at BBN Laboratories Inc., Massachusetts, to interconnect cluster of heterogeneous computers on high-speed LANs (Local Area Networks). It supports three types of objects: *primal objects* (bound forever to the host that created them), *migrating objects* (basis for system reconfiguration-load balancing to improve performance), and *replicated objects* (to achieve survivability).

Object-Oriented Programming has made long lasting changes in programming methodology. The old style of programming referred to as structured programming is now dead. OOP has emerged as the winner. All new operating systems and development tools will support OOPs and make the life of the programmer easier and the life of the program longer. Revolutionary features of modern operating systems such as Object Linking and Embedding (OLE) in Microsoft Windows have given rise to the Common Object Model (COM), which is expected to become a standard and leading Object-Oriented Operating System.

Review Questions

1.1 What is a software crisis ? Justify the need for a new programming paradigm. Explain how object-oriented paradigm overcomes this software crisis.

1.2 What is object-oriented paradigm ? Explain the various features of OO paradigm.

1.3 Define the following terms related to OO paradigm:
a) Encapsulation b) Data abstraction c) Inheritance d) Multiple Inheritance e) Polymorphism f) Message Passing g) Extensibility h) Persistence i) Delegation j) Containership k) Genericity l) Abstract Data Types m) Objects n) Classes

1.4 What are the programming paradigms currently available ? Explain their features with programming languages supporting them.

1.5 Compare structured and OO Programming paradigms.

1.6 What are the elements of Object-Oriented Programming ? Explain its key components such as objects and classes with examples.

1.7 Write an object representation (pictorial) of Student class.

1.8 Explain multiple views of an object with a suitable example.

1.9 What is the difference between inheritance and delegation ? Illustrate with examples.

1.10 List different methods of realizing polymorphism and explain them with examples.

1.11 What are the steps involved in OO Programming ? Explain its message communication model.

1.12 List some popular OOP Languages and compare their object-oriented features.

1.13 Which is the first object-oriented language ? Explain the heritage of C++.

1.14 What is Java ? Why is this language gaining popularity now-a-days ?

1.15 Discuss the merits and demerits of object-oriented methodologies.

1.16 What is software reuse ? What is the difference between reuse and porting ? What are the factors influencing the software reuse ?

1.17 Identify reusable components in software and discuss how OOPs helps in managing them.

1.18 Justify "Objects hold the key." List some promising areas of applications of OOPs. Discuss how object-oriented paradigm affects different elements of computing such as hardware architectures, operating systems, programming environments, and applications ?

2

Moving from C to C++

2.1 Introduction

C++ has borrowed many features from other programming languages. It includes the commenting style from BCPL, the class concept with derived classes and virtual functions from Simula 67. It owes the concept of operator overloading and freedom to place definitions wherever necessary, to Algol 108, while the template facility and inline functions were borrowed from Ada. The concept of parametrized modules is borrowed from Clu programming language.

This chapter is a guideline for C programmers to transit from C to C++ programming without really bothering about C++'s OOP features. Mastering *non-class* features of C++ will provide impetus to the user to appreciate the influence of object oriented concepts over the conventional style of programming. Even if the programmers are not interested in OO programming, the other benefits, which are essential for structured programming with C, can be found in a more powerful form in C++. For instance, features such as strict prototyping as demanded by the compiler and others such as function overloading, single-line comment, function templates, etc., greatly improve productivity of the programmer. The various non-OOP features supported in C++ have greater role to play while writing OOP based programs.

2.2 Hello World

Similar to C, C++ programs must contain a function called `main()`, from which execution of the program starts. The function `main()` is designated as the starting point of the program execution and it is defined by the user. It cannot be overloaded and its syntax type is implementation dependent. Therefore, the number of arguments and their data-type is dependent on the compiler. The most popularly used format for defining the function `main()` is shown below:

```
void main()
{
    ....
    // Program Body
    ....
}
```

The traditional beginner's C program, usually called *Hello World*, is listed in `hello.c`. It has one of the heavily used header file `stdio.h`, included for supporting standard I/O operations. The `printf` statement outputs the string message `Hello World` on the console. The function body consists of statements for creating data storage variables called *local variable* and executable statements. Note that although the program execution starts from the `main()`, the data variables defined by it are not visible to any other function. With all the pieces of the program in place, a *driver* is needed to initialize and start things. The function `main()` serves as a driver function.

```
/* hello.c: printing Hello World message */
#include <stdio.h>
void main()
{
    printf( "Hello World" );
}
```

Run:

```
Hello World
```

The standard C library function `printf()` sends characters to the standard output device. The *Hello World* program will also work in C++, since it supports the ANSI-C function library. However, the program could be rewritten using C++ streams. The C++ equivalent of the Hello World program is listed in the program `hello.cpp`.

```
// hello.cpp: printing Hello World message
#include <iostream.h>
void main()
{
    cout << "Hello World";
}
```

Run:

```
Hello World
```

The header file `iostream.h` supports streams programming features by including predefined stream objects. The C++'s stream insertion operator, `<<` sends the message `"Hello World"` to the predefined console object, `cout`, which in turn prints on the console. The Hello World program in C++ is shown in Figure 2.1 for the purpose of comparative analysis.

```
1: // hello.cpp: printing Hello World message ————    comment

2: #include <iostream.h> ————    preprocessor directive

3: void main( ) ————    function declarator

4: { ————    function begin

5:    cout << "Hello World"; ————    body of the function main

6: } ————    function end
```

Figure 2.1: Hello World program in C++

The various components of the program `hello.cpp`, shown in Figure 2.1, are discussed in the following section:

First Line - Comment Line

The statement which starts with symbols // (i.e., two slash characters one after another without a space) is treated as comment. Hence the compiler ignores the complete line starting from the // character **pair**.

Although comments do not contribute to the runtime of a program, when used properly, they are the most valuable part of a piece of source code.

The word cpp, in the program hello.cpp, is an acronym for CPlusPlus (C++). The compiler will recognize program as a C++ program only when it has an extension cpp. (However, the extension is compiler dependent and most of the compilers assume cpp as default extension. Some C++ compilers such as GNU under UNIX system, expect program files to have cc as an extension).

Second Line - Preprocessor Directive

The second line is a preprocessor directive. The preprocessor directive

```
#include <iostream.h>
```

includes all the statements of the header file iostream.h. It contains instructions and predefined constants that will be used in the program. It plays a role similar to that of the header file stdio.h of C. The header file iostream.h contains declarations that are needed by the cout and cin stream objects. There are a number of such preprocessor directives provided by the C++ library, and they have to be included depending on the built-in functions used in the program. In addition, the users can also write preprocessor directives and declare them in the beginning of the program (usually, but they can be declared anywhere in the program). In effect, these directives are processed before any other executable statements in the source file of the program by the compiler.

Third Line - Function Declarator

The third line in the program is

```
void main()
```

Similar to a C program, the C++ program also consists of a set of functions. Every C++ program must have one function with name main, from where the execution of the program begins. The name main is a special word (not a reserved word) and must not be invoked anywhere by the user. The names of the functions (except main) are coined by the programmer. The function name is followed by a pair of parentheses which may or may not contain arguments. In this case, there are no arguments, but still the parentheses pair is mandatory. Every function is supposed to return a value, but the function in this example does not return any value. Such function names must be preceded by the reserved word void.

Fourth Line - Function Begin

The function body in a C/C++ program, is enclosed between two flower brackets. The opening flower bracket ({) marks the beginning of a function. All the statements in a function, which are listed after this brace can either be executable or non-executable statements.

Fifth Line - Function Body

The function body contains a statement to display the message Hello World. The output statement cout is pronounced as C-out (meaning Console Output). It plays a role similar to that of the printf() in C. The first statement in the main() body (of course it is the last statement in the main() body in this case)

```
cout << "Hello World";
```

prints the message "Hello World" on the standard console output device (VDU, video display unit by default). It plays the role of the statement

```
printf( "Hello World" );
```

as in the hello.c program.

Sixth Line - Function End

The end of a function body in a C/C++ program is marked by the closing flower bracket (}). When the compiler encounters this bracket, it is replaced by the statement,

```
return;
```

which transfers control to a caller. In this program, the last line actually marks the end of program and control is transferred to the operating system on termination of the program.

Compilation Process

The C++ program hello.cpp, can be entered into the system using any available text editor. Some of the most commonly available editors are Norton editor (ne), edline, edit, vi (most popular editor in UNIX environment). The program coded by the programmer is called the *source code*. This source code is supplied to the compiler for converting it into the *machine code*.

C++ programs make use of libraries. A library contains the object code of standard functions. The object code of all functions used in the program have to be combined with the program written by the programmer. In addition, some *start-up code* is required to produce an executable version of the program. This process of combining all the required object codes and the start-up code is called *linking* and the final product is called the *executable code*.

Most of the modern compilers support sophisticated features such as multiple window editing, mouse support, on-line help, project management support, etc. One such compiler is Borland C++. It can be invoked through command-line or integrated development environment (refer to Borland C++ developers guide).

Command Line Compilation

Most of the compilers support the command line compilation of a program. All the required arguments are passed to the compiler from the command line. For the purpose of discussion, consider the Borland C++ compiler. (However this process is implementation dependent. For more details, refer to the manual supplied by the compiler vendor.)

The command-line compiler is invoked by issuing the command:

```
tcc filename.cpp   (in the case of Turbo C++)
bcc filename.cpp   (in the case of Borland C++)
```

at the DOS prompt. It creates an object file filename.obj, and an executable file filename.exe. In the case of multiple file compilation, they must be compiled through -c option to create only the object file as follows:

```
tcc/bcc -c filename.cpp
```

The linker is invoked to link multiple object files and to create an executable file through the explicit issue of the linking command:

```
tlink filename1.obj  filename2.obj <library name>
```

The library file can also be passed as a parameter to the linker for binding functions defined in it. To create the executable of hello.cpp, issue the command bcc hello.cpp at the MS-DOS prompt.

2.3 Streams Based I/O

C++ supports a rich set of functions for performing input and output operations. The syntax of using these I/O functions is totally consistent, irrespective of the device with which I/O operations are performed. C++'s new features for handling I/O operations are called streams. Streams are abstractions that refer to data flow. Streams in C++ are classified into

- Output Streams
- Input Streams

Output Streams

The output streams allow to perform write operations on output devices such as screen, disk, etc. Output on the standard stream is performed using the `cout` object. C++ uses the bit-wise left-shift operator for performing console output operation. The syntax for the standard output stream operation is as follows:

        cout << variable;

The word `cout` is followed by the symbol <<, called the insertion or put-to operator, and then with the items (variables/constants/expressions) that are to be output. Variables can be of any basic data type. The use of `cout` to perform an output operation is shown in Figure 2.2.

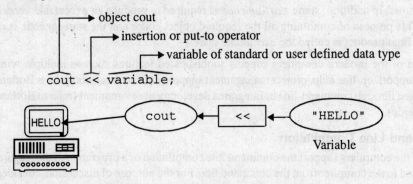

Figure 2.2:   Output with cout operator

The following are examples of stream output operations:

1.   cout << "Hello World";
2.   int age;
         cout << age;
3.   float weight;
         cout << weight;
4.   double area;
         cout << area;
5.   char code;
         cout << code;

More than one item can be displayed using a single `cout` output stream object. Such output operations in C++ are called *cascaded output operations*. For example, output of the age of a person along with some message can be performed by `cout` as follows:

        cout << "Age = " << age;

The `cout` object will display all the items from left to right. Hence, in the above case, it prints the message string "Age = " first, and then prints the value of the variable `age`. C++ does not enforce any restrictions on the maximum number of items to be output. The complete syntax of the standard output streams operation is as follows:

```
cout << variable1 << variable2 << .. << variableN;
```

The object `cout` must be associated with at least one argument. Like `printf`, a constant value can also be sent as an argument to the `cout` object. Following are some valid output statements

```
cout << 'H';
cout << "Hello";
cout << 420;
cout << 90.25;
cout << 1234567;
cout << " ";  // will display blank
cout << "\n"; // prints new line
cout << x << " " << y;
```

The last output statement prints the value of the variable x followed by a blank character, and then the value of the variable y.

The program `output.cpp` demonstrates the various methods of using `cout` for performing output operation.

```
// output.cpp: display contents of variables of different data types
#include <iostream.h>
void main()
{
   char sex;
   char *msg = "C++ cout object";
   int age;
   float number;
   sex = 'M';
   age = 24;
   number = 420.5;
   cout << sex;
   cout << " " << age << " " << number;
   cout << "\n" << msg << endl;
   cout << 1 << 2 << 3 << endl;
   cout << number+1;
   cout << "\n" << 99.99;
}
```

Run

```
M 24 420.5
C++ cout object
123
421.5
99.99
```

The item `endl` in the statement

```
cout << "\n" << msg << endl;
```

serves the same purpose as "\n" (linefeed and carriage return) and is known as a *manipulator*. It may be noticed that there is no mention of the data types in the I/O statements as in C. Hence, I/O statements of C++ are easier to code and use. C++, as a superset of C, supports all functions of C, however, they are not used in the above C++ program.

Input Streams

The input streams allow to perform read operation with input devices such as keyboard, disk, etc. Input from the standard stream is performed using the cin object. C++ uses the bit-wise right-shift operator for performing console input operation. The syntax for standard input streams operation is as follows:

```
cin >> variable;
```

The word cin is followed by the symbol >> (extraction operator) and then with the variable, into which the input data is to be stored. The use of cin in performing an input operation is shown in Figure 2.3.

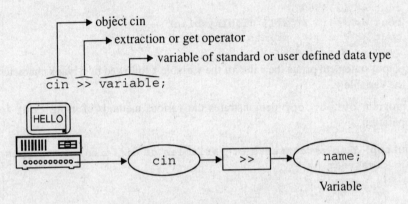

Figure 2.3:   Input with cin operator

The following are examples of stream input operations:

1.   int age;
        cin >> age;

2.   float weight;
        cin >> weight;

3.   double area;
        cin >> area;

4.   char code;
        cout >> code;

5.   char name[20];
        cin >> name;

Input of more than one item can also be performed using the cin input stream object. Such input operations in C++ are called *cascaded input operations*. For example, reading the name of a person followed by the age, can be performed by the cin as follows:

```
cin >> name >> age;
```

The cin object will read all the items from left to right. Hence, in the above case, it reads the name of the person as a string (until first blank) first, and then the age of person into the variable age. C++ does not impose any restrictions on the number of items to be read. The complete syntax of the standard input streams operation is as follows:

```
cin >> variable1 >> variable2 >> .. >> variableN;
```

The object cin, must be associated with at least one argument. Like scanf(), constant values cannot be sent as an argument to the cin object. Following are some valid input statements:

```
    cin >> i >> j >> k;
    cin >> name >> age >> address;
```

The program read.cpp demonstrates the various methods of using cin for performing input operation.

```
// read.cpp: data input through cin object
#include <iostream.h>
void main()
{
    char name[25];
    int age;
    char address[25];
    // read data
    cout << "Enter Name: ";
    cin >> name;
    cout << "Enter Age: ";
    cin >> age;
    cout << "Enter Address: ";
    cin >> address;
    // output data
    cout << "The data entered are:" << endl;
    cout << "Name = " << name << endl;
    cout << "Age = " << age << endl;
    cout << "Address = " << address;
}
```

Run

```
Enter Name: Rajkumar
Enter Age: 24
Enter Address: C-DAC-Bangalore
The data entered are:
Name = Rajkumar
Age = 24
Address = C-DAC-Bangalore
```

Performing I/O operations through the cout and cin are analogous to the printf and scanf of the C language, but with different syntax specifications. The following are two important points to be noted about the stream operations.

♦ Streams do not require explicit data type specification in I/O statement.

♦ Streams do not require explicit address operator prior to the variable in the input statement.

In scanf and printf functions, format strings are necessary, while in the cin stream format specification is not necessary, and in the cout stream format, specification is optional. Format-free input and output are special features of C++, which make I/O operations comfortable for beginners. The input stream cin accepts both numbers and characters, when the variables are given in the normal form. The function scanf requires ampersand (&) symbol to be prefixed to a numeric or a character variable, (whereas, the string variables can be given as they are). One must, therefore, carefully follow the syntax requirements in coding the different statements.

Another point to be noticed is that, the operator << , is the same as the left-shift bit-wise operator and the operator >>, is the same as the right-shift bit-wise operator used in C and also in C++. In C++, operators can be overloaded, i.e., the same operator can perform different activities depending on the context (types of data-items with which they are associated). The cout is a predefined object in C++, which corresponds to the output stream, and cin is an object in the input stream. Different objects are instructed to do specified jobs.

2.4 Single Line Comment

C++ has borrowed the new commenting style from Basic Computer Programming Language (BCPL), the predecessor of the C language. In C, comment(s) is/are enclosed between /* and */ character pairs. It can be either used for single line comment or multiple line comment.

Single line comment runs across only one line in a source program. The statement below is an example of single line comment:

```
/* I am a single line comment */
```

Multiple line comment runs across two or more lines in a source program. The statement below is an example of multiple line comment.

```
/* I am a multiple line comment.
   Hope you got it. */
```

Apart from the above style of commenting, C++ supports a new style of commenting. It starts with two forward slashes i.e., // (without separation by spaces) and ends with the end-of-line character. The syntax for the new style of C++ comment is shown in Figure 2.4.

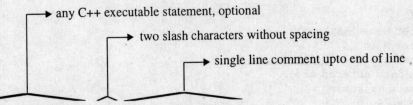

any C++ executable statement, optional

two slash characters without spacing

single line comment upto end of line

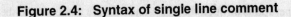

```
[any C++ statement] // I am a C++ comment
```

Figure 2.4:   Syntax of single line comment

The following examples illustrate the syntax of C++ comments:

```
int acc;                // Account Number
acc = acc + 1;          // adding new account number for new customer
```

In C, the above two statements are written as

```
int acc;                /* Account Number */
acc = acc + 1;          /* adding new account number for new customer */
```

The above examples of comments indicate that, C++ commenting style is easy and quicker for single line commenting. Although, C++ supports C style of commenting, it is advisable to use the C style for commenting multiple lines and the C++ style for commenting a single line.

Some typical examples of commenting are listed below:

1.   `// this is a new style of comment in C++`
2.   `/* this is an old style of comment in C++ */`
3.   `// style of comment runs to the end of a line`
4.   `/* runs to any number of lines but hard to type and takes up more space`
         `and coding time also. */`
5. (i)   `/* Here is a comment followed by an  executable statement */ a = 100;`
   (ii) `// Here is a comment followed by a non-executable statement  a = 100;`

The statement (i) has a comment followed by an executable statement a = 100; but, the statement (ii) is entirely treated as a commented line.

Large programs become hard to understand even by the original author (programmer), after some time has passed. Even a few well-placed comments which explain *why* and *what* of a variable, expression, statement, or block, help tremendously. Comments that simply restate the nature of a line of code, obviously do not add much value, but comments which explain the algorithm are the mark of a good programmer.

Comments are integral part of any program and they help in program coding and maintenance. The compiler completely ignores comments, therefore, they do not slow down the execution speed, nor do they increase the size of the executable program. Comments should be used liberally in a program and they should be written during the program development, but not as an after-thought activity.

The program simpint.cpp for computing the simple interest demonstrates how comments aid in the understanding and improving redability of the source code.

```cpp
// simpint.cpp: Simple interest computation
#include <iostream.h>
void main()
{
    // data structure definition
    int principle;     // principle amount
    int time;          // time in years
    int rate;          // rate of interest
    int SimpInt;       // Simple interest
    int total;         // total amount to be paid back after 'time' years
    // read all the data required to compute simple interest
    cout << "Enter Principle Amount: ";
    cin >> principle;
    cout << "Enter Time (in years): ";
    cin >> time;
    cout << "Enter Rate of Interest: ";
    cin >> rate;
    // compute simple interest and display the results
    SimpInt = (principle * time * rate) / 100;
    cout << "Simple Interest = ";
    cout << SimpInt;
    // total amount = principle amount + simple interest
    total = principle + SimpInt;
    cout << "\nTotal Amount = ";
    cout << total;
}
```

Run

```
Enter Principle Amount: 1000
Enter Time (in years): 2
Enter Rate of Interest: 5
Simple Interest = 100
Total Amount = 1100
```

2.5 Literals—Constant Qualifiers

Literals are constants, to which symbolic names are associated for the purpose of readability and ease of handling standard constant values. C++ provides the following three ways of defining constants:

+ `#  define` preprocessor directive
+ enumerated data types
+ `const` keyword

The variables in C can be created and initialized with a constant value at the point of its definition. For instance, the statement

```
float PI = 3.1452;
```

defines a variable named PI, and is assigned with the floating-point numeric constant value 3.1452. It is known that the constant value does not change. In the above case, the variable PI is considered as a constant, whose value does not change throughout the life of the program (complete execution-time). However, an accidental change of the value of the variable PI is not restricted by C. C++ overcomes this by supporting a new constant qualifier for defining a variable, whose value cannot be changed once it is assigned with a value at the time of variable definition. The qualifier used in C++ to define such variables is the `const` qualifier. The syntax of defining variables with the constant qualifier is shown in Figure 2.5. Note that if `DataType` is ommitted, it is considered as `int` by default.

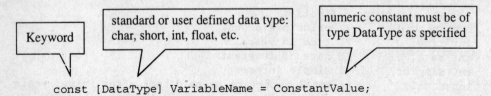

```
const [DataType] VariableName = ConstantValue;
```

Figure 2.5: Syntax of constant variable definition

The following examples illustrate the declaration of the constant variables:

+ `const float PI = 3.1452;`
+ `const int TRUE = 1;`
+ `const int FALSE = 0;`
+ `const char *book_name = "OOPs with C++";`

The program `area.cpp`, illustrates the declaration and the use of constant variables.

```
// area.cpp: area of a circle
#include <iostream.h>
const float PI = 3.1452;
```

```
void main()
{
   float radius;
   float area;
   cout << "Enter Radius of Circle: ";
   cin >> radius;
   area = PI * radius * radius;
   cout << "Area of Circle = " << area;
}
```

Run

```
Enter Radius of Circle: 2
Area of Circle = 12.5808
```

In the above program, the use of the statement such as

```
     PI = 2.3;
```

to modify a constant type variable leads to the compilation error: *Cannot modify a const object*

Thus, the keyword const, can be used before a type to indicate that the variable declared is constant, and may therefore not appear on the left side of the assignment (=) operator. In C++, the const qualifier can be used to indicate the parameters that are to be treated as read-only in the function body.

Consider the C program disp.c, having the function to display any string passed to it.

```
/* disp.c:  display message in C */
#include <stdio.h>
#include <string.h>
void display( char *msg )
{
   printf( "%s", msg );
   /* modify the message */
   strcpy( msg, "Misuse" );
}
void main()
{
   char string[15];
   strcpy( string, "Hello World" );
   display( string );
   printf( "\n%s", string );
}
```

Run

```
Hello World
Misuse
```

The function display(), is supposed to output the input string argument passed to it onto the console. But accidental use of a statement such as

```
     strcpy( msg, "Misuse" );
```

in display() modifies the input argument. This modification is also reflected in the calling function; (see the second message in the output) the string argument is a pointer type and any modification in function will also be reflected in the calling function. Such accidental errors can be avoided by defining the input parameter with the `const` qualifier. The C++ program `disp.cpp` illustrates the mechanism of overcoming the problem of modifying constant variables.

```
// disp.cpp:  display message in C++
#include <stdio.h>
#include <string.h>
void display( const char *msg )
{
    cout << msg;
    /* modify the message */
    // strcpy( msg, "Misuse" ); this produces a compilation error
}
void main()
{
    char string[15];
    strcpy( string, "Hello World" );
    display( string );
    cout << endl << string;
}
```

Run
```
Hello World
Hello World
```

The use of a statement such as,

```
        strcpy( msg, "Misuse" );
```

in `display()` leads to a compilation error. Thus, reminding the programmer regarding the accidental modification of read-only type variables will protect from common programming errors.

2.6 Scope Resolution Operator ::

C++ supports a mechanism to access a global variable from a function in which a local variable is defined with the same name as a global variable. It is achieved using the *scope resolution operator*. The syntax for accessing a global variable using the scope resolution operator is shown in Figure 2.6.

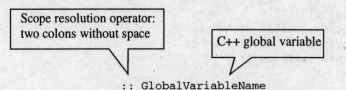

```
        :: GlobalVariableName
```

Figure 2.6:   Syntax of global variable access

The global variable to be accessed must be preceded by the scope resolution operator. It directs the compiler to access a global variable, instead of one defined as a local variable. The program `global.cpp` illustrates the access mechanism to the global variable `num` from the function `main()`, which has a local variable by the same name. Thus, *the scope resolution operator permits a program to reference an identifier in the global scope that has been hidden by another identifier with the same name in the local scope.*

```
// global.cpp: global variables access through scope resolution operator
#include <iostream.h>
int num = 20;
void main()
{
    int num = 10;
    cout << "Local = " << num;           // local variable
    cout << "\nGlobal = " << ::num;      // global variable
    cout << "\nGlobal+Local = " << ::num+num;  // both local & global use
}
```

Run

```
Local = 10
Global = 20
Global+Local = 30
```

The program loop.cpp illustrates the accessing of local and global variables within a for loop. It also shows mixing of the single-line comment statement within a single executable statement.

```
// loop.cpp: local and global variables in a loop
#include <iostream.h>
int counter = 50;                    // global variable
int main ()
{
    register int  counter;           // local variable
    for(counter = 1;                 // this refers to the
        counter < 10;                // local variable
        counter++)
    {
        cout << endl <<              // print new line followed by
                ::counter            // global variable
                /                    // divided by
                counter;             // local variable
    }
    return( 0 );
}
```

Run

```
50
25
16
12
10
8
7
6
5
```

2.7 Variable Definition at the Point of Use

In C, local variables can only be defined at the top of a function, or at the beginning of a nested block. In C++, local variables can be created at any position in the code, even between statements. Furthermore, local variables can be defined in some statements, just prior to their usage. The program `var1.cpp` defines the variable in the `for` statement and its scope continues even after the `for` statement.

```
// var1.cpp: defining variables at the point of use
#include <iostream.h>
int main()
{
    // variable i cannot be referred before 'for' statement
    for ( int i = 0; i < 5; i++ ) // variable i is defined and used here
        cout << i << endl;
    cout << i;   // i visible after the 'for' statement also
    return( 0 );
}
```

Run

```
0
1
2
3
4
5
```

In `main()`, the statement

```
for ( int i = 0; i < 5; i++ )
```

creates the variable `i` inside the `for` statement. The variable does not exist prior to the statement, but continues to be available as a local integer variable even after the block scope of the `for` statement. The statement outside the `for` loop

```
cout << i;
```

refers to the variable created in the `for` loop.

The program `def2.cpp` illustrates the scope of variables and the usage of scope resolution operator.

```
// def2.cpp: Variable scope demonstration
#include <iostream.h>
int a = 10; // global variable
void main()
{
    cout << a << "\n";      // uses global variable
    int a = 20;
    {
        int a = 30;
        cout << a << "\n";   // uses locally defined variable within a block
        cout << ::a << "\n"; // uses global variable
    } // variable a defined within a block goes out of scope here
    cout << a << "\n";      // uses local variable a defined near main()
    cout << ::a << "\n";     // uses global variable
}
```

Run

```
10
30
10
20
10
```

The definition of variables at any position in the code can reduce code readablity. Therefore local variables should be defined at the beginning of a function, following the first {, or they should be created at *intuitively right* places.

2.8 Variable Aliases—Reference Variables

C++ supports one more type of variable called reference variable, in addition to the value variable and pointer variables of C. Value variables are used to hold some numeric values; pointer variables are used to hold the address of (pointer to) some other value variables. Reference variable behaves similar to both, a value variable and a pointer variable. In the program code, it is used similar to that of a value variable, but has an action of a pointer variable. In other words, a reference variable acts as an alias (alternative name) for the other value variables. Thus, *the reference variable enjoys the simplicity of value variable and power of the pointer variable.* It does not provide the flexibility supported by the pointer variable. Unlike pointer variable, when a reference is bound to a variable, then its binding cannot be changed. All the accesses made to the reference variable are same as the access to the variable, to which it is bound. The general format of declaring the reference variable is shown in Figure 2.7.

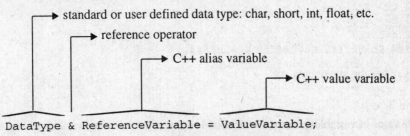

Figure 2.7:   Syntax of reference variable declaration

The reference variable must be initialized to some variable only at the point of its declaration. Initialization of reference variable after its declaration causes compilation error. Hence, reference variables allow to create alias (another name) of existing variables. The following examples illustrate the concept of reference variables.

```
1.      char & ch1 = ch;       // ch1 is an alias of char ch
2.      int & a = b;           // a is an alias of int b
3.      float & x = y;
4.      double & height = length;
5.      int &x = y[100];       // x is an alias of y[100] element
6.      int n;
        int *p = &n;
        int &m = *p;
```

These declarations cause m to refer n, which is pointed to by the pointer variable p.

7.   `int &num = 100;        // invalid`

This statement causes compilation error; constants cannot be made to be pointed to by a reference variable. Hence the rule, *no alias for constant value*.

Reference variables are not bounded to a new memory location, but to the variables to which they are aliases. For instance, the reference variable height is bound to the same memory location to which the value variable length is bound. The program refvar.cpp, illustrates the use of reference variables.

```
// refvar.cpp: reference variable for aliasing
#include <iostream.h>
void main()
{
  int a = 1, b = 2, c = 3;
  int &z = a;    // variable z becomes alias of a
  cout << "a=" << a << " b=" << b << " c=" << c << " z=" << z << endl;
  z = b;         // changes value of a to the value of b
  cout << "a=" << a << " b=" << b << " c=" << c << " z=" << z << endl;
  z = c;         // changes value of a to the value of c
  cout << "a=" << a << " b=" << b << " c=" << c << " z=" << z << endl;
  cout<<"&a=" << &a << " &b=" <<&b << "&c=" << &c << " &z=" << &z << endl;
}
```

Run
```
a=1 b=2 c=3 z=1
a=2 b=2 c=3 z=2
a=3 b=2 c=3 z=3
&a=0xfff4 &b=0xfff2 &c=0xfff0 &z=0xfff4
```

In main(), the statements
```
        z = b;
        z = c;
```
assign the value of variables b and c to the variable a since, the reference variable z is its alias variable. It can be observed that, in the last line of the above program output, the memory addresses of the variables a and z are same. The reference variables are bound to memory locations at compile time only. Consider the following statements:
```
        int n;
        int *p = &n;
        int &m = *p;
```
Here m refers to n, which is pointed to by the variable p. The compiler actually binds the variable m to n but not to the pointer. If pointer p is bound to some other variable at runtime, it does not affect the value referenced by m and n. It is illustrated in the program reftest.cpp.

```
// reftest.cpp: testing of reference binding
#include <iostream.h>
void main()
{
  int n = 100;
  int *p = &n;
```

```
int &m = *p;    // m is bound to n
cout << "n = " << n << " m = " << m << " *p = " << *p << endl;
int k = 5;
p = &k;  // pointer value is changed
k = 200;
// is there change in m value ?
cout << "n = " << n << " m = " << m << " *p = " << *p << endl;
}
```

Run

```
n = 100 m = 100 *p = 100
n = 100 m = 100 *p = 200
```

In main(), the statement

```
        p = &k;  // pointer value changed
```

changes the pointer value of p, but does not effect the reference variable m and the variable n.

2.9 Strict Type Checking

C++ is a strongly-typed language and it uses very strict type checking. A prototype must be known for each function which is called, and the call must match the prototype. The prototype provides information of the type and number of arguments passed and it also specifies the return type (if any) of the function. In C++, function prototyping is compulsory if the definition is not placed before the function call whereas, in C, it is optional. The program max.cpp for computing the maximum of two numbers illustrates the need for the function prototype.

```
// max.cpp: maximum of two numbers
#include <iostream.h>
int main ()
{
   int x, y;
   cout << "Enter two integers: ";
   cin >> x >> y;
   cout << "Maximum = " << max( x, y ); // Error max.cpp 11:...
   return 0;
}
int max( int a, int b )
{
   if( a > b )
      return a;
   else
      return b;
}
```

Compilation of the above program produces the following errors:

```
Error max.cpp 11: Function 'max' should have a prototype in function main()
```

C++ checks all the parameters passed to a function against its prototype declaration during compilation. It produces errors if there is a mismatch in argument types and this can be overcome by placing the prototype of the function max() before it is invoked. The modified program of max.cpp is listed in newmax.cpp, which is compiled without any errors.

```
// newmax.cpp: maximum of two numbers
#include <iostream.h>
int max( int a, int b );        // prototype of max
void main ()
{
   int x, y;
   cout << "Enter two integers: ";
   cin >> x >> y;
   cout << "Maximum = " << max( x, y );
}
int max( int a, int b )
{
   if( a > b )
      return a;
   else
      return b;
}
```

Run

```
Enter two integers: 10 20
Maximum = 20
```

The advantages of strict type checking is that the compiler warns the users if a function is called with improper data types. It helps the user to identify errors in a function call and increases the reliability of a program. The program swap_err.cpp shows notification of the compiler, when improper data type parameters are passed to the function. The program swap_err.cpp illustrates the detection of the statement calling the function with improper data items.

```
// swap_err.cpp: swap integer values by reference
#include <iostream.h>
void swap( int * x, int * y )
{
   int t;    // temporarily used in swapping
   t = *x;
   *x = *y;
   *y = t;
}
void main()
{
   int a, b;
   swap( &a, &b );       // OK
   float c, d;
   swap( &c, &d );       // Errors
}
```

The compilation of the above program produces the following errors:

Error swap_err.cpp 20: Cannot convert 'float *' to 'int *' in function main()
Error swap_err.cpp 20: Type mismatch in parameter 'x' in call to 'swap(int *,int *)' in function main()
Error swap_err.cpp 20: Cannot convert 'float *' to 'int *' in function main()
Error swap_err.cpp 20: Type mismatch in parameter 'y' in call to 'swap(int *,int *)' in function main()

The above errors are produced due to the following statement in `main()`

```
swap( &c, &d );      // Compilation Errors
```

Because the expressions `&c` and `&d` passed to `swap()` are not pointers to integer data type. When a call to a function is made, the C++ compiler checks its parameters against the parameter types declared in the function prototype. The compiler flags errors if improper arguments are passed.

2.10 Parameters Passing by Reference

A function in C++ can take arguments passed by value, by pointer, or by reference. The arguments passed by reference is an enhancement over C. A copy of the actual parameters in the function call is assigned to the formal parameters in the case of pass-by-value, whereas the address of the actual parameters is passed in the case of pass-by-pointer. In the case of pass-by-reference, an alias (reference) of the actual parameters is passed. Mechanism of parameter linkage is shown in Figure 2.8.

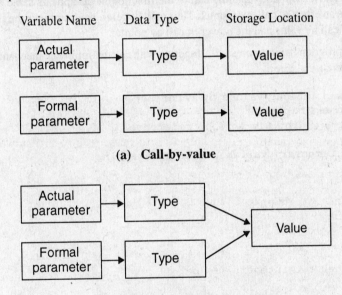

Figure 2.8:   Parameter passing mechanism

Consider an example of swapping two numbers to illustrate the mechanism of parameter passing by reference. The function definition with pointer type parameters is listed below:

```
void swap( int * p, int * q ) // by pointers
{
    int t;
    t = *p;
    *p = *q;
    *q = t;
}
```

A call to the function `swap()`

```
swap( &x, &y )
```

has effect on the values of x and y i.e, it exchanges the contents of variables x and y. The above swap(..) function can be redefined by using a new parameter passing scheme, call by reference, as follows:

```
void swap( int & x, int & y ) // by reference
{
    int t;
    t = x;
    x = y;
    y = t;
}
```

A call to the function swap()

```
    swap( x, y );
```

with integer variables x and y, has effect on the values of x and y variables. It exchanges the contents of the variables x and y. The body and the call to the function swap appears same as that of call-by-value case, but has an effect of call-by-pointer. Thus, call by reference combines the flexibility (ease of programming) of call by value and the power of call by pointer.

The complete program having swap(..) function with call-by-reference mechanism for parameter passing is listed in swap.cpp.

```
// swap.cpp: swap integer values by reference
#include <iostream.h>
void swap( int & x, int & y ) // by reference
{
    int t;     // temporary variable used in swapping
    t = x;
    x = y;
    y = t;
}
void main()
{
    int a, b;
    cout << "Enter two integers <a, b>: ";
    cin >> a >> b;
    swap( a, b );
    cout << "On swapping <a, b>: " << a << " " << b;
}
```

Run

```
Enter two integers <a, b>: 2 3
On swapping <a, b>: 3 2
```

In main(), the statement

```
    swap( a, b );
```

is translated into

```
    swap( & a, & b );
```

internally during compilation; the prototype of the function

```
    void swap( int & x, int & y ) // by reference
```

indicates that the formal parameters are of reference type and hence, they must be bound to the memory location of the actual parameter. Thus, any access made to reference formal parameters in `swap()` refers to the actual parameters. The statements

```
t = x;
x = y;
y = t;
```

in the body of `swap()` function, internally (as treated by the compiler) have the following meaning,

```
t = *x;          // store the value pointed by x into t
*x = *y;         // store the value pointed by y into location pointed by x
*y = t;          // store the value hold by 't' into location pointed by y
```

because, the formal parameters are of reference type and therefore, the compiler treats them similar to pointers, but does not allow the modification of the address stored in them.

Void Argument List

A function prototype in C with an empty argument list, such as

```
extern void func ();
```

implies that the argument list of the declared function is not prototyped; the compiler will not be able to warn against improper argument usage. To declare a function in C which has no arguments, the keyword `void` is used, as indicated:

```
extern void func (void);
```

In C++, the above two declarations are equivalent. Because C++ maintains strict type checking, an empty argument list is interpreted as the absence of any parameter.

2.11 Inline Functions

Function execution involves the overhead of jumping to and from the calling statement. Trading of this overhead in execution time is considerably large whenever a function is small, and hence in such cases, inline functions can be used. A function in C++ can be treated as a macro if the keyword `inline` precedes its definition. The syntax of representing the `inline` function is shown in Figure 2.9.

Keyword, function qualifier

```
inline ReturnType FunctionName (Parameters)
{
    // body of a main function
}
```

Figure 2.9: Syntax of inline function

Example: An inline function to find square of a number is as follows:

```
inline float square( float x )
{
    x = x * x;
    return( x );
}
```

The significant feature of `inline` functions is that there is no explicit function call; the function body is substituted at the point of inline function call. Thereby, the runtime overhead for function linkage mechanism is reduced. The program `square.cpp` uses an inline function in the computation of the square of a number.

```
// square.cpp: square of a number using inline function
#include <iostream.h>
inline float square( float x )
{
    x = x * x;
    return( x );
}
void main()
{
    float num;
    cout << "Enter a Number <float>: ";
    cin >> num;
    cout << "Its Square = " << square( num );
}
```

Run

```
Enter a Number <float>: 5.5
Its Square = 30.25
```

In `main()`, the statement

```
        cout << "Its Square = " << square( num );
```

invokes the `inline` function `square(..)`. It will be suitably replaced by the instruction(s) of the `square(..)` function body by the compiler. The execution time of the function `square(..)` is less than the time required to establish a linkage between the function *caller* (calling function) and the *callee* (called function). This process involves the operation of saving the actual parameters and function return address onto the stack, followed by a call to the function. On return, the stack must be cleaned to restore the old status. This process is costlier in comparison to having square computation instruction within a program itself instead of a function. Thus, support of `inline` functions allow to enjoy the flexibility and benefits of modular programming, while at the same time delivering computational speedup of macros. Functions having small body do not increase the code size even though they are physically substituted at the point of a call; there is no code for function linkage mechanism. Hence, it is advisable to define functions having small function body as inline functions.

2.12 Function Overloading

A *word* is said to be overloaded when it has two or more distinct meanings. The intended meaning of any particular use is determined by its context. In C++, two or more functions can be given the same name provided each has a unique signature (in either the number or data type of their arguments).

In C++, it is possible to define several functions with the same name, but which perform different actions. It helps in reducing the need for unusual function names, making code easier to read. The functions must only differ in the argument list. For example

```
        swap( int, int );      // prototype
        swap( float, float );  // prototype
```

From a user's view point, there is only one function performing swapping of numbers.

Consider the C program show.c having multiple show() functions for displaying input messages to illustrate the importance of function overloading.

```c
/* show.c: display different types of information with different functions */
#include <stdio.h>
void show_integer( int val )
{
    printf ("Integer: %d\n", val);
}
void show_double( double val )
{
    printf ("Double: %lf\n", val);
}
void show_string( char *val )
{
    printf ("String: %s\n", val);
}
int main ()
{
    show_integer( 420 );
    show_double( 3.1415 );
    show_string( "Hello World\n!" );
    return( 0 );
}
```

Run

```
Integer: 420
Double: 3.141500
String: Hello World
!
```

The above program has the following three different functions

```c
        void show_integer( int val );
        void show_double( double val );
        void show_string( char *val );
```

performing the same operations, but on different data types. Logically, all the three functions display the value of the input parameters. It has unusual names such as show_integer, show_double, etc., making the task of programming difficult and recalling function names although all of them perform the same operation logically. In C++, this difficulty is circumvented by using the feature of the function name overloading. All the functions performing the same operation must differ in input arguments data-type or in the number of arguments. The program show.cpp equivalent of C's show.c is written using function overloading features.

```cpp
// show.cpp: display different types of information with same function
#include <iostream.h>
void show( int val )
{
    cout << "Integer: " << val << endl;
}
```

```
void show( double val )
{
    cout << "Double: " << val << endl;
}
void show( char *val )
{
    cout << "String: " << val << endl;
}
int main ()
{
    show( 420 );                    // calls show( int val );
    show( 3.1415 );                 // calls show( double val );
    show( "Hello World\n!" );       // calls show( char *val );
    return( 0 );
}
```

Run

```
Integer: 420
Double: 3.1415
String: Hello World
!
```

In the above program, three functions named show() are defined, which only differ in their argument lists: int, double, or char*. The functions have the same name. The definition of several functions with the same name is called *function overloading*.

It is interesting to note the way in which the C++ compiler implements function overloading. Although, the functions share the same name in the source text (as in the example above, show()), the compiler (and hence the linker) uses different names. The conversion of a name in the source file to an internally used name is called *name mangling*. For instance, the C++ compiler might convert the name void show(int) to the internal name VshowI, while an analogous function with a char* argument might be called VshowCP. The actual names which are used internally depend on the compiler and are not relevant to the programmer, except where these names shown in the example, a listing of the contents of a function library.

A few remarks concerning function overloading are the following:

♦ The usage of more than one function with the same name, but quite different actions should be avoided. In the above example, the functions show() are still somewhat related (they print information on the screen). However, it is also quite possible to define two functions, say lookup(), one of which would find a name in a list, while the other would determine the video mode. In this case, the two functions have nothing in common except their name. It would therefore be more practical to use names which suggest the action; say, findname() and getvidmode().

♦ C++ does not allow overloaded functions to only differ in their return value. The reason is that processing (testing) of a function return value is always left to the programmer. For instance, the fragment

```
    printf ("Hello World!\n");
```
holds no information concerning the return value of the function printf() (The return value is, in this case, an integer value that states the number of printed characters. This return value is practically

never inspected.). Two functions printf() which differ in their return type could therefore, not be distinguished by the compiler.

♦ Function overloading can lead to surprises. For instance, imagine a usage of a statement such as

```
show( 0 );
```

in the program show.cpp; it is difficult to predict which one of the above three show() functions is invoked. The zero could be interpreted here as a NULL pointer to a char, i.e., a (char*)0, or as an integer with the value zero. C++ will invoke the function expecting an integer argument, which might not be what one expects.

2.13 Default Arguments

In a C++ function call, when one or more arguments are omitted, the function may be defined to take default values for omitted arguments by providing the default values in the function prototype. These arguments are supplied by the compiler when they are not specified by the programmer explicitly. The program prnstr.cpp illustrates the passing of default arguments to function.

```
// prnstr.cpp: default arguments and message printing
#include <iostream.h>
void showstring( char *str = "Hello World!\n" )
{
    cout << str;
}
int main ()
{
    showstring( "Here is an explicit argument\n" );
    showstring();   // in fact this says: showstring ("Hello World!\n");
    return 0;
}
```

Run

```
Here is an explicit argument
Hello World!
```

In main(), when the compiler encounters the statement

```
showstring();
```

it is replaced by the statement

```
showstring( "Hello World!\n" );
```

internally. When the function parameter is missing, the compiler substitutes the default parameter in that place.

The possibility of omitting arguments in situations where default arguments are defined is elegant; the compiler will supply the missing arguments, when they are not specified. The code of the program by no means becomes shorter or more efficient. Functions may be defined with more than one default argument.

Default arguments must be known to the compiler prior to the invocation of a function with default arguments. It reduces the burden of passing arguments explicitly at the point of a function call. The program defarg1.cpp illustrates the concept of default arguments.

```
// defarg1.cpp: Default arguments to functions
#include <iostream.h>
void PrintLine( char = '-', int = 70 );
void main()
{
  PrintLine();              // uses both default arguments
  PrintLine( '!' );         // assumes 2nd argument as default
  PrintLine( '*', 40 );     // ignores default arguments
  PrintLine( 'R', 55 );     // ignores default arguments
}
void PrintLine( char ch, int RepeatCount )
{
  int i;
  cout << endl;
  for( i = 0; i < RepeatCount; i++ )
    cout << ch;
}
```

Run

```
----------------------------------------------------------------------
!!!!!!!!!!!!!!!!!!!!!!!!!!!!!!!!!!!!!!!!!!!!!!!!!!!!!!!!!!!!!!!!!!!!!!!!!!
****************************************
RRRRRRRRRRRRRRRRRRRRRRRRRRRRRRRRRRRRRRRRRRRRRRRRRRRRRRRR
```

The feature of default arguments can be utilized to enhance the functionality of the program, without the need for modifying the old code referencing to functions. For instance, the function in the above program

```
        void PrintLine( char = '-', int = 70 );
```

prints a line with default character '-' in case it is not passed explicitly. This function can be enhanced to print multiple number of lines, whose new prototype is

```
        void PrintLine( char = '-', int = 70, int = 1 );
```

It may be noted that in the new function, the last parameter specifies the number of lines to be printed and by default, it is 1. Therefore, the old code referring to this function need not be modified and new statements can be added without affecting the functionality. The program defarg2.cpp has extended the capability of defarg1.cpp program.

```
/* defarg2.cpp: Default arguments to functions
            Extending the functionality of defarg1.cpp module */
#include <iostream.h>
void PrintLine( char = '-', int = 70, int = 1 );
void main()
{
  PrintLine();              // uses both default arguments
  PrintLine( '!' );         // assumes 2nd argument as default
  PrintLine( '*', 40 );     // ignores default arguments
  PrintLine( 'R', 55 );     // ignores default arguments
  // new code, Note: old code listed above is unaffected
  PrintLine( '&', 25, 2 );
}
```

```
void PrintLine( char ch, int RepeatCount, int nLines )
{
    int i, j;
    for( j = 0; j < nLines; j++ )
    {
        cout << endl;
        for( i = 0; i < RepeatCount; i++ )
            cout << ch;
    }
}
```

Run
```
--------------------------------------------------------------------
!!!!!!!!!!!!!!!!!!!!!!!!!!!!!!!!!!!!!!!!!!!!!!!!!!!!!!!!!!!!!!!!!!!!!!!!!
********************************************
RRRRRRRRRRRRRRRRRRRRRRRRRRRRRRRRRRRRRRRRRRRRRRRRRRRRRRRRRR
&&&&&&&&&&&&&&&&&&&&&&&&&
&&&&&&&&&&&&&&&&&&&&&&&&&
```

The following statements in the above two programs

```
PrintLine();              // uses both default arguments
PrintLine( '!' );         // assumes 2nd argument as default
PrintLine( '*', 40 );     // ignores default arguments
PrintLine( 'R', 55 );     // ignores default arguments
```

are the same. Although, the functionality of the function `PrintLine`, is enhanced in `defarg2.cpp` program, the old code referring to it remains unaffected in terms of its functionality; the compiler supplies the last argument as 1, thereby the new function does the same operation as that of the old one. Thus, default arguments feature can be potentially utilized in extending the function without modifying the old code. Note that all arguments in a multiple argument function need not have default values.

2.14 Keyword `typedef`

The keyword `typedef` is allowed in C++, but no longer necessary, when it is used as a prefix in `enum`, `struct`, or `union` declarations. This is illustrated in the following example:

```
struct somestruct
{
    int a;
    double d;
    char string [80];
};
```

When a `struct`, `enum`, or any other compound type is defined, the tag of this type can be used as type name (`somestruct` is the tag in the above example). For instance, the statement

```
somestruct  what;
```

defines the structure variable `what`. In C, the same variable is defined as

```
struct somestruct  what;
```

Thus, the use of keyword `struct` in the structure variable is default. In C++, the members of the structure variables are accessed similar to C. The statement

```
what.d = 3.1415;
```

assigns the numeric value 3.1415 to d, which is a member of the structure variable what. The structure declaration and its use in the definition of variables is illustrated in the program date1.cpp.

```
// date1.cpp: displaying birth date of the authors
#include <iostream.h>
struct date
{                        //specifies a structure
   int  day;
   int month;
   int year;
};
void main()
{
   date d1 = { 26, 3, 1958 };
   date d2 = { 14, 4, 1971 };
   date d3 = { 1, 9, 1973 };
   cout << "Birth Date of the First Author: ";
   cout << d1.day << "-" << d1.month << "-" << d1.year << endl;
   cout << "Birth Date of the Second Author: ";
   cout << d2.day << "-" << d2.month << "-" << d2.year << endl;
   cout << "Birth Date of the Third Author: ";
   cout << d3.day << "-" << d3.month << "-" << d3.year << endl;
}
```

Run

```
Birth Date of the First Author: 26-3-1958
Birth Date of the Second Author: 14-4-1971
Birth Date of the Third Author: 1-9-1973
```

2.15 Functions as a Part of a `struct`

Structures in C++ have undergone major revisions. Like C structures, C++ structures also provide a mechanism to group together data of different types, into one unit belonging to the same family. In addition to this, C++ allows to associate functions as a part of a structure. Thus, C++ structures provide a true mechanism to handle data abstraction. This is the first concrete example of the definition of an object, as described previously. An object is a structure containing all involved code and data. The general syntax of the C++ structure is:

```
struct StructureName
{
   public:
      // data and functions
   private:
      // data and functions
   protected:
      // data and functions
};
```

The structure has two types of members: data members and member functions. Functions defined within a structure, operate on any member of the structure. The keywords public, private, and protected are called *access specifiers*. If none of these keywords appear in the structure declaration, *all the members of the structure have public access.* The private and protected members of a structure can be accessed only within the structure. Public members of a structure are accessible to both member functions and its instances (structure variables). Internal functions of a structure are privileged code and they can see all the features of a structure, but external code can see only the public features.

A definition of the structure `point` is given in the code fragment below. In this structure, two `int` data fields and one function `draw()` are declared.

```
struct point
{
    int  x, y;           // coordinates
    void draw (void);    // drawing function
};
```

A similar structure could be a part of the painting program used to represent a pixel in the drawing. The following are the points to be noted about structures:

♦ The function `draw()`, which occurs in the structure body is only a declaration. The actual code of the function, or in other words, the actions to be performed by the function are located elsewhere in the code section of the program. Member function can also be defined within the body of a structure.

♦ The size of the structure `point` is just two integers. Though a function is declared in the structure, its size remains unaffected. The compiler implements this behavior by allowing the function `draw()` to be known only in the context of the `point` structure.

The point structure could be used as follows:

```
point a, b;       // two points on the screen
a.x = 0;          // define first dot
a.y = 10;         // and draw it
a.draw ();
b = a;            // copy a to b
b.y = 20;         // redefine y-coordinate
b.draw ();        // and draw it
```

The function `draw()`, which is a part of the structure, is selected in a manner similar to the selection of data fields; i.e., using the field selector operator (.) with value structures or `->` with pointers to structures.

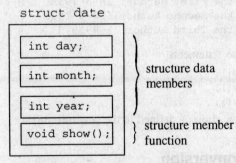

Figure 2.10:   Date structure having function show()

The idea behind this syntactical construction is that several structures may contain functions with the same name. For instance, a structure representing a circle might contain three integer values; two values for the coordinates of the center of the circle and one value for the radius. Analogous to the point structure, a draw() could be declared in the circle structure which would draw the circle.

The program date2.cpp is C++ equivalent of the earlier program date1.cpp. It illustrates the concept of associating functions operating on structure members as shown in Figure 2.10. The structure date has both the data members and functions operating on them. The user accesses the member functions additionally, when compared to C's structure using the *dot operator*.

```cpp
// date2.cpp: displaying birth date of the authors
#include <iostream.h>
struct date
{                       //specifies a structure
   int  day;
   int month;
   int year;
   void show()
   {
      cout << day << "-" << month << "-" << year << endl;
   }
};
void main()
{
   date d1 = { 26, 3, 1958 };
   date d2 = { 14, 4, 1971 };
   date d3 = { 1, 9, 1973 };
   cout << "Birth Date of the First Author: ";
   d1.show();
   cout << "Birth Date of the Second Author: ";
   d2.show();
   cout << "Birth Date of the Third Author: ";
   d3.show();
}
```

Run
```
Birth Date of the First Author: 26-3-1958
Birth Date of the Second Author: 14-4-1971
Birth Date of the Third Author: 1-9-1973
```

In main(), the statements
```
d1.show();
d2.show();
d3.show();
```
invoke the function show() defined in the structure date.

2.16 Type Conversion

The basic data types can be used with great flexibility in assignments and expressions, due to the implicit type conversion facility provided, whereas with the user-defined data types, the same can be achieved through explicit type conversion (the type cast operator). The syntax of type conversion specification in C and C++ is shown in Figure 2.11.

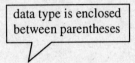

| data type is enclosed between parentheses | variable name is enclosed between parentheses |

```
    (DataType) Variable            DataType (Variable)
    Ex: (int)age,(float)weight     Ex: int(age),float(weight)
```

     (a) Type casting in C   **(b) Type casting in C++**

Figure 2.11:   Syntax of data type casting in C and C++

Consider the following statements

```
float weight;
int age;
weight = age;
```

where `weight` is of type `float` and `age` is of type `int`. Here, the compiler calls a special routine to convert the contents of `age`, which is represented in an integer format, to a floating-point format, so that it can be assigned to `weight`. The compiler has built-in routines for conversion of basic data types such as char to integer, float to double, etc. The feature of the compiler that performs data conversion without the user intervention, is known as *implicit type conversion*.

The compiler can be instructed explicitly to perform type conversion using the type conversion operators known as type cast operator. For instance, to convert `int` to `float`, the statement is

```
weight = (float) age;
```

where the keyword `float` is enclosed between braces. Here, `float` enclosed between braces is the *type casting operator*. In C++, the above statement can also be expressed in a more readable form as

```
weight = float( age );
```

The explicit conversion of `float` to `int` uses the same built-in routine as implicit conversions. The program `cast.cpp` illustrates the explicit type casting in C++.

```
// cast.cpp: new style of typecasting in C++
# include <iostream.h>
void main()
{
   int a;
   float b = 420.5;
   cout << "int(10.4) = " << int( 10.4 ) << endl;
   cout << "int(10.99) = " << int( 10.99 ) << endl;
   cout << "b = " << b << endl;
   a = int( b );
   cout << "a = int(b) = " << a << endl;
   b = float( a ) + 1.5;
   cout << "b = float(a)+1.5 = " << b;
}
```

Run

```
int(10.4) = 10
int(10.99) = 10
b = 420.5
a = int(b) = 420
b = float(a)+1.5 = 421.5
```

2.17 Function Templates

Templates provide a mechanism for creating a single function possessing the capability of several functions, which differ only in their parameters and local variables data type. Such a function is called *function template*. It permits writing one source declaration that can produce multiple functions differing only in their data types. The general format of a template function is depicted in Figure 2.12. A function generated from a function template is known as *template function*, which is created by the compiler internally and is transparent to the user.

Keyword for declaring function template

name of the template data-type

Function parameters of type template, primitive or user-defined

```
template < class T1, class T2, ..>
ReturnType  FunctionName   ( Arguments of type T1 and T2, ... )
{
   // local variables of type T1, T2, or any other
   //  function body, operating on variables of type T1, T2
   //  and other variables
}
```

Figure 2.12:   Syntax of function template

The syntax of template function is similar to a normal function, except that it uses variables whose data types are not known until they are invoked. Such unknown data types (generic data types) are resolved by the compiler and are expanded to the respective data types (depending on the data type of actual parameters in a function call statement). A call to a template function is similar to that of a normal function. It can be called with arguments of any data-type. The complier will create functions internally without the user intervention, depending on the data types of the input parameters. The function template for finding the maximum of two numbers is shown below:

```
template <class T>
T max( T a, T b )
{
   if( a > b )
      return a;
   else
      return b;
}
```

The program `mswap.cpp` illustrates the need for function templates. It defines multiple `swap` functions for swapping the values of different data types.

```
// mswap.cpp: Multiple swap functions
#include <iostream.h>
void swap( char & x, char & y ) // pass by reference
{
    char t;  // temporary used in swapping
    t = x;
    x = y;
    y = t;
}
void swap( int & x, int  & y ) // pass by reference
{
    int t;   // temporary used in swapping
    t = x;
    x = y;
    y = t;
}
void swap( float & x, float & y ) // pass by reference
{
    float t; // temporary used in swapping
    t = x;
    x = y;
    y = t;
}
void main()
{
    char ch1, ch2;
    cout << "Enter two Characters <ch1, ch2>: ";
    cin >> ch1 >> ch2;
    swap( ch1, ch2 ); // compiler calls swap( char &a, char &b );
    cout << "On swapping <ch1, ch2>: " << ch1 << " " << ch2 << endl;
    int a, b;
    cout << "Enter two integers <a, b>: ";
    cin >> a >> b;
    swap( a, b );  // compiler calls swap( int &a, int &b );
    cout << "On swapping <a, b>: " << a << " " << b << endl;
    float c, d;
    cout << "Enter two floats <c, d>: ";
    cin >> c >> d;
    swap( c, d );  // compiler calls swap( float &a, float &b );
    cout << "On swapping <c, d>: " << c << " " << d;
}
```

Run

```
Enter two Characters <ch1, ch2>: R K
On swapping <ch1, ch2>: K R
Enter two integers <a, b>: 5 10
On swapping <a, b>: 10 5
Enter two floats <c, d>: 20.5 99.5
On swapping <c, d>: 99.5 20.5
```

The above program has three swap functions

```
        void swap( char & x, char  & y );
```

```
        void swap( int & x, int  & y );
        void swap( float & x, float & y );
```

whose logic for swapping is same. Such functions can be defined as template functions without redefining it for every data type. The program gswap.cpp makes all those functions as templates and
avoids the overhead of writing the same pattern of code again and again, operating on different data
types.

```
// gswap.cpp: generic function for swapping
#include <iostream.h>
template <class T>
void swap( T & x, T & y ) // by reference
{
   T t;  // temporary used in swapping, template variable
   t = x;
   x = y;
   y = t;
}
void main()
{
   char ch1, ch2;
   cout << "Enter two Characters <ch1, ch2>: ";
   cin >> ch1 >> ch2;
   swap( ch1, ch2 );//compiler creates and calls swap( char &a, char &b );
   cout << "On swapping <ch1, ch2>: " << ch1 << " " << ch2 << endl;
   int a, b;
   cout << "Enter two integers <a, b>: ";
   cin >> a >> b;
   swap( a, b );  // compiler creates and calls swap( int &x, int &y );
   cout << "On swapping <a, b>: " << a << " " << b << endl;
   float c, d;
   cout << "Enter two floats <c, d>: ";
   cin >> c >> d;
   swap( c, d );  // compiler creates and calls swap(float &x, float &y );
   cout << "On swapping <c, d>: " << c << " " << d;
}
```

Run

```
Enter two Characters <ch1, ch2>: R K
On swapping <ch1, ch2>: K R
Enter two integers <a, b>: 5 10
On swapping <a, b>: 10 5
Enter two floats <c, d>: 20.5 99.5
On swapping <c, d>: 99.5 20.5
```

In main(), when the compiler encounters the statement

```
        swap( ch1, ch2 );
```

calling the swap template function with char type variables, it creates an internal function of type

```
        swap( char &a, char &b );
```

The compiler automatically identifies the data type of the arguments passed to the template function,
creates a new function, and makes an appropriate call. The process of compiling a template function is

totally invisible to the user. Similarly, the compiler translates the following calls

```
swap( a, b );  // compiler creates swap( int &x, int &y );
swap( c, d );  // compiler creates swap( float &x, float &y );
```

into appropriate functions (if necessary), and calls them based on their input parameter data types.

Template Function Overloading

A template function can be overloaded in two ways - (i) by other functions of its name or (ii) by other template functions of the same name. Overloading resolution for functions and template functions can be done in the following three steps:

- If an exact match for the function is found, call it.
- If a function can be generated from a function template matching exactly, then call the generated function.
- If a function can be found by trying ordinary overloading resolution techniques then call it;
- If no match is found, report an error.

2.18   Runtime Memory Management

Whenever an array is defined, a specified amount of memory is set aside at compile time, which may not be utilized fully or may not be sufficient. If a situation arises in which the amount of memory required is unknown at compile time, the memory allocation can be performed during execution. Such a technique of allocating memory during runtime on demand is known as *dynamic memory allocation*.

C++ provides the following two special operators to perform memory management dynamically.

- `new` operator for dynamic memory allocation
- `delete` operator for dynamic memory deallocation

The memory management functions such as `malloc()`, `calloc()`, and `free()` in C, have been improved and evolved in C++ as the `new` and `delete` operators to accomplish dynamic memory allocation and deallocation respectively.

new Operator

The `new` operator offers dynamic storage allocation similar to the standard library function `malloc`. It is particularly designed keeping OOP in mind and throws an exception if memory allocation fails. The general format of the `new` operator is shown in Figure 2.13.

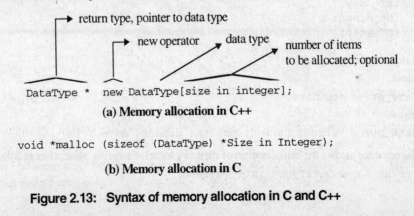

(a) **Memory allocation in C++**

```
void *malloc (sizeof (DataType) *Size in Integer);
```

(b) **Memory allocation in C**

Figure 2.13:   Syntax of memory allocation in C and C++

The C++ statement

```
PtrVar = new DataType[ IntegerSize ];
```

is equivalent to C's

```
PtrVar = (DataType *) malloc( sizeof( DataType ) * IntegerSize );
```

The operator new allocates a specified amount of memory during runtime and returns a pointer to that memory location. It computes the size of the memory to be allocated by

```
sizeof( DataType ) * IntegerSize
```

where DataType can be a standard data type or a user defined data type. IntegerSize can be an integer expression, which specifies the number of elements in the array. The new operator returns NULL, if memory allocation is unsuccessful.

The following examples illustrate the allocation of memory to various data types.

1.      ```
        int *a;
        a = new int[ 100 ];
        ```

is equivalent to C's

```
a = (int *) malloc( sizeof( int ) * 100 );
```

It creates a memory space for an array of 100 integers. a[0] will refer to the first element, a[1] to the second element, and so on

2.      ```
        float *b;
        b = new float[ size ];      // size is integer variable
        ```

is equivalent to

```
b = (float *) malloc( sizeof( float ) * size );
```

3.      ```
        double *d;
        d = new double[ size ];     // size is integer variable
        ```

is equivalent to

```
d = (double *) malloc( sizeof( double ) * size );
```

4.      ```
        char *city;
        city = new char[ city_name_size ]; // city_name_size is int variable
        ```

is equivalent to

```
city = (char *) malloc( sizeof( char ) * city_name_size );
```

5.      ```
        struct date
        {                       //specifies a structure
            int  day;
            int month;
            int year;
        };
        date *date_ptr;
        ```

The statement

```
date_ptr = new date;
```

is equivalent to

```
date_ptr = (struct date *) malloc( sizeof( date ) );
```

The new operator allows the initialization of memory locations during allocation as follows:

```
PtrVar = new DataType( init_value );
```
```

where `init_value` specifies the value to be initialized to a dynamically created element. Note that, `DataType` is optional. It is illustrated by the following examples:

```
int *a = new( 100 );
float *rate = new( 5.5 );
```

The first statement creates a memory for an integer and initializes it with 100 and the second statement creates a memory location for float and initializes it with 5.5.

`delete` Operator

The `new` operator's counterpart, `delete`, ensures the safe and efficient use of memory. This operator is used to return the memory allocated by the `new` operator back to the memory pool. Memory thus released, will be reused by other parts of the program. Although, the memory allocated is returned automatically to the system, when the program terminates, it is safer to use this operator explicitly within the pointer. This is absolutely necessary in situations where local variables pointing to the memory get destroyed when the function terminates, leaving memory inaccessible to the rest of the program. The syntax of the `delete` operator is shown in Figure 2.14.

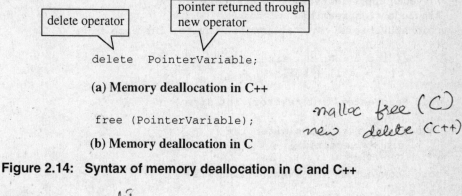

delete operator

pointer returned through new operator

```
delete    PointerVariable;
```

(a) Memory deallocation in C++

```
free (PointerVariable);
```

malloc free (C)
new delete (C++)

(b) Memory deallocation in C

Figure 2.14:   Syntax of memory deallocation in C and C++

The C++ statement   _seperates_ .

```
delete PtrVar;
```

is equivalent to C's

```
free( PtrVar );
```

where `PtrVar` holds the pointer returned by the memory allocation functions such as `new` operator and `malloc()` function. The memory allocated using the `new` operator or `malloc()` function should be released by the `delete` operator and `free()` function respectively.

It should be noted that, by deallocating the memory, the pointer variable does not get deleted and the address value stored in it does not change. However, this **address** becomes invalid, as the returned memory will be used up for storing entirely different data.

The following examples illustrate the use of the `delete` **operator** in releasing memory allocated in the earlier memory allocation examples.

1.   `delete a;`

is equivalent to C's

```
free( (int *) a );
```

2.   delete b;
is equivalent to
       free((float *) b);

3.   delete d;
is equivalent to
       free((double *) d);

4.   delete city;
is equivalent to
       free((char *) city);

5.   delete date_ptr;
is equivalent to
       free((struct date *) date_ptr);

The program `vector.cpp` illustrates the concept of dynamic allocation and deallocation using new and `delete` operators.

```cpp
// vector.cpp: addition of two vectors
#include <iostream.h>
void AddVectors( int *a, int *b, int *c, int size )
{
   for( int i = 0; i < size; i++ )
     c[i] = a[i] + b[i];
}
void ReadVector( int *vector, int size )
{
   for( int i = 0; i < size; i++ )
     cin >> vector[i];
}
void ShowVector( int *vector, int size )
{
   for( int i = 0; i < size; i++ )
     cout << vector[i] << " ";
}
void main()
{
   int vec_size;
   int *x, *y, *z;
   cout << "Enter Size of Vector: ";
   cin >> vec_size;
   // allocate memory for all the three vectors
   x = new int[ vec_size ];   // x becomes array of size vec_size
   y = new int[ vec_size ];   // y becomes array of size vec_size
   z = new int[ vec_size ];   // z becomes array of size vec_size
   cout << "Enter elements of vector x: ";
   ReadVector( x, vec_size );
   cout << "Enter elements of vector y: ";
   ReadVector( y, vec_size );
   AddVectors( x, y, z, vec_size ); // z = x+y
```

```
    cout << "Summation Vector z = x + y: ";
    ShowVector( z, vec_size );
    // free memory allocated to all the three vectors
    delete x;    // memory allocated to x is released
    delete y;    // memory allocated to y is released
    delete z;    // memory allocated to z is released
}
```

Run

```
Enter Size of Vector: 5
Enter elements of vector x: 1 2 3 4 5
Enter elements of vector y: 2 3 1 0 4
Summation Vector z = x + y: 3 5 4 4 9
```

In main(), the following statements

```
    x = new int[ vec_size ];    // x becomes array of size vec_size
    y = new int[ vec_size ];    // y becomes array of size vec_size
    z = new int[ vec_size ];    // z becomes array of size vec_size
```

allocate memory of size vec_size (integer value read previously) to the integer pointer variables x, y, and z respectively. It is equivalent to defining an array of size vec_size statically but the size of the array must be known at compile time. This inflexibility of array definition is circumvented by using dynamic allocation known as programmer-controlled memory management. The following statements

```
    delete x;    // memory allocated to x is released
    delete y;    // memory allocated to y is released
    delete z;    // memory allocated to z is released
```

release the memory of size vec_size (integer value read previously) allocated to the integer pointer variables x, y, and z respectively. An array defined statically is released automatically by the system whenever the array goes out of scope. But dynamically allocated arrays must be explicitly released by the delete operator.

Comments

Most of the concepts introduced in this chapter serve as a quick introduction to enhancements made to C++ language apart from another notable enhancement that is object-oriented programming support. All the material covered in this chapter are discussed in detail in later relevant chapters. This chapter is mainly aimed at those who are familiar with C and want a quick introduction to C++ language. It allows them to extrapolate from the material in this chapter and similarly from the next chapter (*C++ at a Glance*) to their own programming needs. Beginners should supplement it by writing small, similar programs of their own. Both groups can use this and the next chapter as a frame to hang on to the more detailed descriptions that begin in Chapter 4.

Review Questions

2.1 What are the enhancements added to C++ apart from the object-oriented features ?

2.2 Compare the traditional beginner's Hello World program written in C and C++.

2.3 List the compilers supporting C++. Explain their compilation features.

2.4 In C/C++, why is the main() function popularly called as the driver function ?

2.5 Enumerate the important features of stream-based I/O and provide a comparative analysis with its

C counterpart statements such as `scanf()` and `printf()`.

2.6 Write an interactive program for computing the roots of a quadratic equation by handling all possible cases. Use streams to perform I/O operations.

2.7 What are the benefits of commenting a program ? Develop a program to illustrate how commenting helps in writing a program, which can be understood by others easily ?

2.8 Why are variables defined with `const` called as read-only variables ? What are its benefits when compared to macros ?

2.9 Justify the need of the scope resolution operator for accessing global variables.

2.10 What are the benefits of defining variables at the point of use ? In the following statement:
```
for( int i = 0; i < 10; i++ )
    xxx;
```
is the variable `i` visible after the termination of loop ?

2.11 What are the differences between reference variables and normal variables ? Why cannot a constant value be initialized to variables of reference type ?

2.12 What are the benefits of strict type checking ? Explain with suitable examples.

2.13 What are the different types of parameter passing methods supported in C++ ? Provide a comparative analysis between pass-by-pointer and pass-by-reference methods.

2.14 What is the difference between inline functions and normal functions ? Write an interactive program with an inline function for finding the maximum value of two numbers.

2.15 What is function overloading ? Explain how it helps in writing well thought-out programs.

2.16 What is name mangling and explain its need ? Is this transparent to the user ?

2.17 Write an interactive program for swapping integer, real, and character type variables without using function overloading. Write the same program by using function overloading features and compare the same with its C counterpart.

2.18 Explain the need of default arguments. Write an interactive program for drawing chart of marks scored by a student in different subjects. A default arguments function has to support statements such as:
```
DrawChart( 50 );
DrawChart( 60, '*' );
DrawChart( 34, '?' );
```
By default, `DrawChart()` draws chart by using star symbols.

2.19 What are the improvements made to the `struct` construct in C++ ? What are the benefits of having functions as a part of the structure declaration. Write an interactive program for processing a student record using structures. All functions manipulating structure variable members must be members of that structure.

2.20 Explain the need for type conversion with suitable examples.

2.21 What are function templates ? What are the differences between function template and template function? Write a program to sort numbers using function templates.

2.22 Explain the constructs supported by C++ for runtime memory management. Write an interactive program processing student's results using C++'s memory management operators.

2.23 Write a program for creating variables of the `date` structure dynamically. Can a pointer variable be used to store data in a memory location pointed to by them, with the binding pointer to a specific location.

3

C++ at a Glance

3.1 Introduction

The C++ language evolved as a result of extensions and enhancements to C. It has efficient memory management techniques, provisions for building new concepts, and a new style of program analysis and design. The reason for retaining C as a subset is its popularity among programmers, and moreover, millions of lines of code already written in C can be directly moved to C++ without rewriting. The other advantages are: the syntax and structure of many statements of C closely resemble the actual operation on the computer's internal registers and allow to produce fast executable code.

The most interesting features of C++ are those which support a new style of programming known as object-oriented programming. It emphasizes on data decomposition rather than algorithm decomposition. OOP is generally useful for any kind of application, but it is particularly suited for interactive computer graphics, simulations, databases, artificial intelligence, high-performance computing, and system programming applications. This chapter presents the first impression of C++ with its features of object-oriented programming.

C++ as an object oriented programming language supports modular programming and enables easy maintainability. The most prominent features of C++ that provide a foundation for data abstraction and object-oriented programming are the following:

- Data Encapsulation and Abstraction: Classes
- Inheritance: Derived Class
- Polymorphism: Operator Overloading
- Friend Functions
- Polymorphism: Virtual Functions
- Generic Classes: Class Templates
- Exception Handling
- Streams Computation

3.2 Data Encapsulation and Abstraction—Classes

Data abstraction is the ability to create user-defined data types for modeling real world objects using built-in data types and a set of permitted operators. Encapsulation is achieved by using the `class`, which combines data and functions that operate on the data. Data hiding is achieved by restricting the members of classes as private or protected.

The object oriented programming technique involves the representation of real world problems in terms of objects. C++ provides a new data structure called *class* whose instance is called *object*. A class consists of procedures or methods and data variables.

Class is the basic construct for creating user-defined data types called abstract data types; in a way it supports encapsulation. Encapsulation allows to combine data and functions that operates on them into a single unit. One or more classes grouped together constitute a program. The program counter1.cpp illustrates various concepts such as classes and objects, encapsulation, and declaration of abstract data types. The program creates a class with one data member and instantiates two objects to demonstrate the features of classes. It simulates the behavior of an upward counter.

```cpp
// counter1.cpp: counter class having upward counting capability
#include <iostream.h>
class counter
{
   private:
      int value;              // counter value
   public:
      counter()               // No argument constructor
      {
         value = 0;           // initialize counter value to zero
      }
      counter( int val )      // Constructor with one argument
      {
         value = val;         // initialize counter value
      }
      ~counter()              // destructor
      {
         cout << "object destroyed" << endl;
      }
      int GetCounter()        // counter Access
      {
         return value;
      }
      void up()   // increment counter
      {
         value = value + 1;
      }
};
void main()
{
   counter counter1;        // calls no argument constructor
   counter counter2 = 1;    // calls one argument constructor
   cout << "counter1 = " << counter1.GetCounter() << endl;
   cout << "counter2 = " << counter2.GetCounter() << endl;
   // update counters, increment
   counter1.up();
   counter2.up();
   cout << "counter1 = " << counter1.GetCounter() << endl;
   cout << "counter2 = " << counter2.GetCounter() << endl;
}
```

Run

```
counter1 = 0
counter2 = 1
counter1 = 1
```

```
counter2 = 2
object destroyed
object destroyed
```

The following section describes the various parts of the program:

♦ **Class,** encloses the data and functions into a single unit. The name of the class is `counter`. The class `counter` can be used as the user-defined data type for defining its variables called objects.

♦ **Data Members,** describe the data in the abstract data types. The data member in the class counter is `value`. A class can have any number of data members.

♦ **Member Functions,** define the permissible operations of the data type (member variables). The class `counter` has the following member functions:

1. `counter()`   : constructor with no argument
2. `counter(int  val)`   : constructor with one argument
3. `~counter()`   : destructor
4. `GetCounter()`   : counter value access interface
5. `up()`   : increment counter

♦ **Constructor,** is a member function having the same name as that of its class and is executed automatically when the class is instantiated (object is created). It is used generally to initialize object data members and allocate the necessary resources to them. The class `counter` has two constructors to initialize the data members of the class.

```
counter()
counter(int)
```

Similar to normal functions, member functions of a class including constructors (but not destructor) differ in their specifications (data types of argument or number of arguments); this feature is called function overloading. The compiler will identify a suitable constructor, whose formal parameters matches with those actual parameters passed to it at the time of creation of objects.

♦ **Destructor,** is a member function having the character ~ (tilde) followed by a function name, which is same as the class name (i.e., `~classname()`) and is invoked automatically when class's object goes out of scope (i.e., the object is no longer needed). It is generally used to reclaim all the resources allocated to the object. The above program has the destructor named `~counter()` in the class `counter`. It is automatically invoked whenever objects go out of scope (when program terminates in the above case). A class can have at the most one destructor.

♦ **Access Specifiers,** control the visibility status of the members of a class. Access specifiers in the above program are the keywords `private` and `public`. The members of the class `counter` declared following the keyword `private` are accessible to only members of its own class. Thus, hiding the data inside a class, so that it is not accessed mistakenly by any function outside the class. Whereas, the members of the class `counter` declared following the keyword `public` are accessible from objects of the class in addition to their own class members.

In the above program, the data member `value` is declared as `private` and member functions are declared as `public`. By default, these are `private`. The explicit declaration `public` means that these functions can be accessed from outside the class.

♦ **Object,** is an instance of a class. The objects created in the program are `counter1` and `counter2` which are the instances of the class `counter`. The first object's data member `value` is initialized using zero-argument constructor, whereas the second object is initialized using one-argument constructor.

The pictorial representation of the class `counter` and invocation of its members by various statements in `main()` is shown in the Figure 3.1a.

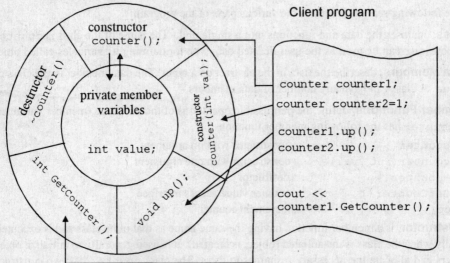

Instances of the class counter

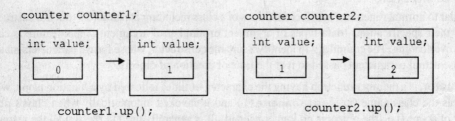

(a) Counter object and member access

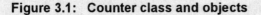

counter1.up();   counter2.up();

(b) Counter objects status

Figure 3.1: Counter class and objects

In `main()`, the statements

```
counter counter1;       // calls no argument constructor
counter counter2 = 1;   // calls 1 argument constructor
```

create two objects called `counter1` and `counter2` of the class `counter`. The first statement invokes no-argument constructor, `counter()` automatically, which initializes its data member `value` to zero, whereas the second statement invokes a single argument constructor, `counter(int)` automatically and initializes its data member `value` to 1 (as mentioned in the statement). The statements

```
counter1.up();
counter2.up();
```

invoke member function `up()` defined in the class `counter` and increment the data member `value` by one. Thus, the two objects `counter1` and `counter2` of the class `counter` have different data values as shown in Figure 3.1b. Each object of the counter class is stored in a separate area in memory.

Classes are syntactically, an extension of structures. The difference is that, all the members of structures are public by default, whereas members of classes are private by default. Class follows the principle of *all the information about a module should be private to the module unless it is specifically declared public*.

Member Functions

The data members of a class must be declared within the body of a class, whereas the member functions of a class can be defined in one of the following ways:

- Inside the class body
- .Outside the class body

The syntax of a member function definition changes depending on whether it is defined inside or outside the class specification. However, irrespective of the location of its definition (inside or outside the class body), the member function must perform the same operation. Therefore, the code inside the function body would be identical in both the cases. The compiler treats member functions defined inside a class as *inline* functions, whereas those defined outside a class are not treated as inline functions. The program `stdclass.cpp` illustrates the mechanism of defining member functions outside the body of the class.

```
// stdclass.cpp: member functions defined outside a body of the class
#include <iostream.h>
#include <string.h>
class student
{
   private:
       int roll_no;           // roll number
       char name[ 20 ];       // name of a student
   public:
       void setdata( int roll_no_in, char *name_in );
       void outdata();
};
// initializing data members
void student::setdata( int roll_no_in, char *name_in )
{
   roll_no = roll_no_in;
   strcpy( name, name_in );
}
// display data members on the console screen
void student::outdata()
{
   cout << "Roll No = " << roll_no << endl;
   cout << "Name = " << name << endl;
}
void main()
{
   student s1;     // first object/variable of class student
   student s2;     // second object/variable of class student
   s1.setdata( 1, "Tejaswi" );    // object s1 calls member function setdata
   s2.setdata( 10, "Rajkumar" ); // calls member function setdata
```

```
    cout << "Student details..." << endl;
    s1.outdata();      // object s1 calls member function outdata
    s2.outdata();      // object s2 calls member function outdata
}
```

Run

```
Student details...
Roll No = 1
Name = Tejaswi
Roll No = 10
Name = Rajkumar
```

In the class student, the prototype of member functions setdata and outdata are declared within the body of the class and they are defined outside the body of the class. In the declarator

        void student::outdata()

student:: indicates that the function outdata(), belongs to the class student and it is a member function of the class student.

3.3 Inheritance—Derived Classes

Inheritance is a technique of organizing information in the hierarchical form. It is similar to a child inheriting the features such as beauty of the mother and intelligence of the father. It is an important feature of object oriented programming that allows to extend and reuse existing code without requiring to rewrite it from scratch. Inheritance involves derivation of new classes from the existing ones, thus enabling the creation of a hierarchy of classes, similar to the concepts of class and subclass in the real world. A new class created using an existing class is called the derived class. This process is called inheritance. The derived class inherits the members - both data and functions of the base class. It can also modify or add to the members of a base class. Inheritance allows a hierarchy of classes to be derived.

Derived classes, inherit data members and member functions from their base classes, and can be enhanced by adding other data members and member functions.

Recall that the program counter1.cpp discussed above, uses the class counter as a general purpose counter variable. A counter could be incremented or decremented. The counter class can be extended to support downward counting. It can be achieved by either modifying the counter class or by deriving a new class called NewCounter from the counter class. The program counter2.cpp is an extended version of the previous program and has two classes, one, counter as a base class and two, NewCounter as a derived class. The private members of a base class cannot be inherited.

C++ supports another access specifier called protected. Its access privileges are similar to private except that they are accessible to its derived classes. Protected access privilege is used when members in base class's section are to be treated as *private* and they must be inheritable by a derived class. The public members of the base class are accessible to the derived class, but the private members of the base class are not. However, the *protected members* of the base class are accessible to the derived class, but they are private to all other classes.

```cpp
// counter2.cpp: new counter having upward and downward counting capability
#include <iostream.h>
class counter
{
    protected:                  // Note: it is private in COUNTER1.CPP
        int value;              // counter value
    public:
        counter()               // No argument constructor
        {
            value = 0;          // initialize counter value to zero
        }
        counter( int val )      // Constructor with one argument
        {
            value = val;        // initialize counter value
        }
        int GetCounter()        // counter Access
        {
            return value;
        }
        void up()       // increment counter
        {
            value = value + 1;
        }
};
// NewCounter is derived from the old class counter publically
class NewCounter: public counter
{
    public:
        NewCounter(): counter()
        {}
        NewCounter( int val ) : counter( val )
        {}
        void down()     // decrement counter
        {
            value = value - 1;   // decrement counter
        }
};
void main()
{
    NewCounter counter1;        // calls no argument constructor
    NewCounter counter2 = 1;    // calls 1 argument constructor
    cout << "counter1 initially = " << counter1.GetCounter() << endl;
    cout << "counter2 initially = " << counter2.GetCounter() << endl;
    // increment counter
    counter1.up();
    counter2.up();
    cout << "counter1 on increment = " << counter1.GetCounter() << endl;
    cout << "counter2 on increment = " << counter2.GetCounter() << endl;
    // decrement counter
    counter1.down();
```

```
counter2.down();
cout << "counter1 on decrement = " << counter1.GetCounter() << endl;
cout << "counter2 on decrement = " << counter2.GetCounter();
}
```

Run

```
counter1 initially = 0
counter2 initially = 1
counter1 on increment = 1
counter2 on increment = 2
counter1 on decrement = 0
counter2 on decrement = 1
```

In the above program, the NewCounter class has its own features to perform counter decrement by using the member functions of the counter. The statement

```
class NewCounter: public counter
```

derives a new class NewCounter known as derived class from the base class counter. The base class counter is publicly inherited by the derived class NewCounter. Hence, the members of counter class that are protected become protected and public become public in the derived class NewCounter. The NewCounter class can treat all the members of the counter class, as though they belong to it.

When an object of the derived class is created, one of the constructors of the base class must be executed before a constructor of the derived class is executed. In the case of destructors, the body of the derived class destructor is executed first followed by that of the base class. The specification of the constructors in the following statements

```
NewCounter(): counter()
NewCounter( int val ) : counter( val )
```

indicate as to which one of the constructors in the base class has to be selected while creating objects of the derived class. If no explicit specification of the base class constructor is made in the derived class constructor, the compiler will select the no-argument constructor of the base class by default as indicated in Figure 3.2.

In main(), the statements

```
NewCounter counter1;        // calls no argument constructor
NewCounter counter2 = 1;    // calls 1 argument constructor
```

create two objects called counter1 and counter2 of the NewCounter class. The first statement invokes the no-argument (default) constructor NewCounter() automatically, which in turn calls the base class constructor counter() to initialize the data member value to zero. Whereas, the second statement invokes the one-argument constructor NewCounter(int) automatically, which in turn calls the base class constructor counter(int) to initialize the data member value to 1 (as mentioned in the statement). Derived class can also initialize its own data members or base class data members explicitly.

The statements

```
counter1.up();
counter2.up();
```

call member function up() of the base class to increment the counter value by one. Whereas the statements

```
counter1.down();
counter2.down();
```

call member function down() of the derived class to decrement the counter value by one. C++ supports derivation of a class from more than one base class, which is called multiple inheritance. Some of the other forms of inheritance supported by C++ are hierarchical, multilevel, hybrid, and multipath.

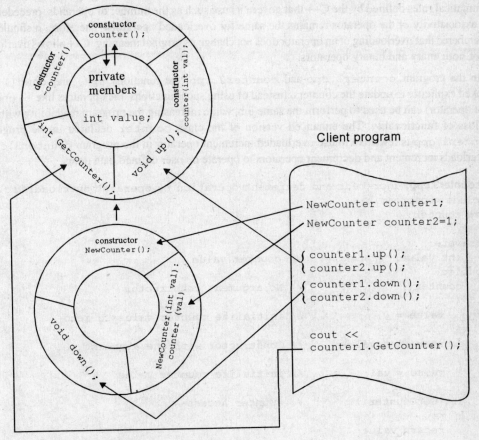

Instances of the class NewCounter

Figure 3.2: NewCounter class and inheritance

3.4 Polymorphism–Operator Overloading

Polymorphism allows a single name/operator to be associated with different operations depending on the type of data passed. In C++, it is realized by using function overloading, operator overloading, and dynamic binding. The operators such as +,-,*,/ etc., dealing with basic data types can be extended to work on user-defined data types by using the facility of operator overloading. Overloaded operators work with user-defined or basic-data types depending upon the type of operands. Operator overloading allows the user to give additional meaning to most operators so that it can be used with the user's own data types, thereby making the data-types easier to use.

Operator overloading, similar to function name overloading, helps to reduce the need for unusual function names, making code easier to understand. It also supports programmer-controlled automatic type conversion, which blend user defined data types, appear and work in the same way as fundamental data types provided by the C++ language.

Operator overloading extends the *semantics* of an operator without changing their *syntax*. The grammatical rules defined by the C++ that govern its use such as the number of operands, precedence, and associativity of the operator remains the same for overloaded operators. Therefore, it should be remembered that overloading of an operator does not change its original meaning. C++ allows overloading of both unary and binary operators.

In the program `counter1.cpp` and `counter2.cpp`, the functions `up()` and `down()` are invoked explicitly to update the counters. Instead of using such functions, the operators like ++ (increment operator) can be used to perform the same job, while increasing the program readability without the loss of functionality. The enhanced version of the class `counter` declared in the program `counter2.cpp` is rewritten to use overloaded increment operator in the program `counter3.cpp`. It overloads increment and decrement operators to operate on user defined data items.

```
// counter3.cpp: increment and decrement operation by operator overloading
#include <iostream.h>
class counter
{
    private:
        int value;                // counter value
    public:
        counter()                 // No argument constructor
        {
            value = 0;            // initialize counter value to zero
        }
        counter( int val )        // Constructor with one argument
        {
            value = val;          // initialize counter value
        }
        int GetCounter()          // counter Access
        {
            return value;
        }
        // overloading increment operator
        void operator++()         // increment counter
        {
            value = value + 1;
        }
        void operator --()        // decrement counter
        {
            value = value - 1;    // decrement counter
        }
};
void main()
{
    counter counter1;             // calls no argument constructor
```

```
counter counter2 = 1;    // calls 1 argument constructor
cout << "counter1 initially = " << counter1.GetCounter() << endl;
cout << "counter2 initially = " << counter2.GetCounter() << endl;
// increment counter
++counter1;
counter2++;
cout << "counter1 on increment = " << counter1.GetCounter() << endl;
cout << "counter2 on increment = " << counter2.GetCounter() << endl;
// decrement counter
--counter1;
counter2--;
cout << "counter1 on decrement = " << counter1.GetCounter() << endl;
cout << "counter2 on decrement = " << counter2.GetCounter();
}
```

Run

```
counter1 initially = 0
counter2 initially = 1
counter1 on increment = 1
counter2 on increment = 2
counter1 on decrement = 0
counter2 on decrement = 1
```

The word operator is a keyword. It is preceded by the return type void. The operator to be overloaded is immediately written after the keyword operator, followed by the void function symbol as operator++(). This declarator syntax informs the compiler to call this member function whenever the ++ operator is encountered, provided its operand is of type counter.

The statement in the class counter

```
void operator ++()       // increment counter
```

overloads the increment operator (++) to operate on the user defined data type. When the compiler encounters statements such as

```
++counter1;
counter2++;
```

it calls the overloaded operator function defined in the user-defined class (see Figure 3.3). The statement in the class counter

```
void operator--()        // decrement counter
```

overloads the decrement operator (--) to operate on objects of the user defined data type. When the compiler encounters statements such as

```
--counter1;
counter2--;
```

it calls the overloaded operator function defined in the user-defined class. It can be observed that the function body of an overloaded and a non-overloaded operator function is same; the only change is in the function prototype and method of calling. For instance, the statement in counter2.cpp

```
counter2.up();
```

can be replaced by a more readable equivalent statement:

```
counter2++;
```

in the above program.

Instances of the class `counter`

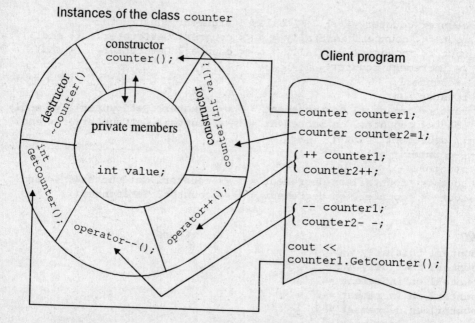

Figure 3.3: Unary operator overloading in counter class

The concept of unary operator overloading also applies equally to binary operators. Addition of two counters without using operator overloading can be performed by a statement such as

```
counter3 = counter1.AddCounter( counter2 );
```

It invokes the member function `AddCounter()` of `counter1` object's class. By overloading the + operator, the above clumsy and dense-looking expression can be represented in a readable and simplified form as:

```
counter3 = counter1 + counter2;
```

A detailed discussion on operator overloading can be found in the chapter on *Operator Overloading*.

3.5 Friend Functions

C++ provides the concept of a *friend class* whose member functions can access the private members of another class. A *friend function* accesses the private data variables of another class. The major difference between an ordinary class function and a friend function is that the ordinary function accesses the object that involves the member function, while a friend function requires objects to be passed by reference or value.

Friend functions play a very important role in operator overloading by providing the flexibility, which is denied by the member functions of a class. It allows overloading of stream operators (<< or >>) for stream computation on user defined data types. The only difference between the friend function and member function is that, the friend function requires all formal arguments to be specified explicitly, whereas the member function takes first formal argument implicitly and the remaining arguments (if any) explicitly. Friend functions can either be used with a unary or binary operator.

Similar to the built-in variables, the user-defined objects can also be read or output using the stream operators: insertion and extraction operators. In the case of the overloaded << operator, the *ostream &* is taken as the first argument of a friend function of a class. The return value of this friend function is of type *ostream &*. Similarly, for overloading the >> operator, the *istream &* is taken as the first argument of a friend function of a class. The return value of this friend function is of type *istream &*. In both the cases, a reference to an object of the current class is taken as a second argument and after storing the result in its second object, its first argument, the istream object would be returned.

The program `counter4.cpp` illustrates the flexibility of overloading the output stream operators and their usage with the user defined objects.

```cpp
// counter4.cpp: overloading stream operator cout << value
#include <iostream.h>
class counter
{
   private:
      int value;              // counter value
   public:
      counter()               // No argument constructor
      {
         value = 0;           // initialize counter value to zero
      }
      counter( int val )      // Constructor with one argument
      {
         value = val;         // initialize counter value
      }
      int GetCounter()        // counter Access
      {
         return value;
      }
      // overloading increment operator
      void operator++()     // increment counter
      {
         value = value + 1;
      }
      // overloading decrement operator
      void operator --()      // decrement counter
      {
         value = value - 1;   // decrement counter
      }
      // overloading binary operator
      counter operator +( counter counter2 );
      friend ostream & operator << ( ostream & Out, counter & counter );
};
// operator function defined outside the class body, hence use :: operator
counter counter::operator +( counter counter2 )
{
   counter temp;
   // value belongs to counter1 and counter2.value is of counter2
   temp.value = value + counter2.value;
```

```
    return temp;
}
// it is just a friend function, it is not a member of counter classes
ostream & operator << ( ostream & Out, counter & counter )
{
    // display all internal data of counter class
    cout << counter.value;
    // return output stream Out for cascading purpose
    return Out;
}
void main()
{
    counter counter1;        // calls no argument constructor
    counter counter2 = 1 ;   // calls 1 argument constructor
    cout << "counter1 initially = " << counter1 << endl;
    cout << "counter2 initially = " << counter2 << endl;
    // increment counter
    ++counter1;
    counter2++;
    cout << "counter1 on increment = " << counter1 << endl;
    cout << "counter2 on increment = " << counter2 << endl;
    // decrement counter
    --counter1;
    counter2--;
    cout << "counter1 on decrement = " << counter1 << endl;
    cout << "counter2 on decrement = " << counter2 << endl;
    counter counter3;        // calls no argument constructor
    counter3 = counter1 + counter2;  // calls operator+(counter)
    cout << "counter3 = counter1+counter2 = " << counter3;
}
```

Run
```
counter1 initially = 0
counter2 initially = 1
counter1 on increment = 1
counter2 on increment = 2
counter1 on decrement = 0
counter2 on decrement = 1
counter3 = counter1+counter2 = 1
```

The contents of the object `counter1` can be displayed by using the statement

```
    cout << counter1;
```

instead of using the statement

```
    cout << counter.GetCounter();
```

This is the same as the use of the stream operator to display the contents of variables of standard data type. The operator member function

```
    ostream & operator << ( ostream & Out, counter & counter );
```

defined in the `counter` class displays the contents of the objects of the `counter` class (see Figure 3.4). The stream classes, *istream* and *ostream* are declared in the `iostream.h` header file.

The input stream operator can also be overloaded to read objects of the `counter` class, whose prototype can be:

```
istream & operator >> ( istream & In, counter & counter );
```

Note that C++ does not allow overloading of operators =, (), [], and -> as friend operator functions. however, they can be overloaded as member operator functions.

Instances of the class `counter`

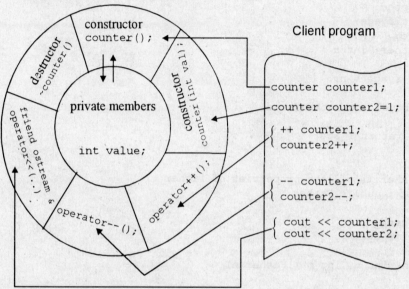

Figure 3.4: Operator overloading and friend functions

3.6 Polymorphism—Virtual Functions

In C++, runtime polymorphism is achieved using virtual functions. Virtual functions facilitate dynamic binding of functions to the appropriate objects. They are the means by which functions of the base class can be overridden by functions of the derived class.

Virtual functions allow derived class to redefine member functions inherited from a base class. General programs can then be written that are obvious to the classes of the objects they manipulate, through dynamic binding. The runtime system will choose the function appropriate to a particular class.

Virtual functions allow programmers to declare functions in a base class that can be redefined in each derived class. When a pointer to the base class is used with a base or derived class object, the object to which it points determines the activation of an appropriate member function call. That is, when a base class pointer points to the object of a derived class, the derived class's member function is selected and when it points to the object of the base class, the base class's member function is selected at runtime.

In C++, calls to virtual member functions are linked at runtime, as a result of which an object's behavior is determined only at runtime. This binding procedure is termed as *late binding*. The keyword `virtual` instructs the compiler that the calls to these member functions are to be linked only at run time. Thus, the choice of member function to be executed depends on the object of a class, the pointer is addressing at runtime. The program `virtual.cpp` illustrates the concept of virtual functions.

```cpp
// virtual.cpp: Binding pointer to base class's object to base or derived
// objects at runtime and invoking respective members if they are virtual
#include <iostream.h>
class Father
{
   protected:
      int f_age;
   public:
      Father( int n )
      {
         f_age = n;
      }
      virtual int GetAge(void)
      {
         return f_age;
      }
};
// Son inherits all the properties of father
class Son : public Father
{
   protected:
      int s_age;
   public:
      Son( int n, int m ):Father(n)
      {
         s_age = m;
      }
      int GetAge(void)
      {
         return s_age;
      }
};
void main()
{
   Father *basep;
   basep = new Father(45);    // pointer to father
   cout << "Father's Age: ";
   cout << basep->GetAge() << endl;  // calls father::GetAge
   delete basep;
   basep = new Son(45, 20);   // pointer to son
   cout << "Son's Age: ";
   cout << basep->GetAge() << endl;  // calls son::GetAge()
   delete basep;
}
```

Run

```
Father's Age: 45
Son's Age: 20
```

In the base class `Father`, the statement

    virtual int GetAge(void)

indicates that, an invocation of `GetAge()` through the pointer to an object must be resolved at runtime based on *which class's object the pointer is pointing to.* A pointer to the object of the base class can be made to point to its derived class.

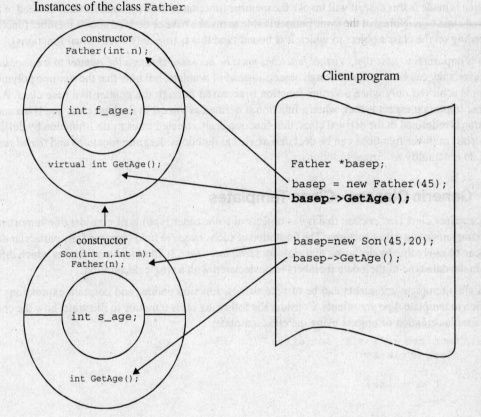

**Figure 3.5: Virtual functions and dynamic binding
(base pointer accessing derived objects)**

In `main()`, the statement

    Father *basep;

creates a pointer variable to the object of the base class `Father` and the statement

    basep = new Father(45);   // pointer to Father

creates an object of the class `Father` dynamically and assigns its address to the pointer `basep`. The statement

    cout << basep->GetAge() << endl; // calls father::GetAge

invokes the member function `GetAge()` of the `Father` class.

Similarly, the statement

```
basep = new Son(45, 20);    // pointer to son
```

creates an object of type class Son dynamically and assigns its address to the pointer basep. The statement

```
cout << basep->GetAge() << endl;  // calls Son::GetAge
```

invokes the member function GetAge() of the class Son (see Figure 3.5). If a call to a non-virtual function is made in this case, it will invoke the member function of the base class Father instead of the derived class Son. Note that the same pointer is able to invoke base or derived class's member function depending on the class's object to which it is bound (and this is true only with virtual functions).

It is important to note that, *virtual functions must be accessed through the pointer to a base class*. However, they can be accessed through objects instead of pointers, but note that the runtime polymorphism is achieved only when a virtual function is accessed through the pointer to a base class. Also another important aspect is that, when a function is defined as virtual in the base class and if the same function is redefined in the derived class, that function is also treated as virtual function by default. Only class member functions can be declared as virtual functions. Regular functions and *friend* functions do not qualify as virtual functions.

3.7 Generic Classes–Class Templates

The container class (i.e., a class that holds objects of some other type) is of considerable importance when implementing data structures. The limitation of such classes to hold objects of any particular data type can be overcome by declaring that class as a *template class*. It allows several classes which differ only in the data type of their data members to be declared with a single declaration.

A class template arguments can be of type strings, function names, and constant expressions, in addition to template type arguments. Consider the following class template to illustrate, how the compiler handles creation of objects using the class templates:

```
template <class T, int size>
class myclass
{
    T arr[size];
    ....
};
```

When objects of template class are created using the statement such as,

```
myclass <float,10> new1;
```

the compiler creates the following class:

```
class myclass
{
    float arr[10];
    ....
};
```

Again if a statement such as,

```
myclass <int, 5> new2;
```

is encountered for creating the object new2, the compiler creates the following class:

```
        class myclass
        {
            int arr[5];
            ....
        };
```

The template declaration of the `vector` class is illustrated in the program `vector.cpp`. It has a data member which is a pointer to an array of generic type `T`. The type `T` can be changed to `int`, `float`, etc., depending on the type of object to be created.

```
// vector.cpp: parameterized vector class
#include <iostream.h>
template <class T>
class vector
{
    T * v;            // changes to int *v, float *v, ..., etc.
    int size;         // size of vector v
  public:
    vector( int vector_size )
    {
       size = vector_size;
       v = new T[ vector_size ];  //e.g., v=new int[ size ],if T is int
    }
    ~vector()
    {
       delete v;
    }
    T & elem( int i )
    {
       if( i >= size )
          cout << endl << "Error: Out of Range";
       return v[i];
    }
    void show();
};
template <class T>
void vector<T>::show()
{
   for( int i = 0; i < size; i++ )
      cout << elem( i ) << ", ";
}
void main()
{
   int i;
   vector <int> int_vect( 5 );
   vector <float> float_vect( 4 );
   for( i = 0; i < 5; i++ )
      int_vect.elem( i ) = i + 1;
   for( i = 0; i < 4; i++ )
      float_vect.elem( i ) = float( i + 1.5 );
   cout << "Integer Vector: ";
   int_vect.show();
```

```
        cout << endl << "Floating Vector:
        float_vect.show();
}
```

Run

```
Integer Vector: 1, 2, 3, 4, 5,
Floating Vector: 1.5, 2.5, 3.5, 4.5,
```

Note that the class template specification is similar to an ordinary class specification except for the prefix `template <class T>` and the use of `T` in place of the data-type. This prefix informs the compiler that the class declaration following it is a template and uses `T` as a type name in the declaration. Thus, the class `vector` becomes a parameterized class with the type `T` as its parameter. The type `T` may be substituted by any data type including the user defined types.

In `main()`, the statements

```
        vector <int> int_vect( 5 );
        vector <float> float_vect( 4 );
```

create the vector objects `int_vect` and `float_vect` to hold vectors of type integer and floating point respectively. Once the objects of class template are created, their usage is same as the objects of non-template classes.

3.8 Exception Handling

An exceptional condition is an error situation that occurs during the normal flow of events and prevents the program from continuing correctly. C++ provides *exception handling mechanism* for handling error conditions that should not be ignored by a caller. Error condition such as division of a number by zero is difficult to predict; however, that can be handled by using exceptions.

C++ offers the following three constructs for handling exceptions:

- ◆ try
- ◆ throw
- ◆ catch

A block of code in which an exception can occur must be prefixed by the keyword `try`. This block of code is called *try-block*. It indicates that the program is prepared for testing the existence of exceptions. If an exception occurs, the program flow is interrupted; call to an exception handler is made if one exists, otherwise, `abort()` is invoked.

The exception handler is indicated by the `catch` keyword and it must be specified immediately after the *try-block*. The keyword `catch` can occur immediately after another `catch`. Each handler will only evaluate an exception that matches, or can be converted to, the type specified in its argument list. Every exception thrown by the program must be caught and processed by the exception handler. If the program fails to provide an exception handler for a thrown exception, the program will call the terminate function.

The mechanism suggests that error handling code must perform the following tasks.

- ◆ Detect the problem causing exception (Hit the exception)
- ◆ Inform that an error has occured (Throw the exception)
- ◆ Receive the error information (Catch the exception)
- ◆ Take corrective actions (Handle the exceptions)

The program `number.cpp` illustrates the mechanism of handling exceptions. It has the class `number` to store an integer number, the member function `read()` to read a number from the console and the member function `div()` to perform the division operation. It raises an exception if an attempt is made to divide a number by zero.

```cpp
// number.cpp: Divide Exceptions, divide by zero exceptions
#include <iostream.h>
class number
{
   private:
      int num;
   public:
      void read()
      {
         cin >> num;
      }
      class DIVIDE {};          // abstract class used in exceptions
      int div( number num2 )
      {
         if( num2.num == 0 )  // check for zero divisor if yes
            throw DIVIDE();    // raise exception
         else
            return num / num2.num;  // compute and return the result
      }
};
int main()
{
   number num1, num2;
   int result;
   cout << "Enter Number 1: ";
   num1.read();
   cout << "Enter Number 2: ";
   num2.read();
   // statements must be enclosed in try block if exception is to be raised
   try
   {
      cout << "trying division operation...";
      result = num1.div( num2 );
      cout << "succeeded" << endl;
   }
   catch( number::DIVIDE )    // exception handler block
   {
      // actions taken in response to exception
      cout << "failed" << endl;
      cout << "Exception: Divide-By-Zero";
      return 1;
   }
   // no exceptions, display result
   cout << "num1/num2 = " << result;
   return 0;
}
```

Run1

```
Enter Number 1: 10
Enter Number 2: 2
trying division operation...succeeded
num1/num2 = 5
```

Run2

```
Enter Number 1: 10
Enter Number 2: 0
trying division operation...failed
Exception: Divide-By-Zero
```

In `main()`, the try-block

```
try
{
    result = num1.div( num2 );
}
```

invokes the member function `div()` to perform the division operation using the function defined in the number class. (See Figure 3.6.)

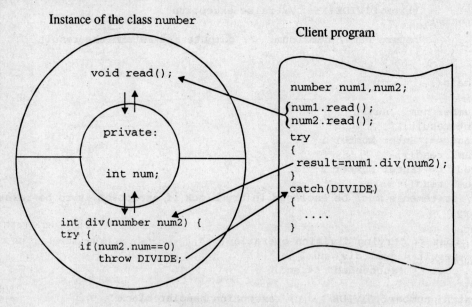

Figure 3.6:   Exception handling in number class

If any attempt is made to divide by zero, the following statement in `div()` member function

```
if( num2.num == 0 )   // check for zero division if yes
    throw DIVIDE();   // raise exception
```

detects the same and raises the exception by passing a nameless object of the `DIVIDE` class. The following block of code in `main()` immediately after the try-block,

```
catch( number::DIVIDE )
{
    cout << "Exception: Divide-By-Zero";
    return 1;
}
```

will catch the exception raised due to a malfunction (divide-by-zero) in the preceding try-block and executes its (catch-block) body. When an exception is raised and if the exception matches with any of the catch's exception type, its catch-block will be executed; otherwise, the program terminates. The execution skips the catch-block and proceeds with the normal operations when no exception is raised.

3.9 Streams Computation

Stream is a name given to the flow of data and it acts as an interface between the program and the input/output devices. Streams provide a consistent interface irrespective of the device with which they operate (see Figure 3.7). For instance, the output operation can be performed either on the console or file; the interface for accessing these devices is the same as shown in the following statements:

```
cout << "Hello World";
outfile << "Hello World";
```

The first statement prints the message Hello World to a standard output device whereas the second statement prints the same in a file to which the variable outfile is the file handler.

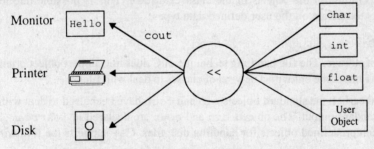

Figure 3.7: Consistent stream computation

Input-output operations in C++ are interpreted as a flow of stream of bytes. The program extracts bytes from the input stream when read operation is initiated and inserts bytes to the output stream when the output has to be performed.

C++ provides the following predefined stream objects (declared in iostream.h):

cin	Standard input (usually keyboard) corresponding to stdin in C.
cout	Standard output (usually screen) corresponding to stdout in C.
cerr	Standard error output (usually screen) corresponding to stderr in C.
clog	A fully-buffered version of cerr (no C equivalent).

The statement

```
cin >> m;
```

reads data from the console (keyboard) and stores it into the variable m. The statement

```
cout << "Hello World" << m;
```

prints the string message followed by the value stored in the variable m onto the console (monitor). The statement,

```
cerr << "Error: Hello World";
```

prints the string message onto the standard error device (usually monitor). The statement,

```
clog << "Log Errors";
```

prints the message to standard error device and displays when the buffer is flushed or \n (new line) character is encountered.

In C++, streams with operator overloading provide a mechanism for filtering. The standard stream operators << and >> do not know anything about the user-defined data types. They can be overloaded to operate on user-defined data items, which comprise operations on basic data items with standard stream operators. For example, consider the statements:

```
cout << counter1;

cin >> counter2;
```

The data-items counter1 and counter2, are the objects of the counter class (see friend.cpp program discussed above). The operators >> or << do not know anything about the objects counter1 and counter2. These are overloaded in the counter class as member functions, which process the attributes of counter objects as if they are basic data-items. Collectively, it appears as if the stream operators are operating on the objects of the class counter. This is possible due to overloading stream operators to operate on the user defined data types.

File Streams

A file is a unit of storage. The file handling technique of C does not support object oriented programming, hence C++ has come out with a new set of classes to deal with files.

As discussed earlier, the standard objects cin and cout have been used to deal with the standard input and the standard output. The objects cin and cout are declared in iostream.h header file. There are no such predefined objects for handling disk files. C++ supports the following classes for handling files:

- ifstream - for handling input files.
- ofstream - for handling output files.
- fstream - for handling files on which both input and output are done.

These classes are designed to manage the disk files and are declared in the fstream.h header file. To use file streams, include the following statement in the program:

```
#include <fstream.h>
```

The general pattern of accessing the data in a file is similar to the stdio.h functions. First, of course, the file has to be opened. In all the three classes, a file can be opened by giving a filename as the first parameter in the constructor itself. For example, the statement,

```
ifstream infile("test.txt");
```

will open the file test.txt for input operation.

The classes ifstream, ofstream, and fstream are derived from the classes istream, ostream, and iostream respectively to handle file streams and file input/output. The ifstream is meant for input files and ofstream for output files; the fstream is meant for both the input and output files.

File Input with ifstream Class

The class ifstream supports input operations. It contains the function open() with the default input mode. Inherits get(), getline(), read(), seekg(), and tellg() functions from istream. The program infile.cpp illustrates the use of ifstream class in file manipulation. It reads the contents of the file sample.in line by line and prints the same on the console.

```cpp
// infile.cpp: reads all the names stored in file 'sample.in'
#include <fstream.h>
#include <process.h>
#include <iostream.h>
void main()
{
    char buff[ 80 ];
    ifstream infile;  // input file
    infile.open("sample.in");  // open file
    if( infile.fail())    // open fail
    {
        cout << "Error: sample.in non-existent";
        exit( 1 );
    }
    while( !infile.eof() )  // until end-of-file do processing
    {
        infile.getline(buff, 80);  // read complete line from file
        cout << buff << endl;
    }
    infile.close();
}
```

Run

```
Rajkumar, C-DAC, India
Bjarne Stroustrup, AT & T, USA
Smrithi, Hyderabad, India
Tejaswi, Bangalore, India
```

The input file sample.in contains the following information before the execution of the program:

```
Rajkumar, C-DAC, India
Bjarne Stroustrup, AT & T, USA
Smrithi, Hyderabad, India
Tejaswi, Bangalore, India
```

In main(), the statement

```
        ifstream infile;                           // input file
```

creates the object infile and the statement

```
        infile.open("sample.in");   // open file
```

opens the file sample.in in the input mode. The statement

```
        if( infile.fail())            // open fail
```

checks for the status of file open operation. If file-open fails, it returns 1, otherwise 0. The statement

```
        while( !infile.eof() )        // until end-of-file, do processing
```

repeats the file reading operation until the end-of-file. And the statement

```
        infile.getline(buff, 80);   // read complete line from file
```

reads a single line from the file or maximum of 80 characters from that line and proceeds to the next line. The statement,

```
        infile.close();
```

closes the file and thus preventing it from further manipulation.

File Output with `ofstream` Class

The class `ofstream` supports output operations. It contains the function `open()` with output mode as default. It inherits `put()`, `seekp()`, `tellp()`, and `write()` functions from `ostream`. The program `outfile.cpp` illustrates the use of the class `ofstream` in the file manipulation. It reads information entered through the keyboard and writes the same into the output file `sample.out`.

```cpp
// outfile.cpp: writes all the input into the file 'sample.out'
#include <fstream.h>
#include <process.h>
#include <iostream.h>
#include <string.h>
void main()
{
   char buff[ 80 ];
   ofstream outfile; // output file
   outfile.open("sample.out");   // open in output mode
   if( outfile.fail())  // open fail
   {
      cout << "Error: sample.out unable to open";
      exit( 1 );
   }
   // loop until input = "end"
   while(1)
   {
      cin.getline(buff, 80);  // read a line from keyboard
      if( strcmp( buff, "end" ) == 0 )
         break;
      outfile << buff << endl;   // write to output file
   }
   outfile.close();
}
```

Run
```
OOP is good
C++ is OOP
C++ is good
end
```

Note: On execution, the file `sample.out` has the following:
```
OOP is good
C++ is OOP
C++ is good
```

In `main()`, the statement

        ofstream outfile;   // output file

creates the object `outfile` and the statement

        outfile.open("sample.out"); // open in output mode

opens the file `sample.out` in output mode. The statement

        if(outfile.fail())   // open fail

checks for the status of file open. If file open fails, it returns 1, otherwise 0. The statement

        outfile << buff << endl;   // write to output file

writes the `buff` contents and new-line character to the output file. The syntax of writing to the disk file resembles the writing to the console.

Guidelines

This chapter has given a glimpse on various prime features of C++. The fundamental construct of C++ i.e., *class* has been used to explain data encapsulation and abstraction features. More details on this can be found in chapters 10 and onwards. Other features discussed are inheritance, polymorphism, friend functions, virtual functions, class templates, exceptions handling, and streams computation.

Review Questions

3.1   State some reasons for C++ gaining popularity over other object-oriented programming languages.

3.2   Date consists of day, month, and year. Can this item be modeled as a class? What are the permissible operations this class needs to support ? Write a complete program having class declaration and the `main()` function to create its objects and manipulate them.

3.3   List the various object-oriented features supported by C++. Explain the constructs supported by C++ to implement them.

3.4   What is inheritance ? What are base and derived classes ? Give a suitable example for inheritance.

3.5   What are the different types of access specifiers supported by C++. Explain with a suitable example.

3.6   What is polymorphism ? Write a program to overload the + operator for manipulating objects of the `Distance` class.

3.7   What are friend functions ? Can they access members of a class directly ? Enhance the Date class such that it allows to read and display its objects using stream operators.

3.8   What are the differences between static binding and late binding ? Explain dynamic binding with a suitable example.

3.9   What are generic classes? Explain how they are useful. Write an interactive program having template-based Distance class. Create two objects: one of type integer and another of type floating-point.

3.10   What are exceptions ? What are the constructs supported by C++ to handle exceptions ?

3.11   What are streams ? Write an interactive program to copy a file to another file. Both source and destination files have to be processed as the objects of file-stream classes.

4

Data Types, Operators and Expressions

4.1 Introduction

Variables and constants are the fundamental elements of any programming language. Variables allow to name memory locations and use that name to access memory contents instead of accessing it through the physical address. Constants are those whose value never change during the execution of the program. Operators are used to specify the type of operation to be carried out on the variables and constants. Expressions combine the variables and constants to produce new values. The type of an object (variable/constant) determines the set of values it can represent and various operations that can be performed on it. When an expression has variables of different types, they need to be coerced (type converted) before their use. It can be either performed by the compiler implicitly, or by the user explicitly. C++ qualifiers allow promotion of any fundamental data type. The precedence and associativity of operators specify the order of evaluation of an expression to generate a valid output.

4.2 Character Set

The C++ character set consists of the upper and lower case alphabets, digits, special characters and white spaces. The alphabets and digits together constitute the alphanumeric set. The complete character set is shown in Table 4.1. The compiler ignores white spaces unless they are a part of a string constant. White spaces are used to separate words (and sometimes to increase the readability of a program), but cannot be embedded in the keywords and identifiers.

```
Alphabets:
    Uppercase:   A B ... Z
    Lowercase:   a b ... z
Digits
    0 1 2 3 4 5 6 7 8 9
Special Characters:
    ,   comma              <   opening angle bracket    >   closing angle bracket
    .   period             _   underscore               (   left parenthesis
    ;   semicolon          $   dollar sign              )   right parenthesis
    :   colon              %   percent sign             [   left bracket
    #   number sign        ?   question mark            ]   right bracket
    '   apostrophe         &   ampersand                {   left brace
    "   quotation mark     ^   caret                    }   right brace
    !   exclamation mark   *   asterisk                 /   slash
    |   vertical bar       -   minus sign               \   blackslash
    ~   tilde              +   plus sign
White space characters:
    blank space                 newline                  carriage return
    formfeed                    horizontal tab           vertical tab
```

Table 4.1:   C++ character set

4.3 Tokens, Identifiers, and Keywords

C++ program consists of many elements, which are identified by the compiler as *tokens*. Tokens supported in C++ can be categorized as keywords, variables, constants, special characters, and operators as shown in Figure 4.1.

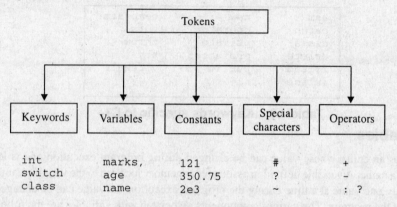

Figure 4.1:   C++ tokens

In a C++ program, every word can be either classified as an identifier, or a keyword. As the name suggests, identifiers are used to identify or name variables, symbolic constants, functions, and so on. Keywords have predefined meanings and cannot be changed by the user. The following rules need to be followed while naming identifiers:

♦ Identifier name is formed by using alphabets, digits, or underscore characters.
♦ Identifier names must begin with an alphabet or underscore character.
♦ The maximum number of characters used in forming an identifier must not exceed 31 characters. Some compilers allow the identifier length to be more than 31 characters, however, only the first 31 characters are significant.
♦ C++ is case sensitive (since the upper and lower case letters are treated differently). For instance, names such as `rate`, `Rate`, and `RATE` are treated as different identifiers. It is a general practice to use lower or mixed case letters to name variables and functions, and upper case to name symbolic constants.
♦ C++ has standard identifiers called *keywords*. Keywords are declared by the C++ language and have a predefined meaning. Hence, they cannot be used for any other purpose other than that specified by the C++ language. The keywords supported by C language are shown in Table 4.2 and they are also available in C++ (C++ is a superset of C).

auto	double	int	struct
break	else	long	switch
case	enum	register	typedef
char	extern	return	union
const	float	short	unsigned
continue	for	signed	void
default	goto	sizeof	volatile
do	if	static	while

Table 4.2:   Keywords common to C and C++

C++ Specific Keywords

There are several keywords specific to C++ which are listed in Table 4.3. These keywords primarily deal with classes, templates, and exception handling. For more details on keywords, refer to Appendix: *C++ Keywords and Operators*.

```
asm          new          template
catch        operator     this
class        private      throw
delete       protected    try
friend       public       virtual
inline
```

Table 4.3:   Keywords specific to C++

4.4 Variables

A variable is an entity whose value can be changed during program execution and is known to the program by a name. A variable definition associates a memory location to the variable name. A variable can hold only one value at a time during the program execution. Its value can be changed during the execution of the program. The various components associated with variables are the following:

- Data type - `char`, `int`, `float`, `date` (user defined), etc.
- Variable name - User view
- Binding address - Machine view
- Value - data stored in memory location

The relation among the above components is shown in Figure 4.2. In the statement

```
    f = 1.8 * c + 32.
```

the symbols f and c are variables.

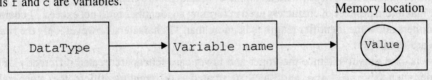

Figure 4.2:   Components of variables

Variable Names

Variable names are identifiers used to name variables. They are the symbolic names assigned to the memory locations. A variable name consists of a sequence of letters and digits, the first one being a letter. The rules that apply to identifiers (given above), also apply to variable names. The following are some valid variable names:

```
i                sum          MAX          min
class_mark       student_name emp_num      fact_recur
classMark        StudentName  rank1 _x1    _num
```

The following are some invalid variable names (with reasons given along side):

a's	illegal character(')
fact recur	blank not allowed
class-mark	illegal character(-)
5root	first character should be a letter
student,rec	comma not allowed

4.5 Data Types and Sizes

C++ supports a wide variety of data types and the programmer can select the type appropriate to the needs of the application. However, storage representation and machine instructions to manipulate each data type differ from machine to machine, although C++ instructions are identical on all machines. C++ supports the following classes of data types:

- Primary (fundamental) data types
- Derived data types
- User-defined data types

The primary data types and their extensions is the subject of this chapter. Derived data types such as arrays and pointers, and user defined data types such as structures and classes are discussed in the later chapters.

C++ language supports the following basic data types:

char	a single byte that can hold one character.
int	an integer.
float	a single precision floating point number.
double	a double precision floating point number.

Further, applying qualifiers to the above basic types yields additional types. A qualifier alters the characteristics such as the size or sign of the data types. The qualifiers that alter the size are short and long. These qualifiers are applicable to integers, and yield two more types:

short int	Integer represented by 16 bits irrespective of machine type.
long int	Integer represented 32 bits irrespective of machine type.

The exact sizes of these data types depend on the compiler as shown in Table 4.4.

Data Type	Data Size (bytes)	Minimum value	Maximum value
char	1	-128	127
short	2	-327868	327867
int	2 (16 bit compiler)	-327868	327867
	4 (32 bit compiler)	-2147483648	2147483647
long	4	-2147483648	2147483647
float	4	-3.4E-38	3.4E+38
double	8	-1.7E-308	1.7E+308
long double	10	-3.4E-4932	1.1E+4932

Table 4.4: Data types and their size

The qualifier long can also be used along with the double precision floating point type:

long double — an extended precision floating point number.

The sign qualifiers are signed and unsigned. The sign qualifiers are applicable to the integer data types (int, short int, and long int) resulting in six additional data types given below:

```
signed short int
unsigned short int
signed int
unsigned int
signed long int
unsigned long int
```

Qualifiers are also applicable to the char data type as follows:

```
signed char
unsigned char
```

Size qualifiers (short and long) cannot be applied to the char and float data types and sign qualifiers (signed and unsigned) cannot be applied to float, double, and long double.

4.6 Variable Definition

A variable must be defined before using it in a program. It reserves memory required for data storage and associates it with a symbolic name. The syntax for defining variables is shown in Figure 4.3. The variable name can be any valid C++ identifier except the reserved words. The data type can be any primitive or user-defined data type such as int, float, double, and so on.

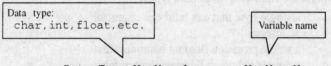

Figure 4.3: Syntax of variable definition

The following are some of the valid variable definition statements:

```
int a;              // a is an integer variable
int b, c, d;        // b, c, and d are valid integer variables
float total, length; // total and length are valid real variables
double sum1, product;  // sum1 and product are valid double variables
```

Variables can be defined at the point of their usage as follows:

```
int c;
cout << "Hello World";
int d = 10;
for( int i = 0; i < 10; i++ )
    cout << i;
```

Note that the variables d and i are defined at the point of their usage.

4.7 Variable Initialization

In C++, a variable can be assigned with a value during its definition, or during the execution of a program. The assignment operator (=) is used in both the cases. A variable can be initialized during its definition using any one of the following syntax:

data-type variable-name = constant-value;
data-type variable-name(constant-value);

This syntax is most commonly used since it avoids chances of using uninitialized variables leading to runtime errors. The following statements initialize variables during their definition:

```
int a = 20;                  // or int a(20);
float c = 1920.9, d = 4.5; // or float c(1920.9), d(4.5);
double g = 123455.56;
```

The value to be initialized to a variable at the time of definition must be known while writing the program i.e., it must be a constant value or must have been assigned at runtime before its definition as follows:

```
int i = 3;
int k = i + 3;
```

A variable which is initialized at its definition is called *value-initialized variable*. However, its value can be modified during the program execution at a later point. When multiple variables are being declared in a single statement, initialization is carried out in the following way:

```
int i = 10, j = 5;
```

The right side of the assignment operator can be any valid expression as given below:

```
int k = i / j;
```

It assigns the value 2 to k if i=10 and j=5.

The variables can be initialized by using any valid expression at runtime. The general format is as follows:

variable-name = expression;

The *expression* can be a constant, variable name, or variables and/or constants connected by using operators (mathematical expression). For example,

```
a = 10;
a = b;
a = c+d-5;
```

where the symbols + and - represent addition and subtraction operation respectively. The program show1.cpp illustrates the initialization of variables in the definition or during its execution.

```cpp
// show1.cpp: variable definition and assignment
#include <iostream.h>
void main()
{
  int a, b;           // integer type variable definition
  int c = 100;        // variable definition and initialization
  float distance;     // floating-point type variable definition
  // initialization during execution time
  a = c;
  b = c + 100;
  distance = 55.9;
  // display contents of the variables
  cout << "a = " << a << "\n";
  cout << "b = " << b << "\n";
  cout << "c = " << c << "\n";
  cout << "distance = " << distance;
}
```

Run

```
a = 100
b = 200
c = 100
distance = 55.9
```

In main(), the statement

```
int c = 100;
```

defines a variable called c and initializes it with the constant integer value 100. The statement

```
a = c;
```

reads the contents of the variable c and assigns it to the variable a. The statement

```
b = c + 100;
```

adds the contents of the variable c with the numeric constant 100, and assigns the result to the variable b. The statement

```
distance = 55.9;
```

assigns the floating-point constant value 55.9 to the variable distance. The statement

```
cout << "a = " << a << "\n";
```

displays a message a = followed by the contents of the variable a and then a newline. Input and output operations in C++ have already been discussed in Chapter 2. For more information refer to the chapter, *Streams Computation with Console*.

4.8 Characters and Character Strings

A character variable can hold a single character. For instance, the statement

```
char code = 'R';
```

assigns the character constant R to the variable code. The value stored in the variable code is the ASCII equivalent of the character R. Note that the character constant is enclosed in a pair of single quotes and each character representation requires 8 bits (one byte).

A sequence of characters is called a string. String constants are enclosed in double-quotes as follows:

```
"Hello World"
```

String constants are useful while conveying some messages to the user. For instance, the statement

```
cout << "I love C++ programming";
```

displays the message indicated by the string constant as follows:

```
I love C++ programming
```

In C++, characters can be treated like integers. A character variable holds one character such as a letter, a digit, or a punctuation mark. These characters are represented in memory by a number, called the code for the character. For example, the code for the letter A may be 65, that for letter B may be 66, and so on.

Actually, any number can represent the letter A, any other number can be used for B and so on, but these numbers should be fixed by a coding convention. For example, when the computer wants the printer to print the letter A, it actually sends the number 65 to the printer. The important point here is that the printer accepts the number 65 and prints the letter A. Hence, the printer must also use the same code to represent character as that is used by the computer. This requirement led to the establishment of a standard called ASCII (American Standard Code for Information Interchange). ASCII codes are widely used all over the world to represent various symbols in a computer.

The program ascii.cpp reads the ASCII code of a character and prints out the symbol associated with the code.

```
// ascii.cpp: ASCII code example
#include <iostream.h>
void main()
{
    int code;
    char symbol;
    cout << "Enter an ASCII code (0 to 127): ";
    cin >> code;   // reads integer value
    symbol = code; // store into character variable
    cout << "The symbol corresponding to " << code  << " is " << symbol;
}
```

Run1

```
Enter an ASCII code (0 to 127): 65
The symbol corresponding to 65 is A
```

Run2

```
Enter an ASCII code (0 to 127): 67
The symbol corresponding to 67 is C
```

In main(), the statement

```
symbol = code;
```

assigns the value of the integer variable code to the character variable symbol. In the output statement

```
cout << "The symbol corresponding to " << code  << " is " << symbol;
```

the character variable code forces cout to display the ASCII symbol corresponding to the value stored in it.

A string in C++ is just a sequence of consecutive characters in memory, the last one being the null character. A null character has an ASCII code 0 and is called the *end-of-string* marker in C++. For instance, consider the following string constant:

```
"I love C++ programming"
```

In memory, it is stored as a sequence of bytes as shown in Figure 4.4. Each location holds ASCII equivalent of the respective character. The null character (a byte with value zero) is placed at the end of the string. It serves to terminate the string. i.e., to mark the end of the string.

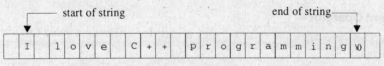

Figure 4.4: String representation in memory

4.9 Operators and Expressions

C++ operators are special characters which instruct the compiler to perform *operation* on some *operands*. Operation instructions are specified by operators, while operands can be variables, expressions, or literal values. Some operators operate on a single operand and they are called *unary operators*. Some operators are indicated before operands and they are called *prefix operators*. Others, indicated after the operand are called *postfix operators*. For instance, expressions ++i or i++ use unary prefix and postfix operators respectively. Most operators are embedded between the two operands, and they are called *infix binary operators*. An expression a+b uses the binary plus operator. C++ has even an operator that takes three operands, called a *ternary operator*. Unification of the operands and the operators results in the formation of *expressions*.

Types of Operators

In C++, operators can be classified into various categories based on their utility and action as follows:

+ Arithmetic operators
+ Relational operators
+ Logical operators
+ Assignment operators
+ Increment and decrement operators
+ Conditional operator
+ Bitwise operators
+ Special operators

An expression is a combination of variables, constants and operators written according to the syntax of the language. In C++, every expression evaluates to a value. i.e., every expression results in some value of a valid data type, that can be assigned to a variable. The following are some of the valid expressions:

```
a+b
a+200+40
c+b*z
z+20
total+20+c/3
```

Expressions having operands of different data types are called *mixed-mode expressions*. Consider the following statements:

```
int a, c;
float d, e;
```

The expression

```
(a+d+e+c)
```

is called *mixed-mode expression,* since it contains variables of types; integer and floating-point.

Assignment Operator =

As in most other languages, the equal (=) sign is used for assigning a value to a variable. It has the following syntax:

variable = expression;

The left hand side has to be a variable (often called *lvalue*) and the right hand side has to be a valid expression (often called *rvalue*). The following are some valid assignment statements:

```
a = 32000;          // rvalue is constant
b = z + 10 * a;     // rvalue is expression
c = sqrt( 20.2 );   // rvalue is function
```

The program temper.cpp illustrates the conversion of temperature value in fahrenheit to centigrade and vice-versa using the following relation:

*fahrenheit = 1.8 * centigrade + 32*

```
// temper.cpp: conversion of centigrade to fahrenheit and vice-versa
#include <iostream.h>
void main()
{
    float c, f;
    cout << "Enter temperature in celsius: ";
    cin >> c;
    f = 1.8 * c + 32;
    cout << "Equivalent fahrenheit = " << f << endl;
    cout << "Enter temperature in fahrenheit: ";
    cin >> f;
    c = (f - 32) / 1.8;
    cout << "Equivalent celsius = " << c;
}
```

Run

```
Enter temperature in celsius: 5
Equivalent fahrenheit = 41
Enter temperature in fahrenheit: 40
Equivalent celsius = 4.444445
```

4.10 Qualifiers

Qualifiers modify the behavior of the variable type, to which they are applied. Qualifiers can be classified into two types:

- ◆ Size qualifiers
- ◆ Sign qualifiers

Consider the variable definition statement:

> int i;

It specifies that i is an integer, which takes both positive and negative values. That is, i is a signed integer by default. The above definition could also be written as:

> signed int i;

Prefixing of the qualifier signed explicitly, is unnecessary, since int data type definitions are signed by default. If the variable i is used to hold only positive values (for example, if it is used to hold the number of students in a class), it can be defined as follows:

> unsigned int i;

Here, the qualifier unsigned is applied to the data type int. This qualifier modifies the behavior of the integer so that a variable of this type always contains a positive value.

int with Size Qualifiers

Size qualifiers alter the size of the basic type. There are two size qualifiers that can be applied to integers (i.e., to the basic type int): short and long. In any ANSI C++ compiler, the sizes of short int, int and long int have the following specification:

- ◆ The size of a short int is 16 bits.
- ◆ The size of an int must be greater than or equal to that of a short int.
- ◆ The size of a long int must be greater than or equal to that of an int.
- ◆ The size of a long int is 32 bits.

In most compilers available on DOS, the size of a short int and an int are the same (16 bits). A long int occupies 32 bits. But in 32-bit compilers such as GNU C/C++, an int and a long int are of the same size (32 bits), while a short int is 16 bits. On the other hand, almost all UNIX compilers have the size of int as 16 bits, int and long int being 32 bits.

sizeof operator

The operator sizeof returns the number of bytes required to represent a data type or variable. It has the following forms:

> *sizeof(data-type)*
> *sizeof(variable)*

The data type can be standard or user defined data type. The following statements illustrate the usage of sizeof operator:

```
int i, j;
float c;
sizeof( int )          returns 2 or 4 depending on compiler implementation
sizeof( float )        returns 4
sizeof( long )         returns 4
sizeof( i )            returns 2 or 4 depending on compiler implementation
sizeof( c )            returns 4
```

The program size.cpp determines the size of an integer and its variants. It uses the function sizeof(), which gives the size of any data type in bytes.

```
// size.cpp: size qualifiers and sizeof operator
#include <iostream.h>
void main()
{
   cout << "sizeof( char ) = " << sizeof(char) << endl;
   cout << "sizeof( short )  = " << sizeof(short) << endl;
   cout << "sizeof( short int ) = " << sizeof(short int) << endl;
   cout << "sizeof( int ) = " << sizeof(int) << endl;
   cout << "sizeof( long ) = " << sizeof(long) << endl;
   cout << "sizeof( long int ) = " << sizeof(long int) << endl;
   cout << "sizeof( float ) = " << sizeof(float) << endl;
   cout << "sizeof( double ) = " << sizeof(double) << endl;
   cout << "sizeof( long double ) = " << sizeof(long double) << endl;
}
```

Run1

```
sizeof( char ) = 1
sizeof( short )  = 2
sizeof( short int ) = 2
sizeof( int ) = 2
sizeof( long ) = 4
sizeof( long int ) = 4
sizeof( float ) = 4
sizeof( double ) = 8
sizeof( long double ) = 10
```

Run2

```
sizeof( char ) = 1
sizeof( short ) = 2
sizeof( short int ) = 2
sizeof( int ) = 4
sizeof( long ) = 4
sizeof( long int ) = 4
sizeof( float ) = 4
sizeof( double ) = 8
sizeof( long double ) = 10
```

Note: The output displayed in *Run1* is generated by executing the program on the DOS system compiled with Borland C++ compiler. *Run2* is generated by executing the program on the UNIX system.

The name of the variable type is passed to the `sizeof` operator in parentheses. The number of bytes occupied by a variable of that type is given by the `sizeof` operator. The `sizeof` operator is very useful in developing portable programs. It is a bad practice to assume the size of a particular type, since its size can vary from compiler to compiler.

The `sizeof` operator also takes variable names and returns the size of the variable given, in bytes. For example, the statements

```
int i;
cout << "The size of i is " << sizeof(i);
```

will output

```
The size of i is 2
```

The result of `sizeof(int)` or `sizeof(i)` will be the same, since i is an int. However, it is a better practice to pass a variable name to the `sizeof` operator; if the data-type of i has to be changed later, then rest of the program need not be modified.

Size qualifiers, as applied to `double`

The type qualifier `long` can also be applied on the data type `double`. A variable of type `long double` has more precision when compared to a variable of type `double`. C++ provides three data types for real numbers: `float`, `double` and `long double`. In any C++ compiler, the precision of a `double` is greater than or equal to that of a `float`, and the precision of a `long double` is greater than or equal to that of a `double`. i.e., precision-wise,

precision of long double >= precision of double >= precision of float

To find out the actual range that a compiler offers, a program(mer) can refer to the constants defined in the header file `float.h`.

Sign Qualifiers

The keywords `signed` and `unsigned` are the two sign qualifiers which inform the compiler whether a variable can hold both negative and positive numbers, or only positive numbers. These qualifiers can be applied to the data types `int` and `char` only. For example, an unsigned integer can be declared as

```
unsigned int i;
```

As mentioned earlier, `signed int` is the same as `int` (i.e., `int` is signed by default). The `char` data type can be treated as either `signed char`, or `unsigned char`, and the exact representation is compiler dependent.

4.11 Arithmetic Operators

The C++ language has both unary and binary arithmetic operators. Unary operators are those, which operate on a single operand whereas, binary operators operate on two operands. The arithmetic operators can operate on any built-in data type. Arithmetic operators and their meaning are shown in Table 4.5. Note that, C++ has no operator for exponentiation. However, a function `pow(x, y)` exists in `math.h` which returns x^y.

Operator	Meaning
+	Addition or unary plus
–	Subtraction or unary minus
*	Multiplication
/	Division
%	Modulo Division

Table 4.5: Arithmetic operators

Unary Minus Operator (Negation)

The unary minus operator can be used to negate the value of a variable. It is also used to specify a negative number; here a minus (-) sign is prefixed to the number. Consider the following examples

1.   `int x = 5;`
         `y = -x;`

The value of x after negation is assigned to y i.e., y becomes -5.

2.   `int x = -5;`
         `sum = -x;`

The value of sum is +5. The unary minus operator has the effect of multiplying its operand by -1.

3. The use of unary + operator does not serve any purpose. However, it can be used as follows:

         `a = +100;`

By default, numeric constants are assumed to be positive.

Binary Operators

Binary arithmetic operators such as +, -, *, etc., require two operands of standard data types. Depending on the data types of the operands, these operators perform either integer or floating-point arithmetic operation.

Integer arithmetic: When the two operands say x and y are defined as integers, any arithmetic operation performed on these operands is called integer arithmetic, which always yields an integer result.

Example:

Let x and y be defined by the statement:

         `int x = 16, y = 5;`

Then the integer arithmetic operations yield the following results:

         `x + y = 21`
         `x - y = 11`
         `x * y = 80`

```
x / y = 3        The result is truncated, the decimal part is discarded.
x % y = 1        The result is the remainder of the integer division. The sign of the result is
                 always the sign of the first operand.
```

In integer division operation, the result is truncated towards the lower value if both the operands are of the same sign, and is dependent on the machine if one of the operands is negative.

Example:

```
6 / 8 = 0
-6 / -8 = 0
-6 / 8 = 0 or -1    The result is machine dependent.
```

Floating-point arithmetic: Floating-point arithmetic involves operands of real type in decimal or exponential notation. The floating point results are rounded off to the number of significant digits specified, and hence the final value is only an approximation of the correct result. The remainder operator % is not applicable to floating point operands.

Example:

Let a and b be defined by the statement

```
float a = 14.0, b = 4.0;
```

and p, q and r be floating point variables; then the floating point arithmetic operations will yield the following results

```
p = a / b = 3.500000
q = b / a = 0.285714
r = a + b = 18.00000
```

Mixed mode arithmetic: In mixed mode arithmetic, if either one of the operands is real, the resultant value is always a real value. For example, 35 / 5.0 = 7.0. Here, since 5.0 is a double constant, 35 is converted to a double and the result is also a double

The expression

```
x % y
```

produces the remainder when x is divided by y (it returns 0 when y divides x exactly). The program modulus.cpp illustrates the use of the *modulus operator.*

```
// modules.cpp:  computation of remainder of division operation
#include <iostream.h>
void main()
{
    int numerator, denominator;
    float result, remainder;
    cout << "Enter numerator: ";
    cin >> numerator;
    cout << "Enter denominator: ";
    cin >> denominator;
    result = numerator / denominator;
    remainder = numerator % denominator;
    cout << numerator << "/" << denominator << " = " << result << endl;
    cout << numerator << "%" << denominator << " = " << remainder;
}
```

Run

```
Enter numerator: 12
Enter denominator: 5
12/5 = 2
12%5 = 2
```

An arithmetic expression without parentheses will evaluate from left to right using the following rules of precedence for operators:

> High priority: * / %
> Low priority: + -

The basic evaluation process requires two passes. During the first pass, the highest priority operators are applied as they are encountered and in the next pass, the low priority operators are applied. Consider the following statement:

```
a = b + c * 5 + d / 2 - 3;
```

When b = 5, c = 2, d = 10, the statement becomes

```
a = 5 + 2 * 5 + 10 / 2 - 3;
```

It is evaluated as follows:

First pass:

```
step 1: a = 5 + 10 + 10 / 2 - 3;
step 2: a = 5 + 10 + 5 - 3;
```

Second pass:

```
step 3: a = 15 + 5 - 3;
step 4: a = 20 - 3;
step 5: a = 17;
```

These evaluation steps are shown in Figure 4.5, which illustrates the hierarchy of operators. When parentheses are used, the expression within the innermost parentheses gains highest priority.

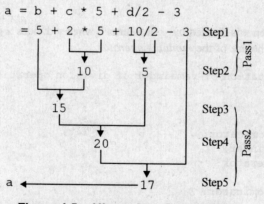

Figure 4.5: Hierarchy of operations

A program for swapping two integer numbers without using a temporary variable, is listed in notemp.cpp. The steps involved are illustrated in Figure 4.6.

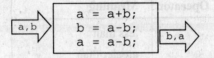

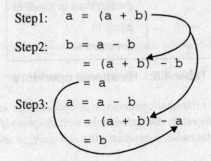

(a) Steps for swapping two numbers

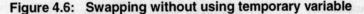

(b) Swapping steps derivations

Figure 4.6: Swapping without using temporary variable

```
// notemp.cpp: swapping two numbers without using temporary variable
#include <iostream.h>
void main()
{
    int a, b;
    cout << "Enter two integers <a, b>: ";
    cin >> a >> b;
    a = a + b;
    b = a - b;
    a = a - b;
    // logic for swapping a and b ends here
    cout << "Value of a and b on swapping in main(): " << a << " " << b;
}
```

Run

```
Enter two integers <a, b>: 10 20
Value of a and b on swapping in main(): 20 10
```

4.12 Relational Operators

A relational operator is used to make comparisons between two expressions. All these operators are binary and require two operands. Logically similar quantities are often compared for taking decisions. These comparisons can be done with the help of relational operators as shown in Table 4.6. Each one of these operators compares its left hand side operand with its right hand side operand. The whole expression involving the relational operator then evaluates to an integer. It evaluates to zero if the condition is false, and non-zero value if it is true.

Operator	Meaning
<	less than
>	greater than
<=	less than or equal to
>=	greater than or equal to
==	equal to
!=	not equal to

Table 4.6:   Relational operators

In order to understand the relational operators, it is necessary to know the basics of an `if` statement. (The `if` statement is elaborately discussed in the next chapter.) If condition-expression is true, it executes the *then-part* only, otherwise, it evaluates the *else-part*, as shown below:

```
if( condition )
    statement1;        // executed when condition is true
else
    statement2;        // executed when condition is false
```

The program `relation.cpp` illustrates the use of the relational operators in taking decisions.

```
// relation.cpp: relational operator usage
#include <iostream.h>
void main()
{
    int my_age, your_age;
    cout << "Enter my age: ";
    cin >> my_age;
    cout << "Enter your age: ";
    cin >> your_age;
    if( my_age == your_age )
        cout << "We are born in the same year.";
    else
        cout << "We are born in different years";
}
```

Run1

```
Enter my age: 25
Enter your age: 25
We are born in the same year.
```

Run2

```
Enter my age: 25
Enter your age: 21
We are born in different years
```

In `main()`, the statement

```
if( my_age == your_age )
```

has the expression `my_age == your_age` as a conditional expression. It returns *true* if `my_age` and `your_age` are equal, otherwise it returns *false*. Note that 0 is treated as *false*, whereas any non-zero value is treated as *true*.

Note that in C++, the operator for testing equality is == (two = signs placed together). One of the most common mistakes is to use a single = sign, to test for equality. For example, consider the statement

```
if( my_age = your_age )
```

The conditional expression evaluates to *true* even if `my_age` and `your_age` are unequal (except when `your_age` is equal to zero). This happens because the result of an assignment operator is the assigned value itself. (Consider `my_age` is 25 and `your_age` is 21.) Here, the value of `your_age` (25) is assigned to `my_age`, and the assignment expression evaluates to 25, which is non-zero. Since any non-zero value is considered to be *true*, the statements following the if (then-part) are executed.

While using the relational operators, the fact whether the numbers being compared are signed or not becomes important. Neglecting this fact can lead to hard-to-find errors. The program `char1.cpp` illustrates the use of `char` type variables as 8-bit integers.

```
// char1.cpp: Using char as an 8-bit integer
#include <iostream.h>
void main()
{
    // Integer value being assigned to a char
    char c = 255;
    char d = -1;
    if( c < 0 )
        cout << "c is less than 0\n";
    else
        cout << "c is not less than 0\n";
    if( d < 0 )
        cout << "d is less than 0\n";
    else
        cout << "d is not less than 0\n";
    if( c == d )
        cout << "c and d are equal";
    else
        cout << "c and d are not equal";
}
```

Run

```
c is less than 0
d is less than 0
c and d are equal
```

In `main()`, the statement

```
if( c == d )
```

treats c and d as equal, although c is assigned with 255 and d is assigned with -1. It is because both of them are treated as signed numbers by default. This can be overcome by explicitly defining variables of type `char` as signed or unsigned while using them as 8-bit integers, as illustrated in the program `char2.cpp`.

```
// char2.cpp: Using char as an 8-bit integer
#include <iostream.h>
void main()
{
    // Integer value being assigned to a char
    unsigned char c = 255;
    char d = -1;
    if( c < 0 )
        cout << "c is less than 0\n";
    else
        cout << "c is not less than 0\n";
    if( d < 0 )
        cout << "d is less than 0\n";
    else
        cout << "d is not less than 0\n";
    if( c == d )
        cout << "c and d are equal";
    else
        cout << "c and d are not equal";
}
```

Run

```
c is not less than 0
d is less than 0
c and d are not equal
```

4.13 Logical Operators

Any expression that evaluates to zero denotes a FALSE logical condition, and that evaluating to non-zero value denotes a TRUE logical condition. Logical operators are useful in combining one or more conditions. C++ has three logical operators shown in Table 4.7.

Operator	Meaning
&&	Logical AND
||	Logical OR
!	Logical NOT

Table 4.7:   Logical operators

The first two operators && and || are binary, whereas the exclamation (!) is a unary operator and is used to negate a condition. The result of logical operations when applied to operands with all possible values, is shown in Table 4.8.

Logical AND: For example, consider the following expression

    a > b && x == 10

The expression on the left is a > b and that on the right is x == 10. The whole expression evaluates to true only if both expressions are true (if a is greater than b as well as x is equal to 10)

T- True, F- False

operand1 a	operand2 b	~a	~b	a && b	a || b
F	F	T	T	F	F
F	T	T	F	F	T
T	F	F	T	F	T
T	T	F	F	T	T

Table 4.8: Truth table for logical operator

Logical OR: Consider the following example involving the | | operator.

```
a < m || a < n
```

The expression is *true* if one of them is *true*, or if both of them are *true* i.e., if the value of a is less than that of m, or if it is less than n. Needless to say, it evaluates to *true* when a is less than m and n.

Logical NOT: The ! (NOT) operator takes a single expression and evaluates to *true* if the expression is *false*, and evaluates to *false* if the expression is *true*. In other words, it just reverses the value of the expression. For example, consider:

```
!( x >= y )
```

It has the same meaning as

```
x < y
```

The ! operator can be conveniently used to replace a statement such as

```
if( a == 0 )
```

by the statement

```
if( !a )
```

The expression ! a evaluates to *true* if the variable a holds zero, *false* otherwise.

The unary negation operator (!) has a higher precedence amongst these, followed by the logical AND (&&) operator and then the logical OR (| |) operator, and are evaluated from left to right.

The logical operator is used to connect various conditions to determine whether a given year is a leap year or not. A year is a leap year if it is divisible by 4 but not by 100, or that is divisible by 400. The program leap.cpp illustrates the use of the modulus operator.

```
// leap.cpp: detects whether year is leap or not
#include <iostream.h>
void main()
{
    int year;
    cout << "Enter any year: ";
    cin >> year;
    if( (year % 4 == 0 && year % 100 != 0 ) || (year % 400 == 0) )
        cout << year << " is a leap year";
    else
        cout << year << " is not a leap year";
}
```

Run1

```
Enter any year: 1996
1996 is a leap year
```

Run2

```
Enter any year: 1997
1997 is not a leap year
```

In main(), the statement

```
if( (year % 4 == 0 && year % 100 != 0 ) || (year % 400 == 0) )
```

can be replaced by

```
if( (!(year % 4) && year % 100 != 0 ) || !(year % 400) )
```

4.14 Bit-wise Operators

The support of bit-wise manipulation on integer operands is useful in various applications. Table 4.9 shows the bit-wise operators supported by C++. To illustrate these operators with examples, assume that a, b and c are defined as integer variables as follows:

```
int a = 13, b = 7, c;
```

Consider the variables a, b, and c as 16-bit integers, and the value stored in a and b have the following representation in the binary form:

> The binary representation of a is 0000 0000 0000 1101
> The binary representation of b is 0000 0000 0000 0111

(The spaces appearing after every 4 bits are only for clarity. Actually, the integers are merely 16 continuous bits.)

Operator	Meaning
&	Bitwise AND
|	Bitwise OR
^	Bitwise EX-OR
~	Bitwise complement
<<	Shift left
>>	Shift right

Table 4.9:   Bit-wise operators

(i) Logical Bit-wise Operators

Logical bit-wise operators perform logical operations such as AND, OR, EX-OR, NOT between corresponding bits of operands (if binary) and negation of bits (if unary).

Unary Operator : One's Complement Operator (~)

The complement operator causes the bits of its operand to be inverted, i.e., 1 becomes 0 and 0 becomes 1. For instance, the largest possible number, which can be stored in an unsigned integer can be found as follows. When one's complement operator is applied on this word holding zero, all the bits will be inverted to ones and a new value becomes the largest possible number. The program `large.cpp` illustrates this conversion process.

```
// large.cpp: detects largest possible unsigned integer
#include <iostream.h>
int main()
{
    unsigned u = 0;
    cout << "Value before conversion: " << u << endl;
    u = ~u;
    cout << "Value after conversion : " << u << endl;
    return 0;
}
```

Run1

```
Value before conversion: 0
Value after conversion : 65535
```

Run2

```
Value before conversion: 0
Value after conversion : 4294967295
```

☞ *Run1* is executed on the MS-DOS based machine using a 16-bit compiler.

Run2 is executed on the UNIX based machine using a 32-bit compiler.

Binary Logical Bit-wise Operators

There are three binary logical bit-wise operators: & (and), | (or) and ^ (exclusive or). The operations are carried out independently on each pair of the corresponding bits in the operands, i.e. the bit 1 of operand1 is logically operated with the bit 1 of operand 2. The operations using these operators are discussed in the following sections.

Bitwise AND: The statement

```
    c = a & b;
```

makes use of the bitwise AND operator. After this statement is executed, each bit in c will be 1 only if the corresponding bits in both a and b are 1. For example, the rightmost bit of both integers is 1, and hence the rightmost bit in c is 1. The next bit is 0 in a and 1 in b. Hence the second bit (from the right) in c is 0. Applying the same reasoning for all the bits in each one of the integers, the value of c after the above statement is executed will be 0000 0000 0000 0101 which, in decimal is 5 and is illustrated below:

Bitwise AND operator: a & b

a	0000 0000 0000 1101
b	0000 0000 0000 0111
a & b	0000 0000 0000 0101

Bitwise OR: The statement

```
    c = a | b;
```

makes use of the bitwise OR operator. After this statement is executed, a bit in c will be 1 whenever at least one of the corresponding bits in either a or b is 1. In the example given below, the value of c will be 0000 0000 0000 1111 i.e., decimal 15 and is illustrated below:

Bitwise OR operator: a I b

```
    a   0000 0000 0000 1101
    b   0000 0000 0000 0111
a | b   0000 0000 0000 1111
```

Bitwise XOR: The statement

```
c = a ^ b;
```

makes use of the bitwise XOR operator. After this statement is executed, a bit in c will be 1 whenever the corresponding bits in a and b differ. So in the example given below, the value of c will be 0000 0000 0000 1010 which, in decimal is 10 and is illustrated below:

Bitwise EX-OR operator: a ^ b

```
    a   0000 0000 0000 1101
    b   0000 0000 0000 0111
a ^ b   0000 0000 0000 1010
```

(ii) Shift Operators

There are two shift operators in C++: left shift (<<) and right shift (>>). These are binary operators and have the following syntax:

```
operand << count      for left shift
operand >> count      for right shift
```

The first operand is the value which is to be shifted. The second is the number of bits by which it is shifted. The left shift operator moves the count number of bits to the left, whereas the right shift operator moves the count number of bits to the right. The leftmost or the rightmost bits are shifted out and are lost.

Left Shift Operator

Consider the statement

```
c = a << 3;
```

The value in the integer a is shifted left by three bit positions. The result is assigned to the integer c. Since the value of a is 0000 0000 0000 1101 the value of c after the execution of the above statement is 0000 0000 0110 1000 (104 in decimal), and is illustrated below:

Left-Shift <<

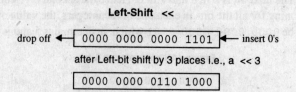

drop off ◄── 0000 0000 0000 1101 ◄── insert 0's

after Left-bit shift by 3 places i.e., a << 3

0000 0000 0110 1000

The three leftmost bits drop off due to the left shift (i.e., they are not present in the result). Three zeros are inserted in the right. The effect of shifting a variable to the left by one bit position is equivalent to multiplying the value by 2. If the initial value of a is 13, shifting left by 3 bit positions yields 13*8=104.

While multiplying a number with a power of 2, considerable savings in execution time can be achieved by using the left bit-shift operator instead of the multiplication operator, since a shift is faster than multiplication.

Right Shift Operator

Consider the statement

```
c = a >> 2;
```

The value of a is shifted right by 2 positions. Since the value of a is 0000 0000 0000 1101 the value of c after the execution of the above statement is 0000 0000 0000 0011 (3 in decimal) and is illustrated below:

Right-Shift >>

insert 0's → | 0000 0000 0000 1101 | → drop off

after right shift by 2 places i.e., a >> 2

| 0000 0000 0000 0011 |

The 2 rightmost bits drop off (are not present in the result), and zeros are inserted in the left. The effect of shifting a variable to the right by one bit position is equivalent to dividing the value by 2 (i.e., divide by 2 and truncate the result). As the initial value of a is 13, shifting it right by 2 bit positions yields the value 3 (the result of dividing 13 by 4 and truncating the result). Note that if the negative number is shifted right, then 1 is inserted at the left for every bit shifted to the right.

The program extract.cpp illustrates the binary operators. It reads an integer and prints the value of a specified bit in the integer. The position of bits are numbered starting with 0 from right to left. For example, to find the value of the second bit of an integer i, it is necessary to shift i to the right by two bits, and take the least significant digit.

```
// extract.cpp: Fishing the nth bit
#include <iostream.h>
void main()
{
    // a is the input integer and n, the bit position to extract
    int a, n, bit;
    cout << "Enter an integer: ";
    cin >> a;
    cout << "Enter bit position to extract: ";
    cin >> n;
    bit = (a >> n) & 1;    // bit is the value of the bit extracted (0 or 1)
    cout << "The bit is " << bit;
}
```

Run

```
Enter an integer: 10
Enter bit position to extract: 2
The bit is 1
```

In main(), the statement

```
bit = (a >> n) & 1;
```

first shifts a to the right by n bits and then masks (clears) all the bits of a except the least significant bit (rightmost bit), retaining the bit which is required. Parentheses are not required in the above statement, since the operator >> has more precedence than & (i.e., in an expression, if both >> and & are present, the >> operator is executed first). Since this fact is not obvious, it is always better to use parentheses in such situations, for the sake of readability.

4.15 Compound Assignment Operators

As discussed earlier, the assignment operator = (equal sign) evaluates the expression on the right and assigns the resulting value to the variable on the left. Other forms of assignment operators exist, which are obtained by combining operators such as +, -, *, etc., with the = sign as follows:

variable operator= expression/constant/function;

For example, expressions such as

```
i = i + 10;
```

in which the variable i on the left hand side is repeated immediately after = sign, and can be rewritten in the compact form as follows:

```
·i += 10;
```

The operator += is known as compound assignment operator. Various possible compound assignment operators are shown in Table 4.10. These operators evaluate the expression on their right, and use the result to perform the corresponding operation on the variable on the left. Note that, only the binary operators can be combined with the assignment operator.

Operator	Usage	Effect
+=	a += exp;	a = a + (exp);
-=	a -= exp;	a = a - (exp);
*=	a *= exp;	a = a * (exp);
/=	a /= exp;	a = a / (exp);
%=	a %= exp;	a = a % (exp);
&=	a &= exp;	a = a & (exp);
|=	a |= exp;	a = a | (exp);
^=	a ^= exp;	a = a ^ (exp);
<<=	a <<= exp;	a = a << (exp);
>>=	a >>= exp;	a = a >> (exp);

Table 4.10:   Compound assignment operators

The statement

variable operator= expression;

is equivalent to

variable = variable operator (expression);

Hence, a statement such as

```
x *= y + 2;
```

is equivalent to

```
x = x * (y + 2);
```

rather than

```
x = x * y + 2;
```

4.16 Increment and Decrement Operators

The C++ language offers two unusual unary operators for incrementing and decrementing variables. These are ++ and -- operators and are known as increment and decrement operators respectively. These operators increase or decrease the value of a variable on which they operate by one. The speciality about them is that they can be used as prefix or postfix and their meaning changes accordingly. When used as a prefix, the value of the variable is incremented/decremented before being used in the expression. But when used as a postfix, it's value is first used in the expression and then the value is incremented/decremented. The syntax of the operators is given below:

> *++VariableName*
> *VariableName++*
> *--VariableName*
> *VariableName--*

The operator ++ adds 1 to the operand and -- subtracts 1 from the operand. The prefix and postfix for increment expressions are shown below:

> ++m   and   m++

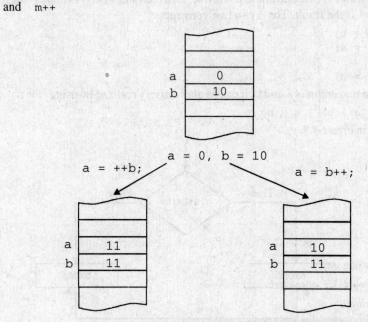

Figure 4.7:   Prefix and postfix increment

Consider the following statements

> ++m;
> m++;

In the above statements, it does not matter whether the increment operator is prefixed or suffixed, it will produce the same result. However, in the following examples, it does make a difference:

> int a = 0, b = 10;

The statement

> a = ++b;

is different from

```
a = b++;
```

In the first case, the value of a after the execution of this statement will be 11, since b is incremented first and then assigned. In the second case, the value of a will be 10, since it is assigned first and then incremented (see Figure 4.7). The value of b in both the cases will be 11. These unary operators have a higher precedence than the binary arithmetic operators. The increment and decrement operators can only be applied to variables; an expression such as (i+j)++ is illegal.

4.17 Conditional Operator (Ternary Operator)

An alternate method to using a simple if-else construct is the conditional expression operator ?;. It is called the ternary operator, which operates on three operands. It has the following syntax:

expression1 ? expression2 : expression3

Here the *expression1* is evaluated first; if it is true, then the value of *expression2* is the result; otherwise, the *expression3* is the result. The if-else construct

```
if(a > b)
    z = a;
else
    z = b;
```

which finds the maximum of a and b; it can be alternatively realized by using

```
z = (a > b) ? a : b;
```

It is illustrated in Figure 4.8.

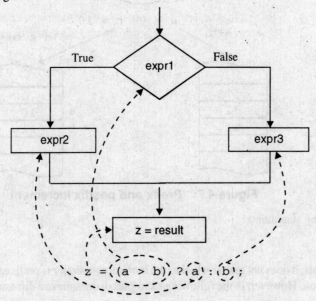

Figure 4.8: Ternary operation evaluation

The program max.cpp reads two integers and displays the value of the larger of the two numbers computed using the ternary operator. If they are equal, then naturally, either of them can be printed.

```
// max.cpp: finding the maximum using the conditional operator
#include <iostream.h>
void main()
{
    int a, b, larger;
    cout << "Enter two integers: ";
    cin >> a >> b;
    larger = a > b ? a : b;
    cout << "The larger of the two is " << larger;
}
```

Run

```
Enter two integers: 10 20
The larger of the two is 20
```

In main(), the statement

```
        larger = a > b ? a : b;
```

has three components. The conditional expression (a > b ? a : b) returns a if a > b, otherwise it returns b. It can be equivalently coded using the if statement as follows:

```
        if( a > b )
            larger = a;
        else
            larger = b;
```

The expressions in the ternary operator can be any valid variable, constant, or an expression. The program oddeven.cpp checks whether the number is odd or even using the ternary operator.

```
// oddeven.cpp: checks whether the number is odd or even
#include <iostream.h>
void main()
{
    int num;
    char *str;
    cout << "Enter the number: ";
    cin >> num;
    cout << "The number " << num << " is ";
    cout << ((num % 2) ? "Odd" : "Even");
    cout << endl << "Enter the number: ";
    cin >> num;
    cout << "The number " << num << " is ";
    (num % 2) ? cout << "Odd" : cout << "Even";
}
```

Run

```
Enter the number: 10
The number 10 is Even
Enter the number: 25
The number 25 is Odd
```

In main(), the statements

```
cout << ((num % 2) ? "Odd" : "Even");
(num % 2) ? cout << "Odd" : cout << "Even";
```

produce the same result. In the first statement, when the input value is 10, it returns the string Even, which is passed to cout for display. The second statement executes

```
cout << "Even"
```

when the input is a even number, otherwise, it executes the first expression

```
cout << "Odd"
```

4.18 Special Operators

Some of the special operators supported by C++ include sizeof, indirection, comma, etc. The sizeof() operator returns the size of the data type or the variable in terms of bytes occupied in memory, as illustrated earlier. Another class of operators is the member selection operators (. and ->) which are used with structures and unions. The indirection and address operators * and & respectively are explained in detail in the later chapters.

Comma Operator

A set of expressions separated by commas is a valid construct in the C++ language. It links the related expressions together. Expressions linked using *comma operator* are evaluated from left to right and the value of the rightmost expression is the result. For example, consider the following statement that makes use of the comma operator.

```
i = (j = 3, j + 2);
```

The right hand side consists of two expressions separated by commas. The first expression is j=3 and the second one is j+2. These expressions are evaluated from left to right. i.e., first the value 3 is assigned to j and then the expression j+2 is evaluated, giving 5. *The value of the entire comma-separated expression is the value of the right-most expression.* In the above example, the value assigned to i would be 5.

Some other typical situations where the comma operator can be used are the following:

```
1. for( int i = 2, j = 10; ..; .. )
2. t = x, x = y, y = t;      // exchanges x and y values
```

4.19 typedef Statement

The typedef statement is used to give new names to existing data types. It allows the user to declare an identifier to represent an existing data type (with enhancement) as shown in the following syntax:

```
typedef type identifier;
```

where *type* refers to an existing data type and identifier refers to the new name given to the data type. For example, the statement,

```
typedef unsigned long ulong;
```

declares ulong to be a new type, equivalent to unsigned long. It can be used just like any standard data type in the program. For example, the statement

```
ulong u;
```

defines u to be of type ulong. Also sizeof(ulong) returns the size of the new variable type in bytes.

4.20 Promotion and Type Conversion

A mixed mode expression is one in which the operands are not of the same type. In this case, the operands are converted before evaluation, to maintain compatibility between data types. It can be carried out by the compiler automatically or by the programmer explicitly.

Implicit Type Conversion

The compiler performs type conversion of data items when an expression consists of data items of different types. This is called implicit or automatic type conversion. The rules followed by the compiler for implicit type conversion is shown in Table 4.11.

Operand1	Operand2	Result
char	int	int
int	long	long
int	float	float
int	double	double
int	unsigned	unsigned
long	double	double
double	float	double

Table 4.11: Automatic type conversion rule table

Consider the following statements to illustrate automatic type conversion

```
float f = 10.0;
int i = 0;
i = f / 3;
```

In this expression, the constant 3 will be converted to a float and then the floating point division will take place, resulting in 3.33333. This (integer to float) type of conversion, where the variable of a lower data type (which can hold lower range of values or has lower precision) is converted to a higher type (which can hold higher range of values or has higher precision) is called *promotion*. But the lvalue is an integer variable, hence, the result of f/3 will be automatically truncated to 3 and the fractional part will be lost. This (float to integer) type of conversion, where the variable of higher type is converted to a lower type is called *demotion*.

The implicit conversions thus occurring are also called *silent conversions* since the programmer is not aware of these conversions. The flexibility of the C++ language, to allow mixed type conversions implicitly, saves a lot of effort on the part of the programmer, but at times, it can give rise to bugs in the program.

The following statement illustrates the process of type conversion:

```
int a, c;
long l;
```

```
float f;
double d;
l = l / a + f * d - d;
```

The variables a and f are type converted to long and double respectively. The process of type conversion leading to data *promotion* or *demotion* while assigning the computed result (if necessary), is shown in Figure 4.9.

```
int a;
long l;
float f;
double d;
```

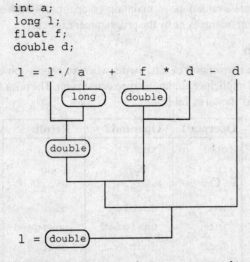

Figure 4.9:   Automatic type conversion

Explicit Type Conversion

Implicit type conversions, as allowed by the C++ language, can lead to errors creeping into the program, if adequate care is not taken. Therefore, the use of explicit type conversion is recommended in mixed mode expressions. It is achieved by typecasting a value of a particular type, into the desired type as follows:

> (*type*) *expression*
> (*type*) *variable_name*

The expression/variable is converted to the given type. Consider the expression:

> (float)i+f

It *type casts* the variable i of type integer to float. Another syntax for type conversion, which is specific to C++ is as follows:

> *type*(*expression*)
> *type*(*variable_name*)

Typecasting can also be used to convert from a higher type to a lower type. For example, if f is a float whose value is 2.7, the expression

> int(f)

evaluates to 2. The program coerce.cpp illustrates the different ways of achieving type conversion.

```
// coerce.cpp: type conversion
#include <iostream.h>
void main()
```

```
{
    int i, j;
    float f;
    i = 12;
    j = 5;
    cout << "when i = " << i << " j = " << j << endl;
    f = i/j;
    cout << "i/j = " << f << endl;
    f = (float)i/j;
    cout << "(float)i/j = " << f << endl;
    f = float(i)/j;
    cout << "float(i)/j = " << f << endl;
    f = i/float(j);
    cout << "i/float(j) = " << f << endl;
}
```

Run

```
when i = 12 j = 5
i/j = 2
(float)i/j = 2.4
float(i)/j = 2.4
i/float(j) = 2.4
```

4.21 Constants

A constant does not change its value during the entire execution of the program. They can be classified as integer, floating point, character, and enumeration constants.

(i) Integer Constants

C++ allows to represent the integer constants in three forms. They are octal, decimal, and hexadecimal.

Octal System (Base 8): Octal numbers are specified with a leading zero, rest of the digits being between 0 and 7. For instance, 0175 is an integer constant specified in octal whose base-10 (decimal) value is 125.

Decimal System (Base 10): It is the most commonly used system. A number in this system is represented by using digits 0-10. For instance, 175 is an integer constant with base 10.

Hexadecimal System (Base 16): Hexadecimal numbers are specified with 0x or 0x in the beginning. The digits that follow 0x must be numbers in the range 0-9 or one of the letters a-f or A-F. For example, 0xa1 is an integer constant specified in hexadecimal whose base-10 or decimal value is 161. 0Xa1 is the same as 0xa1, or 0xA1. i.e., either a lower case or an upper case x can be used.

A size or sign qualifier can be appended at the end of the constant. The suffix u is used for unsigned int constants, l for long int constants and s for signed int constants. It can be represented either in upper case or lower case.

Examples:

1. Unsigned integer constants

```
56789U
56789u
```

2. Long integer constants

```
7689909L
76899091
0675434L  (A long integer constant specified in octal).
0x34ADL   (A long integer constant specified in hexadecimal).
0xf4A3L   (A long integer constant in hexadecimal with upper and lower case letters).
```

3. The suffixes can be combined, as illustrated in the following unsigned long integer constants. The suffixes can be specified in any order.

```
6578890994Ul
6578890994ul
```

(ii) Floating Point Constants

Floating point constants have a decimal point, or an exponent sign, or both.

Decimal notation: Here the number is represented as a whole number, followed by a decimal point and a fractional part. It is possible to omit digits before and after the decimal point.

Examples of valid floating point constants:

```
125.45  241.   .976  -.71   +.5
```

Exponential notation: Exponential notation is useful in representing numbers whose magnitudes are very large or very small. The exponential notation consist of a mantissa and an exponent. The exponent is positive unless preceded by a minus sign. The number 231.78 can also be written as 0.23178e3, representing the number $0.23178*10^3$. The sequence of digits 23178 in this case after the decimal point is called the mantissa, and 3 is called the exponent.

For example, the number 75000000000 can be written as 75e9 or 0.75e11. Similarly , the number 0.00000000045 can be written as 0.45e-9.

(i) The following examples are valid constants

```
2000.0434
3.4e4
3E8
```

(ii) The following are some invalid constants.

```
2,000.0434    - comma not allowed.
3.4E.4        - exponent must be an integer.
3e 8          - blank not allowed.
```

Normalized exponential representation is one in which the value of the mantissa is adjusted to a value between 0.1 and 0.99, for example, the number 75000000000 is written as 0.75e11

The rules governing exponential representation of the real constants are given below:

- The mantissa is either a real number expressed in decimal notation or an integer.
- The mantissa can be preceded by a sign.
- The exponent is an integer preceded by an optional sign.
- The letter e can be written in lowercase or uppercase.
- Embedded white space is not allowed.

By default, real constants are assumed to be double. Suffixes f or F can be used to specify the float values. For example, 0.257 is assumed to be a double constant, while 0.257f is a float constant.

The character l or L can be used to specify long double values. For example, 0.257L is a long double constant.

(iii) Character Constants

A character constant is enclosed in single quotes.

Examples: Valid character constants: 'a' '5' '\n'.
Invalid character constants: 'ab' '54'.

Note that multiple characters can also exist within single quotes. The compiler will not report any error. The value of the constant however, depends upon the compiler used. This notation of having multiple characters in single quotes is practically never used.

Inside the single quotes, a backslash character starts an escape sequence. \xhh specifies a character constant in hexadecimal, where h is any hexadecimal digit. The hexadecimal digits hh gives the ASCII value of the character. For example, the character constant \x07 represents the BELL character. The complete list of escape sequences is shown in Table 4.12.

Operator	Meaning
\a	Beep
\b	Backspace
\f	Formfeed
\n	Newline
\t	Horizontal tab
\\	Backslash
\'	Single quote
\"	Double quote
\v	Vertical tab
\?	Question mark
\0	Null
\0ooo	Code specified in octal
\xhh	Code specified in hexadecimal

Table 4.12: Escape sequences

The escape sequence \0xxx specifies a character constant in octal, where 0 denotes any octal digit. As before, xxx is the ASCII value of the number specified in octal. For example, the ASCII code of K is 75. The character constant \0113 specifies this character in octal. The program beep.cpp generates the beep sound using the escape sequence. The escape sequence \x07 (can be \7) in the cout can be replaced by \a.

```
// beep.cpp: generating beep sound
#include <iostream.h>
void main()
{
    cout << '\x07';  // computer generates sound
}
```

Run

Note: You will hear a beep sound.

Examples:

(i) `cout << "\\ is a backslash.";` will print as follows:

   `\ is a backslash.`

(ii) `cout << "This \" is a double quote.";` will print

   `This " is a double quote.`

(iv) String Literals

A string literal is a sequence of characters enclosed in double quotes. The characters may be letters, numbers, escape sequences, or blank space. To make it easier, string constants are concatenated at compile time. For example, the strings:

   `"C++ is the best"` and,

   `"C++ is "  "the best"` are the same.

An important difference: `'A'` and `"A"`

The notations `!A'` and `"A"` have an important difference. The first one (`'A'`) is a character constant, while the second (`"A"`) is a string constant. The notation `'A'` is a constant occupying a single byte containing the ASCII code of the character A. The notation `"A"` on the other hand, is a constant that occupies two bytes, one for the ASCII code of A and the other for the null character with value 0, that terminates all strings. The statement

   `char ch = 'R';`

assigns ASCII code of the character R to the variable ch, whereas the statement

   `char *str = "Hello OOPs!";`

assigns the starting address of the string Hello OOPs! to the variable str.

4.22 Declaring Symbolic Constants—Literals

Literals are constants to which symbolic names are associated for the purpose of readability and ease of handling. C++ provides the following three ways of defining constants:

   ◆ # define preprocessor directive
   ◆ enumerated data types
   ◆ const keyword

The keyword const is already discussed in the chapter 2. The following section discusses macros and enumerated data types.

#define Preprocessor Directive

The preprocessor directive #define, associates a constant value to a symbol and is visible throughout the module in which it is defined. The symbols defined using #define are called *macros*. The syntax of #define directive is

   `#define SymbolName ConstantValue`

Examples:

   `# define MAX_VAR 100`

```
# define PI 3.1452
# define NAME "Rajkumar"
```

The preprocessor will replace all the macro symbols used in the program by their values before starting the compilation operation. For instance, the statement,

```
area = PI * radius * radius;
```

is translated as,

```
area = 3.1452 * radius * radius;
```

by the processor if there exist a preprocessor directive,

```
#define PI 3.1452
```

in the program and before the statement referencing to it. The definition of macros can be superseded by a new definition. For instance, the symbol PI can be redeclared as,

```
#define PI (22/7)
```

The program city.cpp illustrates the superseding of the value of old macro symbol by a new declaration.

```
// city.cpp: superseding of macros
#include <iostream.h>
#define CITY "Bidar"
void which_city();
void main()
{
    cout << "Earlier City: ";
    cout << CITY << endl;
#define CITY "Bangalore"
    cout << "New City: ";
    cout << CITY << endl;
    which_city();
}
void which_city()
{
    cout << "City in Function: ";
    cout << CITY;
}
```

Run

```
Earlier City: Bidar
New City: Bangalore
City in Function: Bangalore
```

In the above program, initially the macro constant CITY is declared with the value "Bidar". The statement in the beginning of the main() function

```
cout << CITY << endl;
```

will print the message

```
Bidar
```

as seen in the output of the program. However, the same statement at the end of main() and in the function which_city() prints the message

```
Bangalore
```

Thus, the most recent declaration of the macro constant will supersede the earlier one. Macro constants behave similar to global variables except that they are visible from the point of their declaration.

The important advantages of using macro symbols include the following:

- Program coding is easier
- Enhances program readability
- Program maintenance is easier

The disadvantage of macro constants is that, they do not support the specification of the data-type in the declaration; any type of value can be assigned (either integer, float, or string).

4.23 Enumerated Data Types

An enumerated data type is a user defined type, with values ranging over a finite set of identifiers called enumeration constants. For example,

```
enum color {red, blue, green};
```

This defines `color` to be of a new data type which can assume the value, `red`, `blue`, or `green`. Each of these is an enumeration constant. In the program, `color` can be used as a new type. A variable of type `color` can have any one of the three values: red, blue or green. For example, the statement

```
color c;
```

defines `c` to be of type `color`. Internally, the C++ compiler treats an enum type (such as color) as an integer itself. The above identifiers `red`, `blue`, and `green` represent the integer values of 0, 1, and 2 respectively. So, the statements

```
c = blue;
cout << "As an int, c has the value " << c;
```

will print

```
As an int, c has the value 1
```

Constant values can be explicitly specified for the identifiers. When the value for one identifier is specified in this manner, the value of the next element is incremented by one (next higher integer). For example, if the definition of `color` is

```
enum color {red = 10, blue, green = 34};
```

then the statement `c = red` will assign the value 10 to c. Thereafter, the statement

```
c = blue;
```

assigns the value 11 to c, and the statement

```
c = green;
```

assigns the value 34 to c. (If no value is specified for `green` in the declaration, it would assume the value 12).

Enumeration is a convenient way to associate constant integers with meaningful names. They have the advantage of generating the values automatically. Use of enumeration constants, in general makes the program easier to read and change at a later date.

Names of different enumeration constants must be distinct. The following example is invalid.

```
enum emotion  {happy, hot, cool};
enum weather  {hot, cold, wet};
```

It is not difficult to see why the above declarations are invalid; the name `hot` has the value 1 in the enum `emotion` and the value 0 in `weather`. In the program, if the name `hot` is used, there is ambiguity as to which value to use. On the other hand, values need not be distinct in the same enumeration. For example, the following declaration is perfectly valid:

```
enum weather {hot, warm = 0, cold, wet};
```

The names hot and warm can be interchangeably used, since both represent the value 0.

Consider the following enumeration statement

```
enum flag { false, true };
```

It declares the identifier flag as an enumerated data type. It can be further used in the definition of enumerated variables as follows:

```
flag flag1;    // holds either false or true
```

In this case, the variable flag1 is defined as an enumerated variable of type flag and always holds the value either true or false as follows:

```
flag1 = true;
```

If an attempt is made to assign any value other than true or false, the compiler generates a warning.

```
flag1 = 3;     // warning: trying to assign integer to flag1
```

Use only enumerated constants with enumerated variables. The multimodule programs color1.cpp and color2.cpp illustrate some critical points on enumerated data types.

```
// color1.cpp: main having enum typedef and calling function from color2.cpp
#include <iostream.h>
typedef enum Color { red, green, blue }; // red = 0, green = 1, and blue = 2
void PrintColor( Color c );
void main()
{
    cout << "Your color choice in color1.cpp module: green" << endl;
    PrintColor( green );    // calls module in color2.cpp
}
```

```
// color2.cpp: prints color name based on color code
#include <iostream.h>
typedef enum Color { red, blue, green }; // red = 0, blue = 1, and green = 2
void PrintColor( Color c )
{
    char *color;
    switch( c )
    {
        case red:    // case 0
            color = "red";
            break;
        case blue:   // case 1
            color = "blue";
            break;
        case green:  // case 2
            color = "green";
            break;
    }
    cout << "Your color choice as per color2.cpp module: " << color;
}
```

Run
```
Your color choice in color1.cpp module: green
Your color choice as per color2.cpp module: blue
```

The modules `color1.cpp` and `color2.cpp` must be compiled and linked together in order to create an executable code. The command to create an executable version of these modules, in the Borland C++ environment is:

```
bcc color1.cpp color2.cpp
```

It creates the executable file `color1.exe`.

The enumeration declaration statement in `color1.cpp`

```
typedef enum Color { red, green, blue };
```

creates three constant symbols red, green, blue with 0, 1, and 2 respectively. It can be written without the use of `typedef` keyword as follows:

```
enum Color { red, green, blue };
```

An enumerated variable can be defined using the statement

```
Color c1;
```

although, the `typedef` keyword is missing. The enumeration declaration statement in `color2.cpp`

```
typedef enum Color { red, blue, green };
```

creates three constant symbols red, blue, green with 0, 1, and 2 respectively. Note that, the enumerated symbol green has the value 1 in the first module `color1.cpp` whereas, it has the value 2 in the module `color2.cpp`. The statement in `color1.cpp`

```
PrintColor( green );    // calls module in color2.cpp
```

invokes the `PrintColor()` defined in the `color2.cpp` module with the enumerated symbol green (whose value is 1 in `color1.cpp`) to print the message green. Instead it prints the message blue; the enumeration declaration in `color2.cpp` declares the symbol green having the value 2 and blue as 1. The value of symbol green in `color1.cpp` is the same as that of the symbol blue in `color2.cpp`. This can be observed from the switch statement with the enumerated variable c in the `color2.cpp` module. Such inconsistent enumeration declaration must be avoided, and they must have the same declaration in all the modules constituting a program. Thus, enumeration variables can be defined in any module, but it is defined according to the enumeration declaration in its own module. Enumerated constants will have the same value as declared in the current module. In the above program, the module `color1.cpp` has enumeration declaration:

```
typedef enum Color { red, green, blue };
```

and the module `color2.cpp` has the enumeration declaration:

```
typedef enum Color { red, blue, green };
```

Note that, in the above declarations, enumeration constants green and blue will have different value in different modules. Such mismatch in declaration will generate wrong results. Therefore, the call

```
PrintColor( green );
```

in the module `color1.cpp` prints blue instead of green.

4.24 Macro Functions

The preprocessor will replace all the macro functions used in the program by their function body before the compilation. The distinguishing feature of macro functions are that there will be no explicit function call during execution, since the function body is substituted at the point of macro call during compilation. Thereby the runtime overhead for function linking or context-switch time is reduced. The directive #define, indicates the start of a macro function as shown in Figure 4.10. The macro function specification spans for a maximum of one line only. However, macro function body can spread to multiple lines if each new line is followed by '\' character.

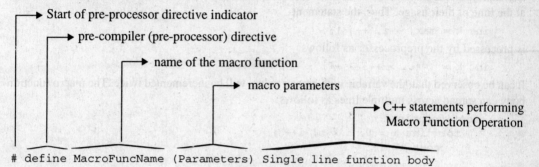

```
# define MacroFuncName (Parameters) Single line function body
```

Figure 4.10: Syntax for declaring macro function

Examples:
```
#define inc( a ) a+1
#define add( a, b ) (a+b)
```

The program maxmacro.cpp illustrates the use of macro function in the computation of the maximum of two numbers.

```
// maxmacro.cpp: maximum of two numbers using macros
#include <iostream.h>
#define max( a, b ) ( a > b ? a : b )
void main()
{
    cout << "max( 2, 3 ) = " << max( 2, 3 ) << endl;
    cout << "max( 10.2, 4.5 ) = " << max( 10.2, 4.5 ) << endl;
    int i = 5, j = 10;
    cout << "i = " << i << endl;
    cout << "j = " << j << endl;
    cout << "On execution of k = max( ++i, ++j );..." << endl;
    int k = max( ++i, ++j );
    cout << "i = " << i << endl;
    cout << "j = " << j << endl;
    cout << "k = " << k << endl;
}
```

Run

```
max( 2, 3 ) = 3
max( 10.2, 4.5 ) = 10.2
i = 5
j = 10
On execution of k = max( ++i, ++j );...
i = 6
j = 12
k = 12
```

In `main()`, the expressions

```
max( 2, 3 )
max( 10.2, 4.5 )
```

invoke the macro function `max()`. Unlike normal functions, macro functions can take parameters of any data type. If arguments are in the form of expressions, they are not evaluated at the point of call, but at the time of their usage. Thus, the statement

```
int k = max( ++i, ++j );
```

is processed by the preprocessor as follows:

```
int k = ( ++i > ++j ? ++i : ++j );
```

It can be observed that, the variable with greater value, will be incremented twice. The macro function body can spread across multiple lines as follows:

```
#define print( n ) \
    for( int i = 0; i < n; i++ ) \
        cout << i;
```

4.25 Operator Precedence and Associativity

Every operator in C++ has a precedence associated with it. Precedence rules help in removing the ambiguity about the order of performing operations while evaluating an expression. The associativity of the operators is also important. Associativity specifies the direction in which the expression is evaluated, while using a particular operator. The precedence and associativity of all the operators including those introduced by C++ are shown in Table 4.13. It is important to note the order of precedence and evaluation (associativity) of operators. Consider the following two statements:

```
int a = 10, b = 15, c = 3, d;
d = a + b * c;
```

In the second statement, first b is multiplied by c, and then the result is added to a and the sum is assigned to d. Multiplication is done before addition, since it has higher precedence than the addition operator. In order to override the precedence, braces can be used. For example, the statement

```
d = (a + b) * c;
```

would add a to b first, multiply the result by c and assign the product to d. Associativity of an operator can be from left-to-right or right-to-left. For example, in the expression

```
d = a - b - c;
```

the leftmost minus is evaluated first and then the second minus is evaluated, causing c to be subtracted from the result. Thus, in case where several operators of the same type appear in an expression without braces, the operators are normally evaluated starting from the leftmost operator, proceeding rightward, hence the minus operator associates from left to right. On the other hand, the assignment operator associates from right to left. For example, in the statement

```
d = a = c;
```

the second (right-most) assignment operator is evaluated first. The variable c is assigned to a and then this value is assigned to d.

Like most programming languages, C++ does not specify the order in which the operands of an operator are evaluated. Such operators are &&, ||, ?:, and ','.) For example, in the statement such as

```
x = g() + h();
```

g() may be evaluated before h() or vice versa; thus if g() or h() alters a variable (global) on which the other depends, then the resultant value of x is dependent on the order of evaluation. Similarly, the order in which function arguments are evaluated is not specified, so the statement

Category	Operator	Operation	Precedence	Associativity
Highest precedence	( ) [ ] -> : : .	Function call Array subscript C++ indirect component selector C++ scope access/resolution C++ direct component selector	1	L→R (left to right)
Unary	! ~ + – ++ -- & * sizeof new delete	Logical negation (NOT) Bitwise (1's) component Unary plus Unary minus Preincrement or postincrement Predecrement or postdecrement Address Indirection (returns size of operand, in bytes) dynamically allocates C++ storage dynamically deallocates C++ storage	2	R→L (right to left)
Member access	.* ->*	dereference dereference	3	L→R
Multiplication	* / %	Multiply Divide Remainder (modulus)	4	L→R
Additive	+ –	Binary plus Binary minus	5	L→R
Shift	<< >>	Shift left Shift right	6	L→R
Relational	< <= > >=	Less than Less than or equal to Greater than Greater than or equal to	7	L→R
Equality	== !=	Equal to Not equal to	8	L→R
Bitwise AND	&	Bitwise AND	9	L→R
Bitwise XOR	^	Bitwise XOR	10	L→R
Bitwise OR	|	Bitwise OR	11	L→R
Logical AND	&&	Logical AND	12	L→R
Logical OR	||	Logical OR	13	L→R
Conditional	?:	(a?x:y means "if a then x, else y")	14	L→R
Assignment	= *= /= %= += -= &= ^= |= <<= >>=	Simple assignment Assign product Assign quotient Assign remainder (modulus) Assign sum Assign difference Assign bitwise AND Assign bitwise XOR Assign bitwise OR Assign left shift Assign right shift	15	R→L
Comma		Evaluate	16	L→R

Table 4.13: Operator precedence and associativity

```
add( ++n, pow( 2, n ) );
```

can produce different results with different compilers. However, *most C++ compilers evaluate function arguments from right to left*. There are cases such as in function calls, nested assignments, increment and decrement operators cause *side effects*—some variable is changed as a by-product of the evaluation of the expression. The (C language and hence, C++) standard intentionally leaves such matters unspecified. When side effects (variable modification) take place within an expression, it is left to the discretion of the compiler, since the best order depends strongly on the machine architecture.

The moral is that developing a code that depends on the order of evaluation, is not a good programming practice in any language. Hence, it is necessary to know what to avoid, but if it is not known how they are treated, the programmer should not be tempted to take advantage of a particular implementation.

Review Questions

4.1 What are variables ? List C++ rules for variable naming.

4.2 Why `output` and `Output` are considered as different identifiers ?

4.3 What are keywords ? List keywords specific to C++. Can these keywords be used as variables ?

4.4 What is a data type ? What are the different data types supported by C++ ?

4.6 What is new about C++ in terms of the variable definition ?

4.7 What is the difference between a character and a character string representation ?

4.8 What is an expression ? Is this different from a statement ? Give reasons.

4.9 List categories of operators supported by C++.

4.10 What are qualifiers ? Illustrate them with examples.

4.11 Develop an interactive program to compute simple and compound interest.

4.12 List evaluation steps for the expression `(a+(b*c))*c+d/2`.

4.13 Write an interactive program to find the largest of two numbers.

4.14 How C++ represents true and false values ? Are the expressions `!a` and `a==0` have the same meaning ? Give reasons.

4.15 Write a program to determine the type of compiler (whether 16 or 32-bit) used to compile it.

4.16 Write a program to multiply and divide a given number by 2 without using `*` and `/` operators.

4.17 Illustrate how compound assignment operators allow to write compact expressions ?.

4.18 What is the effect of the following expressions if `i=1` and `j=4` ?
   a) `i++`   b) `j = j++;`   c) `j = ++j;`   d) `i+++j`   e) `i = i+++++j;`

4.19 Write an interactive program to find elder among *you* and *me* using the ternary operator.

4.20 What is the outcome of the statement: `a=(a=10,a++,a--);` if a holds the value 5 initially.

4.21 What is type conversion ? What are the differences between silent and explicit type conversion? Write type conversion steps required for evaluating the statement:
   `z=i+b+j-k/4;` (where i and j are ints, b is float, and k is double, and z is long type).

4.22 What are escape sequences ? Write a program to output messages in double quotes.

4.23 What are macros ? Write a program to find the minimum of two numbers using macros. What is the output of the statement: `a = min( ++a, ++b);`   (if a = 2 and b = 4).

4.24 What is operator precedence ? Arrange the following operators in the order of their precedence:
   `-, *, +, (), ^, !, ++, --, |, ||, &, /,` and `&&`

4.25 What is the significance of the associativity of operators ? What is the order of evaluation of the operator `? :` in the statement
   `a = i > j ? i : j;`

5

Control Flow

5.1 Introduction

In real-world, several activities are initiated (sequenced), or repeated based on some decisions. Such activities can be programmed by specifying the order in which computations are carried out. Flow control is the way a program causes the flow of execution to advance and branch based on changes in the data state. Branching, iteration, dispatch, and function calls are all different forms of *flow control*. Flow control in C++ is nearly identical to those in C. Many C programs can be converted quite easily to C++ because of this similarity. The C++ language offers a number of control flow statements: `for`, `while`, `do-while`, `if-else`, `else-if`, `switch`, `goto`. Although all of them can perform operations such as looping or branching, each one of them is convenient for a particular requirement. The control flow statements can be broadly categorized as, branching and looping statements.

Branching Statements

Branching statements alter sequential execution of program statements. Following are the branching statements supported by C++:

     (a) `if` statement
     (b) `if-else` statement
     (c) `switch` statement
     (d) `goto` statement

Among all the above statements, `goto` is the only unconditional branching statement.

Looping Statements

Loops cause a section of code to be executed repeatedly until a termination condition is met. The following are the looping statements supported in C++:

     (a) `for` statement
     (b) `while` statement
     (c) `do-while` statement

The `goto` statement can be used for looping, but its use is generally avoided as it leads to haphazard code and also increases the chances of error.

5.2 Statements and Block

An expression such as a = 1000, x++, or cout << "Hi", when followed by the semicolon, becomes a statement. For example, the following

```
a = 1000;
x++;
cout << "Hi";
```

are treated as C++ statements. In C++, the semicolon is a statement terminator, rather than a separator as in Pascal.

C++ allows grouping of statements, which have to be treated as an entity and the resulting group is called *compound statement* or *block*. It consists of declarations, definitions, and statements enclosed within braces { and } as follows:

```
{
    int a;
    int b = 10;
    a = b + 100;
    . . . .
}
```

Note that, there is no semicolon after the right brace that ends a block. A block is syntactically equivalent to a single statement. Any variable defined within a block is local to the block and it is not visible outside the block. Blocks are very useful when branching or looping action is to be applied on a set of statements depending on a particular decision. Examples illustrating the use of a block will be discussed later.

5.3 `if` Statement

The `if` construct is a powerful decision making statement which is used to control the sequence of the execution of statements. It alters the sequential execution using the following syntax:

> *if(test-expression)*
>   *statement;*

The test-expression should always be enclosed in parentheses. If test-expression is true (nonzero), then the statement immediately following it is executed. Otherwise, control passes to the next statement following the `if` construct. The control flow in the `if` statement is shown in Figure 5.1.

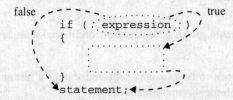

Figure 5.1:   Control flow in if statement

Notice that there is no `then` keyword following the test expression, as there is in BASIC and Pascal. The program `age1.cpp` illustrates the use of `if` statement for making a decision.

```
// age1.cpp: use of if statement
#include <iostream.h>
void main()
{
    int age;
    cout << "Enter your age: ";
    cin >> age;
    if( age > 12 && age < 20 )
        cout << "you are a teen-aged person. good!";
}
```

Run1

```
Enter your age: 15
you are a teen-aged person. good!
```

Run2

```
Enter your age: 20
```

In `main()`, the statement

```
if( age > 12 && age < 20 )
```

first evaluates the test expression and executes the if-part only when it is true. In *Run1*, the input data entered is 15 which lies between 13 and 19 and hence, the statement

```
cout << "you are a teen-aged person. good!";
```

gets executed. Whereas, in *Run2*, the input data is 20 which does not lie within this range and hence, the control proceeds to the next statement.

Compound Statement with `if`

In the `if` construct, the if-part can be represented by a compound statement as follows:

```
if(test-expression)
{
    statement 1;
    statement 2;
}
```

In this case, when test-expression is true, the statements enclosed within the curly braces, representing a compound statement, are executed. The program `age2.cpp` illustrates the use of the compound-if statement.

```
// age2.cpp: use of if statement and data validation
#include <iostream.h>
void main()
{
    int age;
    cout << "Enter your age: ";
    cin >> age;
    if( age < 0 )
    {
        cout << "I am sorry!" << endl;
        cout << "age can never be negative";
        return;    // terminate program
    }
    if( age > 12 && age < 20 )
        cout << "you are a teen-aged person. good!";
}
```

Run

```
Enter your age: -10
I am sorry!
age can never be negative
```

In `main()`, the statement

```
if( age < 0 )
```

validates the input data and accordingly takes action. It terminates the program after issuing the warning message, when the input data is negative.

The program `large.cpp` illustrates the use of multiple decision statements to compute the maximum of three numbers.

```
// large.cpp: find the largest of three numbers
#include <iostream.h>
void main()
{
    float  a, b, c, big;
    cout << "Enter three floating-point numbers: ";
    cin >> a >> b >> c;
    // computing the largest of three numbers
    big = a;
    if(b > big)
        big = b;
    if(c > big)
        big = c;
    cout << "Largest of the three numbers = " << big;
}
```

Run

```
Enter three floating-point numbers: 10.2 15.6 12.8
Largest of the three numbers = 15.6
```

5.4 `if-else` Statement

The `if-else` statement will execute a single statement or a group of statements, when the test expression is true. It does nothing when the test expression fails. C++ provides the `if-else` construct to perform some action even when the test expression fails. The control flow in the `if-else` statement is shown in Figure 5.2.

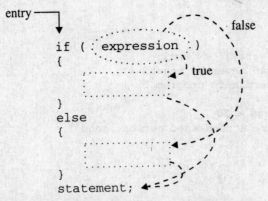

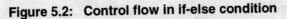

Figure 5.2:   Control flow in if-else condition

When test-expression is true (nonzero), the if-part is executed and control passes to the next statement following the `if` construct. Otherwise, the else-part is executed and control passes to the next statement. The program `age3.cpp` illustrates the use of the `if-else` statement.

```
// age3.cpp: use of if..else statement
#include <iostream.h>
void main()
{
    int age;
    cout << "Enter your age: ";
    cin >> age;
    if( age > 12 && age < 20 )
        cout << "you are a teen-aged person. good!";
    else
        cout << "you are not a teen-aged person.";
}
```

Run1

Enter your age: <u>15</u>
you are a teen-aged person. good!

Run2

Enter your age: <u>20</u>
you are not a teen-aged person.

In `main()`, the statement

```
        if( age > 12 && age < 20 )
```

generates different types of output depending on the input values. If the test expression is true, the statement

```
        cout << "you are a teen-aged person. good!";
```

is executed. Otherwise, the statement

```
        cout << "you are not a teen-aged person.";
```

in the else-part is executed.

Compound Statement with `if-else`

In the `if-else` construct, the if-part, or else-part, or both can have a compound statement as follows:

```
        if( test-expression)
        {
            statement 1;
            statement 2;
        }
        else
        {
            statement 3;
            statement 4;
        }
```

The program `lived.cpp` illustrates the use of the compound `if-else` statements.

```
// lived.cpp: single if statement validates input data
#include <iostream.h>
void main()
{
   float years, secs;
   cout << "Enter your age in years: ";
   cin >> years;
   if( years < 0 )
     cout << "I am sorry! age can never be negative" << endl;
   else
   {
     secs = years * 365 * 24 * 60 * 60;
     cout << "You have lived for " << secs << " seconds";
   }
}
```

Run1

```
Enter your age in years: -1
I am sorry! age can never be negative
```

Run2

```
Enter your age in years: 25
You have lived for 7.884e+08 seconds
```

5.5 Nested if-else Statements

Multi-way decisions arise when there are multiple conditions and different actions to be taken under each condition. A multi-way decision can be written by using if-else constructs in the else-part as follows:

> *if(test-expression1)*
>   *statement1;*
> *else*
>   *if(test-expression2)*
>   *statement2;*
>   *else*
>   *if(test-expression3)*
>   *statement3;*

Here, if test-expression1 is true, the whole chain is terminated. Only if test-expression1 is found false, the chain of events continue. At any stage if an expression is true, the remaining chain will be terminated. The program age4.cpp illustrates the use of nested if-else statements.

```
// age4.cpp: use of if..else..if statement
#include <iostream.h>
void main()
{
   int age;
   cout << "Enter your age: ";
   cin >> age;
   if( age > 12 && age < 20 )
```

```
        cout << "you are a teen-aged person. good!";
    else
        if( age < 13 )
            cout << "you will surely reach teen-age.";
        else
            cout << "you have crossed teen-age!";
}
```

Run1

```
Enter your age: 16
you are a teen-aged person. good!
```

Run2

```
Enter your age: 25
you have crossed teen-age!
```

In the above program, the nested if-else statement takes decisions based on the input data and displays appropriate messages for any given input. It proceeds to match the input data with various conditions when the earlier condition fails to decide the fate of the input data. Note that in case of nested if-else statements, the else statement is always associated with the corresponding inner most if statement.

Indentation

In all the above examples, the statements inside the if construct are indented. The C++ language, however, does not expect indentation of statements. It is done merely for improving program readability. The importance of indenting becomes evident during the usage of nested if statements (if statements within other if statements; any number of nested-if statements are allowed). For example, consider the following if statement

```
        if( a > b ) if( .a > c ) big = a;
        else big = c;
```

The above statement is perfectly valid as far as the compiler is concerned, but it is very difficult for the programmer to decipher it. An indented version of this is listed below:

```
        if( a > b )
            if( a > c )
                big = a;
            else
                big = c;
```

From the above code it can be observed that, indentation enhances the readability of the code and helps in understanding the flow of control with ease.

Nested if-else statements can be conveniently replaced by a new construct called switch. It allows to choose among several alternatives; it is.dealt later in this chapter.

5.6 for Loop

The for loop is useful while executing a statement a fixed number of times. Even here, more than one statement can be enclosed in curly braces to form a compound statement. The control flow in the for loop is shown in Figure 5.3.

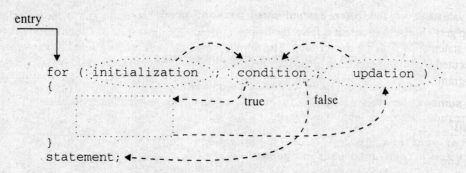

Figure 5.3:   Control flow in for loop

The for statement is a compact way to express a loop. All the four parts of a loop are in close proximity with the for statement. The *initialization part* is executed only once. Next the *test condition* is evaluated. If the test evaluates to false, then the next statement after the for loop is executed. If the *test expression* evaluates to true, then after executing the *body* of the loop, the *update part* is executed. The test is evaluated again and the whole process is repeated as long as the test expression evaluates to true as illustrated in the program count1.cpp.

```
// count1.cpp: display numbers 1..N using for loop
#include <iostream.h>
void main()
{
    int n;
    cout << "How many integers to be displayed: ";
    cin >> n;
    for( int i = 0; i < n; i++ )
       cout << i << endl;
}
```

Run

```
How many integers to be displayed: 5
0
1
2
3
4
```

In main(), the statement

```
    for( int i = 0; i < n; i++ )
        cout << i << endl;
```

has four components. The first three components enclosed in round braces and separated by semicolons are the following:

```
    int i = 0
    i < n
    i++
```

The first component int i = 0 is called the *initialization expression* and is executed only once prior to the statements within the for loop. The second component i < n is called the *test expression* and is evaluated every time before execution of the loop body. If this expression is true, the statement in the loop gets executed. In case it is false, the loop terminates and the control of execution is transferred to the statement following the for loop. The third component i++, is called *update expression*, and is executed after every execution of the statement in the loop. The fourth component is the loop-body. The program sumsq1.cpp, finds the sum and the sum of squares of the first 15 positive even integers.

```cpp
// sumsq1.cpp: sum of first 15 even numbers and their squares' sum
#include<iostream.h>
void main()
{
    int i;
    int sum = 0, sum_of_squares = 0;
    for( i = 2; i <= 30; i += 2 )
    {
        sum += i;
        sum_of_squares += i*i;
    }
    cout << "Sum of first 15 positive even numbers = " << sum << endl;
    cout << "Sum of their squares = " << sum_of_squares;
}
```

Run

```
Sum of first 15 positive even numbers = 240
Sum of their squares = 4960
```

In main(), the statement

```
for( i = 2; i <= 30; i += 2 )
```

increments the loop variable i by 2 using the update expression

```
i += 2
```

The body of the loop consists of multiple statements, forming a compound statement. The for loop counts from 2 to 30 in steps of two. It is just as easy for a loop to count down, from 30 to 2, as illustrated in the program sumsq2.cpp.

```cpp
// sumsq2.cpp: sum of first 15 even numbers and their squares' sum
#include<iostream.h>
void main()
{
    int i;
    int sum = 0, sum_of_squares = 0;
    for( i = 30; i >= 2; i -= 2 )
    {
        sum += i;
        sum_of_squares += i*i;
    }
    cout << "Sum of first 15 positive even numbers = " << sum << endl;
    cout << "Sum of their squares = " << sum_of_squares;
}
```

Run

```
Sum of first 15 positive even numbers = 240
Sum of their squares = 4960
```

Notice the changes: the value of i is initialized to 30, the test expression involves the >= condition instead of the <= as in the previous example, and the update expression i -= 2 decrements the value of i. But the output in this case is identical to the first.

The *comma operator* is especially useful in for loops. The initialization, test, or update part having multiple expressions can be be separated by commas. For instance,

```
for( i = 0, j=-5; i < 25; i++, j-- )
{
    cout << i << " " << j;
}
```

Another interesting feature of the for loop is that any of the three components (the initialization, test and the update components) may be left out, however, the separating semicolons must be present. The variants of the for loop are shown in Figures 5.4.

Keyword
Initialization expression
Test expression
Update expression

(i) `for ( j = 0 ; j < 25 ; j++ )` ⟶ ✘ No semicolon here
        `statement ;`   Single-statement body

(ii) `for ( j = 0 ;   j < 15 ;   j++ )` ⟶ ✘ No semicolon here
        `{`
        `    statement ;`
        `    .....`   ⎫ Compound statement body
        `    statement ;`   ⎭
        `}`

(iii) `for( j = 0 ; j < 25 ; j++ ) ;` ⟶ Has the same effect as j = 25;

(iv) `for( i = 0 ,j = 10 ; j < 25; j++, i-- )` ⟶ Multiple initialization and
        `cout << i << j;`   multiple update using
                                                             comma operator

(v) `for( ; j < 25; j++ )` ⟶ Initialization expression
        `cout << j;`   not used

(vi) `for( ; ; j++)` ⟶ Initialization and test
        `cout << j;`   expressions not used

(vii) `for( ; ; )` ⟶ Initialization, test, update
        `cout << "I cannot stop.";`   expressions not used

Figure 5.4:   Variants of for loop

The program noinit.cpp, prints the first 10 multiples of 5, in which the for loop has only the test component.

```
// noinit.cpp: for loop without initialization and updation
#include <iostream.h>
```

```
void main()
{
   int i = 1;
   for( ; i<=10; )
   {
      cout << i*5 << " ";
      ++i;
   }
}
```

Run

5 10 15 20 25 30 35 40 45 50

In main(), the statement

```
      int i = 1;
```

is introduced before the for loop. Also, instead of the update expression, i is incremented inside the for loop body. Note again that the C++ language does not require the user to indent statements in a for loop. The lines are indented merely for enhancing program appearance (readability).

The nested for loops are used extensively in developing programs for solving matrix multiplication, numerical analysis, sorting, and searching problems. The program pyramid.cpp illustrates the use of nested for loops in generating a pyramid of numbers.

```
// pyramid.cpp: constructs pyramid of digits
#include <iostream.h>
void main()
{
   int p, m, q, n;
   cout << "Enter the number of lines: ";
   cin >> n;
   for(p = 1; p <= n; p++)
   {
      // To print spaces
      for(q = 1; q <= n-p; q++)
         cout << "    ";
      // To print numbers
      m = p;
      for(q = 1; q <= p; q++)
      {
         cout.width(4);
         cout << m++;
      }
      m = m - 2;
      for(q = 1; q < p; q++)
      {
         cout.width(4);
         cout << m--;
      }
      cout << endl;
   }
}
```

Run
```
Enter the number of lines: 5
                    1
                2   3   2
            3   4   5   4   3
        4   5   6   7   6   5   4
    5   6   7   8   9   8   7   6   5
```

5.7 while loop

The while loop is used when the number of iterations to be performed are not known in advance. The control flow in the while loop is shown in Figure 5.5. The statements in the loop are executed if the test condition is true and the execution continues as long as it remains true. The program count2.cpp illustrates the use of the while loop to perform the same function as the for loop.

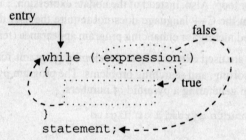

Figure 5.5: Control flow in while loop

```cpp
// count2.cpp: display numbers 1..N using while loop
#include <iostream.h>
void main()
{
    int n;
    cout << "How many integers to be displayed: ";
    cin >> n;
    int i = 0;
    while( i < n )
    {
        cout << i << endl;
        i++;
    }
}
```

Run
```
How many integers to be displayed: 5
0
1
2
3
4
```

The `while` loop is often used when the number of times the loop has to be executed is unknown in advance. It is illustrated in the program `average1.cpp`.

```
// average1.cpp: find the average of the marks
#include <iostream.h>
void main()
{
    int i, sum = 0, count = 0, marks;
    cout << "Enter the marks, -1 at the end...\n";
    cin >> marks;
    while( marks != -1 )
    {
        sum += marks;
        count++;
        cin >> marks;
    }
    float average = sum / count;
    cout << "The average is " << average;
}
```

Run

```
Enter the marks, -1 at the end...
80
75
82
74
-1
The average is 77
```

The first `cin` statement, just before the while loop, reads the marks scored in the first subject and stores in the variable `marks`, so that the statement inside the loop can have some valid data to operate. The `cin` statement inside the loop reads the marks scored in the other subjects one by one. When -1 is entered, the condition

> `marks != -1`

evaluates to false in the while loop. So, the while loop terminates and the program execution proceeds with the statement immediately after the while loop, which in the above program is

> `average = sum / count;`

Consider the case when the user inputs -1 as the first marks. The condition in the while statement evaluates to false, and the statements inside the loop are not executed at all. In this case, the value of `count` continues to be zero, so, while computing the `average` it leads to division by zero causing a run-time error. This can be prevented by using the `if` statement as follows:

> `if( count != 0 )`
> `    average = sum / count;`

The above statement can also be written as

> `if( count )`
> `    average = sum / count;`

Any expression whose value is nonzero is treated as true. The program `binary.cpp` illustrates such situations. It uses the while construct to convert a binary number to its decimal equivalent. The shift-left operator `<<` is used for shifting bits stored in a variable in this program.

```
// bin2deci.cpp: conversion of binary number to its decimal equivalent
#include <iostream.h>
void main()
{
    int binary, decimal = 0, digit, position = 0;
    cout << "Enter the binary number: ";
    cin >> binary;
    // converting binary to decimal
    while( binary )
    {
        digit = binary % 10; // extract binary bit
        decimal += digit << position; // newvalue = oldvalue + 2^position
        binary /= 10;  // advance to next bit
        position += 1; // advance to next bit position
    }
    cout << "Its decimal equivalent = " << decimal;
}
```

Run

```
Enter the binary number: 111
Its decimal equivalent = 7
```

5.8 do..while Loop

Sometimes, it is desirable to execute the body of a while loop at least once, even if the test expression evaluates to false during the first iteration. In effect, this requires testing of termination expression at the end of the loop rather than the beginning as in the while loop. So the do-while loop is called a bottom tested loop. The loop is executed as long as the test condition remains true. The control flow in the do..while loop is shown in Figure 5.6. Note the semicolon (;) following the while statement at the bottom.

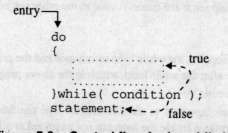

Figure 5.6: Control flow in do..while loop

The program count3.cpp illustrates the use of the do..while loop.

```
// count3.cpp: display numbers 1..N using do..while loop
#include <iostream.h>
void main()
{
    int n;
    cout << "How many integers to be displayed: ";
    cin >> n;
    int i = 0;
```

```
    do
    {
       cout << i << endl;
       i++;
    } while( i < n );
}
```

Run

```
How many integers to be displayed: 5
0
1
2
3
4
```

To realize the usefulness of the do..while construct, consider the following problem: The user has to be prompted to press m or f. In reality, the user can press any key other than m or f. In such a case, the message has to be shown again, and the users should be allowed to re-enter one of the two options. An ideal construct to handle such a situation is the do..while loop as illustrated in the program dowhile.cpp.

```
// dowhile.cpp: do..while loop for asking data until it is valid
#include <iostream.h>
void main()
{
   char inchar;
   do
   {
      cout << "Enter your sex (m/f): ";
      cin >> inchar;
   } while( inchar != 'm' && inchar != 'f' );
   if( inchar == 'm' )
      cout << "So you are male. good!";
   else
      cout << "So you are female. good!";
}
```

Run

```
Enter your sex (m/f): d
Enter your sex (m/f): b
Enter your sex (m/f): m
So you are male. good!
```

In main(), the do..while loop keeps prompting for the user input until the character m for male or f for female is entered. Such validation of data is very important while handling sensitive and critical data.

The solution to certain problems inherently requires data validation only after some operation is performed as illustrated in the program pal.cpp. It checks if the user entered number is a palindrome using the do-while construct.

```
// pal.cpp: to check for a palindrome
#include<iostream.h>
void main()
{
    int n, num, digit, rev = 0;
    cout << "Enter the number: ";
    cin >> num;
    n = num;
    do
    {
        digit = num % 10;
        rev = rev * 10 + digit;
        num /= 10;
    } while( num != 0 );
    cout << "Reverse of the number = " << rev << endl;
    if(n == rev)
        cout << "The number is a palindrome\n";
    else
        cout << "The number is not a palindrome\n";
}
```

Run1

```
Enter the number: 123
Reverse of the number = 321
The number is not a palindrome
```

Run2

```
Enter the number: 121
Reverse of the number = 121
The number is a palindrome
```

5.9 `break` Statement

A break construct terminates the execution of loop and the control is transferred to the statement immediately following the loop. The term *break* refers to the act of breaking out of a block of code. The control flow in `for`, `while`, and `do-while` loop statements with `break` statement embedded within their body is shown in Figure 5.7.

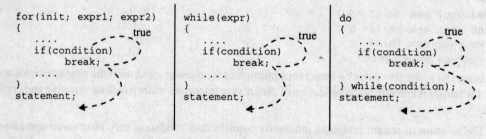

Figure 5.7:   break statements in loops

The program `average1.cpp` discussed earlier has the following code:

```
cin >> marks;
while( marks != -1 )
{
    sum += marks;
    count++;
    cin >> marks;
}
```

It computes the sum of marks entered by the user and maintains their count. This segment of code can be replaced by the following piece of code using the `break` statement:

```
while( 1 )
{
    cin >> marks;
    if( marks == -1 )
        break;
    sum += marks;
    count++;
}
```

Note that it avoids the use of two `cin` statements. Whenever -1 is input, the condition `marks==-1` evaluates to true, and the `break` statement is executed, which leads to the termination of loop. Control passes to the statement following the `while` construct. Observe that the condition in the `while` loop has been specified as 1 (one) which is nonzero and hence is always true. The condition specifies an infinite loop, but the `break` prevents such a situation. The above segment of code can also be replaced by the following `for` loop segment:

```
for( ;; )
{
    cin >> marks;
    if( marks == -1 )
        break;
    sum += marks;
    count++;
}
```

Note that, when test-expression is not mentioned in the `for` loop, it is implicitly treated as true causing an infinite loop condition. However, it does not lead to an infinite loop as the `break` statement takes over the responsibility of loop termination. In general, the `break` statement causes control to pass to the statement following the innermost enclosing `for`, `while`, `do-while`, or `switch` statement. The same action can also be achieved by using `do..while` loop as follows:

```
do
{
    cin >> marks;
    if( marks == -1 )
        break;
    sum += marks;
    count++;
} while( 1 );
```

The program `average2.cpp` illustrates the use of `break` in loop statements. It performs the same operation as that of the program `average1.cpp`.

```
// average2.cpp: find the average of the marks
#include <iostream.h>
void main()
{
    int i, sum = 0, count = 0, marks;
    cout << "Enter the marks, -1 at the end...\n";
    while( 1 )
    {
        cin >> marks;
        if( marks == -1 )
            break;
        sum += marks;
        count++;
    }
    float average = sum / count;
    cout << "The average is " << average;
}
```

Run

```
Enter the marks, -1 at the end...
80
75
82
74
-1
The average is 77
```

5.10 `switch` Statement

The `switch` statement provides a clean way to dispatch to different parts of a code based on the value of a single variable or expression. It is a multi-way decision-making construct that allows choosing of a statement (or a group of statements) among several alternatives. The control flow in the switch statement is shown in Figure 5.8. The `switch` statement is mainly used to replace multiple if-else sequence which is hard-to-read and hard-to-maintain.

The expression following the `switch` keyword is an integer valued expression. The value of this expression decides the sequence of statements to be executed. Each sequence of statements begins with the keyword `case` followed by a constant integer. (Note that constant characters may also be specified). Control is transferred to the statements following the case label whose constant is equal to the value of the expression in the `switch` statement. The `default` part is optional in the `switch` statement. The keyword `break` is used to delimit the scope of the statements under a particular case.

```
switch( option )
{
    case 1: cout << "Option # 1 entered";
        break;
    case 2: cout << "Option # 2 entered";
        break;
    default: cout << "Invalid option entered";
}
```

In the above segment, if option is 1, then the first cout will be executed and the control will pass to the next statement after the switch. Otherwise, the rest of the case statement will be evaluated in the same way. If none of them match, then the last cout with the default will be executed.

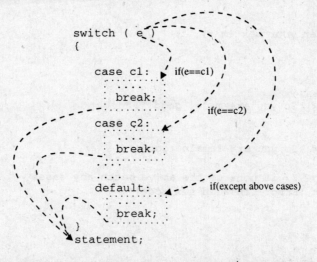

Figure 5.8: Control flow in switch statement

The break statement is essential for the correct realization of the switch structure. It causes exit from the switch structure after the case statements are executed. The break can be omitted in which case the control falls through to the next case statements. For example, omitting the break statement in the first case statement will cause both the case 1 and case 2's body to be executed. The break statements can be omitted when the same operation is to be performed for a number of cases as illustrated below:

```
switch( ch )
{
    case 'a':
    case 'e':
    case 'i':
    case 'o':
    case 'u': ++ vowel;
        break;
    case ' ': ++ spaces;
        break;
    default : ++ consonant;
}
```

In the above segment, when the contents of ch is equal to a vowel character, the statement

```
++vowel;
```

is executed.

The different cases and the default keyword may appear in any order. The program sex2.cpp illustrates the use of switch construct in replacing the nested if-else statements.

```
// sex2.cpp: use of switch statement
#include <iostream.h>
void main()
{
   char ch;
   cout << "Enter your sex (m/f): ";
   cin >> ch;
   switch( ch )
   {
      case 'm':
         cout << "So you are male. good!";
         break;
      case 'f':
         cout << "So you are female. good!";
         break;
      default:    // if none of the above match any cases
         cout << "Error: Invalid sex code!";
   }
}
```

Run1

```
Enter your sex (m/f): m
So you are male. good!
```

Run2

```
Enter your sex (m/f): b
Error: Invalid sex code!
```

5.11 continue Statement

The continue statement skips the remainder of the current iteration and initiates the execution of the next iteration. When this statement is encountered in a loop, the rest of the statements in the loop are skipped, and the control passes to the condition, which is evaluated, and if true, the loop is entered again. The continue statement has the following syntax:

```
        continue;
```

The control flow in for, while, and do..while loops with continue statement embedded within their body is shown in Figure 5.9.

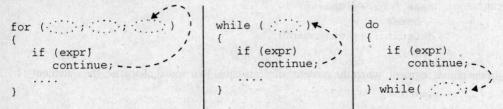

Figure 5.9:   Operational flow with continue statement

The program sumpos.cpp accepts an indefinite number of values from the keyboard and prints the sum of only the positive numbers. It demonstrates the use of break and continue statements.

```
// sumpos.cpp: sum of positive numbers
#include <iostream.h>
void main()
{
    int num, total = 0;
    do
    {
        cout << "Enter a number (0 to quit): ";
        cin >> num;
        if( num == 0 )
        {
            cout << "end of data entry." << endl;
            break;        // terminates loop
        }
        if( num < 0 )
        {
            cout << "skipping this number." << endl;
            continue; // skips next statements and transfers to start of loop
        }
        total += num;
    } while(1);
    cout << "Total of all +ve numbers is " << total;
}
```

Run

```
Enter a number (0 to quit): 10
Enter a number (0 to quit): 20
Enter a number (0 to quit): -5
skipping this number.
Enter a number (0 to quit): 10
Enter a number (0 to quit): 0
end of data entry.
Total of all +ve numbers is 40
```

In do..while loop of the above program, on encountering break, control is transferred outside the loop. On encountering continue, control is transferred to the while condition which is always true (nonzero). Figure 5.10 shows action differences between break and continue statements in loops. The break and continue statements must be judiciously used and their indiscriminate use can hamper the clarity of the logic.

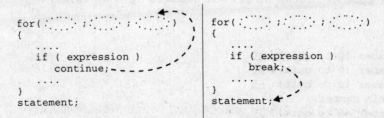

Figure 5.10: Control flow for continue and break

5.12 goto Statement

The C++ language also provides the much abused goto statement for branching unconditionally to any part of a program . A debate on whether the use of the goto construct in structured programming is essential or not, is purely academic, but practically, the goto, is never necessary and therefore is not used by many programmers. However, there are certain places where the use of goto becomes mandatory. For instance, to exit from some deeply nested loops, goto can be used. The general format of a goto statement is:

        goto label;

Here label is an identifier used to label the target statement to which the control should be transferred. Control may be transferred to any other statement within the current function. The target statement must be labeled and the label must be followed by a colon. The target statement will appear as

        label: statement;

Note that the declaration of the label symbol is not required. The program jump.cpp is equivalent to the program sumpos.cpp discussed above. It uses goto statement instead of the break statement.

```cpp
// jump.cpp: sum of positive numbers using goto construct
#include <iostream.h>
void main()
{
   int num, total = 0;
   do
   {
      cout << "Enter a number (0 to quit): ";
      cin >> num;
      if( num == 0 )
      {
         cout << "end of data entry." << endl;
         goto dataend;     // transfer to dataend position
      }
      if( num < 0 )
      {
         cout << "skipping this number." << endl;
         continue; // skips next statements and transfers to start of loop
      }
      total += num;
   } while(1);
   dataend: cout << "Total of all +ve numbers is " << total;
}
```

Run

```
Enter a number (0 to quit): 10
Enter a number (0 to quit): 20
Enter a number (0 to quit): -5
skipping this number.
Enter a number (0 to quit): 10
Enter a number (0 to quit): 0
end of data entry.
Total of all +ve numbers is 40
```

Any loop (`for`, `while`, or `do..while`) statement can be replaced by an if statement coupled with a `goto` statement. But this, of course makes the program unreadable. On the other hand, there are situations wherein `goto` statement can make the flow of control more obvious. For example, the following segment determines whether two arrays `x` and `y` have an element in common or not. The element `x` has `n` elements and `y` has `m` elements.

```
for( i = 0; i < n; i++ )
    for( j = 0; j < m; j++ )
        if( x[ i ] == y[ j ] )
            goto found;
// Element not found
...
found:
// Element found
...
```

Except in cases such as the one cited above, the use of the `goto` statement must be avoided.

It is possible to use `goto` statement to jump from outside a loop to inside the loop body, but it is logically incorrect. Hence, goto jumps shown in Figure 5.11 would cause problems and therefore must be avoided.

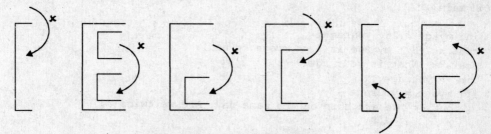

Figure 5.11: Invalid goto's

5.13 Wild Statements

It is very difficult to detect semantic errors in a program when semicolons are used improperly with loops. One such case is illustrated in the program `age5.cpp`

```
// age5.cpp: if statement with wrong usage of syntax
#include <iostream.h>
void main()
{
    int age;
    cout << "Enter your age: ";
    cin >> age;
    if( age > 12 && age < 20 );
        cout << "you are a teen-aged person. good!";
}
```

Run1

```
Enter your age: 14
you are a teen-aged person. good!
```

Run2

```
Enter your age: 50
you are a teen-aged person. good!
```

In main(), the statement

```
        if( age > 12 && age < 20 );
```

effectively does nothing; observe the semicolon after the condition statement. The program displays the same message for any type of input data. Whether the input age lies in range of teenage or not, it produces the message

```
        you are a teen-aged person. good!
```

See *Run2* output which shows even 50 year aged person as teen-aged!

Equality Test

The program agecmp.cpp is written for comparing ages of two persons. It prints the illogical message except for some typical value.

```
// agecmp.cpp: age comparison
#include <iostream.h>
void main()
{
    int myage = 25, yourage;
    cout << "Hi! my age is " << myage << endl;
    cout << "What is your age ? ";
    cin >> yourage;
    if( myage = yourage )
        cout << "We are born on the same day. Are we twins!";
}
```

Run1

```
Hi! my age is 25
What is your age ? 25
We are born on the same day. Are we twins!
```

Run2

```
Hi! my age is 25
What is your age ? 10
We are born on the same day. Are we twins!
```

Run3

```
Hi! my age is 25
What is your age ? 0
```

The statement in main()

```
        if( myage = yourage )
```

has the expression myage = yourage. It assigns the contents of the variable yourage, to myage. It is evaluated to true, for all nonzero values of yourage and hence, the program prints the same message except for zero input value. The programmer must be careful while writing the statement, which checks for the equality of data.

Review Questions

5.1 Discuss the need of control flow statements in C++.

5.2 What are the differences between break and continue statements ? Develop an interactive program which illustrates the differences.

5.3 Justify that "goto statement cannot be used to transfer control from outside to inside the loop"

5.4 Write an interactive program to print a given integer in the reverse order. For instance, 1234 should be printed as 4321.

5.5 Write an optimized algorithm (program) to print the first N prime numbers, where N is a number accepted from the keyboard.

5.6 Write a program to print the sum of all squares between 1 and N, where N is a number accepted from the keyboard. i.e., $1 + 4 + \ldots + (N*N)$.

5.7 Develop a program to find the roots of a quadratic equation. Use switch statements to handle different values of the discriminant $(b^2-4*a*c)$.

5.8 State which of the following statements are TRUE or FALSE. Give reasons.

(a) Use of goto helps in developing structured programming.

(b) In if statement, if the if condition fails, else-part is executed.

(c) The value -1 is treated as false.

(d) The switch statement can have more than one matching cases.

(e) The break statement terminates the execution of the loop.

(f) Explicit transfer of control from outside the loop to inside is logically correct.

(g) The use of an expression such as a = b as a test expression is not encouraged.

5.9 Write a program to compute the exponential value of a given number x using the series:

$$e(x) = 1+x+x^2/2!+x^3/3!+\ldots$$

5.10 Write an interactive program for computing the *factorial* of a number using the while loop.

5.11 Write a program to generate reverse pyramid of digits.

5.12 Write an interactive program to compute the *cosine* of a number using the series:

$$\cos(x)=1-x^2/2!+x^4/4!-x^6/6!+\ldots$$

5.13 Write an interactive program to compute the area of a triangle for the following cases:

a) for 3 sides of a triangle (a, b, and c):

```
p = a + b + c;
s = (a + b + c)/2;
area = sqrt((double)(s*(s-a)*(s-b)*(s-c)));
```

b) for right angle triangle: `area = (base*height)/2;`

5.14 Write a program to print the multiplication table using do..while loop.

5.15 Write an interactive program to draw a histogram of marks scored in different subjects as follows:

```
subject1: *********************** (50%)
subject2: ********************************* (72%)
```

5.16 Write a program to print a conversion chart of various currencies as shown in the table below:

```
------------------------------------------------------------
  US $       Rs       Dinar     Yen       Pound
------------------------------------------------------------
  ....       ....      ....      ....      ....
------------------------------------------------------------
```

6

Arrays and Strings

6.1 Introduction

An array is a group of logically related data items of the same data-type addressed by a common name, and all the items are stored in contiguous (physically adjacent) memory locations. For instance, the statement

```
int marks[10];
```

defines an array by the name marks that can hold a maximum of ten elements. The individual elements of an array are accessed and manipulated using the array name followed by their index. The marks scored in the first subject is accessed as marks[0] and the marks scored in the 10th subject as marks[9]. In this case, a sequence of ten integers representing the marks are stored one after another in memory. A sequence of characters is called *string*. It can be used for storing and manipulating text such as words, names, and sentences. The arrays can be used to represent a vector, matrix, etc., as shown in Figure 6.1.

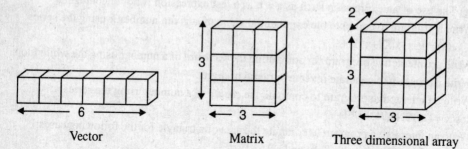

Vector   Matrix   Three dimensional array

Figure 6.1: Single and multidimensional arrays

6.2 Operations on Arrays

To see the usefulness of arrays, consider the problem of reading the ages of five persons and computing the average age. Five variables need to be defined for storing the age of five persons and they have to be read and processed using distinct statements as illustrated in the program age1.cpp.

```cpp
// age1.cpp: multiple variables to handle data which are logically same
#include <iostream.h>
void main()
{
  int age1, age2, age3, age4, age5;
  float sum = 0;
```

```
    cout << "Enter person 1 age: ";
    cin >> age1;
    sum += age1;
    cout << "Enter person 2 age: ";
    cin >> age2;
    sum += age2;
    cout << "Enter person 3 age: ";
    cin >> age3;
    sum += age3;
    cout << "Enter person 4 age: ";
    cin >> age4;
    sum += age4;
    cout << "Enter person 5 age: ";
    cin >> age5;
    sum += age5;
    cout << "Average age = " << sum/5;
}
```

Run

```
Enter person 1 age: 23
Enter person 2 age: 40
Enter person 3 age: 30
Enter person 4 age: 27
Enter person 5 age: 25
Average age = 29
```

The above program uses distinct statements to read and add the age of each person. The resulting value of summation is stored in the variable sum. Finally, the average age is computed by dividing the sum by 5. A program written in this style is very clumsy, and difficult to enhance. If there are a large number of individuals, the number of statements increase proportionately. A more elegant approach is to use an array type variable to store the age of persons, and process them using loops as illustrated in the program age2.cpp.

```
// age2.cpp: arrays to handle data which are of the same type
#include <iostream.h>
void main()
{
    int age[5];            // array definition
    float sum = 0;
    for( int i = 0; i < 5; i++ )
    {
        cout << "Enter person " << i+1 << " age: ";
        cin >> age[i];     // reading array elements
    }
    for( i = 0; i < 5; i++ )
        sum += age[i];     // array manipulation
    cout << "Average age = " << sum/5;
}
```

Run

```
Enter person 1 age: 23
```

```
Enter person 2 age: 40
Enter person 3 age: 30
Enter person 4 age: 27
Enter person 5 age: 25
Average age = 29
```

Handling arrays involve array definition, array initialization, and accessing elements of an array. In main(), the statement

```
int age[5];
```

defines an array of five elements of integer type with the name age. It reserves 5*sizeof(int) bytes of memory space for storing the five integer numbers. The statement

```
cin >> age[i];
```

reads each integer value and stores it in the array element indexed by the variable i. Here, the variable i is known as the *array index* or *subscript* and hence, arrays are popularly called *subscripted variables*. Note that an array of N elements has indexes in the range 0 to N-1. The statement

```
sum += age[i];
```

accesses the contents of the $(i+1)^{th}$ element of the array age and adds it to the variable sum.

Array Definition

Like other normal variables, the array variable must be defined before its use. The syntax for defining an array is shown in Figure 6.2.

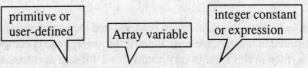

```
DataType ArrayName[array_size],...;
```

Figure 6.2:   Array definition

In the definition, the array name must be a valid C++ variable, followed by an integer value enclosed in square braces. The integer value indicates the maximum number of elements the array can hold. The following are some valid array definition statements:

```
int marks[100];            // integer array of size 100
float salary[25];          // floating-point array of size 25
char name[50];             // character array of size 50
int a[10], b[12], c[25];   // defines three arrays
double d1, num[10];        // defines a variable and double array
```

The last statement indicates that a normal variable and array can be defined in a single statement. The representation of an array defined using the statement

```
int age[5];
```

is shown in Figure 6.3 by assuming that each element of the array (i.e., each integer) occupies two bytes.

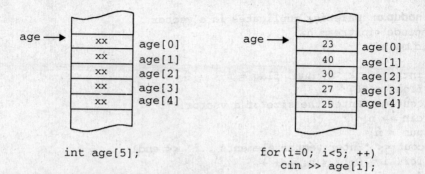

Figure 6.3:   Storage representation for an array

Accessing Array Elements

Once an array variable is defined, its elements can be accessed by using an index. The syntax for accessing array elements is shown in Figure 6.4.

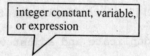

Figure 6.4:   Accessing an array element

To access a particular element in the array, specify the array name followed by an integer constant or variable (array index) enclosed within square braces. The array index, indicates the element of the array, which has to be accessed. For instance, the expression

```
age[4]
```

accesses the 5th element of the array age. Note that, in an array of N elements, the first element is indexed by zero and the last element of an array is indexed by N-1. The loop used to read the elements of the array is:

```
for( int i = 0; i < 5; i++ )
{
    cout << "Enter person " << i+1 << " age: ";
    cin >> age[i];
}
```

The variable i varies from 0 to N-1 (i.e., 0 to 4 in the above segment). Statements such as,

```
age[i]++;
```

can be used to increment the value of the ith item in the array age and hence the following,

```
age[i] = 11;
age[3] = 25;
```

are valid statements. Note that, *the expression* age[i] *can also be represented as* i[age]; *similarly, the expression* age[3] *is equivalent to* 3[age].

The program nodup.cpp illustrates the manipulation of a vector. It reads a vector and removes all duplicate elements in that vector. The vector is adjusted after removing all the duplicate elements.

```
// nodup.c: Deleting duplicates in a vector
#include <iostream.h>
void main()
{
    int i, j, k, n, num, flag = 0;
    float a[50];
    cout << "Enter the size of a vector: ";
    cin >> n;
    num = n;
    cout << "Enter vector elements ..." << endl;
    for( i = 0; i < n; i++ )
    {
        cout << "a[" << i << "] = ? ";
        cin >> a[i];
    }
    // removing duplicates
    for (i = 0; i < n - 1; i++)
        for (j = i + 1; j < n; j++)
        {
            if( a[i] == a[j] )    // duplicate found
            {
                // remove duplicate and adjust vector and its size
                n = n - 1;
                for (k = j; k < n; k++)
                    a[k] = a[k+1];
                flag = 1;    // vector has duplicates
                j = j - 1;
            }
        }
    if( flag )
    {
        cout << "vector has " << num-n << " duplicate element(s).\n";
        cout << "Vector after removing duplicates ...\n";
        for( i = 0; i < n; i++ )
            cout << "a[" << i << "] = " << a[i] << endl;
    }
    else
        cout << "vector has no duplicate elements";
}
```

Run

```
Enter the size of a vector: 6
Enter vector elements ...
a[0] = ? 1
a[1] = ? 5
a[2] = ? 6
a[3] = ? 8
a[4] = ? 5
a[5] = ? 9
vector has 1 duplicate element(s).
Vector after removing duplicates ...
```

```
a[0] = 1
a[1] = 5
a[2] = 6
a[3] = 8
a[4] = 9
```

Initialization at Definition

Arrays can be initialized at the point of their definition as follows:

data-type array-name[*size*] = { *list of values separated by comma* };

For instance, the statement

```
int age[ 5 ] = { 19, 21, 16, 1, 50 };
```

defines an array of integers of size 5. In this case, the first element of the array age is initialized with 19, second with 21, and so on as shown in Figure 6.5. A semicolon always follows the closing brace. The array size may be omitted when the array is initialized during array definition as follows:

```
int age[] = { 19, 21, 16, 1, 50 };
```

In such cases, the compiler assumes the array size to be equal to the number of elements enclosed within the curly braces. Hence, in the above statement, the size of the array is considered as five.

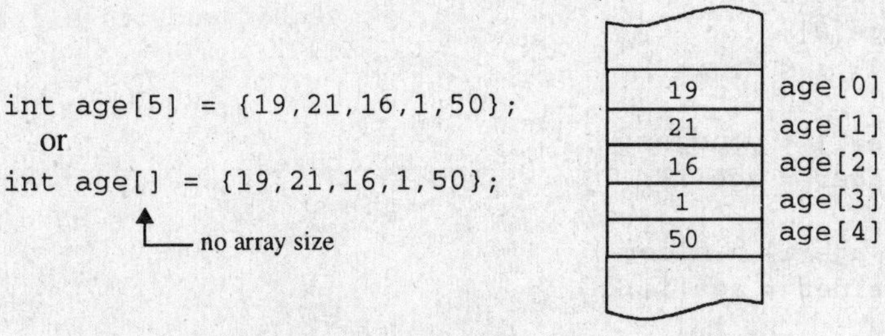

```
int age[5] = {19,21,16,1,50};
   or
int age[] = {19,21,16,1,50};

      └─── no array size
```

19	age[0]
21	age[1]
16	age[2]
1	age[3]
50	age[4]

Figure 6.5:   Array initialization at its definition

Caution! No Array Bound Validation

C++ does not support bound checking i.e., it does not check for the validity of the array index value while accessing the array elements. If the program tries to store something beyond the size of an array, neither the compiler nor the run-time will indicate the error. Such a situation may cause overwriting of data or code leading to fatal errors. Therefore, the programmer has to take extra care to use indexes within the array limits. For example, consider the following program:

```
void main()
{
    int age[ 40 ];
    age[ 50 ] = 11;
    age[ 50 ]++;
}
```

It defines age to be an array of 40 integers, and then modifies the 51st element! The compiler does not consider such an access as illegal and produces the executable code. Execution of such programs can behave in an unpredictable manner. Detecting such errors in a program is a difficult and time consuming task. Thus, it is the responsibility of the programmer to see that the value of an array index is within the array bounds while accessing an array element.

6.3 Array Illustrations

The program `elder.cpp` finds the age of the eldest and youngest person in a family. It reads the ages of all the members of a family stores them in an array and then scans the array to find out the required information.

```cpp
// elder.cpp: finding youngest and eldest person age
#include <iostream.h>
void main()
{
   int i, n;
   float age[25], younger, elder;
   cout << "How many persons are there in list <max-25> ? ";
   cin >> n;
   for( i = 0; i < n; i++ )
   {
      cout << "Enter person" << i+1 << " age: ";
      cin >> age[i];
   }
   // finding youngest and eldest person age begins here
   younger = age[0];
   elder = age[0];
   for (i = 1; i < n; i++)
   {
      if( age[i] < younger )
         younger = age[i];
      else
         if( age[i] > elder )
            elder = age[i];
   }
   // finding younger and elder person ends here
   cout << "Age of eldest person is " << elder << endl;
   cout << "Age of youngest person is " << younger;
}
```

Run

```
How many persons are there in list <max-25> ? 7
Enter person1 age: 25
Enter person2 age: 4
Enter person3 age: 45
Enter person4 age: 18
Enter person5 age: 35
Enter person6 age: 23
Enter person7 age: 32
Age of eldest person is 45
Age of youngest person is 4
```

Bubble Sort

A classical bubble sort is the first standard sorting algorithm most programmers learn to code. It has gained popularity because it is intuitive, easy to write and debug, and consumes little memory. In each pass, the first two items in a list are compared and placed in the correct order. Items two and three are then compared and reordered, followed by items three and four, then four and five, and so on. The sort continues until a pass with no swap occurs. High-value items near the beginning of a list (as shown in Figure 6.6) move to their correct position rapidly and are called turtles, because they move only one position with each pass. The program bubble.cpp illustrates the implementation of the bubble sort.

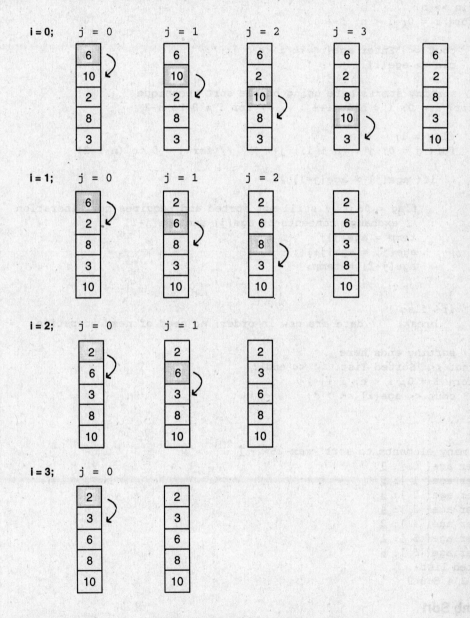

Figure 6.6: Trace of Bubble Sort

```
// bubble.cpp: sorting of numbers using bubble sorting
#include <iostream.h>
void main()
{
   int i, j, n, age[25], flag, temp;
   cout << "How many elements to sort <max-25> ? ";
   cin >> n;
   for( i = 0; i < n; i++ )
   {
      cout << "Enter age[ " << i << " ]: ";
      cin >> age[i];
   }
   // sorting starts here using bubble sort technique
   for( i = 0; i < n-1; i++ )     // for i = 0 to n-2
   {
      flag = 1;
      for( j = 0; j < (n-1-i); j++ )    // for j = 0 to (n-i-2)
      {
         if( age[j] > age[j+1] )
         {
            flag = 0;    // still not sorted and requires next iteration
            // exchange contents of age[j] and age[j+1]
            temp = age[j];
            age[j] = age[j+1];
            age[j+1] = temp;
         }
      }
      if( flag )
         break;  // data are now in order; no need of next iteration
   }
   // sorting ends here
   cout << "Sorted list..." << endl;
   for( i = 0; i < n; i ++ )
      cout << age[i] << " ";
}
```

Run

```
How many elements to sort <max-25> ? 7
Enter age[ 0 ]: 3
Enter age[ 1 ]: 5
Enter age[ 2 ]: 9
Enter age[ 3 ]: 4
Enter age[ 4 ]: 2
Enter age[ 5 ]: 1
Enter age[ 6 ]: 6
Sorted list...
1 2 3 4 5 6 9
```

Comb Sort

Comb sort is a generalization of the bubble sort that permits comparison of non-adjacent items. It retains the simplicity of a bubble sort, but with a dramatic increase in speed. Consider a sample list of 100 elements to be arranged in the ascending order. In this method elements are compared to sort them and the space between the elements to be compared is known as the *gap*. (For instance, the gap in bubble sort is one.) A gap of 80 would compare elements 1 and 81, 2 and 82, ..., and 20 and 100, and switch pairs when appropriate. Such a pass would take 20 comparisons rather than the 99 of an equivalent bubble sort. The benefit is that the swap could move the elements as much as 80 notches closer to their final destination. It is found that the ideal way to select the next gap is to divide the previous gap by 1.3 (which is known as the *shrinking factor*). The shrinking factor 1.3 has been experimentally found out to be the optimal value. The gap value remains constant once it reaches 1. A bubble sort is converted into comb sort by the following process:

- Initialize the gap with 1 in the inner loop.
- Initialize the gap size and the dimension of the list.
- Recalculate the gap with the do-loop by dividing the previous gap by 1.3, taking the integer part and using the result or 1, whichever is greater.
- Repeat the loop until the gap is 1 and the switch counter is 0, indicating that the sort operation is completed.

The program comb.cpp illustrates the implementation of the comb sort. The only difference between bubble sort and comb sort is that, in bubble sort, the turtles (data) crawl whereas in comb sort they jump. Successively shrinking the gap is analogous to combing long, tangled hair—stroking first with fingers alone, then with a pick comb that has widely spaced teeth, followed by finer combs with progressively closer teeth. Comb sort has a similar shrinking effect on the gap (hence, the name comb sort). Each stroke presorts the list (i.e., it kills or winds up some turtles). Therefore, by the time the gap declines to unity (a Bubble sort), all the elements are so close to their final position that applying a bubble sort at this stage is efficient.

```
// comb.cpp: sorting of numbers using comb sorting
#define SHRINKINGFACTOR 1.3
#include <iostream.h>
void main()
{
    int i, j, n, age[25], flag, temp;
    cout << "How many elements to sort <max-25> ? ";
    cin >> n;
    for( i = 0; i < n; i++ )
    {
        cout << "Enter age[ " << i << " ]: ";
        cin >> age[i];
    }
    // sorting starts here using comb sort technique
    int size = n;
    int gap = size;    // gap is initialized to size i.e, length of a list
    do
    {
        gap = (int) (float(gap)/SHRINKINGFACTOR);
        switch( gap )
        {
            case 0:
                gap = 1; // the smallest gap is 1 as in bubble sort
                break;
```

```
        case 9:
        case 10:
            gap = 11;
            break;
    }
    flag = 1;
    int top = size - gap;
    for( i = 0; i < top; i++)
    {
        j = i+gap;
        if( age[i] > age[j] )
        {
            flag = 0;    // still not sorted and requires next iteration
            // exchange contents of age[i] and age[j]
            temp = age[i];
            age[i] = age[j];
            age[j] = temp;
        }
    }
} while( !flag || gap > 1 );
// sorting ends here
cout << "Sorted list..." << endl;
for( i = 0; i < n; i ++ )
    cout << age[i] << " ";
}
```

Run

```
How many elements to sort <max-25> ? 7
Enter age[ 0 ]: 3
Enter age[ 1 ]: 5
Enter age[ 2 ]: 9
Enter age[ 3 ]: 4
Enter age[ 4 ]: 2
Enter age[ 5 ]: 1
Enter age[ 6 ]: 6
Sorted list...
1 2 3 4 5 6 9
```

Although the algorithm for comb sort and shell sort appear to be very similar (both use a gap and a shrink factor), they do in fact perform differently. The shell sort does a complete sort (until there are no more swaps to be made) for each gap size. comb sort makes only a single pass for each gap size--it can be thought of as a more optimistic version of the shell sort. There are other differences that result from this optimism: The ideal shrink factor for shell sort is 1.7, compared with 1.3 of comb sort. The complexity obtained by plotting sorting time against the list of size n, for shell sort, appears as a step function of $(n*\log_2 n*\log_2 n)$, whereas for comb sort it approximates to a flatter curve of $(n * \log_2 n)$.

6.4 Multi-dimensional Arrays

Most of the scientific data can be easily modeled using multi-dimensional arrays. Such representations allow manipulation of data easily and even allow the programmer to write simple and efficient programs. Matrix is a two dimensional array and two subscripts are required to access each element.

Definition

A multidimensional array is defined as follows:

> *data-type array-name*[*s1*][*s2*]...[*sn*];

For instance, the statement

```
int axis[3][3][2];
```

defines a three-dimensional array with the array-name `axis`.

The general format for defining a two-dimensional array is

> *data-type array-name*[*row-size*][*column-size*];

For instance, the statements

```
int marks[4][3];
float b[3][3];
```

define arrays named `marks` and `b` respectively. The expression `marks[0][0]`, accesses the first element of the matrix `marks` and `marks[3][2]` accesses the last row and last column. The expression `b[2][1]`, accesses the 3rd row and 2nd column element of the `b` matrix. The representation of a two-dimensional array in memory is shown in Figure 6.7.

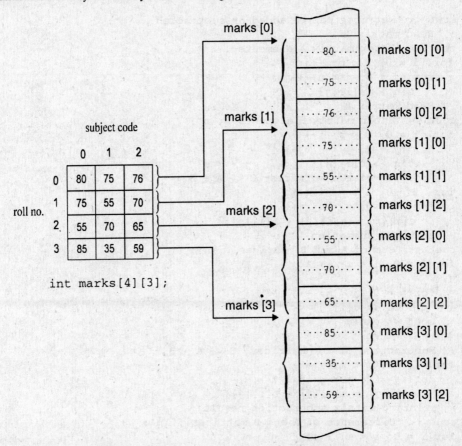

Figure 6.7: Two dimensional array to store marks

Accessing two Dimensional Array Elements

The elements of a two dimensional array can be accessed by the following statement

```
marks[i][j]
```

where i refers to the row number and j refers to the column number. The subscripts must be integer constants or variables or they can be expressions generating integer results. The program matrix.cpp illustrates the use of two dimensional arrays in matrix addition and subtraction.

```cpp
// matrix.cpp: addition and subtraction of matrices
#include <iostream.h>
void main()
{
  int a[5][5], b[5][5], c[5][5];
  int i, j, m, n, p, q;
  cout << "Enter row and column size of A matrix: ";
  cin >> m >> n;
  cout << "Enter row and column size of B matrix: ";
  cin >> p >> q;
  if((m == p) && (n == q)) // check if matrices can be added
  {
    cout << "Matrices can be added or subtracted...\n";
    // Read matrix A
    cout << "Enter matrix A elements...\n";
    for( i = 0; i < m; ++i )
       for( j = 0; j < n; ++j )
          cin >> a[i][j];
    // Read matrix B
    cout << "Enter matrix B elements...\n";
    for( i = 0; i < p; i++ )
       for( j = 0; j < q; j++ )
          cin >> b[i][j];
    // Addition of two matrices: C <- A + B
    for( i = 0; i < m; i++ )
       for( j = 0; j < n; j++ )
          c[i][j] = a[i][j] + b[i][j];
    // printing summation
    cout << "Sum of A and B matrices...\n";
    for(i = 0; i < m; ++i)
    {
       for(j = 0; j < n; ++j)
          cout << c[i][j] << "   ";
       cout << endl;
    }
    // Subtraction of two matrices: C <- A - B
    for( i = 0; i < m; i++ )
       for( j = 0; j < n; j++ )
          c[i][j] = a[i][j] - b[i][j];
    // printing matrix subtraction result
    cout << "Difference of A and B matrices...\n";
    for(i = 0; i < m; ++i)
```

```
    {
        for(j = 0; j < n; ++j)
        {
            cout.width( 2 );
            cout << c[i][j] << "  ";
        }
        cout << endl;
    }
}
}
```

Run

```
Enter row and column size of A matrix: 3 3
Enter row and column size of B matrix: 3 3
Matrices can be added or subtracted...
Enter matrix A elements...
1 2 3
4 3 1
3 1 2
Enter matrix B elements...
3 2 1
3 3 2
1 2 1
Sum of A and B matrices...
4   4   4
7   6   3
4   3   3
Difference of A and B matrices..
-2    0    2
 1    0   -1
 2   -1    1
```

Initialization at Definition

A two-dimensional array can be initialized during its definition as follows:

> *data-type matrix-name[row-size][col-size]* = {
>> { *elements of first row* },
>> { *elements of second row* },
>>
>> ....
>> { *elements of n-1 row* }
> };

For instance, the statement

```
int a[3][3] =
{
{ 1, 2, 3 },
{ 4, 3, 1 },
{ 3, 1, 2 }
};
```

defines two dimensional array of order 3x3 and initializes all its elements. The first subscript (size of the row) can be omitted. Hence, the above definition can be replaced by

```
int a[][3] =
{
    { 1, 2, 3 },
    { 4, 3, 1 },
    { 3, 1, 2 }
};
```

The inner braces can be omitted, permitting the numbers to be written in one continuous sequence as follows:

```
int a[][3] = { 1, 2, 3, 4, 3, 1, 3, 1, 2 };
```

It has the same effect as the earlier definitions, but it suffers from readability.

6.5 Strings

Strings are used in programming languages for storing and manipulating text, such as words, names, and sentences. It is represented as an array of characters and the end of the string is marked by the NULL ('\0') character. String constants are enclosed in double quotes. For instance,

```
"Hello World"
```

is a string. A string is stored in memory by using the ASCII codes of the characters that form the string. The representation of the string Hello World in memory is shown in Figure 6.8.

character string terminated by a null character '\0'

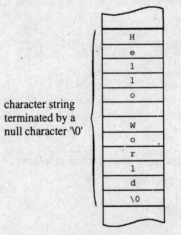

Figure 6.8:   String representation in memory

Definition

An array of characters representing a string is defined as follows:

```
char array-name[size];
```

As usual, the size of the array must be an integer value. For instance, the statement

```
char name[50];
```

defines an array and reserves 50 bytes of memory for storing a set of characters. The length of this string cannot exceed 49 since, one storage location must be reserved for storing the end of the string marker. The program name.cpp defines an array and uses it to store characters.

```
// name.cpp: read and display string
#include <iostream.h>
void main()
{
    char name[50]; // string definition
    cout << "Enter your name <49-max>: ";
    cin >> name;
    cout << "Your name is " << name;
}
```

Run

```
Enter your name <49-max>: Archana
Your name is Archana
```

In main(), the statement

```
        cin >> name;
```

reads characters and stores them into the variable name. The statement

```
        cout << "Your name is " << name;
```

outputs the contents of the string variable name.

Initialization at the Point of Definition

The string variable can be initialized at the point of its definition as follows:

char array-name[size] = { *list of values separated by comma* };

For instance, the statement

```
        char month[] = { 'A','p','r','i','l', 0 };
```

defines the string variable and assigns the character 'A' to month[0], 'p' to month[1],.., 0 to month[5]. The end of the string in the above statement can also be represented as follows:

```
        char month[] = { 'A','p','r','i','l', '\0' };
```

C++ offers another style for initializing an array of characters. For instance, the statement

```
        char month[] = "April";
```

has the same effect as the above statements. In this case, the characters of the string are enclosed in a pair of double quotes. The compiler takes care of storing the ASCII codes of the characters of the string in memory, and also stores the NULL terminator at the end.

Special characters can also be embedded within a string as illustrated in the program succ.cpp. When manipulated using C++ I/O operators, they are interpreted as special characters and action is taken according to their predefined meaning.

```
// succ.cpp: string with special characters
#include <iostream.h>
void main()
{
    char msg[] = "C to C++\nC++ to Java\nJava to ...";
    cout << "Please note the following message: " << endl;
    cout << msg;
}
```

```
Please note the following message:
C to C++
C++ to Java
Java to ...
```

Note that the characters \ and n used in the string definition

```
    char msg[] = "C to C++\nC++ to Java\nJava to ...";
```

are treated as a new line character.

6.6 Strings Manipulations

C++ has several built-in functions such as `strlen()`, `strcat()`, `strlwr()`, etc., for string manipulation. To use these functions, the header file `string.h` must be included in the program using the statement

```
    #include <string.h>
```

String Length

The string function `strlen()` returns the length of a given string. A string constant or an array of characters can be passed as an argument. The length of the string excludes the end-of-string character (NULL). The `strlen.cpp` illustrates the use of `strlen()` and user defined function to find the length of the string.

```
// strlen.cpp: computing length of string
#include <iostream.h>
#include <string.h>
void main()
{
    char s1[25];
    cout << "Enter your name: ";
    cin >> s1;
    cout << "strlen( s1 ): " << strlen(s1) << endl;
}
```

```
Enter your name: Smrithi
strlen( s1 ): 7
```

String Copy

The string function `strcpy()` copies the contents of one string to another. It takes two arguments, the first argument is the destination string array and the second argument is the source string array. The source string is copied into the destination string. The program `strcpy.cpp` illustrates the use of `strcpy()` to copy a string.

```
// strcpy.cpp: copying string
#include <iostream.h>
#include <string.h>
void main()
{
    char s1[25], s2[25];
```

```
    cout << "Enter a string: ";
    cin >> s1;
    strcpy( s2, s1 );
    cout << "strcpy( s2, s1 ): " << s2;
}
```

Run

```
Enter a string: Garbage
strcpy( s2, s1 ): Garbage
```

String Concatenation

The string function `strcat()` concatenates two strings resulting in a single string. It takes two arguments, which are the destination and source strings. The destination and source strings are concatenated and the resultant string is stored in the destination (first) string. The program `strcat.cpp` illustrates the use of `strcat()` to concatenate two strings.

```
// strcat.cpp: string concatenation
#include <iostream.h>
#include <string.h>
void main()
{
    char s1[40], s2[25];
    cout << "Enter string s1: ";
    cin >> s1;
    cout << "Enter string s2: ";
    cin >> s2;
    strcat( s1, s2 );
    cout << "strcat( s1, s2 ): " << s1;
}
```

Run

```
Enter string s1: C
Enter string s2: ++
strcat( s1, s2 ): C++
```

String Comparison

The string function `strcmp()` compares two strings, character by character. It accepts two strings as parameters and returns an integer, whose value is

- < 0 if the first string is less than the second
- $== 0$ if both are identical
- > 0 if the first string is greater than the second

Whenever two corresponding characters in the string differ, the string which has the character with the higher ASCII value is greater. For example, consider the strings `hello` and `Hello!!`. The first character itself differs. The ASCII code for h is 104, while the ASCII code for H is 72. Since the ASCII code of h is greater, the string `hello` is greater than the string `Hello!`. Once a differing character is found, there is no need to compare remaining characters in the string. The program `strcmp.cpp` illustrates the use of `strcmp()` to compare two strings.

```
// strcmp.cpp: string concatenation
#include <iostream.h>
#include <string.h>
void main()
{
   char s1[25], s2[25];
   cout << "Enter string s1: ";
   cin >> s1;
   cout << "Enter string s2: ";
   cin >> s2;
   int status = strcmp( s1, s2 );
   cout << "strcmp( s1, s2 ): ";
   if( status == 0 )
      cout << s1 << " is equal to " << s2;
   else
      if( status > 0 )
         cout << s1 << " is greater than " << s2;
      else
         cout << s1 << " is less than " << s2;
}
```

Run
```
Enter string s1: Computer
Enter string s2: Computing
strcmp( s1, s2 ): Computer is less than Computing
```

String to Upper/Lower Case

The functions `strlwr()` and `strupr()` convert a string to lower-case and upper-case respectively and return the address of the converted string. The program uprlwr.cpp illustrates the conversion of string to lower and upper cases.

```
// uprlwr.cpp: converting string to upper or lower case
#include <iostream.h>
#include <string.h>
void main()
{
   char s1[25], temp[25];
   cout << "Enter a string: ";
   cin >> s1;
   strcpy( temp, s1 );
   cout << "strupr( temp ): " << strupr( temp ) << endl;
   cout << "strlwr( temp ): " << strlwr( temp ) << endl;
}
```

Run
```
Enter a string: Smrithi
strupr( temp ): SMRITHI
strlwr( temp ): smrithi
```

6.7 Arrays of Strings

An array of strings is a two dimensional array of characters and is defined as follows:

       char array-name[row_size][column_size];

For instance, the statement

       `char person[10][15];`

defines an array of string which can store names of 10 persons and each name cannot exceed 14 characters; 1 character is used to represent the end of a string. The name of the first person is accessed by the expression `person[0]`, and the second person by `person[1]`, and so on. The individual characters of a string can also be accessed. For instance, the first character of the first person is accessed by the expression `person[0][0]` and the fifth character in the 3rd person's name is accessed by `person[2][4]`. The program `names.cpp` illustrates the manipulation of an array of strings.

```
// names.cpp: array of strings storing names of the persons
#include <iostream.h>
#include <string.h>
const int LEN = 15;
void main()
{
   int i, n;
   char person[10][LEN];
   cout << "How many persons ? ";
   cin >> n;
   for( i = 0; i < n; i++ )
   {
      cout << "Enter person" << i+1 << " name: ";
      cin >> person[i];
   }
   cout<< "----------------------------------------------------------------\n";
   cout << "P#    Person Name   Length   In lower case  In UPPER case\n";
   cout<< "----------------------------------------------------------------\n";
   for( i = 0; i < n; i++ )
   {
      cout.width( 2 );
      cout << i+1;
      cout.width( LEN );
      cout << person[i] << "     ";
      cout.width( 2 );
      cout << strlen( person[i] ) << "     ";
      cout.width( LEN );
      cout << strlwr(person[i]);
      cout.width( LEN );
      cout << strupr(person[i]) << endl;
   }
   cout<< "----------------------------------------------------------------\n";
}
```

Run

```
How many persons ? 5
```

```
Enter person1 name: Anand
Enter person2 name: Viswanath
Enter person3 name: Archana
Enter person4 name: Yadunandan
Enter person5 name: Mallikarjun
------------------------------------------------------------
P#    Person Name   Length   In lower case   In UPPER case
------------------------------------------------------------
1           Anand   5               anand           ANAND
2       Viswanath   9           viswanath       VISWANATH
3         Archana   7             archana         ARCHANA
4      Yadunandan   10          yadunandan      YADUNANDAN
5      Mallikarjun  11         mallikarjun     MALLIKARJUN
------------------------------------------------------------
```

An array of string can be initialized at the point of its definition as follows:

char array-name[row_size][column_size] = { *"row1 string"*, *"row2-string"*, ... };

It can also be defined as

char array-name[row_size][column_size] =
    { { *row1 string characters*}, { *row2 string characters*}, .. };

For instance, the statement

```
char person[][12]={"Anand","Viswanath","Archana","Yadunandan","Mallikarjun"};
```

defines an array of strings and initializes them at the point of definition (see Figure 6.9 for the memory representation). The above statement is equivalent to

```
char person[5][12]={"Anand","Viswanath","Archana","Yadunandan","Mallikarjun"};
```

The second dimension must be specified explicitly in the array definition, otherwise, the compiler generates an error message. However, the first dimension can be skipped; the compiler computes this value based on the number of values specified in the initialization list. This rule applies only when the initialization appears at the point of definition.

	0	1	2	3	4	5	6	7	8	9	10	11	
0	A	n	a	n	d	\0							person[0]
1	V	i	s	w	a	n	a	t	h	\0			person[1]
2	A	r	c	h	a	n	a	\0					person[2]
3	Y	a	d	u	n	a	n	d	a	n	\0		person[3]
4	M	a	l	l	i	k	a	r	j	u	n	\0	person[4]

Figure 6.9:   Array of strings representation in memory

6.8 Evaluation Order / Undefined Behaviors

The order of evaluation of sub-expressions within an expression is undefined. Consider the following segment of code:

```
int i = 0;
v[i] = i++;
```

The second statement can be evaluated either as:

```
v[0] = 0;
```

or

```
v[1] = 0;
```

The compiler can generate better code in the absence of restrictions on the expression evaluation order. It can take advantage of underlying hardware architecture and generate the most optimal code. The compiler can warn about such ambiguities. Unfortunately, most compilers do not report a warning about such ambiguities.

The operators

```
&&  ||
```

guarantees that their left-hand side operand is evaluated first before their right-hand side operand. For instance, in the statement,

```
x = (y = 5, y+1);
```

the expression (y = 5, y+1), the comma operator first assigns 5 to y and then evaluates the right-hand side operand and the resulting value 6 is assigned to the x variable. Note that the sequencing operator comma (,) is logically different from the comma used to separate arguments in a function call. Consider the following statements:

```
f1( a[i], i++ );     // two arguments
f2( (a[i], i++) );   // one argument
```

The call of f1() has two arguments, a[i] and i++, and the order of evaluation of the argument is undefined. However, most compilers follow evaluation of arguments at a function call from right to left. The function

```
f1( int a, int b )
{
    cout << a << " " << b;
}
```

when invoked as

```
f1( a[i], i++ );
```

where a[] = { 1, 2, 3, 4, 5 } and i = 0. The output will be 2 and 0. The parameters evaluated are passed in the following order:

1. The contents of the variable i whose value is 0 is assigned to b, and then the expression i++ will be evaluated, thereby i becomes 1.

2. The value of a[i] (now i holds the value 1) is 2 and is assigned to the variable a.

Review Questions

6.1 What are arrays ? Explain how they simplify programming with suitable examples.

6.2 Explain how comb sort algorithm is superior over bubble sort. What is their time complexity. Hint: time complexity is measured in terms of number of elements compared, since comparison operation is the active operation in any sorting algorithm.

6.3 What are the side-effects of the following statements:

```
int a[100];
```

```
a[0] = 20;
a[100] = 200;
cout << a[101];
a[-1] = 5;
cout << a[-1];
```

Does the compiler reports an error when illegal accesses are made to an array ?

6.4 What are multi-dimensional arrays ? Explain their syntax and mechanism for accessing their elements.

6.5 Write an interactive program for calculating grades of N students from 3 tests and present the result in the following format:

```
-----------------------------------------------------------------
    Sl.NO.              SCORES            AVERAGE       GRADE
-----------------------------------------------------------------
    XX            XX  XX  XX                XX            X
-----------------------------------------------------------------
```

6.6 Write a program for computing the norm of the matrix.

6.7 Can arrays be initialized at the point of their definition ? If yes, explain its syntax with suitable examples ?

6.8 Write a program to find the symmetry of the matrix.

6.9 What are strings ? Are they standard or derived data type ? Write an interactive program to check whether a given string is palindrome or not. What happens if the end-of-string character is missing ?

6.10 Write a program to sort integer numbers using shell sort and compare its time complexity with that of the comb sort.

6.11 Write a program for computing mean(m), variance, and standard deviation(s) of a set of numbers using the following formulae:

$$\text{mean} = m = \frac{1}{n} \sum_{i=1}^{n} x_i$$

$$\text{variance} = \frac{1}{n} \sum_{i=1}^{n} (x_i - m)^2$$

$$s = \sqrt{\text{variance}}$$

6.12 Write a program to find the transpose of a matrix. (The transpose can be obtained by interchanging the elements of rows and columns).

6.13 Write a program to find the saddle points in a matrix. It is computed as follows: Find out the smallest element in a row. The saddle point exists in a row if an element is the largest element in that corresponding column. For instance, consider the following matrix:

```
 7   5   6
10   2   3
 1   3   3
```

The saddle point results are as listed below:

In row 1, saddle point exists at column 2.

In row 2, saddle point does not exist.

In row 3, saddle point does not exist.

6.14 Write an interactive program to multiply two matrices and print the result in a matrix form.

7

Modular Programming with Functions

7.1 Introduction

It is difficult to implement a large program even if its algorithm is available. To implement such a program with ease, it should be split into a number of independent tasks, which can be easily designed, implemented, and managed. This process of splitting a large program into small manageable tasks and designing them independently is popularly called *modular programming* or *divide-and-conquer technique*. Large programs are more prone to errors and it is difficult to locate and isolate errors that creep into them. A repeated group of instructions in a program can be organized as a *function*. It can be invoked instead of having the same pattern of code wherever it is required as shown in Figure 7.1.

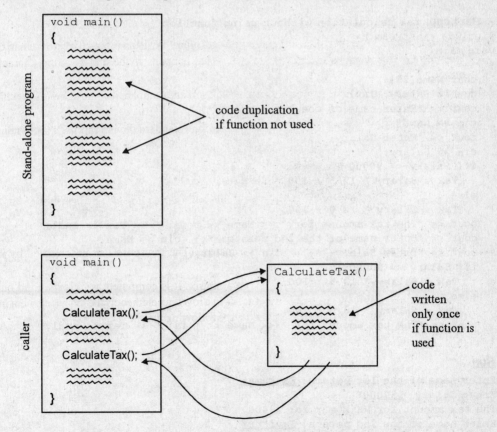

Figure 7.1: Functions for eliminating redundancy of code

A function is a set of program statements that can be processed independently. A function can be invoked which behaves as though its code is inserted at the point of the function call. The communication between a *caller* (calling function) and *callee* (called function) takes place through parameters. The functions can be designed, developed, and implemented independently by different programmers. The independent functions can be grouped to form a software library. Functions are independent because variable names and labels defined within its body are local to it. The use of functions offer flexibility in the design, development, and implementation of the program to solve complex problems. The advantages of functions include the following:

◆ Modular programming
◆ Reduction in the amount of work and development time
◆ Program and function debugging is easier
◆ Division of work is simplified due to the use of divide-and-conquer principle
◆ Reduction in size of the program due to code reusability
◆ Functions can be accessed repeatedly without redevelopment, which in turn promotes reuse of code
◆ *Library of functions* can be implemented by combining well designed, tested, and proven functions

The program `tax1.cpp` computes the tax amount of two persons based on their annual salary without the use of functions.

```
// tax1.cpp: tax calculation without using function
#include <iostream.h>
void main()
{
   char Name[25];
   double Salary, Tax;
   cout << "Enter name of the 1st person: ";
   cin >> Name;
   cout << "Enter Salary: ";
   cin >> Salary;
   if( Salary <= 90000 )
      Tax = Salary * 12.5 / 100;
   else
      Tax = Salary * 18.0 / 100;
   cout << "The tax amount for " << Name << " is: " << Tax << endl;
   cout << "Enter name of the 2nd person: ";   cin >> Name;
   cout << "Enter Salary: ";    cin >> Salary;
   if( Salary <= 90000 )
      Tax = Salary * 12.5 / 100;
   else
      Tax = Salary * 18.0 / 100;
   cout << "The tax amount for " << Name << " is: " << Tax << endl;
}
```

Run

```
Enter name of the 1st person: Rajkumar
Enter Salary: 130000
The tax amount for Rajkumar is: 23400
Enter name of the 2nd person: Savithri
Enter Salary: 90000
The tax amount for Savithri is: 11250
```

Multiple copies of the same pattern of code can be eliminated by grouping repeated statements together to generate a function `CalculateTax()`, as illustrated in the program `tax2.cpp`.

```
// tax2.cpp: tax calculation using function
#include <iostream.h>
void CalculateTax()
{
   char Name[25];
   double Salary, Tax;
   cout << "Enter name of the person: ";
   cin >> Name;
   cout << "Enter Salary: ";
   cin >> Salary;
   if( Salary <= 90000 )
      Tax = Salary * 12.5 / 100;
   else
      Tax = Salary * 18.0 / 100;
   cout << "The tax amount for " << Name << " is: " << Tax << endl;
}
void main()
{
   CalculateTax();
   CalculateTax();
}
```

Run
```
Enter name of the person: Rajkumar
Enter Salary: 130000
The tax amount for Rajkumar is: 23400
Enter name of the person: Savithri
Enter Salary: 90000
The tax amount for Savithri is: 11250
```

In `main()`, the statement
```
      CalculateTax();
```
is invoked twice to calculate tax for two persons. It computes the tax amount and displays it. The same function can be invoked to calculate tax amounts for a large number of people using a loop construct.

7.2 Function Components

Every function has the following elements associated with it:

  ◆ Function declaration or prototype.
  ◆ Function parameters (formal parameters)
  ◆ Combination of function declaration and its definition.
  ◆ Function definition (function declarator and a function body).
  ◆ return statement.
  ◆ Function call.

A function can be executed using a *function call* in the program. The various components associated with functions are shown in Figure 7.2.

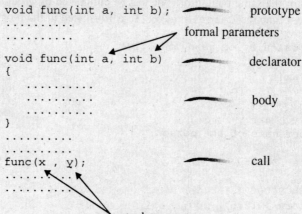

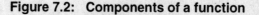

Figure 7.2:   Components of a function

The program `max1.cpp` illustrates the various components of a function. It computes the maximum of two integer numbers.

```
// max1.cpp: maximum of two integer numbers
#include <iostream.h>
int max( int x, int y );        // prototype
void main()                     // function caller
{
   int a, b, c;
   cout << "Enter two integers <a, b>: ";
   cin >> a >> b;
   c = max( a, b );             // function call
   cout << "max( a, b): " << c << endl;
}
int max( int x, int y )         // function definition
{
   // all the statements enclosed in braces forms body of the function
   if( x > y )
      return x;                 // function return
   else
      return y;                 // function return
}
```

Run

```
Enter two integers <a, b>: 20 10
max( a, b ): 20
```

As discussed earlier, `main()` is a function, so it is not surprising that `max()` which is also a function, appears similar to `main()`. The only special feature about `main()` is that it is always executed first. It does not matter whether `main()` is the first function in the program listing or is placed elsewhere in the program; it will always be the first one to execute.

There are five elements involved in using a function: the function prototype, the function definition, the function call, the function parameters, and the function return.

Function Prototype

The first function related statement in `max1.cpp` is the function prototype. This is the line before the beginning of `main()`:

```
int max( int x, int y );        // prototype
```

It provides the following information to the compiler:

- The name of the function,
- The type of the value returned (optional; default is an integer),
- The number and the types of the arguments that must be supplied in a call to the function.

Function prototyping is one of the key improvements added to the C++ functions. When a function call is encountered, the compiler checks the function call with its prototype so that correct argument types are used. The compiler informs the user about any violations in the actual parameters that are to be passed to a function.

A function prototype is a declaration statement which has the following syntax:

```
ret_val function_name( argument1, argument2, ... , argumentn );
```

The `ret_val` specifies the datatype of the value in the return statement. The function can return any data-type; if there is no return value, a keyword `void` is placed before the function name. In a function without any return value, a dummy return statement can be included before the closing brace. A program can have more than one `return` statements. (Note: `return` is a keyword. The statement `return 0;` is sufficient in place of the `return(0);`). The number of arguments to a function can be fixed or variable. The function declaration terminates with a semicolon.

Consider the prototype statement

```
int max( int x, int y );        // prototype
```

It informs the compiler that the function `max` has two arguments of type integer (the list of data types separated by commas form the argument list). The function `max()` returns an integer value; the compiler knows how many bytes to retrieve and how to interpret the value returned by the function. Function declarations are also called *prototype*, since they provide a model or blue print for the function. C++ makes prototyping mandatory if functions are defined after the function `main`. C++ assumes `void` type in case no arguments are specified in the argument list; the default return type is an integer.

Function Definition

The function itself is referred to as function definition. The first line of the function definition is known as *function declarator* and is followed by the *function body*. Figure 7.3 shows that the declarator and the function body make up the function definition. The declarator and declaration must use the same function name, the number of arguments, the arguments type and the return type. No other function definitions are allowed within a function definition.

The body of the function is enclosed in braces. C++ allows the definition to be placed anywhere in the program. If the function is defined before its invocation, then its prototypes declaration is optional.

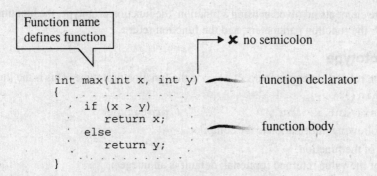

Figure 7.3:   Function definition

Function Call

A function is a dormant entity, which gets life only when a call to the function is made. A function call is specified by the function name followed by the arguments enclosed in parentheses and terminated by a semicolon. The return type is not mentioned in the function call. For instance, in the function main() of the program max1.cpp, the statement

```
c = max( a, b );              // function call
```

invokes the function max() with two integer parameters. Executing the call statement causes the control to be transferred to the first statement in the function body and after execution of the function body the control is returned to the statement following the function call. The max() returns the maximum of the parameters a and b. The return value is assigned to the local variable c in main().

Function Parameters

The parameters specified in the function call are known as *actual parameters* and those specified in the function declarator are known as *formal parameters*. For instance, in main(), the statement

```
c = max( a, b );                    // function call
```

passes the parameters (actual parameters) a and b to max(). The parameters x and y are formal parameters. When a function call is made, a one-to-one correspondence is established between the actual and the formal parameters. In this case, the value of the variable a is assigned to the variable x and that of b is assigned to y. The scope of formal parameters is limited to its function only.

Function Return

Functions can be grouped into two categories: functions that do not have a return value (void functions) and functions that have a return value. The statements

```
return x;                      // function return
```
and
```
return y;                      // function return
```

in function max() are called function return statements. The caller must be able to receive the value returned by the function (but not mandatory). In the statement

```
c = max( a, b );                  // function call
```

the value returned by the function max() is assigned to the local variable c in main(). Figure 7.4 shows the function max() returning a value to the caller.

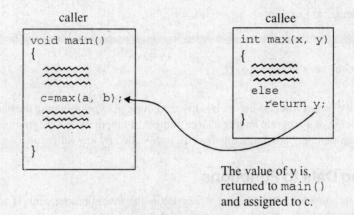

The value of y is,
returned to main()
and assigned to c.

Figure 7.4:   Function returning a value

The return statement in a function need not be at the end of the function. It can occur anywhere in the function body and as soon as it is encountered, execution control will be returned to the caller.

A function that does not return anything is indicated by the keyword void. It has the following form:

```
void FunctionName( ParameterList )
{
   statement(s);
   return;  // return is optional
}
```

In void functions, the use of return statement is optional.

Elimination of the Function Prototype

The function declaration can be eliminated by defining the function before calling it. The program max2.cpp illustrates this concept.

```cpp
// max2.cpp: maximum of two integer numbers
#include <iostream.h>
int max( int x, int y )            // function definition
{
   // all the statements enclosed in braces forms body of the function
   if( x > y )
      return x;                    // function return
   else
      return y;                    // function return
}
void main()                        // function caller
{
   int a, b, c;
   cout << "Enter two integers <a, b>: ";
   cin >> a >> b;
   c = max( a, b );                // function call
```

```
cout << "max( a, b): " << c << endl;
}
```

Run
```
Enter two integers <a, b>: 20 10
max( a, b): 20
```

The definition of max() occurs before it is invoked in main(), eliminating the need for a function prototype. In the case of a program having a large number of functions, the programmer has to arrange the functions, such that they are defined before they are called by any other function.

7.3 Passing Data to Functions

The entity used to convey the message to a function is the function argument. It can be a numeric constant, a variable, multiple variables, user defined data type, etc.

Passing Constants as Arguments

The program chart1.cpp illustrates the passing of a numeric constant as an argument to a function. This constant argument is assigned to the formal parameter which is processed in the function body.

```
// chart1.cpp: Percentage chart by passing numeric value
#include <iostream.h>
void PercentageChart( int percentage );
void main()
{
   cout << "Sridevi :   ";
   PercentageChart( 50 );
   cout << "Rajkumar:  ";
   PercentageChart( 84 );
   cout << "Savithri:  ";
   PercentageChart( 79 );
   cout << "Anand    :  ";
   PercentageChart( 74 );
}
void PercentageChart( int percentage )
{
   for( int i = 0; i < percentage/2; i++ )
     cout << '\xCD';       // double line character (see ASCII table)
   cout << endl;
}
```

Run
```
Sridevi :  =========================
Rajkumar:  ==========================================
Savithri:  =======================================
Anand   :  =====================================
```

In main(), the statement
```
   PercentageChart( 84 );
```
invokes the function PercentageChart with the integer constant 84 to draw a chart. It draws a

horizontal line, made up of the double-line graphic character (`'\xCD'`) on the screen.

In the function definition, the variable name `percentage` is placed between the parentheses following the function name `PercentageChart`. The invocation of this function by the statement

```
PercentageChart( 84 );
```

ensures that the numeric constant 84 is assigned to the variable `percentage` as shown in Figure 7.5.

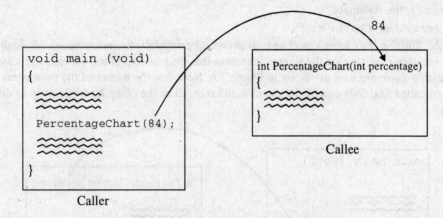

Figure 7.5: Passing value to a function

Passing Variables as Arguments

Similar to constants, variables can also be passed as arguments to a function. The program `chart2.cpp` illustrates the mechanism of passing a variable as an argument to a function.

```cpp
// chart2.cpp: Percentage chart by passing variables
#include <iostream.h>
void PercentageChart( int percentage );
void main()
{
    int m1, m2, m3, m4;
    cout << "Enter percentage score of Sri, Raj, Savi, An: ";
    cin >> m1 >> m2 >> m3 >> m4;
    cout << "Sridevi :  ";
    PercentageChart( m1 );
    cout << "Rajkumar:  ";
    PercentageChart( m2 );
    cout << "Savithri:  ";
    PercentageChart( m3 );
    cout << "Anand   :  ";
    PercentageChart( m4 );
}
void PercentageChart( int percentage )
{
    for( int i = 0; i < percentage/2; i++ )
        cout << '\xCD';        // double line character (see ASCII table)
    cout << endl;
}
```

Run

```
Enter percentage score of Sri, Raj, Savi, An: 55 92 83 67
Sridevi :  ============================
Rajkumar:  ====================================================
Savithri:  =========================================
Anand   :  ================================
```

In main(), the statement

```
        PercentageChart( m2 );
```

invokes the function PercentageChart. It draws a horizontal line, made up of the double-line graphic character ('xCD') on the screen. It ensures that the contents of the variable m2 is assigned to the variable percentage as shown in Figure 7.6. Note that the names of the parameters in the calling and called functions can be the same or different, since the compiler treats them as different variables.

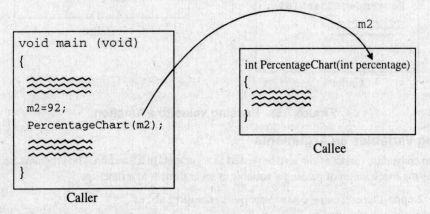

Figure 7.6:   Variable used as argument

Passing Multiple Arguments

C++ imposes no limitation on the number of arguments that can be passed to a function. The program chart3.cpp passes two arguments to the function PercentageChart(), whose purpose is to draw various style charts on the screen.

```
// chart3.cpp: Percentage chart by passing multiple variables
#include <iostream.h>
void PercentageChart( int percentage, char style );
void main()
{
    int m1, m2, m3, m4;
    cout << "Enter percentage score of Sri, Raj, Savi, An: ";
    cin >> m1 >> m2 >> m3 >> m4;
    cout << "Sridevi :  ";
    PercentageChart( m1, '*' );
    cout << "Rajkumar:  ";
```

```
   PercentageChart( m2, '\xCD' );
   cout << "Savithri:  ";
   PercentageChart( m3, '~');
   cout << "Anand    : ";
   PercentageChart( m4, '!' );
}
void PercentageChart( int percentage, char style )
{
   for( int i = 0; i < percentage/2; i++ )
      cout << style;
   cout << endl;
}
```

Run

```
Enter percentage score of Sri, Raj, Savi, An: 55 92 83 67
Sridevi : ***************************
Rajkumar: ================================================
Savithri: ~~~~~~~~~~~~~~~~~~~~~~~~~~~~~~~~~~~~~~~~~~
Anand   : !!!!!!!!!!!!!!!!!!!!!!!!!!!!!!!!!!!!
```

The process of passing two parameters is similar to passing a single parameter. The value of the first *actual* parameter in the *caller* (calling function) is assigned to the first *formal* parameter in the *callee* (called function), and the value of the second actual parameter is assigned to the second formal parameter, as shown in Figure 7.7. Of course, more than two parameters can be passed in the same way.

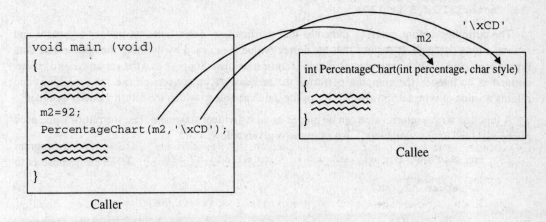

Figure 7.7: Multiple arguments passed to a function

7.4 Function Return Data Type

The return value can be a constant, a variable, a user-defined data structure, a general expression (reducible expressions), a pointer to a function or a function call (in which case the call must return a value). C++ does not place any restriction on the type of return value, except that it cannot be an array (a pointer to an array can be returned. A function can return an array that is a part of a structure).

```
// ifact.cpp: factorial computation Returns a long integer value
#include <iostream.h>
long fact( int n )
{
   long result;
   if( n == 0 )
      result = 1;    // factorial of zero is one
   else
   {
      result = 1;
      for( int i = 2; i <= n; i++ )
         result = result * i;
   }
   return result;
}
void main( void )
{
   int n;
   cout << "Enter the number whose factorial is to be found: ";
   cin >> n;
   cout << "The factorial of " << n << " is " << fact(n) << endl;
}
```

Run

```
Enter the number whose factorial is to be found: 5
The factorial of 5 is 120
```

The definition before `main()` indicates that the function `fact` takes an integer argument and returns a long datatype. It ensures that the correct value is returned by defining the appropriate data type (i.e, a `long` variable) and placing it in the return statement. Suppose that the variable `result` was defined as an integer, the compiler performs the necessary type conversion (i.e., to type long) and returns a value of type `long`, irrespective of the data variable to which the return value is assigned.

A function with a return value can be placed as an individual statement (i.e., the return value need not be assigned to any variable(s)). An example is given below.

```
int SumTwo( int n1, int n2 )    // n1 and n2 are the parameters
{
    return n1 + n2;
}
```

When a function has nothing specific to return or take, it is indicated by `void`. Typically, such functions are called `void` functions. The following is the prototype of a `void` function:

```
void func( void );
```

However, the keyword `void` is optional. C++ maintains strict type checking and an empty argument list is interpreted as the absence of any parameters.

Limitation of `return`

A key limitation of the `return` statement is that it can be used to return only *one item* from a function. An alternative method to overcome this limitation is to use parameters as a media of communication between calling and called functions.

7.5 Library Functions

Library functions are shipped along with the compilers. They are predefined and pre-compiled into library files, and their prototypes can be found in the files with .h (called header files) as their extension in the include directory. The definitions are available in the form of object codes in the files with .lib (called library files) as their extension in the lib directory. In order to make use of a library function, include the corresponding header file. Once the header file is included, any function available in that library can be invoked. The linker will add such functions to a calling program by extracting them from an appropriate function library. Some of the library calls are sqrt(), pow() (declared in the header file math.h), strlen(), strcat(), strcpy(), and strncpy() (declared in string.h). In case of user defined functions, the prototype and definitions of the functions must be a part of a program module. The program namelen.cpp illustrates the use of library functions.

```
// namelen.cpp: use of string library functions
#include <iostream.h>
#include <string.h>          // string function header file
void main()
{
   char name[ 20 ];
   cout << "Enter your name: ";
   cin >> name;
   int len = strlen( name ); // strlen returns the length of name
   cout << "Length of your name = " << len;
}
```

Run

```
Enter your name: Rajkumar
Length of your name = 8
```

Note that, the statement

```
      #include <string.h>
```

informs the compiler to include the prototypes of the string related functions. The statement

```
      int len = strlen( name );
```

invokes the library function strlen and assigns the length of the string stored in the variable name to the variable len.

The calls may be mathematical, such as sin(), cos(), log10() or may even include functions to round a value or truncate a resultant value. The program maths.cpp accesses mathematical functions.

```
// maths.cpp : Use of library function calls to round and truncate a result
#include <iostream.h>
#include <math.h>
void main(void)
{
   float num, num1, num2;
   cout << "Enter any fractional number: ";
   cin >> num;
   num1 = ceil( num );   // rounds up
```

```
    num2 = floor( num ); // rounds down
    cout << "ceil( " << num << " ) = " << num1 << endl;
    cout << "floor( " << num << " ) = " << num2 << endl;
}
```

Run1
```
Enter any fractional number: 2.9
ceil( 2.9 ) = 3
floor( 2.9 ) = 2
```

Run2
```
Enter any fractional number: 2.1
ceil( 2.1 ) = 3
floor( 2.1 ) = 2
```

Library functions improve the program design, reduce debugging and testing time, thereby reducing the amount of work needed for the development of the program. These functions are certainly better programmed, tested, and well proved. Hence, the use of library functions increases the program reliability and reduces the complexity.

7.6 Parameter Passing

Parameter passing is a mechanism for communication of data and information between the calling function (caller) and the called function (callee). It can be achieved either by passing the value or address of the variable. C++ supports the following three types of parameter passing schemes:

- Pass by Value
- Pass by Address
- Pass by Reference (only in C++)

The parameters used to transfer data to a function are known as *input-parameters* and those used to transfer the result to the caller are known as *output-parameters*. The parameters used to transfer data in both the directions are called *input-output parameters*.

Parameters can be classified as formal parameters and actual parameters. The formal parameters are those specified in the function declaration and function definition. The actual parameters are those specified in the function call. The following conditions must be satisfied for a function call:

- the number of arguments in the function call and the function declarator must be the same.
- the data type of each of the arguments in the function call should be the same as the corresponding parameter in the function declarator statement. However, the names of the arguments in the function call and the parameters in the function definition can be different.

Pass by Value

The default mechanism of parameter passing is called pass by value. Pass-by-value mechanism does not change the contents of the argument variable in the calling function (caller), even if they are changed in the called function (callee); because the content of the actual parameter in a caller is copied to the formal parameter in the callee. The formal parameter is stored in the local data area of the callee. Changes to the parameter within the function will effect only the copy (formal parameters), and will have no effect on the actual argument. It is illustrated in the program swap1.cpp. Most of the functions discussed earlier fall under the category *pass-by-value* parameter passing.

```
// swap1.cpp: swap integer values by value
#include <iostream.h>
void swap( int x, int y )
{
   int t;    // temporary used in swapping
   cout<<"Value of x and y in swap before exchange: "<< x <<" "<< y << endl;
   t = x;
   x = y;
   y = t;
   cout<<"Value of x and y in swap after exchange: "<< x <<" " << y << endl;
}
void main()
{
   int a, b;
   cout << "Enter two integers <a, b>: ";
   cin >> a >> b;
   swap( a, b );
   cout << "Value of a and b on swap( a, b ) in main(): " << a << " " << b;
}
```

Run

```
Enter two integers <a, b>: 10 20
Value of x and y in swap before exchange: 10 20
Value of x and y in swap after exchange: 20 10
Value of a and b on swap( a, b ) in main(): 10 20
```

In main(), the statement

```
    swap( x, y )
```

invokes the function swap() and assigns the contents of the actual parameters a and b to the formal parameters x and y respectively. In the swap() function, the input parameters are exchanged, however it is not reflected in the caller; actual parameters a and b do not get modified (see Figure 7.8).

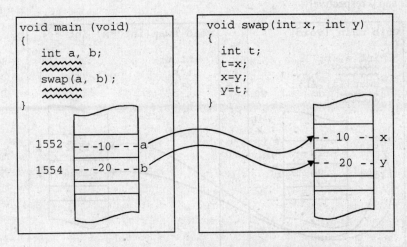

Figure 7.8: Parameter passing by value

Pass by Address

C++ provides another means of passing values to a function known as pass-by-address. Instead of passing the value, the address of the variable is passed. In the function, the address of the argument is copied into a memory location instead of the value. The de-referencing operator is used to access the variable in the called function.

```cpp
// swap2.cpp: swap integer values by pointers
#include <iostream.h>
void swap( int * x, int * y )
{
    int t;   // temporary used in swapping
    t = *x;
    *x = *y;
    *y = t;
}
void main()
{
    int a, b;
    cout << "Enter two integers <a, b>: ";
    cin >> a >> b;
    swap( &a, &b );
    cout << "Value of a and b on swap( a, b ): " << a << " " << b;
}
```

Run

```
Enter two integers <a, b>: 10 20
Value of a and b on swap( a, b ): 20 10
```

In `main()`, the statement

```
    swap( &x, &y )
```

invokes the function `swap` and assigns the address of the actual parameters `a` and `b` to the formal parameters `x` and `y` respectively.

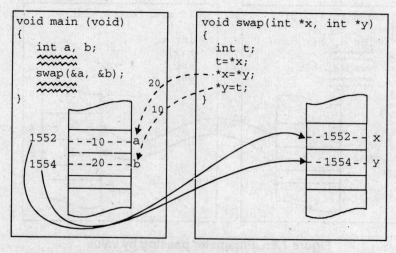

Figure 7.9: Parameter passing by address

In swap(), the statement

```
t = *x;
```

assigns the contents of the memory location pointed to by the pointer (address) stored in the variable x (It is effectively accessing the contents of the actual variable a in the caller. Similarly, the parameter y holds the address of the parameter b. Any modification to the memory contents using these addresses will be reflected in the caller; the actual parameters a and b get modified (see Figure 7.9).

Pass by Reference

Passing parameters by reference has the functionality of pass-by-pointer and the syntax of call-by-value. Any modifications made through the formal pointer parameter is also reflected in the actual parameter. Therefore, the function body and the call to it is identical to that of call-by-value, but has the effect of call-by-pointer.

To pass an argument by reference, the function call is similar to that of call by value. In the function declarator, those parameters, which are to be received by reference must be preceded by the & operator. The reference type formal parameters are accessed in the same way as normal value parameters. However, any modification to them will also be reflected in the actual parameters. The program swap3.cpp illustrates the mechanism of passing parameters by reference.

```
// swap3.cpp: swap integer values by reference
#include <iostream.h>
void swap( int & x, int & y )
{
   int t;    // temporary used in swapping
   t = x;
   x = y;
   y = t;
}
void main()
{
   int a, b;
   cout << "Enter two integers <a, b>: ";
   cin >> a >> b;
   swap( a, b );
   cout << "Value of a and b on swap( a, b ): " << a << " " << b;
}
```

Run

```
Enter two integers <a, b>: 10 20
Value of a and b on swap( a, b ): 20 10
```

In main(), the statement

```
swap( a, b );
```

is translated into

```
swap( & a, & b );
```

internally during compilation. The function declarator

```
void swap( int & a, int & b )
```

indicates that the formal parameters are of reference type and hence, they must be bound to the memory location of the actual parameter. Thus, any access made to the reference formal parameters in the `swap()` function refers to the actual parameters. The following statements in the body of the `swap()` function:

```
t = x;
x = y;
y = t;
```

(as treated by the compiler) have the following interpretation internally:

```
t = *x;  // store the value pointed by x into t
*x = *y; // store the value pointed by y into location pointed by x
*y = t;  // store the value hold by 't' into location pointed by y
```

This is because, the formal parameters are of reference type and therefore the compiler treats them similar to pointers but does not allow the modification of the pointer value (cannot be made to point to some other variable). Changes made to the formal parameters x and y reflect on the actual parameters a and b (see Figure 7.10).

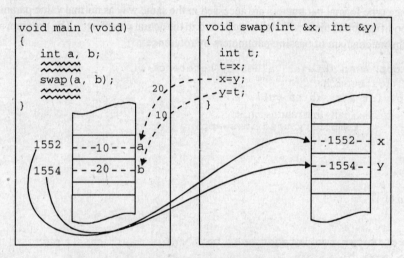

Figure 7.10:   Parameter passing by reference

The following points can be noted about reference parameters:

♦ A reference can never be null, it must always refer to a legitimate object (variable).

♦ Once established, a reference can never be changed so as to make it point to a different object.

♦ A reference does not require any explicit mechanism to dereference the memory address and access the actual data value.

Note

Procedures can be implemented using functions. A function with no return value can be treated similar to a procedure of Pascal. The main difference between using functions and procedures in C++ (or C) is that function can be placed on the right side of the '=' (assignment) and on either side of == (equal) operator. Procedures (function with no return values) cannot be used with these operators. The return value from the function can be directly passed to cout for display, whereas procedures cannot be used in the cout statement.

Niceties of Parameter Passing

Pass by address/reference is also used when the size of the user defined data-structure is large, since a large number of arguments cannot be accommodated in the limited stack space. Consider the following declaration:

```
struct LargeStruct
{
    char Name[30];
    unsigned int Age, Sex;
    char Address[50];
    enum MartialStatus { Married, Unmarried } Ms;
};
```

If a variable of the above structure type is passed by value, 85 bytes of data movement between the caller space and a function stack space is required. If it is passed by address, it just requires 4 bytes movement and thus reduces the function context switching overhead.

7.7 Return by Reference

A function that returns a reference variable is actually an alias for the referred variable. This method of returning references is used in operator overloading to form a cascade of member function calls specified in a single statement. For example,

```
cout << i << j << endl;
```

is a set of cascaded calls that returns a reference to the object cout. The program ref.cpp illustrates the function return value by reference.

```
// ref.cpp: return variable by reference
#include <iostream.h>
int & max( int & x, int & y );        // prototype
void main()
{
    int a, b, c;
    cout << "Enter two integers <a, b>: ";
    cin >> a >> b;
    max( a, b ) = 425;
    cout<<"The value of a and b on execution of max(a,b) = 425; ..." << endl;
    cout << "a = " << a << " b = " << b;

}
int & max( int & x, int & y )    // function definition
{
    // all the statements enclosed in braces form body of the function
    if( x > y )
        return x;                     // function return
    else
        return y;                     // function return
}
```

Run1

Enter two integers <a, b>: <u>1 2</u>

```
The value of a and b on execution of max(a, b) = 425; ...
a = 1 b = 425
```

Run2

```
Enter two integers <a, b>: 2 1
The value of a and b on execution of max(a, b) = 425; ...
a = 425 b = 1
```

In `main()`, the statement

```
        max( a, b ) = 425;
```

invokes the function max. It returns the reference to the variable holding the maximum value and assigns the value 425 to it (see *Run2*). Since the return type of the max() is int &, it implies that the call to max() can appear on the left-hand side of an assignment statement. Therefore, the above statement is valid and assigns 425 to a if it is larger, otherwise, it is assigned to b.

7.8 Default Arguments

Normally, a function call should specify all the arguments used in the function definition. In a C++ function call, when one or more arguments are omitted, the function may be defined to take default values for the omitted arguments by providing the *default values* in the function prototype.

Parameters without default arguments are placed first, and those with default values are placed later (because of the C++ convention of storing the arguments on the stack from right to left). Hence the feature of default arguments allows the same function to be called with fewer arguments than defined in the function prototype.

To establish a default value, the function prototype or the function definition (when functions are defined before being called) must be used. The compiler checks the function prototype/declarator with the arguments in the function call to provide default values (if available) to those arguments, which are omitted. The arguments specified in the function call explicitly always override the default values specified in the function prototype/declarator. In a function call, all the trailing missing arguments are replaced by default arguments as shown in Figure 7.11.

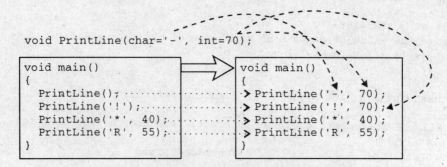

**Figure 7.11: Preprocessor handling missing arguments
at function call using default arguments**

When a function is called by omitting some arguments, they are supplied by the compiler implicitly. The code of the program by no means becomes shorter or more efficient, but it provides high flexibility on programming. Functions may be defined with more than one default argument.

Default arguments must be known to the compiler prior to the invocation of a function. It reduces the burden of passing arguments explicitly at the point of the function call. The program defarg1.cpp illustrates the concept of default arguments.

```
// defarg1.cpp: Default arguments to functions
#include <iostream.h>
void PrintLine( char = '-', int = 70 );
void main()
{
   PrintLine();           // uses both default arguments
   PrintLine( '!' );      // assumes 2nd argument as default
   PrintLine( '*', 40 );  // ignores default arguments
   PrintLine( 'R', 55 );  // ignores default arguments
}
void PrintLine( char ch, int RepeatCount )
{
   int i;
   cout << endl;
   for( i = 0; i < RepeatCount; i++ )
      cout << ch;
}
```

Run

```
---------------------------------------------------------------------
!!!!!!!!!!!!!!!!!!!!!!!!!!!!!!!!!!!!!!!!!!!!!!!!!!!!!!!!!!!!!!!!!!!!!!!!!!
****************************************
RRRRRRRRRRRRRRRRRRRRRRRRRRRRRRRRRRRRRRRRRRRRRRRRRRRRRRRRR
```

In main(), when the compiler encounters the statement

        PrintLine();

it is replaced by the statement

        PrintLine('-', 70);

internally by substituting the missing arguments. Similarly, the statement

        PrintLine('!');

is replaced by

        PrintLine('!',70);

Note that in the first statement both the arguments are default arguments and in the second case only the missing argument (second argument) is replaced by its default value.

The feature of default arguments can be utilized in enhancing the functionality of the program without the need for modifying the old code referencing to functions. For instance, the function in the above program

        void PrintLine(char = '-', int = 70);

prints a line with default character '-' in case it is not passed explicitly. This function can be enhanced to print multiple lines using the new prototype:

        void PrintLine(char = '-', int = 70, int = 1);

In this new function, the last parameter specifies the number of lines to be printed and by default, it is

1. Therefore, the old code referring to this function need not be modified and new statements can be added without affecting the functionality. The program `defarg2.cpp` extends the capability of `defarg1.cpp` program.

```
// defarg2.cpp: extending the functionality without modifying old calls
#include <iostream.h>
void PrintLine( char = '-', int = 70, int = 1 );
void main()
{
    PrintLine();              // uses both default arguments
    PrintLine( '!' );         // assumes 2nd argument as default
    PrintLine( '*', 40 );     // ignores default arguments
    PrintLine( 'R', 55 );     // ignores default arguments
    // new code, Note: old code listed above is unaffected
    PrintLine( '&', 25, 2 );
}
void PrintLine( char ch, int RepeatCount, int nLines )
{
    int i, j;
    for( j = 0; j < nLines; j++ )
    {
        cout << endl;
        for( i = 0; i < RepeatCount; i++ )
            cout << ch;
    }
}
```

Run

```
!!!!!!!!!!!!!!!!!!!!!!!!!!!!!!!!!!!!!!!!!!!!!!!!!!!!!!!!!!!!!!!!!!!!!!!!!!
**************************************
RRRRRRRRRRRRRRRRRRRRRRRRRRRRRRRRRRRRRRRRRRRRRRRRRRRRRRRR
&&&&&&&&&&&&&&&&&&&&&&&&&
&&&&&&&&&&&&&&&&&&&&&&&&&
```

The following statements in the above two programs

```
    PrintLine();              // uses both default arguments
    PrintLine( '!' );         // assumes 2nd argument as default
    PrintLine( '*', 40 );     // ignores default arguments
    PrintLine( 'R', 55 );     // ignores default arguments
```

are the same. Though the functionality of `PrintLine()` is enhanced in the program `defarg2.cpp`, the old code referring to it remains unaffected in terms of its functionality; the compiler supplies the last argument as 1, and thereby the new function does the same operation as that of the old one. Thus, the C++ feature of default arguments can be potentially utilized in extending a function without modifying the old code.

A default argument can appear either in the function prototype or definition. Once it is defined, it cannot be redefined. It is advisable to define default arguments in the function prototype so that it is known to the compiler at the time of compilation. Variable names may be omitted while assigning default values in the prototype.

7.9 Inline Functions

Function calls involve branching to a specified address, and returning to the instruction following the function call. That is, when the program executes a function call instruction, the CPU stores the memory address of the instruction following the function call, copies the arguments of the function call onto the stack, and finally transfers control to the specified function. The CPU then executes the function code, stores the function return value in a predefined memory location/register, and returns control to the calling function. This constitutes an overhead in the execution time of the program. This overhead is relatively large if the time required to execute a function is less than the context switch time.

C++ provides an alternative to normal function calls in the form of inline functions. Inline functions are those whose function body is inserted in place of the function call statement during the compilation process. With the inline code, the program will not incur any context switching overhead. The concept of inline functions is similar to *macro functions* of C. Hence, inline functions enjoy both the flexibility and power offered by normal functions and macro functions respectively.

An inline function definition is similar to an ordinary function except that the keyword `inline` precedes the function definition. The syntax for defining an inline function is shown in Figure 7.12..

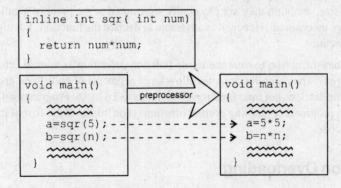

Figure 7.12:   Inline function and its expansion

The significant feature of inline functions is: there is no explicit function call and body is substituted at the point of `inline` function call, thereby, the run-time overhead for function linkage mechanism is reduced. The program `square.cpp` uses `inline` function to compute the square of a number.

```
// square.cpp: square of a number using inline function
#include <iostream.h>
inline int sqr( int num )
{
    return num*num;
}
void main()
{
    float n;
    cout << "Enter a number: ";
    cin >> n;
    cout << "Its Square = " << sqr( n ) << endl;
```

```
    cout << "sqr( 10 ) = " << sqr( 10 );
}
```

Run

```
Enter a number: 5
Its Square = 25
sqr( 10 ) = 100
```

In main, the statement

```
        cout << "Its Square = " << square( num );
```

invokes the `inline` function `square(..)`. It will be suitably replaced by the instruction(s) of the body of the function `square(..)` by the compiler. The execution time of the function `square(..)` is less than the time required to establish a linkage between the caller (calling function) and callee (called function). Execution of a normal function call involves the operation of saving actual parameter and function return address onto the stack followed by a call to the function. On return, the stack must be cleaned to restore the original status. This process is costly when compared to having square computation instructions within a caller's body. Thus, `inline` functions enjoy the flexibility and modularity of functions and at the same time achieve computational speedup. Functions having small body do not increase the code size, although they are physically substituted at the point of a call; there is no code for function linkage mechanism. Hence, it is advisable to declare the functions having a small function body as inline functions.

The compiler has the option to treat the inline function definition as normal functions (a warning message is displayed). The compiler does not allow large segments of code to be grouped as `inline` functions. The compiler does not treat functions with loops as `inline`. Programs with inline functions execute faster than programs containing normal functions (non inline) at the cost of increase in the size of the executable code.

7.10 Function Overloading

Function polymorphism, or function overloading is a concept that allows multiple functions to share the same name with different argument types. Function polymorphism implies that the function definition can have multiple forms. Assigning one or more function body to the same name is known as *function overloading* or *function name overloading*.

The program `swap4.cpp` illustrates the need for function overloading. It has multiple functions for swapping numbers of different data types but with different names.

```
// swap4.cpp: multiple swap functions with different names
#include <iostream.h>
void swap_char( char & x, char & y )
{
    char t;  // temporary used in swapping
    t = x;
    x = y;
    y = t;
}
```

```
void swap_int( int & x, int  & y )
{
   int t;    // temporary used in swapping
   t = x;
   x = y;
   y = t;
}
void swap_float( float & x, float & y )
{
   float t; // temporary used in swapping
   t = x;
   x = y;
   y = t;
}
void main()
{
   char ch1, ch2;
   cout << "Enter two Characters <ch1, ch2>: ";
   cin >> ch1 >> ch2;
   swap_char( ch1, ch2 );
   cout << "On swapping <ch1, ch2>: " << ch1 << " " << ch2 << endl;
   int a, b;
   cout << "Enter two integers <a, b>: ";
   cin >> a >> b;
   swap_int( a, b );
   cout << "On swapping <a, b>: " << a << " " << b << endl;
   float c, d;
   cout << "Enter two floats <c, d>: ";
   cin >> c >> d;
   swap_float( c, d );
   cout << "On swapping <c, d>: " << c << " " << d;
}
```

Run

```
Enter two Characters <ch1, ch2>: R K
On swapping <ch1, ch2>: K R
Enter two integers <a, b>: 5 10
On swapping <a, b>: 10 5
Enter two floats <c, d>: 20.5 99.5
On swapping <c, d>: 99.5 20.5
```

The above program has three different functions:

```
        void swap_char( char & x, char & y )
        void swap_int( int & x, int  & y )
        void swap_float( float & x, float & y )
```

performing the same activity, but on different data types. Logically, all the three functions display the value of the input parameters. It has names such as `swap_char`, `swap_int`, `swap_float`, etc., making the task of programming difficult and creating the need to remember function names, which perform the same operation. In C++, this difficulty is circumvented by using the feature of overloading the function.

In C++, two or more functions can be given the same name provided the signaturè (parameters count or their data types) of each of them is unique either in the number or data type of their arguments. It is possible to define several functions having the same name, but performing different actions. It helps in reducing the need for unusual function names, making the code easier to read. The functions must only differ in the argument list. For example

```
swap( int, int );    // prototype
swap( float, float ); // prototype
```

From user's view point, there is only one operation which performs swapping numbers of different data types.

All the functions performing the same operation must differ in terms of the input argument data-types or number of arguments. The program swap5.cpp illustrates the benefits of function overloading.

```
// swap5.cpp: multiple swap functions, function overloading
#include <iostream.h>
void swap( char & x, char & y )
{
   char t;  // temporarily used in swapping
   t = x;
   x = y;
   y = t;
}
void swap( int & x, int & y )
{
   int t;   // temporarily used in swapping
   t = x;
   x = y;
   y = t;
}
void swap( float & x, float & y )
{
   float t; // temporarily used in swapping
   t = x;
   x = y;
   y = t;
}
void main()
{
   char ch1, ch2;
   cout << "Enter two Characters <ch1, ch2>: ";
   cin >> ch1 >> ch2;
   swap( ch1, ch2 ); // compiler calls swap( char &a, char &b );
   cout << "On swapping <ch1, ch2>: " << ch1 << " " << ch2 << endl;
   int a, b;
   cout << "Enter two integers <a, b>: ";
   cin >> a >> b;
   swap( a, b );  // compiler calls swap( int &a, int &b );
   cout << "On swapping <a, b>: " << a << " " << b << endl;
```

```
    float c, d;
    cout << "Enter two floats <c, d>: ";
    cin >> c >> d;
    swap( c, d );  // compiler calls swap( float &a, float &b );
    cout << "On swapping <c, d>: " << c << " " << d;
}
```

Run

```
Enter two Characters <ch1, ch2>: R K
On swapping <ch1, ch2>: K R
Enter two integers <a, b>: 5 10
On swapping <a, b>: 10 5
Enter two floats <c, d>: 20.5 99.5
On swapping <c, d>: 99.5 20.5
```

In the above program, three functions named swap() are defined, which only differ in their argument data types: char, int, or float. In main(), when the statement

```
    swap( ch1, ch2 );
```

is encountered, the compiler invokes the swap() function which takes character type arguments. This decision is based on the data type of the arguments. (see Figure 7.13).

Figure 7.13: Function overloading

It is interesting to note the way in which the C++ compiler implements function overloading. Although the functions share the same name in the source text (as in the example above, swap), the compiler (and hence the linker) uses quite different names. The conversion of a name in the source file to an internally used name is called *name mangling*. It can be performed as follows: the C++ compiler might convert the name void swap(int &, int &) to the internal name say VshowI, while an analogous function with a char* argument might be called VswapCP. The actual names, which are internally used, depend on the compiler and are transparent to the programmer.

Another typical example program of function overloading is illustrated in show.cpp.

```
// show.cpp: display different types of information with same function
#include <iostream.h>
```

```
void show( int val )
{
    cout << "Integer: " << val << endl;
}
void show( double val )
{
    cout << "Double. " << val << endl;
}
void show( char *val )
{
    cout << "String: " << val << endl;
}
int main ()
{
    show( 420 );                    // calls show( int val );
    show( 3.1415 );                 // calls show( double val );
    show( "Hello World\n!" );       // calls show( char *val );
    return( 0 );
}
```

Run

```
Integer: 420
Double: 3.1415
String: Hello World
!
```

The following remarks can be made on function overloading:

◆ The use of more than one function with the same name, but having different actions should be avoided. In the above example, the functions show() are somewhat related (they print information on the screen). However, it is also possible to define two functions, say lookup(); one of which would find a name in a list, while the other would determine the video mode. In this case, the two functions have nothing in common except their name. It would, therefore, be more practical to use names such as findname() and getvidmode(), which suggest the action they perform.

◆ C++ does not permit overloading of functions differing only in their return value. The reason is that it is always the programmer's choice to inspect or ignore the return value of a function. For instance, the fragment

```
        printf("Hello World!\n");
```

holds no information concerning the return value of the function printf(). (The return value in this case is an integer, which states the number of printed characters. This return value is practically never inspected). Two functions printf(), which would only differ in their return types and hence they are not distinguished by the compiler.

◆ Function overloading can lead to surprises. For instance, imagine the usage of statements

```
        show( 0 );
        show( NULL );
```

where there are multiple overloaded functions as in the program show.cpp. The zero could be interpret d here as a NULL pointer to a char, i.e., a (char*) 0, or as an integer with the value zero. C++ will invoke the function expecting an integer argument, which might not be what the user expects.

7.11 Function Templates

C++ allows to create a single function possessing the capabilities of several functions, which differ only in the data types. Such a function is known as *function template* or *generic function*. It permits writing one source declaration that can produce multiple functions differing only in the data types. The syntax of function template is shown in Figure 7.14.

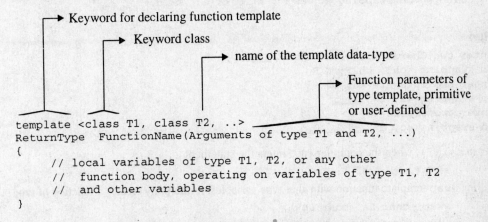

```
template <class T1, class T2, ..>
ReturnType  FunctionName(Arguments of type T1 and T2, ...)
{
      // local variables of type T1, T2, or any other
      //  function body, operating on variables of type T1, T2
      //  and other variables
}
```

Figure 7.14: Syntax of function template

The program swap5.cpp has functions with the same code pattern (same function body but operating on different data types). The program swap6.cpp illustrates, declaring a single function template from which all those functions having the same pattern of code, but operating on different data types can be created.

```
// swap6.cpp: multiple swap functions, function overloading
#include <iostream.h>

template <class T>
void swap( T & x, T & y )
{
   T t;  // temporarily used in swapping, template variable
   t = x;
   x = y;
   y = t;
}
void main()
{
   char ch1, ch2;
   cout << "Enter two Characters <ch1, ch2>: ";
   cin >> ch1 >> ch2;
   swap( ch1, ch2 ); // compiler creates and calls swap( char &x, char &y );
   cout << "On swapping <ch1, ch2>: " << ch1 << " " << ch2 << endl;
   int a, b;
   cout << "Enter two integers <a, b>: ";
   cin >> a >> b;
```

```
swap( a, b );  // compiler creates and calls swap( int &x, int &y );
cout << "On swapping <a, b>: " << a << " " << b << endl;
float c, d;
cout << "Enter two floats <c, d>: ";
cin >> c >> d;
swap( c, d );  // compiler creates and calls swap( float &x, float &y );
cout << "On swapping <c, d>: " << c << " " << d;
}
```

Run

```
Enter two Characters <ch1, ch2>: R K
On swapping <ch1, ch2>: K R
Enter two integers <a, b>: 5 10
On swapping <a, b>: 10 5
Enter two floats <c, d>: 20.5 99.5
On swapping <c, d>: 99.5 20.5
```

In main(), when the compiler encounters the statement

```
swap( ch1, ch2 );
```

calling swap template function with char type variables, it internally creates a function of type

```
swap( char &a, char &b );
```

The compiler automatically identifies the data type of the arguments passed to the template function, creates a new function and makes an appropriate call. The process by which the compiler handles function templates is totally invisible to the user. Similarly, the compiler converts the following calls

```
swap( a, b );  // compiler creates and calls swap( int &x, int &y );
swap( c, d );  // compiler creates and calls swap( float &x, float &y );
```

into equivalent functions and calls them based on their parameter data types.

For more details on function templates, refer to the chapter: *Generic Programming with Templates*.

7.12 Arrays and Functions

The arrays are passed by reference or by address. To pass an array to a function, it is sufficient to pass the address of the first element of the array. The program sort.cpp illustrates the concept of passing array type parameters to a function.

```
// sort.cpp: function to sort elements of an array
#include <iostream.h>
enum boolean { false, true };
void swap( int & x, int  & y )
{
   int t;    // temporary used in swapping
   t = x;
   x = y;
   y = t;
}
void BubbleSort( int * a, int size )
{
   boolean swapped = true;
```

```
    for( int i = 0; ( i < size - 1 ) && swapped; i++ )
    {
        swapped = false;
        for( int j = 0; j < ( size - 1 ) - i; j++ )
            if( a[ j ] > a[ j + 1 ] )
            {
                swapped = true;
                swap( a[ j ], a[ j + 1 ] );
            }
    }
}
void main( void )
{
    int a[25];
    int i, size;
    cout << "Program to sort elements..." << endl;
    cout << "Enter the size of the integer vector <max-25>: ";
    cin >> size;
    cout << "Enter the elements of the integer vector..." << endl;
    for( i = 0; i < size; i++ )
        cin >> a[i];
    BubbleSort( a, size );
    cout << "Sorted Vector:" << endl;
    for( i = 0; i < size; i++ )
        cout << a[i] << "  ";
}
```

Run

```
Program to sort elements...
Enter the size of the integer vector <max-25>: 5
Enter the elements of the integer vector...
8
6
9
3
2
Sorted Vector:
2  3  6  8  9
```

In main(), the statement

```
    BubbleSort( a, size );
```

invokes the sorting function by passing the address of the array variable a and the value of the variable size to it. Hence, any modification made to the elements of the array a will be reflected in the caller.

7.13 C++ Stack

The medium for communication between a caller and the callee is the stack, which is used to store function parameters, return address, local variables, etc. When the function is invoked, the information such as return address and parameters, are pushed onto the stack by the function linkage mechanism;

these values are pushed onto or popped from the stack using the C convention for parameter passing. The argument values are pushed in order, from right to left. When they are popped out, the topmost value stored in the stack will be passed to the first parameter in the function parameter list. The order of storing the function parameters in the stack when the statement

```
func( a, b, c, d );
```

is invoked is shown in Figure 7.15. Note that, the Pascal convention of parameter passing is to push parameters from left to right when a function is invoked. Knowledge of parameter passing convention is essential while doing mixed language programming.

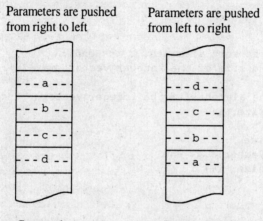

Function call: `func(a, b, c, d);`

Parameters are pushed from right to left   Parameters are pushed from left to right

C++ stack   Pascal stack

Figure 7.15: Parameter passing and Stack

The program `funcstk.cpp` demonstrates the concept of storing and retrieving the elements from the stack.

```
// funcstk.cpp: C++ convention of using stack
#include <iostream.h>
void Func( j, k )
{
   cout<<"In the function the argument values are " << j<< " .. "<<k<< endl;
}
int main( void )
{
   int i = 99;
   Func( ++i, i );
}
```

Run
```
In the function the argument values are 100 .. 99
```

The output of the program is not 100 .. 100 as expected, because of the C convention for passing parameters. In the function call, first the value of right-most parameter i, which is 99 will be pushed onto the stack, and will be followed by ++i; i.e., 100. Hence, the stack will have 99 at the bottom and 100 at the top. Hence, the statement

```
Func( ++i, i );
```

assigns the value 100 and 99 to the formal parameters j and k respectively.

7.14 Scope and Extent of Variables

Every variable in a program has some memory associated with it. Memory for variables are allocated and released at different points in the program. For example, in case of normal local variables defined in functions, memory is allocated when the function starts execution and released when the function returns. A variable defined outside all function bodies is called a global variable. Its extent is the entire life-span of the program. *The period of time during which the memory is associated with a variable is called the extent of the variable.* Consider the following function

```
void func()
{
    int i;
    i = 10;
}
```

Allocation of memory to the integer variable i is the process of deciding the memory locations to be occupied by i. The memory of such local variables is allocated in the program stack when the function func() is invoked. Naturally, the memory that was allocated to i is released when the function terminates, and that memory space is available for use. Identifiers defined in a function are not accessible outside that function and hence, their extent is limited to life of that function. However, there are exceptions (static variables). For instance, consider the following segment of a program code:

```
void func()
{
    int i;
    i = 10;
}
void main()
{
    i = 20;
    func();
    i = 30;
}
```

When this program is compiled, the statements,

```
i = 20;
i = 30;
```

lead to compilation errors; the variable i is not visible inside the main(). So the definition of the identifier i is valid only inside the func(). *The region of source code over which the definition of an identifier is visible is called the scope of the identifier.* The scope of the variable i defined in func() is limited to this function only. If the statement

```
int i;
```

is defined in the beginning of main(), then no errors occur, but nevertheless, the variable i in the func() and that in function main() are different. Modifications to one variable do not affect the other variables. Note that the scope of the variable defined in main() is limited to main() only, whereas its extent is entire life-span (execution time) of the program. The program variable.cpp illustrates the scope and extent of local and global variables.

```
// variable.cpp: scope and extent of different variable
#include <iostream.h>
int g = 100;  // global variable
void func1()
{
   int g = 50; // local variable
   cout << "Local variable g in func1(): " << g << endl;
}
void func2()
{
   cout << "In func2() g is visible, since it is global." << endl;
   cout << "Incrementing g in func..." << endl;
   g++;  //accesses global variable
}
void main()
{
   cout << "In main g is visible here, since it is global.\n";
   cout << "Assigning 20 to g in main...\n";
   g = 20;      // accesses global variable
   cout << "Calling func1...\n";
   func1();
   cout << "func1 returned. g is " << g << endl;
   cout << "Calling func2...\n";
   func2();
   cout << "func2 returned. g is " << g << endl;
}
```

Run
```
In main g is visible here, since it is global.
Assigning 20 to g in main...
Calling func1...
Local variable g in func1(): 50
func1 returned. g is 20
Calling func2...
In func2() g is visible, since it is global.
Incrementing g in func...
func2 returned. g is 21
```

The global variable g is visible to all functions (entire file) and its *extent* is the entire execution time of the program. The scope and extent of local variable g of func1() is limited to its function body.

The scope of a variable can confirm to a block, a function, a file, or an entire program (in case of multimodule file). The variables defined within a block can be accessed only within that block. The program block1.cpp illustrates the block scope of variables.

```
// block.cpp:  illustration of the variables scope in blocks
.#include <iostream.h>
int main( void )
{
    int i = 144; .
    cout << "i = " << i;
    {
        /* nested block*/
        int k = 12;
        cin >> k;
        i = i % k ;
    }
    if( i == 0 )
        cout << " i is a divisor of " << k; // Error: k undefined in main()
    return 0;
}
```

Reference to variable k in the main block results in a compile-time error: *Undefined symbol k in the function main ()*; the variable k is declared inside the nested block within main (). The memory space for the variable k is allocated when the execution of the block starts, and released when execution reaches the end of the nested block. When a variable is accessed, the compiler first checks for its existence in the current block, and then moves outwards if it does not exist in the current block; this process continues until the global definition. The function can access the identifiers in the parameter list, the local definitions and the global definitions (if any).

7.15 Storage Classes

The period of time during which memory is associated with a variable is called the extent of the variable. It is characterized by storage classes. The storage class of a variable indicates the allocation of storage space to the variable by the compiler. Storage classes define the extent of a variable. C++ supports the following four types of storage classes:

- auto
- register
- extern
- static

The syntax for defining variables with explicit storage class is shown in Figure 7.16. The storage classes except extern are used for defining variables; extern is used for declaration of variables. The scope and extent of auto and register storage class is the same. The scope of static variables is limited to its block (maximum to a file), but its extent is throughout the execution time of the program (does not matter whether it is local or global type).

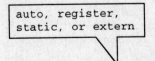

StorageClass DataType Variable1,....;

Figure 7.16: Storage classes and variable declaration

Declaration Versus Definition

A declaration informs the compiler about the existence of the data or a function some where in the program. A definition allocates the storage location. In C++, a piece of data or function can be declared in several different places, but there must only be one definition. Otherwise, the linker will complain (generates multiple definition error) while uniting all the object modules, if it encounters more than one definition for the same function or piece of data. Almost all C and C++ programs require declarations. Therefore, it is essential for the programmer to understand the correct way to write a declaration. As far as data is concerned, except `extern` storage class, all others define data i.e., they not only direct the compiler, but also allocate resource for a variable.

Auto Variables

By default, all the variables are defined as auto variables. They are created when the function/block is entered and destroyed when the function/block is terminated. The memory space for local auto variables is allocated on the stack. The global auto variables are visible to all the modules of a program, and hence, they cannot be defined many times unlike the declarations.

Register Variables

The allocation of CPU (processor) registers to variables, speeds up the execution of a program; memory is not referred when such variables are accessed. The number of variables, which can be declared as `register` are limited (typically two or three), within any function or as global variables (else they are treated as auto variables). A program that uses register variables executes faster when compared to a similar program without register variables. It is possible to find out the allocation of register variables only by executing and comparing the timing performance of the program (perceptible in large programs). It is the responsibility of the compiler to allot register variables. In case the compiler is unable to do so, these variables are treated as auto variables. It is advisable to define frequently used variables, such as loop indices, as `register` variables. It is illustrated in the program `regvar.cpp`.

```
// regvar.cpp: use of register variable as loop index
#include <iostream.h>
#include <string.h>
void main()
{
   char name[30];
   register int i;       // register variable
   cout << "Enter a string: ";
   cin >> name;
   cout << "The reverse of the string is: ";
   for( i = strlen( name )-1; i >= 0; i-- )
      cout << name[i];
}
```

Run1
```
Enter a string: mahatma
The reverse of the string is: amtaham
```

Run2
```
Enter a string: malayalam
```

```
The reverse of the string is: malayalam
```

Static Variables

The static storage class allows to define a variable whose scope is restricted to either a block, a function, or a file (but not all files in multimodule program) and extent is the life-span of a program. The memory space for local static and global variables is allocated from the *global heap*. Static variables that are defined within a function remember their values from the previous call (i.e., the values to which they are initialized or changed before returning from the function). The static variables defined outside all functions in a file are called *file static variables*. They are accessible only in the file in which they are defined. The program count.cpp illustrates the use of function static local variables.

```cpp
// count.cpp: use of static variables defined inside functions
#include <iostream.h>
void PrintCount( void )
{
   static int Count = 1; // Count is initialized only on the first call
   cout << "Count = " << Count << endl;
   Count = Count + 1;    // The incremented value of Count is retained
}
void main( void )
{
   PrintCount();
   PrintCount();
   PrintCount();
}
```

Run
```
Count = 1
Count = 2
Count = 3
```

The output of the program is a sequence of numbers starting with 1, rather than a string of 1's. The initialization of static variable Count is performed only in the first instance of the function call. In successive calls to the function, the variable Count has the same value as it had before the termination of the most recent call. However, these static variables are not accessible from other parts of the program.

Extern global variables are global to the file in which they are defined. They are used when the same global variable is referenced in each one of the files and these variables must be independent of each other across files. The use of global variables is not recommended, since they do not allow to achieve function independence which is one of the basic ideas of modular programming.

Extern Variables

When a program spans across different files, they can share information using global variables. Global variables must be defined only once in any of the program module and they can be accessed by all others. It is achieved by declaring such variables as extern variables. It informs the compiler that such variables are defined in some other file. Consider a program having the following files:

```
// file1.cpp: module one defining global variable
int done;    // global variable definition
void func1()
{
    ....
    ....
}
void disp()
{
    ....
    ....
}
// file2.cpp: module two of the project
extern int done;    // global variable declaration
void func3
{
    ....
    ....
}
```

In file1.cpp, the statement

```
        int done;
```

defines the variable done as a global variable. In file2.cpp, the statement

```
        extern int done;
```

declares the variable done and indicates that it is defined in some other file. Note that the definition of the variable done must appear in any one of the modules, whereas extern declaration can appear in any or all modules of a program. When the linker encounters such variables, it binds all references to the same memory location. Thus, any modification to the variable done is visible to all the modules accessing it.

If the global variable done is defined as static, it can be again defined in other modules since the linker treats each as a different variable. Such global static variables have scope restricted to a file and extent is equal to the entire life-span of the program. The auto and static global variables are used mainly in managing large multimodule software project. Note that, the memory space for global variable is allocated from the global heap memory.

7.16 Functions with Variable Number of Arguments

C++ functions such as vfprintf() and vprintf() accept variable argument lists in addition to taking a number of fixed (known) parameters. The va_arg, va_end, and va_start macros provide access to these argument lists in the standard form. They are used for stepping through a list of arguments when the called function does not know the number and types of the arguments being passed. The header file stdarg.h declares one type (va_list) and three macros (va_start, va_arg, and va_end).

The syntax of macros handling variable number of arguments are the following:

```
        #include <stdarg.h>
        void va_start(va_list ap, lastfix);
```

```
type va_arg(va_list ap, type);
void va_end(va_list ap);
```

va_list: This array holds information needed by va_arg and va_end. When a called function takes a variable argument list, it declares a variable ap of type va_list.

va_start: This routine (implemented as a macro) sets ap to point to the first of the variable arguments being passed to the function. va_start must be used before the first call to va_arg or va_end. The macro va_start takes two parameters: ap and lastfix. ap is a pointer to the variable argument list. lastfix is the name of the last fixed parameter passed to the caller.

va_arg: This routine (also implemented as a macro) expands to an expression that has the same type and value as the next argument being passed (one of the variable arguments). The variable ap to va_arg should be the same ap that va_start initialized. Note that because of default promotions, char, unsigned char, or float types cannot be used with va_arg.

When va_arg is used first time, it returns the first argument in the list. Every successive use of va_arg, returns the next argument in the list. It does this by first dereferencing ap, and then incrementing ap to point to the following item. va_arg uses the type to perform both the dereferencing and to locating the following item. Each time va_arg is invoked, it modifies ap to point to the next argument in the list.

va_end: This macro helps the called function to perform a normal return. va_end might modify ap in such a way that it cannot be used unless va_start is recalled. va_end should be called after va_arg has read all the arguments; failure to do so might cause a program to behave erratically.

Return Value: va_start and va_end return no values; va_arg returns the current argument in the list (the one that ap is pointing to).

The syntax of function receiving variable number of arguments is:

```
ReturnType Func( arg1, [arguments], ... );
```

It is same as the normal function except for the last three dots, which indicates that the function is of type variable arguments. The program add.cpp illustrates the use of variable number of arguments.

```
// add.cpp: variable number of arguments to a function
#include <iostream.h>
#include <stdarg.h>
int add( int argc, ... )
{
   int num, result;
   va_list args;
   va_start( args, argc );    // link to variable arguments
   result = 0;
   for(int i=0; i < argc; i++)
   {
      num = va_arg( args, int );    // get argument value
      result += num;
   }
   va_end( args );       // end of arguments
   return result;
}
```

```
void main()
{
    int sum1, sum2, sum3;
    sum1 = add( 3, 1, 2, 3 );
    cout << "sum1 = " << sum1 << endl;
    sum2 = add( 1, 10 );
    cout << "sum2 = " << sum2 << endl;
    sum3 = add( 0 );
    cout << "sum3 = " << sum3 << endl;
}
```

Run
```
sum1 = 6
sum2 = 10
sum3 = 0
```

The function declarator (prototype)
```
    int add( int argc, ... )
```
indicates that it takes one known argument and the remaining are unknown number of arguments. The three dots indicate that the function takes variable arguments, to which a chain has to be built. In add() function, the statement
```
    va_list args;
```
creates a pointer variable named args. The macro call statement
```
    va_start( args, argc );    // link to variable arguments
```
links variable arguments to the variable args. The variable args is the last known argument and those that follow are variable arguments. The statement
```
    num = va_arg( args, int );    // get argument value
```
accesses the argument of type integer and assigns to the variable num. Later, args is updated to point to the next argument. The statement
```
    va_end( args );        // end of arguments
```
indicates the end of access to variable arguments using args. In main(), the statement
```
    sum1 = add( 3, 1, 2, 3 );
```
invokes the function add() and the first argument is a known argument indicating the number of variable arguments.

The last argument in the list of variable number of arguments must be established by the user. Another way of indicating the end of variable arguments is illustrated in the program sum.cpp.

```
// sum.cpp: variable arguments example
#include <iostream.h>
#include <stdarg.h>
// calculate sum of a 0 terminated list
void sum(char *msg, ...)
{
    int total = 0;
    va_list ap;
    int arg;
```

```
    va_start(ap, msg);
    while ((arg = va_arg(ap,int)) != 0) {
        total += arg;
    }
    cout << msg << total;
    va_end(ap);
}

int main(void)
{
    sum("The total of 1+2+3+4 is ", 1,2,3,4,0);
    return 0;
}
```

Run
```
The total of 1+2+3+4 is 10
```

In main(), the statement
```
        sum("The total of 1+2+3+4 is ", 1,2,3,4,0);
```
invokes the variable argument function. The function sum() is designed such that when a zero valued argument is encountered, it is understood that no more arguments exists for further processing. Hence, the last argument 0 (zero) in this case, is the end-of-argument indicator. The programmer has full freedom for selecting suitable end-of-argument indicator.

7.17 Recursive Functions

Many of the scientific operations are expressed using recurrence relations. C++ allows the programmers to express such a relation using functions. A function that contains a function call to itself, or a function call to a second function which eventually calls the first function is known as a recursive function. The recursive definition for computing the factorial of a number can be expressed as follows:

$$fact(n) = \begin{cases} 1 \text{ if } n = 0 \\ n * fact(n-1), \text{ otherwise} \end{cases}$$

Recursion, as the name suggests, revolves around a function recalling itself. Recursive functions are those, in which there is atleast one function call to itself (there can be more than one call to itself as in the *tower of hanoi* algorithm). The recursive approach of problem solving substitutes the given problem with another problem of the same form in such a way that the new problem is simpler than the original.

Two important conditions which must be satisfied by any recursive function are:
1. Each time a function calls itself it must be nearer, in some sense, to a solution.
2. There must be a decision criterion for stopping the process or computation.

Recursive functions involve the overhead of saving the return address, formal parameters, local variables upon entry, and restore these parameters and variables on completion.

Factorial of a Number

The program rfact.cpp computes the factorial of a number. It has a recursive function fact() which implements the above stated definition of recursion.

```
// rfact.cpp: factorial of a number using recursion
#include <iostream.h>
void main( void )
{
   int n;
   long int fact( int );    // prototype
   cout << "Enter the number whose factorial is to be found: ";
   cin >> n;
   cout << "The factorial of " << n << " is " << fact(n) << endl;
}
long fact( int num )
{
   if( num == 0 )
      return 1;
   else
      return num * fact( num - 1 );
}
```

Run

```
Enter the number whose factorial is to be found: 5
The factorial of 5 is 120
```

Tower of Hanoi

Tower of hanoi is a historical problem, which can be easily expressed using recursion. There are N disks of decreasing size stacked on one needle, and two other empty needles. It is required to stack all the disks onto a second needle in the decreasing order of size. The third needle can be used as a temporary storage. The movement of the disks must conform to the following rules:

1. Only one disk may be moved at a time
2. A disk can be moved from any needle to any other
3. At no time, a larger disk rests upon a smaller one.

The program `hanoi.cpp` implements the tower of hanoi problem. The physical model of a tower of hanoi problem is shown in Figure 7.17.

```
// hanoi.cpp: Tower of hanoi simulation using recursion
#include <iostream.h>
void main( void )
{
   unsigned int nvalue;
   char source  = 'L', intermediate = 'C', destination = 'R';
   void  hanoi( unsigned int, char, char, char );
   cout << "Enter number of disks: ";
   cin >> nvalue;
   cout << "Tower of Hanoi problem with " << nvalue << " disks" << endl;
   hanoi( nvalue, source, intermediate, destination );
}
void hanoi( unsigned n, char left, char mid, char right )
{
   if(n != 0)
   {
```

```
    // Move n-1 disks from starting needle to intermediate needle
    hanoi( n-1, left, right, mid );
    // Move disk n from start to destination
    cout<< "Move disk " << n << " from " << left<<" to " << right <<endl;
    // Move n-1 disks from intermediate needle to destination needle
    hanoi( n-1, mid, left, right );
  }
}
```

Run

```
Enter number of disks: 3
Tower of Hanoi problem with 3 disks
Move disk 1 from L to R
Move disk 2 from L to C
Move disk 1 from R to C
Move disk 3 from L to R
Move disk 1 from C to L
Move disk 2 from C to R
Move disk 1 from L to R
```

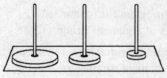

Initial Configuration

Move 1

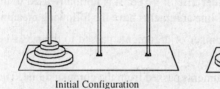

Move 2

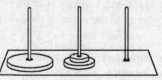

Move 3

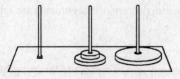

Move 4

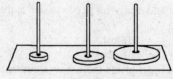

Move 5

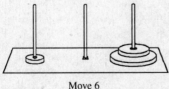

Move 6

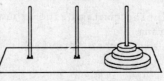

Move 7

Figure 7.17:   Tower of Hanoi

7.18 Complete Syntax of `main()`

The function `main()` takes three input parameters called command-line arguments. These are passed from the point of program execution (usually operating system shell or command interpreter). The general format of the `main()` function is shown in Figure 7.18

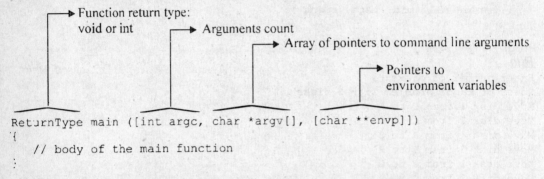

```
ReturnType main ([int argc, char *argv[], [char **envp]])
{
    // body of the main function
    :
```

Figure 7.18:   Syntax of the main function

The return type of the `main` function must be either `int` or `void`. It is normally used to indicate the status of the program termination. The command-line arguments have the following meaning:

argc: argument count, holds the value of the number of arguments passed to the `main()` function and its value is always positive.

argv: argument vector, holds pointers to the arguments passed from the command line. The meaning of various elements of the `argv` vector is as follows:

```
argv[ 0 ] = pointer to the name of the executable program file (command)
argv[ 1 ] .. argv[ argc - 1 ] = pointers to argument strings
```

envp: environment parameter, holds pointers to environment variables set in the operating system during the program execution. It includes path and environment parameters. It is optional and not a ANSI specification.

When the command `disp hello` is issued at the system prompt, the arguments are set as follows:

```
argc = 2
argv[ 0 ] = "disp"
argv[ 1 ] = "hello"
```

The program `args.cpp` prints the list of arguments passed to it. To execute this program, issue the command args Hello World at the system prompt.

```
// args.cpp: printing command line arguments
#include <iostream.h>
void main( int argc, char *argv[] )
{
    int i;
    cout << "Argument Count = " << argc;
    cout << "\nProgram Name = " << argv[ 0 ];
    cout << "\nArgument Vectors Are:\n";
    for ( i = 0; i < argc; i++ )
        cout << argv[i] << "\n";
}
```

Run

```
Argument Count = 3
Program Name = D:\CPP_SRC\MC2CPP.C02\ARGS.EXE
Argument Vectors Are:
D:\CPP_SRC\MC2CPP.C02\ARGS.EXE
Hello
World
```

Program Execution Status

Normally, after the complete execution of the program, it exits from the main() function itself. However, programs can be terminated from anywhere within the program. The return type of the main function can be used by the system to decide whether the program terminates with successful execution or not. The return statement in main()

```
        return 0;    // program return type
```

or the exit() statement anywhere in the program

```
        exit( 0 )
```

terminates the program with the program execution status as zero. The general convention is that, the return value 0 is treated as a successful execution of the program and nonzero value is interpreted as unsuccessful execution of the program. The method of identifying this return value from outside the program (from where it is invoked), depends on the operating system environment in which the program is executed. For instance, under MS-DOS operating system, the system sets the environment variable errorlevel to the value returned by the programmer. The user can inspect the value held by the errorlevel variable to decide the status of program execution. The program fullmain.cpp displays the command line arguments and environment variables.

```
// fullmain.cpp: prints command line arguments and environment variables
#include <iostream.h>
int main( int argc, char **argv, char **envp )
{
    cout << "The number of command line arguments is: " << argc << endl;
    cout << "The command line arguments are as follows" << endl;
    for( int i = 0; i < argc; i++ )
        cout << "argv[" << i << "] : " << argv[i] << endl;
    cout << "The environment variables are:" << endl;
    i = 0;
    while( *envp[i] )
        cout << envp[i++] << endl;
    return 0;
}
```

Run

```
The number of command line arguments is: 3
The command line arguments are as follows
argv[0] : C:\CPP_SRC\FUNCTION.C07\FULLMAIN.EXE
argv[1] : Hello
argv[2] : World
The environment variables are:
COMSPEC=C:\COMMAND.COM
PROMPT=$p$g
PATH=C:\BC4\BIN;C:\EXCEEDW\PATHWAY;C:\BC4\BIN;C:\WINDOWS;C:\DOS;C:\PATHWAY;
```

Review Questions

7.1 What is modular programming and what are its benefits ? Explain the same with a C++ example.

7.2 Explain different components of a C++ program with a suitable example program.

7.3 What are the differences between actual parameters and formal parameters ?

7.4 What are caller and callee ? List the various components causing the overhead of function invocation.

7.5 What are library functions ? Explain how they ease program development. What are the different categories of functions supported by C++ library ?

7.6 What is parameter passing ? Explain parameter passing schemes supported by C++.

7.7 Develop a function to sort numbers using bubble sort technique. Write a driver function also.

7.8 What are the differences between parameter passing by value and passing by address ?

7.9 What are the benefits of pass by reference method of parameter passing over pass by pointer ?

7.10 What are default arguments ? Write a program to compute tax. A *tax compute* function takes two arguments: amount and tax percentage. Default tax percentage is 15% of income.

7.11 State whether the following statements are valid or not ? Give reasons.
```
tax_amount( int amount, int percentage = 15 );   // prototype
tax_amount( , 5 );
show( char ch = 'A', int count = 3 );   // prototype
show( , 2 );
show( , );
show();
```

7.11 What are inline functions ? Write an inline function for finding minimum of two numbers.

7.12 What is function overloading ? Write overloaded functions for computing area of a triangle, a circle, and a rectangle. Develop a driver function.

7.13 What are function templates ? Write a template based program for sorting numbers.

7.14 What is the difference between parameter passing in C++ and Pascal ? What is the result of:
```
sum = add( i++, a[i] ); // if i=1 and a[] = { 5, 10, 15, 20 }
```

7.15 Define terms: scope and extent. Explain different storage classes supported by C++. Also explain there scope and extent.

7.16 Write a program having a variable argument function to multiply input numbers.

7.17 What are recursive functions ? Write a program to find the gcd of two numbers using the following Euclid's recursive algorithm.
$$gcd(m,n) = \begin{cases} gcd(n, m) & \text{if } n > m \\ m & \text{if } n = 0 \\ gcd(n, m \% n), & \text{otherwise} \end{cases}$$

7.18 Write a program for adding integer parameters passed as command line arguments.

7.19 Write a program to generate fibonacci series using the following recursive algorithm:
$$fib(n) = \begin{cases} 0 \text{ if } n = 0 \\ 1 \text{ if } n = 1 \\ fib(n-1)+fib(n-2), \text{ otherwise} \end{cases}$$

7.20 Implement a recursive binary serach using *divide and conquer* technique.

8
Structures and Unions

8.1 Introduction

Structures combine logically related data items into a single unit. The data items enclosed within a structure are known as members and they can be of the same or different data types. Hence, a structure can be viewed as a heterogeneous user-defined data type. It can be used to create variables, which can be manipulated in the same way as variables of standard data types. It encourages better organization and management of data in a program.

8.2 Structure Declaration

The declaration of a structure specifies the grouping of various data items into a single unit without assigning any resources to them. The syntax for declaring a structure in C++ is shown in Figure 8.1.

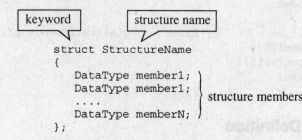

Figure 8.1: Structure declaration

The structure declaration starts with the structure header, which consists of the keyword `struct` followed by a tag. The tag serves as a structure name, which can be used for creating structure variables. The individual members of the structure are enclosed between the curly braces and they can be of the same or different data types. The data type of each variable is specified in the individual member declarations. Like all data structure declarations, the closing brace is terminated with a semicolon.

Consider a student database consisting of student roll number, name, branch, and total marks scored. A structure declaration to hold this information is shown below:

```
struct Student
{
    int roll_no;
    char name[25];
    char branch[15];
    int marks;
};
```

The data items enclosed between flower brackets in the above structure declaration are called *structure elements* or *structure members*. Student is the name of the structure and is called *structure tag*. Note that, some members of Student structure are integer type and some are character array type. The description of various components of the structure Student is shown in Figure 8.2.

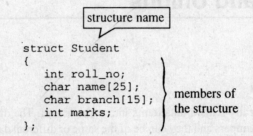

```
struct Student
{
    int roll_no;
    char name[25];
    char branch[15];
    int marks;
};
```

Figure 8.2:   Declaration of structure Student

The individual members of a structure can be variables of built-in data types, pointers, arrays, or even other structures. All member names within a particular structure must be different. However, member names may be the same as those of variables declared outside the structure. The individual members cannot be initialized inside the structure declaration. For example, the following declaration is invalid:

```
struct Student
{
    int roll_no = 0;    // Error: initialization not allowed here
    char name[25];
    char branch[15];
    int marks;
};
```

8.3 Structure Definition

The declaration of a structure will not serve any purpose without its definition. It only acts as a blueprint for the creation of variables of type struct (structure). The structure definition creates structure variables and allocates storage space for them. Structure variables can be created at the point of structure declaration itself, or by using the structure tag explicitly as and when required. The most commonly used syntax for structure definition is shown in Figure 8.3.

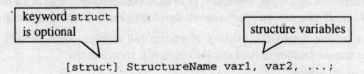

```
[struct] StructureName var1, var2, ...;
```

Figure 8.3:   Syntax of structure definition

The use of the keyword struct in the structure definition statement is optional. The following statements create variables of the structure Student declared earlier:

```
struct Student s1;
or
Student s1;
```

Figure 8.4 shows the storage of the members of the structure Student.

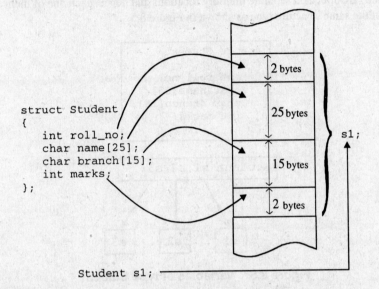

Student s1;

Figure 8.4: Storage organisation when structure variable is defined

The structure variables can be created during the declaration of a structure as follows:

```
struct Student
{
    int roll_no;
    char name[25];
    char branch[15];
    int marks;
} s1;
```

In the above declaration, Student is the structure tag, while s1 is a variable of type Student. If variables of this structure type are not defined later in the program, then the tag name Student can be omitted as shown below:

```
struct
{
    int roll_no;
    char name[25];
    char branch[15];
    int marks;
} s1;
```

It is not a good practice, to have both declaration and definition in the same statement.

Multiple variables of a structure can be created using a single statement as follows:

```
struct Student s1, s3, s4;
```

or

```
Student s1, s3, s4;
```

All these instances are allocated separate memory locations and hence, each one of them are independent variables of the same structure type as shown in Figure 8.5.

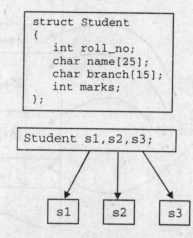

```
struct Student
{
    int roll_no;
    char name[25];
    char branch[15];
    int marks;
};
```

```
Student s1,s2,s3;
```

| s1 | s2 | s3 |

Figure 8.5:   Variables of type Student

8.4 Accessing Structure Members

C++ provides the period or dot (.) operator to access the members of a structure independently. The dot operator connects a structure variable and its member. The syntax for accessing members of a structure variable is shown in Figure 8.6.

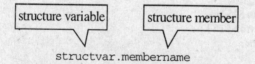

| structure variable | | structure member |

```
structvar.membername
```

Figure 8.6:   Accessing a structure member using dot operator

Here, `structvar` is a structure variable and `membername` is one of its members. Thus, the dot operator must have a structure variable on its left and a legal member name on its right. Consider the following statement:

```
Student s1;
```

Each member of the structure variable `s1` can be accessed using the dot operator as follows:

`s1.roll_no`	will access `s1`'s `roll_no`
`s1.name`	will access `s1`'s `name`
`s1.branch`	will access `s1`'s `branch`
`s1.marks`	will access `s1`'s `marks`

The following are valid operations on the structure variable s1:

```
s1.roll_no = 5;
cin >> s1.roll_no;
strcpy( s1.name, "Mangala" );
cout << s1.name;
strcpy( s1.branch, "Computer" );
```

Accessing members of a structure using structure tag is not allowed. Hence, a statement such as

```
Student.roll_no = 5; // Error: Student is not a structure variable
```

is invalid; structure name Student is a data type like int, and not a variable. Just as int = 10 is invalid, Student.roll_no = 5 is invalid.

The program student1.cpp illustrates the various concepts discussed in the earlier sections such as structure declaration, definition, and accessing members of a structure.

```
// student1.cpp: processing of student data using structures
#include <iostream.h>
// structure declaration
struct Student
{
   int roll_no;
   char name[25];
   char branch[15];
   int marks;
};
void main()
{
   Student s1;     // structure definition
   cout << "Enter data for student..." << endl;
   cout << "Roll Number ? ";
   cin >> s1.roll_no;       // accessing structure member
   cout << "Name ? ";
   cin >> s1.name;
   cout << "Branch ? ";
   cin >> s1.branch;
   cout << "Total Marks <max-325> ? ";
   cin >> s1.marks;
   cout << "Student Report" << endl;
   cout << "---------------" << endl;
   // process student data
   cout << "Roll Number: " << s1.roll_no << endl;
   cout << "Name: " << s1.name << endl;
   cout << "Branch: " << s1.branch << endl;
   cout << "Percentage: " << s1.marks*(100.0/325) << endl;
}
```

Run

```
Enter data for student...
Roll Number ? 5
Name ? Mangala
```

```
Branch ? Computer
Total Marks <max-325> ? 290
Student Report
--------------
Roll Number: 5
Name: Mangala
Branch: Computer
Percentage: 89.230769
```

Precedence of the DOT operator

The dot operator is a member of the highest precedence group, and its associativity is from left to right. Hence, the expression such as ++stvar.membern is equivalent to ++(stvar.membern), implying that the unary operator will act only on a particular member of the structure and not the entire structure.

8.5 Structure Initialization

Similar to the standard data types, structure variables can be initialized at the point of their definition. Consider the following structure declaration:

```
struct Student
{
    int roll_no;
    char name[25];
    char branch[15];
    int marks;
};
```

A variable of the structure Student can be initialized during its definition as follows:

```
Student s1 ={ 5, "Mangala", "Computer", 290 };
```

The initial values for the components of the structure are placed in curly braces and separated by commas. The members of the variable s1, roll_no, name, branch, and marks are initialized to 5, "Mangala", "Computer", and 290 respectively (see Figure 8.7).

The program days.cpp illustrates the initialization of the members of a structure at the point of a structure variable definition.

```
// days.cpp: structure members initialization at the point of definition
#include <iostream.h>
// structure declaration
struct date
{
    int day;
    int month;
    int year;
};
void main()
{
    date d1 = { 14, 4, 1971 };
    date d2 = { 3, 7, 1996 };
```

```
    cout << "Birth date: ";
    cout << d1.day <<"-"<< d1.month <<"-"<< d1.year;
    cout << endl << "Today date: ";
    cout << d2.day <<"-"<< d2.month <<"-"<< d2.year;
}
```

Run

```
Birth date: 14-4-1971
Today date: 3-7-1996
```

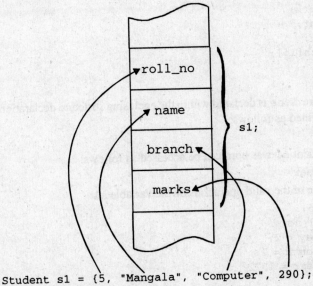

Student s1 = {5, "Mangala", "Computer", 290};

Figure 8.7: Structure members' initialization during definition

8.6 Nesting of Structures

A member of a structure may itself be a structure. Such nesting enables building of very powerful data structures. The Student structure can be enhanced to accomodate the date of birth of a student. The new member birthday is a structure of type date by itself as shown below:

```
struct date
{
    int day;
    int month;
    int year;
};
struct Student
{
    int roll_no;
    char name[25];
    struct date birthday;
    char branch[15];
    int marks;
};
```

The structure to be embedded must be declared before its use. Another way of declaring a nested structure is to embed member structure declaration within the declaration of a new structure as follows:

```
struct Student
{
    int roll_no;
    char name[25];
    struct date
    {
        int day;
        int month;
        int year;
    } birthday;
    char branch[15];
    int marks;
};
```

The embedded structure `date` is declared within the enclosing structure declaration. A variable of type `Student` can be defined as follows:

```
Student s1;
```

The year in which the student `s1` was born can be accessed as follows:

```
s1.birthday.year
```

The following are the some of the valid operations on the variable `s1`:

```
s1.roll_no = 5;
cin >> s1.roll_no;
s1.birthday.day = 2;
s1.birthday.month = 2;
s1.birthday.year = 1972;
```

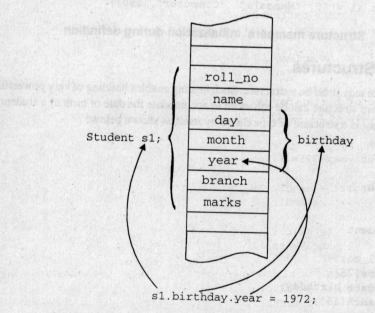

Figure 8.8:   Accessing members of nested structures

The dot operator accessing a member of the nested structure birthday using the statement

```
s1.birthday.year = 1972;
```

is shown in Figure 8.8. The program student2.cpp illustrates the declaration, definition, and processing of nested structure members.

A statement such as

```
s1.date.day = 2;     // error
```

is invalid, because a member of the nested structure must be accessed using its variable name.

```cpp
// student2.cpp: processing of student data using structures
#include <iostream.h>
// structure declaration
struct date
{
   int day;
   int month;
   int year;
};
struct Student
{
   int roll_no;
   char name[25];
   struct date birthday;       // structure within a structure
   char branch[15];
   int marks;
};
void main()
{
   Student s1;     // structure definition
   cout << "Enter data for student..." << endl;
   cout << "Roll Number ? ";
   cin >> s1.roll_no;         // accessing structure member
   cout << "Name ? ";
   cin >> s1.name;
   cout << "Enter date of birth <day month year>: ";
   cin >> s1.birthday.day >> s1.birthday.month >> s1.birthday.year;
   cout << "Branch ? ";
   cin >> s1.branch;
   cout << "Total Marks <max-325> ? ";
   cin >> s1.marks;
   cout << "Student Report" << endl;
   cout << "--------------" << endl;
   // process student data
   cout << "Roll Number: " << s1.roll_no << endl;
   cout << "Name: " << s1.name << endl;
   cout << "Birth day: ";
   cout<<s1.birthday.day <<"-"<< s1.birthday.month<<"-"<<s1.birthday.year;
   cout << endl << "Branch: " << s1.branch << endl;
   cout << "Percentage: " << s1.marks*(100.0/325) << endl;
}
```

Run

```
Enter data for student...
Roll Number ? 9
Name ? Savithri
Enter date of birth <day month year>: 2 2 1972
Branch ? Electrical
Total Marks <max-325> ? 295
Student Report
--------------
Roll Number: 9
Name: Savithri
Birth day: 2-2-1972
Branch: Electrical
Percentage: 91.076923
```

8.7 Array of Structures

It is possible to define an array of structures; each array element is similar to a variable of that structure. The syntax for defining an array of structures and accessing its members using an index, is shown in Figure 8.9.

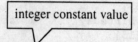

```
StructureName ArrayName[size];
```

(a) Array of structures definition

```
ArrayName[index]
```

(b) Accessing a particular array element

```
ArrayName[index].MemberName
```

(c) Accessing a particular member

Figure 8.9:   Array of structures and member access

The following examples illustrate the concepts of defining arrays of structures and manipulating their members. Consider the structure declaration given below:

```
struct Student
{
    int roll_no;
    char name[25];
    struct date birthday;
    char branch[15];
    int marks;
};
```

An array of the above structure can be defined as follows:

```
Student s[10];
```

The variable s is a 10 element array of structures of the type Student. The 5th structure can be accessed as follows:

```
s[4];    // arrays are numbered from 0 to n-1
```

The following statements access members of the structure array elements:

```
s[4].name;          // access the name of 5th structure
s[0].marks[5];      // access 6th character of 1st structure
&s[2].name          // address of 3rd s structure member name
```

Another method of defining an array of structures is as follows:

```
struct Student
{
    int roll_no;
    char name[25];
    struct date birthday;
    char branch[15];
    int marks;
} s[10];
```

More than one array of structure variables can be defined in a single statement as follows:

```
Student class1[10], class2[15];
```

It defines two arrays of structure variables class1 and class2 of size 10 and 15 respectively. Each element of the class1 will be a structure of type Student. The program student3.cpp illustrates the method of processing of an array of structures.

```
// student3.cpp: processing of student data using structures
#include <iostream.h>
struct Student
{
    int roll_no;
    char name[25];
    char branch[15];
    int marks;
};
void main()
{
    // data definitions of 10 students
    Student s[10];
    int n;
    cout << "How many students to be processed <max-10>: ";
    cin >> n;
    // read student data
    for( int i = 0; i < n; i++ )
    {
        cout << "Enter data for student " << i+1 << "..." << endl;
        cout << "Roll Number ? ";
        cin >> s[i].roll_no;
        cout << "Name ? ";
```

```
        cin >> s[i].name;
        cout << "Branch ? ";
        cin >> s[i].branch;
        cout << "Total Marks <max-325> ? ";
        cin >> s[i].marks;
    }
    cout << "Students Report" << endl;
    cout << "----------------" << endl;
    // process student data
    for( i = 0; i < n; i++ )
    {
        cout << "Roll Number: " << s[i].roll_no << endl;
        cout << "Name: " << s[i].name << endl;
        cout << "Branch: " << s[i].branch << endl;
        cout << "Percentage: " << s[i].marks*(100.0/325) << endl;
    }
}
```

Run

```
How many students to be processed <max-10>: 2
Enter data for student 1...
Roll Number ? 5
Name ? Mangala
Branch ? Computer
Total Marks <max-325> ? 290
Enter data for student 2...
Roll Number ? 9
Name ? Shivakumar
Branch ? Electronics
Total Marks <max-325> ? 250
Students Report
---------------
Roll Number: 5
Name: Mangala
Branch: Computer
Percentage: 89.230769
Roll Number: 9
Name: Shivakumar
Branch: Electronics
Percentage: 76.923077
```

Initialization of Array of Structures

An array of structures can be initialized in the same way as a single structure and hence, the discussion regarding the initialization of a single structure is still relevant. This is illustrated by the following example:

```
Student s[5] = {
    2, "Tejaswi", "CS", 200,
    3, "Laxmi H", "IT", 215,
    5, "Bhavani", "Electronics", 250,
    7, "Anil",    "Civil", 215,
```

```
        9, "Savithri", "Electrical", 290
    };
```

The variable s is an array of 5 elements of type Student. Thus, structure element s[0] will be assigned the first set of values, s[1] the second set of values, etc. Note that there are 5 sets of values in the initialization, which are placed in different rows for clarity. The values are separated by commas and enclosed within braces, with the closing brace being followed by a semicolon. To improve the readability of the program code, it is advisable to enclose the individual sets of values within braces as shown below:

```
Student s[5] = {
    { 2, "Tejaswi",  "CS", 200 },
    { 3, "Laxmi",    "IT", 215 },
    { 5, "Bhavani",  "Electronics", 250 },
    { 7, "Anil",     "Civil", 215 },
    { 9, "Savithri", "Electrical", 290 }
};
```

The program student4.cpp illustrates the initialization of an array of structures at the point of its definition.

```cpp
// student4.cpp: array of structures and their initialization
#include <iostream.h>
struct Student
{
    int roll_no;
    char name[25];
    char branch[15];
    int marks;
};
int const STUDENTS_COUNT = 5;
void main()
{
    // data definitions of 10 students
    Student s[ STUDENTS_COUNT ] = {
        { 2, "Tejaswi", "CS", 285 },
        { 3, "Laxmi", "IT", 215 },
        { 5, "Bhavani", "Electronics", 250 },
        { 7, "Anil", "Civil", 215 },
        { 9, "Savithri", "Electrical", 290 }
    };
    cout << "Students Report" << endl;
    cout << "---------------" << endl;
    // process student data
    for( int i = 0; i < STUDENTS_COUNT; i++ )
    {
        cout << "Roll Number: " << s[i].roll_no << endl;
        cout << "Name: " << s[i].name << endl;
        cout << "Branch: " << s[i].branch << endl;
        cout << "Percentage: " << s[i].marks*(100.0/325) << endl;
    }
}
```

Run

```
Students Report
---------------
Roll Number: 2
Name: Tejaswi
Branch: CS
Percentage: 87.6923
Roll Number: 3
Name: Laxmi
Branch: IT
Percentage: 66.1538
Roll Number: 5
Name: Bhavani
Branch: Electronics
Percentage: 76.9231
Roll Number: 7
Name: Anil
Branch: Civil
Percentage: 66.1538
Roll Number: 9
Name: Savithri
Branch: Electrical
Percentage: 89.2308
```

Operations Involving the Assignment Operator

The individual structure member can be used in an assignment statement just like any other ordinary variable. It is illustrated in the following statements:

```
s[1].marks = 290;    // marks set to 290
s[1].marks += 5;     // marks is incremented by 5
```

Notice that only the individual structure members are accessed, and not the entire structure. If the structure member is itself a structure, then the embedded structure's member is accessed as follows:

```
s[1].birthday.day
```

It accesses the member day of the structure variable birthday embedded in the 2nd element of the array of structure variable s. The assignment operator can also be used to copy variables of the same structure. For instance, the statement,

```
s1 = s2;
```

copies contents of s2 to s1, which are variables of the student structure. It is performed by copying each member transparently. Array of structure elements can also be copied as follows:

```
s[2] = s[1];
s[i] = s[j];
```

If a structure has members of type pointers, then only the address stored in that pointer member is copied and hence, such members still point to that pointed to by the source variable. In such a situation, make sure that memory is allocated, and explicitly copy the elements pointed to by the pointers. If this is not done, it might result in a dangling reference. It happens when the destination variable releases memory and the source variable continue to exist. (*Dangling reference:* it refers to a situation when a pointer to the memory item continues to exist, but memory allocated to that item is released. *Garbage memory*: it indicates that the memory item continues to exist but the pointer to it is lost; it happens when memory is not released explicitly.)

8.8 Structures and Functions

Structure variables may be passed to functions just like any other variables. It is also possible for functions to return structure variables through the use of the `return` statement. Note that any number of structure variables can be passed to the function as arguments in the function call, but only one structure variable can be returned from the function by the return statement. The program `student5.cpp` illustrates the passing of structure parameters and returning of a structure value.

```cpp
// student5.cpp: structure data type parameter passing
#include <iostream.h>
struct Student
{
    int roll_no;
    char name[25];
    char branch[15];
    int marks;
};
// reads data of type Student and returns
Student read()
{
    Student dull;
    cout << "Roll Number ? ";
    cin >> dull.roll_no;
    cout << "Name ? ";
    cin >> dull.name;
    cout << "Branch ? ";
    cin >> dull.branch;
    cout << "Total Marks <max-325> ? ";
    cin >> dull.marks;
    return dull;   // returning structure variables
}
// displays contents of the structure Student
void show( Student genius )   // takes structure type parameter
{
    cout << "Roll Number: " << genius.roll_no << endl;
    cout << "Name: " << genius.name << endl;
    cout << "Branch: " << genius.branch << endl;
    cout << "Percentage: " << genius.marks*(100.0/325) << endl;
}
void main()
{
    // data definitions of 10 students
    Student s[10];
    int n;
    cout << "How many students to be processed <max-10>: ";
    cin >> n;
    // read student data
    for( int i = 0; i < n; i++ )
    {
        cout << "Enter data for student " << i+1 << "..." << endl;
```

```
        s[i] = read();
    }
    cout << "Students Report" << endl;
    cout << "----------------" << endl;
    // process student data
    for( i = 0; i < n; i++ )
        show( s[i] );
}
```

Run

```
How many students to be processed <max-10>: 2
Enter data for student 1...
Roll Number ? 3
Name ? Smrithi
Branch ? Genetics
Total Marks <max-325> ? 295
Enter data for student 2...
Roll Number ? 10
Name ? Bindhu
Branch ? MCA
Total Marks <max-325> ? 300
Students Report
----------------
Roll Number: 3
Name: Smrithi
Branch: Genetics
Percentage: 90.7692
Roll Number: 10
Name: Bindhu
Branch: MCA
Percentage: 92.3077
```

Passing Structure to a Function

In main(), the statement

```
        show( s[i] );
```

passes a parameter of type structure Student to show() using the *pass-by-value* mechanism. All the members of the structure s[i] are assigned to respective members of the formal structure-parameter genius in the function show(). Any modification to the members of the structure variable genius in show() will not be reflected in the actual parameter s[i].

Returning Structure from Function

Similar to variables of the standard data types, a variable of a structure type can be assigned to another variable of the same type. It is performed by using the assignment operator, which copies all the members by a one-to-one correspondence.

In main(), the statement

```
        s[i] = read();
```

invokes read() and assigns all the members of a structure returned by read() to the structure variable s[i]. Here all the members are copied to the destination variable on a member-by-member basis as shown in Figure 8.10.

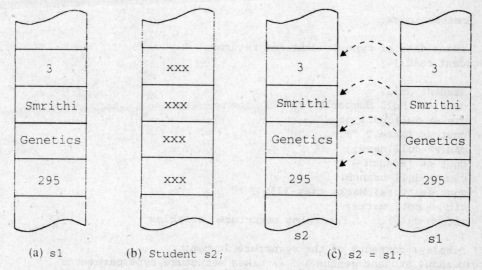

(a) s1   (b) Student s2;   (c) s2 = s1;

Figure 8.10:   Structure assignment -- copied on a member-by-member basis

Passing an Array of Structures to Functions

Passing an array of structures to functions involves the same syntax and properties like passing any array to a function. Pass by reference method is employed and consequently, any changes made to the structures by the function are visible throughout the program. The program student6.cpp illustrates the passing an array of structures to a function.

```
// student6.cpp: passing array of structures
#include <iostream.h>
struct Student
{
    int roll_no;
    char name[25];
    char branch[15];
    int marks;
};
// return index to a structures which holds student details who
// scores highest marks in the university examination
int HighestMarks( Student s[], int count )
{
    int index, big;
    big = s[0].marks;
    index = 0;
    for( int i = 1; i < count; i++ )
    {
        if( s[i].marks > big )
        {
            big = s[i].marks;
```

```
            index = i;
        }
    }
    return index;
}
// reads data of type Student and returns
Student read()
{
    Student dull;
    cout << "Roll Number ? ";
    cin >> dull.roll_no;
    cout << "Name ? ";
    cin >> dull.name;
    cout << "Branch ? ";
    cin >> dull.branch;
    cout << "Total Marks <max-325> ? ";
    cin >> dull.marks;
    return dull;   // returning structure variables
}
// displays contents of the structure Student
void show( Student genius )    // takes structure type parameter
{
    cout << "Roll Number: " << genius.roll_no << endl;
    cout << "Name: " << genius.name << endl;
    cout << "Branch: " << genius.branch << endl;
    cout << "Percentage: " << genius.marks*(100.0/325) << endl;
}
void main()
{
    // data definitions of 10 students
    Student s[10];
    int n, id;
    cout << "How many students to be processed <max-10>: ";
    cin >> n;
    // read student data
    for( int i = 0; i < n; i++ )
    {
        cout << "Enter data for student " << i+1 << "..." << endl;
        s[i] = read();
    }
    id = HighestMarks( s, n );
    cout << "Details of student scoring highest marks..." << endl;
    show( s[id] );
}
```

Run

```
How many students to be processed <max-10>: 3
Enter data for student 1...
Roll Number ? 3
Name ? Smrithi
```

```
Branch ? Genetics
Total Marks <max-325> ? 295
Enter data for student 2...
Roll Number ? 15
Name ? Rajkumar
Branch ? Computer
Total Marks <max-325> ? 315
Enter data for student 3...
Roll Number ? 7
Name ? Laxmi
Branch ? Electronics
Total Marks <max-325> ? 255
Details of student scoring highest marks...
Roll Number: 15
Name: Rajkumar
Branch: Computer
Percentage: 96.9231
```

In main(), the statement

```
        id = HighestMarks( s, n );
```

invokes the function HighestMarks() and finds the student with the highest marks. It accepts two arguments, the first is an array of structures and the second argument is an integer which denotes the number of students. The index of the student record with the highest marks is found by this function and returned to its caller (in this case, main() is the caller).

8.9 Data Type Enhancement Using typedef

C++ provides a facility called type definition by which new type names can be created. This is accomplished by using the typedef keyword as shown in Figure 8.11.

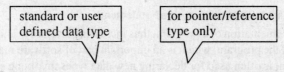

```
        typedef ExistingTypeName [*/&] NewTypeName;
```

Figure 8.11: Enhancing existing data types

ExistingTypeName is the name of an existing data type, and NewTypeName is the new user defined data type. Notice that a new user defined data type is created only from the existing data types such as int, float, struct, etc. The following examples illustrate the concepts introduced.

```
        typedef int Length;
```

Length now becomes a synonym for int and variables can be defined using the new type name. Length denotes a type name like int and is not a variable. Consider the following statement:

```
        Length len1, len2;
```

The above statement defines two variables of type integer and is equivalent to

```
        int len1, len2;
```

Note that the operations possible on the variables `len1` and `len2` are precisely. the same as the operations permitted on integer variables defined using the keyword `int`. Consider the following set of statements.

```
typedef int emprec[10];
emprec person1, person2;
```

The type `emprec` is now a new data type which is a 10 element array of integer quantities. `person1` and `person2` are two variables of this new type and each variable is a 10 element array of integer quantities. The following are valid expressions:

```
person1[3]              access the 4th element of person1
person1                 access the starting address of person1
&person1[0]             access the starting address of person1
```

The `typedef` statement for defining string data type is

```
typedef char * String;
```

It can be used as follows:

```
String name;
```

It is equivalent to

```
char * name;
```

The `typedef` can be used to create reference type (alias) integer data type as follows:

```
typedef int & INTREF;
```

Aliases for variables can be created using `INTREF` as follows:

```
INTREF b = c;
```

It is effectively equivalent to

```
int &b = c;
```

Benefits of the typedef statement

There are several important uses of the `typedef` statement:

◆ It helps in effective documentation of a program, thus increasing its clarity. This in turn enhances the ease of maintenance of the program, which is an important part of software management.
◆ The `typedef` statement is often used for declaring new data types involving structures. A new data type representing the structure is declared using the `typedef` keyword. Since all structure declarations in C++ are `typedef` by default, explicit use of the `struct` keyword during structure variable definition is optional. It is used explicitly when the structure's pointer or alias type is to be created. The usage of the `typedef` statement is illustrated below:

```
typedef struct tag
{
    type member1;
    type member2;
    . . .
    type membern;
} [*/&] NewDataType;
```

Consider the following declarations:

```
struct date
{
```

```
            int day;
            int month;
            int year;
        };
    typedef date * DATEPTR;
```

The type name DATEPTR can be used to define a pointer to the structure date as follows:

```
        DATEPTR dp;
```

It is equivalent to

```
        date * dp;
```

• The third important use of the typedef statement is its usage in writing portable programs. The sizes of different data types are dependent on the compiler. For instance, the size of an integer is two bytes on a 16-bit compiler and four bytes on a 32-bit compiler. Portability is achieved by type-declaring an integer as follows:

```
        typedef long int INT;
```

In the program, use definitions such as

```
        INT a, b;
```

instead of the statement

```
        int a, b;
```

to increase the portability of a program.

8.10 Structures and Encapsulation

Structures in C++ have undergone a major revision. Like C structures, C++ structures also provide a mechanism to group together data of different types into a single unit. In addition to this, C++ allows to associate functions as part of a structure. Thus, C++ structures provide a true mechanism to handle data abstraction. Such structures have two types of members: data members and member functions. (See Figure 8.12) Functions defined within a structure can operate on any member of the structure.

The program complex.cpp illustrates the concept of associating functions operating on the structure members. The functions enclosed within a structure can access data or other member functions directly. Similar to the data members, member functions can be accessed using the dot operator.

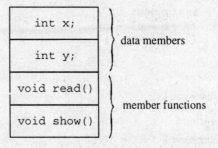

Figure 8.12:   Functions as a part of C++ structures

```
// complex.cpp: functions as a part of C++ structures
#include <iostream.h>
#include <math.h>
struct complex
{
   int x;       // real part
   int y;       // imaginary part
   void read()
   {
      cout << "Real part ? ";
      cin >> x;
      cout << "Imaginary part ?";
      cin >> y;
   }
   void show( char *msg )
   {
      cout << msg << x;
      if( y < 0 )
         cout << "-i";
      else
         cout << "+i";
      cout << fabs(y) << endl;
   }
   void add( complex c2 )
   {
      x += c2.x;
      y += c2.y;
   }
};
void main()
{
   complex c1, c2, c3;
   cout << "Enter complex number c1 .." << endl;
   c1.read();
   cout << "Enter complex number c2 .." << endl;
   c2.read();
   c1.show( "c1 = " );
   c2.show( "c2 = " );
   c3 = c1;    // assignment
   c3.add( c2 );  // c3 = c3 + c2;
   c3.show( "c3 = c1 + c2 = " );
}
```

Run

```
Enter complex number c1 ..
Real part ? 1
Imaginary part ?2
Enter complex number c2 ..
Real part ? 3
Imaginary part ? 4
c1 = 1+i2
```

```
c2 = 3+i4
c3 = c1 + c2 = 4+i6
```

In `main()`, the statement

```
    c1.read();
```

invokes the member function `read()`, defined in the structure `complex`. The data members of the variable `c1` are assigned with the input values. The statement,

```
    c1.show( "c1 = " );
```

displays data members with suitable messages. The statement,

```
    c3 = c1;    // assignment
```

assigns the contents of all the data members of the variable `c1` to corresponding members of `c2`. The statement,

```
    c3.add( c2 );  // c3 = c3 + c2;
```

adds the contents of the variable `c2` to `c3`.

Note that, structures and classes in C++ exhibit the same set of features except that structure members are public by default, whereas class members are private by default. Most of the C++ programmers prefer to use a class to group data and functions; a structure to group only data which are logically related. Hence, through out this book, a construct called `class` (instead of `struct`) is used as a means for implementing OOP concepts. More details on classes can be found in the chapter: *Classes and Objects*.

8.11 Unions

A union allows the overlay of more than one variable in the same memory area. Normally, each and every variable is stored in a separate location and as a result, each one of these variables have their own addresses. Often, it is found that the variables used in a program appear only in a small portion of the source code. Consider the following situation to illustrate the benefits of union data type:

Suppose, a string of 200 bytes is needed to store *filename* in the first 500 lines of the code only, and another string of 400 bytes is needed to use as *buffer* in the rest of the code (that is from the 500th line onwards) Note that, no part of the code will access both the variables simultaneously. In such a situation, it would be a waste of memory if two arrays of 200 bytes and 400 bytes are defined; it requires 600 bytes of memory. The union provides a means by which the memory space can be shared, and only 400 bytes of memory is needed.

Declaring a Union

In terms of declaration syntax, the union is similar to a structure as shown in Figure 8.13. The method used to declare a structure is adopted to declare a union. A `union` data type is like a structure, except that it allows to define variables, which share storage space. Note the only change is the substitution of the keyword `struct` by the keyword `union`. The rest of the discussion regarding the declaration is the same as that given for the structure (i.e., even functions can be a part of union).

The compiler will allocate sufficient storage to accommodate the largest element in the union. Unlike a structure, members of a union variable occupy the same locations in memory (starting at the zero offsets). Thus, updating one member will *overwrite* the other. Elements of a `union` type variable are accessed in the same manner as the elements of a structure.

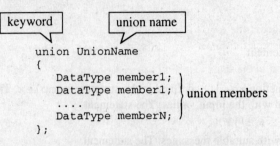

Figure 8.13:   Union declaration

The memory space required for defining a variable of the union is:

```
max( sizeof(member1), sizeof( member2), ..., sizeof(memberN) )
```

That is, the member of biggest size should fit in the common memory space.

Defining Variables

Union variables can be defined at the point of union declaration or can be defined separately as and when required. Consider the following declaration:

```
union X                          // union declaration
{
    int a;
    char ch;
    double b;
};
```

The variables of the above union X can be defined as follows:

```
union X x1;
```

The storage space required to represent the variable x1 is max(sizeof(int), sizeof(char), sizeof(double)). At any point of time, the union variable can hold data of any one of its members. It is the responsibility of the programmer to decide to which of its members the data stored in the union variable is meaningful.

Member Access

Members of the union can be accessed using either the dot or the arrow (->) operator. It is similar to accessing the structure variable. Consider the following declaration:

```
union person
{
    char name[25];
    int idno;
    float salary;
};
```

The variables of the above union person can be defined as follows:

```
union person var1,*var2;  // var1 is value variable, var2 is pointer
```

The statement to assign the address of a variable var1 to the pointer variable var2 is as follows:

```
var2 = &var1;
```

The individual members can be accessed as follows:

```
var1.name              access the name
```

```
var1.idno       access the idno
var2->salary    access the salary
```

The members can be assigned in the same way as the members of a structure. For instance,

```
var1.idno = 20;
strcpy( var1.name, "Vijayashree" );
```

the content of the members of the union variable var1 can be displayed as follows:

```
cout << var1.name;
```

The program union.cpp illustrates the usage of union to share the storage space.

```cpp
// union.cpp: union of two strings
#include <iostream.h>
#include <string.h>
union Strings
{
  char filename[200];
  char output[400];
};
void main()
{
  Strings s;
  //.....
  strcpy( s.filename, "/cdacb/usr1/raj/oops/microkernel/pserver.cpp" );
  cout << "filename: " << s.filename << endl;
  //.....
  //.....
  strcpy(s.output,"OOPs is a most complex entity ever created by humans");
  cout << "output: " << s.output << endl;
  cout << "Size of union Strings = " << sizeof( Strings );
}
```

Run

```
filename: /cdacb/usr1/raj/oops/microkernel/pserver.cpp
output: OOPs is a most complex entity ever created by humans
Size of union Strings = 400
```

8.12 Differences between Structures and Unions

Structures and unions have the same syntax in terms of their declaration and definition of their variables. However, they differ in the amount of storage space required for their storage and the scope of the members.

Memory Allocation

The amount of memory required to store a structure variable is the sum of the size of all the members. On the other hand, in the case of unions, the amount of memory required is always equal to that required by its largest member. The program sudiff.cpp illustrates the memory requirements for variables of the structure and union types.

```
// sudiff.cpp: memory requirement for structures and unions
#include <iostream.h>
struct
{
    char name[25];
    int idno;
    float salary;
} emp;
union
{
    char name[25];
    int idno;
    float salary;
} desc;

void main()
{
    cout << "The size of the structure is " << sizeof(emp) << endl;
    cout << "The size of the union is " << sizeof(desc) << endl;
}
```

Run

```
The size of the structure is 31
The size of the union is 25
```

Operations on Members

Only one member of a union can be accessed at any given time. This is because, at any instant, only one of the union variables can be active. The general rule for determining the active member is: *only that member which is updated can be read*. At this point, the other variables will contain meaningless values. It is the responsibility of the programmer to keep track of the active members, The program uaccess.cpp illustrates accessing of a union variable and its members.

```
// uaccess.cpp: accessing of union members
#include <iostream.h>
#include <string.h>
union emp
{
    char name[25];
    int idno;
    float salary;
};
void show( union emp e )
{
    cout << "Employee Details ..." << endl;
    cout << "The name is " << e.name << endl;
    cout << "The idno is " << e.idno << endl;
    cout << "The salary is " << e.salary << endl;
}
```

```
void main()
{
    union emp e;    // or emp e;
    strcpy(e.name, "Rajkumar");
    show( e );
    e.idno = 10;
    show( e );
    e.salary = 9000;
    show( e );
}
```

Run

```
Employee Details ...
The name is Rajkumar
The idno is 24914
The salary is 2.83348e+26
Employee Details ...
The name is
The idno is 10
The salary is 2.82889e+26
Employee Details ...
The name is
The idno is -24576
The salary is 9000
```

The status of the variable e after execuion of each one of the following:

       1. `strcpy(e.name, "Rajkumar");`
       2. `e.idno = 10;` and
       3. `e.salary = 9000;`

is shown in Figure 8.14a, 8.14b, 8.14c respectively. Note that, access of *non active* members will lead to meaningless values.

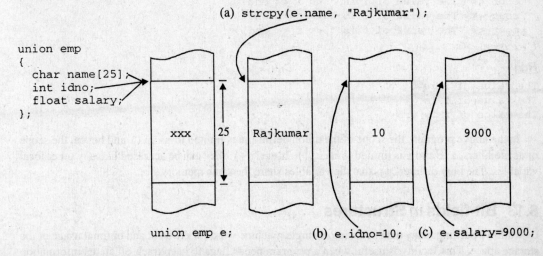

Figure 8.14:   Union variable initialization

Operation on Unions

In addition to the features discussed above, the union has all the features provided by the structure except for minor changes, which is a consequence of the memory sharing capabilities of the union. This is made evident by the following legal operations.

- A union variable can be assigned to another union variable, if their tags are same.
- A union variable can be passed to a function as a parameter.
- The address of the union variable can be extracted by using the address-of operator (&). This union pointer can be passed to functions.
- A function can return a union or a pointer to the union.

Performing operations on the unions as a whole, for example, arithmetic or comparison operations are illegal.

Scope of a Union

The members of a union have the same scope as the union itself. It is illustrated in the program uscope.cpp. The union definition having no tag or instance variable is called *anonymous union*.

```
// uscope.cpp: scope of union declaration
#include <iostream.h>
void main()
{
  union          // anonymous union definition
  {
    int i;
    char c;
    float f;
  };
  i = 10;
  c = 9;
  f = 4.5;
  cout << "The value of i is " << i << endl;
  cout << "The value of c is " << c << endl;
  cout << "The value of f is " << f << endl;
}
```

Run

```
The value of i is 0
The value of c is
The value of f is 4.5
```

In the above program, the scope of the union definition is limited to main() and hence, the scope of its members, i, c and f is limited to main(). In main(), they can be accessed like any other local variables. The only difference is that the variables share the same memory.

8.13 Bit-fields in Structures

C++ allows packing many data items into a single machine word for efficient and optimal usage of the storage space. This facility is useful when a program needs flags to keep track of status information related to various activities. Consider a program, which stores information about a person including the following:

- ◆ Are you possessing any formal degree ?
- ◆ Are you employed ?
- ◆ Single or married ?
- ◆ Male or Female ?
- ◆ Are you a teenage ?
- ◆ Are you Indian ?

The simplest way of achieving the above task is to define six integer variables, each keeping the status of one item. This method requires `6*sizeof(int)` bytes of memory locations. Another mechanism of achieving it is through the use of bit masks (macros) as follows:

```
#define DEGREE    01
#define EMPLOYED  02
#define MARRIED   04
#define MALE      08
#define TEENAGE   16
#define INDIAN    32
```

Note that, the numbers must be powers of two, so that they can act as masks corresponding to the relevant bit positions, thus accessing the bits by shifting, masking, and complementing. For instance, the statement

```
flags |= DEGREE;
```

sets the first bit to 1 and the statement

```
flags &= ~MARRIED;
```

clears the second bit indicating that a person is unmarried. The conditional statement

```
if( flags & MARRIED )
  cout << "Married person";
else
  cout << "Unmarried person";
```

is valid. These idioms (mode of expressions) are easily prone to errors. As an alternative to this mechanism, C++ offers the capability of defining and accessing fields within a word directly rather than by bitwise logical operators. A *bit-field* or *field* in short, is a set of adjacent bits within a single implementation-defined storage unit called a *word*. The syntax of field definition and access is based on structures. For instance, the above `#define` statements could be replaced by the definition of six fields as follows:

```
struct
{
    unsigned int is_degree  : 1;
    unsigned int is_employed: 1;
    unsigned int is_married : 1;
    unsigned int is_male    : 1;
    unsigned int is_teenage : 1;
    unsigned int is_indian  : 1;
} flags;
```

It defines a variable called `flags` which contains six single-bit fields. The number following the colon represents the field width. The fields declared are of type `unsigned int` (can be `int`) to ensure that they are unsigned quantities.

The Individual fields are referenced in the same way as other structure members. For instance,

```
flags.is_married
```

expression accesses the contents of its corresponding bit. Fields act like integers and can be used in arithmetic expressions just like other integers. Thus, the previous examples can be written more naturally as follows:

```
flags.is_degree = 1;
```

sets the first bit to 1 and the statement

```
flags.is_married = 0;
```

clears the second bit, indicating that a person is unmarried. The conditional statement

```
if( flags.is_married )
   cout << "Married person";
else
   cout << "Unmarried person";
```

is valid.

Consider the following declaration which illustrates bit-fields of larger width:

```
struct with_bits
{
    unsigned first : 5;
    unsigned second : 9;
};
```

The identifier with_bits is a structure containing 2 members: first and second. The member first is an integer with 5 bits, and second is an integer with 9 bits. Both the numbers can be stored in a single 16-bit entity (even though they add up to 14 bits, a 14-bit entity cannot exist in memory), rather than two separate integers. It is illustrated in the program share.cpp.

```
// share.cpp: union and structure combined
#include <iostream.h>
struct with_bits
{
   unsigned first : 5;
   unsigned second : 9;
};
void main()
{
   union
   {
     with_bits b;
     int i;
   };
   i = 0;          // Both first and second are cleared to 0
   cout << "On i = 0: b.first = " << b.first << " b.second = "<< b.second;
   b.first = 9;    // first is set to 9; second remains 0
   cout << endl << "b.first = 9: ";
   cout << "b.first = " << b.first << " b.second = " << b.second;
}
```

Run

```
On i = 0: b.first = 0 b.second = 0
b.first = 9: b.first = 9 b.second = 0
```

In `main()`, the union defines two variables `b` and `i`, and they are stored in the same memory location. In a way, they can act as aliases. The statement,

```
i = 0;
```

clears the complete word and inturn clears members of the structure `with_bits`. The statement

```
b.first = 9;
```

updates only the first 5-bits of the word. Note: *the maximum size of each bit-field is sizeof (int)*.

Review Questions

8.1   What are structures ? Justify their need with an illustrative example.

8.2   Why structures are called heterogeneous data-types ?

8.3   Explain storage organization of structure variables.

8.4   Write an interactive program, which processes date of birth using structures. Enhance the same supporting processing of multiple students date of birth.

8.5   Write a short note on passing structure type variables to a function, and suitability of different parameter passing schemes in different situations.

8.6   Develop a program for processing admission report. Use a structure which has elements representing information such as roll number, name, date of birth (nested structure), branch allotted. The functions processing members of a structure must be a part of a structure. The format of report is as follows:

```
------------------------------------------------------------------
  Roll.no.          Name             Date of Birth      Branch Allotted
------------------------------------------------------------------
  xx          xxxxxxxxxxxxxxx         dd/mm/yy           xxxxxxxx
------------------------------------------------------------------
```

8.7   What are unions? Write a program to illustrate the use of the union.

8.8   What are the differences between structures and unions.

8.9   Write an interactive program to process complex numbers. It has to perform addition, subtraction, multiplication, and division of complex numbers. Print results in x+iy form.

8.10 Write a union declaration for representing register model of x86 family of microprocessors. Note that general purpose registers such as AX are also accessed by lower and higher word registers AH and AL respectively.

8.11 Consider the following structure declaration:

```
struct institution
{
    struct teacher {
        int empl_no;
        char name[20];
    };
    struct student  {
        int roll_no;
        char name[15];
    };
};
```

What is the `sizeof(institution)`, `sizeof(teacher)`, and `sizeof(student)`?

9

Pointers and Runtime Binding

9.1 Introduction

The use of pointers offers a high degree of flexibility in the management of data. Knowledge of memory organization plays a very important role for understanding the concept of pointers. As the name implies, pointer refers to the address identifying a programming element (data or function). Interestingly, the system main memory is organized into code and data area as shown in Figure 9.1. Although in many situations programming can be done without the use of pointers, their usage enhances the capability of the language to manipulate data. Dynamic memory allocation is a programming concept wherein the use of pointers becomes indispensable. For instance, to read the marks of a set of students and store them for processing, an array can be defined as follows:

```
float marks[100];
```

But this method limits the maximum number of students (to 100), which must be decided during the development of the program. On the other hand, by using dynamic allocation, the program can be designed so that the limit for the maximum number of students is restricted only by the amount of memory available in the system. The real power of C++ (of course C) lies in the proper use of pointers.

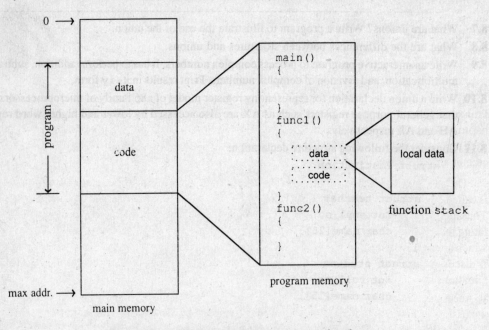

Figure 9.1: Primary memory organization

Memory is organized in the form of a sequence of byte-sized (8-bits per byte) locations or *storage cells* containing either program code or data. These bytes are numbered starting from zero onwards. The number associated with each cell (byte location) is known as its address or memory location. A pointer is an entity, which contains a memory address. In effect, a pointer is a number, which specifies a location in memory. The key concepts and terminology associated with memory organization are the following:

♦ Each byte in the memory is associated with a unique address.

♦ An address is a sequence of binary digits (0 or 1) of fixed length, used for labeling a byte in the memory.

♦ Address is a positive integer ranging from 0 to maximum addressing capability of the microprocessor (for instance, 8086 processor has 20-address lines and hence, it can address upto 2^{20} locations:1 MB).

♦ Every element (data or program code) that is loaded into memory is associated with a valid range of addresses. i.e., each variable and function in the program starts at a particular location and spans across consecutive addresses from that point onwards depending upon the size of the data item.

♦ The number of bytes accessed by a pointer depends on the data type of an item to which it is a pointer.

The address stored in a pointer variable can be relative or absolute. Most of the modern systems use the relative addressing mode to access memory, by default. In relative addressing mode, an address consists of two components: the *base* (or the segment) and the *offset* address. The base or segment address designates a specific region of memory, and the offset specifies the distance of the desired memory location from the beginning of the segment. The effective address is computed by combining both the segment and offset values. In absolute mode, the address stored in a pointer is itself the effective address, and hence, memory can be directly accessed using this address. Note that, relative addressing requires mapping of logical address (offset) to physical address.

It is not always necessary to be aware of the segments and offsets while programming in C++, unless the pointer is used to hold the address of any device specific information. For instance, in IBM-PC and its compatibles, the display memory is located at the segment and offset value, 0xb800:0000. (The display memory address changes from one video mode to another.)

9.2 Pointers and their Binding

Pointer is defined as a variable used to store memory addresses. It is similar to any other variable and has to be defined before using it, to hold an address. Just like, an integer variable can hold only integers, each pointer variable can hold only pointer to a specific data type such as int, char, float, double, etc., or any user defined data type).

The allocation of memory space for data structure (storage) during the course of program execution is called dynamic memory allocation. Dynamic variables so-created can only be accessed with pointers. Thus, pointers offer tremendous flexibility in the creation of dynamic variables, accessing and manipulating the contents of memory location and releasing the memory occupied by the dynamic variables, which are no longer needed. (A more detailed account of dynamic memory allocation and de-allocation is discussed in the later sections of this chapter.) The usage of the pointer is essential in the following situations:

♦ Accessing array elements.

♦ Passing arguments to functions by address when modification of formal arguments are to be reflected on actual arguments.

- Passing arrays and strings to functions.
- Creating data structures such as linked lists, trees, graphs, etc.
- Obtaining memory from the system dynamically.

9.3 Address Operator &

All the variables defined in a program (including pointer variables) reside at specific addresses. It is possible to obtain the address of a program variable by using the address operator &(ampersand). When used as a prefix to the variable name, the & operator returns the address of that variable. The program getaddr.cpp illustrates the use of the & operator.

```
// getaddr.cppc: use of '&' operator to access address
#include <iostream.h>
void main()
{
  // define and initialize three integer variables
  int a = 100;
  int b = 200;
  int c = 300;
  // print the address and contents of the above variables
  cout << "Address " << &a << " contains value " << a << endl;
  cout << "Address " << &b << " contains value " << b << endl;
  cout << "Address " << &c << " contains value " << c << endl;
}
```

Run
```
Address 0xfff4 contains value 100
Address 0xfff2 contains value 200
Address 0xfff0 contains value 300
```

In main(), the statement
```
        cout << "Address " << &a << ". contains value " << a << endl;
```
displays the address and contents of the variable a. The expression &a returns the address of the variable a. It should, however, be noted that the addresses printed by the above program, depend on the current configuration of a system. This is because the memory occupied by the program's variables depend on several factors such as memory management scheme, memory model, and the current status of the memory contents.

The output shows the addresses of the variables in hexadecimal notation, and they are in the decreasing order. From this, it is evident that *all automatic variables are created in the program's stack area and that the stack always grows from a higher to a lower memory address*. Further, each of the addresses differ from others by exactly two bytes, since integer variables are allocated 2 bytes of memory. The sizeof() operator can be used to determine the number of bytes allocated to each type of variable. The integer is the fundamental data type and hence its size depends on the processor word size, compiler, and operating system memory manager. For instance, the size of an integer data type in MS-DOS based machines is two bytes, whereas in UNIX based machines it is four bytes.

Sufficient care must be taken to avoid any kind of confusion between the following:
- unary address operator & which precedes a variable name.
- binary logical operator & which performs a bit-wise AND operation.

9.4 Pointer Variables

Pointers are also variables and hence, they must be defined in a program like any other variable. Rules for variable names and declaring pointers are the same as for any other data type. This naturally gives rise to questions about the data type of a pointer, size of memory allocated to a pointer and the format for defining different types of pointers.

Pointer Definition

When a pointer variable is defined, the C++ compiler needs to know the type of variable the pointer points to. The syntax of pointer variable definition is shown in Figure 9.2.

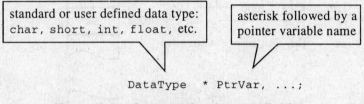

```
DataType  * PtrVar, ...;
```

Figure 9.2:   Syntax of pointer definition

`DataType` could be a primitive data type or user defined structure (such as structures and classes). The `PtrVar` could be any valid C++ variable name. The character star (*) following the `DataType` informs the compiler that the variable `PtrVar` is a pointer variable. The pointer so created can hold the address of any variable of the specified type. Some typical pointer definitions are:

```
int *int_ptr;    // int_ptr is a pointer to an integer
char *ch_ptr;    // ch_ptr is a pointer to a character
Date *d_ptr;     // d_ptr is a pointer to user defined data type
```

The pointer variable must be bound to a memory location. It can be achieved either by assigning the address of a variable, or by assigning the address of the memory allocated dynamically. The address of a variable can be assigned to a pointer variable as follows:

```
int_ptr = &marks;
```

where the variable `marks` is of type integer.

Pointer to characters (a string) can be defined as follows:

```
char *msg;
```

It can be initialized at the point of definition as follows:

```
char *msg = "abcd..xyz";
```

Or, it can also be initialized during execution as follows:

```
msg = "abcd..xyz";
```

Dereferencing of Pointers

Dereferencing is the process of accessing and manipulating data stored in the memory location pointed to by a pointer. The operator * (asterisk) is used to dereference pointers in addition to creating them. A pointer variable is dereferenced when the *unary operator* * (in this case, it is called as the *indirection operator*) is prefixed to the pointer variable or pointer expression. Any operation that is performed on the dereferenced pointer directly affects the value of the variable it points to. The syntax for *dereferencing pointers* is shown in Figure 9.3.

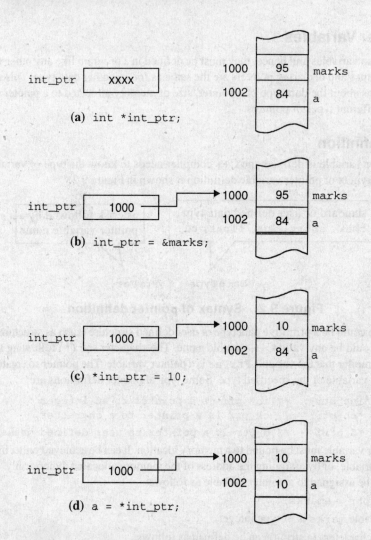

Figure 9.3:   Pointers binding and dereferencing

Consider the statement

```
int_ptr = &marks;
```

It stores the address of the variable `marks` in the pointer variable `int_ptr`. The contents of the variable `marks` can be displayed using the following statement:

```
cout << *int_ptr;
```

Effectively, the above statement achieves the same result as the statement

```
cout << marks;
```

Thus, accessing information using pointers is called indirect addressing. It refers to accessing information, whose address is stored in a special type of variable, which is a pointer variable.

The contents of memory locations can be modified by using a pointer variable as follows:

```
*int_ptr = 25;
```

It assigns the value 25 to the memory location pointed to by the variable `int_ptr`. The contents of the memory location can be read by using the pointer variable as follows:

```
a = *int_ptr;
```

It assigns the contents of the memory location pointed to by the address stored in the variable `int_ptr` to the variable `a` of type integer. The program `initptr.cpp` illustrates the mechanism of pointer variable definition, binding and dereferencing.

```
// initptr.cpp: pointer (address variables) usage demonstration
#include <iostream.h>
void main ()
{
    int *iptr;         // pointer to integer, figure 9.4a
    int var1, var2;    // two integer variables, figure 9.4b
    var1 = 10;         // figure 9.4c
    var2 = 20;         // figure 9.4d
    iptr = &var1;      // figure 9.4e
    cout << "Address and contents of var1 is " << iptr << " and " << *iptr;
    iptr = &var2;      //   figure 9.4f
    cout<<"\nAddress and contents of var2 is " << iptr << " and " << *iptr;
    *iptr = 125;       // figure 9.4g
    var1 = *iptr + 1;  // figure 9.4h
}
```

Run

```
Address and contents of var1 is 0x1f8afff4 and 10
Address and contents of var2 is 0x1f8afff2 and 20
```

In `main()`, the first statement

```
    int *iptr;
```

specifies that `iptr` is a pointer to an integer. The asterisk prefixed to the variable name specifies that `iptr` is a pointer variable. The data type `int` specifies that `iptr` can point to any integer type item(s) stored in the main memory. The statement

```
    int *iptr;            // pointer to integer, figure 9.4a
```

could also be written as

```
    int* iptr;
```

It makes no difference as far as the compiler is concerned. But there are certain advantages in following the former convention (i.e., placing the * closer to the variable name). The compiler always associates the * with the pointer variable name rather than the data type, thus allowing both pointer variable type and non-pointer variable of a particular data type to be defined in a single definition. Thus, the following statements

```
    int *iptr;         // pointer to integer, figure 9.4a
    int var1, var2;    // two integer variables, figure 9.4b
```

are valid. They can also be written in a single equivalent statement as follows:

```
    int *iptr, var1, var2;
```

An asterisk must be prefixed to the name of each pointer variable to define multiple pointers using a single statement. For instance, the statement,

```
float  *f1, *f2, *f3;
```

defines f1, f2, and f3 as pointers to float variables.

The program `initptr.cpp` has highlighted the following important facts about pointers:

- The asterisk (*) used as an *indirection operator* has a different meaning from the asterisk used while defining pointer variables.
- Indirection allows the contents of a variable to be accessed and manipulated without using the name of the variable.

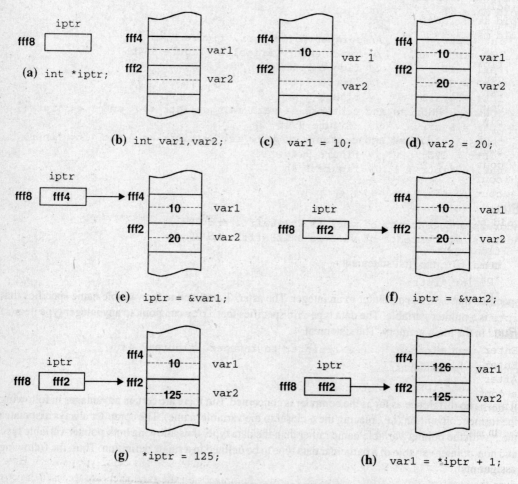

Figure 9.4:   Dereferencing of pointers

All variables that can be accessed directly (by their names) can also be accessed indirectly by means of pointers. The power of pointers becomes evident in situations, where indirect access is the only way to access variables in memory. Figure 9.4 gives a pictorial representation of accessing a variable using a pointer.

Pointers and Parameter Passing

Pointers provide a two way communication between the service requester and service provider. It is achieved by passing the address of the actual parameters instead of their contents. Any modification done to formal variables in the function will be automatically reflected in the actual parameters when they are passed by address. A program to swap two numbers is listed in swap.cpp.

```
// swap.cpp: swap 2 numbers using pointers
#include <iostream.h>
void swap(float *, float *);
void main()
{
    float a, b;
    cout << "Enter real number <a>: ";
    cin >> a;
    cout << "Enter real number <b>: ";
    cin >> b;
    // Pass address of the variables whose values are to be swapped
    swap(&a, &b);    // figure 9.6a
    cout << "After swapping ......\n";
    cout << "a contains " << a << endl;
    cout << "b contains " << b;
}
void swap( float *pa, float *pb ) // function to swap two numbers
{
    float temp;
    temp = *pa;    // figure 9.6b
    *pa  = *pb;    // figure 9.6c
    *pb  = temp;   // figure 9.6d
}
```

Run

```
Enter real number <a>: 10.5
Enter real number <b>: 20.9
After swapping ......
a contains 20.9
b contains 10.5
```

In main(), the statement

```
        swap(&a, &b);
```

assigns addresses of the actual parameters to the formal parameters, which are of type pointers. However, they are manipulated differently (see Figure 9.5). In main(), the parameters are accessed directly with their names whereas in swap(), they are accessed using the *indirection operator*.

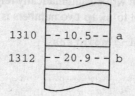

```
1310  --10.5--  a
1312  --20.9--  b
```

Figure 9.5: Data addressing in different perspectives

In swap(), accessing contents of the memory location pointed to by the variable pa, actually accesses the contents of the variable a. Similarly, accessing the contents of the memory location pointed to by the variable pb actually access the contents of the variable b. Hence, swapping the contents of memory using pointer variables pa and pb along with the indirection operator will in fact exchange the contents of the actual parameters a and b (passed by caller) as shown in Figure 9.6.

9.5 Void Pointers

Pointers defined to be of a specific data type cannot hold the address of some other type of variable i.e., it is syntactically incorrect in C++ to assign the address of (say) an integer variable to a pointer of type float. Consider the following definitions

```
float *f_ptr; // pointer to float
int   my_int; // integer variable
```

The assignment of incompatible variable address to a pointer variable in a statement such as

```
f_ptr = &my_int;
```

results in compilation error. Such type-compatibility problems can be overcome by using a general-purpose pointer type called *void pointer*. The format for declaring a *void pointer* is as follows:

```
void *v_ptr;  // define a pointer to void
```

It uses the reserved word void for specifying the type of the pointer. Pointers defined in this manner do not have any type associated with them and can hold the address of any type of variable. The following are some valid C++ statements:

```
void *vd_ptr;
int *it_ptr;
int  invar;
char chvar;
float flvar;
vd_ptr = &invar;  // valid
vd_ptr = &chvar;  // valid
```

```
vd_ptr = &flvar;   // valid
it_ptr = &invar;   // valid
```

The following are some invalid statements:

```
it_ptr = &chvar;   // invalid
it_ptr = &flvar;   // invalid
```

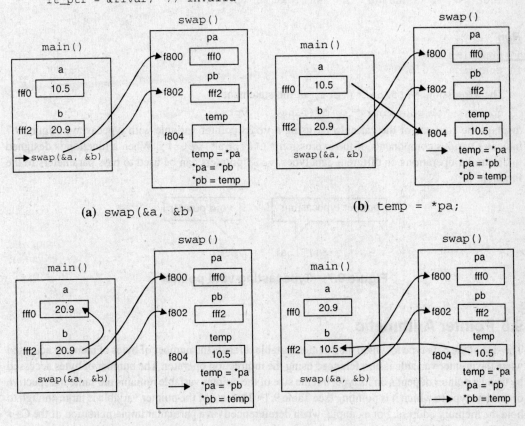

Figure 9.6: Swapping of two numbers.

Pointers to void cannot be directly dereferenced like other pointer variables using the *indirection operator*. Prior to dereferencing a pointer to void, it must be suitably typecasted to the required data type. The program voidptr.cpp illustrates the typecasting of void pointers while accessing memory locations pointed to by them.

```
// voidptr.cpp: the use of void pointers to hold pointer of any type
#include <iostream.h>
void main()
{
    int i1 = 100;     // define and initialize int i1 to 100
```

```
float f1 = 200.5; // define and initialize float f1 to 200.50
void *vptr;        // define pointer to void
vptr = &i1;        // pointer assignment
cout << "i1 contains " << *((int *) vptr) << endl;
vptr = &f1;        // pointer assignment
cout << "f1 contains " << *((float *) vptr);
}
```

Run
```
i1 contains 100
f1 contains 200.5
```

The expression *((float*)vptr) in the statement

```
cout << "f1 contains " << *((float *) vptr);
```

displays the contents of the variable f1 using a void pointer variable with typecasting. Figure 9.7 indicates various components of the expression *((float*)vptr)). When a function is designed to do similar operations on different data types, void pointers can be used to pass parameters to the function.

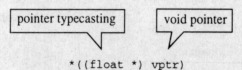

Figure 9.7:   Typecasting void pointer

9.6 Pointer Arithmetic

The size of the data type to which the pointer variable refers is the number of bytes of memory accessed when the pointer variable is dereferenced using the indirection operator. The number of bytes accessed by using a pointer depends on its type, but the size of the pointer variable remains the same irrespective of the data type to which it is pointing (see Table 9.1). The size of the pointer variable is large enough to hold the memory address. For example, when dereferenced (in a particular implementation of the C++ compiler—on 16-bit system),

- ◆ a pointer to an integer accesses 2 bytes of memory
- ◆ a pointer to a char accesses 1 byte of memory
- ◆ a pointer to a float accesses 4 bytes of memory
- ◆ a pointer to a double accesses 8 bytes of memory

The C++ language allows arithmetic operations to be performed on pointer variables. It is, however, the responsibility of the programmer to see that the result obtained by performing pointer arithmetic is the address of relevant and meaningful data.

The arithmetic operators available for use with pointers can be classified as

- ◆ Unary operators : ++ (increment) and -- (decrement).
- ◆ Binary operators : + (addition) and - (subtraction).

Data type	Data size	Pointer type	
		near	far
char	1	2	4
short	2	2	4
int	2 (16-bit compiler) 4 (32-bit compiler)	2	4
long	4	2	4
float	4	2	4
double	8	2	4

Table 9.1:   Size of data types and their pointers

The following are some of the examples of pointer arithmetic:

```
int a, b, *p, *q;
p = -q;                   // Illegal use of pointer
p <<= 1;                  // Illegal use of pointer
p = p - b;                // Valid
p = p - q;                // Invalid: Nonportable pointer conversion
p = (int *)(p - q);       // Valid
p = p - q - a;            // Invalid: Nonportable pointer conversion
p = (int *)(p - q) - a;   // Valid
p = p + a;                // Valid
p = p + q;                // Invalid pointer addition
p = p + q + a;            // Invalid pointer addition
p = p * q;                // Illegal use of pointer
p = p * a;                // Illegal use of pointer
p = p / q;                // Illegal use of pointer
p = p / b;                // Illegal use of pointer
p = a / p;                // Illegal use of pointer
a = *p ** q;              // Valid and it is same as a = (*p) * (*q);
```

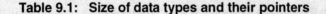

The C++ compiler takes into account the size of the data type being pointed, while performing arithmetic operations on a pointer. For example, if a pointer to an integer is incremented using the ++ operator (preceding or succeeding the pointer), then the initial address contained in the pointer is incremented by two and not one, assuming that an integer occupies two bytes in memory. Similarly, incrementing a pointer to float causes the initial address contained in the float pointer to be actually incremented by 4 and not 1 (if the size of the float variable is 4 on the machine). In general, a pointer to some type, d_type (where d_type can be primitive or user defined data type), when incremented by an integral value i, has the following effect:

```
(current address in pointer) + i * sizeof(d_type)
```

Consider the following statements:

```
float *sum;
char *name;
```

A statement such as

```
sum++; or ++sum;
```

advances the pointer variable sum to point to the next element. If the pointer variable sum holds the address 1000, on execution of the above statement, the variable sum will hold the address (1000+4) = 1004 since the size of float is 4 bytes. Similarly, when a statement such as

```
name++; or ++name;
```

is executed, and if the pointer variable name points to address 2000 earlier, then it will hold the address (2000+1), since the size of char is one byte. This concept applies to all arithmetic operations performed on pointer variables.

When a pointer variable is incremented, its value actually gets incremented by the size of the type to which it points. For example, let pi be a pointer to an integer defined with the statement

```
int* pi;
```

Also, let pi point to the memory location 1020. i.e., the number 1020 is stored in the pointer pi. Now, a statement which increments pi, such as

```
pi++;
```

will add two to pi, making it 1022 (assuming that the size of an integer is 2 bytes). This makes pi point to the next integer. Similarly, the statement

```
pi--;
```

will decrement the value of pi by 2. The pointer arithmetic on different types is shown in Table 9.2.

Pointer variable	Pointer value	Pointer increment	Pointer value after increment
char * a;	10	a++;/++a; a=a+3;	11(a+sizeof (char)) 13(a+sizeof (char)*3)
int * b;	10	b++;/++b; b=b+2;	12(b+sizeof (int)) 14(b+sizeof (int)*2)
long * c;	10	c++;/++c; c=c+3;	14(c+sizeof (long)) 22(c+sizeof (long)*3)
float * d;	10	d++;/++d; d=d+2;	14(d+sizeof (float)) 18(d+sizeof (float)*2)
double * e;	10	e++;/++e; e=e+2;	18(e+sizeof (double)) 26(e+sizeof(double)*2)

Table 9.2: Pointer arithmetic

Pointer arithmetic becomes significant for accessing and processing array elements efficiently (a more detailed account of array processing with pointers is taken up later in this chapter). Note that pointer arithmetic cannot be performed on void pointers without typecasting, since they have no type associated with them.

The elements of an array can be efficiently accessed by using a pointer. The program ptrarr1.cpp illustrates the use of pointer holding the address of arrays and pointer arithmetic in manipulating large amount of data stored in sequence.

```
// ptrarr1.cpp: smallest in an array of 'n' elements using pointers
#include <iostream.h>
void main()
{
   int i,n, small, *ptr, a[50];
   cout  << "Size of the array ? ";
   cin >> n;
   cout << "Array elements ?\n";
   for (i = 0; i < n; i++)
      cin >> a[i];
   //  assign address of a[0] to pointer 'ptr'. This can be done in two
   // way: 1. ptr = &a[0];  2. ptr = a;
   ptr = a;
   // contents of a[0] assigned to small
   small = *ptr;
   // pointer points to next element in the array i.e., a[1]
   ptr++;
   // loop n-1 times to search for smallest element in the array
   for (i = 1; i < n; i++)
   {
      if(small > *ptr)
         small = *ptr;
      ptr++;   // pointer is incremented to point to a[i+1]
   }
   cout << "Smallest element is " << small;
}
```

Run

```
Size of the array ? 5
Array elements ?
4 2 6 1 9
Smallest element is 1
```

In main(), the statement

```
      ptr = a;
```

assigns the address of the 0th element of the array to the integer pointer ptr. Hence, the statement

```
      small = *ptr;
```

effectively assigns the value of a[0] to the variable small. When ptr is incremented, the value stored in ptr is incremented by sizeof(int) (i.e., = 2 in DOS and = 4 in UNIX) to point to the next element of the array.

It is interesting to note that the name of the array represents the starting address of the array i.e., it is the address of the first element in the array. Hence, the expression a[i] can also be represented by the expression *(a+i).

9.7 Runtime Memory Management

C++ provides two special operators new and delete to perform memory allocation and deallocation at runtime respectively. These operators with their syntax and suitable examples are already discussed in the earlier chapter on *Moving from C to C++*. An additional discussion on new operator follows:

The new operator must always be supplied with a data type in place of type-name. Items surrounded by angle brackets are optional. The syntax of new operator is as follows:

```
<::> new <new-args> type-name <(initializer)>
<::> new <new-args> (type-name) <(initializer)>
```

The components present in the syntax has the following meaning:

◆ :: operator, invokes the global version of new.

◆ new-args can be used to supply additional arguments to new. It is used when the program has an overloaded version of new that matches the optional arguments.

◆ initializer, if present, is used to initialize the memory.

A request for non-array allocation uses the appropriate operator new() function. Any request for array allocation will call the appropriate operator new[]() function. Selection of the operator is done as follows:

◆ By default, the operator new[]() calls the operator new()

◆ If a class Type has an overloaded version of operator new[](), arrays of Type will be allocated using Type::operator new[]()

◆ If a class Type has an overloaded version of new and it is not the array allocation operator new[](), then the arrays of Type will be allocated using Type::operator new()

◆ If none of the above cases apply, the global ::operator new() is used.

More details on dynamic objects is discussed in later chapters.

Handling Errors for the new Operator

The new operator offers dynamic storage allocation similar to the standard library function malloc. It is particularly designed keeping OOPs in mind and throws an exception if the allocation fails. For more details on handling exceptions raised by the new operator, refer to the chapter on *Exception Handling*.

The user can define a function to be invoked when the new operator fails. The new operator can be informed about the new-handler function, by using set_new_handler() and pass a pointer to the new-handler. The new operator can be configured to return NULL on failure as follows:

```
set_new_handler(0).
```

It sets the handler to NULL so that the new operator returns NULL when it fails to allocate the requested amount of memory and thus exhibiting the behavior of the standard function malloc(). The program newhand.cpp illustrates the mechanism of handling the failure of memory allocation.

```
// newhand.cpp: new operator memory allocation test
#include <iostream.h>
#include <process.h>
#include <new.h>
void main(void)
{
```

```
    int * data;
    int size;
    set_new_handler( 0 );
    cout << "How many bytes to allocate: ";
    cin >> size;
    if( (data = new int[ size ]) )
        cout << "Memory allocation success, address = " << data;
    else
    {
        cout << "Could not allocate. Bye ...";
        exit(1);
    }
    delete data;
}
```

Run1

```
How many bytes to allocate: 100
Memory allocation success, address = 0x16be
```

Run2

```
How many bytes to allocate: 30000
Could not allocate. Bye ...
```

Note: A request for allocation of 0 bytes returns a non-null pointer. Repeated requests for zero-size allocations return distinct, non-null pointers.

9.8 Pointers to Pointers

C++ allows programmers to define a pointer to pointers, which offers flexibility in handling arrays, passing pointer variables to functions, etc. The syntax for defining a pointer to pointer is:

```
        DataType  **PtrToPtr;
```

which uses two * symbols (placed one beside the other). It implies that PtrToPtr is a pointer-to-a-pointer addressing a data object of type DataType. This feature is often used for representing two dimensional arrays. The program ptr2ptr.cpp illustrates the format for defining and using a pointer to another pointer.

```
// ptr2ptr.cpp: definition and use of pointers to pointers
#include <iostream.h>
void main(void)
{
    int *iptr;        // iptr as a pointer to an integer, figure 9.8a
    int **ptriptr;    // Defines pointer to int pointer, figure 9.8b
    int data;         // Some integer location, figure 9.8c
    iptr = &data;     // iptr now points to data, figure 9.8d
    ptriptr = &iptr;  // ptriptr points to iptr, figure 9.8e
    *iptr = 100;      // Same as data = 100, figure 9.8f
    cout << "The variable 'data' contains " << data << endl;
    **ptriptr = 200;  // Same as data = 200, figure 9.8g
    cout << "The variable 'data' contains " << data << endl;
    data = 300;       // figure 9.8h
```

```
    cout << "ptriptr is pointing to " << **ptriptr << endl;
}
```

Run

```
The variable 'data' contains 100
The variable 'data' contains 200
ptriptr is pointing to 300
```

In main(), the statement

        int **ptriptr;

creates a pointer variable which holds a pointer to another pointer variable. The statement

        ptriptr = &iptr;

assigns address of the pointer variable iptr to ptriptr. The value pointed by iptr can also be accessed by ptriptr as follows:

        **ptriptr

The expression **ptriptr effectively accesses the contents of the variable data. The various operations on the pointer to a pointer are shown in Figure 9.8.

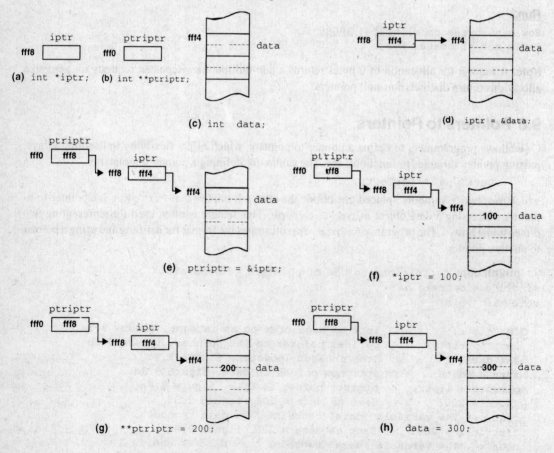

Figure 9.8:   Pointers to pointer and dereferencing

Passing Address of a Pointer

When a pointer variable is defined, a memory location for the pointer is allocated, but it will not be initialized. Before using the pointer variable, it should be initialized. If the pointer variable has to be initialized in a function other than where it is defined, then the pointer's address has to be passed to the function. The contents of the *pointer to a pointer* variable can be used to access or modify the pointer type formal variable. The program big.cpp illustrates passing the address of a pointer, so that the pointer can be made to point to a desired variable (in this program, it is the biggest of two integers).

```
// big.cpp: program to find the biggest number using pointers
#include <iostream.h>
void FindBig(int *pa, int *pb, int **pbig)
{
   // compare the contents of *pa and *pb and assign their address to pbig
   if( *pa > *pb )
      *pbig = pa;
   else
      *pbig = pb;
}
void main()
{
   int a, b, *big;
   cout << "Enter two integers: ";
   cin >> a >> b;
   FindBig( &a, &b, &big );
   cout << "The value as obtained from the pointer: " << *big;
}
```

Run

```
Enter two integers: 10 20
The value as obtained from the pointer: 20
```

In main(), the statement

```
      FindBig( &a, &b, &big );
```

passes a, b, and big variables by address. It assigns the address of the variable a or b to the pointer variable big. In FindBig(), the statement

```
      *pbig = pa;
```

effectively stores the address of the variable a in the pointer variable big, which is defined in the main() function.

9.9 Array of Pointers

An array of pointers is similar to an array of any predefined data type. As a pointer variable always contains an address, an array of pointers is a collection of addresses. These can be addresses of ordinary isolated variables or addresses of array elements. The elements of an array of pointers are stored in the memory just like the elements of any other kind of array. All rules that apply to other arrays also apply to the array of pointers.

The syntax for defining an array of pointers is the same as array definition, except that the array name is preceded by the star symbol during definition as follows:

DataType *ArrayName[ARRSIZE];

An array of pointers is useful for holding a pointer to a list of strings. They can be utilized in implementing algorithms involving excessive data movements. It is a traditional style to sort data, by data movement. This method of sorting incurs much overhead in terms of both the time and space complexity, as it requires temporary space for exchanging the data between the records and has excessive data movement. This is especially true if the size of the data being sorted is large. Pointers can be utilized to perform the same with much flexibility and less overhead. In this method, instead of data exchange, pointers are exchanged to accomplish the same task. The program `sortptr.c` illustrates a method of sorting data without swapping their contents.

```cpp
// sortptr.cpp: sorting of strings by pointer movement
#include <iostream.h>
#include <string.h>
// bubble sort algorithm based sorting function. It speeds up sorting
// by exchanging the pointers instead of heavy data movement
void SortByPtrExchange( char ** person, int n )
{
   int i, j, flag;
   char *temp;
   for( i = 0; i < n-1; i++ )     // for i = 0 to n-2
   {
      flag = 1;
      for( j = 0; j < (n-1-i); j++ )    // for j = 0 to (n-i-2)
      {
         if( strcmp( person[j], person[j+1] ) > 0 )
         {
            flag = 0;   // still not sorted and requires next iteration
            // exchange pointers
            temp = person[j];
            person[j] = person[j+1];
            person[j+1] = temp;
         }
      }
      if( flag )
         break; // data are in sorted order now; no need of next iteration
   }
}
void main()
{
   int i, n = 0;
   char *person[100];
   char choice;
   do
   {
      person[n] = new char[40];   // allocate space for a string
      cout << "Enter Name: ";
      cin >> person[n++];
      cout << "Enter another (y/n) ? ";
      cin >> choice;
   } while( choice == 'y' );
```

```
    cout << "Unsorted list: ";
    for( i = 0; i < n; i ++ )
        cout << endl << person[i];
    SortByPtrExchange( person, n );
    cout << endl << "Sorted list: ";
    for( i = 0; i < n; i ++ )
        cout << endl << person[i];
    // release memory allocated
    for( i = 0; i < n; i++ )
        delete person[i];
}
```

Run

```
Enter Name: Tejaswi
Enter another (y/n) ? y
Enter Name: Prasad
Enter another (y/n) ? y
Enter Name: Prakash
Enter another (y/n) ? y
Enter Name: Sudeep
Enter another (y/n) ? y
Enter Name: Anand
Enter another (y/n) ? n
Unsorted list:
Tejaswi
Prasad
Prakash
Sudeep
Anand
Sorted list:
Anand
Prakash
Prasad
Sudeep
Tejaswi
```

In main(), the statement

```
        person[n] = new char[40];
```

allocates 40 bytes of memory to the $(n+1)^{th}$ element and stores its memory address in the array of pointers to strings indexed by n. The statement

```
        SortByPtrExchange( person, n );
```

invokes the sorting function by passing the array of pointers and *data count* as actual parameters. Note that, array is passed to a function just by mentioning its name. This is equivalent to passing an entire array; the address of the first element of an array can be used to access any element in the array by using offset values. The data sorted by SortByPtrExchange() do not change their physical location (see Figure 9.9). The effect of sorting is seen when strings are accessed using pointers in a sequence.

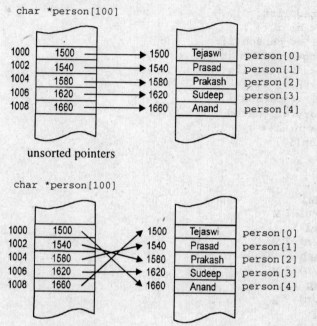

Figure 9.9:   Sorting using pointers

Precedence of * and [ ] Operators

In C++, the notations `*p[3]` and `(*p)[3]` are different since `*` operator has a lower precedence than [ ] operator. The following examples illustrate the difference between these two notations:

1. `int *data[10];`

    It defines an array of 10 pointers. The increment operation such as

    ```
    data++; or ++data;
    ```

is invalid; the array variable data is a constant pointer.

2. `int (*data)[10];`

    It defines a pointer to an array of 10 elements. The increment operation such as

    ```
    data++; or ++data;
    ```

is invalid; the variable data will point beyond 10 integers, i.e., `10 *sizeof(int)` will be added to the variable data. The program `show.cpp` illustrates the use of defining a pointer to a matrix having arbitrary number of rows and fixed number of columns.

```
//show.cpp: matrix of unknown number of rows and known number of columns
#include <iostream.h>
void show( int a[][3], int m )
{
  int (*c)[3];   // pointer to an array of 3 elements
  c = a;
  for( int i = 0; i < m; i++ )
  {
```

```
        for( int j = 0; j < 3; j++ )
            cout << c[i][j] << " ";
        cout << endl;
    }
}
void main()
{
    int c[2][3]={{1,2,3}, {4,5,6}};
    show(c, 2);
}
```

Run

```
1 2 3
4 5 6
```

In `show()`, the statement

```
        int (*c)[3];
```

defines a pointer to an array of three elements. It is useful for processing two dimensional array parameter declared with unknown number of rows. The statement

```
        c = a;
```

assigns the address of a two dimensional array having three columns. The variable c allows to access all the array elements in the same way as a matrix. It allows pointer increment operations such as

```
        c++; or ++c;
```

It increments pointer by `3*sizeof(int)`.

9.10 Dynamic Multi-dimensional Arrays

Pointers permit the creation of multi-dimensional arrays dynamically so that the amount of memory required by the array can be determined at runtime depending on the problem size. A two dimensional array can be thought of as a collection of a number of one dimensional arrays each representing a row. The 2D array is stored in memory in the row major form and it can be created dynamically using the following steps:

1. Define a pointer to pointers matrix variable: `int **p;`

2. Allocate memory for storing pointers to all rows of a matrix:

```
    p = new int *[ row ];
```

3. Allocate memory for all column elements:

```
    for( int i = 0; i < row; i++ )
        p[i] = new int[ col ];
```

The model of a dynamic matrix is shown in Figure 9.10. It is possible to access the two dimensional array elements using pointers in the same way as the one-dimensional array. Each row of the two dimensional array is treated as one dimensional array. The name of the array indicates the starting address of the array. The expressions `arrayname[i]` and `(arrayname+i)` point to the ith row of the array. Therefore, `*(arrayname+i)+j` points to the jth element in the ith row of the array. The subscript j actually acts as an offset to the base address of the ith row. The two dimensional dynamic matrix elements can also be accessed by using the notation `a[i][j]`.

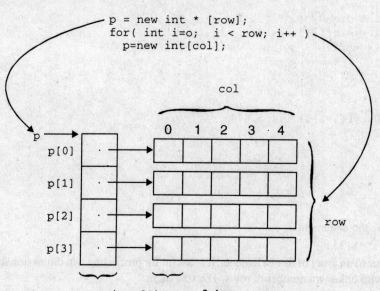

```
p = new int * [row];
for( int i=o;   i < row; i++ )
    p=new int[col];
```

col

0 1 2 3 · 4

p

p[0]

p[1]

p[2]

p[3]

row

sizeof(int) = 2 bytes
sizeof(int*) = 2 bytes, near pointer
            = 4 bytes, far pointer

Figure 9.10:   Model of dynamic matrix

```cpp
// matrix.cpp: matrix manipulation and dynamically resource allocation
#include <iostream.h>
#include <process.h>
int **MatAlloc( int row, int col )
{
    int **p;
    p = new int *[ row ]; ·
    for( int i = 0; i < row; i++ )
        p[i] = new int[ col ];
    return p;
}
void MatRelease( int **p, int row )
{
    for( int i = 0; i < row; i++ )
        delete p[i];
    delete p;
}
void MatRead(int **a, int row, int col )
{
    int i, j;
    for( i = 0; i < row; i++ )
        for( j = 0; j < col; j++ )
        {
            cout << "Matrix[" << i << "," << j << "] = ? ";
```

```
            cin >> a[i][j];
      }
}
// multiplication of matrices, c3.mul(c1, c2): c3 = c1*c2
void MatMul( int **a, int m, int n, int **b, int p, int q, int **c )
{
   int i, j, k;
   if( n != p )
   {
     cout << "Error: Invalid matrix order for multiplication";
     exit( 1 );
   }
    for( i = 0; i < m; i++ )
      for( j = 0; j < q; j++ )
      {
         c[i][j] = 0;
         for( k = 0; k < n; k++ )
            c[i][j] += a[i][k] * b[k][j];
      }
}
void MatShow( int **a, int row, int col )
{
   int i, j;
   for( i = 0; i < row; i++ )
   {
      cout << endl;
      for( j = 0; j < col; j++ )
         cout << a[i][j] << " ";
   }
}
void main()
{
   int **a, **b, **c;
   int m, n, p, q;
   cout << "Enter Matrix A details..." << endl;
   cout << "How many rows ? ";
   cin >> m;
   cout << "How many columns ? ";
   cin >> n;
   a = MatAlloc( m, n );
   MatRead( a, m, n );
   cout << "Enter Matrix B details..." << endl;
   cout << "How many rows ? ";
   cin >> p;
   cout << "How many columns ? ";
   cin >> q;
   b = MatAlloc( p, q );
   MatRead( b, p, q );
   c = MatAlloc( m, q );
   MatMul( a, m, n, b, p, q, c );
```

```
   cout << "Matrix C = A * B ...";
   MatShow( c, m, q );
}
```

Run

```
Enter Matrix A details...
How many rows ? 3
How many columns ? 2
Matrix[0,0] = ? 1
Matrix[0,1] = ? 1
Matrix[1,0] = ? 1
Matrix[1,1] = ? 1
Matrix[2,0] = ? 1
Matrix[2,1] = ? 1
Enter Matrix B details...
How many rows ? 2
How many columns ? 3
Matrix[0,0] = ? 1
Matrix[0,1] = ? 1
Matrix[0,2] = ? 1
Matrix[1,0] = ? 1
Matrix[1,1] = ? 1
Matrix[1,2] = ? 1
Matrix C = A * B ...
2 2 2
2 2 2
2 2 2
```

Three-dimensional Array

A three dimensional array can be thought of as an array of two dimensional arrays. Each element of a three dimensional array is accessed using three subscripts, one for each dimension.

As usual, the array name points to the base address of the three dimensional array. The array name with a single subscript i contains the base address of the ith two-dimensional array. Hence arrayname[i] or (arrayname+i) is the address of the ith two dimensional array. The expression arrayname[i][j] or *(arrayname+i)+j represents the base address of the jth row in the ith two dimensional array. Similarly, the expression *(*(arrayname+j)+k) points to the kth element in the jth row in the ith two dimensional array. The program 3ptr.cpp illustrates these concepts.

```
// 3ptr.cpp: pointer to 3-dimensional arrays
#include <iostream.h>
void main()
{
   int arr[2][3][2] ={ {{2,1},{3,6},{5,3}}, {{0,9},{2,3},{5,8}}};
   cout << arr << endl;
   cout << *arr << endl;
   cout << **arr << endl;
   cout << ***arr << endl;
```

```
cout << arr+1 << endl;
cout << *arr+1 << endl;
cout << **arr+1 << endl;
cout << ***arr+1 << endl;
for( int i=0; i < 2; i++ )
{
    for( int j=0; j < 3; j++ )
    {
        for( int k=0; k < 2; k++ )
        {
            cout << "arr[" << i << "][" << j << "][" << k << "] = ";
            cout << *(*(*(arr+i)+j)+k) << endl;
        }
    }
}
}
```

Run

```
0xffb8
0xffb8
0xffb8
2
0xffc4
0xffbc
0xffba
3
arr[0][0][0] = 2
arr[0][0][1] = 1
arr[0][1][0] = 3
arr[0][1][1] = 6
arr[0][2][0] = 5
arr[0][2][1] = 3
arr[1][0][0] = 0
arr[1][0][1] = 9
arr[1][1][0] = 2
arr[1][1][1] = 3
arr[1][2][0] = 5
arr[1][2][1] = 8
```

The array arr will be stored in memory as shown in Figure 9.11. In the above program, the array name arr is the base address of the three dimensional array. The expression *arr is the base address of the 0th two dimensional array, **arr is the 0th row in the 0th two dimensional array and ***arr contains the value stored in the 0th column and 0th row of the 0th two dimensional array. The expression arr+1 is the base address of the 1st two dimensional array, *arr+1 is the address of the 1st row in the 0th two dimensional array, **arr+1 gives the address of 0th row and 1st column of a zero dimensional array, ***arr+1 adds 1 to its current value (2) obtained from the 0th element in the 0th row of the 0th two dimensional array. The expression within the for loop prints the contents of the three dimensional array in the order in which they are stored in memory.

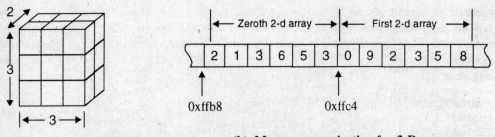

(a) Three dimensional array   (b) Memory organisation for 3-D array

Figure 9.11: Pointer to 3-dimensional arrays

9.11 Pointer Constants

As mentioned earlier, the name of an array holds the starting address of the array. Hence if arr[3] is an array of any data type, then the name of the array arr is the address of (and does not point to) the 0th element of the array and arr+1 is the address of the 1st element of the array. If arr is a pointer, then arr+i cannot be replaced by an expression arr++ executing i times. Using the increment operator with it (the name of the array) is incorrect as the starting address of the array has been placed in the code directly by the compiler, thus making the array name a constant. The array name does not have any storage location allocated unlike a pointer variable which itself has a storage location. Hence, performing an increment operation on the address of the array (which is a constant) is like performing the increment operation; 5++, which is meaningless. The program ptrinc.cpp illustrates these concepts.

```
// ptrinc.cpp: pointers can be incremented but not an array
#include <iostream.h>
void main()
{
   int ia[3] = { 2, 5, 9 };
   int *ptr=ia;
   for( int i = 0; i < 3; i++ )
   {
      //  cout << *(ia++);   error, array address of ia cannot be changed
      cout << " " << *ptr++;  // note: pointer update
   }
}
```

Run

```
2 5 9
```

In the above program, the elements of the array are accessed using the pointer ptr which is assigned the starting address of the array ia. The pointer variable ptr is incremented every time to point to the next element. The expression ia++ is incorrect.

9.12 Pointers and String Functions

Like arrays, pointers holding address of strings are widely used for manipulating strings. C++'s library or user defined functions can be used for manipulating strings. These functions assume the character \0 as the end-of-string indicator and hence, it is not considered as part of a string data. Therefore to store a string of length L, allocate (L+1) bytes of memory. A pointer to the string is passed to these functions instead of the entire string. The program strfunc.cpp illustrates string manipulations using strandard and user defined functions.

```
// strfunc.cpp: user defined string processing functions
#include <iostream.h>
#include <string.h>
// user defined string processing functions prototype
int my_strlen( char *str );
void my_strcpy( char *s2, char *s1 );
void my_strcat( char *s2, char *s1 );
int my_strcmp( char *s1, char *s2 );
void main()
{
    char temp[100], *s1, *s2, *s3;
    cout << "Enter string1: ";
    cin >> temp;
    s1 = new char[ strlen(temp)+1 ];
    my_strcpy( s1, temp );
    cout << "Enter string2: ";
    cin >> temp;
    s2 = new char[ strlen(temp)+1 ];
    my_strcpy( s2, temp );
    cout << "Length of string1: " << my_strlen( s1 ) << endl;
    s3 = new char[ strlen(s1) + my_strlen(s2) + 1 ];
    my_strcpy( s3, s1 );
    my_strcat( s3, s2 );
    cout << "Strings' on concatenation: " << s3 << endl;
    cout << "String comparison using ..." << endl;
    cout << "   Library function: " << strcmp( s1, s2 ) << endl;
    cout << "   User's function: " << my_strcmp( s1, s2 ) << endl;
    delete s1;
    delete s2;
    delete s3;
}
int my_strlen( char *str )
{
    char *ptr = str;
    while( *ptr != '\0' )    // move ptr to end of string
        ++ptr;
    return ptr-str;  // address of last character - starting address = length
}
void my_strcpy( char *s2, char *s1 )
{
    while( *s1 != '\0' )
        *s2++ = *s1++;
    *s2 = '\0'; // copy end of string
}
```

```
void my_strcat( char *s2, char *s1 )
{
    // move end of string
    while( *s2 != '\0' )
        s2++;
    // append s1 to s2
    while( *s1 != '\0' )
        *s2++ = *s1++;
    *s2 = '\0'; // copy end of string
}
int my_strcmp( char *s1, char *s2 )
{
    // compare as long as they are equal
    while( *s1 == *s2 && (*s1 != NULL || *s2 != NULL) )
    {
        s1++;
        s2++;
    }
    return *s1 - *s2;
}
```

Run

```
Enter string1: Object
Enter string2: Oriented
Length of string1: 6
Strings' on concatenation: ObjectOriented
String comparison using ...
    Library function: -16
    User's function: -16
```

9.13 Environment Specific Issues

Pointer variables, like other variables are also allocated memory whenever they are defined. The size of the memory allocated (in bytes) to a pointer variable depends on whether the pointer just holds the offset part of the address, or both the segment and offset values. The memory model in which the program is compiled also influences the size of the pointer variables used in that program. C++ compilers (such as Borland or Microsoft C++) running under DOS environment support six different memory models, each of which determines the amount of memory allocated to the program's data and code (see Table 9.3).

Normally, all pointers defined in a program in the small model contain only the offset part of the address. Such pointers are known as *near pointers,* for which two bytes of memory are allocated. The use of near pointers limits the programmer to access only those memory locations, which lie within a single segment only. (The maximum size of a segment is 64 KB). This limitation can be overcome by the use of pointers, which are capable of holding both the segment as well as the offset part of an address. Such pointers are called *far pointers,* for which four bytes of memory is allocated. It is possible to access any memory location, using far pointers. The far pointers can be defined (even in a small memory model) by using the keyword far as follows:

```
int far *ifarptr;  // defines a far pointer to int
```

```
char far *cfarptr; // defines a far pointer to char
```

In the compact and large models, the data area can be more than 64K but any single data structure (like array or structure) should be smaller than 64 KB. For example, if an array is defined as `int far *ary;`, then `ary` will have both a segment and an offset part, but when pointer arithmetic is done, only the offset part is used and not the segment part. If `ary = 0x5437:0xfffe` and it is incremented then `ary` will become `0x5437:0x0000` i.e., the offset part wraps around and the segment part remains unchanged, hence any single data structure should be less than 64 K. However, such limitations are overcome in other memory models such as *huge*.

Memory model	Segment			Pointer	
	Code	Data	Stack	Code	Data
Tiny	64K			near	near
Small	64K	64K		near	near
Medium	1MB	64K		far	near
Compact	64K	1MB		near	far
Large	1MB	1MB		far	far
Huge	1MB	64K each	64K each	far	far

Table 9.3:   Memory models

C++ compilers in MS-DOS normally provide three specialized, predefined macros viz., `MK_FP`, `FP_SEG`, and `FP_OFF` for use with `far` and `huge` pointers. The `MK_FP` macro takes two unsigned integer input arguments which are the segment and the offset addresses of the location to be accessed and returns a value that can be used to initialize a `far` or `huge` pointer variable. Here is an example for initializing a `far` pointer variable.

```
char far *cptr;  // define a far pointer variable
. . .
cptr = (char far *) MK_FP( 0xb800, 0x0000 );
```

It causes the `far` pointer `cptr` to point to a byte which resides in segment `0xb800` (in hex) and at an offset `0x0000` (in hex). Note that, the `macro` function `MK_FP` returns a `far` pointer to `void` which must be typecasted suitably before its use.

The macros `FP_SEG` and `FP_OFF` require a `far` pointer as their only input argument, and they return the segment and offset parts of the address contained in that `far` pointer. The three macros mentioned above become available by including the header file `dos.h`.

The program `farptr.cpp` defines a `far` pointer to a character, initializes it with an arbitrary address (say segment = `0xb800` and offset= `0x0000`), extracts and prints the segment and offset of the same pointer. It also prints the ASCII character residing at the address `b800:0000`.

```
// farptr.cpp: far pointers and related macros to access display memory
#include <dos.h>
#include <iostream.h>
void main()
{
```

```
    char ch;
    char far *cptr;    // define far pointer to character
    unsigned int seg_val, off_val;
    // initialize far pointer
    cptr = (char far *) MK_FP( 0xb800, 0x0000 );
    // fetch segment address from far pointer
    seg_val = FP_SEG(cptr);
    // fetch offset address from far pointer
    off_val = FP_OFF(cptr);
    ch = *cptr;
    cout << "Character at 0xb800:0x0000 = " << ch << endl;
    cout << "Segment part of cptr = " << hex << seg_val << endl;
    cout << "Offset part of cptr = " << hex << off_val << endl;
}
```

Run

```
Character at 0xb800:0x0000 = S
Segment part of cptr = b800
Offset part of cptr = 0
```

Note: The ASCII character printed by the above program will be the same as the first character on the top left corner of the monitor. It is because the address b8000:0000 is a location in the video memory, which holds the ASCII value of the character appearing in the top left corner in the text mode.

9.14 Pointers to Functions

A pointer-to-function can be defined to hold the starting address of a function, and the same can be used to invoke a function. It is also possible to pass addresses of different functions at different times thus making the function more flexible and abstract. The syntax of defining a pointer to a function is shown in Figure 9.12.

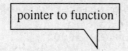

```
ReturnType (*PtrToFn)(arguments_if_any);
```

Figure 9.12:   Syntax of defining pointer to function

The definition of a pointer to a function requires the function's return type and the function's argument list to be specified along with the pointer variable. It should be remembered that the function prototype or definition should be known before its address is assigned to a pointer.

Once a pointer to a function is defined, it can be used to point to any function which matches with the return type and the argument-list stated in the definition of the pointer to a function. Consider a statement such as

```
    int (*any_func)(int, int)
```

It defines the variable any_func as a pointer to a function. The variable any_func can point to any function that takes two integer arguments and returns a single integer value. For instance, it can point to the following functions:

```
    int min( int a, int b );
```

```
int max( int a, int b );
int add( int x, int y );
```

Address of a Function

The address of a function can be obtained by just specifying the name of the function without the trailing parentheses. The following statements assign address of the functions to pointer to the function variable `any_func` since prototype of all of them is same:

```
any_func = min;
any_func = max;
any_func = add;
```

Invoking a Function using Pointers

The syntax for invoking a function using a pointer to a function is as follows:

> (*PtrToFn)(arguments_if_any);

> or

> PtrToFn(arguments_if_any);

Consider the following pointer to functions

```
int (*pfunc1)( int );
float (*pfunc2)( float, float );
```

If these hold addresses of an appropriate function, the statements

```
(*pfunc1)( 2 );
(*pfunc2)( 2.5, a );
pfunc1( i );
```

invoke functions pointed to by them. The parameters can be constants or variables.

In the definition of pointers to functions, the pointer variable along with the symbol * plays the role of the function name. Hence, while invoking functions using pointers, the function name is replaced by the pointer variable. The program `rfact.cpp` illustrates this concept.

```
// rfact.cpp: pointer to function and its use
#include <iostream.h>
long fact( int num )
{
   if( num == 0 )
      return 1;
   else
      return num * fact( num - 1 );
}
void main( void )
{
   int n;
   long (*ptrfact)(int);      // definition of pointer to function
   ptrfact = fact;            // address of function to pointer assignment
   cout << "Enter the number whose factorial is to be found: ";
   cin >> n;
   long f1 = (*ptrfact)(n);
   cout << "The factorial of " << n << " is " << f1 << endl;
   cout << "The factorial of " << n+1 << " is " << ptrfact(n+1) << endl;
}
```

Run

```
Enter the number whose factorial is to be found: 5
The factorial of 5 is 120
The factorial of 6 is 720
```

In the above program, a pointer `ptrfact` is defined to point to a function which takes an integer argument and returns an integer value. Then the address of the function `fact` is assigned to the pointer `ptrfact`. The function `fact` computes the factorial of a given positive integer. The function `fact` is invoked using the pointer variable `ptrfact`.

Recursive call to `main()`

When an attempt is made to invoke `main()` within a program, generally compilers generate an error message such as:

```
        cannot call main from within the program
```

Because in C++, `main()` cannot be invoked recursively; however it is compiler dependent. The following operations cannot be performed on `main()`:

- `main()` cannot be invoked recursively.
- `main()` cannot be overloaded
- `main()` cannot be declared inline
- `main()` cannot be declared static

The first restriction can be violated by using a pointer to functions. The program `rmain.cpp` invokes `main()` recursively using a pointer to functions.

```
// rmain.cpp: recursive call to main() using a pointer to functions
#include <iostream.h>
void main()
{
    void (*p)();
    cout << "Hello...";
    p = main;
    (*p)();
}
```

Run

```
Hello...Hello...Hello...Hello...Hello...Hello...Hello...Hello...Hello...Hello...
```

The above program generates `Hello...` message indefinite number of times. It stops when stack overflow occurs. In `main()`, the statements

```
        p = main;
        (*p)();
```

assign the address of `main` to the pointer `p` and transfer control to `main()` using pointer to a function respectively.

Passing Function Address

The address of a function can be passed as an argument to functions, either by a function name or a pointer holding the address of a function. The program `passfn.cpp` illustrates these concepts. It takes two integer parameters and returns the largest and smallest among them.

```
// passfn.cpp: passing pointer to function type parameters
#include <iostream.h>
int small( int a, int b )
{
    return a < b ? a : b;
}
int large( int a, int b )
{
    return a > b ? a : b;
}
int select( int (*fn)(int, int), int x, int y )
{
    int value = fn( x, y );
    return value;
}
void main( void )
{
    int m, n;
    int (*ptrf)(int, int);     // definition of pointer to function
    cout << "Enter two integers: ";
    cin >> m >> n;
    int high = select( large, m, n );   // function as parameter
    ptrf = small;
    int low = select( ptrf, m, n );     // pointer to function as parameter
    cout << "Large = " << high << endl;
    cout << "Small = " << low;
}
```

Run

```
Enter two integers: 10 20
Large = 20
Small = 10
```

In the above program, the function declarator

```
        int select( int (*fn)(int, int), int x, int y )
```

indicates that it takes the pointer to a function as the first parameter and the remaining two integer parameters. In `main()`, the statement

```
        int high = select( large, m, n );   // function as parameter
```

passes the address of the function `large()` and two integer variables as actual parameters. The pointer to the function parameter `large` operates on the last two parameters m and n and returns an integer result. Similarly, the statement

```
        int low = select( ptrf, m, n );     // pointer to function as parameter
```

passes a pointer to a function variable `ptrf` (note that, `ptrf` is initialized to the address of `small()`). Such a mechanism is useful in selecting the type of operation to be performed at runtime.

9.16 Pointers to Constant Objects

Consider the statement

```
        const int* pi;   // it is the same as: int const * pi;
```

It defines `pi` as a pointer to a constant integer. Let `pi` be initialized by the statement

```
int i[ 20 ];
pi = i;
```

i.e., `*pi` would refer to the integer `i[0]`. Due to the definition of `pi` (which, as mentioned above, is `const int* pi;`), statements such as

```
*pi = 10; or even pi[ 10 ] = 20;
```

are invalid. It results in compile time errors. But `pi` itself can be changed. i.e., a statement such as

```
pi++;
```

is perfectly valid. Such pointers can be used as character pointers, when the pointer has to be passed to a function for printing. It is a good practice to code such a function for instance, `print()` as follows:

```
void print( const char* str )
{
    cout << str;
}
```

It accepts a const `char  *` (pointer to constant character). The string being pointed to cannot be modified. This is a safety measure, since it avoids accidental modification of the string passed to the function. In the function, the pointer `str` can be changed and a statement such as

```
str++;.
```

is valid. But this does not affect the calling procedure, since the pointer is passed by value.

9.17 Constant Pointers

The statement

```
int* const pi = i;
```

defines a constant pointer to an integer (assume that `i` is an integer array). In this case, the use of a statement such as

```
*pi = 10;
```

is perfectly valid, but others that modify the pointer, such as

```
pi++;
```

are invalid and result in compile time errors.

A pointer definition such as

```
const int* const pi = i;
```

will disallow any modifications to `pi` or the integer to which `pi` is referencing. (Assume as before that `i` is an integer array).

9.18 Pointer to Structures

A pointer can also hold the address of user defined data types such as structures. Similar to pointers to standard data types, pointers to user defined data types can be initialized with address of statically or dynamically created data items. Note that in C++, structures can combine both the data and functions operating on it into a single unit. Both the data and function members of structure are accessed in the same way. The syntax for defining pointer to structures is shown in Figure 9.13.

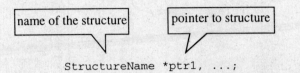

$$StructureName \text{ *ptr1, ...;}$$

Figure 9.13:   Syntax of defining pointer to structure

The syntax for accessing members of a structure using a structure pointer is as follows:

StructPtrVar->MemberName;

The symbol -> is called the *arrow operator.* (The dot operator connects a structure with a member of the structure; the arrow operator connects a pointer with a member of the structure). The program bdate.cpp illustrates the mechanism of creating user defined data type variables dynamically.

```cpp
// bdate.cpp: displaying birth date of the authors
#include <iostream.h>
struct date
{                        //specifies a structure
   int day;
   int month;
   int year;
   void show()
   {
      cout << day << "-" << month << "-" << year << endl;
   }
};
void read( date *dp )
{
   cout << "Enter day: ";
   cin >> dp->day;
   cout << "Enter month: ";
   cin >> dp->month;
   cout << "Enter year: ";
   cin >> dp->year;
}
void main()
{
   date d1, *dp1, *dp2;
   cout << "Enter birth date of boy..." << endl;
   read( &d1 );
   // read date2
   dp2 = new date;    // allocate memory dynamically
   cout << "Enter birth date of girl..." << endl;
   read( dp2 );
   cout << "Birth date of boy: ";
   dp1 = &d1;          // dp1 points to statically allocated structure
   dp1->show();
   cout << "Birth date of girl: ";
   dp2->show();
```

```
        delete dp2;        // release memory
}
```

Run

```
Enter birth date of boy...
Enter day: 14
Enter month: 4
Enter year: 71
Enter birth date of girl...
Enter day: 1
Enter month: 4
Enter year: 72
Birth date of boy: 14-4-71
Birth date of girl: 1-4-72
```

In main(), the statement

```
        date d1, *dp1, *dp2;
```

creates variable d1 and two pointers of type structure date. The statement,

```
        dp2 = new date;    // allocate memory dynamically
```

creates the structure date type item dynamically and stores its address in a pointer variable dp2. The statement

```
        dp1 = &d1;         // dp1 points to statically allocated structure
```

assigns the address of statically created variable d1 to the pointer variable dp1. The statement,

```
        dp1->show();
```

accesses the member function show() of date using the pointer variable dp1. The statement

```
        delete dp2;
```

releases the memory allocated to the pointer variable dp2.

Arithmetic Operations on Pointer to structures

Consider the statement

```
        data *d1;
```

It defines the pointer variable d1 to the structure date. The statement

```
        ++d1->day;
```

increments the contents of the member variable day and not d1. However, the statement

```
        (++d1)->day;
```

increments d1 first, and then accesses day. The statement

```
        d1++->day;
```

increments d1 after accessing the member variable day. The statement

```
        d1++; or ++d1;
```

increments d1 by sizeof(date).

Self Referential Structure

A structure having references to itself is called a self-referential structure. It is useful for implementing data structures such as linked list, trees, etc. A linked list consists of structures related to each other through pointers. The self referential pointer in the structure points to the next node of a list. The organization of a linked list is shown in Figure 9.14.

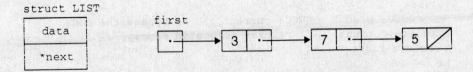

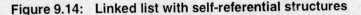

Figure 9.14:   Linked list with self-referential structures

The program `list.cpp` illustrates the manipulation of a linked list. It supports `create`, `delete`, and `display` operations on the linked list. The structure `LIST` is a *self referential* structure, since it has a pointer to the next node as one of the data items.

```cpp
// list.cpp: self referential structure-linked list
#include <iostream.h>
#include <new.h>
#include <process.h>
#define SUCC( node ) node->next
struct LIST
{
   int data;   // node data
   LIST *next; // pointer to next node
};
// creates node using data and returns pointer to first node of the list
LIST * InsertNode( int data, LIST *first )
{
   LIST *newnode;
   newnode = new LIST;         // allocate memory for node
   if( newnode == NULL )
   {
     cout << "Error: Out-of-memory" << endl;
     exit( 1 );
   }
   newnode->data = data;       // Initialize list data member
   SUCC( newnode ) = first;    // new node becomes first node
   return newnode;
}
// deletes node whose data matches input data and returns updated list
LIST * DeleteNode( int data, LIST *first )
{
   LIST *current, *pred; // work space for insertion
   if( !first )
   {
     cout << "Empty list" << endl;
     return first;
   }
   for(pred=current=first;current; pred=current,current = SUCC( current ))
      if( current->data == data )
      {
         // node found, release this node
         if( current == first )     // if node to be deleted is first node
           first = SUCC( current );// then update list pointer
```

```cpp
            else
               SUCC( pred ) = SUCC( current );   // bypass the node
            delete current;   // release allocated memory
            return first;
        }
    return( first );
}
// Display list
void DisplayList( LIST *first )
{
    LIST *list;
    for( list = first; list;. list = SUCC( list ) )
        cout << "->" << list->data;
    cout << endl;
}
void main()
{
    LIST *list = NULL;    // list is empty
    int choice, data;
    set_new_handler( 0 );    // makes new to return to NULL if it fails
    cout << "Linked-list manipulations program...\n";
    while(1)
    {
        cout << "List operation, 1- Insert, 2-Display, 3-Delete, 4-Quit: ";
        cin >> choice;
        switch( choice )
        {
            case 1:
                cout << "Enter data for node to be created: ";
                cin >> data;
                list = InsertNode( data, list );
                break;
            case 2:
                cout << "List contents: ";
                DisplayList( list );
                break;
            case 3:
                cout << "Enter data for node to be delete: ";
                cin >> data;
                list = DeleteNode( data, list );
                break;
            case 4:
                cout << "End of Linked List Computation !!.\n";
                return;
            default:
                cout << "Bad Option Selected\n";
                break;
        }
    }
}
```

Run

```
Linked-list manipulations program...
List operation, 1- Insert, 2-Display, 3-Delete, 4-Quit: 1
Enter data for node to be created: 5
List operation, 1- Insert, 2-Display, 3-Delete, 4-Quit: 1
Enter data for node to be created: 7
List operation, 1- Insert, 2-Display, 3-Delete, 4-Quit: 1
Enter data for node to be created: 3
List operation, 1- Insert, 2-Display, 3-Delete, 4-Quit: 2
List contents: ->3->7->5
List operation, 1- Insert, 2-Display, 3-Delete, 4-Quit: 3
Enter data for node to be delete: 7
List operation, 1- Insert, 2-Display, 3-Delete, 4-Quit: 2
List contents: ->3->5
List operation, 1- Insert, 2-Display, 3-Delete, 4-Quit: 4
End of Linked List Computation !!.
```

In main(), the statement

```
list = InsertNode( data, list );
```

takes an integer type data and a pointer to the first node as input parameters. It returns a pointer to the updated linked list. Initially, the second parameter has to be set to NULL indicating a empty linked list.

The statement

```
list = DeleteNode( data, list );
```

deletes a node which matches with the parameter data and returns the address of the first node in the linked list to the pointer list. The statement

```
DisplayList( list );
```

prints the data information contents of a linked list on the console.

9.19 Wild Pointers

Pointers have to be handled very carefully since, issues associated with them are confusing. Especially, the scope and extent of a data object, to which a pointer is pointing to is a crucial aspect. Pointers exhibit wild behavior if these crucial issues are not taken into consideration while accessing data. A pointer becomes a *wild pointer* when it is pointing to an unallocated memory or when it is pointing to a data item whose memory is already released. Side effects of such pointers are creation of *garbage memory* and *dangling reference*. The memory becomes *garbage memory* when a pointer pointing to a memory object (data item) is lost; i.e., it indicates that the memory item continues to exist, but the pointer to it is lost; it happens when memory is not released explicitly. A memory access using a pointer is known as *dangling reference when* a pointer to the memory item continues to exist, but memory allocated to that item is released; i.e., accessing memory object, for which no memory is allocated. Pointers become wild pointers under the following situations:

- When a pointer is uninitialized
- Pointer modification
- Pointer referencing to a data which is destroyed

(1) *When pointer is uninitialized*: It contains an illegal address and it is difficult to predict the outcome

of a program. For instance, in the definition

```
int *p;
```

it is impossible to predict which integer value the pointer p is pointing to. The pointer wild1.cpp illustrates accessing data through the uninitialized variables.

```
// wild1.cpp: accessing uninitialized pointer
#include <iostream.h>
void main()
{
    int *p;  // pointer is uninitialized
    for( int i = 0; i < 10; i++ )
        cout << p[i] << " "; // accessing uninitialized pointer
}
```

Run (under MS-DOS)

```
0 21838 19532 17184 17736 19267 0 14 0 -1
```

Run (under UNIX)

```
-2130509557 73728 8192 0 105384 8224 0 0 -1139793920 -80506873
```

It can be observed that, the output generated by the program is different from system to system. The use of a statement such as

```
p[1] = 10;
```

might modify some sensitive data pertaining to a system leading to corruption of the whole system or the program may behave erratically. Under UNIX system, such errors will lead to segment violation error as illustrated in the program wild2.cpp.

```
// wild2.cpp: assigning data using uninitialized pointers
#include <iostream.h>
#include <string.h>
void main()
{
    char *name;
    strcpy( name, "Savithri " );  // assigning without memory allocation
    cout << name;
}
```

Run (under MS-DOS)

```
Savithri Null pointer assignment
```

Run (under UNIX)

```
Segmentation fault (core dumped)
```

In main(), the statement

```
strcpy( name, "Savithri " );
```

assigns the string "Savithri " to a pointer to string, for which memory is not allocated. From the output, it can be noted that, in the UNIX environment the program immediately terminates by core dumping when such a situation is detected. Hence, use a statement such as

```
name = new char[ 10 ];
```

to avoid such runtime errors before trying to store anything in the memory.

(2) *Pointer modification*: The inadvertent storage of a new address in a pointer variable is referred to as pointer modification. This situation will occur when some other wild pointer modifies the address of a valid pointer. It transforms a valid pointer to a wild pointer.

(3) *Pointer referencing to a data which is destroyed*. In this case, the pointer tries to access memory object or item which no longer exists. It is illustrated in the program wild3.cpp.

```
// wild3.cpp: assigning destroyed object
#include <iostream.h>
#include <string.h>
char * nameplease();
char * charplease();
void main()
{
   char *p1, *p2;
   p1 = nameplease();
   p2 = charplease();
   cout << "Name = " << p1 << endl;
   cout << "Char = " << p2 << endl;
}
char * nameplease()
{
   char name[] = "Savithri ";
   return name;
}
char * charplease()
{
   char ch;
   ch = 'X';
   return &ch;
}
```

Run
```
Name = SavivN'
Char = i
```

In the function nameplease(), invoked by the statement

```
        p1 = nameplease();
```

when the address of the variable name is returned, the control comes out of the function nameplease() and hence, the variable name dies (since it is an auto variable). Thus p1 would contain the address of the variable which does not exist. In effect, this is a situation of dangling reference. In such a situation the compiler issues a warning such as

    Suspicious pointer reference

    or
    Returning a reference to a local object

It implies that a pointer or reference to a local (auto) variable/object should never be returned. As soon as the function is terminated, the memory assigned to the local variable is released or gets destroyed, and any reference or pointer points to some invalid data. However, returning a copy (return by value) of a local variable/object is valid.

Another important point to be noted is that, avoid storing the address of a variable or an object into a pointer in the inner block, and using the same in the outer block. The program `wild4.cpp` illustrates the wild pointer accessing garbage location.

```
// wild4.cpp: out of scope of a block variable access
#include <iostream.h>
#include <string.h>
void main()
{
   char *p1;
   {
     char name[] = "Savithri ";
     p1 = name;
   }
   // do some processing here
   cout << "Name = " << p1 << endl;
}
```

Run

```
Name = Savith@$!
```

In `main()`, the statement

```
      cout << "Name = " << p1 << endl;
```

accesses the data pointed to by the pointer variable `p1`. The variable `p1` is assigned to point to the variable `name` defined within an inner block. When the execution of this block is completed, all the variables are destroyed and hence, accessing of data stored in the variable `name` becomes invalid data. In some situation, the programs might execute properly, but they may corrupt other program's data and lead to system crash.

The above discussion also holds good for pointer to objects. Like variables, whenever objects goes out of scope, they are destroyed. Referencing such objects is like accessing invalid-data variable and hence, such reference should be avoided.

Review Questions

9.1   What are pointers ? What are the advantages of using pointers in programming ? Explain *addressing mode* required to access memory locations using pointers.

9.2   Under what situations, the use of pointers is indispensable ?

9.3   Write a program to print address of the variables defined by the following statement:
```
int a, b = 10;
float c = 2, d;
```

9.4   Explain the syntax for defining pointer variables. How different are these from normal variables?

9.5   What is dereferencing of pointers ? Write a program to dereference the pointer variables in the following statements (print value pointed to by pointer variables):
```
int *a; double *b;
a = &i; b = &f;
```

9.6   What are the differences between passing parameters by value and by pointers ? Give examples.

9.7 What are the different arithmetic operations that can be performed on pointer variables ? Consider the following definitions:

```
int *a, *b, c; float *e; char *p;
```

The pointer variables a, b, and c are initially pointing to memory locations 100, 150, and 50 (assume) respectively. What is the address stored in the pointer variable (a, b, and c) on execution of the following statements ?

```
a++;
b = --a;
cout << *b++;
cout << *++p;
e++;
a = &c;
```

9.8 Consider the following definitions:

```
int *a, *b, c; float *e; char *p; int i1, *ip;
char ch; long l; double *d; long double lb;
```

What is the return value of sizeof() operator when applied to the variables created by the above statements individually? For instance, the return value of sizeof(int) or sizeof(i1) is 2 (in DOS) and 4 (in UNIX). Comment on such differences.

9.9 What is runtime memory management ? What support is provided by C++ for this and how does it differs from C's memory management ?

9.10 Write a program for finding the smallest and largest in a list of N numbers. Accept the value of N at runtime and allocate the necessary amount of storage for storing numbers.

9.11 Write an interactive program for manipulation of matrices. Support addition, subtraction, and multiplication operations on them. Create matrices dynamically.

9.12 Write a program for sorting names of persons by swapping pointers instead of data. Use Comb sort algorithm for sorting. (Comb sort is explained in the chapter *Arrays and Strings*).

9.13 Explain syntax for defining pointers to functions. Write a program which supports the following:

```
a = compute( sin, 1.345 );
b = compute( log, 150 );
c = computer( sqrt, 4.0 );
```

9.14 Consider the function show(), which is defined as follows:

```
void show( int a, int b, int c)
{
    cout << a  << " " << b << " " << c;
}
int *i, j;
i = &j;
j = 2;
int k[] = { 1, 2, 3 };
```

What is the output of the following statements: (Note that actual parameters are evaluated from right to left while assigning them to formal parameters)

```
show( *i, j, *k );
show( *i, *i++, *i);
show( *k, *k++, *k++ );
```

9.15 What are the differences between pointers to constants and constant pointers ? Give examples.

9.16 Write a program for creating a linked list and support insertion and deletion operations on it.

Nodes of linked list have to be modeled using nested structures.

9.19   Define the following: (a) Wild pointers (b) Garbage (c) Dangling reference. Consider the following program:

```
#include <iostream.h>
void main()
{
    int * a;
    const int *b;
    int *const p;
    int c = 2, d = 3;
    cout << a;  b = &c; p = &d;
    *b = 10;
    b = new int;
    *b = 10;
    delete b;
    cout << *b;
    a = new int[10];
    a[9] = 20;
    a[10] = 30;
    a = new int[5];
    a++;
    ++b;
    cout << *a;
}
```

Observe the above program carefully and find out where all garbage, dangling reference, and wild pointers exist. Identify statements which are treated as errorneous by the compiler.

9.20   Write the function `locate(s,pattern)`, which returns -1 if the string `pattern` does not exist in `s`, otherwise returns location at which it is found.

9.21   Consider the following statements:

```
char *name;
chat str[20];
name = new char[ strlen(str)+1 ];
strcpy( name, str );
```

Why one more extra byte is allocated to the string `name` ? What will happen if one extra byte is not allocated ? What is the effect of the following statements during runtime:

```
char *s;
cin >> s;
```

Does the second statement leads to any runtime error ? Give reasons.

10

Classes and Objects

10.1 Introduction

Object-oriented programming paradigm is playing an increasingly significant role in the design and implementation of software systems. It simplifies the development of large and complex software systems and helps in the production of software, which is modular, easily understandable, reusable, and adaptable to changes. The object-oriented approach centers around modeling the real world problems in terms of objects (*data decomposition*), which is in contrast to older, more traditional approaches that emphasize a function oriented view, separating data and procedures (*algorithm decomposition*). Object oriented modeling is a new way of visualizing problems using models organized around the real-world concepts. Objects are the result of programming methodology rather than a language.

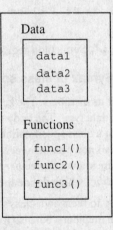

Figure 10.1: Class grouping data and functions

Object-oriented programming constructs modeled out of data types called *classes*. Defining variables of a class data type is known as a *class instantiation* and such variables are called *objects*. (Object is an instance of a class.) A class encloses both the *data* and *functions* that operate on the data, into a *single unit* as shown in Figure 10.1. The variables and functions enclosed in a class are called *data members* and *member functions* respectively. Member functions define the permissible operations on the data members of a class.

Placing data and functions together in a single unit is the central theme of object-oriented programming. The programmers are entirely responsible for creating their own classes and can also have access to classes developed by the software vendors.

Classes are the basic language construct of C++ for creating the user defined data types. They are syntactically an extension of structures. The difference is that, all the members of structures are *public by default* whereas, the members of classes are *private by default*. Class follows the principle that *the information about a module should be private to the module unless it is specifically declared public*.

10.2 Class Specification

C++ provides support for defining classes, which is a significant feature that makes C++ an object oriented language. In C terms, a class is the natural evolution of a structure. Classes contain not only data but also functions. The functions are called member functions and define the set of operations that can be performed on the data members of a class. Thus, a class can be described as a collection of data members along with member functions. This property of C++, which allows association of data and functions into a single unit is called *encapsulation*. Sometimes, classes may not contain any data members or member functions (and such classes are called as *empty classes*). The syntax of a class specification is shown in Figure 10.2.

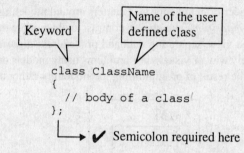

```
class ClassName
{
    // body of a class
};
```

Keyword

Name of the user defined class

✔ Semicolon required here

Figure 10.2:   Syntax of class specification

The class specifies the type and scope of its members. The keyword `class` indicates that the name which follows (`ClassName`) is an abstract data type. The body of a class is enclosed within the curly braces followed by a semicolon—the end of a class specification. The body of a class contains declaration of variables and functions, collectively known as *members*. The variables declared inside a class are known as *data members,* and functions are known as *member functions*. These members are usually grouped under two sections, *private* and *public*, which define the visibility of members.

The private members are accessible only to their own class's members. On the other hand, public members are not only accessible to their own members, but also from outside the class. The members in the beginning of class without any access specifier are private by default. Hence, the first use of the keyword `private` in a class is optional. A class which is totally *private* is hidden from the external world and will not serve any useful purpose.

The following declaration illustrates the specification of a class called `student` having `roll_no` and name as its data members:

```
class student
{
    int roll_no;        // roll number
    char name[ 20 ];    // name of a student
    public:
```

```
            void setdata( int roll_no_in, char *name_in )
            {
               roll_no = roll_no_in;
               strcpy( name, name_in );
            }
            void outdata()
            {
               cout << "Roll No = " << roll_no << endl;
               cout << "Name = " << name << endl;
            }
      };
```

A class should be given some meaningful name, (for instance, `student`) reflecting the information it holds. The class name `student` becomes a new data type identifier, which satisfies the properties of *abstraction*; it can be used to define instances of `class` data type. The class `student` contains two data members and two member functions. The data members are private by default while both the member functions are public as specified. The member function `setdata()` can be used to assign values to the date members `roll_no` and `name`. The member function `outdata()` can be used for displaying the value of data members. The data members of the class `student` cannot be accessed by any other function except member functions of the `student` class. It is a general practice to declare data members as *private* and member functions as *public*. Three different notations for representation of the `student` class is shown in Figure 10.3.

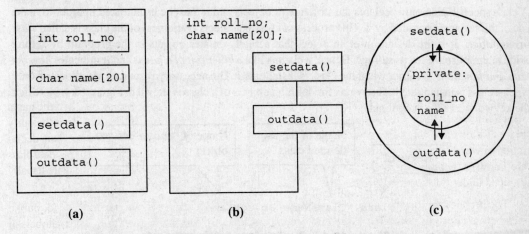

Figure 10.3:   Different representations of the class student

The name of data and member functions of a class can be the same as those in other classes; the members of different classes do not conflict with each other. Essentially, a class identifies all the data members associated with its declaration. The following example illustrates this concept:

```
      class Person
      {
         private:
            char name[20];
            int age;
            ......
      };
```

The data member name appears in the student class and in the Person class declarations, but their scope is limited to their respective classes. However, *more than one class with the same class-name in a program is an error, whether the declarations are identical or not*. A class can have multiple member functions (but not data members) with the same name as long as they differ in terms of *signature* ; this feature is known as *method overloading*.

Like structures, the data members of the class cannot be initialized during their declaration, but they can be initialized by its member functions as follows:

```
class GeoObject
{
    ....
    float x, y = 5;    // Error: data members cannot be initialized here
    void SetOrigin()   // set point to origin
    {
        x = y = 0.0;
    }
};
```

The data members x or y of the class GeoObject cannot be initialized at the point of their declaration, but, they can be initialized in member functions as indicated in the SetOrigin() member function.

10.3 Class Objects

A class specification only declares the structure of objects and it must be instantiated in order to make use of the services provided by it. This process of creating objects (variables) of the class is called *class instantiation*. It is the definition of an object that actually creates objects in the program by setting aside memory space for its storage. Hence, a class is like a *blueprint of a house* and it indicates *how the data and functions are used* when the class is instantiated. The necessary resources are allocated only when a class is instantiated. The syntax for defining objects of a class is shown in Figure 10.4. Note that the keyword class is optional.

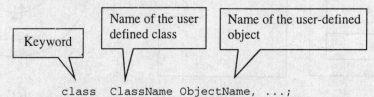

```
class  ClassName ObjectName, ...;
```

Figure 10.4: Syntax for creating objects

An example of class instantiation for creating objects is shown below:

```
class student s1;
    or
student s1;
```

It creates the object s1 of the class student. More than one object can be created with a single statement as follows:

```
class student s1, s2, s3, s4;
    or
student s1, s2, s3, s4;
```

It creates multiple objects of the class student.

The definition of an object is similar to that of a variable of any primitive data type. Objects can also be created by placing their names immediately after the closing brace like in the creation of the structure variables. Thus, the definition

```
class student
{
    ....
    ....
} s1, s2, s3, s4;
```

creates objects s1,s2,s3, and s4 of the class student. In C++, the convention of defining objects at the point of class specification is rarely followed; the user would like to define the objects as and when required, or at the point of their usage.

An object is a *conceptual entity* possessing the following properties:

◆ it is identifiable.
◆ it has features that span a local state space.
◆ it has operations that can change the status of the system locally, while also inducing operations in peer objects.
◆ it refers to a thing, either a tangible or a mental construct, which is identifiable by the users of the target system.

10.4 Accessing Class Members

Once an object of a class has been created, there must be a provision to access its members. This is achieved by using the member access operator, dot (.). The syntax for accessing members (data and functions) of a class is shown in Figure 10.5.

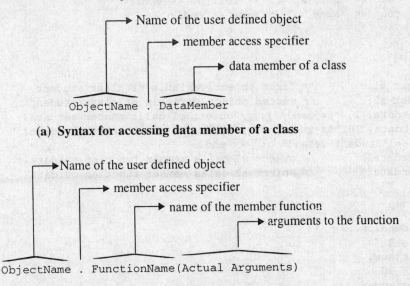

(a) Syntax for accessing data member of a class

(b) Syntax for accessing member function of a class

Figure 10.5: Syntax for accessing class members

If a member to be accessed is a function, then a pair of parentheses is to be added following the function name. The following statements access member functions of the object s1, which is an instance of the student class:

```
s1.setdata( 10, "Rajkumar" );
s1.outdata();
```

The program student.cpp illustrates the declaration of the class student with the operations on its objects.

```
// student.cpp: member functions defined inside the body of the student class
#include <iostream.h>
#include <string.h>
class student
{
  private:
      int roll_no;          // roll number
      char name[ 20 ];      // name of a student
  public:
      // initializing data members
      void setdata( int roll_no_in, char *name_in )
      {
         roll_no = roll_no_in;
         strcpy( name, name_in );
      }
      // display data members on the console screen
      void outdata()
      {
         cout << "Roll No = " << roll_no << endl;
         cout << "Name = " << name << endl;
      }
};
void main()
{
   student s1;         // first object/variable of class student
   student s2;         // second object/variable of class student
   s1.setdata( 1, "Tejaswi" ); // object s1 calls member setdata()
   s2.setdata( 10,"Rajkumar" ); //object s2 calls member setdata()
   cout << "Student details..." << endl;
   s1.outdata();       // object s1 calls member function outdata()
   s2.outdata();       // object s2 calls member function outdata()
}
```

Run
```
Student details...
Roll No = 1
Name = Tejaswi
Roll No = 10
Name = Rajkumar
```

The various actions performed on objects of the class student are portrayed in Figure 10.6 with the client object accessing the services provided by the class student.

In main(), the statements

```
student s1;      // first object/variable of class student
student s2;      // second object/variable of class student
```

create two objects called s1 and s2 of the student class. The statements

```
s1.setdata( 1, "Tejaswi" ); //object s1 calls member function setdata
s2.setdata( 10,"Rajkumar" ); //object s2 calls member function setdata
```

initialize the data members of the objects s1 and s2. The object s1's data member roll_no is assigned 1 and name is assigned Tejaswi. Similarly, the object s2's data member roll_no is assigned 10 and name is assigned Rajkumar.

Instance of the class student

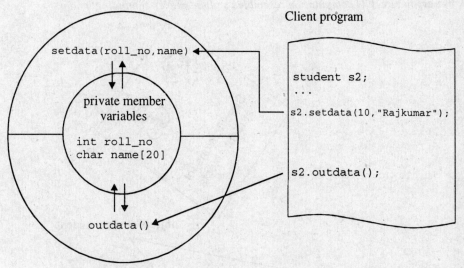

Figure 10.6:   Student object and member access

The statements

```
s1.outdata();      // object s1 calls member function outdata
s2.outdata();      // object s2 calls member function outdata
```

call their member outdata() to display the contents of data members namely, roll_no and name of student objects s1 and s2 in succession. Thus, the two objects s1 and s2 of the class student have different data values as shown in Figure 10.7.

Client-Server Model

In conventional programming languages, *a function is invoked on a piece of data* (function-driven communication), whereas in an OOPL (object-oriented programming language), *a message is sent to an object* (message-driven communication) i.e., conventional programming is based on *function abstraction* whereas, object oriented programming is based on *data abstraction*.

The object accessing its class members resembles a client-server model. A client seeks a service whereas, a server provides services requested by a client. In the above example, the class student resembles a *server* whereas, the objects of the class `student` resemble *clients*. They make calls to the server by sending messages. In the statement

    s2.setdata(10, "Rajkumar"); // object s2 calls member function setdata

the object `s2` sends the message `setdata` to the server with the parameters `10` and `Rajkumar`. As a server, the member function `setdata()` of the class `student` performs the operation of setting the data members according to the messages sent to it. Similarly, the statement

    s2.outdata();

can be visualized as sending message (`outdata`) to object `s2`'s class to display object contents. The term message is commonly used in OOPs terminology to provide an illusion of objects as discrete entities, and a user communicates with them by calling their member functions as shown in Figure 10.8. Thus, by its very nature, *OO computation resembles a client-server computing model*.

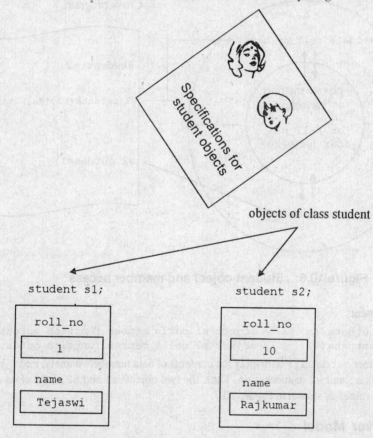

objects of class student

    student s1;

roll_no
1

name
Tejaswi

    student s2;

roll_no
10

name
Rajkumar

Figure 10.7:   Two objects of the class student

In OOPs, the process of programming involves the following steps:

- Creation of classes for defining objects and their behaviors.
- Creation of class objects; class declaration acts like a blueprint for which physical resources are not allocated.
- Establishment of communication among objects through message passing.

Similar to the real world objects, OO objects also have a life cycle. They can be created and destroyed *automatically* whenever necessary. Communication between the objects can take place as long as they are alive (active). Communication among the objects takes place in the same way as people pass messages to one another. The concept of programming with *message passing model* is an efficient way of modeling real-world problems on computers.

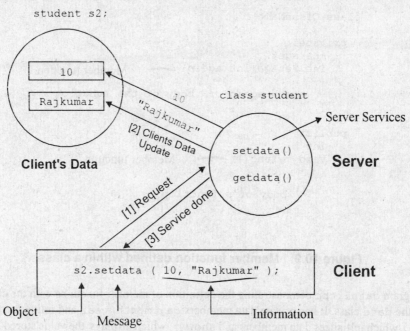

Figure 10.8:   Client-Server model for message communication

A message for an object is interpreted as a request for execution of a procedure. The subroutine or function is invoked soon after receiving the message and the desired results are generated within an object. It comprises the name of an object, the name of a function, and the information to be sent to an object.

10.5 Defining Member Functions

The data members of a class must be declared within the body of the class, whereas the member functions of the class can be defined in any one of the following ways:

- Inside the class specification
- Outside the class specification

The syntax of a member function definition changes depending on whether it is defined inside or outside the class specification. However, irrespective of the location of their definition (inside or outside a class), the member function must perform the same operation. Therefore, the code inside the function body would be identical in both the cases. The compiler treats these two types of function definitions in a different manner.

Member Functions Inside the Class Body

The syntax for specifying a member function declaration is similar to a normal function definition except that it is enclosed within the body of a class and is shown in Figure 10.9. All the member functions defined within the body of a class are treated as inline by default except those members having looping statements such as for, while, etc., and it also depends on compilers.

```
class ClassName
{
  private:
     int age;
     int SetAge(int agein)  ———   Member function
     {
        age = agein; // body of the function
     }
        . . .
  public:
     int b;
     void myfunc()  ———   Member function
     {

        // body of a function

     }
};
```

Figure 10.9:   Member function defined within a class

The program date1.cpp demonstrating the definition of member functions with the class specification of the date class. It has private data members day, month, year and inline member functions, set() which initializes data members and show(), which displays the value stored in the data members.

```
// date1.cpp: date class with member functions defined inside a class
#include <iostream.h>
class date
{
   private:
      int  day;
      int month;
      int year;
   public:
      void set( int DayIn, int MonthIn, int YearIn )
      {
         day = DayIn;
         month = MonthIn;
         year = YearIn;
      }
      void show()
      {
         cout << day << "-" << month << "-" << year << endl;
      }
};
```

```
void main()
{
   date d1, d2, d3;      // date objects d1, d2, and d3 creation
   // set date of births
   d1.set( 26, 3, 1958 );
   d2.set( 14, 4, 1971 );
   d3.set( 1, 9, 1973 );
   cout << "Birth Date of the First Author: ";
   d1.show();
   cout << "Birth Date of the Second Author: ";
   d2.show();
   cout << "Birth Date of the Third Author: ";
   d3.show();
}
```

Run

```
Birth Date of the First Author: 26-3-1958
Birth Date of the Second Author: 14-4-1971
Birth Date of the Third Author: 1-4-1972
```

Member functions defined inside a class are considered as *inline* functions by default thus, offering both advantages and limitations of inline functions. However, in some implementations, member functions having loop instructions such as for, while, do..while, etc., are not treated as inline functions. The compiler produces a warning message if an attempt is made to define inline member functions with loop instructions. Normally, functions with a small body are defined inside the class specification. In the above student class specification, the functions set() and show() are treated as *inline* functions by the compiler.

Member Functions Outside the Class Body

Another method of defining a member function is to declare *function prototype* within the body of a class and then define it outside the body of a class. Since the functions defined outside the class specification have the same syntax as normal functions, there should be a mechanism of binding the functions to the class to which they belong. This is done by using the *scope resolution operator*(::). It acts as an *identity-label* to inform the compiler, the class to which the function belongs. The general format of a member function definition is shown in Figure 10.10. This form of syntax can be used with members defined either inside or outside the body of a class, but member functions defined outside the body of a class must follow this syntax.

```
class ClassName
{
   . . . .
      ReturnType MemberFunction(arguments);  ———  function prototype
   . . . .                     ┌──► user defined class name
};                   ┌─────────┘  ┌──► Scope resolution operator
                     └────────────┘
ReturnType ClassName :: MemberFunction ( arguments )
{
   // body of the function
}
```

Figure 10.10:   Member function definition outside a class declaration

The label ClassName:: informs the compiler that the function MemberFunction is the member of the class ClassName. The scope of the function is restricted to only the objects and other members of the class. The program date1.cpp having member functions inside the body of the date class is modified to date2.cpp which defines member functions outside the body of a class.

```cpp
// date2.cpp: date class with member functions defined outside the class body
#include <iostream.h>
class date
{
   private:
      int day;
      int month;
      int year;
   public:
      void set( int DayIn, int MonthIn, int YearIn ); //declaration
      void show();     // declaration
};
void date::set( int DayIn, int MonthIn, int YearIn )   //definition
{
   day = DayIn;
   month = MonthIn;
   year = YearIn;
}
void date::show()      // definition
{
   cout << day << "-" << month << "-" << year << endl;
}
void main()
{
   date d1, d2, d3;      // date objects d1, d2, and d3 creation
   // set date of births
   d1.set( 26, 3, 1958 );
   d2.set( 14, 4, 1971 );
   d3.set( 1, 9, 1973 );
   cout << "Birth Date of the First Author: ";
   d1.show();
   cout << "Birth Date of the Second Author: ";
   d2.show();
   cout << "Birth Date of the Third Author: ";
   d3.show();
}
```

Run

```
Birth Date of the First Author: 26-3-1958
Birth Date of the Second Author: 14-4-1971
Birth Date of the Third Author: 1-4-1972
```

Consider the member functions set and show defined in the above program:

```cpp
void date::set( int DayIn, int MonthIn, int YearIn )
{
   day = DayIn;
   ....
}
```

```
void date::show()
{
    cout << day << "-" << month << "-" << year << endl;
}
```

In the above definitions, the label `date::` informs the compiler that the functions `set` and `show` are the members of the `date` class. It can access all the members (date and functions) of the `date` class and also global data items and functions if necessary. Some of the special characteristics of the member functions are the following.

- A program can have several classes and they can have member functions with the same name. The ambiguity of the compiler in deciding *which function belongs to which class* can be resolved by the use of membership label (`ClassName::`), the scope resolution operator.
- Private members of a class, can be accessed by all the members of the class, whereas non-member functions are not allowed to access. However, friend functions (discussed later) can access them.
- Member functions of the same class can access all other members of their own class without the use of dot operator.
- Member functions defined as `public` act as an interface between the service provider (server) and the service seeker (client).
- A class can *have* multiple member functions with the same name as long as they differ in terms of argument specification (data type or number of arguments).

10.6 Outside Member Functions as `inline`

OOP provides feature of separating policy from the mechanism. Policy provides guidelines for defining specification whereas mechanism provides guidelines for design and implementation. It is a good practice to declare the class specification first and then implement class member functions outside the class specification. The inline member functions are a group of member functions that decrease the overhead involved in accessing member functions and make the usage of member functions more efficient. An *inline member function* is treated like a *macro*; any call to this function in a program is replaced by the function itself. This is called *inline expansion*. By this, the overhead incurred in the transfer of control by the function call and the function return statements are cut down. Note that inline functions are also called *open subroutines* since they get expanded at the point of a call whereas, normal functions are called *closed subroutines* since only call to a function exists at the point of their call. A member function prototype defined within a class is declared without any special keyword.

C++ treats all the member functions that are defined within a class as *inline* functions and those defined outside as *non-inline* (outline). Member function declared outside the class declaration can be made inline by prefixing the `inline` to its definition as shown in Figure 10.11.

Keyword : indicates function defined outside a class body is inline

```
inline ReturnType ClassName :: FunctionName(arguments)
{
    // body of Inline function
}
```

Figure 10.11:   Inline function definition outside the class declaration

The keyword `inline` acts as a function qualifier. The modified program of `date2.cpp` is listed in `date3.cpp`, making all the member functions of the class `date` as inline member functions.

```
// date3.cpp: date class with member functions defined outside as inline
#include <iostream.h>
class date
{                              // specifies a structure
   private:
      int day;
      int month;
      int year;
   public:
      void set( int DayIn, int MonthIn, int YearIn ); //declaration
      void show();  // declaration
};
inline void date::set( int DayIn, int MonthIn, int YearIn )
{
   day = DayIn;
   month = MonthIn;
   year = YearIn;
}
inline void date::show()   // definition
{
   cout << day << "-" << month << "-" << year << endl;
}
void main()
{
   date d1, d2, d3;     // date objects d1, d2, and d3 creation
   // set date of births
   d1.set( 26, 3, 1958 );
   d2.set( 14, 4, 1971 );
   d3.set( 1, 4, 1972 );
   cout << "Birth Date of the First Author: ";
   d1.show();
   cout << "Birth Date of the Second Author: ";
   d2.show();
   cout << "Birth Date of the Third Author: ";
   d3.show();
}
```

Run

```
Birth Date of the First Author: 26-3-1958
Birth Date of the Second Author: 14-4-1971
Birth Date of the Third Author: 1-4-1972
```

In the above program, the member functions `set()` and `show()` of the class `date` are considered as inline member functions defined outside the body of the class `date`. They are explicitly defined as inline functions with the use of the *inline* qualifier. The use of the `inline` qualifier in the statements

```
      inline void date::set( int DayIn, int MonthIn, int YearIn )
      inline void date::show()
```

inform the compiler to treat the member functions set and show as inline functions. The method of invoking inline member functions is the same as those of the normal functions. In main(), the statements

```
d1.set( 26, 3, 1958 );
d2.show();
```

will be replaced by the function itself since the function is an inline function. Note that, the inline qualifier is tagged to the inline member function at the point of its definition.

The feature of inline member functions is useful only when they are short. Declaring a function having many statements as inline is not advisable, since it will make the object code of a program very large. However, some C++ compilers judge (determine) whether a given function can be appropriately sized to *inline expanded*. If the function is too large to be expanded, it will not be treated as inline. In this case, declaring a function inline will not guarantee that the compiler will consider it as an inline function.

When to Use inline Functions

The following are simple thumb rules in deciding as to when inline functions should be used:

- In general, inline functions should not be used.
- Defining inline functions can be considered once a fully developed and tested program runs too slowly and shows *bottlenecks* in certain functions. A *profiler* (which runs the program and determines where most of the execution time is spent) can be used in deciding such an optimization.
- Inline functions can be used when member functions consist of one very simple statement such as the return statement in date::getday(), which can be implemented as follows:

```
inline int date::getday()    // definition
{
    return day;
}
```

- It is only useful to implement an inline function if the time spent during a function call is more compared to the function body execution time. An example, where an inline function has no effect at all is the following:

```
inline void date::show()    // definition
{
    cout << day << "-" << month << "-" << year << endl;
}
```

The above function, which is presumed to be a member of the class date for the sake of argument, contains only one statement; but takes relatively a long time to execute. In general, functions which perform input and output operation spend a considerable amount of time. The effect of conversion of the function show() to inline would lead to reduction in execution time.

Inline functions have one disadvantage: the actual code is inserted by the compiler and therefore it should be known at compile-time. Hence, an inline function cannot be located in a run-time library. Practically, an inline function is placed near the declaration of a class, usually in the same header file. It results in a header file having the declaration of a class with its implementation visible to the user.

10.7 Accessing Member Functions within the Class

A member function of a class is accessed by the objects of that class using the dot operator. A member function of a class can call any other member function of its own class irrespective of its privilege and this situation is called *nesting* of member functions. The method for calling member functions of one's own class is similar to calling any other standard (library) functions as illustrated in the program nesting.cpp.

```cpp
// nesting.cpp: A member function accessing another member function
#include <iostream.h>
class NumberPairs
{
    int num1, num2;      // private by default
    public:
        void read()
        {
            cout << "Enter First Number: ";
            cin >> num1;
            cout << "Enter Second Number: ";
            cin >> num2;
        }
        int max()          // member function
        {
            if( num1 > num2 )
                return num1;
            else
                return num2;
        }
        // Nesting of member function
        void ShowMax()
        {
            // calls member function max()
            cout << "Maximum = " << max();
        }
};
void main()
{
    NumberPairs n1;
    n1.read();
    n1.ShowMax();
}
```

Run

```
Enter First Number: 5
Enter Second Number: 10
Maximum = 10
```

The class NumberPairs has the member function ShowMax() having the statement

```cpp
cout << "Maximum = " << max();
```

It calls the member function max() to compute the maximum of class data members num1 and num2.

10.8 Data Hiding

Data is hidden inside a class, so that it cannot be accessed even by mistake by any function outside the class, which is a key feature of OOP. C++ imposes a restriction to access both the data and functions of a class. It is achieved·by declaring the data part as *private*. All the data and functions defined in a class are private by default. But for the sake of clarity, the items are declared as private explicitly. Normally, data members are declared as *private* and member functions are declared as *public*. This is illustrated in the program part.cpp.

```cpp
// part.cpp: class hiding vehicle details
#include <iostream.h>
class part
{
   private:            // private members
      int ModelNum;   // model number
      int PartNum;    // part number
      float cost;     // cost of a part
   public:             // public members
      void SetPart( int mn, int pn, float c )
      {
         ModelNum = mn;
         PartNum = pn;
         cost = c;
      }
      void ShowPart()
      {
         cout << "Model: " << ModelNum << endl;
         cout << "Number: " << PartNum << endl;
         cout << "Cost: " << cost << endl;
      }
};
void main()
{
   part p1, p2;   // objects p1 and p2 of class part are defined
   // Values are passed to their object
   p1.SetPart( 1996, 23, 1250.55 );
   p2.SetPart( 2000, 243, 2354.75 );
   // Each object display their values
   cout << "First Part Details ..." << endl;
   p1.ShowPart();
   cout << "Second Part Details ..." << endl;
   p2.ShowPart();
}
```

Run

```
First Part Details ...
Model: 1996
Number: 23
Cost: 1250.550049
Second Part Details ...
Model: 2000
```

```
Number: 243
Cost: 2354.75
```

In the above program, the data fields ModelNum, PartNum, and cost of the class part cannot be accessed by direct references using p1.ModelNum, p1.PartNum, and p1.cost respectively. When a class is used, its declaration must be available. Thus, a user of the class is presented with a description of the class. The internal details of the class, which are not essential to the user are not presented to him. This is the concept of *information hiding* or *data encapsulation*. As far as the user is concerned, the knowledge of accessible data and member functions of a class is enough. These interfaces, usually called the *user interface methods*, specify their abstracted functionality. Thus, to the user, a class is like a black box with a characterized behavior.

The purpose of data encapsulation is to prevent accidental modification of information of a class. It is achieved by imposing a set of rules—the manner in which a class is to be manipulated and the data and functions of the class can be accessed. The following are the three kinds of users of a class:

◆ A class member, which can access all the data members and functions of its class.
◆ Generic users, which define the instance of a class.
◆ Derived classes, which can access members based on privileges.

Each user has different access privileges to the object. A class differentiates between access privileges by partitioning its contents and associating each one of them with any one of the following keywords:

◆ private
◆ public
◆ protected

These keywords are called *access-control specifiers*. All the members that follow a keyword (upto another keyword) belong to that type. If no keyword is specified, then the members are assumed to have private privilege. The following specification of a class illustrates these concepts:

```
class PiggyBank
{
    int Money;                       // Private by default
    void Display()                   // Private by default
    {
        ...
    }
    private:                         // Private by declaration
        int AccNumber;
    public:
        int code;                    // Public
        void SetData(int a, int b)   // Public
        {
            ...
        }
    protected:
        int PolicyCode;              // Protected
        void GetPolicyCode()         // Protected
        {
            ...
        }
};
```

In the above declaration, the members `Money`, `AccNumber`, and `Display()` will be of type `private`; the members `code` and `SetData()` will be of type `public`; and the members `PolicyCode` and `GetData()` will be of type `protected`.

Data hiding is mainly designed to protect well-intentioned programmers from honest mistakes. It protects access to the data according to the design decision made while designing a class. Programmers who really want to figure out a way to access highly protected data such as private, will find it hard to do so even by accident. *There are mechanisms to access even private data using friends, pointer to members, etc. from outside the class.*

Private Members

The private members of a class have strict access control. Only the member functions of the same class can access these members. The private members of a class are inaccessible outside the class, thus, providing a mechanism for preventing accidental modifications of the data members. It is illustrated in Figure 10.12. Strictly speaking, information hiding is implemented only partially, the private members can still be accessed. Access control in C++ has the objective of reducing the likelihood of bugs and enhancing consistency. Since the basic intention of declaring a class is to use it in a program, the class should have atleast one member that is not private.

```
class Person
{                          → Note: colon here
    private :    ━━━━━     access specifier
    // private members
    .....
    int age;     ━━━━━     private data
    int getage(); ━━━━━    private function
    ....
};

Person p1;
a=p1.age;   ✘ cannot access private data
p1.getage(); ✘ cannot access private function
```

Figure 10.12: Private members accessibility

The following example illustrates the situation when all the members of a class are declared as private:

```
class Inaccessible
{
    int x;
    void Display()
    {
        cout << "\nData = " << x;
    }
};
void main()
{
    Inaccessible obj1;      // Creating an object.
    obj1.x = 5;             // Error: Invalid access.
    obj1.Display();         // Error: Invalid access.
}
```

The class having all the members with private access control is of no use; there is no means available to communicate with the external world. Therefore, classes of the above type will not contribute anything to the program.

Protected Members

The access control of the protected members is similar to that of private members and has more significance in inheritance. Hence, detailed discussion on this is postponed to the chapter on *Inheritance*. Access control of protected members is shown in Figure 10.13.

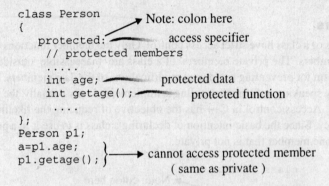

```
class Person              Note: colon here
{
    protected:            access specifier
    // protected members
    .....
    int age;              protected data
    int getage();         protected function
    ....
};
Person p1;
a=p1.age;          }
p1.getage();       }      cannot access protected member
                              ( same as private )
```

Figure 10.13:   Protected members accessibility

Public Members

The members of a class, which are to be visible (accessible) outside the class, should be declared in *public* section. All data members and functions declared in the public section of the class can be accessed without any restriction from anywhere in the program, either by functions that belong to the class or by those external to the class. Accessibility control of public members is shown in Figure 10.14.

```
class Person
{                         Note: colon here
    public:               access specifier
    // public members
    .....
    int age;              public data
    int getage();         public function
    ....
};
Person p1;
a=p1.age;   ✔ can access public data
p1.getage();  ✔ can access public function
```

Figure 10.14:   Public members accessibility

10.9 Access Boundary of Objects Revisited

Hierarchy of access, in which privilege code can see the whole structure of an object, but external code can see only the public features. The access-limit of members within a class, or from objects of a class is shown in Table 10.1 and Figure 10.15.

Access Specifier	Accessible to	
	Own class Members	Objects of a Class
`private:`	Yes	No
`protected:`	Yes	No
`public:`	Yes	Yes

Table 10.1: Visibility of class members

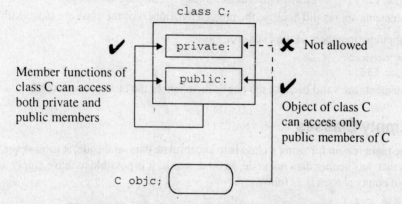

Figure 10.15: Class member accessibility

The following declaration of a class illustrates the visibility limit of the various class members:

```
class MyClass
{
    private:
        int a;
        void f1()
        {
            //can refer to data members a, b, c and functions f1, f2, and f3
        }
    protected:
        int b;
        void f2()
        {
            //can refer to data member a, b, c and functions f1, f2, and f3
        }
    public:
        int c;
        void f3()
        {
            //can refer to data member a, b, c and functions f1, f2, and f3
        }
};
```

Consider the statements

```
MyClass objx; // objx is an object of class MyClass
int d;        // temporary variable d
```

They define an object `objx` and an integer variable `d`. The accessibility of members of the class `MyClass` through the object `objx` is illustrated in the following section.

1. Accessing private members of the class `MyClass`:

```
d = objx.a; // Error: 'MyClass::a' is not accessible
objx.f1();  // Error: 'MyClass::f1()' is not accessible
```

Both the statements are invalid because the private members of the class are inaccessible.

2. Accessing protected members of the class `MyClass`:

```
d = objx.b; // Error: 'MyClass::b' is not accessible
objx.f2();  // Error: 'MyClass::f2()' is not accessible
```

Both the statements are invalid because the protected members of the class are inaccessible.

3. Accessing public members of the class `MyClass`:

```
d = objx.c; // OK
objx.f3();  // OK
```

Both the statements are valid because the public members of the class are accessible.

10.10 Empty Classes

Although the main reason for using a class is to encapsulate data and code, it is however, possible to have a class that has neither data nor code. In other words, it is possible to have empty classes. The declaration of empty classes is as follows:

```
class xyz { };
class Empty { };
class abc
{
};
```

During the initial stages of development of a project, some of the classes are either not fully identified, or not fully implemented. In such cases, they are implemented as empty classes during the first few implementations of the project. Such empty classes are also called as *stubs*. The significant usage of empty classes can be found with exception handling; it is illustrated in the chapter *Exception Handling*.

10.11 Pointers within a Class

The size of data members such as vectors when defined using arrays must be known at compile time itself. In this case, vector size cannot be increased or decreased irrespective of the requirement. This inflexibility of arrays can be overcome by having a data member for storing vector elements whose size can be dynamically changed during runtime. The program `vector.cpp` facilitates the creation of the vector of varying size during runtime. It has a pointer member instead of an array member. The size of the vector is varied by creating an object whose vector size is known only at runtime.

```
// vector.cpp: vector class with array dynamically allocated
#include <iostream.h>
class vector
{
```

```
      int *v;  // pointer to a vector
      int sz;  // size of a vector
   public:
      void VectorSize( int size )  // allocate memory dynamically
      {
         sz = size;
         v = new int[ size ];    // dynamically allocate vector
      }
      void read();
      void show_sum();
      void release()    // release memory allocated
      {
         delete v;
      }
};
void vector::read()
{
   for( int i = 0; i < sz; i++ )
   {
      cout << "Enter vector[ " << i << " ] ? ";
      cin >> v[i];
   }
}
void vector::show_sum()
{
   int sum = 0;
   for( int i = 0; i < sz; i++ )
      sum += v[i];
   cout << "Vector Sum = " << sum;
}
void main()
{
   vector v1;
   int count;
   cout << "How many elements are there in vector: ";
   cin >> count;
   v1.VectorSize( count );    // set vector size
   v1.read();
   v1.show_sum();
   v1.release();              // free vector resources
}
```

Run

```
How many elements are there in vector: 5
Enter vector[ 0 ] ? 1
Enter vector[ 1 ] ? 2
Enter vector[ 2 ] ? 3
Enter vector[ 3 ] ? 4
Enter vector[ 4 ] ? 5
Vector Sum = 15
```

In main(), the statement
```
    vector v1;
```
creates an object v1 of the class vector and the statement
```
    v1.VectorSize( count );    // set vector size
```
allocates the required amount (specified by the parameter count) of memory, dynamically for vector elements storage. The last statement
```
    v1.release();
```
releases the memory allocated to the pointer data member v of the vector class. The operation of dynamic allocation of memory to data members can be at best realized by defining *constructor* and *destructor* functions. (More details can be found in the chapter *Object Initialization and Cleanup*).

10.12 Passing Objects as Arguments

It is possible to have functions which accept objects of a class as arguments, just as there are functions which accept other variables as arguments. Like any other data type, an object can be passed as an argument to a function by the following ways:

- pass-by-value, a copy of the entire object is passed to the function
- pass-by-reference, only the address of the object is passed implicitly to the function
- pass-by-pointer, the address of the object is passed explicitly to the function

In the case of *pass-by-value*, a copy of the object is passed to the function and any modifications made to the object inside the function is not reflected in the object used to call the function. Whereas, in *pass-by-reference* or *pointer*, an address of the object is passed to the function and any changes made to the object inside the function is reflected in the actual object. The parameter passing by reference or pointer is more efficient since, only the address of the object is passed and not a copy of the entire object.

Passing Objects by Value

The program distance.cpp illustrates the use of objects as function arguments in *pass-by-value* mechanism. It performs the addition of distance in feet and inches format.

```
// distance.cpp: distance manipulation in feet and inches
#include <iostream.h>
class distance
{
  private:
    float feet;
    float inches;
  public:
    void init( float ft, float in )
    {
      feet = ft;
      inches = in;
    }
    void read()
    {
      cout << "Enter feet: ";   cin >> feet;
      cout << "Enter inches: "; cin >> inches;
    }
```

```
        void show()
        {
           cout << feet << "-" << inches << '\"';
        }
        void add( distance d1, distance d2 )
        {
           feet = d1.feet + d2.feet;
           inches = d1.inches + d2.inches;
           if( inches >= 12.0 )
            {
                // 1 foot = 12.0 inches
                feet = feet + 1.0;
                inches = inches - 12.0;
            }
        }
};
void main()
{
    distance d1, d2, d3;
    d2.init( 11.0, 6.25 );
    d1.read();
    cout << "d1 = ";  d1.show();
    cout << "\nd2 = ";   d2.show();
    d3.add( d1, d2 ); // d3 = d1 + d2
    cout << "\nd3 = d1+d2 = ";  d3.show();
}
```

Run

```
Enter feet: 12.0
Enter inches: 7.25
d1 = 12'-7.25"
d2 = 11'-6.25"
d3 = d1+ d2 = 24'-1.5"
```

In main(), the statement

```
        d3.add( d1, d2 ); // d3 = d1 + d2
```

invokes the member function add() of the class distance by the object d3, with the object d1 and d2 as arguments. It can directly access the feet and inches variables of d3. The members of d1 and d2 can be accessed only by using the dot operator (like d1.feet and d1.inches) within the add() member. Figure 10.16 shows the two objects d1 and d2 being added together with the result stored in the recipient object d3. Any modification made to the data members of the objects d1 and d2 are not visible to the caller's actual parameters.

Passing Objects by Reference

Accessibility of the objects passed by reference is similar to those passed by value. Modifications carried out on such objects in the called function will also be reflected in the calling function. The method of passing objects as reference parameters to a function is illustrated in the program account.cpp. Given the account numbers and the balance of two accounts, this program transfers a specified sum from one of these accounts to the other and then, updates the balance in both the accounts.

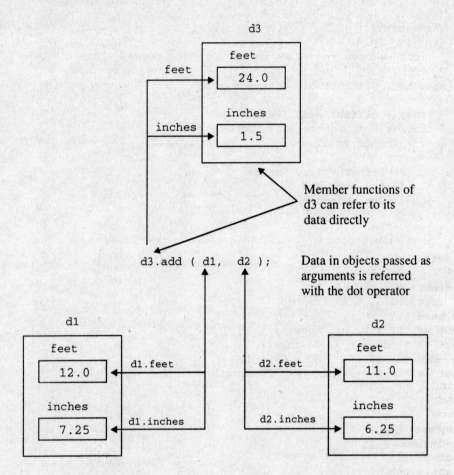

Figure 10.16:   Objects of the distance class as parameters

```cpp
// account.cpp: passing objects as parameters to functions
#include<iostream.h>
class AccClass
{
   private:                 // class data members
      int accno;
      float balance;
   public:                  // class function members
      void getdata()
      {
         cout << "Enter the account number for acc1 object: ";
         cin >> accno;
         cout << "Enter the balance: ";
         cin >> balance;
      }
```

```
    void setdata( int accIn )
    {
        accno = accIn;
        balance = 0;
    }
    void setdata( int accIn, float balanceIn )
    {
        accno = accIn;
        balance = balanceIn;
    }
    void display()
    {
        cout << "Account number is: " << accno << endl;
        cout << "Balance is: " << balance << endl;
    }
    void MoneyTransfer( AccClass & acc, float amount );
};
// acc1.MoneyTransfer( acc2, 100 ),transfers 100 rupees from acc1 to acc2
void AccClass::MoneyTransfer( AccClass & acc, float amount )
{
    balance = balance - amount;    // deduct money from source
    acc.balance = acc.balance + amount; // add money to destination
}
void main()
{
    int trans_money;
    AccClass acc1, acc2, acc3;
    acc1.getdata();
    acc2.setdata( 10 );
    acc3.setdata( 20, 750.5 );
    cout << "Account Information..." << endl;
    acc1.display();
    acc2.display();
    acc3.display();
    cout << "How much money is to be transferred from acc3 to acc1: ";
    cin >> trans_money;
    acc3.MoneyTransfer(acc1,trans_money); //transfers money from acc3 to acc1
    cout << "Updated Information about accounts..." << endl;
    acc1.display();
    acc2.display();
    acc3.display();
}
```

Run

```
Enter the account number for acc1 object: 1
Enter the balance: 100
Account Information...
Account number is: 1
Balance is: 100
Account number is: 10
Balance is: 0
```

```
Account number is: 20
Balance is: 750.5
How much money is to be transferred from acc3 to acc1: 200
Updated Information about accounts...
Account number is: 1
Balance is: 300
Account number is: 10
Balance is: 0
Account number is: 20
Balance is: 550.5
```

In main(), the statement

```
acc3.MoneyTransfer( acc1, trans_money );
```

transfers the object acc1 by reference to the member function MoneyTransfer(). It is to be noted that when the MoneyTransfer() is invoked with acc1 as the object parameter, the data members of acc3 are accessed without the use of the class member access operator, while the data members of acc1 are accessed by using their names in association with the name of the object to which they belong. An object can also be passed to a non-member function of the class and that can have access to the public members only through the objects passed as arguments to it.

Passing Objects by Pointer

The members of objects passed by pointer are accessed by using the -> operator, and they have similar effect as those passed by value. The above program requires the following changes if parameters are to be passed by pointer:

1. The prototype of the member function MoneyTransfer() has to be changed to:

```
void MoneyTransfer( AccClass * acc, float amount );
```

2. The definition of the member function MoneyTransfer() has to be changed to:

```
void AccClass::MoneyTransfer( AccClass & acc, float amount )
{
    balance = balance - amount;    // deduct money from source
    acc->balance = acc->balance + amount; // add money to destination
}
```

3. The statement invoking the member function MoneyTransfer() has to be changed to:

```
acc3.MoneyTransfer( &acc1, trans_money );
```

10.13 Returning Objects from Functions

Similar to sending objects as parameters to functions, it is also possible to return objects from functions. The syntax used is similar to that of returning variables from functions. The return type of the function is declared as the return object type. It is illustrated in the program complex.cpp.

```
// complex.cpp: Addition of Complex Numbers, class complex as data type
#include <iostream.h>
#include <math.h>
class complex
{
  private:
    float real;    // real part of complex number
    float imag;    // imaginary part of complex number
```

```
    public:
        void getdata()
        {
            cout << "Real Part ? ";
            cin >> real;
            cout << "Imag Part ? ";
            cin >> imag;
        }
        void outdata( char *msg )      // display number in x+iy form
        {
            cout << msg << real;
            if( imag < 0 )
                cout << "-i";
            else
                cout << "+i";
            cout << fabs(imag) << endl;
        }
        complex add( complex c2 );    // addition of complex numbers
};
complex complex::add( complex c2 )  // add default and c2 objects
{
    complex temp;                     // object temp of complex class
    temp.real = real + c2.real;       // add real parts
    temp.imag = imag + c2.imag;       // add imaginary parts
    return( temp );                   // return complex object
}
void main()
{
    complex c1, c2, c3;        // c1, c2, and c2 are objects of complex
    cout << "Enter Complex Number c1 .." << endl;
    c1.getdata();
    cout << "Enter Complex Number c2 .." << endl;
    c2.getdata();
    c3 = c1.add( c2 );         // add c1 and c2 assign to c3
    c3.outdata( "c3 = c1.add( c2 ): " );
}
```

Run

```
Enter Complex Number c1 ..
Real Part ? 1.5
Imag Part ? 2
Enter Complex Number c2 ..
Real Part ? 3
Imag Part ? -4.3
c3 = c1.add( c2 ): 4.5-i2.3
```

In main(), the statement

```
        c3 = c1.add( c2 );       // add c1 and c2 assign to c3
```

invokes the function add() of the class complex by passing the object c2 as a parameter. The statement in this function,

```
        return( temp );          // return complex object
```

returns the object temp as a return object.

10.14 Friend Functions and Friend Classes

The concept of encapsulation and data hiding dictate that non-member functions should not be allowed to access an object's private and protected members. The policy is, *if you are not a member you cannot get it*. Sometimes this feature leads to considerable inconvenience in programming. Imagine that the user wants a function to operate on objects of two different classes. At such times, it is required to allow functions outside a class to access and manipulate the private members of the class. In C++, this is achieved by using the concept of *friends*.

One of the convenient and a controversial feature of C++ is allowing non-member functions to access even the private members of a class using friend functions or friend classes. It permits a function or all the functions of another class to access a different class's private members. The accessibility of class members in various forms is shown in Figure 10.17.

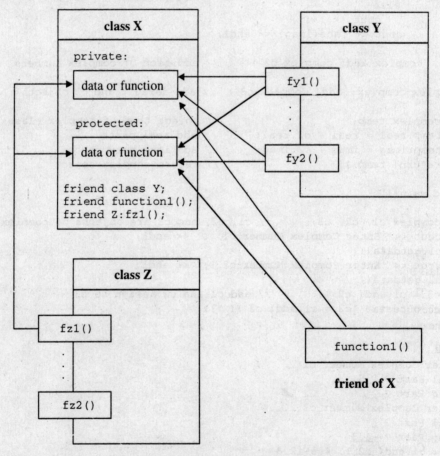

Figure 10.17: Class members accessibility in various forms

The function declaration must be prefixed by the keyword `friend` whereas the function definition must not. The function could be defined anywhere in the program similar to any normal C++ function. The functions that are declared with the keyword `friend` are called *friend functions*. A function can be a friend to multiple classes. A friend function possesses the following special characteristics:

✓

- The scope of a friend function is not limited to the class in which it has been declared as a friend.
- A friend function cannot be called using the object of that class; it is not in the scope of the class. It can be invoked like a normal function without the use of any object.
- Unlike class member functions, it cannot access the class members directly. However, it can use the object and the dot operator with each member name to access both the private and public members.
- It can be either declared in the private part or the public part of a class without affecting its meaning.

Consider the following skeleton of the program code to illustrate friend functions.

```
class A
{
    private:
        int value; // value is private data
    public:
        void setval( int v )
        { value = v;    }
        int getval ()
        { return( value );   }
};
// function decrement: tries to alter A's private data
void decrement( A &a )
{
    a.value--;       // Error:: not allowed to access private data
}
class B              // class B: tries to access A's private data
{
    public:
        void touch (A &a)
        { a.value++; }
};
```

This code will not compile, since the function decrement() and the function touch() of the class B attempt to access a private data member of the class A.

The function can be allowed explicitly to access A's data and class B members can be allowed to access the class A's data. To accomplish this, the offending classless function decrement() and the class B are declared to be friends of the class A as illustrated in the following code:

```
class A
{
    public:
        friend class B;  // B is my friend, I trust him
        friend void decrement (A &what);  // decrement() is also a good pal

};
```

Concerning friendship between classes, the following should be noted:

- Friendship is not mutual by default. That is, once B is declared as a friend of A, this does not give A the right to access the private members of the class B.
- Friendship, when applied to program design, is an escape mechanism which creates exceptions to the rule of data hiding. Usage of friend classes should, therefore, be limited to those cases where it is absolutely essential.

Bridging Classes with Friend Functions

Consider a situation of operating on objects of two different classes. In such a situation, friend functions can be used to bridge the two classes. It is illustrated in the program `friend1.cpp`. The syntax of defining friend non-member function is shown in Figure 10.18.

```
class Testclass
{
    int num1, num2;
    ......
    public:
        // public members
                              → keyword
        friend  float  sum ( Testclass obj );
    ......
};
          ┌──────→ ✘ No friend keyword
          │     ┌──────→ ✘ No scope resolution operator, Testclass :: sum cannot be made
          │     │
    float  sum (Testclass obj) ──→ private data member
    {
        float result;
        result = obj.num1 + obj.num2;
        return result;
    }
```

Figure 10.18:   Friend function of a class

```
// friend1.cpp: Normal function accessing object's private members
#include <iostream.h>

class two;  // advance declaration like function prototype
class one
{
  private:
      int data1;
  public:
      void setdata( int init )
      {
          data1 = init;
      }
      friend int add_both( one a, two b );   // friend function
};
class two
{
  private:
      int data2;
  public:
      void setdata( int init )
      {
          data2 = init;
      }
      friend int add_both( one a, two b );  // friend function
};
```

```
// friend function of class one and two
int add_both( one a, two b )
{
    return a.data1 + b.data2;   // a.data1 and b.data2 are private
}
void main()
{
    one a;
    two b;
    a.setdata( 5 );
    b.setdata( 10 );
    cout << "Sum of one and two: " << add_both( a, b );
}
```

Run

```
Sum of one and two: 15
```

The above program, contains two classes named `one` and `two`. To allow the normal function `add_both()` to have an access to private data members of objects of these classes, it must be declared as a friend function. It has been declared with the `friend` keyword in both the classes as:

```
        friend int add_both( one a, two b );
```

This declaration can be placed either in the private or the public section of the class.

An object of each class has been passed as an argument to the function `add_both()`. Being a friend function, it can access the private members of both classes through these arguments.

Observe the following declaration at the beginning of the program

```
        class two;  // advance declaration like function prototype
```

It is necessary, since a class cannot be referred until it has been declared before the class `one`. It informs the compiler that the class `two`'s specification will appear later.

Though friend functions add flexibility to the language and make programming convenient in certain situations, they are controversial; it goes against the philosophy that only member functions can access a class's private data. Friend functions should be used sparingly. If a program uses many friend functions, it can easily be concluded that there is a basic flaw in the design of a program and it would be better to redesign such programs. However, friend functions are very useful in certain situations. One such example is when a friend is used to increase the versatility of overloaded operators, which will be discussed in the chapter *Operator Overloading*.

Friend functions are useful in the following situations:

- Function operating on objects of two different classes. This is the ideal situation where the friend function can be used to bridge two classes.
- Friend functions can be used to increase the versatility of overloaded operators.
- Sometimes, a friend allows a more obvious syntax for calling a function, rather than what a member function can do.

Friend Classes

Friend functions permit an exception to the rules of data encapsulation. The `friend` keyword allows a function, or all the functions of another class to manipulate the private members of the original class. The syntax of declaring *friend* class is shown in Figure 10.19.

```
class boy
{
    private: ———   private specifier
        int income1;
        int income2;
    public: ———    public specifier
        int gettotal()
        {
            return income1 + income2;
        }

    friend class girl; //class girl can access private members
};
class girl
{
    // all the members of class girl can access attributes of boy
    ......
    public:
        int girlfunc(boy b1)
        {
            result = b1.income1+b1.income2;
            return result;
        }
        void show()
        {
            boy b1;
            cout << "Income1: " << b1.income1;  // private data of boy
        }
};
```

private data of class boy

private data of class boy

Figure 10.19:   girl class is a friend of class boy

All the member functions of one class can be friend functions of another class. The program friend2.cpp demonstrates the method of bridging classes using friend class.

```
// friend2.cpp: class girl is declared as a friend of class boy
#include <iostream.h>
// forward declaration of class girl; is optional
class boy
{
    private:      // private members
        int income1;
        int income2;
    public:
        void setdata( int in1, int in2 )
        {
            income1 = in1;
            income2 = in2;
        }
    friend class girl;  // class girl can access private data
};
```

```
class girl
{
   int income; // income is private data member
   public:
      int girlfunc( boy b1 )
      {
         return b1.income1+b1.income2;
      }
      void setdata( int in )
      {
          income = in;
      }
      void show()
      {
          boy b1;
          b1.setdata( 100, 200 );
          cout << "boy's Income1 in show(): " << b1.income1 << endl;
          cout << "girl's income in show(): " << income << endl;
      }
};
void main()
{
   boy b1;
   girl g1;
   b1.setdata( 500, 1000 );
   g1.setdata( 300 );
   cout << "boy b1 total income: " << g1.girlfunc(b1) << endl;
   g1.show();
};
```

Run
```
boy b1 total income: 1500
boy's Income1 in show(): 100
girl's income in show(): 300
```

The statement in the class boy

```
        friend class girl;  // class girl can access private data members
```

declares that all the member functions of the class girl are friend functions of class boy but not the other way. (Thus in C++, class girl, the friend class of the class boy, does not mean that the class boy is the friend of the class girl). The objects of the class girl can access all the members of the class boy irrespective of their access privileges.

The function show() in the girl class

```
        cout << "boy's Income1 in show(): " << b1.income1 << endl;
```

accesses the private data member income1 of the boy class.

Class Friend to a Specified Class Member

When only specific member function of one class should be friend function of another class, it must be specified explicitly using the scope resolution operator as shown in Figure 10.20. The function girlfunc() is a member function of class girl and a friend of class boy.

```
class boy
{
    private:
        int income1;          ———  private specifier
        int income2;
    public:
        int gettotal()        ——  public specifier
        {
            return income1 + income2;
        }
                              ——→  class name to which this function is a member
    friend girl :: girlfunc(boy b1);  // class girl's girlfunc() is allowed to
};                                    // access data and functions of class boy

class girl
{
    public:                                   private data members of class boy
        int girlfunc( boy b1 )
        {
            result = b1.income1 + b1.income2;
            return result;
        }
        void show () // cannot access private members of boy
        {
            boy b1;   // only public members can be accessed
        }
};
```

Figure 10.20:   Member function to which class boy is a friend

In the class `girl`, only function `girlfunc()` is allowed to access the private data and functions of the class boy. So only this function could be specifically made a friend in the class `boy` as illustrated in the program `friend3.cpp`.

```
// friend3.cpp: specific member function class girl is friend of boy
#include <iostream.h>
class boy; // advance declaration like function prototype
class girl
{
    int income; // income is private data member
    public:
    int girlfunc( boy b1 );
    void setdata( int in )
    {
        income = in;
    }
    void show()
    {
        cout << "girl income: " << income;
    }
};
```

```
class boy
{
   private:         // private members
      int income1;
      int income2;
   public:
      void setdata( int in1, int in2 )
      {
         income1 = in1;
         income2 = in2;
      }
      // only this function can access private data of boy
      friend int girl::girlfunc( boy b1 );
};
// only this function can access private data of the boy class
int girl::girlfunc( boy b1 )
{
   return b1.income1+b1.income2;
}
void main()
{
   boy b1;
   girl g1;
   b1.setdata( 500, 1000 );
   g1.setdata( 300 );
   cout << "boy b1 total income: " << g1.girlfunc(b1) << endl;
   g1.show();
}
```

Run

```
boy b1 total income: 1500
girl income: 300
```

The null-body class declaration statement,

```
        class boy; // advance declaration like function prototype
```

appears in the beginning of the program; a class cannot be referred until it has been declared before the class girl. It informs the compiler that the class boy is defined later. The statement in the class boy

```
        friend int girl::girlfunc( boy b1 );
```

declares that only member function girlfunc() of the class girl can access private data and member functions of the class boy.

10.15 Constant Parameters and Member Functions

Certain member functions of a class, access the class data members without modifying them. It is advisable to declare such functions as const (constant) functions. The syntax for declaring const member functions is shown in Figure 10.21. A const member function is used to indicate that it does not alter the data fields of the object, but only inspects them.

```
ReturnType FunctionName(arguments) const
```

Figure 10.21: Syntax of declaring a constant member function

A member function, which does not alter any data members in the class can be declared as const member function. The following statements illustrate the same:

```
    void showname() const;
    float divide() const;
```

The qualifier const is suffixed to the function in both the declaration and the definition. The compiler will generate an error message if such functions attempt to alter the class data members. The concept of constant member functions is illustrated in the program constmem.cpp.

```cpp
// constmem.cpp: person class with const member functions
#include <iostream.h>
#include <string.h>
class Person
{
  private:
    char *name;            // name of person
    char *address;         // address field
    char *phone;           // telephone number
  public:
    void init();
    void clear();
    // functions to set fields
    void setname(char const *str);
    void setaddress(char const *str);
    void setphone(char const *str);
    // functions to inspect fields
    char const *getname(void) const;
    char const *getaddress(void) const;
    char const *getphone(void) const;
};
// initialize class data members to NULL
inline void Person::init()
{
  name = address = phone = 0;
}
// release memory allocated to class data members
inline void Person::clear()
{
  delete name;
  delete address;
  delete phone;
}
```

```cpp
// interface functions set...()
void Person::setname( char const *str )
{
   if( name )
      delete name;
   name = new char[ strlen(str) + 1 ];
   strcpy( name, str );
}
void Person::setaddress( char const *str )
{
   if( address )
      delete address;
   address = new char[ strlen(str) + 1 ];
   strcpy( address, str );
}
void Person::setphone( char const *str )
{
   if( phone )
      delete phone;
   phone = new char[ strlen(str) + 1 ];
   strcpy( phone, str );
}
inline char const *Person::getname() const
{
   return name;
}
inline char const *Person::getaddress() const
{
   return address;
}
inline char const *Person::getphone() const
{
   return phone;
}
void printperson( Person const &p )
{
   if( p.getname() )
      cout << "Name    : " << p.getname() << endl;
   if( p.getaddress() )
      cout << "Address: " << p.getaddress() << endl ;
   if( p.getphone() )
      cout << "Phone   : " << p.getphone() << endl;
}
void main()
{
   Person p1, p2;
   p1.init();
   p2.init();
   p1.setname( "Rajkumar" );
   p1.setaddress( "E-mail: raj@cdacb.ernet.in" );
```

```
    p1.setphone( "90-080-5584271" );
    printperson( p1 );
    p2.setname( "Venugopal K R" );
    p2.setaddress( "Bangalore University" );
    p2.setphone( "-not sure-" );
    printperson( p2 );
    p1.clear();
    p2.clear();
}
```

Run

```
Name    : Rajkumar
Address : E-mail: raj@cdacb.ernet.in
Phone   : 90-080-5584271
Name    : Venugopal K R
Address : Bangalore University
Phone   : -not sure-
```

As illustrated in this program, the keyword const occurs following the argument list of functions. Again the following *Const-Rule* applies: *whichever appears before the keyword const must not alter its contents and if any attempt is made to alter data, the compiler issues an error message.* The same specification must be repeated in the definition of member functions:

```
char const *Person::getname() const
{
    return name;
}
```

A member function, which is declared and defined as const, should not alter any data fields of its class. In other words, a statement like

```
        name = 0;
```

in the above const function getname() would lead to a compilation error.

The formal parameter to the function

```
        void printperson( Person const &p )
```

is declared as a constant object. The private data members, by specification itself cannot be modified. If the object parameter is declared as const, even its public data members cannot be modified. Thus the function printperson() can only read public data members, but cannot modify them.

The purpose of const functions lies in the fact that C++ allows const objects to be created. For such objects only the const member, which does not modify them has to be called. The only exception to the rule are the constructors and destructors: these are called *automatically*. This feature is comparable to the definition of a variable int const max=10; such a variable may be initialized on its definition. Analogously, the constructor can initialize its object at the definition, but subsequent assignments cannot be performed. Generally, it is good to declare member functions which do not modify their object to be const.

10.16 Structures and Classes

Structures and classes in C++ are given the same set of features. For example, structures may also be used to group data as well as functions. In C++, the difference between structures and classes is that by default, structure members have public accessibility, whereas class members have private access control unless otherwise explicitly stated. The declaration for a structure in C++ is similar to a class specification. It is illustrated in the following declaration:

```
class complex

    private:          // private part
       float real;      // real part of complex number
       float imag;      // imaginary part of complex number
    public:             // public part
       void getdata();
       void outdata( char *msg );
       complex AddComplex( complex c2 );
};
```

A similar structure may be created as shown below:

```
struct complex
{
    private:          // private part
       float real;      // real part of complex number
       float imag;      // imaginary part of complex number
    public:             // public part
       void getdata();
       void outdata( char *msg );
       complex AddComplex( complex c2 );
};
```

The above declarations of class and structure can be written without any loss of meaning as follows:

```
class complex
{
    // by default private part, the keyword private is omitted
    float real;      // real part of complex number
    float imag;      // imaginary part of complex number
    public:          // public part
       void getdata();
       void outdata( char *msg );
       complex AddComplex( complex c2 );
};
```

Thus, in the absence of the keyword private, the members of a class are treated as private till another access-specifier keyword (private or public) is encountered. However, in a structure, the members are treated as public by default. It is illustrated in the following declaration:

```
struct complex
{
    // by default public, the keyword public is omitted
    void getdata();
    void outdata( char *msg );
    complex AddComplex( complex c2 );
    private:          // private part
       float real;      // real part of complex number
       float imag;      // imaginary part of complex number
};
```

Note: Most programmers prefer to use a class to group data as well as functions, a structure to group only data, following the conventions of C. It is advisable to use the keywords `private` and `public` explicitly in the declaration of classes and structures to improve readability of the program code.

10.17 Static Data and Member Functions

Earlier examples of classes have shown that, each object of a class has its own set of public or private data. Each public or private function then accesses the object's own version of the data. In some situations, it is desirable to have one or more common data fields, which are accessible to all objects of the class. An example of such a situation is keeping the status of how many objects of a class are created and how many of them are currently active in the program. Another example is a flag variable, which states whether some specific initialization has occurred; only the first object of the class performs the initialization and then sets the flag to *done*.

Such situations are analogous to C code, where several functions need to access the same variable. A common solution in C is to define all these functions in one source file and to declare the variable as static: the variable name is then not known beyond the scope of the source file. This approach is quite valid, but does not agree with the philosophy of one data or function per program having multiple source files. Another C-like solution is to create the variable in question with unusual names such as `__MYFLAG`, `_6ULDV8`, etc., with the hope that other parts of the program (libraries, link modules, etc.) do not make use by defining these variables by accident. Neither the first, nor the second C-like solution is elegant. C++ therefore allows static data and functions, which are common to all objects of a class.

Static Data Member Definition

In Turbo C++ version 1.0, static data members were not required to be explicitly defined. When the linker finds undefined static data, it would automatically define them and allocate storage for them instead of generating errors, but both new versions of Turbo C++ and Borland C++ insist on the explicit definition; no other way to define a static data exists. The syntax of defining static data member of a class is shown in Figure 10.22.

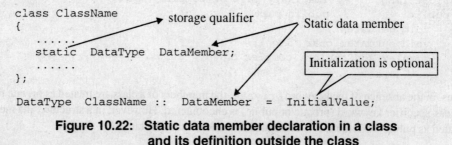

Figure 10.22:   Static data member declaration in a class and its definition outside the class

The static data members can be initialized during their definition outside all the member functions, in the same way as global variables are initialized. The definition and initialization of a static data member usually occur in one of the source files of the class functions. The statement which defines and initializes the variable `MyClass::count` (`count` is a data member of `MyClass`) is always valid whether `count` is declared private, public or protected inside the class `MyClass`. The reason is that static data members accessed in this way are essentially global data.

Private static data members

When a data member is required to be accessible to more than one function, the normal procedure adopted in a function-oriented language is to declare it as an external variable. But this technique may be dangerous as it exposes external data variable to accidental modification, which may have undesirable effects on the efficient and reliable working of the program.

C++ provides an elegant solution to that problem in the form of static data members. The usual technique that is adopted is to declare the static data member in the private section of a class. Thus, effective data hiding is achieved, as the data is only accessible through the member functions, while providing access to all the objects of that class. This is illustrated in the program count.cpp.

```
// count.cpp: counts how many calls are made to a member function set()
#include <iostream.h>
class MyClass
{
    static int count; // static member
    int number;
    public:
        // initializes object's member and increments function call
        void set( int num )
        {
            number = num;
            ++count;
        }
        void show()
        {
            cout << "\nNumber of calls made to 'set()' through any object: "
                << count;
        }
};
// static member count is shared by all the objects of class MyClass
int MyClass::count = 0; // definition and initialization of a data member
void main()
{
    MyClass obj1;
    obj1.show();
    obj1.set( 100 );
    obj1.show();
    MyClass obj2, obj3;
    obj2.set( 200 );
    obj2.show(); //same result even with obj1.show and obj3.show();
    obj2.set( 250 );
    obj3.set( 300 );
    obj1.show(); //same result even with obj2.show and obj3.show();
}
```

Run

```
Number of calls made to 'set()' through any object: 0
Number of calls made to 'set()' through any object: 1
Number of calls made to 'set()' through any object: 2
Number of calls made to 'set()' through any object: 4
```

Omission of the statement

```
int MyClass::count = 0;
```

in the above program would generate linking error although program is compiled successfully. This is because the statement in the class `MyClass`

```
static int count;
```

would not have been defined anywhere and it is a static variable within a class. Hence, an error would be generated if a value is assigned to `count` without any memory being allocated to it. It is possible to omit initialization of a static member variable when it is defined, as shown below:

```
int MyClass::count;
```

Irrespective of whether the data member is private, public or protected, it must always be defined using the scope resolution operator. Static variables act like a bridge between objects of the same class. The linker allocates storage for a static member when the variable is defined even if no objects are actually created from the class.

Access Rules for Static Data Members

The public static data members can be accessed using the scope resolution operator or through objects with member access operator. Using the scope resolution operator is a completely new notation for member access. However, the accessibility of private static data members is same as that of normal private members.

The static data members which are declared public are similar to *normal* global variables. They can be addressed by the program by prefixing class name and scope resolution operator. It is illustrated in the following code fragment:

```
class Test
{
   public:
      static int public_int;
   private:
      static int private_int;
};
void main()
{
   Test::public_int = 145;   // ok
   Test::private_int = 12;   // wrong, do not touch the private data members
   Test myobj;
   myobj.public_int = 145;   // ok
   myobj.private_int = 12;   // wrong, do not access the private data member
}
```

The static data member `public_int` defined in the class `Test` can be accessed using the scope resolution operator prefixed by its class name as follows:

```
Test::public_int = 145;          // ok
```

Whereas, the data member `private_int` cannot be accessed using the scope resolution operator. Therefore, the statement

```
Test::private_int = 12; // wrong, do not touch the private data members
```

leads to a compilation error. Objects accessing the static data member access the same data that is accessed by using the scope resolution operator. The statement

```
myobj.public_int = 145;        // ok
```

refers to the public static data member. However, a private static data member cannot be accessed either by using the scope resolution or the dot operator.

Static Member Functions

Besides static data, C++ allows the definition of static functions. These static functions can access only the static members (data or function) declared in the same class; *non-static* data are unavailable to these functions. Static member functions declared in the public part of a class declaration can be accessed without specifying an object of the class. It is illustrated in the program dirs.cpp.

```
// dirs.cpp: static data and member functions of a class
#include <iostream.h>
#include <string.h>
class Directory
{
   public:
      // the static string
      static char path [];    // declaration
      // constructors, destructors etc. not shown here
      // here's the static public function
      static void setpath( char const *newpath );
};
// the static function
void Directory::setpath (char const *newpath)
{
   strcpy( path, newpath );
}
// definition of the static variable
char Directory::path [199] = "/usr/raj";    // definition
void main ()
{
   // static data member access, which is defined as public
   cout << "Path: " << Directory::path << endl;
   // Alternative (1): calling setpath() without
   // an object of the class Directory
   Directory::setpath ("/usr");
   cout << "Path: " << Directory::path << endl;
   // Alternative (2): with an object
   Directory dir;
   dir.setpath ("/etc");
   cout << "Path: " << dir.path;
}
```

Run

```
Path: /usr/raj
Path: /usr
Path: /etc
```

Static member functions can also be defined in the private region of a class. Such private static member functions can access only static data members and can invoke static member functions. The following points should be noted about static members:

- Only one copy of static data member exists for all the instances of a class.
- Static member functions can access only static members of its class.
- Static data members must be defined and initialized like global variables, otherwise the linker generates errors.
- Static members defined as public can either be accessed through the scope resolution operator as

      ClassName::MemberName

  or it can be accessed through the object of a class as

      ObjectName.MemberName

That is, static members can be accessed using only the class name, without referring to a particular object.

10.18   Class, Objects and Memory Resource

When a class is declared, memory is not allocated to the data members of the class. Thus, there exists a template, but data members cannot be manipulated unless an instance of this class is created by defining an object. It might give an impression that when an object of a particular class is created, memory is allocated to both its data members and member functions. This is partly true. When an object is created, memory is allocated only to its data members and not to member functions.

Member functions are created and stored in memory only once when a class specification is declared. All objects of that class have access to the same area in the memory where the member functions are stored. It is also logically true as the member functions are the same for all objects and there is no point in allocating a separate copy for each and every object created using the same class specification. However, separate storage is allocated for every object's data members since they contain different values. It allows different objects to handle their data in a manner that suits them.

The organization of memory resource for the objects is depicted in Figure 10.23. It can be observed that N objects of the same class are created and data members of those objects are stored in distinct memory locations, whereas the member functions of `object1` to `objectN` are stored in the same memory area. Thus, each object has a separate copy of data members and the different objects share the member functions among them. It is simpler to visualize each object as containing both its own data and functions. But the knowledge of what happens behind the scene is useful in estimating the time and space complexity of a program during its execution.

Static Data Members

Whenever a class is instantiated, memory is allocated to the created object. But there exists an exception to this rule. Storage space for data members which are declared as `static` is allocated only once during the class declaration. Subsequently, all objects of this class have access to this data member, i.e., all instances of the class access the same data member. When one of them modifies the static data member, the effect is visible to all the instances of the class.

The organization of memory resource for the object's `static` data members is shown in Figure 10.24. It can be observed that in the N objects of the same class, *automatic* data members (of each object) are stored in distinct memory locations, whereas *static* data members (of all objects) are stored in the same memory locations. Thus each object has a separate copy of the automatic data members and they share static data members among them.

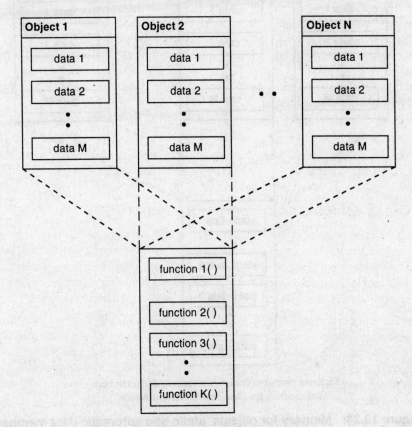

Separate memory for object's data members
Shared memory for class functions

Figure 10.23:   Memory for objects' data and function members

A static data member is allocated a fixed area of storage at link time, like a global variable, but the variable's identifier is accessed only using the scope resolution operator with the class name. Thus static data is useful when all the objects of the same class must share a common item of information having same characteristics as non-static members. It is visible only within the class, but its extent (lifespan) is the entire program execution period.

Data members are generally allocated with the same storage class. If an object is declared `auto`, all its data is `auto`; static objects have static data members. Static data members are an *exception* to this rule; when an object is created, memory is not allocated to its static members (if there are any), because this would cause multiple copies of the static data member appear in every object.

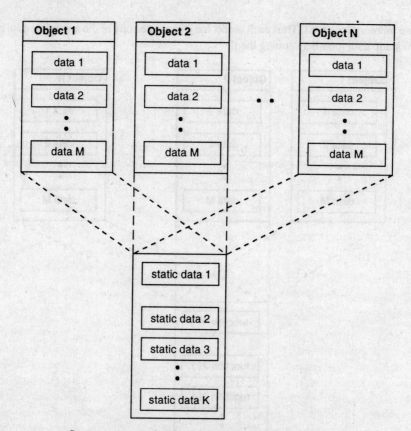

Separate memory for class's automatic data members
Shared memory for class's static data members

Figure 10.24:   Memory for objects' static and automatic data members

10.19 Class Design Steps

As pointed out by the designer of C++, Dr. Bjarne Stroustrup, "Considering designing a single class is typically not a good idea. Concepts do not exist in isolation; rather, a concept is defined in the context of other concepts. Similarly, a class does not exist in isolation, but is declared together with logically related classes. Such a set is often called a class library or a component. Sometimes all classes in a component constitute a single class hierarchy, sometimes they do not."

The set of classes in a component is united by some logical criteria, often by a component style and by a reliance on common services. A component is thus the unit of design, documentation, ownership, and often reuse. However, to use any part of a component, one needs to understand the logical criteria that define the component, the conventions and style embodied in the design of the components and its documentation, and the common services (if any).

The design of a component is a challenging task. It can be easily handled by breaking it into steps so that focus can be placed on the various sub-tasks in a logical and complete way. (Unlike structured programming, OOPs concentrates on data decomposition instead of algorithm decomposition.) However, there is no one right method for component design, Here is a series of steps that have worked well in the design of components with most designers:

[1]. Find the concepts/classes and their most fundamental relationships.

[2]. Refine the classes by specifying the sets of operations on them.

a. Classify these operations. In particular, consider the needs for construction, copying, and destruction. C++ features for defining such operations are discussed in the chapter on *Object Initialization and Cleanup.*

b. Provide standard interface. It must provide the same look and feel of standard data types to user defined data types. C++ has constructs for defining such standard interfaces and are discussed in the chapter on *Operator Overloading.*

c. Consider minimalism, completeness, and convenience.

[3]. Refine the classes by specifying their dependencies on other classes:

a. Inheritance. (Discussed in the chapter on *Inheritance.*)

b. Use dependencies.

[4]. Specify the interfaces for the classes.

a. Separate functions into private, public, and protected operations.

b. Specify the exact type of the operations on the classes.

Note that these steps are iterative in nature and hence, several sequences over these steps are required to produce a design code. It is advisable to design these classes as template classes as discussed in the chapter *Generic Programming with Templates.* The error handling model adopted in these classes must use exceptions to report runtime errors; discussed in the chapter *Exception Handling.* Once objects are created dynamically, there must be provision to invoke operations on these objects dynamically. These features are discussed in the chapter *Virtual Functions.* Apart from the class design steps, a true object-oriented development passes through object-oriented analysis, design, testing, etc., phases; discussed in the chapter *OO Analysis, Design and Development.*

Review Questions

10.1 What is a class ? Describe the syntax for declaring a class with examples.

10.2 What are the differences between structures and classes in C++ ?

10.3 What are objects ? Describe the syntax for defining objects with examples. Explain how C++ supports encapsulation and data abstraction.

10.4 Write a program illustrating class declaration, definition, and accessing class members.

10.5 Explain the client-server model of object communication.

10.6 The University requires an interactive student database package that permits one to keep track of the dynamic student population in the campus. This database maintains at the minimum, a student's name, roll-no, marks of three *hardcore* subjects and three *softcore* subjects. The information about any student can come at any time.
(a) What kind of data structure is suited for the above implementation and why ?
(b) Give the class specification.
(c) Given a student's roll-no, how do we determine the marks scored by the student ?

10.7 What are the guidelines that need to be followed for deciding whether to make the member functions inline or not ?

10.8 What is the difference between member functions defined inside and outside the body of a class? How are inline member functions defined outside the body of a class ?

10.9 What is data hiding ? What are the different mechanisms for protecting data from the external users of a class's objects ?

10.10 What are empty classes ? Can instances of empty class be created ? Give reasons.

10.11 Write a program for adding two vectors (which are objects of the class Vector). Use dynamic data members instead of arrays for storing vector elements.

10.12 Explain the different methods of passing object parameters.

10.13 Write an interactive program for manipulating objects of the Distance class. Support member functions for adding and subtracting distance members of two objects.

10.14 What are friend functions and friend classes ? Write a normal function which adds objects of the complex number class. Declare this normal function as friend of the Complex class.

10.15 Write a program for processing objects of the Student class. Declare member functions such as show() as read-only member functions.

10.16 Bring out the differences between auto and static storage class data members. Can static member functions of a class access all types of members of a class. Give reasons. What are the access rules for accessing static members ?

10.17 Discuss memory requirements for classes, objects, data members, member functions, static and non-static data members.

10.18 Why object-oriented programming approach is the preferred form of programming over other approaches.

10.19 Write a program for manipulating coordinates in Rectangle coordinate system. Represent points as objects. The class Point must include members such as x and y (as data members), and add(), sub(), angle(), etc. (as member functions).

10.20 Write a program for manipulating coordinates in Polar coordinate system. Represent points as objects. The class Polar must include data members such as radius and theta, and member functions such as add(), sub(), angle(), etc.

10.22 Explain steps involved in designing class components as suggested by the C++ designer.

11

Object Initialization and Cleanup

11.1 Class Revisited

A class encapsulates both data and functions manipulating them into a single unit. It can be further used as an abstract data type for defining a class instance called object. As with standard data types, there must exist a provision to initialize objects of a class during their definition itself. Consider an example of the class bag having two data members: contents to hold fruits and ItemCount to hold the number of items currently stored in the bag. It has interface functions such as SetEmpty(), put(), and show() whose usage is illustrated in the program bag.cpp.

```
// bag.cpp: Bag into which fruits can be placed
#include <iostream.h>
const int MAX_ITEMS = 25;  // Maximum number of items that a bag can hold
class Bag
{
   private:
      int contents[MAX_ITEMS];   // bag memory area
      int ItemCount;             // Number of items present in a bag
   public:
      // sets ItemCount to empty
      void SetEmpty()
      {
          ItemCount = 0;              //When you purchase a bag, it will be empty
      }
      void put( int item )        // puts item into bag
      {
          contents[ ItemCount++ ] = item; // counter update
      }
      void show();
};
// display contents of a bag
void Bag::show()
{
   for( int i = 0; i < ItemCount; i++ )
      cout << contents[i] << " ";
   cout << endl;
}
void main()
{
   int item;
   Bag bag;
   bag.SetEmpty();    // set bag to empty
```

```
    while( 1 )
    {
       cout<<"Enter Item Number to be put into the bag <0-no item>: ";
       cin >> item;
       if( item == 0 )    // items ends, break
          break;
       bag.put( item );
       cout << "Items in Bag: ";
       bag.show();
    }
}
```

Run

```
Enter Item Number to be put into the bag <0-no item>: 1
Items in Bag: 1
Enter Item Number to be put into the bag <0-no item>: 3
Items in Bag: 1 3
Enter Item Number to be put into the bag <0-no item>: 2
Items in Bag: 1 3 2
Enter Item Number to be put into the bag <0-no item>: 4
Items in Bag: 1 3 2 4
Enter Item Number to be put into the bag <0-no item>: 0
```

In main(), the statement

```
    Bag bag;
```

creates the object bag without initializing the ItemCount to 0 automatically. However, it is performed by a call to the function SetEmpty() as follows:

```
    bag.SetEmpty();    // set bag to empty
```

According to the philosophy of OOPs, when a new object such as bag is created, it will naturally be empty. To provide such a behavior in the above program, it is necessary to invoke the member function SetEmpty explicitly. In reality, when a bag is purchased, it might contain some items placed inside the bag as gift items. Such a situation in C++ can be simulated by

```
    Bag bag1 = 2;
```

It creates the object bag and initializes it with 2, indicating that the bag is sold with two gift items. It resembles the procedure of initialization of a built-in data type during creation, i.e., there must be a provision in C++ to initialize objects during creation itself.

It is therefore clear that OOPs must provide a support for initializing objects when they are created, and destroy them when they are no longer needed. Hence, a class in C++ may contain two special member functions dealing with the internal workings of a class. These functions are the *constructors* and the *destructors*. A constructor enables an object to initialize itself during creation and the destructor destroys the object when it is no longer required, by releasing all the resources allocated to it. These operations are called *object initialization* and *cleanup* respectively.

11.2 Constructors

A constructor is a special member function whose main operation is to allocate the required resources such as memory and initialize the objects of its class. A constructor is distinct from other member functions of the class, and it has the same name as its class. It is executed automatically when a class is instantiated (object is created). It is generally used to initialize object member parameters and allocate the necessary resources to the object members. The constructor has no return value specification (not even void). For instance, for the class Bag, the constructor is Bag::Bag().

The C++ run-time system makes sure that *the constructor of a class is the first member function to be executed automatically when an object of the class is created.* In other words, the constructor is executed everytime an object of that class is defined. Normally constructors are used for initializing the class data members. It is of course possible to define a class which has no constructor at all; in such a case, the run-time system calls a dummy constructor (i.e., which performs no action) when its object is created. The syntax for defining a constructor with its prototype within the class body and the actual definition outside it, is shown in Figure 11.1. Similar to other members, the constructor can be defined either within, or outside the body of a class. It can access any data member like all other member functions but cannot be invoked explicitly and must have public status to serve its purpose. The constructor which does not take arguments explicitly is called *default constructor*.

```
class ClassName
{
        ..... // private members
        public :              must be public
             // public members
             ClassName ( ) ;                Constructor prototype
};                          no return type nor void
ClassName :: ClassName( )           Constructor definition
{
        // constructor body definition
}
```

Figure 11.1: Syntax of constructor

The initialization may entail calling functions, allocating dynamic storage, setting variables to specific values, and so on. Since the constructor is executed every time an object is created, it can be used to assign initial values to the data members of the object. It will reduce the burden on the programmer to specifically initialize the data within each object that is created and hence, prevent errors. These constructors do not have any return type, since they are invoked during the creation of objects transparently. But they can have as many arguments as necessary.

The program newbag.cpp has a counter, which can be used to count events or objects placed in a bag. Since the counter has to start from zero value and count upwards, a mechanism is required by which the counter can be set to zero as soon as it is created. An appropriate solution to this situation, is to use a constructor.

```
// newbag.cpp: Bag into which fruits can be placed with constructor
#include <iostream.h>
const int MAX_ITEMS = 25;  // Maximum number of items that a bag can hold
class Bag
{
    private:
        int contents[MAX_ITEMS];   // bag memory area
        int ItemCount;                // Number of items present in a bag
```

```
    public:
        // sets ItemCount to empty
        Bag()                    // constructor
        {
            ItemCount = 0;          // When you purchase a bag, it will be empty
        }
        void put( int item )      // puts item into bag
        {
            contents[ ItemCount++ ] = item; // item into bag, counter update
        }
        void show();
};
// display contents of the bag
void Bag::show()
{
    for( int i = 0; i < ItemCount; i++ )
        cout << contents[i] << " ";
    cout << endl;
}
void main()
{
    int item;
    Bag bag;
    while( 1 )
    {
        cout << "Enter Item Number to be put into the bag <0-no item>: ";
        cin >> item;
        if( item == 0 )    // items ends, break
            break;

        bag.put( item );
        cout << "Items in Bag: ";
        bag.show();
    }
```

Run

```
ter Item Number to be put into the bag <0-no item>: 1
ems in Bag: 1
ter Item Number to be put into the bag <0-no item>: 3
ems in Bag: 1 3
ter Item Number to be put into the bag <0-no item>: 2
ems in Bag: 1 3 2
ter Item Number to be put into the bag <0-no item>: 4
ms in Bag: 1 3 2 4
er Item Number to be put into the bag <0-no item>: 0
```

n main(), the class instantiation statement

```
    Bag bag;
```

tes the object bag and initializes ItemCount to zero by invoking the no-argument constructor

```
       Bag::Bag()
```
automatically. In the earlier program bag.cpp, these actions are performed by the following statements

```
       Bag bag;
       bag.SetEmpty();     // set bag to empty
```
First, the object bag is created and then, SetEmpty() is explicitly invoked to initialize the data member ItemCount to zero.

When an object is a local non-static variable in a function, the constructor Bag() is called when the function is invoked. When an object is a global or a static variable, the constructor Bag() is invoked before the execution of main() as illustrated in the program test1.cpp.

```
// test1.cpp: a class Test with a constructor function
#include <iostream.h>
class Test
{
   public:              // 'public' function:
      Test();           // the constructor
};
Test::Test()            // here is the definition
{
   cout << "constructor of class Test called" << endl;
}
// and here is the test program:
Test  G;                // global object
void func()
{
   Test L;              // local object in function func()
   cout << "here's function func()" << endl;
}
void main()
{
   Test X;              // local object in function main()
   cout << "main() function" << endl;
   func ();
}
```

Run

```
constructor of class Test called     (global object G)
constructor of class Test called     (object X in main())
main() function
constructor of class Test called     (object L in func())
here's function func()
```

The output produced by the program is as desired (see **_Run_** - the text in parentheses indicates comment). The program shows how a class Test is defined, which consists of only one function: the constructor. The constructor performs only one action; a message is printed. The program contains three objects of the class Test: first a global object, second a local object in main(), and third another local object in func().

A constructor has the following characteristics:

- It has the same name as that of the class to which it belongs.
- It is executed automatically whenever the class is instantiated.
- It does not have any return type.
- It is normally used to initialize the data members of a class.
- It is also used to allocate resources such as memory, to the dynamic data members of a class.

11.3 Parameterized Constructors

Constructors can be invoked with arguments, just as in the case of functions. The argument list can be specified within braces similar to the argument-list in the function. Constructors with arguments are called *parameterized constructors*. The distinguishing characteristic is that the name of the constructor functions have to be the same as that of its class name. In the earlier program `newbag.cpp`, another constructor with arguments could have been provided with one integer value to initialize the data members `ItemCount` and `contents[]`. The syntax of parameterized constructors and their access is shown in Figure 11.2.

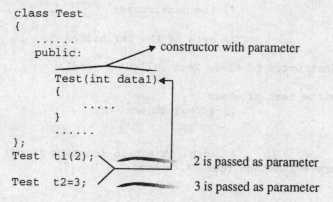

Figure 11.2: **Parameterized constructor**

Since C++ allows function overloading, a constructor with arguments can co-exist with another constructor without arguments. The class `Bag` would thus have two constructors. The usage of a constructor with arguments is illustrated in the modified program `giftbag.cpp` of `newbag.cpp`. The object is initialized during its creation.

```
// giftbag.cpp: Bag which has some items when gifted
#include <iostream.h>
const int MAX_ITEMS = 25;  // Maximum number of items that a bag can hold
class Bag
{
   private:
      int contents[MAX_ITEMS];   // bag memory area
      int ItemCount;             // Number of items present in a bag
```

```
    public:
       // sets ItemCount to empty, it is gifted as empty bag
       Bag()                    // constructor without arguments
       {
           ItemCount = 0;
       }
       Bag( int item )          // constructor with arguments
       {
           contents[ 0 ] = item;   // when bag is gifted, it'll have some items
           ItemCount = 1;
       }
       void put( int item ) // puts item into bag
       {
           contents[ ItemCount++ ] = item; // item into bag, counter update
       }
       void show();
};
// display contents of a bag
void Bag::show()
{
    if( ItemCount )
       for( int i = 0; i < ItemCount; i++ )
           cout << contents[i] << " ";
    else
       cout << "Nil";
    cout << endl;
}
void main()
{
    int item;
    Bag bag1;          // uses Bag::Bag() constructor
    Bag bag2 = 4;  // uses Bag::Bag( int item ) constructor
    cout << "Gifted bag1 initially has: ";
    bag1.show();
    cout << "Gifted bag2 initially has: ";
    bag2.show();
    while( 1 )
    {
       cout << "Enter Item Number to be put into the bag2 <0-no item>: ";
       cin >> item;
       if( item == 0 )   // items ends, break
           break;
       bag2.put( item );
       cout << "Items in bag2: ";
       bag2.show();
    }
}
```

Run

```
Gifted bag1 initially has: Nil
```

```
Gifted bag2 initially has: 4
Enter Item Number to be put into the bag2 <0-no item>: 1
Items in bag2: 4 1
Enter Item Number to be put into the bag2 <0-no item>: 2
Items in bag2: 4 1 2
Enter Item Number to be put into the bag2 <0-no item>: 3
Items in bag2: 4 1 2 3
Enter Item Number to be put into the bag2 <0-no item>: 0
```

The `Bag` class has two constructors. The first constructor does not have any arguments. The next constructor has a single argument. The statement

>   `Bag bag1;`

creates the object `bag1` and initializes its data member `ItemCount` by invoking the no-argument constructor `Bag::Bag()`. The next statement

>   `Bag bag2 = 4;`

creates the object `bag2` and sets its data members `ItemCount` to 1 and `contents` to 4 by invoking the one-argument constructor `Bag::Bag( int item )`. The concept of having multiple constructors and their invocation based on suitable arguments during the creation of objects `bag1` and `bag2` with user interface is shown in Figure 11.3.

Instances of the class `Bag`

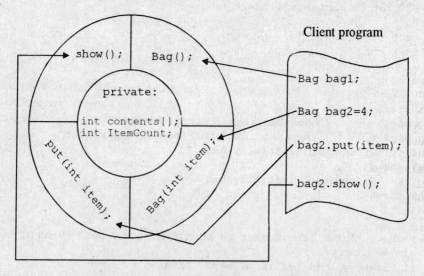

Figure 11.3:   Bag class and parameterized constructor

When a constructor is declared not to accept any arguments, it is called a *default constructor*. It is invoked when the object is instantiated with no arguments. The constructor `Bag()` is a default constructor. Since a default constructor takes no arguments, it follows that each class can have only one default constructor. The operation of the default constructor function is usually to initialize data, used subsequently by other member functions. It can also be used to allocate the necessary resources such as memory, dynamically.

11.4 Destructor

When an object is no longer needed it can be destroyed. A class can have another special member function called the *destructor*, which is invoked when an object is destroyed. This function complements the operation performed by any of the constructors, in the sense that, it is invoked when an object ceases to exist. For objects which are local non-static variables, the destructor is called when the function in which the object is defined is about to terminate. For static or global variables, the destructor is called before the program terminates. Even when a program is interrupted using an exit() call, the destructors are called for all objects which exist at that time.

The syntax of the destructor is shown in Figure 11.4. Destructor is a member function having the character ~(tilde) followed by the name of its class and brackets (i.e., ~classname()). It is invoked automatically to reclaim all the resources allocated to the object when the object goes out of scope and is no longer needed.

```
class ClassName
{
     .....   // private members
     public :  ────   must be public
            // public members
          ~ ClassName();  ────  Destructor prototype
};        ↑ └───────►Tilde character, destructor returns nothing

ClassName :: ~ ClassName()  ────  Destructor definition
{
     // destructor body definition
}
```

Figure 11.4: Syntax of destructor

Similar to constructors, a destructor must be declared in the public section of a class so that it is accessible to all its users. Destructors have no return type. It is incorrect to even declare a void return type. *A class cannot have more than one destructor.* The program test.cpp illustrates the use of destructors.

```
// test.cpp: a class Test with a constructor and destructor
#include <iostream.h>
class Test
{
   public:              // 'public' function:
      Test();           // the constructor
      ~Test();          // the destructor
};
Test::Test()                  // here is the definition of constructor
{
   cout << "constructor of class Test called" << endl;
}
Test::~Test()                 // here is the definition of destructor
{
   cout << "destructor of class Test called" << endl;
}
```

```
void main()
{
    Test x;      // constructor is called while creating
    cout << "terminating main()" << endl;
}  // object x goes out of scope, destructor is called
```

Run

```
constructor of class Test called
terminating main()
destructor of class Test called
```

An interesting aspect of constructors and destructors is illustrated in the program count.cpp. It keeps track of the number of objects created and how many of them are still alive.

```
// count.cpp: counts how many objects are created and how may are alive
#include <iostream.h>
int nobjects = 0;     // number of objects of the class MyClass
int nobj_alive = 0;   // number of objects present of the class MyClass
class MyClass
{
    public:
      MyClass()        // increments objects count
      {
        ++nobjects;     // add to total
        ++nobj_alive;   // add to the active
      }
      ~MyClass()  // decrements active objects count
      {
        --nobj_alive;   // deduct one from active objects list
      }
      void show()
      {
          cout << "Total number of objects created: " << nobjects << endl;
          cout<<"Number of objects currently alive: "<<nobj_alive << endl;
      }
};
void main()
{
    MyClass obj1;
    obj1.show();
    {  // new block
      MyClass obj1, obj2;
      obj2.show();    // can be obj1.show()
    }  // obj1 and obj2 goes out of scope, hence deleted
    obj1.show();
    MyClass obj2, obj3;
    obj2.show();    // can be obj1.show() or obj3.show()
}
```

Run

```
Total number of objects created: 1
Number of objects currently alive: 1
```

```
Total number of objects created: 3
Number of objects currently alive: 3
Total number of objects created: 3
Number of objects currently alive: 1
Total number of objects created: 5
Number of objects currently alive: 3
```

The constructor in the above program increments the global variables nobjects and nobj_alive, by one. Whenever an object is created, the constructor is invoked automatically and counters are updated to maintain the object's statistics. The destructor decrements only the count variable nobj_alive by one. Whenever objects go out of scope, the destructor is invoked automatically and the counters will get updated (decremented). The status can be retrieved by using the member function show() of the class MyClass. It prints the same message irrespective of the object invoking it; (it uses global data, which remains the same irrespective of the object's message).

The following rules need to be considered while defining a destructor for a given class:

♦ The destructor function has the same name as the class but prefixed by a tilde (~). The tilde distinguishes it from a constructor of the same class.

♦ Unlike the constructor, the destructor does not take any arguments. This is because there is only one way to destroy an object.

♦ The destructor has neither arguments, nor a return value.

♦ The destructor has no return type like the constructor, since it is invoked automatically whenever an object goes out of scope.

♦ There can be only one destructor in each class. This is essentially a violation of the rule that a function can take arguments, thereby making function overloading impossible.

11.5 Constructor Overloading

An interesting feature of the constructors is that a class can have multiple constructors. This is called *constructor overloading*. All the constructors have the same name as the corresponding class, and they differ only in terms of their signature (in terms of the number of arguments, or data types of their arguments, or both) as illustrated in the program account.cpp.

```
// account.cpp: passing objects as parameters to functions
#include<iostream.h>
class AccClass
{
    private:              // class data members
        int accno;
        float balance;
    public:               // class function members
        AccClass()        // Constructor no.1
        {
            cout << "Enter the account number for acc1 object: ";
            cin >> accno;
            cout << "Enter the balance: ";
            cin >> balance;
        }
```

```
        AccClass(int an)       // Constructor no.2
         {
            accno = an;
            balance = 0.0 ;
         }
        AccClass(int acval, float bal)    // Constructor no.3
         {
            accno = acval;
            balance = bal;
         }
        void display()
         {
            cout << "Account number is: " << accno << endl;
            cout << "Balance is: " << balance << endl;
         }
        void MoneyTransfer( AccClass & acc, float amount );
};

// acc1.MoneyTransfer( acc2, 100 ),transfers 100 rupees from acc1 to acc2
void AccClass::MoneyTransfer( AccClass & acc, float amount )
{
   balance = balance - amount;   // deduct money from source
   acc.balance = acc.balance + amount; // add money to destination
}
void main()
{
   int trans_money;
   AccClass acc1;                       // uses constructor 1
   AccClass acc2( 10 );                 // uses constructor 2
   AccClass acc3( 20, 750.5 );          // uses constructor 3
   cout << "Account Information..." << endl;
   acc1.display();
   acc2.display();
   acc3.display();
   cout << "How much money is to be transferred from acc3 to acc1: ";
   cin >> trans_money;
   // transfer trans_money from acc3 to acc1
   acc3.MoneyTransfer( acc1, trans_money );
   cout << "Updated Information about accounts..." << endl;
   acc1.display();
   acc2.display();
   acc3.display();
}
```

Run

```
Enter the account number for acc1 object: 1
Enter the balance: 100
Account Information...
Account number is: 1
Balance is: 100
Account number is: 10
```

```
Balance is: 0
Account number is: 20
Balance is: 750.5
How much money is to be transferred from acc3 to acc1: 200
Updated Information about accounts...
Account number is: 1
Balance is: 300
Account number is: 10
Balance is: 0
Account number is: 20
Balance is: 550.5
```

In case of a class having multiple constructors, a constructor is invoked during the creation of an object depending on the number and type of arguments passed. The default constructor can also be defined along with other constructors, if necessary. The invocation of different constructors during the creation of an object of the class AccClass is shown in Figure 11.5.

```
class AccClass
{
    ......
    public:                    overloaded constructors
    . .  AccClass();
       AccClass( int an );
         AccClass( int acval, float bal );
         ......
};
AccClass acc1;
AccClass acc2( 10 )
AccClass acc3( 20, 750, 5 );
```

Figure 11.5: Constructor overloading

In this program, whenever a new account is created, one of the three steps is chosen:

- If no arguments are passed, then the program prompts the user for an account number and balance by invoking the no-argument constructor, AccClass().

- If only an int argument, is provided, then the account number is initialized with the value passed as an input argument while, the balance is set to 0.0 by invoking the one-argument constructor AccClass(int).

- If both an int as well as a float argument is provided, then the account number is set to the int value while the balance is set to the float value by invoking the two-argument constructor, AccClass(int, float).

Differences between Constructors and Destructors

The following are the differences between constructors and destructors:

- Arguments cannot be passed to destructors.
- Only one destructor can be declared for a given class as a consequence of the fact that destructors cannot have arguments and hence, destructors cannot be overloaded.
- Destructors can be virtual, while constructors cannot be virtual. More details can be found in the chapter *Virtual Functions*.

11.6 Order of Construction and Destruction

The possibility of defining constructors with arguments, offers an opportunity to monitor (examine) the exact moment at which an object is created or destroyed during the execution of a program. This has been illustrated in the program, test2.cpp using the Test class.

```
// test2.cpp: the class Test with a constructor and destructor function
#include <iostream.h>
#include <string.h>
class Test
{
   private:
      char *name;
   public:                     // 'public' function:
      Test();                  // the constructor
      Test( char *msg );       // one-argument constructor
      ~Test();
};
Test::Test()                   // here is the
{                              // definition
   name = new char[ strlen("unnamed")+1 ];
   strcpy( name, "unnamed" );
   cout << ."Test object 'unnamed' created" << endl;
}
Test::Test( char *NameIn )
{
   name = new char[ strlen(NameIn)+1 ];
   strcpy( name, NameIn );
   cout << "Test object " << NameIn << " created" << endl;
}
Test::~Test ()
{
   cout <<"Test object " << name << " destroyed" << endl;
   delete name;               // release memory
}
// and here is the test program:
Test  g("global");                      // global object
void func()
{
   Test l("func");                      // local object in function func()

   cout << "here's function func()" << endl;
}
void main()
{
   Test x("main");                      // local object in function main()
   func ();
   cout << "main() function - termination" << endl;
}
```

Run
```
Test object global created
Test object main created
Test object func created
here's function func()
Test object func destroyed
main() function - termination
Test object main destroyed
Test object global destroyed
```

By defining objects of the class Test with specific names, the construction and destruction of these objects can be monitored. In the above program, global objects are created first, hence the statement

```
        Test g("global");
```
creates the object g and initializes its member name to "global". In func(), the statement

```
        Test l("func");
```
creates the local object l and initializes its member name to "func". In main(), the statement

```
        Test x("main"); // local object in function main()
```
creates the local object x and initializes its member name to "main".

The object which goes out of scope is immediately destroyed. In the above program, the function func() terminates first and hence, the local object l is destroyed first, which can also be observed from the program output. Secondly, the object x is destroyed during the termination of the function main(). Finally, the global object g is destroyed. When more than one object is created globally, or locally, they are destroyed in the reverse chronological order (*object created most recently is the first one to be destroyed*).

11.7 Constructors with Default Arguments

Like any other function in C++, constructors can also be defined with default arguments. If any arguments are passed during the creation of an object, the compiler selects the suitable constructor with default arguments. The program complex1.cpp illustrates the usage of default arguments during the creation of objects of the complex type class.

```
// complex1.cpp: default arguments to complex class
#include <iostream.h>
#include <math.h>
class complex
{
   private:
      float real;    // real part of complex number
      float imag;    // imaginary part of complex number
   public:
      complex()      // constructor 0
      {
         real = imag = 0.0;
      }
```

```
        complex( float real_in, float imag_in = 0.0 )    // constructor1
        {
            real = real_in;
            imag = imag_in;
        }
        void show( char *msg )         // display complex number in x+iy form
        {
            cout << msg << real;
            if( imag < 0 )
                cout << "-i";
            else
                cout << "+i";
            cout << fabs(imag) << endl;
        }
        complex add( complex c2 ); // Addition of complex numbers
};
// temp = default object + c2;
complex complex::add( complex c2 )      // add default and c2 complex objects
{
    complex temp;                       // object temp of complex class
    temp.real = real + c2.real;         // add real parts
    temp.imag = imag + c2.imag;         // add imaginary parts
    return( temp );                     // return complex object
}
void main()
{
    complex c1( 1.5, 2.0);   // uses constructor1
    complex c2( 2.2 );       // uses constructor1 with default imag value
    complex c3;              // uses constructor0
    c1.show("c1 = ");
    c2.show("c2 = ");
    c3 = c1.add( c2 );       // add c1 and c2 assign to c3
    c3.show( "c3 = c1.add( c2 ): ");
}
```

Run

```
c1 = 1.5+i2
c2 = 2.2+i0
c3 = c1.add( c2 ): 3.7+i2
```

The constructor complex(), in the class complex is declared as

```
        complex( float real_in, float imag_in = 0.0 )    // constructor1
```

The default value of the argument imag_in is zero. Then, the statement in main(),

```
        complex c2( 2.2 );
```

passes only one parameter explicitly to the constructor. The compiler treats this statement as,

```
        complex c2( 2.2, 0.0 );
```

by assuming the second argument to have default argument value (image_in = 0.0) specified at the declaration of the constructor. However, the statement,

```
        complex c1( 1.5, 2.0);
```

assigns 1.5 to `real_in` and 2.0 to `imag_in`. If the actual parameter is explicitly specified, it overrides the default value. As stated earlier, the missing arguments must be the trailing ones. The invocation of a constructor with default arguments while creating objects of the class `complex` is shown in Figure 11.6.

```
class complex
{
    ......
    ......
    public:
        complex();
        complex(float real_in,float imag_in=6.0);
        ......
};
complex c1(1.5,2.0);
complex c2(2.2);
complex c3;
```

Figure 11.6:   Default arguments to constructor

Suppose the specification of the constructor `complex(float,float)` is changed to,

```
complex( float real_in = 0.0, float imag_in = 0.0 )
```

in the above program, it causes ambiguity while using a statement such as,

```
complex c1;
```

The confusion is whether to call the no-argument constructor,

```
complex::complex()
```

or the two argument default constructor

```
complex::complex( float = 0.0, float = 0.0 )
```

Hence, such a specification should be avoided. If no constructors are defined, the compiler tries to generate a default constructor. This default constructor simply allocates storage to build an object of its class. A constructor that has all default arguments is similar to a default (no-argument) constructor, because it can be called without any explicit arguments. This may also lead to errors as shown in the following program segment:

```
class X
{
    int value;
    public:
        X()
        {
            value=0;
        }
        X(int i=0)
        {
            value=i;
        }
};
```

```
void main()
{
    X c;      // Error: This leads to errors as compiler will not be
              // able to decide which constructor should be called
    X c1(4); // OK
}
```

Trying to create an object of the class X without any arguments, will cause an error as two different constructors satisfy the requirement. Hence, the statement,

```
    X c;
```

causes the ambiguity whether to call X::X() or X::X(int i= 0). In this, if the default constructor is removed, the program works properly.

11.8 Nameless Objects

C++ not only supports the creation of named objects, but also the creation of unnamed objects. In the object creation statement, the name of an object need not be mentioned. The general format for instantiating nameless objects is shown in Figure 11.7.

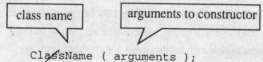

ClassName (arguments);

Figure 11.7:   Syntax of creating nameless objects

In the above syntax, the name of the object is not mentioned. However, the method of passing arguments to a constructor, and the procedure for creating the nameless object is similar to the procedure for creating named objects. Passing arguments to an object is optional and if no-arguments are mentioned, a default constructor of the class is invoked. If arguments are mentioned in the object creation statement, C++ invokes a constructor of the class that matches with the argument types. After execution of the constructor, nameless objects are immediately destroyed and the destructor of the class is invoked as a part of the object cleanup activity. Hence, the scope of a nameless object is limited only to the statement in which it is created.

The feature of nameless object creation is useful in functions returning an object. The program noname.cpp demonstrates the creation of nameless objects.

```
// noname.cpp: Nameless object creation
#include <iostream.h>
class nameless
{
    int a;
    public:
        nameless()
        {
            cout << "Constructor" << endl;
        }
```

```
    ~nameless()
    {
        cout << "Destructor" << endl;
    }
};
void main()
{
    nameless(); // nameless object is created as well as destroyed here
    nameless n1;
    nameless n2;
    cout << "Program terminates" << endl;
}
```

Run

```
Constructor    <— nameless()
Destructor     <— nameless()
Constructor    <— nameless n1()
Constructor    <— nameless n2()
Program terminates
Destructor     <— during program termination
Destructor     <— during program termination
```

From the output it is observed that the first two output statements are generated by the statement

```
    nameless(); // nameless object is created as well as destroyed here
```

It can be observed that, a nameless object is created and destroyed at the same point. But this is not the case with named objects. The statements,

```
    nameless n1;
    nameless n2;
```

create the named objects n1 and n2 and they are destroyed during the termination of the program.

11.9 Dynamic Initialization through Constructors

Object's data members can be dynamically initialized during runtime, even after their creation. The advantage of this feature is that it supports different initialization formats using overloaded constructors. It provides flexibility of using different forms of data at runtime depending upon the user's need.

Consider an example of naming persons. Some persons have only the first name (person name), some have the first and second name (person name and surname), and others have all the three (person name, surname, and third name). The program name.cpp illustrates the use of objects for holding names and constructing them at runtime using dynamic initialization.

```
// name.cpp: object with different name pattern
#include <iostream.h>
#include <string.h>
class name
{
    private:
        char first[15];   // first name
        char middle[15];  // middle name
```

```cpp
        char last[15];     // last name
   public:
     name()    // constructor0
      {
        // initialize all string pointers to NULL
        first[0] = middle[0] = last[0] = '\0';
      }
     name( char *FirstName );    // constructor1
     name( char *FirstName, char *MiddleName );  // constructor2
      //constructor3
     name( char *FirstName, char *MiddleName, char *LastName );
     void show( char *msg );
};
inline name::name( char *FirstName )
{
   strcpy( first, FirstName );
   middle[0] = last[0] = '\0';   // others to NULL
}
inline name::name( char *FirstName, char *MiddleName )
{
   strcpy( first, FirstName );
   strcpy( middle, MiddleName );
   last[0] = '\0';                // others to NULL
}
name::name( char *FirstName, char *MiddleName, char *LastName )
{
   strcpy( first, FirstName );
   strcpy( middle, MiddleName );
   strcpy( last, LastName );
}
void name::show( char *msg )
{
   cout << msg << endl;
   cout << "First Name: " << first << endl;
   if( middle[0] )
      cout << "Middle Name: " << middle << endl;
   if( last[0] )
      cout << "Last Name: " << last << endl;
}
void main()
{
   name n1, n2, n3;  // constructor0
   n1 = name( "Rajkumar" );                 // constructor1
   n2 = name( "Savithri", "S" );            // constructor2
   n3 = name( "Venugopal", "K", "R" );      // constructor3
   n1.show( "First person details..." );
   n2.show( "Second person details..." );
   n3.show( "Third person details..." );
};
```

Run

```
First person details...
First Name: Rajkumar
Second person details...
First Name: Savithri
Middle Name: S
Third person details...
First Name: Venugopal
Middle Name: K
Last Name: R
```

The program has four constructors. The arguments to the last three constructors are passed during runtime. The user input is used to initialize the `name` class's objects in one of the following form:

- No name at all: `default` constructor (constructor0) is invoked
- The first name: constructor1 is invoked
- The first and second name: constructor2 is invoked
- The first, second, and third name: constructor3 is invoked

The compiler selects an appropriate constructor while creating objects by choosing one that matches the input values. For instance, in the situation

```
n2 = name( "Savithri", "S" );            // constructor2
```

the compiler selects the two argument constructor

```
name( char *FirstName, char *MiddleName );  // constructor2
```

which matches the call for initializing the object `n2`'s data members.

11.10 Constructors with Dynamic Operations

A major application of constructors and destructors is in the management of memory allocation during runtime. It will enable a program to allocate the right amount of memory during execution for each object when the object's data member size is not the same. Allocation of memory to objects at the time of their construction is known as *dynamic construction*. The allocated memory can be released when the object is no longer needed (goes out of scope) at runtime and is known as *dynamic destruction*. The program `vector1.cpp` shows the use of `new` and `delete` operators during object creation and destruction respectively.

```
// vector1.cpp: vector class with array dynamically allocated
#include <iostream.h>
class vector
{
    int *v;  // pointer to a vector
    int sz;  // size of a vector
  public:
    vector( int size )   // constructor
    {
      sz = size;
      v = new int[ size ];    // dynamically allocate vector
    }
```

```
    ~vector()          // destructor
    {
        delete v;      // release vector memory
    }
    void read();
    void show_sum();
};
void vector::read()
{
    for( int i = 0; i < sz; i++ )
    {
        cout << "Enter vector[ " << i << " ] ? ";
        cin >> v[i];
    }
}
void vector::show_sum()
{
    int sum = 0;
    for( int i = 0; i < sz; i++ )
        sum += v[i];
    cout << "Vector Sum = " << sum;
}
void main()
{
    int count;
    cout << "How many elements are in the vector: ";
    cin >> count;
    // create an object of vector class and compute sum of vector elements
    vector v1( count );
    v1.read();
    v1.show_sum();
}
```

Run

```
How many elements are in the vector: 5
Enter vector[ 0 ] ? 1
Enter vector[ 1 ] ? 2
Enter vector[ 2 ] ? 3
Enter vector[ 3 ] ? 4
Enter vector[ 4 ] ? 5
Vector Sum = 15
```

In main(), the statement,

```
    vector v1( count );
```

creates the object v1 of the class vector dynamically of the size specified by the variable count (it is also read at runtime). The function read() accepts elements of the vector from the console and show_sum() computes the sum of all the vector elements and prints the same on the console.

The following points can be emphasized on dynamic initialization of objects.

♦ A constructor of the class makes sure that the data members are initially 0-pointers (NULL).

- A constructor with parameters allocates the right amount of memory resources. .
- A destructor releases all the allocated memory.

11.11 Copy Constructor

The parameters of a constructor can be of any of the data types except an object of its own class as a value parameter. Hence declaration of the following class specification leads to an error.

```
class X
{
    private:
    ...
    ...
    public:
        X ( X obj );   // Error: obj is value parameter
        ...
};
```

However, a class's own object can be passed as a reference parameter. Thus the class specification shown in Figure 11.8 is valid.

```
class X
{
    ......                     reference to an object of the class X
    public:
    X()
    X( X &obj );               copy constructor
    X(int a );
};
```

Figure 11.8:   Copy constructor

Such a constructor having a reference to an instance of its own class as an argument is known as *copy constructor*.

The compiler copies all the members of the user-defined source object to the destination object in the assignment statement, when its members are statically allocated. The data members, which are dynamically allocated must be copied to the destination object explicitly. It can be performed by either using the assignment operator, or the copy constructor. Consider the following statements,

```
vector v1( 5 ), v2( 5 );
v1 = v2;            // operator = invoked
vector v3 = v2;     // copy constructor is invoked
```

Assuming that v1 and v2 are the predefined objects of the class vector. The statement

```
v1 = v2;
```

will not invoke the copy constructor even though v1 and v2 are the objects of class vector. It must cause the compiler to copy the data from v2, member-by-member, into v1. This is the task of the assignment operator. For more details on assignment operator overloading refer to the chapter on *Operator Overloading*. The next statement,

```
vector v3 = v2;
```

initializes one object with another object during definition. The data members of v2 are copied member-by-member, into v3. It is the default action performed by the copy constructor. The statement,

        vector v3(v2)

is treated in the same way as the statement,

        vector v3 = v2;

by the compiler.

The default actions performed by the compiler are insufficient if data members of an object are dynamically changeable. It can be overcome by overriding these default actions. The program vector2.cpp illustrates the concept of overriding default operations performed by an user-defined copy constructor.

```cpp
// vector2.cpp: copy constructor for vector elements copying
#include <iostream.h>
class vector
{
      int * v;     // pointer to vector
      int size;    // size of vector v
   public:
      vector( int vector_size )
      {
         size = vector_size;
         v = new int[ vector_size ];
      }
      vector( vector &v2 );
      ~vector()
      {
         delete v;
      }
      int & elem( int i )
      {
         if( i >= size )
         {
            cout << endl << "Error: Out of Range";
            return -1;     // illegal access
         }
         return v[i];
      }
      void show();
};
// copy constructor, vector v1 = v2;
vector::vector( vector &v2 )
{
   cout << "\nCopy constructor invoked";
   size = v2.size;              // size of v1 is equal to size of v2
   v = new int[ v2.size ];      // allocate memory of the vector v1
   for( int i = 0; i < v2.size; i++ )
      v[i] = v2.v[i];
}
```

```
void vector::show()
{
    for( int i = 0; i < size; i++ )
        cout << elem( i ) << ", ";
}
void main()
{
    int i;
    vector v1( 5 ), v2( 5 );
    for( i = 0; i < 5; i++ )
        v2.elem( i ) = i + 1;
    v1 = v2;              // copy constructor is not invoked
    vector v3 = v2;       // copy constructor is invoked, vector v3(v2)
    cout << "\nvector v1: ";
    v1.show();
    cout << "\nvector v2: ";
    v2.show();
    cout << "\nvector v2: ";
    v3.show();
}
```

Run

```
Copy constructor invoked
vector v1: 1, 2, 3, 4, 5,
vector v2: 1, 2, 3, 4, 5,
vector v2: 1, 2, 3, 4, 5,
```

A copy constructor copies the data members from one object to another. The function also prints the message (copy constructor invoked) to assist the user in keeping track of its execution. The copy constructor takes only one argument, an object of the type vector, passed by reference. The prototype is

```
        vector( vector &v2 );
```

It is essential to use a reference in the argument of a copy constructor. It should not be passed as a value; if an argument is passed by value, its copy constructor would call itself to copy the actual parameter to the formal parameter. This process would go on-and-on until the system runs out of memory. Hence, in a copy constructor, the argument must always be passed by reference, preventing creation of copies. A copy constructor also gets invoked when the arguments are passed by value to functions, and when values are returned from functions. If an object is passed by value, the argument on which the function operates is created using a copy constructor. If an object is passed by address, or reference, the copy constructor would not be invoked, since, in such a case, copies of the objects need not be created. When an object is returned from a function, the copy constructor is invoked to create a copy of the value returned by the function.

11.12 Constructors for Two-dimensional Arrays

A class can have multidimensional arrays as data members. Their size can be either statically defined or dynamically varied during runtime. A matrix class can be designed to contain data members for storing matrix elements, which are created dynamically. The program matrix.cpp illustrates the method of constructing a matrix of size MarRow x MaxCol. It has member functions to perform various matrix operations such as addition, subtraction, etc. The destructor releases memory allocated to the matrix whenever an object of the class `matrix` goes out of scope.

```cpp
// matrix.cpp: Matrix manipulation class with dynamic resource allocation
#include <iostream.h>
#include <process.h>
const int TRUE = 1;
const int FALSE = 0;
class matrix
{
   private:
      int MaxRow;     // number of rows
      int MaxCol;     // number of columns
      int **p; // pointer to 2 dimensional array
   public:
      matrix()
      {
         MaxRow = 0; MaxCol = 0;
         p = NULL;
      }
      matrix( int row, int col );
      ~matrix();
      void read();
      void show();
      void add( matrix &a, matrix &b );
      void sub( matrix &a, matrix &b );
      void mul( matrix &a, matrix &b );
      int eql( matrix &b );
};
matrix::matrix( int row, int col )     // constructor
{
   MaxRow = row;
   MaxCol = col;
   p = new int *[ MaxRow ];    // dynamic allocation
   for( int i = 0; i < MaxRow; i++ )
      p[i] = new int[ MaxCol ];
}
matrix::~matrix()                       // destructor
{
   for( int i = 0; i < MaxRow; i++ )
      delete p[i];
   delete p;
}
// addition of matrices, c3.add(c1, c2): c3 = c1+c2
void matrix::add( matrix &a, matrix &b )
{
   int i, j;
   MaxRow = a.MaxRow;
   MaxCol = a.MaxCol;
```

```
   if( a.MaxRow != b.MaxRow || a.MaxCol != b.MaxCol )
   {
      cout << "Error: Invalid matrix order for addition";
      exit( 1 );
   }
   for( i = 0; i < MaxRow; i++ )
      for( j = 0; j < MaxCol; j++ )
         p[i][j] = a.p[i][j] + b.p[i][j];
}
// summation of matrices, c3.sub(c1, c2): c3 = c1-c2
void matrix::sub( matrix &a, matrix &b )
{
   int i, j;
   MaxRow = a.MaxRow;
   MaxCol = a.MaxCol;
   if( MaxRow != b.MaxRow || MaxCol != b.MaxCol )
   {
      cout << "Error: Invalid matrix order for subtraction";
      exit( 1 );
   }
   for( i = 0; i < MaxRow; i++ )
      for( j = 0; j < MaxCol; j++ )
         p[i][j] = a.p[i][j] - b.p[i][j];
}
// multiplication of matrices, c3.mul(c1, c2): c3 = c1*c2
void matrix::mul( matrix &a, matrix &b )
{
   int i, j, k;
   MaxRow = a.MaxRow;
   MaxCol = b.MaxCol;
   if( a.MaxCol != b.MaxRow )
   {
      cout << "Error: Invalid matrix order for multiplication";
      exit( 1 );
   }
   for( i = 0; i < a.MaxRow; i++ )
      for( j = 0; j < b.MaxCol; j++ )
      {
         p[i][j] = 0;
         for( k = 0; k < a.MaxCol; k++ )
            p[i][j] += a.p[i][k] * b.p[k][j];
      }
}
// compare matrices
int matrix::eql( matrix &b )
{
   int i, j;
   for( i = 0; i < MaxRow; i++ )
      for( j = 0; j < MaxCol; j++ )
         if( p[i][j] != b.p[i][j] )
            return 0;
```

```
    return 1;
}
void matrix::read()
{
   int i, j;
   for( i = 0; i < MaxRow; i++ )
      for( j = 0; j < MaxCol; j++ )
      {
         cout << "Matrix[" << i << "," << j << "] = ? ";
         cin >> p[i][j];
      }
}
void matrix::show()
{
   int i, j;
   for( i = 0; i < MaxRow; i++ )
   {
      cout << endl;
      for( j = 0; j < MaxCol; j++ )
         cout << p[i][j] << " ";
   }
}
void main()
{
   int m, n, p, q;
   cout << "Enter Matrix A details..." << endl;
   cout << "How many rows ? ";
   cin >> m;
   cout << "How many columns ? ";
   cin >> n;
   matrix a( m, n );
   a.read();
   cout << "Enter Matrix B details..." << endl;
   cout << "How many rows ? ";
   cin >> p;
   cout << "How many columns ? ";
   cin >> q;
   matrix b( p, q );
   b.read();
   cout << "Matrix A is ...";
   a.show();
   cout << endl << "Matrix B is ...";
   b.show();
   matrix c( m, n );
   c.add( a, b );
   cout << endl << "C = A + B...";
   c.show();
   matrix d( m, n );
   d.sub( a, b );
   cout << endl << "D = A - B...";
```

```
   d.show();
   matrix e( m, q );
   e.mul( a, b );
   cout << endl << "E = A * B...";
   e.show();
   cout << endl << "(Is matrix A equal to matrix B) ? ";
   if( a.eql( b ) )
      cout << "Yes";
   else
      cout << "No";
}
```

Run

```
Enter Matrix A details...
How many rows ? 3
How many columns ? 3
Matrix[0,0] = ? 2
Matrix[0,1] = ? 2
Matrix[0,2] = ? 2
Matrix[1,0] = ? 2
Matrix[1,1] = ? 2
Matrix[1,2] = ? 2
Matrix[2,0] = ? 2
Matrix[2,1] = ? 2
Matrix[2,2] = ? 2
Enter Matrix B details...
How many rows ? 3
How many columns ? 3
Matrix[0,0] = ? 1
Matrix[0,1] = ? 1
Matrix[0,2] = ? 1
Matrix[1,0] = ? 1
Matrix[1,1] = ? 1
Matrix[1,2] = ? 1
Matrix[2,0] = ? 1
Matrix[2,1] = ? 1
Matrix[2,2] = ? 1
Matrix A is ...
2 2 2
2 2 2
2 2 2
Matrix B is ...
1 1 1
1 1 1
1 1 1
C = A + B...
3 3 3
3 3 3
3 3 3
D = A - B...
```

```
1 1 1
1 1 1
1 1 1
E = A * B...
6 6 6
6 6 6
6 6 6
(Is matrix A equal to matrix B) ? No
```

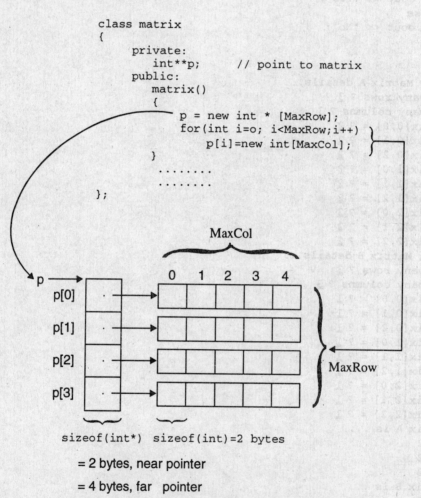

```
                    class matrix
                    {
                        private:
                           int**p;         // point to matrix
                        public:
                           matrix()
                           {
                              p = new int * [MaxRow];
                              for(int i=o; i<MaxRow;i++)
                                 p[i]=new int[MaxCol];
                           }
                           ........
                           ........
                    };
```

sizeof(int*) sizeof(int)=2 bytes

= 2 bytes, near pointer

= 4 bytes, far pointer

Figure 11.9: Constructor creating matrix dynamically

The constructor first creates a *vector pointer* to a list of integers of size MaxRow. It then allocates an integer type vector of size MaxCol pointed to by each element p[i]. Figure 11.9 shows the allocation of memory for the elements of a matrix whose size is MaxRow x MaxCol dynamically.

11.13 Constant Objects and Constructor

C++ allows to define constant objects of user-defined classes similar to constants of standard data types. The syntax for defining a constant object is shown in Figure 11.10.

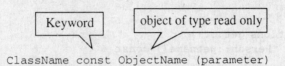

ClassName const ObjectName (parameter)

Figure 11.10: Constant object creation

The data members of a constant object can be initialized only by a constructor, as a part of object creation procedure. Once a constant object is created, no member functions of its class can modify its data members. They can only read the contents of the data member. Such data members are termed as *read-only data members* and the object is termed as *constant,* or *read-only object.* The const objects behave like a ROM (Read Only Memory) of a computer. In such a memory, the data is stored during their fabrication, like constant objects are initialized only by a constructor during its creation. It is illustrated in the program person.cpp.

```
// person.cpp: person class with const member functions
#include <iostream.h>
#include <string.h>
class Person
{
    private:
        char *name;             // name of person
        char *address;          // address field
        char *phone;            // telephone number
    public:
        Person( char *NameIn, char *AddressIn, char *PhoneIn );
        ~Person();
        // functions to set fields
        void Person::changename( char const *NameIn );
        // functions to inspect fields
        char const *getname(void) const;
        char const *getaddress(void) const;
        char const *getphone(void) const;
};
// constructor
void Person::Person( char *NameIn, char *AddressIn, char *PhoneIn )
{
    name = new char[ strlen( NameIn )+1];
    strcpy( name, NameIn );
    address = new char[ strlen( AddressIn )+1];
    strcpy( address, AddressIn );
    phone = new char[ strlen( PhoneIn )+1];
    strcpy( phone, PhoneIn );
}
```

```
// destructor, release memory allocated to class data members
inline void Person::~Person()
{
   delete name;
   delete address;
   delete phone;
}
// interface functions get...()
inline char const *Person::getname() const
{
   return name;
}
inline char const *Person::getaddress() const
{
   return address;
}
inline char const *Person::getphone() const
{
   return phone;
}
void Person::changename( char const *NameIn )
{
   if( name )
      delete name;
   name = new char[ strlen( NameIn )+1 ];
   strcpy( name, NameIn );
}
void printperson( Person const &p )
{
   if( p.getname() )
      cout << "Name   : " << p.getname() << endl;
   if( p.getaddress() )
      cout << "Address: " << p.getaddress() << endl ;
   if( p.getphone() )
      cout << "Phone  : " << p.getphone() << endl;
}
void main()
{
   Person const me("Rajkumar","E-mail: raj@cdacb.ernet.in",
        "91-080-5584271");
   printperson( me );
   Person you( "XYZ", "-not sure-", "-not sure-" );
   cout << "You XYZ by default..." << endl;
   printperson( you );
   you.changename( "ABC" );
   cout << "You XYZ changed to ABC ..." << endl;
   printperson( you );
}
```

Run

```
Name   : Rajkumar
Address: E-mail: raj@cdacb.ernet.in
```

```
Phone : 91-080-5584271
You XYZ by default...
Name   : XYZ
Address: -not sure-
Phone  : -not sure-
You XYZ changed to ABC ...
Name   : ABC
Address: -not sure-
Phone  : -not sure-
```

The above program shows how a constant object of the class `Person` can be defined. At the point of the definition of an object, the data fields are initialized (this is the action of the constructor). Following the definition,

```
Person const me("Rajkumar", "raj@cdacb.ernet.in", "91-080-5584271");
```

it would be illegal to try to redefine the name, address, or phone number for the object `me`; hence, the statement

```
me.setname("Bill Gates");
```

would not be accepted by the compiler. Generally, it is a good habit to define objects and member functions, which do not modify their data as constant type.

11.14 Static Data Members with Constructors and Destructors

Each object of a class has its own public or private data members, which are accessible only to its member functions. In certain situations, it is desirable to have one or more common data fields, which are accessible to all the objects of the class. An example of such a situation is to keep track of the status of *how many objects of a class* are created and *how many of them* are currently active in the program. Based on the number of objects present, some specific initialization has to be performed; only the first object of the class would then perform the initialization and set the flag to *done*.

The use of static data members with constructors and destructors is illustrated by the program `graph.cpp`. It has a class called `Graphics`, which defines the communication of a program with a graphics device (such as EGA or VGA screen). The initial preparation of the device, i.e., switching from text mode to graphics mode, is an action of the constructor and depends on a static flag variable `nobjects`. The variable `nobjects` simply counts the number of objects of the class `Graphics` present at that time. Similarly, the destructor of a class may switch back from graphics mode to text mode when the last graphical object ceases to exist.

```
// graph.cpp: keeps count of how many objects are created
#include <iostream.h>
class Graphics
{
   private:
      // counter of number of objects
      static int nobjects;
      // hypothetical functions to switch to graphics
      // mode or back to text mode
      void setgraphicsmode ()
      {}
```

```
      void settextmode ()
      {}
  public:
    // constructor, destructor
    Graphics ();
    ~Graphics ();
    //other interface is not shown here,to draw lines, or circles etc.
    int get_count() const
    {
        return nobjects;
    }
};
// the constructor
Graphics::Graphics ()
{
   if (! nobjects)
      setgraphicsmode ();
   nobjects++;
}
// the destructor
Graphics::~Graphics ()
{
   nobjects-;
   if (! nobjects)
      settextmode ();
}
void my_func()
{
   Graphics obj;  // nobject is incremented by its constructor
   cout<<"\nNo. of Graphics Object's while in my_func = "<<obj.get_count();
}  // obj goes out of scope, destructor is called
// the static data member
int Graphics::nobjects = 0; //global:if not defined generates linker error
void main()
{
   Graphics obj1;
   cout<<"No. of Graphics Object's before my_func = "<<obj1.get_count();
   my_func();
   cout<<"\nNo. of Graphics Object's after my_func = "<<obj1.get_count();
   Graphics obj2, obj3, obj4;
   cout<<"\nValue of static member nobjects after all 3 more objects...";
   cout << "\nIn obj1 = " << obj1.get_count();
   cout << "\nIn obj2 = " << obj2.get_count();
   cout << "\nIn obj3 = " << obj3.get_count();
   cout << "\nIn obj4 = " << obj4.get_count();
}
```

Run

```
No. of Graphics Object's before my_func = 1
No. of Graphics Object's while in my_func = 2
```

```
No. of Graphics Object's after my_func = 1
Value of static member nobjects after all 3 more objects...
In obj1 = 4
In obj2 = 4
In obj3 = 4
In obj4 = 4
```

The purpose of the variable nobjects is to count the number of objects of the class Graphics, which exist at a given time. When the first object is created, the graphics device is initialized. When the last object is destroyed, the switch from graphics mode to text mode is made. The statement

```
        int Graphics::nobjects = 0;
```

defines and initializes the static data member. If this statement is missing, the linker will generate the error: undefined Graphics::nobjects symbol.

It is obvious that when the class Graphics defines more than one constructor, each constructor would need to increment the variable nobjects and possibly would have to initialize the graphics mode. The constructor

```
        Graphics::Graphics ()
```

increments the variable nobjects by one and the destructor

```
        Graphics::~Graphics ()
```

decrements the variable nobjects by one. Therefore, for every object created, the variable nobjects is incremented by one and whenever an object of the class Graphics goes out of scope, the variable nobjects is decremented by one.

11.15 Nested Classes

The power of abstraction of a class can be increased by including other class declarations inside a class. A class declared inside the declaration of another class is called *nested class*. Nested classes provide classes with non-global status. Host and nested classes follow the same access rules for members that exist between non-nested classes. Nested classes could be used to hide specialized classes and their instances within a host class.

A member of a class may itself be a class. Such nesting enables building of very powerful data structures. The Student class can be enhanced to accommodate the date of birth of a student. The new member data type date is a class by itself as shown below:

```
    class Student
    {
        private:
            int roll_no;
            char name[25];
            char branch[15];
            int marks;
        public:
            class date
            {
                int day;
                int month;
                int year;
```

```
    public:
        date()
        {
          ... // initializing members of date class
        }
        read();
        ..... // other member functions of date class
} birthday;    // instance of the nested date class
Student()
{
    ....// initialize members of Student class
}
~Student()
{
    ....
}
read()
{
    //read members of Student class's object including 'birthday'
    cin >> roll_no;
    ....
    birthday.read();   // accessing member of a nested class date
}
    .... // other member functions of Student class
};
```

The embedded class date is declared within the enclosing class declaration. An object of type Student can be defined as follows:

```
    Student s1;
```

The year in which the student s1 was born can be accessed as follows:

```
    s1.birthday.year
```

A statement such as,

```
    s1.date.day = 2;      // error
```

is invalid, because members of the nested class must be accessed using its object name.

The feature of nesting of classes is useful while implementing powerful data structures such as linked lists and trees. For instance, the stack data structure can be implemented having a node data member which is an instance of another class (node class).

Review Questions

11.1   What are constructors and destructors ? Explain how they differ from normal functions.

11.2   What are the differences between default and parameterized constructors ?

11.3   What are copy constructors and explain their need ?

11.4   What is the order of construction and destruction of objects ?

11.5   What are read-only objects ? What is the role of constructor in creating such objects ?

11.6   State which of the following statements are TRUE or FALSE. Give reasons.

(a) Constructors must be explicitly invoked.

(b) Constructors defined in private section are useful.

(c) Constructors can return value.

(d) Destructors are invoked automatically.

(e) Destructors take input parameters.

(f) Destructors can be overloaded.

(g) Constructors cannot be overloaded.

(h) Constructors can take default arguments.

(i) Data members of nameless objects can be initialized using constructors only.

(j) Constructors can allocate memory during runtime.

(k) A class member function can take its class's objects as value arguments.

(l) Constant objects can be initialized by using constructors only.

(m) Data members of a class can be initialized at the point of their definition.

11.7 Consider a class called MyArray having pointer to integers as its data member. Its objects must appear like arrays, but they must be dynamically re-sizable. Write a program to illustrate the use of constructors in MyArray class.

11.8 Write a program to model Time class using constructors.

11.9 Distinguish between the following two statements:
```
String name( "Smrithi" );
String name = "Smrithi";
```

11.10 Declare a class called String. It must have constructors which allow definition of objects in the following form: (The class String has data member str of type char *)
```
String name1;        // str points to NULL
String name2 = "Minu"; // one-argument constructor is invoked
String name3 = name2; //one-argument constructor taking String object
```
Write a program to model String class and to manipulate its objects. The destructor must release memory allocated to the str data member by its counterpart.

11.11 Create a class, which keeps track of the number of its instances. Use static data member, constructors, and destructors to maintain updated information about active objects.

Dynamic Objects

12.1 Introduction

C++ takes the middle ground between languages (such as C and Pascal) which support dynamic memory allocation (discussed in the chapter *Pointers and Runtime Binding*) and languages (like Java), in which all variables are dynamically allocated. C++ supports creation of objects with scoped lifetimes (stack-based objects) and with arbitrary lifetimes (heap-based objects). Stack-based objects are managed by the compiler implicitly, whereas heap-based objects are managed by the programmers explicitly.

C++ is different from C because it not only allocates memory for an object, but also initializes them. Thus when a dynamic object is created, it creates a *live object*, and not just a chunk of memory big enough to hold the object. It is initialized with necessary data at runtime. Unlike dynamic memory allocation which just allocates memory, dynamic object creation supported by C++ allocates and initializes objects at runtime.

A class can be instantiated at runtime and objects created by such instantiation are called *dynamic objects*. The lifetime of dynamic objects in C++ (which is allocated from heap memory—the free store) is managed explicitly by the program. The program must guarantee that each dynamic object is deleted when it is no longer needed, and certainly before it becomes garbage. (There is no garbage collection in standard C++, and few programs can afford to produce garbage.) For each dynamic allocation, a policy that determines the objects's lifetime must be found by the programmer and implemented. These policies used in managing dynamic objects will be discussed at the end of this chapter. The lifetime of an object in C++ is the interval of time it exists by occupying memory. Creation and deletion of objects as and when required, offers a great degree of flexibility in programming.

Objects with scoped lifetimes are created in the stack memory. Stack memory is a store house which holds local variables or objects, and whenever they go out of scope, the memory allocated for them in the stack is released automatically. *Objects with arbitrary lifetimes* are created in the heap memory. These dynamic objects can be created or destroyed as and when required, explicitly by the programmer. The operators new and delete used with standard data type variable's management can also be used for creating or destroying objects at runtime respectively.

12.2 Pointers to Objects

The C++ language defines two operators which are specific for the allocation and deallocation of memory. These operators are new and delete. The new operator is used to create dynamic objects and delete operator is used to release the memory allocated to the dynamic object by the new operator. A pointer to a variable can be defined to hold the address of an object, which is created statically or dynamically. Such pointer variables can be used to access data or function members of a class using the * or -> operators.

Pointer to Object Definition

Pointers can be used to hold addresses of objects, just as they can hold addresses of primitive and user-defined data items. The need for using pointers to objects becomes clear when objects are to be created while the program is being executed, which is an instance of dynamic allocation of memory. The new operator can also be used to obtain the address of the allocated memory area besides allocating storage area to the objects of the given class. Thus, the address returned by the new operator may be used to initialize a pointer to an object.

The general format for defining a pointer to an object is shown in Figure 12.1, which is similar to the way in which pointers to other data types are declared and defined. A pointer can be made to point to an existing object, or to a newly created object using the new operator. The address operator & can be used to get the address of an object, which is defined statically during the compile time. In the following statement

```
ptr_to_object = & object;
```

The & operator in the expression &object returns the address of the object and the same is initialized to a pointer variable ptr_to_object.

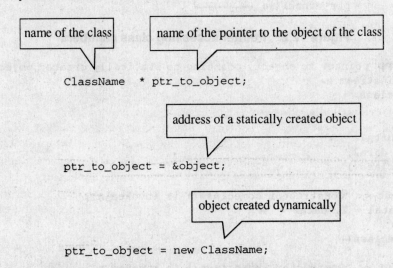

```
ClassName  * ptr_to_object;
```

```
ptr_to_object = &object;
```

```
ptr_to_object = new ClassName;
```

Figure 12.1: Syntax of defining pointer to object

Accessing Members of Objects

In order to utilize a pointer to an object, it is necessary to have some means by which the members of that object can be accessed and manipulated. As in the case of pointers to structures, there are two approaches to referring and accessing the members of an object whose address resides in a pointer. The operator -> can also be used to access member of an object using a pointer to objects. The expression to access a class member using pointer is as follows:

```
pointer_to_object -> member_name
```
or
```
*pointer_to_object.member_name
```

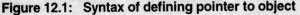

The member to be accessed through the object pointer can be either a data, or function member (see

Figure 12.2). The program `ptrobj1.cpp` illustrates the definition of pointers to objects and their usage in accessing members of a class.

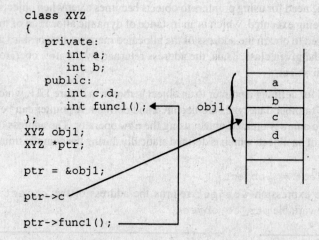

```
class XYZ
{
    private:
        int a;
        int b;
    public:
        int c,d;
        int func1();  ◄────    obj1
};
XYZ obj1;
XYZ *ptr;

ptr = &obj1;

ptr->c

ptr->func1();  ────────
```

Figure 12.2:   Pointer accessing class members

```cpp
// ptrobj1.cpp: pointer to object, pointing to statically created objects
#include <iostream.h>
class someclass
{
   public:
      int data1;
      char data2;
      someclass()
      {
         cout << "Constructor someclass() is invoked\n";
         data1 = 1, data2 = 'A';
      }
      ~someclass()
      {
         cout << "Destructor ~someclass() is invoked\n";
      }
      void show()
      {
         cout << "data1 = " << data1;
         cout << " data2 = " << data2 << endl;
      }
};
void main(void)
{
   someclass *ptr;        // define a pointer to object of class someclass
   someclass object1;     // object of type someclass created statically
   ptr = &object1;
   cout << "Accessing object through object1.show()..." << endl;
```

```
    object1.show();
    cout << "Accessing object through ptr->show()..." << endl;
    ptr->show();   // it can be *ptr.show();
}
```

Run

```
Constructor someclass() is invoked
Accessing object through object1.show()...
data1 = 1 data2 = A
Accessing object through ptr->show()....
data1 = 1 data2 = A
Destructor ~someclass() is invoked
```

In main(), the statement,

> ptr = &object1;

assigns the address of the object object1 of the class someclass to the pointer ptr. The statement

> ptr->show();
>
> or
>
> *ptr.show()

invokes the member function show() of the object pointed to by the pointer ptr. It points to the object1, and hence executes the function show() of the respective class.

Creating and Deleting Dynamic Objects

A dynamic object can be created by the execution of a new operator expression. The syntax for creating a dynamic object using the new operator is as follows:

> *new ClassName*

It returns the address of a newly created object. The returned address of an object can be stored in a variable of type pointer to object (ptr_to_object) as follows:

> *ptr_to_object = new ClassName;*

While creating a dynamic object, *if a class has the default constructor, it is invoked as a part of object creation activity.* Once a pointer is holding the address of a dynamic object, its members can be accessed by using -> operator.

The entity that executes the new expression is the dynamic object's creator. The creator may be a (member) function, an object, or a class. The creator of a dynamic object must be in a position to fully determine the object's lifetime. The creator cannot be inferred from the source code alone. Although, the creator is determined by the intent of the programmer, the language constrains the choice. In the program ptrobj1.cpp, the function main() is the creator of the object pointed to by variable ptr_to_object and hence, it is responsible for destroying it.

The syntax of the delete operator releasing memory allocated to dynamic object is as follows:

> *delete ptr_to_object;*

It destroys the object pointed to by ptr_to_object variable. It also *invokes the destructor of the class if it exists as a part of object destruction activity* before releasing memory allocated to an object by the new operator.

The program `ptrobj2.cpp` illustrates the binding of dynamic objects' address to a pointer variable. The pointer defined is initialized with the address returned by the new operator, which actually creates the object.

```cpp
// ptrobj2.cpp: pointer to object, pointing to dynamically created objects
# include <iostream.h>
class someclass
{
   public:
      int data1;
      char data2;
      someclass()
      {
        cout << "Constructor someclass() is invoked\n";
        data1 = 1, data2 = 'A';
      }
     ~someclass()
      {
        cout << "Destructor ~someclass() is invoked\n";
      }
      void show()
      {
        cout << "data1 = " << data1;
        cout << " data2 = " << data2 << endl;
      }
};
void main(void)
{
   someclass *ptr;        // define a pointer to object of class someclass
   cout << "Creating dynamic object..." << endl;
   ptr = new someclass;  // object created dynamically
   cout << "Accessing dynamic object through ptr->show()..." << endl;
   ptr->show();
   cout << "Destroying dynamic object..." << endl;
   delete ptr;            // object destroyed dynamically
}
```

Run

```
Creating dynamic object...
Constructor someclass() is invoked
Accessing dynamic object through ptr->show()...
data1 = 1 data2 = A
Destroying dynamic object...
Destructor ~someclass() is invoked
```

In `main()`, the statement

```
      ptr = new someclass;  // object created dynamically
```

creates the *nameless object* of the class someclass dynamically and assigns its address to the object pointer ptr. It executes the constructor of the class someclass automatically during the creation of dynamic objects. The default argument constructor initializes the data members data1 and data2.

These data can be referenced by other member functions of its class. The statement

```
ptr->show();
```

invokes the member function show() of the object pointed to by the pointer variable ptr. It points to the object of the class someclass and hence, executes its member function show() as illustrated in Figure 12.3.

When the dynamic object pointed to by the variable ptr goes out of scope, the memory allocated to that object is not released automatically. It must be performed explicitly as follows:

```
delete ptr;
```

The above statement releases the memory allocated to the dynamically created object by the new operator. In addition to this, it also invokes the destructor function ~someclass() to perform cleanup of resources allocated to the object's data members. In this class, object data members are not allocated with any resources dynamically and hence, no need to release them explicitly.

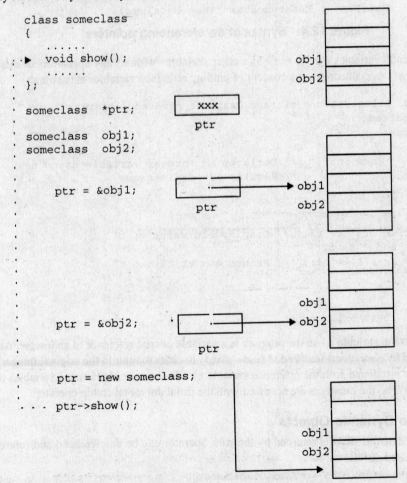

Figure 12.3:   Object pointers and dynamic binding

Whenever it is necessary to determine the size of the memory area allocated to an object by the new operator, the `sizeof` operator may be used. For instance, the expression `sizeof(someclass)` returns the number of bytes required for the creation of an object of the class `someclass`.

Dereferencing Pointers

As the new operator returns a pointer to an area of memory that holds an object, it should be possible to refer to the original object by dereferencing the pointer. This method of memory allocation requires the use of both, the indirection operator * and the reference operator &. The general format for such a declaration is shown in Figure 12.4.

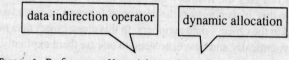

```
DataType & ReferenceVar=*(new DataType);
```

Figure 12.4:   Syntax of dereferencing pointers

Such reference variables can be used like other variables without any special mechanism. The program `useref.cpp` illustrates the concept of binding reference variables at runtime.

```cpp
// useref.cpp: Illustrates a variant usage of reference operator
#include <iostream.h>
void main(void)
{
    int & t1 = *(new int);   // Declares an integer variable using new
    int t2, t3;              // Regular int definitions
    t1 = t3 = 5;
    t2 = 10;
    t1 = t1 + t2;
    cout << "Sum of " << t3;  // Display old value of t1
    cout << " and " << t2 ;
    cout << " is : " << t1;   // Prints sum of t1 and t2
}
```

Run

```
Sum of 5 and 10 is : 15
```

Observe that the variable `t1` in the program is a variable of type reference to an integer. Also, the pointer returned by new is dereferenced, `*(new int)`, in order to refer to the original integer object which is finally associated with the reference variable `t1`. In the case of reference variables to class objects or structures, the members are accessed with the usual dot membership operator.

Reference to Dynamic Objects

The address of dynamic objects returned by the new operator can be dereferenced and reference to them can be created as follows:

```
ClassName &RefObj = *(new ClassName);
```

The reference to object `RefObj` can be used as a normal object; the memory allocated to such objects cannot be released except during the termination of the program. The program `refobj.cpp` illustrates the dereferencing of objects using reference pointers.

```
// refobj.cpp: reference to dynamic objects
#include <iostream.h>
#include <string.h>
class student
{
  private:
     int roll_no;          // roll number
     char name[ 20 ];      // name of a student
  public:
     // initializing data members
     void setdata( int roll_no_in, char *name_in )
     {
        roll_no = roll_no_in;
        strcpy( name, name_in );
     }
     // display data members on the console screen
     void outdata()
     {
        cout << "Roll No = " << roll_no << endl;
        cout << "Name = " << name << endl;
     }
};
void main()
{
  student &s1 = *(new student); // reference to a dynamic object
  s1.setdata( 1, "Savithri" );
  s1.outdata();
  student &s2 = *(new student); // reference to a dynamic object
  s2.setdata( 2, "Bhavani" );
  s2.outdata();
  student s3;
  s3.setdata( 3, "Vani" );
  student &s4 = s3;    // reference to static object
  s3.outdata();
  s4.outdata();
}
```

Run

```
Roll No = 1
Name = Savithri
Roll No = 2
Name = Bhavani
Roll No = 3
Name = Vani
Roll No = 3
Name = Vani
```

In main(), the statement

```
        student &s1 = * (new student);
```

creates a dynamic object of the class student and binds it to the reference variable s1. The expression * (new student) creates a dynamic object. The memory allocated to such objects cannot be released except during the termination of the program. The statement

```
s1.setdata( 1, "Savithri" );
```

accesses the member `setdata()` in the same way as normal objects accesses. The statement

```
student &s4 = s3;
```

creates the reference to normal object with the name `s4`. Note that, reference objects are accessed in the same way whether normal, or dynamic type objects.

12.3 Live Objects

The operator `new` allocates memory big enough to store an object and initializes it with the required data. Objects created dynamically with their data members initialized during creation are known as *live objects*. To create a live object, constructor must be invoked automatically which performs initialization of data members. Similarly, the destructor for an object must be invoked automatically before the memory for that object is deallocated. The syntax for creating a live object is as follows:

```
ptr_to_object = new ClassName( parameters )
```

A class whose live object is to be created must have *atleast one constructor*. The number of parameters passed specified at the point of creation of dynamic objects can be zero or more. If no arguments are specified, the default constructor (constructor with zero arguments) will be invoked automatically. If a class has more than one constructor, the constructor that matches with the parameters specified is invoked for initialization of the dynamic object. Note that there is no special syntax for releasing memory allocated to the objects, which are created and initialized by passing parameters. Hence, the syntax for destroying live objects is the same as that of normal dynamic objects.

The program `student3.cpp` illustrates the creation of *live* objects and their manipulation. It has a class called student having three constructor functions for initializing static or dynamic objects. The information required for initializing some dynamic objects is passed as parameters and some are initialized with information read at runtime.

```
// student3.cpp: manipulation of live objects
#include <iostream.h>
#include <string.h>
class student
{
   private:
      int roll_no;         // roll number
      char *name;          // name of a student
   public:
      // initializing data members using constructors
      student()    // constructor 0
      {
         char flag, str[50];
         cout << "Do you want to initialize the object (y/n): ";
         cin >> flag;
         if( flag == 'y' || flag == 'Y' )
         {
           cout << "Enter Roll no. of student: ";
           cin >> roll_no;
```

```
            cout << "Enter Name of student: ";
            cin >> str;
            name = new char[ strlen(str)+1 ];   // dynamic initialization
            strcpy( name, str );
        }
        else
        {
            roll_no = 0;
            name = NULL;
        }
    }
    student( int roll_no_in )  // constructor 1
    {
        roll_no = roll_no_in;
        name = NULL;
    }
    student( int roll_no_in, char *name_in )   // constructor 2
    {
        roll_no = roll_no_in;
        name = new char[ strlen(name_in)+1 ];
        strcpy( name, name_in );
    }
    ~student()
    {
        if( name )
            delete name;   // release memory allocated to name member
    }
    void set( int roll_no_in, char *name_in )
    {
        student( roll_no_in, name_in );
    }
    // display data members on the console screen
    void show()
    {
        if( roll_no )  // if( roll_no != 0 )
            cout << "Roll No: " << roll_no << endl;
        else
            cout << "Roll No: (not initialized)" << endl;
        if( name )   // if( name != NULL )
            cout << "Name: " << name << endl;
        else
            cout << "Name: (not initialized)" << endl;
    }
};
void main()
{
    student *s1, *s2, *s3, *s4;
    s1 = new student;    // will be initialized during run time by the user
    s2 = new student;    // will be initialized during run time by the user
    s3 = new student( 1 );  // partially live object
    s4 = new student( 2, "Bhavani" ); // fully live object
```

```
    cout << "Live objects contents..." << endl;
    // display contents of all live objects
    s1->show();
    s2->show();
    s3->show();
    s4->show();
    // release the memory allocated to dynamic objects s1, s2, s3, and s4
    delete s1;
    delete s2;
    delete s3;
    delete s4;
}
```

Run

```
Do you want to initialize the object (y/n): n
Do you want to initialize the object (y/n): y
Enter Roll no. of student: 5
Enter Name of student: Rekha
Live objects contents...
Roll No: (not initialized)
Name: (not initialized)
Roll No: 5
Name: Rekha
Roll No: 1
Name: (not initialized)
Roll No: 2
Name: Bhavani
```

In main(), the statement

```
    student *s1, *s2, *s3, *s4;
```

creates pointer variables to objects of the class student. The statements

```
    s1 = new student;
    s2 = new student;
```

create two objects dynamically and store their addresses in the variable s1 and s2 respectively. These objects are initialized by invoking the default constructor which reads the data entered by the user at runtime. The statement

```
    s3 = new student( 1 );
```

creates an object and initializes its first data member by invoking the one-argument constructor. The object s3 is partially initialized object. The statement

```
    s4 = new student( 2, "Bhavani" );
```

creates an object named s4 and initializes all its data members by invoking the two-argument constructor. The member function show() of the class student is invoked for all the objects pointed to by s1, s2, s3, and s4 to display students' roll number and their name. All the objects created in this program are destroyed explicitly by using delete operator. The destructor is invoked automatically for each one of these objects to release the memory allocated to their string data member name. For instance, the statement,

```
    delete s2;
```

releases the memory allocated to the object pointed to by s2 and also invokes the destructor to cleanup.

12.4 Array of Objects

C++ allows the user to create an array of any data type including user-defined data types. Thus, an array of variables of a class data type can also be defined, and such variables are called an array of objects. An array of objects is often used to handle a group of objects, which reside contiguously in the memory. Consider the following class specification:

```
class student
{
    private:
        int roll_no;        // roll number
        char name[ 20 ];    // name of a student
    public:
        void setdata( int roll_no_in, char *name_in );
        void outdata();
};
```

The identifier `student` is a user-defined data type and can be used to create objects that relate to students of different courses. The following definition creates an array of objects of the `student` class:

```
student science[10]; // array of science course students
student medical[5];  // array of medical course students
student engg[25];    // array of engineering course students
```

The array `science` contains ten objects, namely `science[0]`, ..,`science[9]` of type student class, the `medical` array contains 5 objects and the `engg` array contains 25 objects.

An array of objects is stored in the memory in the same way as a multidimensional array created at compile time. The representation of an array of `engg` objects is shown in Figure 12.5. Note that, only the memory space for data members of the objects is created; member functions are stored separately and shared by all the objects of `student` class.

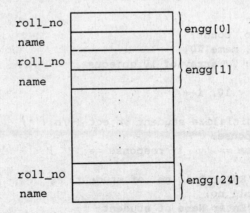

Figure 12.5: Storage for data items in an array of objects

An array of objects behaves similar to any other data-type array. The individual element of an array of objects is referenced by using its index, and member of an object is accessed using the *dot* operator.

For instance, the statement

```
engg[i].setdata( 10, "Rajkumar" );
```

sets the data members of the ith element of the array engg. Similarly, the statement

```
engg[i].outdata();
```

will display the data of the ith element of the array engg[i]. The program student1.cpp illustrates the use of the array of objects.

```cpp
// student1.cpp: array of student data type
#include <iostream.h>
#include <string.h>
class student
{
   private:
      int roll_no;          // roll number
      char name[ 20 ];      // name of a student
   public:
      // initializing data members
      void setdata( int roll_no_in, char *name_in )
      {
         roll_no = roll_no_in;
         strcpy( name, name_in );
      }
      // display data members on the console screen
      void outdata()
      {
         cout << "Roll No = " << roll_no << endl;
         cout << "Name = " << name << endl;
      }
};
void main()
{
   int i, roll_no, count;
   char response, name[20];
   student s[10]; // array of 10 objects
   count = 0;
   for( i = 0; i < 10; i++ )
   {
      cout << "Initialize student object (y/n): ";
      cin >> response;
      if( response == 'y' || response == 'Y' )
      {
         cout << "Enter Roll no. of student: ";
         cin >> roll_no;
         cout << "Enter Name of student: ";
         cin >> name;
         s[i].setdata( roll_no, name );
         count++;
      }
```

```
        else
            break;
    }
    cout << "Student details..." << endl;
    for( i = 0; i < count; i++ )
        s[i].outdata();
}
```

Run
```
Initialize student object (y/n): y
Enter Roll no. of student: 1
Enter Name of student: Rajkumar
Initialize student object (y/n): y
Enter Roll no. of student: 2
Enter Name of student: Tejaswi
Initialize student object (y/n): y
Enter Roll no. of student: 3
Enter Name of student: Savithri
Initialize student object (y/n): n
Student details...
Roll No = 1
Name = Rajkumar
Roll No = 2
Name = Tejaswi
Roll No = 3
Name = Savithri
```

In main(), the statement

```
    student s[10];
```

creates an array of 10 possible objects of the student class. It should be clearly understood that an array of objects allow better organization of the program instead of having 10 different variables and each one of them is the object of the student class. Note that the subscripted notation used for object is similar to the manner in which arrays of other data types are usually handled. The statement

```
    s[i].outdata();
```

executes the outdata() member function in the student class for the ith object of the s array.

12.5 Array of Pointers to Objects

An array of pointers to objects is often used to handle a group of objects, which need not necessarily reside contiguously in memory, as in the case of a static array of objects. This approach is more flexible, in comparison with placing the objects themselves in an array, because objects could be dynamically created as and when they are required. The syntax for defining an array of pointers to objects is the same as any of the fundamental types. The program student2.cpp illustrates the concept of array of pointers to objects.

```
// student2.cpp: array of pointers to student
#include <iostream.h>
#include <string.h>
```

```
class student
{
   private:
      int roll_no;          // roll number
      char name[ 20 ];      // name of a student
   public:
      // initializing data members
      void setdata( int roll_no_in, char *name_in )
      {
         roll_no = roll_no_in;
         strcpy( name, name_in );
      }
      // display data members on the console screen
      void outdata()
      {
         cout << "Roll No = " << roll_no << endl;
         cout << "Name = " << name << endl;
      }
};
void main()
{
   int i, roll_no, count;
   char response, name[20];
   student * s[10];    // array of pointers to objects
   count = 0;
   for( i = 0; i < 10; i++ )
   {
      cout << "Create student object (y/n): ";
      cin >> response;
      if( response == 'y' || response == 'Y' )
      {
         cout << "Enter Roll no. of student: ";
         cin >> roll_no;
         cout << "Enter Name of student: ";
         cin >> name;
         s[i] = new student;  // dynamically creating objects
         s[i]->setdata( roll_no, name );
         count++;
      }
      else
         break;
   }
   cout << "Student details..." << endl;
   for( i = 0; i < count; i++ )
      s[i]->outdata();
   for( i = 0; i < count; i++ )   // release memory allocated to all objects
      delete s[i];
}
```

Run

```
Create student object (y/n): y
```

```
Enter Roll no. of student: 1
Enter Name of student: Rajkumar
Create student object (y/n): Y
Enter Roll no. of student: 2
Enter Name of student: Tejaswi
Create student object (y/n): y
Enter Roll no. of student: 3
Enter Name of student: Savithri
Create student object (y/n): n
Student details...
Roll No = 1
Name = Rajkumar
Roll No = 2
Name = Tejaswi
Roll No = 3
Name = Savithri
```

In main(), the statement

```
student * s[10];
```

creates an array of pointers of 10 possible student objects. It should be clearly understood that the space required for an array of 10 pointers to student objects is certainly less than the space for an array of 10 student objects. Hence, the student class objects are created by the program as and when they are needed (see Figure 12.6).

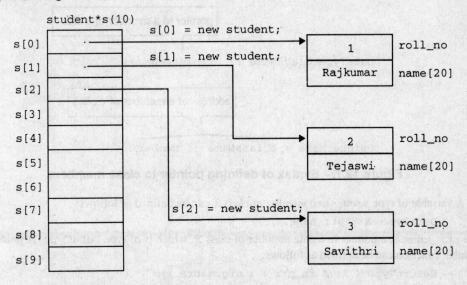

Figure 12.6:   Array of pointers to objects and dynamic binding

Note that the subscripted notation used for object pointers is similar to the manner in which arrays of other data types are usually handled. Thus, s[count] is same as *(s + count) in the program. Similarly the statement

```
s[i]->outdata();
```

executes the outdata() member function in the student class for the ith object of the s array. Pointers to objects could be effectively used to create and manipulate data structures like linked-lists, stacks, queues, etc.

12.6 Pointers to Object Members

Whenever an object is created, memory is allocated to it. The data defining the object is held in the space allocated to it, i.e., the data and member functions of the object reside at specific memory locations subsequent to the creation of the object. Thus, a pointer to an object member can be obtained by applying the address-of operator (&) to a fully qualified class member-name (which may be a data item or a member function). A fully qualified member name is used to refer to a member of a class without any ambiguity. For instance, the declaration

```
<class_name>::<member_name>;
```

is a fully qualified declaration naming the member <member_name> of the class <class_name>. Preceding the above member reference with an & operator causes the address of the member <member_name> of the class <class_name> to be returned.

Members of a class can be accessed using either pointer to an object, or pointer to members itself. The address of a member can be obtained by using the address operator (&) to a *fully qualified* member name of a class similar to variables. A pointer to class members is declared using the operator : :* with the class name. The syntax for defining the pointer to class members is shown in Figure 12.7.

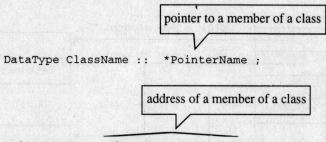

Figure 12.7:   Syntax of defining pointer to class members

A variable of type *pointer to a member of class X* can be defined as follows:

```
DataType  X::*ptr_name;
```

The ptr_name is a pointer to a data member of class X, which is of type DataType. A pointer to a member function can be defined as follows:

```
ReturnType ( X::* fn_ptr ) ( arguments );
```

It defines a pointer variable fn_ptr as a pointer to a member function of the class X which takes one or more arguments as specified by arguments and returns a value of type ReturnType. Consider the following specification of the class X:

```
class X
{
    private:
        int y;
```

```
        public:
            int a;
        public:
            int b;
            int init( int z );
    };
```

A pointer to the member a or b is defined as follows:

```
    int X::*ip;
```

The address of the member a can be assigned by

```
    ip = &X::a;
```

Similarly, the address of the member b can be assigned by

```
    ip = &X::b;
```

The address of the member a can also be assigned to a pointer during its definition as

```
    int X::*ip = &X::a;
```

The pointer variable ip, acts like the class member so that it can be invoked with a class object. In the above statement, the phrase X::* implies *pointer-to-member of the class* X. The phrase &X::a implies *address of the member* a *of the class* X.

The address of the private member y cannot be assigned by using the statement

```
    ip = &X::y;
```

Private members have the same access control privilege even with a pointer to the class members.

Normal pointer variable cannot be used as a pointer to the class member. Hence, the statement

```
    int *ptr = &X::a;
```

is invalid; The pointer and the variable have meaning only when they are associated with the class to which they belong. The scope resolution operator must be applied to both the pointer and the member.

Like pointers to data members, pointers to member functions can also be defined and invoked using the dereferencing operators. A pointer to the member function init() is defined as follows:

```
    int (X::*init_ptr)(int);
```

The address of the member init() can be assigned by

```
    init_ptr = &X::init;
```

to the pointer variable init_ptr. The different methods of accessing class members is shown in Figure 12.8.

Access through Objects

C++ provides operator, .* (dot-star) exclusively for use with pointers to members called *member dereferencing operator*. This operator is used to access class members using a pointer to members and it must be used with the objects of the class. The following statement,

```
    X obj1;
```

creates the object obj1 of the class X. Using the pointer variable ip, the following statement accesses the data member variable.

```
    obj1.*ip = 20;       // if ip is bound to a, it is same as the obj1.a;
    cout << obj1.*ip;
    int k = obj1.*ip;
```

Member functions can also be accessed using the operator `.*` as follows:

```
(obj1.*init_ptr)( 5 );       // same as the obj1.init() call
int k = (obj1.*init_ptr)( 5 );
```

The general format can be deduced to the following:

```
(object-name.*pointer-to-member-function)(arguments);
```

In such calls, the parentheses must be used explicitly, since the precedence of `()` is higher than the dereferencing `.*` operator.

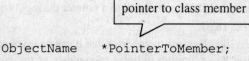

ObjectName . Member

(a) Common way of accessing a class member

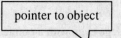

pointer to class member

ObjectName   *PointerToMember;

(b) Accessing class member through its pointer

pointer to object

PointerToObject -> Member;

(c) Accessing class member through the pointer to object

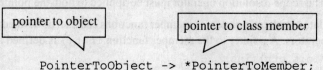

pointer to object   pointer to class member

PointerToObject -> *PointerToMember;

(d) Accessing class member through the pointer to object and member

Figure 12.8:   Different ways of accessing class members

Access through Object Pointers

C++ provides another operator `->*` for use exclusively with pointers to members called member dereferencing operator. This operator is used to access a member using a pointer to it with *pointer to the object*. The following statement

```
X obj1;
X *pobj;
```

create the object `obj1` of the class X and the pointer `pobj` to the objects of the class X. Using the pointer variable `ip` (defined earlier), the following statements access the member variables.

```
pobj->*ip = 20;       // accesses a if ip is bound to data member a
cout << pobj->*ip;    // display data member a
int k = pobj->*ip;    // k = data member a's contents
```

Member functions can also be accessed using the operator ->* as follows.

```
(pobj.*init_ptr)( 5 );
int k = (pobj->*init_ptr)( 5 );
```

The general format can be deduced to the following

```
(pointer-to-object->*pointer-to-member-function)(arguments);
```

In such calls, the parentheses must be used explicitly, since the precedence of () is higher than the dereferencing ->* operator. The program ptrmemb.cpp illustrates the concept of a pointer to class members.

```cpp
// ptrmemb.cpp: pointer to class members
#include <iostream.h>
class X
{
   private:
      int y;   // through pointer it cannot be accessed
   public:   // all public members can be accessed through pointers
      int a;
      int b;
      int init( int z )
      {
         a = z;
         return z;
      }
};
void main()
{
   X obj;
   int X::*ip; // pointer to data member
   ip = &X::a; // address of data member a is assigned to pointer
   // access through object
   obj.*ip = 10;
   cout << "a in obj, after obj.*ip = 10 is " << obj.*ip << endl;
   X *pobj; // pointer to object of the class X
   pobj = &obj;
   // access through object pointer
   pobj->*ip = 10;
   cout << "a in obj, after pobj->*ip = 10 is " << pobj->*ip << endl;
   int (X::*ptr_init)(int);   // pointer to member function
   ptr_init = &X::init; // pointer to member function init()
   // access through object
   (obj.*ptr_init)(5);
   cout << "a in obj, after (obj.*ptr_init)(5) = " << obj.a << endl;
   // access through object pointer
   (pobj->*ptr_init)(5);
   cout << "a in obj, after (pobj->*ptr_init)(5) = " << obj.a << endl;
}
```

**Run**

```
a in obj, after obj.*ip = 10 is 10
```

```
a in obj, after pobj->*ip = 10 is 10
a in obj, after (obj.*ptr_init)(5) = 5
a in obj, after (pobj->*ptr_init)(5) = 5
```

Access Through Friend Functions

The friend functions can access private data members of a class although it is not in the scope of the class. Similarly, members of any access privilege can be accessed using pointers to members. Both the dereferencing operators .* and ->* can be used to access class members. The program friend.cpp illustrates the concept of accessing class members through pointers from friend functions.

```
// friend.cpp: friend functions and pointer to members
#include <iostream.h>
class X
{
   private:
      int a;
      int b;
   public:
      X()
      {
         a = b = 0;
      }
      void SetMembers( int a1, int b1 )
      {
         a = a1;
         b = b1;
      }
      friend int sum( X x );
};
int sum( X objx )
{
   int X::*pa = &X::a;      // pointer to member a
   int X::*pb = &X::b;      // pointer to member b
   X *pobjx = &objx;        // pointer to object of the class X
   int result;
   // the member a is accessed through objects
   // and the member b is accessed through object pointer
   result = objx.*pa + pobjx->*pb;  // sum a and b;
   return result;
}
void main()
{
   X objx;
   void (X::*pfunc) (int, int);
   pfunc = &X::SetMembers;
   (objx.*pfunc)(5, 6);       // equivalent to objx.SetMembers(5, 6)
   cout << "Sum = " << sum( objx ) << endl;
   X *pobjx;                  // pointer to object of the class X
   pobjx = &objx;
   (pobjx->*pfunc)(7, 8);     // equivalent to pobjx->SetMembers(5, 6)
```

```
    cout << "Sum = " << sum( objx ) << endl;
}
```

Run
```
Sum = 11
Sum = 15
```

12.7 Function `set_new_handler()`

The C++ run-time system makes sure that when memory allocation fails, an error function is activated. By default, this function returns the value 0 to the caller of new, so that the pointer which is assigned by new is set to zero. The error function can be redefined, but it must comply with a few prerequisites, which are, unfortunately, compiler-dependent.

The function `set_new_handler()`, sets the function to be called when a request for memory allocation through the operator `new()` function cannot be satisfied. Its prototype is

```
    void ( * set_new_handler(void (* my_handler)() )) ();
```

If new() cannot allocate the requested memory, it invokes the handler set by `set_new_handler()`. The user defined function, `my_handler()` should specify the actions to be taken when `new()` cannot satisfy a request for memory allocation.

If `my_handler()` returns, `new()` will again attempt to satisfy the request. Ideally, `my_handler` would release the memory and return. `new()` would then be able to satisfy the request and the program would continue. However, if `my_handler()` cannot provide memory for `new()`, `my_handler` must terminate the program. Otherwise, an infinite loop will be created.

The default handler is reset by `set_new_handler(0)`. Preferably, it is advisable to overload the `new()` to take appropriate actions as per the application requirement.

The function `set_new_handler` returns the old handler, if it has been defined. By default, no handler is installed. The user-defined argument function, `my_handler`, should not return a value.

The program memhnd.cpp demonstrates the implementation of user-defined function (in Borland C++) to handle memory resource shortage error.

```
// memhnd.cpp: user-defined handler to handle out-of-memory issue
#include <iostream.h>
#include <new.h>
#include <process.h>
void out_of_memory ()
{
    cout << "Memory exhausted, cannot allocate";
    exit( 1 );   // terminate the program
}
void main ()
{
    int *ip;
    long total_allocated = 0L;
    // install error function
    set_new_handler( out_of_memory );
```

```
// eat up all memory
cout << "Ok, allocating.." << endl;
while (1)
{
    ip = new int [100];
    total_allocated += 100L;
    cout << "Now got a total of " << total_allocated << " bytes" << endl;
}
}
```

Run

```
Ok, allocating..
Now got a total of 100 bytes
Now got a total of 200 bytes
.....
.....
Now got a total of 29900 bytes
Memory exhausted, cannot allocate
```

The advantage of an allocation error function lies in the fact that once installed, new can be used without bothering whether the memory allocation has succeeded or not: upon failure, the error function is automatically invoked and the program terminates. It is a good practice to install a new handler in each C++ program, even when the actual code of the program does not allocate memory. Memory allocation can also fail in code which is not directly visible to the programmer, e.g., when streams are used or when strings are duplicated by low-level functions.

Most often, even standard C functions, which allocate memory such as strdup(), malloc(), realloc(), etc., trigger (invoke) the new handler when the memory allocation fails. That is, once a new handler is installed, such functions can be used in a C++ program without testing for errors. However, compilers exit where the C functions do not trigger the new handler.

12.8 this Pointer

It is observed that a member function of a given class is always invoked in the context of some object of the class; there is always an *implicit substrate* (implicitly defined) for the function to act on. C++ has a keyword this to address this substrate (it is not available in the static member functions) . The keyword this is a pointer variable, which always contains the address of the object in question. The this pointer is implicitly defined in each member function (whether public or private); therefore, it appears as if each member function of the class Test contains the following declaration:

```
extern Test *this;
```

Every member function of a class is born with a pointer called this, which points to the object with which the member function is associated.

Thus, member function of every object has access to a pointer named this, which points to the object itself. When a member function is invoked, it comes into existence with the value of this set to the address of the object for which it is called. The this pointer can be treated like any other pointer to an object. Using a this pointer, any member function can find out the address of the object of which it is a member. Method of accessing a member of a class from within a class using this pointer is shown in Figure 12.9.

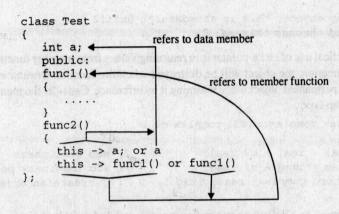

Figure 12.9:   Accessing class members using this pointer

The this pointer can also be used to access the data in the object it points to. The program this.cpp illustrates the working of this pointer.

```
// this.cpp: accessing data members through this pointer
#include <iostream.h>
class Test
{
    private:
        int a;
    public:
        void setdata( int init_a )
        {
            a = init_a;        // normal way to set data
            cout<<"Address of my object, this in setdata(): "<< this <<endl;
            this->a = init_a; // another way to set data
        }
        void showdata()
        {
            // normal way to show data
            cout << "Data accessed in normal way: " << a << endl;
            cout<<"Address of my object, this in showdata(): "<< this<<endl;
            // data access through this pointer
            cout << "Data accessed through this->a: " << this->a;
        }
};
void main()
{
    Test my;
    my.setdata( 25 );
    my.showdata();
}
```

Run

```
Address of my object, this in setdata(): 0xfff2
Data accessed in normal way: 25
```

```
Address of my object, this in showdata(): 0xfff2
Data accessed through this->a: 25
```

A more practical use of this pointer is in returning values from member functions. When an object is local to the function, the object will be destroyed when the function terminates. It necessitates the need for a more permanent object while returning it by reference. Consider the member function add() of the class complex:

```
complex complex::add( complex c2 )
{
    real = real + c2.real;        // add real parts
    imag = imag + c2.imag;        // add imaginary parts
    return complex( real, imag );  // create an object and return
}
```

It adds the object c2 to a default object and returns the updated default object by explicitly creating a nameless object using the statement

```
    return complex( real, imag );
```

It can be replaced by the statement

return *this;

without the loss of functionality. The modified definition of add() appears as follows:

```
complex complex::add( complex c2 )
{
    real = real + c2.real;        // add real parts
    imag = imag + c2.imag;        // add imaginary parts
    return *this;
}
```

Since this is a pointer to the object of which the function is a member, *this naturally refers to the object pointed to by this pointer. The statement

```
    return *this;
```

returns this object by value.

For a given class X, in each one of its member functions, the pointer this is implicitly declared as

```
    X *const this;
```

and initialized to point to the object for which the member function is invoked. As the pointer this is declared as * const, it cannot be changed for a particular object ensuring that the access to the object is not lost, even accidentally. However, the value of this is different for every individual object declared or created in the program. The compiler treats this as a keyword (reserved word) as a result of which it cannot be explicitly declared. Further, it (the compiler) also places a restriction which prevents the keyword this from being used outside a class member function body.

12.9 Self-Referential Classes

Many of the frequently used dynamic data structures like stacks, queues, linked-lists, etc., use self-referential members. Classes can contain one or more members which are pointers to other objects of the same class. This pointer holds an address of the next object in a data structure. Such a feature is essential for implementing dynamic data structures such as linked lists, stack, trees, etc.

Linked List

A list having node, which is a pointer to the next node in a list is called linked list. The pictorial representation of a linked list having pointer to the next object of the same class is shown in Figure 12.10. The program listed in list.cpp implements a linked list of integers using such a self-referential class. The program uses a pointer called this pointer.

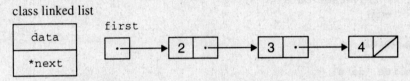

Figure 12.10: Linked list with self-referential classes

```
// list.cpp: Linked list having self reference
#include <iostream.h>
#include <process.h>
// linked list class
class list
{
   private:
     int data;     // data of a node
     list *next;   // pointer to next node
   public:
     list()
     {
        data = 0;
        next = NULL;
     }
     list(int dat)
     {
        data = dat;
        next = NULL;
     }
   ~list() {}
   int get() { return data; }
   void insert(list *node);       // Inserts new node at list
   friend void display(list *);   // Display list
};
// Inserts node. If list empty the first node is created else the
// new node is inserted at the end of a list
void list::insert( list *node )
{
   list *last = this;   // this node pointer to catch last node
   while( last->next )  // if node-next != NULL, it is not last node
     last = last->next;
   last->next = node;   // make last node point to new node
}
// Displays the doubly linked list in both forward and reverse order by
// making use of the series of next and prev pointers.
```

```
void display( list *first )
{
   list *traverse;
   cout << "List traversal yields: ";
   // scan for all the elements
   for( traverse = first; traverse; traverse = traverse->next )
     cout << traverse->data << ", ";
   cout << endl;
}
void main(void)
{
   int choice, data;
   list *first = NULL;  // initially points to NULL
   list *node;     // pointer to new node to be created
   while( 1 )
   {
      cout << "Linked List..." << endl;
      cout << "1.Insert" << endl;
      cout << "2.Display" << endl;
      cout << "3.Quit" << endl;
      cout << "Enter Choice: ";
      cin >> choice;
      switch (choice)
      {
         case 1:
            cout << "Enter Data: ";
            cin >> data;
            node = new list( data );
            if( first == NULL )
               first = node;
            else
               first->insert( node );
            break;
         case 2:
            display( first );
            break; // Display list.
         case 3:
            exit( 1 );
         default:
            cout << "Bad option selected" << endl;
         continue;
      }
   }
}
```

Run

```
Linked List...
1.Insert
2.Display
3.Quit
```

```
Enter Choice: 1
Enter Data: 2
Linked List...
1.Insert
2.Display
3.Quit
Enter Choice: 2
List traversal yields: 2,
Linked List...
1.Insert
2.Display
3.Quit
Enter Choice: 1
Enter Data: 3
Linked List...
1.Insert
2.Display
3.Quit
Enter Choice: 1
Enter Data: 4
Linked List...
1.Insert
2.Display
3.Quit
Enter Choice: 2
List traversal yields: 2, 3, 4,
Linked List...
1.Insert
2.Display
3.Quit
Enter Choice: 3
```

The use of a self-referential class is inevitable in the above program, since each node in the stack has a pointer to another node of its own type, which is its predecessor (in the case of the stack).

Several problems whose solutions are based on the use of data structures like trees, graphs and lists make extensive use of self-referential class.

Doubly Linked List

Using this pointer when referring to a member of its own class is often unnecessary, as illustrated earlier; the major use of the this pointer is for writing member functions that manipulate pointers directly. The doubly linked list has two pointer nodes: one pointing to the next node in the list and another pointing to the previous node in the list. The pictorial representation of a doubly linked list is shown in Figure 12.11.

The program dll.cpp makes use of the data structure, doubly linked list, illustrating the typical use of the this pointer at relevant points. The this pointer is particularly used as a pointer to the first node while traversing through the entire list.

class doubly
linked list   first

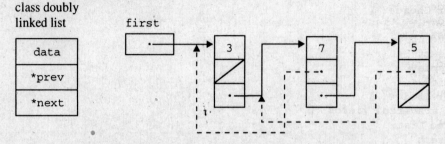

Figure 12.11:   Doubly linked list representation

```cpp
// dll.cpp: doubly linked list
#include <iostream.h>
#include <process.h>
class dll                // doubly linked list class
{
   private:
     int data;      // data of a node
     dll *prev;     // pointer to previous node
     dll *next;     // pointer to next node
   public:
     dll()
     {
        data = 0;
        prev = next = NULL;
     }
     dll( int data_in )
     {
        data = data_in;
        prev = next = NULL;
     }
     ~dll()
     {
        cout << "->" << data;
     }
     int get() { return data; }
     void insert(dll *node);          // Inserts new node at list
     friend void display(dll *);      // Display list
     void FreeAllNodes();
};
// Inserts node. If list empty the first node is created else the
// new node is inserted immediately after the first node.
void dll::insert( dll *node )
{
   dll *last;
   // find out last node. this points to first node
   for( last = this; last->next; last = last->next );
   // insert new node at the end of list
```

```
      node->prev = last;
      node->next = last->next;
      last->next = node;
}
void dll::FreeAllNodes()
{
   cout << "Freeing the node with data: ";
   // this points to first node, use it to release all the nodes
   for( dll *first = this; first; first = first->next )
      delete first;
}
// Displays the doubly linked list in both forward and reverse order making
// use of the series of next and prev pointers.
void display( dll *first )
{
   dll *traverse = first;
   if( traverse == NULL)
   {
      cout << "Nothing to display !" << endl; // along the list.
      return;
   }
   else
   {
      cout << "Processing with forward -> pointer: ";
      // scan for all the elements in forward direction
      for( ;traverse->next; traverse = traverse->next )
         cout << "->" << traverse->data;
      // display last element
      cout << "->" << traverse->data << endl;
      cout << "Processing with backward <- pointer: ";
      // scan for all the elements in reverse direction
      for( ;traverse->prev; traverse = traverse->prev )
            cout << "->" << traverse->data;
      // display first element
      cout << "->" << traverse->data << endl;
   }
}
dll * InsertNode( dll *first, int data )
{
   dll *node;
   node = new dll( data );
   if( first == NULL )
      first = node;
   else
      first->insert( node );
   return first;
}
void main( void )
{
   int choice, data;
```

```
    dll *first = NULL;    // initially points to NULL
    cout << "Double Linked List Manipulation..." << endl;
    while( 1 )
    {
       cout << "Enter Choice ([1] Insert, [2] Display, [3] Quit): ";
       cin >> choice;
       switch (choice)
       {
          case 1:
             cout << "Enter Data: ";
             cin >> data;
             first = InsertNode( first, data );
             break;
          case 2:
             display( first );
             break; // Display list.
          case 3:
             first->FreeAllNodes();   // release all nodes
             exit( 1 );
          default:
             cout << "Bad option selected" << endl;
          continue;
       }
    }
}
```

Run

```
Double Linked List Manipulation...
Enter Choice ([1] Insert, [2] Display, [3] Quit): 1
Enter Data: 3
Enter Choice ([1] Insert, [2] Display, [3] Quit): 2
Processing with forward -> pointer: ->3
Processing with backward <- pointer: ->3
Enter Choice ([1] Insert, [2] Display, [3] Quit): 1
Enter Data: 7
Enter Choice ([1] Insert, [2] Display, [3] Quit): 2
Processing with forward -> pointer: ->3->7
Processing with backward <- pointer: ->7->3
Enter Choice ([1] Insert, [2] Display, [3] Quit): 1
Enter Data: 5
Enter Choice ([1] Insert, [2] Display, [3] Quit): 2
Processing with forward -> pointer: ->3->7->5
Processing with backward <- pointer: ->5->7->3
Enter Choice ([1] Insert, [2] Display, [3] Quit): 0
Bad option selected
Enter Choice ([1] Insert, [2] Display, [3] Quit): 3
Freeing the node with data: ->3->7->5
```

Besides handling dynamic data structures, the this pointer finds extensive application in the following contexts:

• Member functions returning pointers to their respective objects.

• Overloaded operators which return object values by reference.
• Virtual functions wherein decisions, as to which version of an overloaded function is to be executed, is taken only during runtime (late binding).

12.10 Guidelines for Passing Object Parameters

The parameters to normal functions or member functions, of a class can be passed either by value, pointer, or reference. However, passing some objects by pointers or reference is much efficient when compared to passing by value even though modification in a callee need not be reflected in the caller. A few guidelines that help in taking decision on choosing appropriate parameter passing scheme are the following:

[1] If a function does not modify an argument, which is a built-in type or a "small" user-defined type (class objects), pass arguments by value. The meaning of "small" refers to data-type, which require few bytes to represent its objects and it is system dependent.

[2] If a function modifies an argument, which is a built-in type, pass arguments by a pointer. It makes processing of data explicit to anyone reading the code, which modifies built-in type variables.

[3] If a function modifies or does not modify a "large" user-defined type, pass arguments by reference. Any function, which modifies private data (and hence protected) of an object must either be a member function, or a friend function. This is justifiable, since the "class" has control over the functions which modify class's private data. In this case, just because the address of an object is handed over to a function does not mean the function can secretly modify the private data of an object. As far as object data members are concerned, it is very clear and straight forward to answer "who has permission to modify this object ?" Hence, it is advisable to pass reference to an object instead of value or a pointer.

Review Questions

12.1   What is the difference between dynamic memory allocation and dynamic objects ?

12.2   Justify the need of object cleanup and initialization facility for creating live objects

12.3   Explain why C++ is treated as the middle ground between static and dynamic binding languages.

12.4   What is the difference between stack based and heap-based objects ?

12.5   What is dereferencing of objects ? Write a program for illustrating the use of object references.

12.6   What are self-referential classes ? Write a program to create an ordered linked list.

12.7   What are live objects ? Write a program to illustrate live objects supporting different ways of creating them. Will an object created using new operator occupy more space than necessary ?

12.8   Write a program to access members of a student class using pointer to object members.

12.9   Justify the need for "allowing pointers to class members accessing private members of a class"

12.10 Explain how memory allocation failure can be handled in C++ ?.

12.11 What is this pointer ? What is your reaction to the statement:
```
delete this;
```
Write a program demonstrating the use of this pointer.

12.12 Write an interactive program for creating a doubly linked list. The program must support ordered insertion and deletion of a node.

13

Operator Overloading

13.1 Introduction

The operators such as +, -, +=, >, >>, etc., are designed to operate only on standard data types in structured programming languages such as C. The + operator can be used to perform the addition operation on integer, floating-point, or mixed data types as indicated in the expression (a+b). In this expression, the data type of the operands a and b on which the + operator is operating, is not mentioned explicitly. In such cases, the compiler implicitly selects suitable addition operation (integer, floating-point, double, etc.,) depending on the data type of operands without any assistance from the programmer. Consider the following statements:

```
int a, b, c;
float x, y, z;
c = a + b;     // 1: integer addition and assignment
z = x + y;     // 2: floating-point addition and assignment
x = a + b;     // 3: integer addition and floating point assignment
```

The operators = and + behave quite differently in the above statements: the first statement does integer addition and assigns the result to c, the second performs floating-point addition and assigns the result to z, and the last performs integer addition and assigns the result to the floating-point variable x. It indicates that, the + operator is overloaded implicitly to operate on operands of any standard data type supported by the language. Unlike C, in C++, such operators can also be overloaded explicitly to operate on operands of user-defined data types. For instance, the statement

```
c3 = AddComplex( c1, c2 );
```

performs the addition of operands c1 and c2 belonging to the user defined data type and assigns the result to c3 (which is also operand of the user defined data type). In C++, by overloading the + operator, the above statement can be changed to an easily readable form:

```
c3 = c1 + c2;
```

It tries to make the user-defined data types behave in a manner similar (and have the same *look and feel*) to the built-in data types, thereby allowing the user to redefine the language itself. Operator overloading, thus allows to provide additional meaning to operators such as +,*, >=,+=,etc., when they are applied to user defined data types. It allows the user to program (develop solution to) the problems as perceived in the real world.

The operator overloading feature of C++ is one of the methods of realizing *polymorphism*. The word polymorphism is derived from the Greek words *poly* and *morphism* (*polymorphism = poly + morphism*). Here, *poly* refers to many or multiple and *morphism* refers to actions, i.e., performing many actions with a single operator. As stated earlier, the + operator performs integer addition if the operands are of integer type and floating point addition if the operands are of real type.

The concept of operator overloading can also be applied to data conversion. C++ offers automatic conversion of primitive data types. For example, in the statement x=a+b, the compiler implicitly converts the integer result to floating-point representation and then assigns to the `float` variable x. But the conversion of user defined data types requires some effort on the part of the programmer. Thus, operator overloading concepts are applied to the following two principle areas:

- Extending capability of operators to operate on user defined data.
- Data conversion.

Operator overloading extends the *semantics* of an operator without changing its *syntax*. The grammatical rules defined by C++ that govern its use such as the number of operands, precedence, and associativity of the operator remain the same for overloaded operators. Therefore, it should be remembered that the overloaded operator should not change its original meaning. However, semantics (meaning) can be changed, but it is advisable to retain the predefined logical meaning.

13.2 Overloadable Operators

C++ provides a wide variety of operators to perform operations on various operands. The operators are classified into *unary* and *binary* operators based on the number of arguments on which they operate. C++ allows almost all operators to be overloaded in which case atleast one operand must be an instance of a class (object). It allows overloading of the operators listed in Table 13.1.

The precedence relation of overloadable operators and their expression syntax remains the same even after overloading. Even if there is a provision to change the operator precedence or the expression syntax, it does not offer any advantage. For instance, it is improper to define a unary division (/) or a binary complement (~), since the change of precedence or syntax leads to ambiguity. For example, defining an operator ** to represent exponentiation as in the case of Fortran language, appears to be obvious, however, interpretation of the expression a**b, leads to confusion; whether to interpret it as a*(*b) or (a)**(b), because, C++ already interprets it as a*(*b).

Operator Category	Operators
Arithmetic	+, -, *, /, %
Bit-wise	&, |, ~, ^
Logical	&&, ||, !
Relational	>, <, ==, !=, <=, >=
Assignment or Initialization	=
Arithmetic Assignment	+=, -=, *=, /=, %=, &=, |=, ^=
Shift	<<, >>, <<=, >>=
Unary	++, --
Subscripting	[]
Function Call	()
Dereferencing	->
Unary Sign Prefix	+, -
Allocate and Free	new, delete

Table 13.1: C++ overloadable operators

13.3 Unary Operator Overloading

Consider an example of class `Index` which keeps track of the index value. The program `index1.cpp` having class members to maintain the index value is listed below:

```
// index1.cpp: Index class with functions to keep track of index value
#include <iostream.h>
class Index
{
    private:
        int value;                     // Index Value
    public:
        Index()                        // No argument constructor
        {
            value = 0;
        }
        int GetIndex()                 // Index Access
        {
            return value;
        }
        void NextIndex()               // Advance Index
        {
            value = value + 1;
        }
};
void main()
{
    Index idx1, idx2;          // idx1 and idx2 are objects of Index class
    // Display index values
    cout << "\nIndex1 = " << idx1.GetIndex();
    cout << "\nIndex2 = " << idx2.GetIndex();
    // Advance Index objects
    idx1.NextIndex();
    idx2.NextIndex();
    idx2.NextIndex();
    // Display index values
    cout << "\nIndex1 = " << idx1.GetIndex();
    cout << "\nIndex2 = " << idx2.GetIndex();
}
```

Run

```
Index1 = 0
Index2 = 0
Index1 = 1
Index2 = 2
```

The function `NextIndex()` advances (increments) the index value. Instead of using such functions, the operators like ++ (increment operator) can be used to perform the same job. It enhances the program readability without the loss of functionality. A new version of the class program `index1.cpp`, is rewritten using overloaded increment operator. The program `index2.cpp` illustrates overloading of ++ operator.

```
// Index2.cpp: Index class with operator overloading
#include <iostream.h>
class Index
{
    private:
        int value;                 // Index Value
    public:
        Index()                    // No argument constructor
        {
            value = 0;
        }
        int GetIndex()             // Index Access
        {
            return value;
        }
        void operator ++()         // prefix or postfix increment operator
        {
            value = value + 1;     // value++;
        }
};
void main()
{
    Index idx1, idx2;          // idx1 and idx2 are objects of Index class
    // Display index values
    cout << "\nIndex1 = " << idx1.GetIndex();
    cout << "\nIndex2 = " << idx2.GetIndex();
    // Advance Index objects with ++ operators
    ++idx1;                    // equivalent to idx1.operator++();
    idx2++;
    idx2++;
    cout << "\nIndex1 = " << idx1.GetIndex();
    cout << "\nIndex2 = " << idx2.GetIndex();
}
```

Run

```
Index1 = 0
Index2 = 0
Index1 = 1
Index2 = 2
```

In main (), the statements

```
++idx1;                    // equivalent to idx1.operator++();
idx2++;
```

invoke the overloaded ++ operator member function defined in the class Index:

```
    void operator ++()         // prefix or postfix increment operator
```

The name of this overloaded function is ++. The word operator is a keyword and is preceded by the return type void. The operator to be overloaded is written immediately after the keyword operator. This declarator informs the compiler to invoke the overloaded operator function ++ whenever the unary increment operator is prefixed or postfixed to an object of the Index class.

The variables idx1 and idx2 are the objects of the class Index. The index value is advanced by using statements such as ++idx1; idx2++; instead of explicitly invoking the member function NextIndex() as in the earlier program. The operator is applied to objects of the Index class. Yet. operator function ++ takes no arguments. It increments the data member value of the Index class's objects. Figure 13.1 shows the Index class representation and invocation of its member functions when they are accessed implicitly (constructor function) or explicitly (other members).

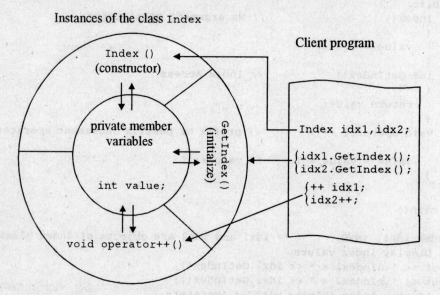

Figure 13.1:   Index class and ++ operator overloading

13.4 operator **Keyword**

The keyword operator facilitates overloading of the C++ operators. The general format of operator overloading is shown in Figure 13.2. The keyword operator indicates that the *operator symbol* following it, is the C++ operator to be overloaded to operate on members of its class. The operator overloaded in a class is known as *overloaded operator function*.

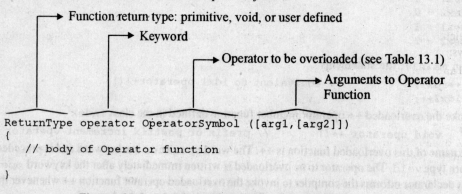

Figure 13.2:   Syntax of operator overloading

Overloading without explicit arguments to an operator function is known as *unary operator overloading* and overloading with a single explicit argument is known as *binary operator overloading*. However, with friend functions, unary operators take one explicit argument and binary operators take two explicit arguments. The syntax of overloading the unary operator is shown in Figure 13.3.

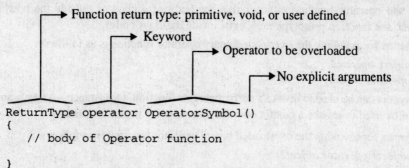

```
ReturnType operator OperatorSymbol()
{
        // body of Operator function

}
```

Figure 13.3: Syntax for overloading unary operator

The following examples illustrate the overloading of unary operators:

(1)	Index operator +();
(2)	int operator -();
(3)	void operator ++();
(4)	void operator --();
(5)	int operator *();

Similar to other member functions of a class, an overloaded operator member function can be either defined within the body of a class or outside the body of a class. The following class specification defines an overloaded operator member function within the body of a class:

```
class MyClass
{
    // class data or function stuff
    int operator++()      // member function definition
    {
        // body of a function
    }
};
```

A skeleton of the same class having the operator member function definition outside its body is as follows:

```
class MyClass
{
    // class data or function stuff
    int operator ++();  // prototype declaration
};
// overloaded member function definition
int MyClass::operator++()
{
    // body of a function
}
```

The process of operator overloading generally involves the following steps:

.1. Declare a class (that defines the data type) whose objects are to be manipulated using operators.
2. Declare the operator function, in the *public* part of the class. It can be either a normal member function or a friend function.
3. Define the operator function either within the body of a class or outside the body of the class (however, the function prototype must exist inside the class body).

The syntax for invoking the overloaded unary operator function is as follows:

>*object operand*
>*operator object*

The·first syntax can be used to invoke a prefix operator function, for instance, `++idx1`, and the second syntax can be used to invoke a postfix operator function, for instance, `idx1++`.

The syntax for invoking the overloaded binary operator function is as follows:

>*object1 operator object2*

For instance, the expression `idx1+idx2` invokes the overloaded member function + of the `idx1` object's class by passing `idx2` as the argument. Note that, in an expression invoking the binary operator function, one of the operands must be the object. The above syntax is interpreted as follows:

>*object1.operator OperatorSymbol(object2)*

Operator Arguments

In `main()` of `index2.cpp` program, `operator++()` is applied to the object of the class `Index` as in the expression `idx2++`; it can be observed that the `operator++()` takes no arguments explicitly. The execution of the expression `idx2++` invokes a member function `operator++()` defined in the class `Index`. In this function, the data members of the object `idx2` are manipulated.

13.5 Operator Return Values

The operator function in the program `index2.cpp` has a subtle defect. An attempt to use an expression such as

>   `idx1 = idx2++;`

will lead to a compilation error like *Improper Assignment*, because the return type of `operator++` is defined as `void` type. The above assignment statement tries to assign the void return type to the object (`idx1`) of the `Index` class. Such an assignment operation can be permitted after modifying the return type of the `operator++()` member function of the `Index` class in the `index2.cpp` program. A program with required modifications is listed in `index3.cpp`.

```
// index3.cpp: Index class with overloaded operator returning an object
#include <iostream.h>
class Index
{
   private:
      int value;              // Index Value
   public:
      Index()                 // No argument constructor
      {
         value = 0;
      }
```

```
      int GetIndex()              // Index Access
      {
         return value;
      }
      Index operator ++()         // Returns Index object
      {
         Index temp;              // temp object
         value = value + 1;       // update index value
         temp.value = value;      // initialize temp object
         return temp;             // return temp object
      }
};
void main()
{
   Index idx1, idx2;  // idx1 and idx2 are objects of class Index
   cout << "\nIndex1 = " << idx1.GetIndex();
   cout << "\nIndex2 = " << idx2.GetIndex();
   idx1 = idx2++;    //returned object of idx2++ is assigned to idx1
   idx2++;                    // returned object of idx2++ is unused
   cout << "\nIndex1 = " << idx1.GetIndex();
   cout << "\nIndex2 = " << idx2.GetIndex();
}
```

Run

```
Index1 = 0
Index2 = 0
Index1 = 1
Index2 = 2
```

In main(), the statement

```
   idx1 = idx2++;    //returned object of idx2++ is assigned to idx1
```

invokes the overloaded operator function and assigns the return value to the object idx1 of the class
Index. The operator ++() function creates a new object of the class Index called temp to be used
as a return value; it can be assigned to another object. The value data member of the implicit object
idx2 is incremented and then assigned to the temp object which is returned to the caller. The returned
object is assigned to the destination object idx1.

13.6 Nameless Temporary Objects

In the program index3.cpp, an intermediate (a temporary) object temp is created as a return object.
A convenient way to return an object is to create a nameless object in the return statement itself. The
program index4.cpp, illustrates the overloaded operator function returning a nameless object.

```
// index4.cpp: Index class with overloaded operator returning nameless object
#include <iostream.h>
class Index
{
   private:
      int value;                  // Index Value
```

```
   public:
      Index()                  // No argument constructor
      { value = 0;  }
      Index( int val )         // Constructor with one argument
      {
         value = val;
      }
      int GetIndex()           // Index Access
      {
         return value;
      }
      Index operator ++() // Returns nameless object of class Index
      {
         value = value + 1;
         return Index( value );   // calls one-argument constructor
      }
};
void main()
{
   Index idx1, idx2;    // idx1 and idx2 are the objects of Index
   cout << "\nIndex1 = " << idx1.GetIndex();
   cout << "\nIndex2 = " << idx2.GetIndex();
   idx1 = idx2++; // return object idx2++ is assigned to object idx1
   idx2++;             // return object idx2++ is unused
   cout << "\nIndex1 = " << idx1.GetIndex();
   cout << "\nIndex2 = " << idx2.GetIndex();
}
```

Run

```
Index1 = 0
Index2 = 0
Index1 = 1
Index2 = 2
```

In the program index3.cpp, the statements used to return an object are the following:

```
      Index temp;
      value = value + 1;
      temp.value = value;
      return temp;
```

In this program, the statements,

```
      value = value + 1;
      return Index( value );
```

perform the same operation as achieved by the above four statements. It creates a nameless object by passing an initialization value. To perform this operation, the following parameterized constructor is added as the constructor member function to the Index class:

```
      Index( int val )
      {
         value = val;
      }
```

13.7 Limitations of Increment/Decrement Operators

The prefix notation causes a variable (of type standard data type) to be updated before its value is used in the expression, whereas the postfix notation causes it to be updated after its value is used. However, the statement (built using user-defined data types and overloaded operator),

```
idx1 = ++idx2;
```

has exactly the same effect as the statement

```
idx1 = idx2++;
```

When ++ and -- operators are overloaded, there is no distinction between the prefix and postfix overloaded operator function. This problem is circumvented in advanced implementations of C++, which provides additional syntax to express and distinguish between prefix and postfix overloaded operator functions. A new syntax to indicate postfix operator overloaded function is:

```
operator ++( int )
```

The program index5.cpp illustrates the invocation of prefix and postfix operator functions. Note that the old syntax is used to overload prefix operator function.

```cpp
// index5.cpp: Index class with overloaded prefix and postfix unary operators
#include <iostream.h>
class Index
{
    private:
        int value;                  // Index Value

    public:
        Index()                     // No argument constructor
        {   value = 0;    }
        Index( int val )            // Constructor with one argument
        {
            value = val;
        }
        int GetIndex()              // Index Access
        {
            return value;
        }
        // Operator overloading for prefix operator
        Index operator ++()
        {
            // Object is created with the ++value, hence object is
            // created with a new value of 'value' and returned
            return Index( ++value );
        }
        // Operator overloading for postfix operator
        Index operator ++(int)
        {
            // Object is created with the value++, hence object is
            // created with old value of 'value' and returned
            return Index( value++ );
        }
```

```
void main()
{
   Index idx1(2), idx2(2), idx3, idx4;

   cout << "\nIndex1 = " << idx1.GetIndex();
   cout << "\nIndex2 = " << idx2.GetIndex();
   idx3 = idx1++;   // postfix increment
   idx4 = ++idx2;   // prefix increment
   cout << "\nIndex1 = " << idx1.GetIndex();
   cout << "\nIndex3 = " << idx3.GetIndex();
   cout << "\nIndex2 = " << idx2.GetIndex();
   cout << "\nIndex4 = " << idx4.GetIndex();
}
```

Run

```
Index1 = 2
Index2 = 2
Index1 = 3
Index3 = 2
Index2 = 3
Index4 = 3
```

In the postfix `operator ++(int)` function, first a nameless object with the old index value is created and then, the index value is updated to achieve the intended operation. The compiler will just make a call to this function for postfix operation, but the responsibility of achieving this rests on the programmer.

The above discussion on *unary plus* overloading is also applicable to overloading of unary decrement and negation operators. It is illustrated by the program `index6.cpp`.

```
// index6.cpp: Index class with unary operator overloading -, ++, and --
#include <iostream.h>
class Index
{
   private:
      int value;              // Index Value
   public:
      Index()                 // No argument constructor
      {   value = 0;   }
      Index( int val )        // Constructor with one argument
      {
         value = val;
      }
      int GetIndex()          // Index Access
      {
         return value;
      }
      Index operator -()      // Negation of Index Value
      {
         return Index( -value );
      }
```

```
        Index operator ++()    // Prefix increment
        {
            ++value;
            return Index( value );
        }
        Index operator --()         // Prefix decrement
        {
            --value;
            return Index( value );
        }
};
void main()
{
    Index idx1, idx2;
    cout << "\nIndex1 = " << idx1.GetIndex();
    cout << "\nIndex2 = " << idx2.GetIndex();
    idx2++;
    idx1 = -idx2;      // negate idx2 and assign to idx1
    ++idx2;
    --idx2;             // prefix decrement
    cout << "\nIndex1 = " << idx1.GetIndex();
    cout << "\nIndex2 = " << idx2.GetIndex();
}
```

Run

```
Index1 = 0
Index2 = 0
Index1 = -1
Index2 = 1
```

Overloading of unary operator does not necessarily mean that it is overloaded to operate on a class's object, which has a single data member. Within the body of a overloaded unary operator function, any amount of data can be manipulated. One of the best example is manipulation of date object data members. A class called date can have three data members day, month, and year. To increment date by one, it may necessitate updation of all the fields on the date class. It depends on the current values of date class's object data members as illustrated in the program mydate.cpp. It has overloaded unary increment operator function to update date object's data members.

```
// mydate.cpp: overloading ++ operator to increment date
#include <iostream.h>
class date
{
    int day;
    int month;
    int year;
    public:
        date()
        {
            day = 0; month = 0; year = 0;
        }
```

```
        date( int d, int m, int y )
        {
            day = d; month = m; year = y;
        }
        void read()
        {
            cout << "Enter date <dd mm yyyy>: ";
            cin >> day >> month >> year;
        }
        void show()
        {
            cout << day << ":" << month << ":" << year;
        }
        int IsLeapYear()
        {
            if( (year % 4 == 0 && year % 100 != 0 ) || (year % 400 == 0) )
                return 1;
            else
                return 0;
        }
        int thisMonthMaxDay()
        {
            int m[12] = { 31, 28, 31, 30, 31, 30, 31, 31, 30, 31, 30, 31 };
            if( month == 2 && IsLeapYear() )
                return 29;  // February month with leap year will have 28 days
            else
                return m[month-1];
        }
        // unary increment operator overloading
        void operator ++()
        {
            ++day;
            // adjust all fields of date according to current day
            // so that they hold valid date
            if( day > thisMonthMaxDay() )
            {
                // set day to 1 and increment month
                day = 1;
                month++;
            }
            if( month > 12 )
            {
                // month to January (1) and increment year
                month = 1;
                year++;
            }
        }
};
void nextday( date & d )
{
    cout << "Date "; d.show();
```

```
    ++d;  // invokes operator function
    cout << " on increment becomes "; d.show();
    cout << endl;
}
void main()
{
    date d1( 14, 4, 1971 );
    date d2( 28, 2, 1992 ); // leap year
    date d3( 28, 2, 1993 );
    date d4( 31, 12, 1995 );
    nextday( d1 );
    nextday( d2 );
    nextday( d3 );
    nextday( d4 );
    date today;
    today.read();
    nextday( today );
}
```

Run

```
Date 14:4:1971 on increment becomes 15:4:1971
Date 28:2:1992 on increment becomes 29:2:1992
Date 28:2:1993 on increment becomes 1:3:1993
Date 31:12:1995 on increment becomes 1:1:1996
Enter date <dd mm yyyy>: 11 9 1996
Date 11:9:1996 on increment becomes 12:9:1996
```

The updation of date requires to take care of conditions such as whether the year is a leap year or not. If it is leap year and month is February, it will have 29 days instead of usual 28 days. Such cases need to be handled explicitly (see the second and third output line in *Run*).

13.8 Binary Operator Overloading

The concept of overloading unary operators applies also to the binary operators. The syntax for overloading a binary operator is shown in Figure 13.4.

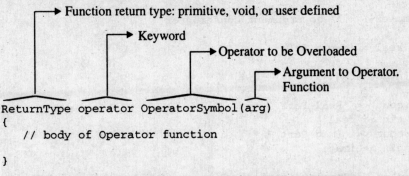

Figure 13.4:   Syntax for overloading a binary operator

The binary overloaded operator function takes the first object as an implicit operand and the second operand must be passed explicitly. The data members of the first object are accessed without using the dot operator whereas, the second argument members can be accessed using the dot operator if the argument is an object, otherwise it can be accessed directly. Note that, the overloaded binary operator function is a member function defined in the first object's class.

The following examples illustrate the overloading of binary operators:

```
complex operator + ( complex c1 );
int operator - ( int a );
void operator * ( complex c1 );
void operator / ( complex c1 );
complex operator += ( complex c1 );
```

Similar to unary operators, binary operators also have to return values so that cascaded assignment expressions can be formed. The programs illustrating the overloading of binary operators are discussed in the following sections.

13.9 Arithmetic Operators

Consider an example involving operations on complex numbers to illustrate the concept of binary operator overloading. Complex numbers consists of two parts: real part and imaginary part. It is represented as $(x+iy)$, where x is the real part and y is the imaginary part. The process of performing the addition operation is illustrated below. Let $c1, c2$, and $c3$ be three complex numbers represented as follows:

$$c1 = x1 + i\ y1;$$
$$c2 = x2 + i\ y2;$$

The operation $c3 = c1 + c2$ is given by
$$c3 = (c1.x1 + c2.x2) + i (c1.y1 + c2.y2);$$

The program complex1.cpp performs addition of complex numbers without operator overloading.

```
// complex1.cpp: Addition of Complex Numbers
#include <iostream.h>
class complex
{
  private:
    float real;      // real part of complex number
    float imag;      // imaginary part of complex number
  public:
    complex()    // no argument constructor
    {
      real = imag = 0.0;
    }
    void getdata()
    {
      cout << "Real Part ? ";
      cin >> real;
      cout << "Imag Part ? ";
      cin >> imag;
    }
    complex AddComplex( complex c2 );    // Add complex numbers
    void outdata( char *msg )            // display complex number
    {
      cout << endl << msg;
```

```
        cout << "(" << real;
        cout << ", " << imag << ")";
    }
};
// adds default and c2 complex objects
complex complex::AddComplex( complex c2 )
{
    complex temp;                    // object temp of complex class
    temp.real = real + c2.real;      // add real parts
    temp.imag = imag + c2.imag;      // add imaginary parts

    return( temp );                  // return complex object
}
void main()
{
    complex c1, c2, c3;     // c1, c2, c3 are object of complex class
    cout << "Enter Complex Number c1 .." << endl;
    c1.getdata();
    cout << "Enter Complex Number c2 .." << endl;
    c2.getdata();
    c3 = c1.AddComplex( c2 );        // add c1 and c2 and assign the result to c3
    c3.outdata( "c3 = c1.AddComplex( c2 ): ");
}
```

Run
```
Enter Complex Number c1 ..
Real Part ? 2.5
Imag Part ? 2.0
Enter Complex Number c2 ..
Real Part ? 3.0
Imag Part ? 1.5
c3 = c1.AddComplex( c2 ): (5.5, 3.5)
```

In main(), the statement

```
        c3 = c1.AddComplex( c2 );
```

invokes the member function AddComplex() of the c1 object's class and adds c2 to it and then the returned result object is assigned to c3. By overloading the + operator, this clumsy and dense-looking statement can be represented in the simplified standard (usual) form as follows:

```
        c3 = c1 + c2;
```

The program complex2.cpp illustrates the overloading of the binary operator + in order to perform addition of complex numbers.

```
// complex2.cpp: Complex Numbers operations with operator overloading
#include <iostream.h>
class complex
{
    private:
        float real;         // real part of complex number
        float imag;         // imaginary part of complex number
```

```
   public:
      complex()                      // no argument constructor
      {
         real = imag = 0.0;
      }
      void getdata()                 // read complex number
      {
         cout << "Real Part ? ";
         cin >> real;
         cout << "Imag Part ? ";
         cin >> imag;
      }
      complex operator + ( complex c2 );  // complex addition
      void outdata( char *msg )      // display complex number
      {
         cout << endl << msg;
         cout << "(" << real;
         cout << ", " << imag << ")";
      }
};
// add default and c2 complex objects
complex complex::operator + ( complex c2 )
{
   complex temp;                     // object temp of complex class
   temp.real = real + c2.real;       // add real parts
   temp.imag = imag + c2.imag;       // add imaginary parts
   return( temp );                   // return complex object
}
void main()
{
   complex c1, c2, c3;      // c1, c2, c3 are object of complex class
   cout << "Enter Complex Number c1 .." << endl;
   c1.getdata();
   cout << "Enter Complex Number c2 .." << endl;
   c2.getdata();
   c3 = c1 + c2; // add c1 and c2 and assign the result to c3
   c3.outdata("c3 = c1 + c2: " ); // display result
}
```

Run

```
Enter Complex Number c1 ..
Real Part ? 2.5
Imag Part ? 2.0
Enter Complex Number c2 ..
Real Part ? 3.0
Imag Part ? 1.5
c3 = c1 + c2: (5.5, 3.5)
```

In the class complex, the operator+() function is declared as follows.

```
complex operator + ( complex c2 );
```
This function takes one explicit argument of type `complex` and returns the result of `complex` type. In a statement such as
```
c3 = c1 + c2;        // c3 = c1.operator+( c2 );
```
it is very important to understand the mechanism of returning a value and relating the arguments of the operator to its objects. When the compiler encounters such expressions, it examines the argument types of the operator. In this case, since the first argument is of type `complex`, the compiler realizes that it must invoke the operator member + () function defined in the `complex` class (Figure 13.5).

Instances of the class `complex`

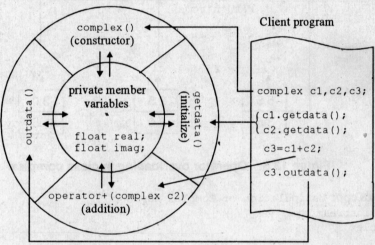

Figure 13.5:   Complex numbers and operator overloading

The argument on the left side of the operator (`c1` in this case) is the object of a class having overloaded operator function as its member function. The object on the right side (`c2` in this case) of the operator is passed as the actual argument to the overloaded operator function. The operator returns a value (complex object `temp` in this case), which can be assigned to another object (c3 in this case) or can be used in other ways (as argument or term in an expression, etc.).

The expression `c1+c2` invokes operator + () member function, `c1` object's data members are accessed directly since, this is the object of which the operator function is a member. The right operand is treated as an argument to the function and its members are accessed using the member access dot operator (as `c2.real` and `c2.imag`).

In the overloading of binary operators, as a rule, the *left-hand* operand is used to invoke the operator function and the *right-hand* operand is passed as an argument to the operator function. The mechanism of handling operands of an overloaded binary operator is illustrated in Figure 13.6.

Similarly, functions can be created to overload other operators to perform addition, subtraction, multiplication, division, etc. The program `complex3.cpp` illustrates the overloading of various arithmetic operators for manipulating complex numbers.

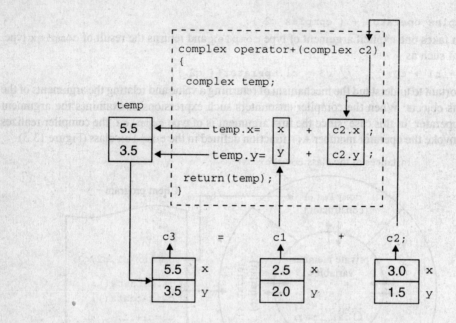

```
complex operator+(complex c2)
{
    complex temp;

    temp.x= x + c2.x ;
    temp.y= y + c2.y ;

    return(temp);
}
```

temp
| 5.5 |
| 3.5 |

c3 = c1 + c2;

c3
| 5.5 | x |
| 3.5 | y |

c1
| 2.5 | x |
| 2.0 | y |

c2
| 3.0 | x |
| 1.5 | y |

Figure 13.6: Operator overloading in class complex

```
// complex3.cpp: Manipulation of Complex Numbers
#include <iostream.h>
class complex
{
  private:
    float real;
    float imag;
  public:
    complex()
    {
        real = imag = 0;
    }
    void getdata()          // read complex number
    {
        cout << "Real Part ? ";
        cin >> real;
        cout << "Imag Part ? ";
        cin >> imag;
    }
    void outdata( char *msg )     // display complex number
    {
        cout << endl << msg;
        cout << "(" << real;
        cout << ", " << imag << ")";
    }
    complex operator + ( complex c2 );
```

```
        complex operator - ( complex c2 );
        complex operator * ( complex c2 );
        complex operator / ( complex c2 );
};
// addition of complex numbers, c3 = c1 + c2
complex complex::operator + ( complex c2 )
{
    complex temp;
    temp.real = real + c2.real;
    temp.imag = imag + c2.imag;
    return( temp );
}
// subtraction of complex numbers, c3 = c1 - c2;
complex complex::operator - ( complex c2 )
{
    complex temp;
    temp.real = real - c2.real;
    temp.imag = imag - c2.imag;
    return( temp );
}
// Multiplication of complex numbers, c3 = c1 * c2
complex complex::operator * ( complex c2 )
{
    complex temp;
    temp.real = real * c2.real - imag * c2.imag;
    temp.imag = real * c2.imag  + imag * c2.real;
    return( temp );
}
// Division of complex numbers, c3 = c1 / c2
complex complex::operator / ( complex c2 )
{
    complex temp;
    float qt;
    qt = c2.real*c2.real+c2.imag*c2.imag;
    temp.real = (real * c2.real + imag * c2.imag)/qt;
    temp.imag = (imag * c2.real- real * c2.imag) /qt;
    return( temp );
}
void main()
{
    complex c1, c2, c3;
    // read complex numbers c1 and c2
    cout << "Enter Complex Number c1 .." << endl;
    c1.getdata();
    cout << "Enter Complex Number c2 .." << endl;
    c2.getdata();
    cout << "Entered Complex Numbers are...";
    c1.outdata( "c1 = " );
    c2.outdata( "c2 = " );
    cout << endl << "Computational results are...";
    c3 = c1 + c2;
```

```
    c3.outdata("c3 = c1 + c2: ");
    c3 = c1 - c2;
    c3.outdata("c3 = c1 - c2: ");
    c3 = c1 * c2;
    c3.outdata("c3 = c1 * c2: ");
    c3 = c1 / c2;
    c3.outdata("c3 = c1 / c2: ");
    c3 = c1 + c2 + c1.+ c2;
    c3.outdata( "c3 = c1 + c2 + c1 + c2: " );
    c3 = c1 * c2 + c1 / c2;
    c3.outdata( "c3 = c1 * c2 + c1 / c2: ");
}
```

Run

```
Enter Complex Number c1 ..
Real Part ? 2.5
Imag Part ? 2.0
Enter Complex Number c2 ..
Real Part ? 3.0
Imag Part ? 1.5
Entered Complex Numbers are...
c1 = (2.5, 2)
c2 = (3, 1.5)
Computational results are...
c3 = c1 + c2: (5.5, 3.5)
c3 = c1 - c2: (-0.5, 0.5)
c3 = c1 * c2: (4.5, 9.75)
c3 = c1 / c2: (0.933333, 0.2)
c3 = c1 + c2 + c1 + c2: (11, 7)
c3 = c1 * c2 + c1 / c2: (5.43333, 9.95)
```

In main(), the statement,

```
        c3 = c1 + c2 + c1 + c2;
```

is evaluated as

```
        ((c1.operator+(c2)).operator+(c1)).operator+(c2);
```

from left to right, since all the operators have the same precedence. However, the statement

```
        c3 = c1 * c2 + c1 / c3;
```

is evaluated as

```
        (c1.operator*(c2)).operator+(c1.operator/(c2))
```

Operators with higher precedence are evaluated first, followed by those with lower precedence.

13.10 Concatenation of Strings

Normally, concatenation of strings is performed by using the library function strcat() explicitly. To illustrate this concept, consider the strings str1 and str2 which are defined as follows:

```
        char str1[50] = "Welcome to ";
        char str2[25] = "Operator Overloading";
```

The strings str1 and str2 are combined, and the result is stored in str1 by invoking the function strcat() as follows:

```
    strcat( str1, str2 );
```

On execution str2 remains unchanged. In C++, such operations can also be performed by defining a string class and overloading the + operator. A statement such as,

```
    str1 = str1 + str2;
```

for concatenation of string, (where str1 and str2 are the objects of a class string) would be perfectly valid. The program string.cpp defines a string class and uses it to concatenate strings.

```cpp
// string.cpp: Concatenation of strings
#include <iostream.h>
#include <string.h>
const int BUFF_SIZE = 50; // length of string
class string               // user defined string class
{
  private:
    char str[BUFF_SIZE];
  public:
    string()               // constructor1 without arguments
    {
      strcpy( str, "" );
    }
    string( char *MyStr )   // constructor2, one argument
    {
      strcpy( str, MyStr );    // MyStr is copied to str
    }
    void echo()     // display string
    {
      cout << str;
    }
    string operator +( string s ) // overloading + operator
    {
      string temp = str;    // creates object and strcpy( temp.str, str );
      strcat( temp.str, s.str ); //  temp.str = temp.str + s.str
      return temp;    // return string object temp
    }
};
void main()
{
  string str1 = "Welcome to ";           // uses constructor2
  string str2 = "Operator Overloading";  // uses constructor2
  string str3;    // uses constructor1, str3.str = NULL
  // display strings of str1, str2, and str3
  cout << "\nBefore str3 = str1 + str2; ..";
  cout << "\nstr1 = ";
  str1.echo();
  cout << "\nstr2 = ";
  str2.echo();
  cout << "\nstr3 = ";
  str3.echo();
  str3 = str1 + str2;  // str1 invokes its operator + function with str2
```

```
// display strings of str1, str2, and str3
cout << "\nAfter str3 = str1 + str2; ..";
cout << "\nstr1 = ";
str1.echo();
cout << "\nstr2 = ";
str2.echo();
cout << "\nstr3 = ";
str3.echo();
}
```

Run

```
Before str3 = str1 + str2; :.
str1 = Welcome to
str2 = Operator Overloading
str3 =
After str3 = str1 + str2; ..
str1 = Welcome to
str2 = Operator Overloading
str3 = Welcome to Operator Overloading
```

The prototype of the string concatenation operator function

```
        string operator +( string s ) // overloading + operator
```

indicates that the + operator takes one argument of type `string` object and returns an object of the same type. The concatenation is performed by creating a temporary `string` object `temp` and initializing it with the first string. The second string is added to first string in the object `temp` using the `strcat()` and finally the resultant temporary string object `temp` is returned. In this case, the length of `str1` plus `str2` should not exceed `BUFF_SIZE`. If it exceeds, then the behavior of the program may be unpredictable. It can be overcome by testing the length of `str1` plus `str2` before concatenating them in the operator + () function of the `string` class and then taking appropriate actions.

13.11 Comparison Operators

Similar to arithmetic operators, the relational operators can be overloaded for comparing the magnitudes of the operands. The relational operators can also operate on the user defined data-types similar to the way they operate on primitive data-types. The program `idxcmp.cpp` demonstrates the overloading of the comparison operator `<` to compare indexes.

```
// idxcmp.cpp: Index comparison with overloading of < operator
#include <iostream.h>
enum boolean { FALSE, TRUE };
class Index
{
   private:
      int value;               // Index Value
   public:
      Index()                  // No argument constructor
      {
         value = 0;
      }
```

```
      Index( int val )           // Constructor with one argument
      {
         value = val;
      }
      int GetIndex()             // Index Access
      {
         return value;
      }
      boolean operator < ( Index idx )   //compare indexes
      {
         return( value < idx.value ? TRUE : FALSE );
      }
};
void main()
{
   Index idx1 = 5;
   Index idx2 = 10;
   cout << "\nIndex1 = " << idx1.GetIndex();
   cout << "\nIndex2 = " << idx2.GetIndex();
   if( idx1 < idx2 )
      cout << "\nIndex1 is less than Index2";
   else
      cout << "\nIndex1 is not less than Index2";
}
```

Run
```
Index1 = 5
Index2 = 10
Index1 is less than Index2
```

The concept of overloading the comparison operator < in the above program is similar to overloading arithmetic operators. The operator function < () returns TRUE or FALSE depending on the magnitudes of the Index operands.

Strings Comparison

The relational operators such as <, >, ==, etc., can be overloaded to operate on strings. These operators return TRUE or FALSE depending on the contents of the string arguments. The program strcmp.cpp illustrates the overloading of relational operators in a string class.

```
// strcmp.cpp: Comparison of strings
#include <iostream.h>
#include <string.h>
const int BUFF_SIZE = 50;    // length of string
enum boolean { FALSE, TRUE };
class string                 // user defined string class
{
   private:
      char str[BUFF_SIZE];
   public:
```

```
        string()                 // constructor without arguments
        {
           strcpy( str, "" );
        }
        void read()              // read string
        {
           cin >> str;
           //  cout << str;
        }
        void echo()     // display string
        {
           cout << str;
        }
        boolean operator < ( string s ) // overloading < operator
        {
           if( strcmp( str, s.str ) < 0 )
              return TRUE;  // str < s.str in lexicographical order
           else
              return FALSE;
        }
        boolean operator > ( string s ) // overloading > operator
        {
           if( strcmp( str, s.str ) > 0 )
              return TRUE;     // str > s.str in lexicographical order
           else
              return FALSE;
        }
        boolean operator == ( char *MyStr ) // overloading == operator
        {
           if( strcmp( str, MyStr ) == 0 )
              return TRUE;   // str and MyStr are same
           else
              return FALSE;
        }
};
void main()
{
   string str1, str2;  // uses constructor 1
   while( TRUE )
   {
      cout << "\nEnter String1 <'end' to stop>: ";
      str1.read();
      if( str1 == "end" )
         break;
      cout << "Enter String2: ";
      str2.read();
      cout << "Comparison Status: ";
      // display comparison status
      // display format: String1 "comparison status <, >, = " String2
      str1.echo();
```

```
        if( str1 < str2 )
            cout << " < ";
        else
            if( str1 > str2 )
                cout << " > ";
            else
                cout << " = ";
        str2.echo();
    }
    cout << "\nBye.!! That's all folks.!";
}
```

Run

```
Enter String1 <'end' to stop>: C
Enter String2: C++
Comparison Status: C < C++
Enter String1 <'end' to stop>: Rajkumar
Enter String2: Bindu
Comparison Status: Rajkumar > Bindu
Enter String1 <'end' to stop>: Rajkumar
Enter String2: Venugopal
Comparison Status: Rajkumar < Venugopal
Enter String1 <'end' to stop>: HELLO
Enter String2: HELLO
Comparison Status: HELLO = HELLO
Enter String1 <'end' to stop>: end
Bye.!! That's all folks.!
```

The overloaded operator functions of the class `string` uses the library function `strcmp()` to compare the two strings. The `strcmp(..)` operates as follows:

- It returns 0 if both the strings are equal
- It returns a negative value if the first string is less than the second one
- It returns a positive value if the first string is greater than the second one

The terms *less than*, *greater than*, or *equal to* are used in lexicographic sense to indicate whether the first string appears before or after the second in the alphabetical order.

The prototype of string comparison function

```
        boolean operator == ( char *MyStr )
```

indicates that the `==` operator takes one argument of type pointer to character and returns TRUE or FALSE depending on the operands weightage in lexicographical order. The `strcmp()` in the function body compares the object's attribute `str` with the argument `MyStr`. From this example, it is understood that the arguments to an overloaded operator need not be of the same data-type, but the overloaded operator must be a *member function of the first object*.

13.12 Arithmetic Assignment Operators

Like arithmetic operators, *arithmetic assignment* operators can also be overloaded to perform an arithmetic operation followed by an assignment operation. Such statements are useful in replacing the expressions involving operations on two operands and storing the result in the first operand. For instance, a statement such as

```
c1 = c1 + c2;
```

can be replaced by

```
c1 += c2;
```

The program `complex4.cpp` illustrates the overloading of arithmetic assignment operators to manipulate complex numbers.

```cpp
// complex4.cpp: Overloading of +=, -=, *=, /= operators for complex class
#include <iostream.h>
class complex
{
  private:
    float real;
    float imag;
  public:
    complex()                 // constructor1
    {
      real = imag = 0;
    }
    void getdata()            // read complex number
    {
      cout << "Real Part ? ";
      cin >> real;
      cout << "Imag Part ? ";
      cin >> imag;
    }
    void outdata( char *msg )     // display complex number
    {
      cout << endl << msg;
      cout << "(" << real;
      cout << ", " << imag << ")";
    }
    void operator += ( complex c2 );
    void operator -= ( complex c2 );
    void operator *= ( complex c2 );
    void operator /= ( complex c2 );
};
// addition of complex numbers, c1 += c2 instead of c1 = c1 + c2;
void complex::operator += ( complex c2 )
{
  real = real + c2.real;
  imag = imag + c2.imag;
}

// subtraction of complex numbers, c1 -= c2, i.e., c1 = c1 - c2;
void complex::operator -= ( complex c2 )
{
  real = real - c2.real;
  imag = imag - c2.imag;
}
```

```
// Multiplication of complex numbers, c1 *= c2, instead of c1 = c1*c2
void complex::operator *= ( complex c2 )
{
    complex old = *this; // *this is an object of type complex

    real = old.real * c2.real - old.imag * c2.imag;
    imag = old.real * c2.imag + old.imag * c2.real;
}

// Division of complex numbers, c1 /= c2, i.e., c1 = c1 / c2
void complex::operator /= ( complex c2 )
{
    complex old = *this;
    float qt;

    qt = c2.real*c2.real+c2.imag*c2.imag;
    real = (old.real * c2.real + old.imag * c2.imag)/qt;
    imag = (old.imag * c2.real - old.real * c2.imag) /qt;
}
void main()
{
    complex c1, c2, c3;

    // read complex numbers c1 and c2
    cout << "Enter Complex Number c1 .." << endl;
    c1.getdata();
    cout << "Enter Complex Number c2 .." << endl;
    c2.getdata();

    cout << "Entered Complex Numbers are...";
    c1.outdata( "c1 = " );
    c2.outdata( "c2 = " );
    cout << endl << "Computational results are...";
    // c3 = c1 + c2
    c3 = c1;
    c3 += c2;
    c3.outdata("let c3 = c1, c3 += c2: ");

    // c3 = c1 - c2
    c3 = c1;
    c3 -= c2;
    c3.outdata("let c3 = c1, c3 -= c2: ");

    // c3 = c1 * c2
    c3 = c1;
    c3 *= c2;
    c3.outdata("let c3 = c1, c3 *= c2: ");

    // c3 = c1 / c2
    c3 = c1;
    c3 /= c2;
    c3.outdata("let c3 = c1, c3 /= c2: ");
}
```

Run

```
Enter Complex Number c1 ..
Real Part ? 2.5
Imag Part ? 2.0
Enter Complex Number c2 ..
Real Part ? 3.0
Imag Part ? 1.5
Entered Complex Numbers are...
c1 = (2.5, 2)
c2 = (3, 1.5)
Computational results are...
let c3 = c1, c3 += c2: (5.5, 3.5)
let c3 = c1, c3 -= c2: (-0.5, 0.5)
let c3 = c1, c3 *= c2: (4.5, 9.75)
let c3 = c1, c3 /= c2: (0.933333, 0.2)
```

Observe the difference between the operator function + () defined in the program complex3.cpp and operator function += () defined in the program complex4.cpp. In the former, a new temporary object of complex type must be created and returned by the function, so that the resultant object can be assigned to a third complex object, as in the statement

```
        c3 = c1 + c2;
```

In the latter, the function operator += () is a member function of the object (destination object's class), which receives the result of computation. Hence, the function operator += () has no return value; it returns void type. Normally, the result of the assignment operation is not required. In a statement, such as,

```
        c3 += c2;
```

the operator alone is used without bothering about the return value.

The use of the arithmetic assignment operator in a complicated statement such as,

```
        c3 = c1 += c2;
```

requires a return value. Such requirements can be satisfied by having the function operator += (), which terminates with the statement such as

```
        return( *this );  or return complex( real, imag );
```

In the first case, the current object is returned and in the latter case, a nameless object is created with initialization and is returned as illustrated in the program complex5.cpp.

```cpp
// complex5.cpp: Overloading of += operator for complex expressions
#include <iostream.h>
class complex
{
   private:
      float real;
      float imag;
   public:
      complex()              // no argument constructor
      {
         real = imag = 0.0;
      }
```

```
      void getdata()          // read complex number
      {
          cout << "Real Part ? ";
          cin >> real;
          cout << "Imag Part ? ";
          cin >> imag;
      }
      complex operator + ( complex c2 );  // complex addition
      void outdata( char *msg )     // display complex number
      {
          cout << endl << msg;
          cout << "(" << real;
          cout << ", " << imag << ")";
      }
      complex operator += ( complex c2 );
};
// addition of complex numbers, c1 += c2 instead of c1 = c1 + c2;
// return complex object *this or build temporary object and return
complex complex::operator += ( complex c2 )
{
   real = real + c2.real;
   imag = imag + c2.imag;
   return( *this );  // *this is current object
}
void main()
{
   complex c1, c2, c3;
   cout << "Enter Complex Number c1 .." << endl;
   c1.getdata();
   cout << "Enter Complex Number c2 .." << endl;
   c2.getdata();

   // Performs 1.  c1 += c2 and 2.  c3 = c1
   c3 = c1 += c2; // c1 += c2 is evaluated first, and assigned to c3
   cout << "\nOn execution of c3 = c1 += c2 ..";
   c1.outdata("Complex c1: ");
   c2.outdata("Complex c2: ");
   c3.outdata("Complex c3: ");
}
```

Run

```
Enter Complex Number c1 ..
Real Part ? 2.5
Imag Part ? 2.0
Enter Complex Number c2 ..
Real Part ? 3.0
Imag Part ? 1.5
On execution of c3 = c1 += c2 ..
Complex c1: (5.5, 3.5)
Complex c2: (3, 1.5)
Complex c3: (5.5, 3.5)
```

13.13 Overloading of `new` and `delete` Operators

The memory allocation operators `new` and `delete` can be overloaded to handle memory resource in a customized way. It allows the programmer to gain full control over the memory resource and to handle resource crunch errors such as *Out of Memory,* within a class. The main reason for overloading these functions is to increase the efficiency of memory management. An application designed to handle memory allocation by itself through overloading can easily detect memory leaks (improper usage). It can also be used to create the illusion of infinite amount of main memory (virtual memory, which exists in effect but not in reality).

The program `resource.cpp` illustrates the overloading of `new` and `delete` operators. The normal call to the `new` operator, such as

```
ptr = new vector;
```

dynamically creates a `vector` object and returns a pointer to that object. The overloaded operator function `new` in the `vector` class not only creates an object, but also allocates the resource for its internal data members.

```
// resource.cpp: Overloading of new and delete operators
#include <iostream.h>
const int ARRAY_SIZE = 10;
class vector
{
   private:
      int *array;     // array is dynamically allocatable data member
   public:
      // overloading of new operator
      void * operator new( size_t size )
      {
         vector *my_vector;
         my_vector = ::new vector;  // it refers to global new, otherwise
                                    // leads to recursive call of vector::new
         my_vector->array = new int[ARRAY_SIZE]; // calls ::new
         return my_vector;
      }
      // overloading of delete operator
      void operator delete( void* vec )
      {
         vector *my_vect;
         my_vect = (vector *) vec;
         delete (int *) my_vect->array;   // calls ::delete
         ::delete vec;     // it refers to global delete, otherwise
                           // leads to recursive call of vector::delete
      }
      void read();
      int sum();
};
void vector::read()
{
   for( int i = 0; i < ARRAY_SIZE; i++ )
   {
      cout << "vector[" << i << "] = ? ";
```

```
        cin >> array[i];
    }
}
int vector::sum()
{
    int sum = 0;
    for( int i = 0; i < ARRAY_SIZE; i++ )
        sum += array[i];
    return sum;
}
void main()
{
    vector *my_vector = new vector;
    cout << "Enter Vector data ..." << endl;
    my_vector->read();
    cout << "Sum of Vector = " << my_vector->sum();
    delete my_vector;
}
```

Run

```
Enter Vector data ...
vector[0] = ? 1
vector[1] = ? 2
vector[2] = ? 3
vector[3] = ? 4
vector[4] = ? 5
vector[5] = ? 6
vector[6] = ? 7
vector[7] = ? 8
vector[8] = ? 9
vector[9] = ? 10
Sum of Vector = 55
```

In main(), the statement

```
        vector *my_vector = new vector;
```

invokes the overloaded operator member function

```
        void * operator new( size_t size )
```

defined in the class vector as

```
        void * operator new( size_t size )
        {
            vector *my_vector;
            my_vector = ::new vector;  // it refers to global new, otherwise
            // leads to recursive call of vector::new
            my_vector->array = new int[ARRAY_SIZE]; // calls ::new
            return my_vector;
        }
```

In the above function, the statement

```
        my_vector = ::new vector;  // it refers to global new, otherwise
```

creates an object of the vector class. If scope resolution operator is not used, the overloaded operator function is called recursively leading to stack overflow. Hence, prefixing of the scope resolution operator to the `new` operator forces to use the standard `new` operator supported by the language instead of the one defined in the program. The class `vector` has a data item of type dynamic array, defined by `int *array`. Another statement in the above function

```
my_vector->array = new int[ARRAY_SIZE]; // calls ::new
```

creates an array and dynamically allocates memory to it.

Similar to the overloaded `new` operator function, the overloaded `delete` operator function handles the process of releasing memory that has been allocated during the dynamic object creation by the `new` operator; it also releases the memory allocated to the internal data-item array through the function call

```
delete my_vector;
```

It invokes the overloaded operator function

```
void operator delete( void* vec )
```

to release the entire memory resource allocated to the `my_vector` object and its data members.

13.14 Data Conversion

Representing the same data in multiple forms is a common practice in scientific computations. It involves the conversion of data from one form to another, for instance, conversion from radian to degree, polar to rectangular, and vice versa. Implicit invocation of the conversion procedure in C++ is achieved by overloading the assignment operator, =. The assignment operator assigns the contents of a variable, the result of an expression, or a constant, to another variable. For example,

```
var1 = var2;        // var1 and var2 are defined as integer variables
```

assigns the value of `var2` to `var1` which are of the same data-type. User defined objects of the same class can also be assigned to one another. In a statement such as

```
c3 = c1 + c2;       // c1, c2, and c3 are objects of complex class
```

the result of addition, which is of type `complex` is assigned to another object `c3` of `complex` class. The assignment of one variable/object to another variable/object, which are of the same data-type is achieved by copying the contents of all member data-items from source object to the destination object. Such operations do not require any conversion procedure for the data-type conversion. In the above expression, the result of (c1+c2) is of the same data-type as that of the destination object `c3`. Hence, the compiler does not require any special instruction from the user to perform the assignment of objects.

Thus, assignment of data items are handled by the compiler with no effort on the part of the user, whether they are basic or user defined provided both source and destination data items are of the same data-type. In case the data items are of different types, data conversion interface function must be explicitly specified by the user. These include conversions between basic and user-defined types or between the user-defined data items of different types.

13.15 Conversion between Basic Data Types

Consider the statement

```
weight = age; // weight is of float type and age is of integer type
```

where `weight` is of type float and `age` is of type integer. Here, the compiler calls a special routine to convert the value of `age`, which is represented in an integer format, to a floating-point format, so that it can be assigned to `weight`. The compiler has several built-in routines for the conversion of basic data types such as `char` to `int`, `float` to `double`, etc. This feature of the compiler, which performs conversion of data without the user intervention is known as *implicit type conversion*.

The compiler can be instructed explicitly to perform type conversion using the type conversion operators known as *typecast operators*. For instance, to convert `int` to `float`, the statement is

```
weight = (float) age;
```

where the keyword `float` enclosed between braces is the typecast operator. In C++, the above statement can also be expressed in a more readable form as

```
weight = float( age );
```

The *explicit conversion* of `float` to `int` uses the same built-in routine as implicit conversion.

13.16 Conversion between Objects and Basic Types

The compiler supports data conversion of only built-in data types supported by the language. The user cannot rely on the compiler to perform conversion from user-defined data types to primitive data types and vice-versa, because the compiler does not know anything about the logical meaning of user defined data types. Therefore, to perform a meaningful conversion, the user must supply the necessary conversion function. In this case, the conversion process can be from basic data types to user-defined data types or from the user-defined data types to basic data types.

The process of conversion between the user-defined type and basic type is illustrated in the program `meter.cpp` listed below. In this example, the user-defined type is the class `Meter`, which represents a unit of length in the MKS measurement system. The basic type is `float`, which is used to represent a unit of length in CGS measurement system.

The conversion between centimeter and meter can be performed by the following relations:

Length in Cms = Length in Meters * 100

Length in Meters = Length in Cms / 100

Where and How the conversion function should exist ?

To convert data from a basic type to a user-defined type, the conversion function should be defined in user-defined object's class in the form of the constructor. This constructor function takes a single argument of basic data-type as shown in Figure 13.7.

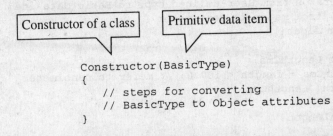

```
Constructor(BasicType)
{
    // steps for converting
    // BasicType to Object attributes
}
```

Constructor of a class   Primitive data item

Figure 13.7:   Conversion function: basic to user-defined

In the case of conversion from a user-defined type to a basic type, the conversion function should be defined in user-defined object's class in the form of the operator function. The operator function is defined as an overloaded basic data-type which takes no arguments. It converts the data members of an object to basic data types and returns a basic data-item. The syntax of such a conversion function is shown in Figure 13.8.

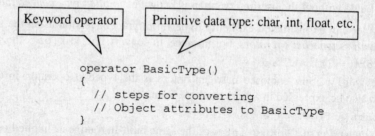

```
operator BasicType()
{
    // steps for converting
    // Object attributes to BasicType
}
```

Figure 13.8: Conversion function: user-defined to basic

In the above syntax, it can be observed that the conversion operator function has no return type specification. However, *it should return* `BasicType` *value*. The program `meter.cpp` illustrates the conversion of the `Meter` class's object to `float` representing centimeter and vice-versa.

```cpp
// meter.cpp: Conversion from Meter to Centimeter and vice-versa
#include <iostream.h>
// Meter class for MKS measurement system
class Meter
{
    private:
        float length;                  // length in meter
    public:
        Meter()                        // constructor0, no arguments
        {
            length = 0.0;
        }
        // Conversion from Basic data-item to user-defined type
        // InitLength is in centimeter unit
        Meter( float InitLength )      // constructor1, one argument
        {
            length = InitLength / 100.0; // centimeter to meter
        }
        // Conversion from user-defined type to Basic data-item
        // i.e., from meter to centimeter
        operator float()
        {
            float LengthCms;
            LengthCms = length * 100.0; // meter to centimeter
            return( LengthCms );
        }
        void GetLength()
        {
            cout << "\nEnter Length (in meters): ";
            cin >> length;
        }
        void ShowLength()
        {
```

```
              cout << "Length (in meter) = " << length;
     }
};

void main()
{
   // Basic to User-defined conversion demonstration Section
   Meter meter1;      // uses constructor0
   float length1;
   cout << "Enter Length (in cms): ";
   cin >> length1;
   meter1 = length1; // converts basic to user-defined, uses constructor1
   meter1.ShowLength();
   // User-defined to Basic conversion demonstration Section
   Meter meter2;  // uses constructor0
   float length2;
   meter2.GetLength();
   length2 = meter2; //converts user-defined to basic, uses operator float()
   cout << "Length (in cms) = " << length2;
}
```

Run

```
Enter Length (in cms): 150.0
Length (in meter) = 1.5
Enter Length (in meters): 1.669
Length (in cms) = 166.900009
```

Basic to User-Defined Data Type Conversion

In main(), the statement

```
       meter1 = length1; // converts basic to user-defined, uses constructor1
```

converts basic data item length1 of float type to the object meter1 by invoking the one-argument constructor:

```
       Meter( float InitLength )     // constructor1, one argument
```

This constructor is invoked while creating objects of the class Meter using a single argument of type float. It converts the input argument represented in centimeters to meters and assigns the resultant value to length data member.

The statements such as

```
       Meter meter1 = 150.0;
       meter1 = length1;
```

invokes the same conversion function. The only difference is, in the case of the first statement, the conversion function is invoked as a part object creation activity, whereas in the case of the second statement, the compiler first searches for the overloaded assignment operator function, and if that is not found, it invokes the one-argument constructor.

The distinction between the function definition and the assignment operator overloading for type conversion is blurred by the compiler; the compiler looks for a constructor if an overloaded = operator function is not available to perform data conversion.

User-Defined to Basic Data Type Conversion

In main(), the statement,

```
length2 = meter2; // convert user-defined to basic, uses operator float()
```

converts the object meter2 to the basic data-item of float type by invoking the overloaded operator function:

```
operator float()
{
    float LengthCms;
    LengthCms = length * 100.0; // meter to centimeter
    return( LengthCms );
}
```

The above conversion function can also be invoked explicitly as follows:

```
length2 = ( float ) meter2;
```

or as

```
length2 = float( meter2 );
```

The compiler searches for the appropriate conversion function. First, the compiler looks for an overloaded = operator. If it does not find one, then it looks for a conversion function and invokes the same implicitly for data conversion.

Conversion between Strings and String Objects

The program strconv.cpp demonstrates the use of a one argument constructor and a conversion function.

```
// strconv.cpp: conversion between basic string (char *) and class string
#include <iostream.h>
#include <string.h>
const int BUFF_SIZE = 50; // length of string
class string                 // user defined string class
{
  private:
    char str[BUFF_SIZE];
  public:
    string()                 // constructor1 without arguments
    {
      strcpy( str, "" );
    }
    string( char *MyStr )    // constructor2, one argument
    {
      strcpy( str, MyStr );     // MyStr is copied to str
    }
    void echo()     // display string
    {
      cout << str;
    }
    // conversion function to convert String object item to char * item
    operator char * () // invoked if destination data-item is char* type
    {
```

```
            return str;
        }
};
void main()
{
    // Conversion from string of type char * to string object
    char msg[20] = "OOPs the Great";
    string str1;    // uses constructor 1
    str1 = msg;     // uses the function 'string( char *MyStr )'
    cout << "str1 = ";
    str1.echo();
    // Conversion from object to char * type
    char *receive;
    string str2 = "It is nice to learn";
    receive = str2;    // uses the function 'operator char * ()'
    cout << "\nstr2 = ";
    cout << receive;
}
```

Run

```
str1 = OOPs the Great
str2 = It is nice to learn
```

In the above example, the one argument constructor

```
        string( char *MyStr )   // constructor2, one argument
        {
            strcpy( str, MyStr );    // MyStr is copied to str
        }
```

converts a normal string defined using char* to an object of class string. The string is passed as an argument to the function; it copies the string MyStr to the str data member of the object.

The conversion will be applied during creation of the string object with initialization or during the assignment of a normal string to the string object. In the statement

```
        string str2 = "It is nice to learn";
```

the conversion of normal string to string object initialization is performed during creation of the object str2. Whereas, in the statement

```
        str1 = msg;    // uses the function 'string( char *MyStr )
```

the conversion of normal string defined as char* type variable msg to string object initialization is performed during assignment. The conversion function

```
        operator char * ()  // invoked if destination data-item is char * type
        {
            return str;
        }
```

is used to convert from a string object to a normal string. It is invoked by the the statement,

```
        receive = str2; // uses the function 'operator char * ()
```

The object str2 can also be passed to the indirection operator << to display a string stored in the data member str as shown in the statement,

```
cout << str2;
```

The object `str2` is passed as an argument to the overloaded output stream operator `<<`. But, it does not know anything about the user-defined object `str2`. This is resolved by the compiler by searching for a function which converts the object to a data-type known to the operator `<< ()`. In this case, the compiler finds the operator function `char* ()`, returning the `char*` type known to the stream operator. If the compiler does not find the conversion function, it reports an error

```
"Operator cannot be applied to these operands in function main()"
```

The program `strconv.cpp` clearly demonstrates the data conversions that take place not only during object creation and in assignment statements, but also in the case of arguments passed to operators (for instance, `<<`) or functions. Incompatible arguments can also be passed to an operator or a function as long as there exists a conversion function. The incompatibility between the formal arguments of the operator function and actual arguments is resolved by the compiler.

13.17 Conversion between Objects of Different Classes

The C++ compiler does not support data conversion between objects of user-defined classes. The data conversion methods: *one-argument constructor* and *conversion function* can also used for conversions among user defined data types. The choice between these two methods for data conversion depends on whether the conversion function should be defined in the source object or destination object. Consider the following skeleton code:

```
ClassA objecta;
ClassB objectb;
.....
objecta = objectb;
```

where `objecta` and `objectb` are the objects of classes `ClassA` and `ClassB` respectively. The conversion method can be either defined in `ClassA` or `ClassB` depending on whether it should be a one-argument constructor or an operator function.

Conversion Routine in Source Object: `operator function`

The conversion routine in the source object's class is implemented as an operator function. The segment of code shown in Figure 13.9 for class declaration demonstrates the method of implementing a conversion routine in the source object's class.

In an assignment statement such as,

```
objecta = objectb;
```

`objectb` is the source object of the class `ClassB` and `objecta` is the destination object of the class `ClassA`. The conversion function `operator ClassA()` exists in the source object's class.

The program `d2r1.cpp` illustrates the concept of defining a conversion routine in the source object. The conversion of an angle between degrees and radians is achieved by the following relations:

♦ Angle in Radian = Angle in Degree * PI / 180.0
♦ Angle in Degree = Angle in Radian * 180.0 / PI,   where PI = 22/7

```
// Destination object class
class ClassA
{
    // ClassA stuff here

};
// Source object class
class ClassB
{
    private:
        // attributes of classB
    public:                              → Destination object's class name

        operator ClassA()                  Conversion operator function
        {
          // program stuff for converting ClassB object
          // to ClassA object attributes
        }
        . . .
        . . .

};
```

Figure 13.9: Conversion routine in source object

```
// d2r1.cpp: Degree to Radian, Conversion Routine in Source class
#include <iostream.h>
const float  PI = 3.141592654;
class Radian
{
    private:
        float rad;                        // radian
    public:
        Radian()                          // constructor0, no arguments
        {
            rad = 0.0;
        }
        Radian( float InitRad )           // constructor1
        {
            rad = InitRad;
        }
        float GetRadian()                 // Access function
        {
            return( rad );
        }
        void Output()                     // Display of radian
        {
            cout << "Radian = " << GetRadian();
        }
};
```

```
class Degree
{
    private:
        float degree;                    // Degree
    public:
        Degree()                         // constructor0, no arguments
        {
            degree = 0.0;
        }
        // radian = degree; conversion routine at the source
        // This function will be called if we try to assign
        // object degree to object of type radian
        operator Radian()
        {
            // convert degree to radian and create an object radian
            // and then return, here radian constructor1 is called
            return( Radian( degree * PI / 180.0 ) );
        }
        void Input()           // Read degree
        {
            cout << "Enter Degree: ";
            cin >> degree;
        }
};
void main( void )
{
    Degree deg1;           // degree using constructor0
    Radian rad1;           // radian using constructor0
    // Read Input values
    deg1.Input();

    rad1 = deg1; // uses 'operator Radian()'

    // display radian and degree
    rad1.Output();
}
```

Run1

```
Enter Degree: 90
Radian = 1.570796
```

Run2

```
Enter Degree: 180
Radian = 3.141593
```

In main(), the statement
```
    rad1 = deg1; // uses 'operator Radian()'
```
assigns the deg1 object of class Degree to the rad1 object of the class Radian. Since both the objects deg1 and rad1 are instances of different classes, the conversion during assignment operation is performed by the member function:

```
operator Radian()
{
    // convert degree to radian and create an object radian
    // and then return, here radian constructor1 is called
    return( Radian( degree * PI / 180.0 ) );
}
```

It is defined in the source object's class Degree; it is chosen by the compiler for converting the object deg1 to rad1 implicitly.

Conversion Routine in Destination Object: constructor function

The conversion routine can also be defined in the destination object's class as a one-argument constructor. The segment of code shown in Figure 13.10 for class declaration demonstrates the method of implementing a conversion routine in the destination object's class.

```
// Source object class
class ClassB
{
    // ClassB stuff here

};
// Destination object class
class ClassA
{
    private:
        // attributes of classA        ──────▶ Destination object's class name
    public:                                   ──────▶ object of a source class

        ClassA(ClassB objectb) ◀━━━━━━━━━           Constructor function
        {

        // program stuff for converting ClassB object
        // to ClassA object attributes
        // Private attributes of ClassB are accessed
        // through its public functions
        ...
        ...
        }

};
```

Figure 13.10:   Conversion routine in destination object

In an assignment statement such as

```
objecta = objectb;
```

objectb is the source object of ClassB and objecta is the destination object of class ClassA. The conversion function (constructor function in this case) ClassA(ClassB objectb) is defined in the destination object's class. The program d2r2.cpp illustrates the concept of defining conversion function in the destination object.

```
// d2r2.cpp: Degree to Radian. Conversion Routine in the Destination object.
#include <iostream.h>
const float  PI = 3.141592654;
```

```
class Degree
{
    private:
        float degree;                  // Degree
    public:
        Degree()                       // constructor0, no arguments
        {
            degree = 0.0;
        }
        float GetDegree()              // Access function
        {
            return( degree );
        }
        void Input()                   // Read degree
        {
            cout << "Enter Degree: ";
            cin >> degree;
        }
};
class Radian
{
    private:
        float rad;                     // radian
    public:
        Radian()                       // constructor0, no arguments
        {
            rad = 0.0;
        }
        float GetRadian()              // Access function
        {
            return( rad );
        }
        // radian = degree: Conversion routine is in destination object's class
        Radian( Degree deg )
        {
            rad = deg.GetDegree() * PI / 180.0;
        }
        void Output()                  // Display of radian
        {
            cout << "Radian = ' << GetRadian();
        }
};
void main( void )
{
    Degree deg1;              // degree using constructor0
    Radian rad1;              // radian using constructor0
    // Read Input values
    deg1.Input();
    rad1 = deg1;             // uses Radian( Degree deg )
    rad1.Output();          // display radian and degree
}
```

Run1
```
Enter Degree: 90
Radian = 1.570796
```

Run2
```
Enter Degree: 180
Radian = 3.141593
```

In main(), the statement

```
rad1 = deg1;  // convert degree to radian, uses Radian( Degree deg )
```

assigns the user-defined object deg1 to another object rad1. Since, the objects deg1 and rad1 are of different types, the conversion during the assignment operation is performed by a member function

```
Radian( Degree deg )
{
    rad = deg.GetDegree() * PI / 180.0;
}
```

defined in the destination object's class Radian as a one-argument constructor. It is chosen by the compiler for converting the object deg1's attributes to rad1's attributes implicitly. The constructor must be able to access the private data members defined in the source object's class. The Degree class defines the following interface function

```
float GetDegree()                     // Access function
{
    return( degree );
}
```

to access the private data members. Note that, the body of the function main() in the program d2r2.cpp is the same as that in the program d2r1.cpp, although the conversion methods have appeared in different forms.

Complete Conversion

The program degrad.cpp illustrates the concept of defining conversion functions in the source or destination object's class. In this program, angles in degrees can be converted to radians or angles in radians can be converted to degrees. The class Degree has conversion functions: constructor function and operator function. A class can have any number of conversion functions as long their signatures are different.

```
// degrad.cpp: Degree to Radian data conversion and vice-versa
#include <iostream.h>
const float  PI = 3.141592654;
class Radian
{
   private:
        float rad;                    // radian
   public:
        Radian()                      // constructor0, no arguments
        {
            rad = 0.0;
        }
```

```
      Radian( float InitRad )     // constructor1, one argument
      {  rad = InitRad;    }
      float GetRadian()            // Access function
      {
         return( rad );
      }
      void Input()                 // Read radian
      {
         cout << "Enter Radian: ";
         cin >> rad;
      }
      void Output()                // Display of radian
      {
         cout << "Radian = " << GetRadian() << endl;
      }
};
class Degree
{
   private:
      float degree;            // Degree
   public:
      Degree()                 // constructor0, no arguments
      {
         degree = 0.0;
      }
      // degree = radian: Conversion routine at the destination
      Degree( Radian rad )     // constructor1, one-argument constructor
      {
         degree = rad.GetRadian() * 180.0 / PI;
      }
      float GetDegree()             // Access function
      {
         return( degree );
      }
      // radian = degree; conversion routine at the source
      operator Radian()
      {
         // convert degree to radian and create an object radian
         // and then return, here radian constructor 1 is called
         return( Radian( degree * PI / 180.0 ) );
      }
      void Input()                 // Read degree
      {
         cout << "Enter Degree: ";
         cin >> degree;
      }
      void Output()                // Display output
      {
         cout << "Degree = " << degree << endl;
      }
};
```

```
void main( void )
{
   Degree deg1, deg2;        // degree using constructor0
   Radian rad1, rad2;        // radian using constructor0
   // degree to radian conversion
   deg1.Input();
   rad1 = deg1;   // convert degree to radian, uses 'operator Radian()'
   rad1.Output();
   // radian to degree conversion
   rad2.Input();
   deg2 = rad2;   // convert radian to degree, uses Degree( Radian rad )
   deg2.Output();
}
Run
Enter Degree: 180
Radian = 3.141593
Enter Radian: 3.142
Degree = 180.023331
```

One-Argument Constructor or Operator Function ?

From the above discussion, it is evident that either the one-argument constructor or the operator function can be used for converting objects of different classes. A wide variety of classes in the form of class libraries are available commercially. But, they are supplied as object modules (machine code in linkable form) and not as source modules. The user has no control over the modification of such classes. This leads to a problem of conversion between the objects defined using the classes supplied by the software vendors and objects defined using the classes declared by the user. This problem can be circumvented by defining a conversion routine in the user-defined classes. It can be a one-argument constructor or a operator function depending on whether the user-defined object is a source or destination object. The thumb rules for deciding where conversion routine has to be defined are the following:

- If the user-defined object is a source object, the conversion routine must be defined as an operator function in the source object's class.
- If the user-defined object is a destination object, the conversion routine must be defined as a one-argument constructor in the destination object's class.
- If both the source and destination object are the instances of user-defined classes, the conversion routine can be placed either in source object's class as a operator function or in destination object's class as a constructor function.

13.18 Subscript Operator Overloading

The subscript operator [ ] can be overloaded to access the attributes of an object. It is mainly useful for bounds checking while accessing elements of an array. Consider the following definition

```
int a[10];
```

An expression such as a[20] is syntactically valid though it is accessing an element beyond the range. Such an illegal access can be detected by overloading subscript operators. The user defined class can overload the [ ] operator and check for validity of accesses to array of objects and permit access to its members only when the index value is valid.

An array of primitive data type can be accessed using integer subscripts only. However, when it is overloaded, it can take parameters other than integer types, i.e., the argument of an operator function [] need not be an integer; it can be of any data type. The program `script.cpp` illustrates the concept of overloading the subscript operator [].

```cpp
// script.cpp: Subscripted operator overloading
#include <iostream.h>
#include <string.h>
typedef struct AccountEntry
{
   int number;       // account number
   char name[25];    // name of account holder
} AccountEntry;
class AccountBook
{
   private:
      int aCount;      // account holders count
      AccountEntry account[10];  // accounts table
   public:
      AccountBook( int aCountIn )  // constructor 1
      {
         aCount = aCountIn;
      }
      void AccountEntry();
      int operator [] ( char * nameIn );
      char * operator [] ( int numberIn );
};
// takes name as input, returns account number
int AccountBook::operator [] ( char *nameIn )
{
   for( int i = 0; i < aCount; i++ )
      if( strcmp( nameIn, account[i].name) == 0 )
       return account[i].number; // found name, return its account number
   return 0;
}
// takes number as input, returns name corresponding to account number
char * AccountBook::operator [] ( int numberIn )
{
   for( int i = 0; i < aCount; i++ )
      if( numberIn == account[i].number )
         return account[i].name;
   return 0;
}
void AccountBook::AccountEntry()
{
   for( int i = 0; i < aCount; i++ )
   {
      cout << "Account Number: ";
      cin >> account[i].number;
      cout << "Account Holder Name: ";
      cin >> account[i].name;
```

```
    }
}
void main()
{
    int accno;
    char name[25];
    AccountBook accounts( 5 ); // account having 5 customers
    cout << "Building 5 Customers Database" << endl;
    accounts.AccountEntry();   // read
    cout << "\nAccessing Accounts Information";
    cout << "\nTo access Name Enter Account Number: ";
    cin >> accno;
    cout << "Name: " << accounts[accno]; //operator [] ( int numberIn )
    cout << "\nTo access Account Number, Enter Name: ";
    cin >> name;
    cout << "Account Number: " << accounts[name];
                                // uses, operator [] ( char *nameIn )
}
```

Run

```
Building 5 Customers Database
Account Number: 1
Account Holder Name: Rajkumar
Account Number: 2
Account Holder Name: Kiran
Account Number: 3
Account Holder Name: Ravishanker
Account Number: 4
Account Holder Name: Anand
Account Number: 5
Account Holder Name: Sindhu
Accessing Accounts Information
To access Name Enter Account Number: 1
Name: Rajkumar
To access Account Number, Enter Name: Sindhu
Account Number: 5
```

In main(), the statement

```
        accounts.AccountEntry();   // read
```

reads a database of five account holders and initializes the object's data members. The statement

```
        cout << "Name: " << accounts[accno]; // operator [] ( int numberIn )
```

uses the function

```
        char * operator [] ( int numberIn );
```

and returns the name of the account holder for a given account number. The statement

```
        cout << "Account Number: " << accounts[name];
```

uses the function

```
        int operator [] ( char *nameIn )
```

and returns the account number corresponding to the name of the given account holder's name. The compiler selects the appropriate function which matches with the actual parameter's data type.

with Friend Functions

a very important role in operator overloading by providing the flexibility denied ...er functions of a class. They allow overloading of stream operators (<< or >>) for stream ...mputation on user defined data types. The only difference between a friend function and member function is that, the friend function requires the arguments to be explicitly passed to the function and processes them explicitly, whereas the member function considers the first argument implicitly. Friend functions can either be used with unary or binary operators. The syntax of operator overloading with friend functions is shown in Figure 13.11.

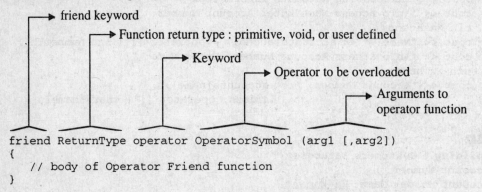

```
friend ReturnType operator OperatorSymbol (arg1 [,arg2])
{
    // body of Operator Friend function
}
```

Figure 13.11:   Syntax of overloading with friend function

The prototype of the friend function must be prefixed with the keyword `friend` inside the class body. The body of friend function can appear either inside or outside the body of a class. It is advisable to define a friend function outside the body of a class. The definition of the friend function outside the body of a class is defined as normal function and is not prefixed with the `friend` keyword. The arguments of the friend functions are generally objects of friend classes. In a friend function, all the members of a class (to which this function is a friend) can be accessed by using its objects. *Friend function is not allowed to access members of a class (to which it is a friend) directly, but it can access all the members including the private members by using objects of that class.* Hence, a friend function is similar to a normal function except that it can access the private members of a class using its objects.

Unary Operator Overloading using Friend Functions

The program `complex6.cpp` illustrates the concept of negation of complex numbers. The negation function returns negated object without modifying the source object.

```
// complex6.cpp: Negation of complex number with Unary Operator
#include <iostream.h>
class complex
{
    private:
        float real;
        float imag;
    public:
        complex()               // no argument constructor
        {
            real = imag = 0.0;
```

```
        }
        void getdata();    // read complex number
        void outdata( char *msg );    // display complex number
        // overloading of unary minus operator to support c2 = - c1
        friend complex operator - ( complex c1 )
        {
            complex c;
            c.real = -c1.real;
            c.imag = -c1.imag;
            return( c );
        }
        void readdata();
};
void complex::readdata()
{
    cout << "Real Part ? ";
    cin >> real;
    cout << "Imag Part ? ";
    cin >> imag;
}
void complex::outdata( char *msg )
{
    cout << endl << msg;
    cout << "(" << real;
    cout << ", " << imag << ")";
}
void main()
{
    complex c1, c2;
    cout << "Enter Complex c1.." << endl;
    c1.readdata();
    c2 = -c1;              // invokes complex operator - ()
    c1.outdata( "Complex c1 : " );
    c2.outdata( "Complex c2 = -Complex c1: " );
}
```

Run

```
Enter Complex c1..
Real Part ? 1.5
Imag Part ? -2.5
Complex c1 : (1.5, -2.5)
Complex c2 = -Complex c1: (-1.5, 2.5)
```

The complex number negation function without a friend is declared as follows:

```
        complex operator - ()
```

In this case, arguments are implicitly assumed. Using the keyword friend, it is declared as follows:

```
        friend complex operator - ( complex c1 )
```

The above friend operator function cannot access members of the class complex directly, unlike its member functions. In main(), the statement

invokes unary operator function, complex operator - ()
1 and assigns it to c2. It returns the negated result without negating
~ject. The object c1 is passed as a value parameter to the negate operator function
~fication to its data members will be reflected in the c1 object.

The negation operation can also be applied to an object to modify its data members. In this case, the same object acts both as a source and a destination object. It is similar to representing a negative number. This can be achieved by passing the object as a reference parameter to the negation operator function so that, the negation of its data members can be also reflected in the calling object. The program complex7.cpp illustrates the concept of negation of complex numbers having the same source and destination operands.

```cpp
// complex7.cpp: Negation of Complex Number with Unary Operator Overloading
#include <iostream.h>
class complex
{
   private:
      float real;
      float imag;
   public:
      complex() { real = imag = 0; }
      void readdata();
      void outdata( char *msg );
      // Note: friend function with explicit reference parameter
      // overloading of unary minus, -c1
      friend void operator - ( complex & c1 ); // definition outside
};
// friend function of the class complex
// Note that, the keyword friend should not prefixed while defining outside
void operator - ( complex & c1 )
{
   c1.real = -c1.real;
   c1.imag = -c1.imag;
}
void complex::readdata()
{
   cout << "Real Part ? ";
   cin >> real;
   cout << "Imag Part ? ";
   cin >> imag;
}
void complex::outdata( char *msg )
{
   cout << endl << msg;
   cout << "(" << real;
   cout << ", " << imag << ")";
}
void main()
{
   complex c1;
```

```
      cout << "Enter Complex c1.." << endl;
      c1.readdata();
      -c1;  // invokes unary operator function, complex operator - ()
      c1.outdata( "Result of -Complex c1: " );
}
```

Run

```
Enter Complex c1..
Real Part ? 1.5
Imag Part ? -2.5
Result of -Complex c1: (-1.5, 2.5)
```

In main(), the statement

```
      -c1;  // invokes unary operator function, complex operator - ()
```

invokes the function

```
      void operator - ( complex & c1 )
```

by passing the object c1 by reference. Thus, the negation of c1 in the function is also reflected in the calling object. Note that, the definition of operator friend function is the same as normal functions.

Binary Operator Overloading using Friend Function

The complex number discussed in the program complex2.cpp can be modified using a friend operator function as follows:

1. Modify the member function prototype as follows:

```
      friend complex operator + ( complex c1, complex c2 )
```

2. Redefine the operator function as follows:

```
      friend complex operator + ( complex c1, complex c2 )
      {
          complex c;
          c.real = c1.real + c2.real;
          c.imag = c1.imag + c2.imag;
          return( c );
      }
```

In the above definition, the input object parameters c1 and c2 are handled explicitly without considering the first argument as an implicit argument. The statement

```
      c3 = c1 + c2;
```

is equivalent to the statement

```
      c3 = operator + ( c1, c2 );
```

The result generated by the friend function is same as that generated by the member function. But, friend functions offer the flexibility of writing an expression as a combination of operands of user defined and primitive data types. For instance, consider the statement

```
      c3 = c1 + 2.0;
```

The expression c1 + 2.0 is made up of the object c1 and a primitive type. In case of an operator member function, both the operands must be of object's data type. When the friend operator functions are used, both the operands need not be instances of user-defined data type. It requires a parameterized constructor taking a primitive data type parameter. The program complex8.cpp illustrates the concept of overloading an operator function as a friend function.

...tion of Complex Numbers with friend feature

```cpp
..ivate:
   float real;
   float imag;
public:
   complex()
   {}
   complex( int realpart )
   {
      real = realpart;
   }
   void readdata()
   {
      cout << "Real Part ? ";
      cin >> real;
      cout << "Imag Part ? ";
      cin >> imag;
   }
   void outdata( char *msg )       // display complex number
   {
      cout << endl << msg;
      cout << "(" << real;
      cout << ", " << imag << ")";
   }
   friend complex operator + ( complex c1, complex c2 );
};
// note that friend keyword and scope resolution operator are not used
complex operator + ( complex c1, complex c2 )
{
   complex c;
   c.real = c1.real + c2.real;
   c.imag = c1.imag + c2.imag;
   return( c );
}

void main()
{
   complex c1, c2, c3 = 3.0;
   cout << "Enter Complex1 c1..:" << endl;
   c1.readdata();
   cout << "Enter Complex2 c2..:" << endl;
   c2.readdata();
   c3 = c1 + c2;
   c3.outdata( "Result of c3 = c1 + c2: " );
   // 2.0 is considered as real part of complex
   c3 = c1 + 2.0;    // c3 = c1 + complex(2.0)
   c3.outdata( "Result of c3 = c1 + 2.0: " );
   // 3.0 is considered as real part of complex
```

```
c3 = 3.0 + c2;    // c3 = complex( 3.0 ) + c2
c3.outdata( "Result of c3 = 3.0 + c2: " );
}
```

Run

```
Enter Complex1 c1..:
Real Part ? 1
Imag Part ? 2
Enter Complex2 c2..:
Real Part ? 3
Imag Part ? 4
Result of c3 = c1 + c2: (4, 6)
Result of c3 = c1 + 2.0: (3, 2)
Result of c3 = 3.0 + c2: (6, 4)
```

In main(), the statement

```
c3 = c1 + 2.0;    // c3 = c1 + complex(2.0)
```

has an expression, which is a combination of the object c1 and the primitive floating point constant 2.0. Though, there is no member function matching this expression, the compiler will resolve this by treating the expression as follows:

```
c3 = c1 + complex( 2.0 );
```

The compiler invokes the single argument constructor and converts the primitive value to a new temporary object (here 2.0 is considered as a real part of the complex number) and passes it to the friend operator function:

```
friend complex operator + ( complex c1, complex c2 )
```

The sum of the object c1 and a new temporary object complex(2.0) is computed and assigned to object c3. The new temporary objects are destroyed immediately after execution of the statement due to which it is created. The above expression can also be written as

```
c3 = 2.0 + c1;
```

Recall that the left-hand operand is responsible for invoking its member function; but this statement has a numeric constant instead of an object. The outcome of either expression is the same, since the compiler treats it as follows:

```
c3 = complex( 2.0 ) + c1;
```

In C++, an object can be used not only to invoke a friend function, but also as an argument to a friend function. Thus, to the friend operator functions, a built-in type operand can be passed either as the first operand or as the second operand.

Overloading Stream Operators using Friend Function

The iostream facility of C++ provides an easy means to perform I/O. The class istream uses the predefined stream cin that can be used to read data from the standard input device. The *extraction* operator >> is used for performing input operations in the iostream library. The *insertion* operator << is used for performing output operations in the iostream library.

Similar to the built-in variables, the user-defined objects can also be read or displayed using the stream operators. In case of the overloaded operator << function, the ostream & is taken as the first argument of a friend function of a class. The return value of this friend function is of type ostream & as shown in Figure 13.12.

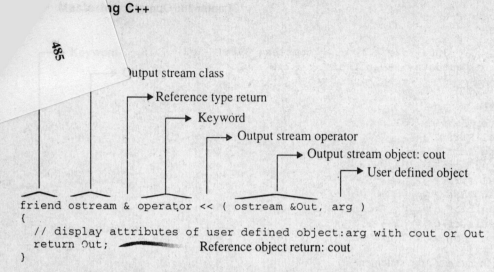

```
friend ostream & operator << ( ostream &Out, arg )
{
    // display attributes of user defined object:arg with cout or Out
    return Out;          Reference object return: cout
}
```

Figure 13.12: Overloading output stream operator as friend function

Similarly, for overloading the >> operator, the `istream &` is taken as the first argument of a friend function of the class. The return value of this friend function is of type `istream &` as shown in Figure 13.13. In both the cases, a reference to an object of the current class is taken as the second argument and the same is returned by reference.

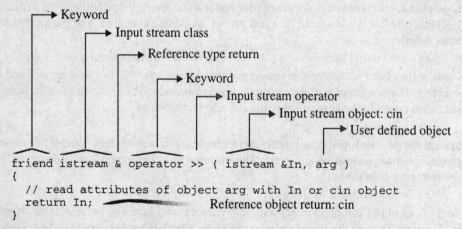

```
friend istream & operator >> ( istream &In, arg )
{
    // read attributes of object arg with In or cin object
    return In;          Reference object return: cin
}
```

Figure 13.13: Overloading input stream operator as friend function

The program complex9.cpp illustrates the flexibility of overloading stream operators and their usage with objects of the user defined data type.

```
// complex9.cpp: Addition of Complex Numbers with stream overloading
#include <iostream.h>
class complex
{
    private:
        float real;
        float imag;
    public:
```

```
        complex() { }
        complex( float InReal )
        {
            real = InReal;
            imag = 0;
        }
        void outdata();
        friend complex operator + ( complex c1, complex c2 )
        {
            complex c;
            c.real = c1.real + c2.real;
            c.imag = c1.imag + c2.imag;
            return( c );
        }
        friend istream & operator >> ( istream &In, complex &c );
        friend ostream & operator << ( ostream &Out, complex &c );
};
istream & operator >> ( istream & In, complex & c )
{
    cout << "Real Part ? ";
    In >> c.real;  // cin >> c.real;
    cout << "Imag Part ? ";
    In >> c.imag;  // cin >> c.imag;
    return In;
}
ostream & operator << ( ostream &Out, complex & c )
{
    Out << "(" << c.real;            // or cout << "Real = " << c.real;
    Out << ", " << c.imag << ")"; // cout in place of Out
    return Out;
}

void main()
{
    complex c1, c2, c3 = 3;
    cout << "Enter Complex1 c1..:" << endl;
    cin >> c1;
    cout << "Enter Complex2 c2..:" << endl;
    cin >> c2;
    c3 = c1 + c2;
    cout << "Result of c3 = c1 + c2: ";
    cout << c3;
    // 2.0 is considered as real part of complex
    c3 = c1 + 2.0;    // c3 = c1 + complex(2.0)
    cout<<endl<<"Result of c3 = c1 + 2.0: "; //c3=c1 + complex(2.0);
    cout << c3;
    // 3.0 is considered as real part of complex
    c3 = 3.0 + c2;
    cout<< endl<<"Result of c3 = 3.0 + c2: "; //c3=complex(3.0)+ c2;
    cout << c3;
}
```

```
   .. ? 2
..er Complex2 c2..:
Real Part ? 3
Imag Part ? 4
Result of c3 = c1 + c2: (4, 6)
Result of c3 = c1 + 2.0: (3, 2)
Result of c3 = 3.0 + c2: (6, 4)
```

In main(), the statements

```
    cin >> c1;
    cin >> c2;
```

read user-defined class's objects c1 and c2 in the same way as built-in data type variables by using the input stream operator. Also, the sum of the complex numbers c1 and c2 stored in c3 is displayed by the statement,

```
        cout << c3;
```

similar to any built-in data item using the output stream operator. The overloaded stream operator functions performing I/O operations with complex numbers are the following:

```
    friend istream & operator >> ( istream &In, complex &c  );
    friend ostream & operator << ( ostream &Out, complex &c  );
```

The classes istream and ostream are defined in the header file iostream.h, which has been included in the program. C++ does not allow overloading of operators listed in Table 13.2 as friend operator functions. They can, however be overloaded as operator member functions.

Operator Category	Operators
Assignment	=
Function call	( )
Subscribing	[ ]
Class Member Access	->

Table 13.2:   Operators that cannot be overloaded as friend operators

13.20 Assignment Operator Overloading

The compiler copies all the members of a user-defined source object to a destination object in an assignment statement, when its members are statically allocated. The data members, which are dynamically allocated must be copied to the destination object explicitly by overloading the assignment operator. Two examples of this process are the assignment operator and the copy constructor. Consider the following statements:

```
    vector v1( 5 ), v2( 5 );
    v1 = v2;    // operator = invoked
```

```
        vector v3 = v2;    // copy constructor is invoked
```
The first statement defines two objects v1 and v2 of the class vector. The second assignment statement
```
        v1 = v2;
```
will cause the compiler to copy the data from v2, member-by-member, into v1. The action is similar to the default operation performed by the assignment operator. The next statement
```
        vector v3 = v2;
```
initializes one object with another object during definition. This statement causes a similar action after creating the new object v3. The data members from v2 are copied member-by-member into v3. This action is similar to the operation performed by the copy constructor, by default.

The default actions performed by the compiler (to perform assignment operation) are insufficient if the object's state is dynamically varying. Such objects can be processed by overriding these default actions. The program vector.cpp illustrates the concept of overriding default actions by the user-defined overloaded assignment operator and copy constructor.

```
// vector.cpp: overloaded assignment operator for vector elements copying
#include <iostream.h>
class vector
{
    int * v;     // pointer to vector
    int size;    // size of vector v
  public:
    vector( int vector_size )
    {
       size = vector_size;
       v = new int[ vector_size ];
    }
    vector( vector &v2 );
    ~vector()
    {
       delete v;
    }
    void operator = ( vector & v2 );
    int & elem( int i )
    {
       if( i >= size )
          cout << endl << "Error: Out of Range";
       return v[i];
    }
    void show();
};
// copy constructor, vector v1 = v2;
vector::vector( vector &v2 )
{
   cout << "\nCopy constructor invoked";
   size = v2.size;              // size of v1 is equal to size of v2
   v = new int[ v2.size ];      // allocate memory of the vector v1
```

```
    for( int i = 0; i < v2.size; i++ )
       v[i] = v2.v[i];
}
// overloading assignment operator, v1 = v2, v1 is implicit
void vector::operator = ( vector & v2 )
{
    cout << "\nAssignment operation invoked";
    // memory is already allocated to the vector and v1.size = v2.size
    for( int i = 0; i < v2.size; i++ )
       v[i] = v2.v[i];
}
void veccor::show()
{
    for( int i = 0; i < size; i++ )
       cout << elem( i ) << ", ";
}
void main()
{
    int i;
    vector v1( 5 ), v2( 5 );
    for( i = 0; i < 5; i++ )
       v2.elem( i ) = i + 1;
    v1 = v2;      // operator = invoked
    vector v3 = v2;    // copy constructor is invoked
    cout << "\nvector v1: ";
    v1.show();
    cout << "\nvector v2: ";
    v2.show();
    cout << "\nvector v2: ";
    v3.show();
}
```

Run

```
Assignment operation invoked
Copy constructor invoked
vector v1: 1, 2, 3, 4, 5,
vector v2: 1, 2, 3, 4, 5,
vector v2: 1, 2, 3, 4, 5,
```

The overloaded = operator function does the job of copying the data members from one object to another. The function also prints a message to assist the user in keeping track of its execution.

The copy constructor

```
      vector( vector &v2 );
```

takes one argument, an object of the type vector, passed by reference. It is essential to pass a reference argument to the copy constructor. It cannot be passed by value. When an argument is passed by value, its copy is constructed using the copy constructor, i.e., the copy constructor would call itself to make this copy. This process would go on until the system runs out of memory. Hence, *arguments to the copy constructor must be always passed by reference, thus preventing creation of copies.* A copy constructor also gets invoked when arguments are passed by value to functions and when values are returned from functions. When an object is passed by value, the argument on which the function operates is created using a copy constructor. If an object is passed by its address or reference, the copy constructor of course would not be invoked, and the copies of the objects are not created. When an object is returned from a function, the copy constructor is invoked to create a copy of the value returned by the function.

13.21 Tracing Memory Leaks

Memory fragmentation can affect program performance, but memory *leaks* frequently cause programs to crash. A memory leak occurs when the user program fails to free an allocated memory block. The new operator can be overloaded to write signature bytes for the blocks it allocates. The meaning of *memory leak* is that dynamic memory being allocated (*new*ed) without being releasing (*delete*d). The executable size quickly outgrows the size of memory in the machine, requiring an undesirable amount of swapping activity. The first step in attacking this problem is to find where memory is being requested, used, and not returned.

Approach

In C++, it is easy to overload the built-in new and delete operators with user-supplied versions and thereby determine when the memory is requested and to which memory location it is bounded. The program mleak.cpp overloads new and delete operators and records the memory location to which the request is bound, in the disk file space.raw. It also records all those bindings that are released using explicit memory free request command.

```
// mleak.cpp: Memory leak tracing
#include <iostream.h>
#include <stdio.h>
#include <process.h>
#include <alloc.h>
#include <string.h>

//global information
static space_debug = 1;    // space_debug switch, ON
FILE * fp_space = NULL;     // file pointer to the debug info
void * operator new( size_t size )
{
   void *ptr;
   if( space_debug )
   {
      if( fp_space == NULL )  // first time call to new or delete
      {
         // open leak debug info file which is unopened
         if( (fp_space = fopen( "space.raw", "w" )) == NULL )
         {
            cout << "Error opening space.raw in write mode";
            exit( 1 );
         }
      }
   }
```

```
      if( (ptr = malloc( size )) == NULL )
      {
         cout << "out of memory space";
         exit( 1 );
      }
   if( space_debug )   // debug switch is ON, store memory info
      fprintf( fp_space, "new( %d ) -> %x\n", size, ptr );
   return ptr;
}
void operator delete( void *ptr )
{
   if( space_debug )
   {
      // open leak debug info file which is unopened
      if( fp_space == NULL )  // first time call to new or delete
      {
         if( (fp_space = fopen( "space.raw", "w" )) == NULL )
         {
            cout << "Error opening space.raw in write mode";
            exit( 1 );
         }
      }
   }
   if( ptr )   // if valid pointer
   {
      free( (char *) ptr );
      if( space_debug )  // debug switch is ON, store memory info
         fprintf( fp_space, "free <- %x\n", ptr );
   }
}
void main()
{
   int *vector;
   char *buffer;
   vector = (int *) new int[ 10 ];
   buffer = (char *) new char[ 6 ];
   for( int i = 0; i < 10; i++ )
      vector[i] = i+1;
   strcpy( buffer, "hello" );
   cout << "vector =  ";
   for( i = 0; i < 10; i++ )
      cout << vector[i] << " ";

   cout << endl << "buffer = " << buffer;
   delete vector;    // vector is deallocated
   fclose( fp_space );
}
```

Run

```
vector =  1 2 3 4 5 6 7 8 9 10
buffer = hello
```

The space_debug variable allows the programmer to decide whether to trace a particular portion of code or not. When tracing is desired it must be set to a nonzero (debug ON) value. When the following statements:

```
vector = (int *) new int[ 10 ];
buffer = (char *) new char[ 6 ];
```

are invoked in the program, the overloaded new operator allocates the requested amount of memory and returns a pointer to the memory location to which it is bound. In addition, it records this memory address to which it is bound, in the disk file space.raw. Similarly, the overloaded delete operator releases the memory pointed to by the input pointer and also records the memory address in the disk file. In the above *Run*, the information recorded in space.raw file is the following:

```
new( 36 ) -> bd2
new( 516 ) -> bfa
new( 36 ) -> e02
new( 516 ) -> e2a
new( 36 ) -> 1032
new( 516 ) -> 105a
new( 10 ) -> 1262
new( 6 ) -> 127a
free <- 1262
free <- bfa
free <- bd2
free <- e2a
free <- e02
free <- 105a
free <- 1032
```

The first six requests are made by the program execution start-up routine. They can be discarded in the memory leak tracing analysis. The seventh and eighth requests are made in the program explicitly. Similarly, the last six memory free requests made by the system, can be discarded during analysis. These requests vary from system to system. The first request to free memory is made by the statement

```
delete vector;     // vector is deallocated
```

The pointer returned for the requests

```
vector = (int *) new int[ 10 ];
buffer = (char *) new char[ 6 ];
```

are the following

```
new( 10 ) -> 1262
new( 6 ) -> 127a
```

By tracing the above allocation address information in the free list, it can be detected that new(6) pointer address is not released, leading to memory leak. In the program it can be observed that, the memory allocated for the variable vector is released explicitly whereas, the memory allocated for the variable buffer is not released. It can also be noticed from the trace of memory debug information.

13.22 Niceties of Operator Overloading and Conversions

Operator overloading and data conversion features of C++ provide an opportunity to the user to redefine the C++ language. Polymorphism feature of C++ is a bonus for the user to customize C++ to their taste. Of course, it can be misused, since C++ does not restrict the user from misusing (exploiting) the feature of operator overloading. Consider an example of overloading the + operator to perform arithmetic on the user-defined objects x, y, and z. The statement,

```
x = y + z;
```

can represent a different meaning as compared with that conveyed by the operation with basic data types. In the body of overloaded function, even if subtraction operation is performed instead of addition, C++ neither signals an error nor restricts such operation. The above operation can also mean concatenation of strings y and z, and storing the result in x (x, y, and z are object's of String class). Thus, operator overloading provides the ability to redefine the building blocks of the language and allows to manipulate the user-defined data-items in a more intuitive and readable way.

The program misuse.cpp illustrates the misuse of the operator overloading feature in C++. The compiler only validates syntax errors but not the semantics.

```
// misuse.cpp: Misuse of operator overloading, performs subtraction instead
//             of addition operation
#include <iostream.h>
class number
{
    private:
        int num;
    public:
        void read()     // number read function
        {
            cin >> num;
        }
        int get()     // private member num access function
        {
            return num;
        }
        // overloaded operator for number addition
        number operator+( number num2 )
        {
            number sum;
            sum.num = num - num2.num;  // subtraction instead of addition
            return sum;
        }
};
void main()
{
    number num1, num2, sum;
    cout << "Enter Number 1: ";
    num1.read();
    cout << "Enter Number 2: ";
    num2.read();
    sum = num1 + num2;    // addition of number
    cout << "sum = num1 + num2 = " << sum.get();
}
```

Run1

```
Enter Number 1: 20
```

```
Enter Number 2: 10
sum = num1 + num2 = 10
```

Run2

```
Enter Number 1: 5
Enter Number 2: 10
sum = num1 + num2 = -5
```

In main(), the statement

```
    sum = num1 + num2;    // addition of number
```

is supposed to perform addition of two numbers num1 and num2, but instead it performs subtraction. The statement in the body of the overloaded operator function number operator+(..)

```
    sum.num = num - num2.num; // instead of addition, subtraction is done
```

performs subtraction instead of addition. Such neglected use of operator overloading is not taken care by the C++ compiler, but it is the responsibility of the programmer.

As operator overloading is only a notational convenience, the language should try to prevent its misuse (but C++ does not prevent). It is indeed said that *the meaning of operators applied to standard data types cannot be redefined. The intent is to make C++ extensible, but not mutable.* Hence, operators cannot be overloaded for enumerations, although it would be sometimes desirable and fully sensible.

Guidelines

It is essential to follow syntax and semantic rules of the language while extending the power of C++ using operator overloading. In fact, operator overloading feature opens up a vast vistas of opportunities for creative programmers (for instance, new and delete can be overloaded to detect memory leaks as illustrated earlier). The following are some guidelines that needs to be kept in mind while overloading any operators to support user defined data types:

1. Retain Meaning

Overloaded operators must perform operations similar to those defined for primitive/basic data types. The operator + can be overloaded to perform subtraction; operator * can be overloaded to perform division operation. However, such definitions should be avoided to retain the intuitive meaning of the operators. For example, the overloaded operator +() function operating on user-defined data-items must retain a meaning similar to addition The operator + could perform the union operation on *set* data type, concatenation on *string* data type, etc.

2. Retain Syntax

The syntactic characteristics and operator hierarchy cannot be changed by overloading. Therefore, overloaded operators must be used in the same way they are used for basic data types. For example, if c1 and c2 are the objects of complex class, the arithmetic assignment operator in the statement

```
    c1 += c2;
```

sets c1 to the sum of c1 and c2. The overloaded version of any operator should do something analogous to the standard definition of the language. The above statement should perform an operation similar to the statement

```
    c1 = c1 + c2;
```

3. Use Functions when Appropriate

An operator must not be overloaded if it does not perform the obvious operation. It should not demand the user's effort in order to identify the actual operation performed by the operator. The main aim of overloading is to make the program code more readable. If the meaning of an operation to be performed by the overloaded operator is unpredictable or doubtful to the user, it is advisable to use a more descriptive and meaningful function name.

4. Avoid Ambiguity

The existence of multiple data conversion routines performing the same operations, places the compiler in an ambiguous state. It does not know which one to select for conversion. For instance, existence of a one-argument constructor in the destination object's class and operator function also in the source object's class performing the same conversion function, confuses the compiler; it does not know which one to select and issues an error message. Therefore, avoid defining multiple routines performing the same operation, which become ambiguous during compilation. The program `confuse.cpp` illustrates the ambiguity which arises when multiple conversion routines exists in a program.

```
// confuse.cpp: conversion routines for object A's to object B
class B;      // forward specification
class A       // source class
{
    // data members of the class A
    public:
      A()
      {}
      // conversion routine in source, operator function
      operator B()
      {
          B b_obj;
          // convert A class's object into class B's object, b_obj
          return b_obj;
      }
      // other member functions of the class A
};
class B       // destination class
{
    // data members of the class B
    public:
      B()
      {}
      // conversion routine in destination, one-argument constructor
      B( A a_obj )
      {
        // convert source class A's object to initialize data members of B
      }
      // other member functions of the class B
};
void main( void )
{
    A a_obj;
```

```
    B b_obj;
    b_obj = a_obj;
    // other operations on objects of the classes A and B if necessary
}
```

In main (), the statement

```
    b_obj = a_obj;
```

leads to the following compilation error:

```
Error confuse.cpp 35: Ambiguity between 'A::operator B()' and 'B::B(A)'
                        in function main()
```

It is because the source object a_obj's class A has operator conversion function and the destination object b_obj's class B also has conversion function in the form of one-argument constructor function.

5. All Operators Cannot be Overloaded

C++ supports a wide variety of operators, but all of them cannot be overloaded (see Table 13.3) to operate in an analogous way on standard operators. These excluded operators are very few compared to the large number of operators, which qualify for overloading.

Operator Category	Operators
Member access	. (dot operator)
Scope resolution	: : (global access)
Conditional	? : (conditional statement)
Pointer to member	*
Size of Data Type	sizeof(..)

Table 13.3: Non-Overloadable C++ operators

An operator such as ? : has an inherent meaning and it requires three arguments. C++ does not support the overloading of an operator, which operates on three operands. Hence, the conditional operator, which is the only ternary operator in the C++ language, cannot be overloaded.

Review Questions

13.1 What is operator overloading ? Explain the importance of operator overloading.

13.2 List the operators that cannot be overloaded and justify why they cannot be overloaded.

13.3 What is operator function ? Describe operator function with syntax and examples.

13.4 Write a program to overload unary operator, say ++ for incrementing distance in FPS system. Describe the working model of an overloaded operator with the same program.

13.5 What are the limitations of overloading unary increment/decrement operator ? How are they overcome ?

13.6 Explain the syntax of binary operator overloading. How many arguments are required in the definition of an overloaded binary operator ?

13.7 Write a program to overload unary operator for processing counters. It should support both upward and downward counting. It must also support operator for adding two counters and storing the result in another counter.

13.8   Write a program to overload arithmetic operators for manipulating vectors.

13.9   Overload new and delete operators to manipulate objects of the Student class. The Student class must contains data members such as char *name, int roll_no, int branch, etc. The overloaded new and delete operators must allocate memory for the Student class object and its data members.

13.10 Design classes called Polar and Rectangle for representing a point in the polar and rectangle systems. Support data conversion function to support statements such as:

        Rectangle r1, r2;   Polar p1, p2;
        r1 = p1;   p2 = r2;

13.11 Write a program to manipulate N student objects. Overload the subscript operator for bounds checking while accessing i^{th} Student object.

13.12 Why is the friend function not allowed to access members of a class directly although its body can appear within the class body ?

13.13 Write a program to overload stream operators for reading or displaying contents of Vector class's objects as follows:

        cin >> v1;   cout << v2;

13.14 Suggest and implement an approach to trace memory leakage.

13.15 State with reasons whether the following statements are TRUE or FALSE:

(a)   Precedence and associativity of overloaded operators can be changed.

(b)   Semantics of overloaded operators can be changed.

(c)   With overloading binary operator, the left and right operands are explicitly passed.

(d)   The overloaded operator functions parameters must be user-defined objects only.

(e)   A constructor can be used to convert a user-defined data types only.

(f)   An object of a class can be assigned to basic type operand.

(g)   Syntax of overloaded operators can be changed.

(h)   The parameter type to overloaded subscript [ ] operator can be of any data type.

(i)   Friend function can access members of a class directly.

(j)   The ternary operator can be overloaded.

(k)   The compiler reports an error if overloaded + operator performs - operation.

13.16 Design classes such that they support the following statements:

        Rupee r1, r2; Dollar d1, d2;
        d1 = r2; // converts rupee (Indian currency) to dollar (US currency)
        r2 = d2; // converts dollar (US currency) to rupee (Indian currency)

Write a complete program which does such conversions according to the world market value.

13.17 Write a program for manipulating linked list supporting node operations as follows:

        node = node + 2;   node = node - 3;

The first statement creates a new node with node information 2 and the second statement deletes a node with node information 3.

13.18 Write a program for creating a doubly linked list. It must support the following operations:

        firstnode = node; firstnode += 10; Node *n = node1 + node2;

The doubly linked list class should have overloaded node creation and deletion operator function should appear in the form of overloaded + and - operator functions respectively.

13.19 Write an interactive operator overloaded program for manipulating matrices. Overload operators such as >>, <<, +, -, *, ==.

13.20 Write an interactive operator overloaded program to manipulate the three-variable polynomial:

$a_n x^n y^n z^n + a_{n-1} x^{n-1} y^{n-1} z^{n-1} + ... + a_1 x^1 y^1 z^1 + a_0$

14

Inheritance

14.1 Introduction

Inheritance is a technique of organizing information in a hierarchical form. It is like a child inheriting the features of its parents (such as beauty of the mother and intelligence of the father). In real world, an object is described by using inheritance. It derives general properties of an object by tracing an inheritance tree from one specific instance, upwards towards the primitive concepts at the root.

Inheritance allows new classes to be built from older and less specialized classes instead of being rewritten from scratch. Classes are created by first inheriting all the variables and behavior defined by some primitive class and then adding specialized variables and behaviors. In object oriented programming, classes encapsulate data and functions into one package. New classes can be built from existing ones, just as a builder constructs a skyscraper out of bricks, stone, and other relatively simple material. *The technique of building new classes from the existing classes is called inheritance.*

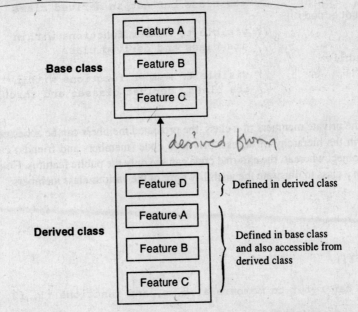

Figure 14.1: Base class and derived class relationship

Inheritance, a prime feature of OOPs can be stated as *the process of creating new classes (called derived classes), from the existing classes (called base classes)*. The derived class inherits all the capabilities of the base class and can add refinements and extensions of its own. The base class remains unchanged. The derivation of a new class from the existing class is represented in Figure 14.1. The derived class inherits the features of the base class (A, B, and C) and adds its own features (D). The arrow in the diagram symbolizes *derived from*. Its direction from the derived class towards the base class, represents that the derived class accesses features of the base class and not vice versa.

A number of terms are used to describe classes that are related through inheritance. A base class is often called the ancestor, parent, or superclass, and a derived class is called the descendent, child, or subclass. A derived class may itself be a base class from which additional classes are derived. There is no specific limit on the number of classes that may be derived from one another, which forms a class hierarchy.

14.2 Class Revisited

C++, not only supports the access specifiers `private` and `public`, but also an important access specifier, `protected`, which is significant in class inheritance. As far as the access limit is concerned, within a class or from the objects of a class, `protected` access-limit is same as that of the `private` specifier. However, the protected specifier has a prominent role to play in inheritance. A class can use all the three visibility modes as illustrated below:

```
class ClassName
{
      private:
        ....        // visible to member functions within
        ....        // its class but not in derived class
      protected:
        ....        // visible to member functions within
        ....        // its class and derived class
      public:
        ....        // visible to member functions within
        ....        // its class, derived classes and through object
};
```

Similar to the private members of a class, the protected members can be accessed only within the class. That is, in the hierarchy of access, privilege code (members and friends) can see the whole structure of an object whereas, the external code can see only the public features. Consider the following definition of a class to illustrate the visibility limit of the various class members:

```
class X
{
   private:
      int a;
      void f1()
      {
      // .. can refer to members a, b, c, and functions f1, f2, and f3
      }
   protected:
      int b;
```

```
        void f2()
        {
        // .. can refer to members a, b, c, and functions f1, f2, and f3
        }
    public:
        int c;
        void f3()
        {
        // .. can refer to members a, b, c, and functions f1, f2, and f3
        }
};
```

The data member a is *private* to class X and is accessible only to members of its own class, that is, member functions f1(), f2(), f3() can access a directly. However, statements outside and even member functions of the derived class are not allowed to access a directly. In addition, the member function f1() can be called only by other members of class X. The statements outside the class cannot call f1(), which is exclusively a private property of the class X.

The data member b and the member function f2() are *protected*. These members are accessible to other member functions of the class X and member functions in a derived class. However, outside the class, protected members have private status. The statements outside the class cannot directly access members b or f2() using the class.

The data member c and the member function f3() are *public*, and may be accessed directly by all the members of the class X, or by members in a derived class, or by objects of the class. *Public members* are always accessible to all users of the class.

The following statements,

```
    X objx;              // objx is an object of class X
    int d;          // temporary variable d
```

define the object objx of the class X and the integer variable d. The member access privileges are illustrated by the following statements referring to the object objx.

1. Accessing private members of the class X

```
        d = objx.a; // Error: 'X::a' is not accessible
        objx.f1();  // Error: 'X::f1()' is not accessible
```

Both the statements are invalid because the private members of a class are inaccessible to the object objx.

2. Accessing protected members of the class X

```
        d = objx.b; // Error: 'X::b' is not accessible
        objx.f2();  // Error: 'X::f2()' is not accessible
```

Both the statements are invalid because the protected members of a class are inaccessible since they are private to the class X.

3. Accessing public members of the class X

```
        d = objx.c; // OK
        objx.f3();  // OK
```

Both the statements are valid because the public members of a class are accessible to statements outside the scope of the class.

acces specifiers

The program bag.cpp uses the access modifier *protected* to hold data members, instead of using the *private* access specifier. It indicates that the protected members are inheritable to derived classes. However, they have the same status as private members in the base class.

```cpp
// bag.cpp: Bag into which fruits can be placed
#include <iostream.h>
enum boolean { FALSE, TRUE };
// Maximum number of items that a bag can hold
const int MAX_ITEMS = 25;
class Bag
{
   protected:                     // Note: not private
      int contents[MAX_ITEMS];    // bag memory area
      int ItemCount;              // Number of items present in a bag
   public:
      Bag()    // no-argument constructor
      {
         ItemCount = 0;    // When you purchase a bag, it will be empty
      }
      void put( int item ) // puts item into bag
      {
         contents[ ItemCount++ ] = item; // item into bag, counter update
      }
      boolean IsEmpty()    // 1, if bag is empty, 0, otherwise
      {
         return ItemCount == 0 ? TRUE : FALSE;
      }
      boolean IsFull()     // 1, if bag is full, 0, otherwise
      {
         return ItemCount == MAX_ITEMS ? TRUE : FALSE;
      }
      boolean IsExist( int item );
      void show();
};
// returns 1, if item is in bag, 0, otherwise
boolean Bag::IsExist( int item )
{
   for( int i = 0; i < ItemCount; i++ )
      if( contents[i] == item )
         return TRUE;
   return FALSE;
}
// display contents of a bag
void Bag::show()
{
   for( int i = 0; i < ItemCount; i++ )
      cout << contents[i] << " ";
   cout << endl;
}
```

```
void main()
{
   Bag bag;
   int item;
   while( TRUE )
   {
      cout << "Enter Item Number to be put into the bag <0-no item>: ";
      cin >> item;
      if( item == 0 )    // end of an item, break
         break;
      bag.put( item );
      cout << "Items in Bag: ";
      bag.show();
      if( bag.IsFull() )
      {
         cout << "Bag Full, no more items can be placed";
         break;
      }
   }
}
```

Run

```
Enter Item Number to be put into the bag <0-no item>: 1
Items in Bag: 1
Enter Item Number to be put into the bag <0-no item>: 2
Items in Bag: 1 2
Enter Item Number to be put into the bag <0-no item>: 3
Items in Bag: 1 2 3
Enter Item Number to be put into the bag <0-no item>: 3
Items in Bag: 1 2 3 3
Enter Item Number to be put into the bag <0-no item>: 1
Items in Bag: 1 2 3 3 1
Enter Item Number to be put into the bag <0-no item>: 0
```

In main(), the statement,

```
      Bag bag;
```

creates the object bag and initializes the data member ItemCount to 0 through a constructor. The statement

```
      bag.put( item );
```

stores the items into the bag. It does not check for the entry of duplicate items into a bag. Any item type can be placed any number of times into a bag and of course, without exceeding the limit or size of bag.

14.3 Derived Class Declaration

A derived class extends its features by inheriting the properties of another class, called base class and adding features of its own. The declaration of a derived class specifies its relationship with the base class in addition to its own features. The syntax of declaring a derived class is shown in Figure 14.2. Note that no memory is allocated to the declaration of a derived class, but memory is allocated when it is instantiated to create objects.

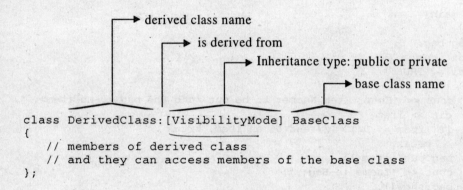

```
class DerivedClass:[VisibilityMode] BaseClass
{
    // members of derived class
    // and they can access members of the base class
};
```

Figure 14.2: Syntax of derived class declaration

The derivation of DerivedClass from the BaseClass is indicated by the colon (:). The VisibilityMode enclosed within the square brackets implies that it is optional. The default visibility mode is private. If the visibility mode is specified, it must be either public or private. Visibility mode specifies whether the features of the base class are *publicly* or *privately inherited*.

The following are the three possible styles of derivation:

```
1.  class D: public B    // public derivation
    {
        // members of D
    };
2.  class D: private B   // private derivation
    {
        // members of D
    };
3.  class D: B           // private derivation by default
    {
        // members of D
    };
```

Inheritance of a base class with visibility mode public, by a derived class, causes public members of the base class to become public members of the derived class and the protected members of the base class become protected members of the derived class. Member functions and objects of the derived class can treat these derived members as though they are defined in the derived class itself. It is known that the public members of a class can be accessed by the objects of the class. Hence, the objects of a derived class can access public members of the base class that are inherited as public using the dot operator. However, protected members cannot be accessed with the dot operator. (See Figure 14.3.)

Inheritance of a base class with visibility mode private by a derived class, causes public members of the base class to become private members of the derived class and the protected members of the base class become private members of the derived class. Member functions and objects of a derived class can treat these derived members as though they are defined in the derived class with the private modifier. Thus objects of a derived class cannot access these members.

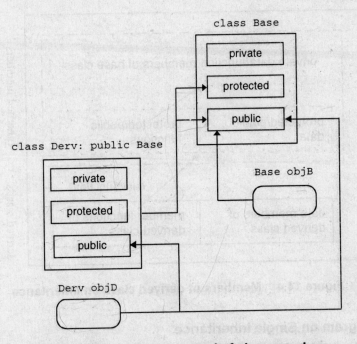

Figure 14.3: Access control of class members

Subsequent derivation of the classes from a *privately* derived class cannot access any members of the grand-parent class. The visibility of base class members undergoes modifications in a derived class as summarized in Table 14.1.

Base class visibility	Derived class visibility	
	Public derivation	**Private derivation**
private	Not Inherited (inherited base class members can access)	Not Inherited (inherited base class members can access)
protected	protected	private
public	public	private

Table 14.1: Visibility of class members

The private members of the base class remain private to the base class, whether the base class is inherited publicly or privately. They add to the data items of the derived class and they are not directly accessible to the member of a derived class. Derived classes can access them through the inherited member functions of the base class (see Figure 14.4).

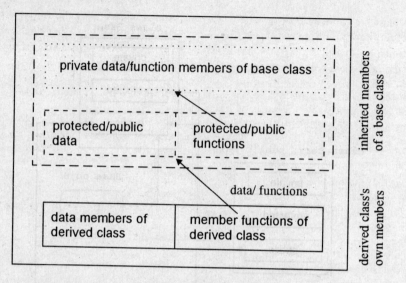

Figure 14.4: Members of derived class on inheritance

A Sample Program on Single Inheritance

A derived class may begin its existence with a copy of its base class members, including any other members inherited from more distantly related classes. *A derived class inherits data members and member functions, but not the constructor or destructor from its base class.* Recall that the program, bag.cpp discussed earlier has the class Bag and its instance, the bag object. A bag could be made empty or filled with items (fruits). The Bag class can be subjected to set operations such as union. intersection, etc.. It can be achieved by either modifying the Bag class or by deriving a new class called Set from the Bag class as shown in Figure 14.5.

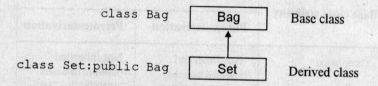

Figure 14.5: Inheritance of bag class

Considering that a large amount of time is spent in the development of the Bag class as well as in testing and debugging, it is not-at-all advisable to extend the Bag class by modifying as it will be impractical to rewrite or modify the original class especially in a large project when many programmers are involved. Also such a change would not be possible if the Bag class is a part of a commercial class library for which no source code is available to the user. Hence, rather than modifying Bag, a new class Set can be derived from it and the required new features can be added. It saves development cost, effort, and time.

The program `union.cpp` demonstrates the mechanism of extending the `Bag` class by using the feature of inheritance. In this case, a new class `Set` is derived from the existing class `Bag` without any modifications. A derived class `Set` inherits all the properties of the class `Bag` and extends itself by adding some of its own features to support set assignment and union operation.

```cpp
// union.cpp: Union of sets. Set class by inheritance of Bag class
#include <iostream.h>
enum boolean { FALSE, TRUE };
const int MAX_ITEMS = 25;  // Maximum number of items that bag can hold
class Bag
{
    protected:                  // Note: not private
        int contents[MAX_ITEMS];  // bag memory area
        int ItemCount;            // number of items present in the bag
    public:
        Bag()                     // no-argument constructor
        {
            ItemCount = 0;     // When you purchase a bag, it will be empty
        }
        void put( int item )      // puts item into bag
        {
            contents[ ItemCount++ ] = item;  // item into bag,counter update
        }
        boolean IsEmpty()         // 1, if bag is empty, 0, otherwise
        {
            return ItemCount == 0 ? TRUE : FALSE;
        }
        boolean IsFull()          // 1, if bag is full, 0, otherwise
        {
            return ItemCount == MAX_ITEMS ? TRUE : FALSE;
        }
        boolean IsExist( int item );
        void show();
};
// returns 1, if item is in bag, 0, otherwise
boolean Bag::IsExist( int item )
{
    for( int i = 0; i < ItemCount; i++ )
        if( contents[i] == item )
            return TRUE;
    return FALSE;
}
// display contents of a bag
void Bag::show()
{
    for( int i = 0; i < ItemCount; i++ )
        cout << contents[i] << " ";
    cout << endl;
}
```

```
class Set: public Bag
{
   public:
      void add( int element )
      {
         if( !IsExist( element ) && !IsFull() )
            put( element );
            // element does not exist in set and it is not full
      }
      void read();
      void operator = (Set s1);
      friend Set operator + ( Set s1, Set s2 );
};
void Set::read()
{
   int element;
   while( TRUE )
   {
      cout << "Enter Set Element <0- end>: ";
      cin >> element;
      if( element == 0 )
         break;
      add( element );
   }
}
void Set::operator = ( Set s2 )
{
   for( int i = 0; i < s2.ItemCount; i++ )
      contents[i] = s2.contents[i];          // access Bag::contents
   ItemCount = s2.ItemCount;
}
Set operator + ( Set s1, Set s2 )
{
   Set temp;
   temp = s1;    // copy all elements of set s1 to temp
   // copy those elements of set s2 into temp, those not exist in set s1
   for( int i = 0; i < s2.ItemCount; i++ )
   {
      if( !s1.IsExist( s2.contents[i] ) ) //if element of s2 is not in s1
         temp.add( s2.contents[i] );       // copy the unique element
   }
   return( temp );
}
void main()
{
   Set s1, s2, s3;    // uses no-argument constructor of Bag class
   cout << "Enter Set 1 elements .." << endl;
   s1.read();
   cout << "Enter Set 2 elements .." << endl;
   s2.read();
   s3 = s1 + s2;
```

```
        cout << endl << "Union of s1 and s2 : ";
        s3.show();      // uses Bag::show() base class
}
```

Run

```
Enter Set 1 elements ..
Enter Set Element <0- end>: 1
Enter Set Element <0- end>: 2
Enter Set Element <0- end>: 3
Enter Set Element <0- end>: 4
Enter Set Element <0- end>: 0
Enter Set 2 elements ..
Enter Set Element <0- end>: 2
Enter Set Element <0- end>: 4
Enter Set Element <0- end>: 5
Enter Set Element <0- end>: 6
Enter Set Element <0- end>: 0
Union of s1 and s2 : 1 2 3 4 5 6
```

In the above program, the Set class has its own features to perform set union by using the member functions of Bag. The statement

```
        class Set: public Bag
```

derives a new class Set from the base class Bag. The base class Bag is *publicly inherited* by the derived class Set. Hence, the members of Bag class, that are *protected* become protected and *public* become public in the derived class Set. The Set class can treat all the members of the Bag class as though they are its own.

The relationship between the base class Bag and the derived class Set has been depicted in Figure 14.5. Remember, that the arrow in the diagram, means *derived from*. The arrow indicates that the derived class Set refers to the data and member functions of the base class Bag, while the base class Bag has no access to the derived class Set.

Access to Constructor

In main(), the statement

```
        Set s1, s2, s3;         // uses no-argument constructor of Bag class
```

creates three objects s1, s2, and s3 of class Set and initializes the ItemCount variable to 0 in all the three objects, even though a constructor does not exist in the derived class Set. Thus, if a constructor is not defined in the derived class, C++ will use an appropriate constructor from the base class. In the above example, there is no constructor defined in the class Set and therefore, the compiler uses the *no-argument constructor*

```
        Bag()                   // no-argument constructor
        {
            ItemCount = 0;  // When you purchase a bag, it will be empty
        }
```

defined in the Bag class. The use of the base class's constructor, in the absence of a constructor in the derived class, exhibits the true nature of inheritance that happens normally in day-to-day life.

Base Class Unchanged

It may be recalled that the base class remains unchanged even if other classes have been derived from it. In `main()` of the program `union.cpp`, objects of type `Bag` could be defined as,

```
Bag bag;        // object of the base class
```

Behaviors of such objects remain the same irrespective of the existence of a derived class such as `Set`.

It should also be noted that inheritance does not work in reverse. The base class and its objects do not know about any classes derived from it. In the example `union.cpp`, the objects of the base class `Bag`, cannot use the function, `operator+()` of the derived class `Set`.

Accessing Base Class Member Functions

The object `s3` of class `Set` also uses the function `show()` from the base class `Bag`. The statement

```
s3.show();      // uses Bag::show() base class
```

in the `main()`, refers to the function `show()`, which does not exist in the derived class `Set`. It is resolved by the compiler by selecting the member function `show()` defined in the base class `Bag`.

14.4 Forms of Inheritance

The derived class inherits some or all the features of the base class depending on the visibility mode and level of inheritance. Level of inheritance refers to the length of its (derived class) path from the root (top base class). A base class itself might have been derived from other classes in the hierarchy. Inheritance is classified into the following forms based on the levels of inheritance and interrelation among the classes involved in the inheritance process:

- Single Inheritance
- Multiple Inheritance
- Hierarchical Inheritance
- Multilevel Inheritance
- Hybrid Inheritance
- Multipath Inheritance

The different forms of inheritance relationship is depicted in Figure 14.6. The pictorial representation of inheritance showing the interrelationship among the classes involved is known as the inheritance tree or class hierarchy. Base classes are represented at higher levels (top of the hierarchy, say root) and derived classes at the bottom of the hierarchy. The arrow directed from the derived class towards the base class, indicates that the derived class accesses features of the base class without modifying it, but not vice versa (Some use convention of representing the arrow in the opposite direction to indicate *inherited from or derived from*).

Single Inheritance: Derivation of a class from only one base class is called single inheritance. The sample program, `union.cpp`, discussed above falls under this category. Figure 14.6a depicts single inheritance.

Multiple Inheritance: Derivation of a class from several (two or more) base classes is called multiple inheritance. Figure 14.6b depicts multiple inheritance.

Hierarchical Inheritance: Derivation of several classes from a single base class i.e., the traits of one class may be inherited by more than one class, is called hierarchical inheritance. Figure 14.6c depicts hierarchical inheritance.

Multilevel Inheritance: Derivation of a class from another *derived class* is called multilevel inheritance. Figure 14.6d depicts multilevel inheritance.

Hybrid Inheritance: Derivation of a class involving more than one form of inheritance is known as hybrid inheritance. Figure 14.6e depicts hybrid inheritance.

Multipath Inheritance: Derivation of a class from other *derived classes*, which are derived from the same base class is called multipath inheritance. Figure 14.6f depicts multipath inheritance.

a) Single inheritance

b) Multiple inheritance

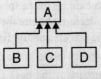

c) Hierarchical inheritance

d) Multilevel inheritance

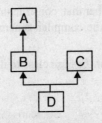

e) Hybrid inheritance

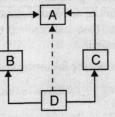

f) Multipath inheritance

Figure 14.6: Forms of inheritance

14.5 Inheritance and Member Accessibility

The examples discussed earlier demonstrated the features of inheritance, which enhances the capabilities of the existing classes without modifying them. It is also observed that the private members of a base class, which cannot be inherited, are overcome by the use of access specifier protected. Accessibility refers to the authorization granted to access the members of a class by using an access specifier or modifier with or without inheritance. It defines the guidelines as to when a member function in the base class can be used by the objects of the derived class.

A protected member can be considered as a hybrid of a private and a public member. Like private members, protected members are accessible only to its class member functions and they are invisible outside the class. Like public members, protected members are inherited by derived classes and are also accessible to member functions of the derived class. The following rules are to be borne in mind while deciding whether to define members as private, protected, or public:

1. A private member is accessible only to members of the class in which the private member is declared. They cannot be inherited.

2. A private member of the base class can be accessed in the derived class through the member functions of the base class.

3. A protected member is accessible to members of its own class and to any of the members in a derived class.

4. If a class is expected to be used as a base class in future, then members which might be needed in the derived class should be declared protected rather than private.

5. A public member is accessible to members of its own class, members of the derived class, and outside users of the class.

6. The private, protected, and public sections may appear as many times as needed in a class and in any order. In case an inline member function refers to another member (data or function), that member must be declared before the inline member function is defined. Nevertheless, it is a normal practice to place the private section first, followed by the protected section and finally the public section.

7. The visibility mode in the derivation of a new class can be either private or public.

8. Constructors of the base class and the derived class are automatically invoked when the derived class is instantiated. If a base class has constructors with arguments, then their invocations must be explicitly specified in the derived class's initialization section. However, no-argument constructor need not be invoked explicitly. Remember that, constructors must be defined in the public section of a class (base and derived) otherwise, the compiler generates the error message: *unable to access constructor*.

Consider the following declarations of the base class to illustrate public and private inheritance:

```
class B     // base class
{
  private:
    int privateB;      // private member of base
  protected:
    int protectedB;    // protected member of base
  public:
    int publicB;       // public member of base
    int getBprivate()
    {
       return privateB;
    }
};
```

Public Inheritance

Consider the following declaration to illustrate the derivation of a new class D from the base class B publicly declared earlier:

```
class D: public B          // publicly derived class
{
  private:
    int privateD;
  protected:
    int protectedD;
  public:
    int publicD;
    void myfunc()
    {
       int a;
```

```
        a = privateB;       // Error: B::privateB is not accessible
        a = getBprivate();  // OK, inherited member accesses private data
        a = protectedB;     // OK
        a = publicB;        // OK
    }
};
```

The member function, myfunc() of the derived class D can access protectedB and publicB inherited from base class B. Since the class B is inherited as public by the derived class D, the status of members protectedB, publicB, getBprivate() remain unchanged in the derived class D. The statements

```
    D objd;             // objd is a object of class D
    int d;              // temporary variable d
```

define the object objd and the integer variable d. Consider the following statements referring to the object objd. Access to the protected member of the base class B in the statement,

```
    d = objd.protectedB; // Error: 'B::protectedB' is not accessible
```

is invalid; protectedB has *protected* visibility status in class D. However the public member of the class B in the statement

```
    d = objd.publicB;       // OK
```

is valid; publicB has public visibility status in class D. The inherited member function, getBprivate() in the statement

```
    d = objd.getBprivate(); //OK, inherited member accesses private data
```

accesses a private data member of the base class.

In a subsequent derivation such as

```
    class X : public D
    {
        public:
            void g();
    };
```

the member function g() in the derived class X may still access members protectedB and publicB and even retains the original protected and public status. Note that, private members of the classes B and D can be accessed through inherited members of the base class.

Private Inheritance

Consider the following declaration to illustrate the derivation of the new class D from the existing base class B privately:

```
class D: private B      // privately derived class
{
    private:
        int privateD;
    protected:
        int protectedD;
    public:
        int publicD;
```

```
void myfunc()
{
    int a;
    a = privateB;        // Error: B::privateB is not accessible
    a = getBprivate();   // OK, inherited member accesses private data
    a = protectedB;      // OK
    a = publicB;         // OK
}
};
```

The member function `myfunc()` of the derived class D may access `protectedB` and `publicB` inherited from the base class B. Since, the base class B is inherited as the private base class of the derived class D, the status of members `protectedB`, `publicB`, and `getBprivate()` become private in the derived class D. The statements

```
D objd;        // objd is a object of class D
int d;         // temporary variable d
```

define the object `objd` and the integer variable d. Consider the following statements referring to the object `objd`. Access to the *protected* member of the base class B in the statement

```
d = objd.protectedB; // Error: B::protectedB is not accessible
```

is invalid; `protectedB` has private visibility status in the class D. Access to the public member of class B in the statement

```
d = objd.publicB;    // Error: B::publicB is not accessible
```

is also invalid; `publicB` has private visibility status in the class D. The use of inherited member function, `getBprivate()` in the statement

```
d = objd.getBprivate(); // Error: getBprivate() is not accessible
```

is invalid; it has become a private member of the derived class D, however, a member function of the derived class can access—`myfunc()` accesses `getBprivate()` function.

In a subsequent derivation such as

```
class X : public D      // X is derived with D as base class
{
    public:
        void g();
};
```

the member function `g()` in X cannot access members `protectedB` and `publicB` since these members have gained `private` visibility status in class D. However, they (including private members of the classes B and D) can be accessed through inherited members of the base class.

Member Functions Accessibility

The various categories of functions which have access to the private and protected members could be any of the following:

- a member function of a class
- a member function of a derived class
- a friend function of a class
- a member function of a friend class

Function Type	Access directly to		
	Private	**Protected**	**Public**
Class Member	Yes	Yes	Yes
Derived class member	No	Yes	Yes
Friend	Yes	Yes	Yes
Friend class member	Yes	Yes	Yes

Table 14.2: Access control to class members

The friend functions and member functions of a friend class have direct access to both the private and protected members of a class. A member function of a class has access to all the members of its own class, be it private, protected, or public. The member functions of a derived class can directly access only the `protected` or `public` members; however they can access the `private` members through the member functions of the base class. Table 14.2 and Figure 14.7 summarizes the scope of access in various situations.

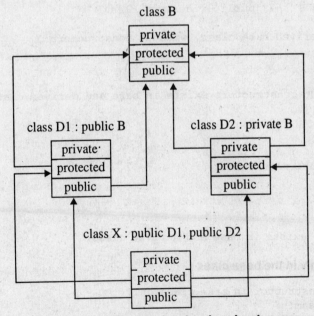

Figure 14.7: Access mechanism in classes

14.6 Constructors in Derived Classes

The constructors play an important role in initializing an object's data members and allocating required resources such as memory. The derived class need not have a constructor as long as the base class has a no-argument constructor. However, if the base class has constructors with arguments (one or more), then it is *mandatory* for the derived class to have a constructor and pass the arguments to the base class constructor. In the application of inheritance, objects of the derived class are usually created instead of the base class. Hence, it makes sense for the derived class to have a constructor and pass arguments to the constructor of the base class. When an object of a derived class is created, the constructor of the base class is executed first and later the constructor of the derived class.

The following examples illustrate the order of invocation of constructors in the base class and the derived class.

1. No-constructors in the base class and derived class

When there are no constructors either in the base or derived classes, the compiler automatically creates objects of classes without any error when the class is instantiated.

```
// cons1.cpp: No-constructors in base class and derived class
#include <iostream.h>
class B       // base class
{
   // body of base class, without constructors
};
class D: public B    // publicly derived class
{
   // body of derived base class, without constructors
   public:
   void msg()
   {
      cout << "No constructors exists in base and derived class" << endl;
   }
};
void main()
{
   D objd; // base constructor
   objd.msg();
}
```

Run

```
No constructors exists in base and derived class
```

2. Constructor only in the base class

```
// cons2.cpp: constructor in base class only
#include <iostream.h>
class B       // base class
{
   public:
```

```
   B()
   {
     cout << "No-argument constructor of the base class B is executed";
   }
};
class D: public B     // publicly derived class
{
   public:
};
void main()
{
   D obj1; // accesses base constructor
}
```

Run

```
No-argument constructor of the base class B is executed
```

3. Constructor only in the derived class

```
// cons3.cpp: constructors in derived class only
#include <iostream.h>
class B      // base class
{
   // body of base class, without constructors
};
class D: public B     // publicly derived class
{
   // body of derived base class, without constructors
   public:
   D()
   {
     cout << "Constructos exists in only in derived class" << endl;
   }
};
void main()
{
   D objd;              // accesses derived constructor
}
```

Run

```
Constructos exists in only in derived class
```

4. Constructor in both base and derived classes

```
// cons4.cpp: constructor in base and derived classes
#include <iostream.h>
class B      // base class
{
   public:
```

```
  B()
  {
   cout<<"No-argument constructor of the base class B executed first\n";
  }
};
class D: public B    // publicly derived class
{
  public:
   D()
   {
    cout<<"No-argument constructor of the derived class D executed next";
   }
};
void main()
{
   D objd;  // access both base constructor
}
```

Run

```
No-argument constructor of the base class B executed first
No-argument constructor of the derived class D executed next
```

5. Multiple constructors in base class and a single constructor in derived class

```
// cons5.cpp: multiple constructors in base and single in derived classes
#include <iostream.h>
class B      // base class
{
   public:
      B() { cout << "No-argument constructor of the base class B"; }
      B(int a) { cout <<"One-argument constructor of the base class B"; }
};
class D: public B    // publicly derived class
{
   public:
      D( int a )
      { cout << "\nOne-argument constructor of the derived class D"; }
};
void main()
{
   D objd( 3 );
}
```

Run

```
No-argument constructor of the base class B
One-argument constructor of the derived class D
```

6. Constructor in base and derived classes without default constructor

The compiler looks for the no-argument constructor by default in the base class. If there is a constructor in the base class, the following conditions must be met:

The base class must have a no-argument constructor

♦ If the base class does not have a default constructor and has an argument constructor, they must be explicitly invoked, otherwise the compiler generates an error.

```
// cons6.cpp: constructor in base and derived class
#include <iostream.h>
class B      // base class
{
   public:
      B(int a) { cout << "One-argument constructor of the base class B";  }
};
class D: public B    // publicly derived class
{
   public:
      D( int a )
      { cout << "\nOne-argument constructor of the derived class D"; }
};
void main()
{
   D objd( 3 );
}
```

The compilation of the above program generates the following error:

     Cannot find 'default' constructor to initialize base class 'B'

This error can be overcome by explicit invocation of a constructor of the base class as illustrated in the program cons7.cpp.

7. Explicit invocation in the absence of default constructor

```
// cons7.cpp: constructor in base and derived classes
#include <iostream.h>
class B      // base class
{
   public:
      B(int a)
      { cout << "One-argument constructor of the base class B"; }
};
class D: public B    // publicly derived class
{
   public:
      D( int a ) : B(a)
      { cout << "\nOne-argument constructor of the derived class D"; }
};
void main()
{
   D objd( 3 );
}
```

Run

```
One-argument constructor of the base class B
One-argument constructor of the derived class D
```

In the derived class D, the statement

```
D( int a ):B(a)
```

defines the derived class constructor D(int a) and calls the constructor of the base class using the special form :B(a). Here, the constructor of B is first invoked with an argument a specified in the constructor function D and then the constructor of D is invoked.

8. Constructor in a multiple inherited class with default invocation

```cpp
// cons8.cpp: constructor in base and derived class, order of invocation
#include <iostream.h>
class B1     // base class
{
   public:
      B1() { cout << "\nNo-argument constructor of the base class B1"; }
};
class B2     // base class
{
   public:
      B2() { cout << "\nNo-argument constructor of the base class B2"; }
};
class D: public B2, public B1     // publicly derived class
{
   public:
      D()
      { cout << "\nNo-argument constructor of the derived class D"; }
};
void main()
{
   D objd;
}
```

Run

```
No-argument constructor of the base class B2
No-argument constructor of the base class B1
No-argument constructor of the derived class D
```

The statement

```
class D: public B2, public B1     // publicly derived class
```

specifies that the class D is derived from the base classes B1 and B2 in order. Hence, constructors are invoked in the order B2(), B1(), and D(); the constructors can be defined with or without arguments.

9. Constructor in a multiple inherited class with explicit invocation

```cpp
// cons9.cpp: constructors with explicit invocation
#include <iostream.h>
class B1     // base class
{
   public:
      B1() {  cout << "\nNo-argument constructor of the base class B1"; }
};
```

```
class B2     // base class
{
   public:
      B2() {  cout << "\nNo-argument constructor of the base class B2"; }
};
class D: public B1, public B2
{
   public:
      D(): B2(), B1()    // explicit call to constructors
      {  cout << "\nNo-argument constructor of the derived class D"; }
};
void main()
{
   D objd;
}
```

Run

```
No-argument constructor of the base class B1
No-argument constructor of the base class B2
No-argument constructor of the derived class D
```

In the above program, the statement

```
        class D: public B1, public B2     // publicly derived class
```

specifies that, the class D is derived from the base classes B1 and B2 in order. The statement

```
        D(): B2(), B1()
```

in the derived class D, specifies that, the base class constructors must be called. However, the constructors are invoked in the order B1(), B2, and D, the order in which the base classes appear in the declaration of the derived class.

10. Constructor in base and derived classes in multiple inheritance

```
// cons10.cpp: constructor in base and derived classes, order of invocation
#include <iostream.h>
class B1     // base class
{
   public:
      B1() { cout << "\nNo-argument constructor of the base class B1"; }
};
class B2     // base class
{
   public:
      B2() { cout << "\nNo-argument constructor of a base class B2"; }
};
class D: public B1, virtual B2        // public B1, private virtual B2
{
   public:
      D(): B1(), B2()
      { cout << "\nNo-argument constructor of the derived class D"; }
};
```

```
void main()
{
    D objd;  // base constructor
}
```

Run

```
No-argument constructor of a base class B2
No-argument constructor of the base class B1
No-argument constructor of the derived class D
```

The statement

```
        class D: public B1, virtual B2      // public B1, private virtual B2
```

specifies that the class D is derived from the base classes B1 and B2. The statement

```
        D():B1(), B2()
```

in the derived class D, specifies that, the base class constructors must be called. However, the constructors are invoked in the order B2(), B1, and D(), instead of the order in which base classes appear in the declaration of the derived class, since, the virtual base class constructors are invoked first followed by an orderly invocation of constructors of other classes.

11. Constructor in multilevel inheritance

```
// cons11.cpp: constructor in base and derived classes, order of invocation
#include <iostream.h>
class B      // base class
{
    public:
        B() { cout << "\nNo-argument constructor of a base class B"; }
};
class D1: public B    // derived class
{
    public:
        D1() { cout << "\nNo-argument constructor of a base class D1"; }
};
class D2: public D1   // publicly derived class
{
    public:
        D2()
        { cout << "\nNo-argument constructor of a derived class D2"; }
};
void main()
{
    D2 objd;  // base constructor
};
```

Run

```
No-argument constructor of a base class B
No-argument constructor of a base class D1
No-argument constructor of a derived class D2
```

The statement

```
class D2: public D1    // publicly derived class
```

specifies that the class D2 is derived from the derived class D1 of B. The constructors are invoked in the order B(), D1(), and D2() corresponding to the order of inheritance.

In the derived class, first the constructors of virtual base classes are invoked, second any non-virtual classes, and finally the derived class constructor. Table 14.3 shows the order of invocation of constructors in a derived class.

Method of Inheritance	Order of Execution
```class D: public B { ... };```	B( ): base constructor D( ): derived constructor
```class D: public B1, public B2 { ... };```	B1( ): base constructor B2( ): base constructor D( ): derived constructor
```class D: public B1, virtual B2 { ... };```	B2( ): virtual base constructor B1( ): base constructor D( ): derived constructor
```class D1: public B { ... }; class D2: public D1 { ... };```	B( ): super base constructor D1( ): base constructor D2( ): derived constructor

Table 14.3: Order of invocation of constructors

14.7 Destructors in Derived Classes

Unlike constructors, destructors in the class hierarchy (parent and child class) are invoked in the reverse order of the constructor invocation. The destructor of that class whose constructor was executed last, while building object of the derived class, will be executed first whenever the object goes out of scope. If destructors are missing in any class in the hierarchy of classes, that class's destructor is not invoked. The program cons12.cpp illustrates the order of invocation of constructors and destructors in handling instances of a derived class.

```
// cons12.cpp: order of invocation of constructors and destructors
#include <iostream.h>
class B1     // base class
{
   public:
      B1() { cout << "\nNo-argument constructor of the base class B1"; }
      ~B1()
      {
         cout << "\nDestructor in the base class B1";
      }
};
class B2     // base class
{
   public:
      B2() { cout << "\nNo-argument constructor of the base class B2"; }
      ~B2()
      {
         cout << "\nDestructor in the base class B2";
      }
};
class D: public B1, public B2     // publicly derived class
{
   public:
      D()
      { cout << '\nNo-argument constructor of the derived class D"; }
      ~D()
      {
         cout << "\nDestructor in the base class D";
      }
};
void main()
{
   D objd;
}
```

Run
```
No-argument constructor of the base class B1
No-argument constructor of the base class B2
No-argument constructor of the derived class D
Destructor in the base class D
Destructor in the base class B2
Destructor in the base class B1
```

Note that, in this program the constructors are invoked in the order of B1 (), B2 (), D () whereas, the destructors are invoked in the order of D (), B2 (), B1 (), which is in reverse order.

In case of dynamically created objects using the new operator, they must be destroyed explicitly by invoking the delete operator. More specialized class's (which are at the bottom of the hierarchy) destructors are called before a more general one (which are at the top of the hierarchy). As usual, no arguments can be passed to destructors, nor can any return type be declared.

14.8 Constructors Invocation and Data Members Initialization

In multiple inheritance, the constructors of base classes are invoked first, *in the order in which they appear in the declaration of the derived class*, whereas in the case of multilevel inheritance, they are executed *in the order of inheritance*. It is the responsibility of the derived class to supply initial values to the base class constructor, when the derived class objects are created. Initial values can be supplied either by the object of a derived class or a constant value can be mentioned in the definition of the constructor. The syntax for defining a constructor in a derived class is shown in Figure 14.8.

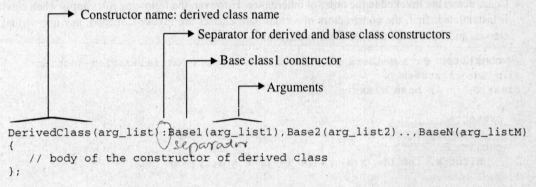

```
DerivedClass(arg_list):Base1(arg_list1),Base2(arg_list2)..,BaseN(arg_listM)
{
    // body of the constructor of derived class
};
```

Figure 14.8: Syntax of derived class constructor

The parameters arg_list1, arg_list2, .., arg_listM are the list of arguments passed to the constructor or they can be any constant value those match with the arguments of the *constructor list* of base classes.

C++ supports another method of initializing the objects of classes through the use of the *initialization list* in the constructor function. It facilitates the initialization of data members by specifying them in the header section of the constructor. The general form of this method is shown in Figure 14.9.

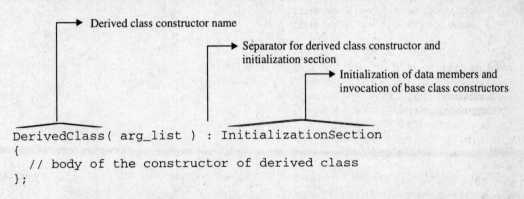

```
DerivedClass( arg_list ) : InitializationSection
{
    // body of the constructor of derived class
};
```

Figure 14.9: Syntax of initialization at derived class constructor

Data member initialization is represented by

```
DataMemberName( value )
```

The data members (DataMemberName) to be initialized are followed by the initialization value enclosed in parentheses (resembles a function call). The value can be arguments of a constructor, expression or other data members. In the initialization section, any parameter of the argument-list can be used as an initialization value. The data member to be initialized must be a member of its own class. The program cons14.cpp illustrates the use of initialization section of the constructor. The following rules must be noted about the initialization and order of invocation of constructors:

- The initialization statements (in the initialization section) are executed in the order of definition of data members in the class.

- Constructors are invoked in the order of inheritance. However, the following rules apply when class is instantiated: first, the constructors of virtual base classes are invoked, second, any non-virtual classes, and finally, the derived class constructor.

```cpp
// cons13.cpp: data members initialization through initialization-section
#include <iostream.h>
class B        // base class
{
   protected:
      int x, y;
   public:
      B(int a, int b): x(a), y(b) {} // x = a, y = b
};
class D: public B      // derived class
{
   private:
      int a, b;
   public:
      D(int p, int q, int r): a(p), B( p, q ), b(r) {}
   void output()
   {
      cout << "x = " << x << endl;
      cout << "y = " << y << endl;
      cout << "a = " << a << endl;
      cout << "b = " << b << endl;
   }
};
void main()
{
   D objb(5, 10, 15);
   objb.output();
}
```

Run

```
x = 5
y = 10
a = 5
b = 15
```

The constructor statement in the class B

```
B(int a, int b): x(a), y(b) {} // x = a, y = b
```

initializes the data members x and y to a and b respectively. The constructor statement in class D

```
D(int p, int q, int r): a(p), B( p, q ), b(r) {}
```

initializes the data members a and b to p and r respectively. It invokes the constructor B (int, int) of the base class B.

Consider the following declaration of class to illustrate the order of initialization:

```
class B       // base class
{
   private:
      int x, y;
   public:
      B(int a, int b): x(a), y(b) {} // x = a, y = b
};
```

Assume, the constructor of the class B is rewritten for illustration and object objb is defined as

```
B objb( 5, 10 );
```

The following examples illustrates the initialization of data members with different formats:

1. B(int a, int b): x(a), y(a+b)

The data member x is assigned the value a and y is assigned the value of the expression (a+b), i.e., x = 5 and y = (5+10) = 15.

2. B(int a, int b): x(a), y(x+b)

The data member x is assigned the value of a and y is assigned the value of the expression (x+b), i.e., x = 5 and y = (5+10) = 15. Note that the newly initialized data member can also be used in further initializations.

3. B(int a, int b): y(a), x(y+b) (result will be wrong)

It produces a wrong result, because, the statement which initializes the data member x is the first one to be executed (x is defined first data member in the class B). Hence the computation x (y+b) (i.e x = y+b) produces a wrong result because the data member y is not yet initialized. The program runtime.cpp illustrates this case. Thus, the order of data members in the initialization list is important.

```
// runtime.cpp: initialization through constructor header
#include <iostream.h>
class B
{
   private:
      int  x, y;
   public:
      B( int a, int b ): y(a), x(y+b) {} // No compilation, but  run-time
      void print()
      {
         cout << x << endl;
         cout << y << endl;
      }
};
```

```
void main()
{
   B b( 2, 3 );
   b.print();
}
```

Run

4211
2

The compiler converts the constructor of the class B into the following form:

```
B( int a, int b )
{
    x = (y+b);
    y = a;
}
```

In the above converted constructor, it should be noted that the statement

```
x = (y+b);
```

refers to the data member y which is still not initialized. Hence, the program produces the wrong result.

14.9 Overloaded Member Functions

The members of a derived class can have the same name as those defined in the base class. An object of a derived class refers to its own functions even if they are defined in both the base class and the derived class. The program cons14.cpp illustrates the overloaded data and member functions in the base and derived classes.

```
// cons14.cpp: overloaded members in base and derived classes
#include <iostream.h>
class B       // base class
{
   protected:
      int x;
      int y;
   public:
      B() {}
      void read()
      {
         cout << "X in class B ? ";
         cin >> x;
         cout << "Y in class B ? ";
         cin >> y;
      };
      void show()
      {
         cout << "X in class B = " << x << endl;
         cout << "Y in class B = " << y << endl;
      }
};
```

```
class D: public B    // publicly derived class
{
   protected:
      int y;
      int z;
   public:
   void read()
      {
        B::read();  // read base class data first
        cout << "Y in class D ? ";
        cin >> y;
        cout << "Z in class D ? ";
        cin >> z;
      };
      void show()
      {
        B::show();  // display base class data first
        cout << "Y in class D = " << y << endl;
        cout << "Z in class D = " << z << endl;
        cout<<"Y of B, show from D = "<< B::y;  //refers to y of class B
      };
};
void main()
{
   D objd;
   cout << "Enter data for object of class D .."  << endl;
   objd.read();
   cout << "Contents of object of class D .." << endl;
   objd.show();
}
```

Run

```
Enter data for object of class D ..
X in class B ? 1
Y in class B ? 2
Y in class D ? 3
Z in class D ? 4
Contents of object of class D ..
X in class B = 1
Y in class B = 2
Y in class D = 3
Z in class D = 4
Y of B, show from D = 2
```

In the derived class, there can also be functions with the same name as those in base class. It results in ambiguity. The compiler resolves the conflict by using the following rule:

If the same member (data/function) exists in both the base class and the derived class, the member in the derived class will be executed.

The above rule is true for derived classes. Objects of the base class do not know anything about the derived class and will always use the base class members. Consider the statements

```
objd.read();
objd.show()
```

in function main(). In the first statement, objd, the object of a class D, invokes the read() function defined in the class D, instead of the read() function of the class B. Similarly, the function show() referenced by the objd uses the function defined in the class D.

Scope Resolution with Overriding Functions

The statement in class D

```
B::read();  // read base class data first
```

refers to the function read() defined in the base class B due to the use of scope resolution operation. Similarly, the statement

```
B::show();  // display base class data first
```

in the function show() of derived class D refers to the show() function of the base class B.

The statement

```
cout << "Y of B, show from D = " << B::y;  // refers to y of class B
```

in the function show() has B::y, which refers to the data member defined in the base class B and not the one defined in the derived class D. These features of C++ demonstrates the creation of powerful functions using primitive functions. The general format of scope resolution for class members is shown in Figure 14.10.

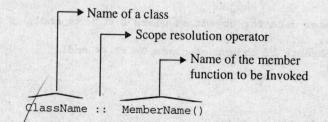

Figure 14.10: Syntax of member function access through scope resolution operator

For instance, as in the following statements

B::read() refers to the member function read() defined in the class B
B::y refers to the data member y defined in the class B

prefixing the class name to the member separated by scope resolution operator :: informs the compiler to call the member function specified in the class B.

Inheritance in the Stack Class

The various programs discussed so far, belong to the category of single Inheritance. Another practical example of inheritance is the stack, which is the most popularly used data-structure in building compilers, execution of recursive programs, allocating storage for local variables, and so on. The stack operates on the principle of Last-In-First-Out, popularly called LIFO policy. The last item entered into the stack is the first one to come out as shown in Figure 14.11.

The program `stack.cpp` has two classes, `Stack` as the base class and `MyStack` as the derived class of `Stack`. The base class `Stack` models a stack as a simple data storage device. It allows to push integers onto the stack and pop them off. However, it has a potential flaw. It does not check for the underflow or overflow that occurs in the manipulation of a stack. The program might not work since data would be placed in memory beyond the end of the `stack[]` array. Trying to pop too many items from the stack results in popping out meaningless data since, it would be reading data from memory locations outside the array.

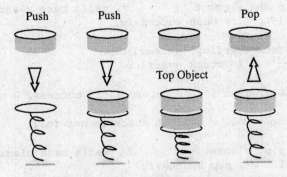

Figure 14.11: Stack operations

The potential flaw, in the class `Stack` can be overcome by developing a new class `MyStack`, a derived class inherited from the old stack class `Stack`. Objects of `MyStack` operate exactly the same way as those of Stack, except that it will issue a warning if an attempt is made to push an item onto a stack which is already full, or try to pop items out of an empty stack.

```cpp
// stack.cpp: Overloading of functions in base and derived classes
#include <iostream.h>
const int MAX_ELEMENTS = 5; // maximum size of stack, you can change this
class Stack                 // base class
{
   protected:               // Note: cannot be private
      int stack[ MAX_ELEMENTS + 1 ]; // for stack[1]..stack[MAX_ELEMENTS]
      int  StackTop;         // It points to current stack top  element
   public:
      Stack()
      {
         StackTop = 0;      // Initially no elements in stack, stack empty
      }
      void push( int element )
      {
         ++StackTop;        // Update StackTop for new entry
         stack[StackTop] = element;    // put element into the stack
      }
      void pop( int &element )
      {
         element = stack[ StackTop ];
         --StackTop;        // Update StackTop to point to next element
      }
};
```

```cpp
// derivation of a new class from the class Stack
class MyStack : public Stack
{
   public:
      int push( int element ) // return 1, if success, 0 otherwise
      {
         if( StackTop < MAX_ELEMENTS )      // if stack is not full
         {
            Stack::push( element );        // calls base class push
            return 1;      // push successful
         }
         cout << "Stack Overflow" << endl;
         return 0;        // stack overflow
      }
      int pop( int & element )   // return 1, if success, 0 otherwise
      {
         if( StackTop > 0 )        // if stack is not full
         {
            Stack::pop( element );        // calls base class pop
            return 1;    // pop successful
         }
         cout << "Stack Underflow" << endl;
         return 0;      // stack underflow
      }
};
void main()
{
   MyStack stack;
   int element;
   // push elements into Stack until it overflows
   cout << "Enter Integer data to put into the stack ..." << endl;
   do
   {
      cout << "Element to Push ? ";
      cin >> element;
   }
   while( stack.push( element ) ); // push and check for overflow
   // pop all elements from stack
   cout << "The Stack Contains ..." << endl;
   while( stack.pop( element ) )
      cout << "pop: " << element << endl;
}
```

Run

```
Enter Integer data to put into the stack ...
Element to Push ? 1
Element to Push ? 2
Element to Push ? 3
Element to Push ? 4
Element to Push ? 5
Element to Push ? 6
```

```
Stack Overflow
The Stack Contains ...
pop: 5
pop: 4
pop: 3
pop: 2
pop: 1
Stack Underflow
```

14.10 Abstract Classes

In order to exploit the potential benefits of inheritance, the base classes are improved or enhanced without modifications, which results in a derived class or inherited class. The objects created often are the instances of a derived class but not of the base class. The base class becomes just the foundation for building new classes and hence such classes are called *abstract base classes* or *abstract classes*. An abstract class is one that has no instances and is not designed to create objects. An abstract class is only designed to be inherited. It specifies an interface at a certain level of inheritance and provides a framework, upon which other classes can be built.

In the previous example (stack.cpp), the class Stack serves as a framework for building the derived classes and it is treated as a member of the derived class MyStack. The abstract class is the most important class and normally exists at the root of the hierarchy; it is a pathway to extending the system. Hence, the class Stack is sometimes loosely called as *abstract class* or *abstract base class*, meaning that no actual instances (objects) of these classes are created. However, abstract classes, in addition to inheritance, have more significance in connection with virtual functions, which will be discussed later in the chapter on *Virtual Functions*.

Abstract classes have other benefits. It provides a framework upon which other classes can be built and need not follow the trick of C (language, C++'s base class) programming. Most of the C programmers follow tricks of creating skeleton code and then copying and modifying the skeleton to create new functionality. One problem with skeleton code is if any modification is done to skeleton code, the changes must be propagated manually throughout the system -- an error prone process at best. In addition, it is difficult to find out whether bugs are in original skeleton or in modified system versions. By using abstract classes, interface can be changed which immediately propagate changes throughout the system with no errors. All changes made by the programmer in the derived classes are shown explicitly in the code, any bugs that show up are almost isolated in the new code.

14.11 Multilevel Inheritance

Derivation of a class from another *derived class* is called multilevel inheritance. It is very common in inheritance that a class is derived from a derived class as shown in Figure 14.12. The class B is the base class for the derived class D1, which in turn serves as a base class for the derived class D2. The class D1 provides a link for the inheritance between B and D2, and is known as *intermediate* base class. The chain B, D1, D2 is known as the *inheritance path*.

A derived class with multilevel inheritance is declared as follows:

```
class B { ... };              // Base class
class D1: public B() // D1 derived from B
```

```
class D2: public D1()        // D2 derived from D1
```
The multilevel inheritance mechanism can be extended to any number of levels.

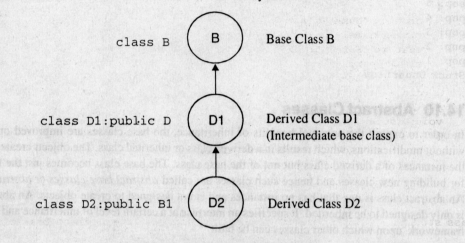

Figure 14.12: Multilevel inheritance

The inheritance relation shown in Figure 14.13 is modeled in the program exam.cpp. It consists of three classes namely, person, student, and exam. Here, the class person is the base class, student is the intermediate base class, and exam is the derived class. The student class inherits the properties of person class whereas, the exam class inherits the properties of the student class (directly) and properties of the person class (indirectly).

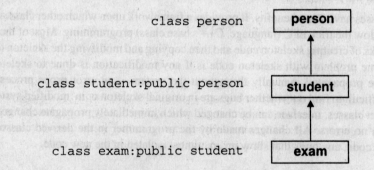

Figure 14.13: Multilevel inheritance

```
// exam.cpp: Models Examination database using Inheritance
#include <iostream.h>
const int MAX_LEN = 25;      // maximum length of name
class person
{
    private:                 // Note: cannot be referred by derived class
        char name[ MAX_LEN ];     // person name
        char sex;                 // person sex, M - male, F - female
        int age;                  // person age
```

```
    public:
       void ReadData()
       {
          cout << "Name ? ";
          cin >> name;
          cout << "Sex ? ";
          cin >> sex;
          cout << "Age ? ";
          cin >> age;
       }
       void DisplayData()
       {
          cout << "Name: " << name << endl;
          cout << "Sex : " << sex << endl;
          cout << "Age : " << age << endl;
       }
};
class student : public person  // publicly derived intermediate-base class
{
    private:
       int RollNo;         // student roll number in a class
       char branch[20];  // branch or subject student is studying
    public:
       void ReadData()
       {
          person::ReadData();  // uses ReadData of person class
          cout << "Roll Number ? ";
          cin >> RollNo;
          cout << "Branch Studying ? ";
          cin >> branch;
       }
       void DisplayData()
       {
          person::DisplayData();  // uses DisplayData of person class
          cout << "Roll Number: " << RollNo << endl;
          cout << "Branch: " << branch << endl;
       }
};
class exam: public student    // derived class
{
    protected:
       int Sub1Marks;
       int Sub2Marks;
    public:
       void ReadData()
       {
          student::ReadData();  // uses ReadData of student class
          cout << "Marks Scored in Subject 1 < Max:100> ? ";
          cin >> Sub1Marks;
          cout << "Marks Scored in Subject 2 < Max:100> ? ";
```

```
            cin >> Sub2Marks;
        }
    void DisplayData()
    {
        student::DisplayData(); // uses DisplayData of student class
        cout << "Marks Scored in Subject 1: " << Sub1Marks << endl;
        cout << "Marks Scored in Subject 2: " << Sub2Marks << endl;
        cout << "Total Marks Scored: " << TotalMarks();
    }
    int TotalMarks()
    {
        return Sub1Marks + Sub2Marks;
    }
};
void main()
{
    exam annual;
    cout << "Enter data for Student ..." << endl;
    annual.ReadData();    // uses exam::ReadData
    cout << "Student details ..." << endl;
    annual.DisplayData();  // exam::DisplayData
}
```

Run

```
Name ? Rajkumar
Sex ? M
Age ? 24
Roll Number ? 9
Branch Studying ? Computer-Technology
Marks Scored in Subject 1 < Max:100> ? 92
Marks Scored in Subject 2 < Max:100> ? 88
Student details ...
Name: Rajkumar
Sex :  M
Age : 24
Roll Number: 9
Branch: Computer-Technology
Marks Scored in Subject 1: 92
Marks Scored in Subject 2: 88
Total Marks Scored: 180
```

In main(), the statements

```
        annual.ReadData();       // uses exam::ReadData
        annual.DisplayData();  // exam::DisplayData
```

refer to the member functions of the class exam, since annual is its object. The statements in
ReadData() function of the class exam

```
        student::ReadData();     // uses ReadData of student class
        student::DisplayData();  // uses DisplayData of student class
```

refers to the functions defined in the student class.

14.12 Multiple Inheritance

A class can be derived by inheriting the traits of two or more base classes. Multiple inheritance refers to the derivation of a class from several (two or more) base classes. It allows the combination of the features of several existing, tested, and well proven classes as a starting point for defining new classes. Multiple inheritance model is shown in Figure 14.14a and its syntax is shown in Figure 14.14b.

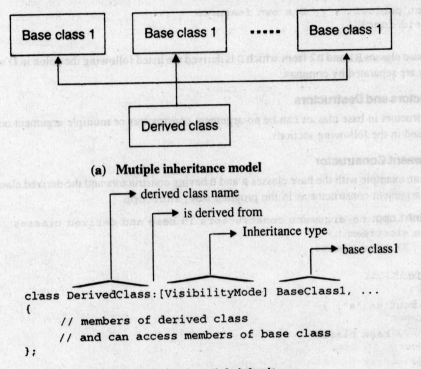

(a) **Mutiple inheritance model**

```
class DerivedClass:[VisibilityMode] BaseClass1, ...
{
    // members of derived class
    // and can access members of base class
};
```

(b) **Syntax of mutiple inheritance**

Figure 14.14: Mutiple inheritance

The default visibility mode is private. If visibility mode is specified, it must be either public or private. In multiple inheritance also, the inheritance of base classes with visibility mode public, implies that the public members of the base class become public members of the derived class and protected members of the base class become protected members of the derived class. Inheritance of base classes with visibility mode private causes both the public and protected members of the base class to become private members of the derived class. However, in both the cases private members of the base class are not inherited and they can be accessed through member functions of the base class.

The following declaration illustrates the concept of multiple inheritance:

```
class D: public B1, public B2  // multiple inheritance
{
    private:
```

```
    int privateD;
    void func1() {}
  protected:
    int protectedD; // D's own features
    void func2()
    { /* Null body function */ }
  public:
    int publicD;   // D's own features
    void func3();
};
```

The base classes B1 and B2 from which D is derived are listed following the colon in D's specification; they are separated by commas.

Constructors and Destructors

The constructors in base classes can be no-argument constructors or multiple argument constructors as discussed in the following sections.

No-Argument Constructor

Consider an example with the base classes A and B having constructors and the derived class C which has a no-argument constructor as in the program mul_inh1.cpp.

```
// mul_inh1.cpp: no-argument constructors in base and derived classes
#include <iostream.h>
class A  // base class1
{
  public:
    A()
    { cout << "a"; }
};
class B  // base class2
{
  public·
    B()
    { cout << "b"; }
};
class C: public A, public B   // derived class
{
  public:
    C()
    { cout << "c"; }
};
void main()
{
  C objc;
}
```

Run

abc

The base class constructors are always executed first, working from the first base class to the last and finally through the derived class constructor. Since the derived class is declared as

```
class C: public A, public B
```

The constructor of the base class A is executed first, followed by the constructor of the class B and finally the constructor of the derived class C. Hence, the above program would print abc on the screen. If classes involved in multiple inheritance have destructors, they are invoked in the reverse order of the constructors invocation.

Passing Parameters to Multiple Constructors

Some or all parameters that are supplied to a derived class constructor may be passed to the base class(es) constructor. Therefore, if any base class constructor has one or more parameters, all classes derived from it must also have constructors with or without parameters. The program mul_inh2.cpp illustrates the base classes A and B having constructors with arguments; their derived class C must also have constructors.

```
// mul_inh2.cpp: constructors with arguments, must be called explicitly
#include <iostream.h>
class A  // base class1
{
   public:
      A( char c )
      { cout << c; }
};
class B  // base class2
{
   public:
      B( char b )
      { cout << b; }
};
class C: public A, public B    // derived class
{
   public:
      C( char c1, char c2, char c3): A( c1 ), B( c2 )
      { cout << c3; }
};
main()
{
   C objc( 'a', 'b', 'c');
}
```

Run
abc

In this case, the parameters c2 and c3 are passed to the constructors of the base classes A and B respectively. The arguments a, b and c are actually passed to the constructors of A, B, and C respectively even though they are parameters to the constructor of the class C. The constructors are executed in the order A, B, and C, hence, the above program would print abc on the screen. In general, parameters can be passed to the constructors of the base class as shown in the following syntax:

```
derived(parameter list):base1(parameter list1), base2(parameter list2), ...
```

The parameter lists of the base classes' constructors may contain any expression that has global scope (e.g., global constants, global variables, dynamically initialized global variables), as well as parameters that were passed to the derived class's constructor. The program mul_inh3.cpp illustrates the handling of constructors with arguments in the base class and the derived class.

```
// mul_inh3.cpp: constructors with arguments, if not called explicitly
#include <iostream.h>
class A  // base class1
{
    public:
        A( char c )
        { cout << c; }
};
class B  // base class2
{
    public:
        B( char b )
        { cout << b; }
};
class C: public A, public B
{
    public:
        C( char c1, char c2, char c3): B( c2 )
        { cout << c3; }
};
main()
{
    C objc( 'a', 'b', 'c' );
}
```

The above program cannot be executed, since the following error is generated during compilation:

```
Error: Cannot find 'A::A()' to initialize base class in function C::C(char,
char, char)
```

If there are constructors in the base class and all of them are of type *constructors with arguments*, they must be explicitly specified in the derived class constructor. Otherwise, the compiler generates a compilation error. However, if a no-argument constructor also exists along with other constructors in base class, the compiler invokes the no-argument constructor as a default. Note that the base classes used in inheritance must preferably have a no-argument constructor.

Ambiguity in Member Access

Ambiguity is a problem that surfaces in certain situations involving multiple inheritance. Consider the following cases:

- Base classes having functions with the same name
- The class derived from these base classes is not having a function with the name as those of its base classes
- Members of a derived class or its objects referring to a member, whose name is the same as those in base classes

These situations create ambiguity in deciding which of the base class's function has to be referred. This problem is resolved using the scope resolution operator as shown in Figure 14.15. The program mul_inh4.cpp illustrates the same.

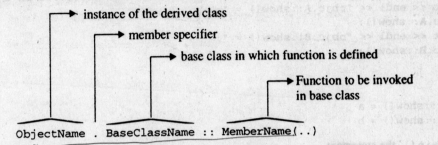

ObjectName . BaseClassName :: MemberName(..)

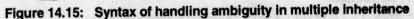

Figure 14.15:   Syntax of handling ambiguity in multiple inheritance

```
// mul_inh4.cpp: overloaded functions in base classes
#include <iostream.h>
class A  // base class1
{
    char ch;    // private data, default
    public:
        A( char c )
        { ch = c; }
        void show()
        {
            cout << ch;
        }
};
class B  // base class2
{
    char ch;    // private data, default
    public:
        B( char b )
        { ch = b; }
        void show()
        {
            cout << ch;
        }
};
class C: public A, public B
{
    char ch;    // private data, default
    public:
        C( char c1, char c2, char c3): A( c1 ), B( c2 )
        {
            ch = c3;
        }
};
```

```
main()
{
    C objc( 'a', 'b', 'c');
    // objc.show();            // Error: Field 'show' is ambiguous in C
    cout << endl << "objc.A::show() = ";
    objc.A::show();
    cout << endl << "objc.B::show() = ";
    objc.B::show();
}
```

Run

```
objc.A::show() = a
objc.B::show() = b
```

In main(), the statement

```
        objc.show(); // Error: Field 'show' is ambiguous in C
```

is ambiguous (whether to choose A::show() or B::show()?) to the compiler resulting in a compilation error. It is resolved using the scope resolution operator as follows.

```
        objc.A::show();
```

refers to the version of show() in the class A, while,

```
        objc.B::show();
```

refers to the function in the class B. Thus, the scope resolution operator circumvents the ambiguity.

The program mul_inh5.cpp illustrates the base and derived classes, which have members with the same name.

```
// mul_inh5.cpp: overloaded functions in base and derived classes
#include <iostream.h>
class A  // base class1
{
    char ch;    // private data, default
    public:
        A( char c )
        { ch = c;  }
        void show()
        {
            cout << ch;
        }
};
class B  // base class2
{
    char ch;    // private data, default
    public:
        B( char b )
        { ch = b; }
        void show()
        {
            cout << ch;
        }
};
```

```
class C: public A, public B
{
    char ch;      // private data, default
    public:
        C( char c1, char c2, char c3): A( c1 ), B( c2 )
        { ch = c3; }
        void show()
        {
            // show(); invokes C::show(), leading to infinite recursion
            A::show();
            B::show();
            cout << ch;
        }
};
main()
{
    C objc( 'a', 'b', 'c');
    cout << "objc.show() = ";
    objc.show();        // refers to show() defined in the derived class C
    cout << endl << "objc.C::show() = ";
    objc.C::show();
    cout << endl << "objc.A::show() = ";
    objc.A::show();
    cout << endl << "objc.B::show() = ";
    objc.B::show();
}
```

Run

```
objc.show() = abc
objc.C::show() = abc
objc.A::show() = a
objc.B::show() = b
```

In main(), the statements

```
        objc.show();
        objc.C::show();
```

refer to the same version of show() defined in the class C, while

```
        objc.A::show();
```

refers to the version of show() defined in the class A, and

```
        objc.B::show();
```

refers to the function defined in the class B. In the derived class C, statements in show()

```
        A::show();
        B::show();
```

refer to the functions defined in the classes A and B respectively.

Example on Multiple Inheritance

Consider a publishing company that publishes and markets books, whose activities are shown in Figure 14.16. Create a class publication that stores the title (string) and price (float) of a publication. Create another class sales that holds an array of three *float*'s so that it can record the sales of a particular publication for the last three months. From these two classes, derive a new class called book that hold pages of integer type. Each of these classes should have the member functions getdata () and display ().

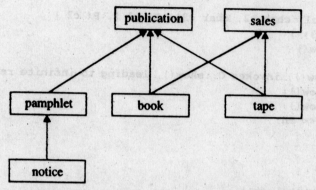

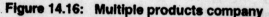

Figure 14.16:   Multiple products company

From the publication and sales classes, derive the tape class, which adds playing time in minutes (type float). Create another class pamphlet from publication, which has no features of its own. Derive a class notice from pamphlet class having data members char whom[20] and member functions getdata () and putdata ().

The program publish1.cpp models the class hierarchy shown in Figure 14.16. Note that, inheritance of the class publication by the classes, pamphlet, book, and tape illustrates the reuse of the code.

```
// publish1.cpp: Multiple products company modeling with multiple inheritance
#include <iostream.h>
class publication     // base class, appears as abstract class
{
   private:
      char title[40];    // name of the publication work
      float price;       // price of a publication
   public:
      void getdata()
      {
         cout << "\tEnter Title: ";
         cin >> title;
         cout << "\tEnter Price: ";
         cin >> price;
      }
      void display()
      {
         cout << "\tTitle = " << title << endl;
         cout << "\tPrice = ' << price << endl;
      }
};
class sales     // base class
{
   private:
```

```
        float PublishSales[3];//sales of a publication for the last 3 months
    public:
        void getdata();
        void display();
};
void sales::getdata()
{
    int i;

    for( i = 0; i < 3; i++ )
    {
        cout << "\tEnter Sales of " << i+1 << " Month: ";
        cin >> PublishSales[i];
    }
}
void sales::display()
{
    int i;
    int TotalSales = 0;

    for( i = 0; i < 3; i++ )
    {
        cout<<"\tSales of "<<i+1 << " Month = " << PublishSales[i] << endl;
        TotalSales += PublishSales[i];
    }
    cout << "\tTotal Sales = " << TotalSales << endl;
}
class book : public publication, public sales    // derived class
{
    private:
        int pages;   // number of pages in a book
    public:
        void getdata() // overloaded function
        {
            publication::getdata();
            cout << "\tEnter Number of Pages: ";
            cin >> pages;
            sales::getdata();
        }
        void display()
        {
            publication::display();
            cout << "\tNumber of Pages = " << pages << endl;
            sales::display();
        }
};
class tape : public publication, public sales    // derived class
{
    private:
        float PlayTime;    // playing time in minutes
```

```
  public:
     void getdata()
     {
        publication::getdata();
        cout << "\tEnter Playing Time in Minute: ";
        cin >> PlayTime;
        sales::getdata();
     }
     void display()
     {
        publication::display();
        cout << "\tPlaying Time in Minute = " << PlayTime << endl;
        sales::display();
     }
};
//for pamphlet class, sales class is not inherited, because, pamphlets
// cannot be sold, they are published for advertisement purpose
class pamphlet : public publication // derived class
{
};
class notice: public pamphlet     // derived, can access publics of pamphlet
{
  private:
     char whom[20];      // notice to all distributors
  public:
     void getdata()
     {
        pamphlet::getdata(); // intern calls getdata of publication
        cout << "\tEnter Type of Distributor: ";
        cin >> whom;
     }
     void display()
     {
        pamphlet::display(); // intern calls display of publication
        cout << "\tType of Distributor = " << whom << endl;
     }
};
void main()
{
  book book1;
  tape tape1;
  pamphlet pamp1;
  notice notice1;
  cout << "Enter Book Publication Data ..." << endl;
  book1.getdata();
  cout << "Enter Tape Publication Data ..." << endl;
  tape1.getdata();
  cout << "Enter Pamphlet Publication Data ..." << endl;
  pamp1.getdata();
  cout << "Enter Notice Publication Data ..." << endl;
  notice1.getdata();
```

```
    cout << "Book Publication Data ..." << endl;
    book1.display();
    cout << "Tape Publication Data ..." << endl;
    tape1.display();
    cout << "Pamphlet Publication Data ..." << endl;
    pamp1.display();
    cout << "Notice Publication Data ..." << endl;
    notice1.display();
}
```

Run

```
Enter Book Publication Data ...
    Enter Title: Microprocessor-x86-Programming
    Enter Price: 180
    Enter Number of Pages: 750
    Enter Sales of 1 Month: 1000
    Enter Sales of 2 Month: 500
    Enter Sales of 3 Month: 800
Enter Tape Publication Data ...
    Enter Title: Love-1947
    Enter Price: 100
    Enter Playing Time in Minute: 10
    Enter Sales of 1 Month: 200
    Enter Sales of 2 Month: 500
    Enter Sales of 3 Month: 400
Enter Pamphlet Publication Data ...
    Enter Title: Advanced-Computing-95-Conference
    Enter Price: 10
Enter Notice Publication Data ...
    Enter Title: General-Meeting
    Enter Price: 100
    Enter Type of Distributor: Retail
Book Publication Data ...
    Title = Microprocessor-x86-Programming
    Price = 180
    Number of Pages = 705
    Sales of 1 Month = 1000
    Sales of 2 Month = 500
    Sales of 3 Month = 800
    Total Sales = 2300
Tape Publication Data ...
    Title = Love-1947
    Price = 100
    Playing Time in Minute = 10
    Sales of 1 Month = 200
    Sales of 2 Month = 500
    Sales of 3 Month = 400
    Total Sales = 1100
Pamphlet Publication Data ...
    Title = Advanced-Computing-95-Conference
```

```
    Price = 10
Notice Publication Data ...
    Title = General-Meeting
    Price = 100
    Type of Distributor = Retail
```

14.13 Hierarchical Inheritance

A well established method of program design is the hierarchical model, which can be modeled better using the concepts of inheritance. Many programming problems fall into this category. Hierarchical model follows a top down approach by breaking up a complex class into simpler constituent classes. In other words, in the hierarchical model, a complex class is conceptualized as being made up of simpler classes. Figure 14.17 illustrates the hierarchical classification of vehicles in a vehicle license department respectively. Hierarchical inheritance resembles the multilevel inheritance, in which only one derived class path is taken into consideration.

In C++, hierarchical programs can be easily converted into class hierarchies. The superclass (base class) includes the features that are common to all the subclasses (derived classes). A subclass is created by inheriting the properties of the base class and adding some of its own features. The subclass can serve as a superclass for the lower level classes again and so on. The program `vehicle.cpp` models the class hierarchy in C++ for the problem shown in Figure 14.17.

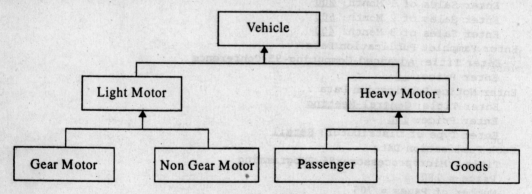

Figure 14.17:   Classification of vehicles

```
// vehicle.cpp: Vehicle Database Hierarchical Model
#include <iostream.h>
const MAX_LEN= 25;    // length of string
class Vehicle
{
  protected:
    char name[ MAX_LEN];     // name of the vehicle
    int WheelsCount;         // number of wheels to vehicle
  public:
    void GetData()
    {
      cout << "Name of the Vehicle ? ";
```

```
            cin >> name;
            cout << "Wheels ? ";
            cin >> WheelsCount;
        }
        void DisplayData()
        {
            cout << "Name of the Vehicle : " << name << endl;
            cout << "Wheels : " << WheelsCount << endl;
        }
};
class LightMotor: public Vehicle
{
    protected:
        int SpeedLimit;
    public:
        void GetData()
        {
            Vehicle::GetData();
            cout << "Speed Limit ? ";
            cin >> SpeedLimit;
        }
        void DisplayData()
        {
            Vehicle::DisplayData();
            cout << "Speed Limit : " << SpeedLimit << endl;
        }
};
class HeavyMotor: public Vehicle
{
    protected:
        int LoadCapacity;    // load carrying capacity
        char permit[MAX_LEN]; // permits: state, country, international
    public:
        void GetData()
        {
            Vehicle::GetData();
            cout << "Load Carrying Capacity ? ";
            cin >> LoadCapacity;
            cout << "Permit Type ? ";
            cin >> permit;
        }
        void DisplayData()
        {
            Vehicle::DisplayData();
            cout << "Load Carrying Capacity : " << LoadCapacity << endl;
            cout << "Permit: " << permit << endl;
        }
};
```

```cpp
class GearMotor: public LightMotor
{
   protected:
      int GearCount;
   public:
      void GetData()
      {
         LightMotor::GetData();
         cout << "No. of Gears ? ";
         cin >> GearCount;
      }
      void DisplayData()
      {
         LightMotor::DisplayData();
         cout << "Gears: " << GearCount << endl;
      }
};
class NonGearMotor: public LightMotor
{
   public:
      void GetData()
      {
         LightMotor::GetData();
      }
      void DisplayData()
      {
         LightMotor::DisplayData();
      }
};
class Passenger: public HeavyMotor
{
   protected:
      int sitting;
      int standing;
   public:
      void GetData()
      {
         HeavyMotor::GetData();
         cout << "Maximum Seats ? ";
         cin >> sitting;
         cout << "Maximum Standing ? ";
         cin >> standing;
      }
      void DisplayData()
      {
         HeavyMotor::DisplayData();
         cout << "Maximum Seats: " << sitting << endl;
         cout << "Maximum Standing: " << standing << endl;
      }
};
```

```
class Goods: public HeavyMotor
{
   public:
      void GetData()
      {
         HeavyMotor::GetData();
      }
      void DisplayData()
      {
         HeavyMotor::DisplayData();
      }
};
void main()
{
   GearMotor vehi1;
   Passenger vehi2;
   // read vehicle data
   cout << "Enter Data for Gear Motor Vehicle ..." << endl;
   vehi1.GetData();
   cout << "Enter Data for Passenger Motor Vehicle ..." << endl;
   vehi2.GetData();
   // display vehicle data
   cout << "Data of Gear Motor Vehicle ..." << endl;
   vehi1.DisplayData();
   cout << "Data of Passenger Motor Vehicle ..." << endl;
   vehi2.DisplayData();
}
```

Run

```
Enter Data for Gear Motor Vehicle ...
Name of the Vehicle ? Maruti-Car
Wheels ? 4
Speed Limit ? 4
No. of Gears ? 5
Enter Data for Passenger Motor Vehicle ...
Name of the Vehicle ? KSRTC-BUS
Wheels ? 4
Load Carrying Capacity ? 60
Permit Type ? National
Maximum Seats ? 45
Maximum Standing ? 60
Data of Gear Motor Vehicle ...
Name of the Vehicle : Maruti-Car
Wheels : 4
Speed Limit : 4
Gears: 5
Data of Passenger Motor Vehicle ...
Name of the Vehicle : KSRTC-BUS
Wheels : 4
Load Carrying Capacity : 60
```

```
Permit: National
Maximum Seats: 45
Maximum Standing: 15
```

14.14 Multipath Inheritance and Virtual Base Classes

The form of inheritance which derives a new class by multiple inheritance of base classes, which are derived earlier from the same base class, is known as *multipath inheritance*. It involves more than one form of inheritance namely multilevel, multiple, and hierarchical as shown in Figure 14.18. The child class is derived from the base classes parent1 and parent2 (multiple inheritance), which them-selves have a common base class grandparent (hierarchical inheritance). The child inherit.. the properties of the grandparent class (multilevel inheritance) via two separate paths as shown by the broken line. The classes parent1 and parent2 are referred to as direct base classes, whereas grandparent is referred to as the indirect base class.

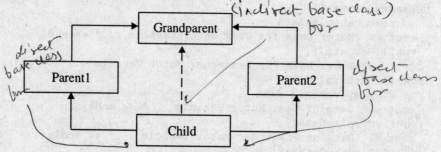

Figure 14.18: Multipath inheritance

Multipath inheritance can pose some problems in compilation. The public and protected members of grandparent are inherited into the child class twice, first, via parent1 class and then via parent2 class. Therefore, the child class would have duplicate sets of members of the grand-parent which leads to ambiguity during compilation and it should be avoided.

C++ supports another important concept called *virtual base classes* to handle ambiguity caused due to the multipath inheritance. It is achieved by making the common base class as a virtual base class while declaring the direct or intermediate classes as shown below:

```cpp
class A
{
   public:
      void func()
      {
          // body of function
      }
};
class B1: public virtual A
{
   // body of class B1
};
```

```
class B2: public virtual A
{
    // body of class B2
};

class D: public B1, public B2
{
    // body of class D
};
```

Consider the statement

```
    objd.func();
```

where `objd` is the object of class `D` and invokes the `func()` defined in the class `A`. If the keyword `virtual` does not exist in the declaration of classes `B1` and `B2`, a call to `func()` leads to the following compilation error:

```
    Error: Member is ambiguous: 'A::func' and 'A::func'
```

C++ takes necessary care to see that only one copy of the class is inherited, when a class is inherited as `virtual` irrespective of the number of paths that exist between the virtual base class and the derived class. The keywords `virtual` and `public` or `protected` may be used in any order.

Consider the processing of the result of student depicted in the Figure 14.19. In this case, the `result` class is derived from the classes `InternalExam` and `ExternalExam`, which are derived classes of the common class `student`. The program `int_ext.cpp` implements the concepts of virtual classes.

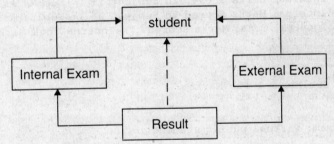

Figure 14.19:   Virtual base classes

```
// int_ext.cpp: Student result based on internal and external marks
//             Multipath Inheritance with virtual classes
#include <iostream.h>
const int MAX_LEN = 25;    // maximum length of name
class student
{
    protected:
        int RollNo;        // student roll number in a class
        char branch[20];   // branch or subject student is studying
    public:
        void ReadStudentData()
        {
            cout << "Roll Number ? ";
```

```
        cin >> RollNo;
        cout << "Branch Studying ? ";
        cin >> branch;
      }
      void DisplayStudentData()
      {
        cout << "Roll Number: " << RollNo << endl;
        cout << "Branch: " << branch << endl;
      }
};
class InternalExam: virtual public student
{
  protected:
      int Sub1Marks;
      int Sub2Marks;
  public:
      void ReadData()
      {
        cout << "Marks Scored in Subject 1 < Max:100> ? ";
        cin >> Sub1Marks;
        cout << "Marks Scored in Subject 2 < Max:100> ? ";
        cin >> Sub2Marks;
      }
      void DisplayData()
      {
        cout<<"Internal Marks Scored in Subject 1: "<<Sub1Marks << endl;
        cout<<"Internal Marks Scored in Subject 2: "<<Sub2Marks << endl;
        cout<<"Internal Total Marks Scored: "<<InternalTotalMarks()<<endl;
      }
      int InternalTotalMarks()
      {
        return Sub1Marks + Sub2Marks;
      }
};
class ExternalExam: virtual public student
{
  protected:
      int Sub1Marks;
      int Sub2Marks;
  public:
      void ReadData()
      {
        cout << "Marks Scored in Subject 1 < Max:100> ? ";
        cin >> Sub1Marks;
        cout << "Marks Scored in Subject 2 < Max:100> ? ";
        cin >> Sub2Marks;
      }
      void DisplayData()
      {
        cout<<"External Marks Scored in Subject 1: "<<Sub1Marks << endl;
```

```
            cout<<"External Marks Scored in Subject 2: "<<Sub2Marks << endl;
            cout<<"External Total Marks Scored: "<<ExternalTotalMarks()<<endl;
        }
      int ExternalTotalMarks()
      {
          return Sub1Marks + Sub2Marks;
      }
};
class result: public InternalExam, public ExternalExam
{
   private:
      int total;
   public:
      int TotalMarks()
      {
          return InternalTotalMarks() + ExternalTotalMarks();
      }
};
void main()
{
   result student1;
   cout << "Enter data for Student1 ..." << endl;
   student1.ReadStudentData();   // virtual resolves ambiguity
   cout << "Enter Internal Marks ..." << endl;
   student1.InternalExam::ReadData();
   cout << "Enter External Marks ..." << endl;
   student1.ExternalExam::ReadData();
   cout << "Student details ..." << endl;
   student1.DisplayStudentData();   // virtual resolves ambiguity
   student1.InternalExam::DisplayData();
   student1.ExternalExam::DisplayData();
   cout << "Total Marks = " << student1.TotalMarks();
}
```

Run

```
Enter data for Student1 ...
Roll Number ? 9
Branch Studying ? Computer-Technology
Enter Internal Marks ...
Marks Scored in Subject 1 < Max:100> ? 80
Marks Scored in Subject 2 < Max:100> ? 85
Enter External Marks ...
Marks Scored in Subject 1 < Max:100> ? 89
Marks Scored in Subject 2 < Max:100> ? 90
Student details ...
Roll Number: 9
Branch: Computer-Technology
Internal Marks Scored in Subject 1: 80
Internal Marks Scored in Subject 2: 85
Internal Total Marks Scored: 165
External Marks Scored in Subject 1: 89
```

External Marks Scored in Subject 2: 90
External Total Marks Scored: 179
Total Marks = 344

Another typical example of virtual classes having their derived classes invoking their base class's constructors is through the initialization section. The program vir.cpp has classes A, B, C, and D representing multi-path inheritance.

```cpp
// vir.cpp: virtual classes with data members initialization
#include <iostream.h>
class A

    protected:
        int x;
    public:
        A()
        {   x = -1; }
        A( int i )
        {   x = i; }
        int geta()
        {   return x; }
};
class B: virtual public A
{
    protected:
        int y;
    public:
        B( int i, int k) : A(i)
        {   y = k;   };
        int getb()
        {   return y;   }
        void show()
        {
            cout << x << " " << geta() << " " << getb();
        }
};
class C:virtual public A
{
    protected:
        int z;
    public:
        C(int i,int k) : A( i )
        {   z = k;   };
        int getc()
        {   return z;   }
        void show()
        {
            cout << x << " " << geta() << " " << getc();
        }
};
```

```
class D: public B,public C
{
    public:
        // invoke A() and then B(i,j) and C(i,j)
        D( int i, int j ) : B(i,j), C(i,j) {}
        void show()
        {
            cout << x << " " << geta() << " " << getb();
            cout << " " << getc() << " " << getc();
        }
};
void main()
{
    D d1( 3, 5 );
    cout << endl << "Object d1 contents: ";
    d1.show();
    B b1( 7, 9 );
    cout << endl << "Object b1 contents: ";
    b1.show();
    C c1( 11, 13 );
    cout << endl << "Object c1 contents: ";
    c1.show();
}
```

Run

```
Object d1 contents: -1 -1 5 5 5
Object b1 contents: 7 7 9
Object c1 contents: 11 11 13
```

In main(), the statement

    B b1(7, 9);

invokes the constructor of the class B

    B(int i, int k) : A(i)

which calls the single argument constructor of the class A and then it executes. Similarly, the statement

    C c1(11, 13);

invokes first the single argument constructor of the class B and then it executes. The first statement in the main() function

    D d1(3, 5);

is supposed to invoke the constructor

    D(int i, int j) : B(i,j), C(i,j) {}

which in turn invokes the constructors of the B and C classes and is expected to produce the results:

    Object d1 contents: 3 3 5 5 5

assuming that the constructor A(i) is invoked, but this has not happened.

According to the inheritance principle, first, the super base class must be instantiated and then followed by the lower level class, finally the one whose object has to be created (No grand child without grand father). When an object of the class D has to be created, first the constructor of the class A is to be invoked. The default no-argument constructor A() is invoked instead of the one-argument constructor. Even if it invokes the one-argument constructor, either through the

```
    B(int i,int k) : A( i )
```

or through the

```
    C(int i,int k) : A( i )
```

it leads to confusion; there are two calls to the constructor which is illegal. It is similar to arguing *father is created before the grand father*, which is neither true in real life nor in C++. Therefore, C++ selects, the no-argument constructor to avoid all these issues. If the constructor of D specification is changed to,

```
    D( int i, int j ) : A(i), B(i,j), C(i,j) {}
```

It produces the result as expected; the one-argument constructor of the super class A is explicitly specified in the initialization section..

14.15 Hybrid Inheritance

There are many situations where more than one form of inheritance is used in designing the class. For example, consider the case of processing the student results as discussed in the program, exam.cpp in multilevel inheritance. Suppose the weightage for a sport is also taken into consideration for finalizing the results. The weightage for sports is stored in a separate class called sports. The new inheritance relationships between various classes would be as shown in Figure 14.20, which indicate both multilevel and multiple inheritance.

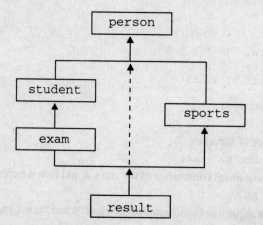

Figure 14.20: Hybrid (multilevel, multipath) inheritance

The inheritance relation shown in Figure 14.20 is modeled in the program sports.cpp. It consists of five classes namely person, student, exam, sports, and result. The class exam is derived by multilevel inheritance. The derivation of the class result from the classes exam and sports exhibits multipath inheritance. Therefore, it has properties of the class person indirectly through two paths: from the exam class and sport class.

```
// sports.cpp: Models student grading based on exam score and sports
#include <iostream.h>
const int MAX_LEN = 25;     // maximum length of name
```

```
class person
{
   private:                 // Note: cannot be referred by derived class
      char name[ MAX_LEN ];      // person name
      char sex;                  // person sex, M - male, F - female
      int age;                   // person age
   public:
      void ReadPerson()
      {
         cout << "Name ? ";
         cin >> name;
         cout << "Sex ? ";
         cin >> sex;
         cout << "Age ? ";
         cin >> age;
      }
      void DisplayPerson()
      {
         cout << "Name: " << name << endl;
         cout << "Sex : " << sex << endl;
         cout << "Age : " << age << endl;
      }
};
class sports: public virtual person.    // note: virtual class
{
   private:
      char name[MAX_LEN];  // name of game
      int score;              // score awarded for result declaration
   protected:
      void ReadData()
      {
         cout << "Game Played ? ";
         cin >> name;
         cout << "Game Score ? ";
         cin >>. score;
      }
      void DisplayData()
      {
         cout << "Sports Played: " << name << endl;
         cout << "Game Score: " << score << endl;
      }
      int SportsScore()
      {
         return score;
      }
};
class student : public virtual person    // note: virtual class
{
   private:
      int RollNo;          // student roll number in a class
```

```cpp
        char branch[20];  // branch or subject student is studying
    public:
        void ReadData()
        {
           cout << "Roll Number ? ";
           cin >> RollNo;
           cout << "Branch Studying ? ";
           cin >> branch;
        }
        void DisplayData()
        {
           cout << "Roll Number: " << RollNo << endl;
           cout << "Branch: " << branch << endl;
        }
};
class exam: public student
{
    protected:
        int Sub1Marks;
        int Sub2Marks;
    public:
        void ReadData()
        {
           cout << "Marks Scored in Subject 1 < Max:100> ? ";
           cin >> Sub1Marks;
           cout << "Marks Scored in Subject 2 < Max:100> ? ";
           cin >> Sub2Marks;
        }
        void DisplayData()
        {
           student::DisplayData(); // uses DisplayData() of student class
           cout << "Marks Scored in Subject 1: " << Sub1Marks << endl;
           cout << "Marks Scored in Subject 2: " << Sub2Marks << endl;
           cout << "Total Marks Scored: " << TotalMarks() << endl;
        }
        int TotalMarks()
        {
           return Sub1Marks + Sub2Marks;
        }
};
class result: public exam, public sports
{
    private:
        int total;
    public:
        void ReadData()
        {
           ReadPerson();          // access person class member
           student::ReadData();
```

```
      exam::ReadData();      // uses ReadData() of exam class
      sports::ReadData();
   }
   void DisplayData()
   {
      DisplayPerson();          // access person class member
      student::DisplayData();
      exam::DisplayData();
      sports::DisplayData();
      cout<<"Overall Performance,(exam+sports): "<<Percentage()<<" %";
   }
   int Percentage()
   {
      return (exam::TotalMarks() + SportsScore())/3;
   }
};
void main()
{
   result student;
   cout << "Enter data for Student ..." << endl;
   student.ReadData();
   cout << "Student details ..." << endl;
   student.DisplayData();
}
```

Run

```
Enter data for Student ...
Name ? Rajkumar
Sex ? M
Age ? 24
Roll Number ? 9
Branch Studying ? Computer-Technology
Marks Scored in Subject 1 < Max:100> ? 92
Marks Scored in Subject 2 < Max:100> ? 88
Sports Played ? Cricket
Game Score ? 85
Student details ...
Name: Rajkumar
Sex : M
Age : 24
Roll Number: 9
Branch: Computer-Technology
Marks Scored in Subject 1: 92
Marks Scored in Subject 2: 88
Total Marks Scored: 180
Sports Played: Cricket
Game Score: 85
Overall Performance, (exam+sports): 88 %
```

14.16 Object Composition–Delegation

Most of us understand concepts such as objects, interfaces, classes, and inheritance. The challenge lies in applying them to build flexible and reusable software. The two most common techniques for reusing functionality in object-oriented systems are *class inheritance* and *object composition*. As explained, inheritance is a mechanism of building a new class by deriving certain properties from other classes. In inheritance, if the class D is derived from the class B, it is said that *D is a kind of B*; the class D has all the properties of B in addition to the features of its own.

A commonly recurring situation is one where objects are used as data members in a class. The use of objects in a class as data members is referred to as *object composition*. Object composition is an alternative to class inheritance. Here, new functionality is obtained by assembling or composing objects to support more powerful functionality. This new approach takes a view that an object can be a collection of many other objects and the relationship is called a *has-a* relationship or *containership*. In OOP, the *has-a* relationship occurs when an object of one class is contained in another class as a data member. In other words, a class can contain objects of other classes as its members (see Figure 14.21).

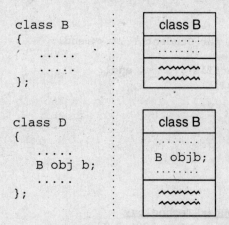

Figure 14.21: Object composition

In the case of inheritance (*kind of* relationship), the constructors of base class are first invoked before the constructor of the derived class. Whereas, in the case of *has-a* relationship, the constructor of the class D is invoked first and then the object of B is created. The concept of creating the member objects first using respective member constructors and then the other ordinary members can also be accomplished in *has-a* relationship by using an *initialization-list* in the constructor of the nested class. Consider the following class declarations

```
class B
{
    // body of a class
};
class D
{
    B ObjectB;      // b is a object of class B
    public:
      D( arg-list ) : ObjectB( arg-list1 );
};
```

where `arg-list` is the list of arguments to be supplied during the creation of objects of the class D. These parameters are used in initializing the members of class D. The `arg-list1` is used to initialize the members of the class B. In this case, first, the constructor of the class B is executed and then the constructor of the class D. The program `nesting.cpp` demonstrates the method of invoking a constructor of another object in a class.

```cpp
// nesting.cpp: Nested class constructor invocation
#include <iostream.h>
class B
{
   public:
      int num;
      B()                // no argument constructor
      { num = 0; }
      B( int a )
      {
         cout << "Constructor B( int a ) is invoked" << endl;
         num = a;
      }
};
class D
{
   int data1;
   B objb;          // object of another class
   public:
      D( int a ): objb( a )   // invokes the constructor of 'objb'
      {
         data1 = a;
      }
      void output()
      {
         cout << "Data in Object of Class D = " << data1 << endl;
         cout<<"Data in Member object of class B in class D = "<<objb.num;
      }
};
void main()
{
   D objd( 10 );
   objd.output();
}
```

Run

```
Constructor B( int a ) is invoked
Data in Object of Class D = 10
Data in Member object of class B in class D = 10
```

Delegation

Delegation is a way of making object composition as powerful as inheritance for reuse. In delegation, two objects are involved in handling a request: a receiving object delegates operations to its `del-egate`. This is analogous to subclasses deferring requests to parent classes. In certain situations, inheritance and containership relationships can serve the same purpose. It is illustrated by the following code:

```
class publication    // base class1
{
    // body of the publication class
};
class sales           // base class2
{
    // body of the sales class

};
```

The book class can be derived from the publication and sales classes using inheritance relationship as follows:

```
class book: public publication, public sales
{
    // body of the book class

};
```

The above functionality can also be achieved by composing objects of the classes publication and sales into the class book as follows:

```
class book
{
    ....
    publication pub; // composition of object of the class publication
    sales market;    // composition of object of the class sales
    ....
};
```

The book class contains instances of the classes publication and sales. The book class delegates its publication and sales issues to instances of the publication and sales classes (see Figure 14.22). Delegation shows that inheritance can be replaced with object composition as a mechanism for code reuse. The program publish2.cpp models the delegation shown in Figure 14.21.

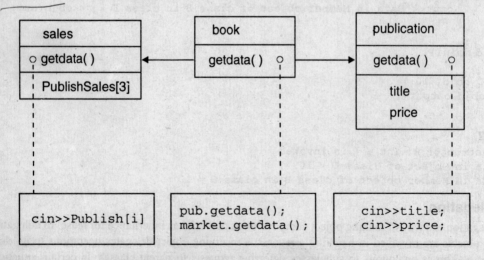

Figure 14.22:   Delegation in publication class

The classes `publication` and `sales` have the same declaration as in inheritance relation but they are used in a different way by the book class. Although containership is an alternative to inheritance and offers the functionality of inheritance, it does not provide flexibility of ownership. Inheritance relationship is simpler to implement and offers a clearer conceptual framework.

```cpp
// publish2.cpp: Publication, Sales details, Objects inside a class
#include <iostream.h>
class publication   // base class, appears as abstract class
{
   private:
      char title[40];    // name of the publication work
      float price;       // price of a publication
   public:
      void getdata()
      {
         cout << "\tEnter Title: ";
         cin >> title;
         cout << "\tEnter Price: ";
         cin >> price;
      }
      void display()
      {
         cout << "\tTitle = " << title << endl;
         cout << "\tPrice = " << price << endl;
      }
};
class sales    // base class
{
   private:
      float PublishSales[3];  //sales of publication for the last 3 months
   public:
      void getdata();
      void display();
};
void sales::getdata()
{
   int i;
   for( i = 0; i < 3; i++ )
   {
      cout << "\tEnter Sales of " << i+1 << " Month: ";
      cin >> PublishSales[i];
   }
}
void sales::display()
{
   int i;
   int TotalSales = 0;
   for( i = 0; i < 3; i++ )
   {
      cout<<"\tSales of " << i+1 <<" Month = " << PublishSales[i] << endl;
```

```
        TotalSales += PublishSales[i];
   }
   cout << "\tTotal Sales = " << TotalSales << endl;
}
class book
{
   private:
      int pages;  // number of pages in a book
   public:
      publication pub;
      sales market;
      void getdata() // overloaded function
      {
         pub.getdata();
         cout << "\tEnter Number of Pages: ";
         cin >> pages;
         market.getdata();
      }
      void display()
      {
         pub.display();
         cout << "\tNumber of Pages = " << pages << endl;
         market.display();
      }
};
void main()
{
   book book1;
   cout << "Enter Book Publication Data ..." << endl;
   book1.getdata();
   cout << "Book Publication Data ..." << endl;
   book1.display();
}
```

Run

```
Enter Book Publication Data ...
   Enter Title: Microprocessor-x86-Programming
   Enter Price: 180
   Enter Number of Pages: 750
   Enter Sales of 1 Month: 1000
   Enter Sales of 2 Month: 500
   Enter Sales of 3 Month: 800
Book Publication Data ...
   Title = Microprocessor-x86-Programming
   Price = 180
   Number of Pages = 705
   Sales of 1 Month = 1000
   Sales of 2 Month = 500
   Sales of 3 Month = 800
```

14.17 When to Use Inheritance ?

The following principles have to be followed to promote the use of inheritance in programming, which leads to code reuse, ease of code maintenance and extension:

- The most common use of inheritance and subclassing is for specialization, which is the most obvious and direct use of the *is-a* rule. If two abstract concepts A and B are being considered, and the sentence *A is a B* makes sense, then it is probably correct in making A as a subclass of B. Examples, *Car is a Vehicle, Triangle is a Shape,* etc.

- Another frequent use of inheritance is to guarantee that classes maintain a certain common interface; that is, they implement the same methods. The parent class can be a combination of implemented operations and operations that are to be implemented in the child classes. Often, there is no interface change between the supertype and subtype - the child implements the behavior described instead of its parent class. This feature has much significance with pure virtual function and will be discussed in the chapter *Virtual Functions*.

- Using generalization technique, a subclass extends the behavior of the superclass to create a more general kind of object. This is often applicable when one is building on a base of existing classes that should not, or cannot be modified.

- While subclassing for generalization modifies or expands on the existing functionality of a class, subclassing for extension adds totally new abilities. Subclassing for extension can be distinguished from subclassing for generalization in derivation. Generalization must override at least one method from the parent, and the functionality is tied to that of the parent whereas extension simply adds new methods to those of the parent, and functionality is less strongly tied to the existing parent methods.

- In subclassing for limitation, the behavior of the subclass is more restricted than the behavior of the superclass. Like subclassing for generalization, subclassing for limitation occurs most frequently when a programmer is building on a base of existing classes that should not or cannot be modified.

- Subclassing for variance is useful when two or more classes have similar implementations, but there does not seem to be any hierarchical relationship between the concepts represented by the classes. Often, however, a better alternative is to factor out the common code into an abstract class, and derive the classes from these common ancestors.

- Subclassing by combination occurs when a subclass represents a combined feature from two or more parent classes.

14.18 Benefits of Inheritance

There are many important benefits that can be derived from the proper use of inheritance. They are code reuse, ease of code maintenance and extension, and reduction in the time to market. The following situations explain benefits of inheritance:

- When inherited from another class, the code that provides a behavior required in the derived class need not have to be rewritten. Benefits of reusable code include increased reliability and a decreased maintenance cost because of sharing of the code by all its users.

- Code sharing can occur at several levels. For example, at a higher level, many users or projects can use the same class. These are referred to as software components. At the lower level, code can be shared by two or more classes within a project.

- When multiple classes inherit from the same superclass, it guarantees that the behavior they inherit will be the same in all cases.

◆ Inheritance permits the construction of reusable software components. Already, several such libraries are commercially available and many more are expected to be available in the near future.

◆ When a software system can be constructed largely out of reusable components, development time can be concentrated on understanding the portion of a new system. Thus, software systems can be generated more quickly and easily by rapid prototyping.

14.19 Cost of Inheritance

Inspite of many benefits of inheritance, it incurs compiler overhead. In inheritance relationship, there are certain members in the base class that are not at all used, however data space is allocated to them. This necessitates the need for specialized inheritance, which is complex to develop. The following are some of the perceived costs of inheritance:

◆ Inherited methods, which must be prepared to deal with arbitrary subclasses, are often slower than specialized codes.

◆ The use of any software library frequently imposes a size penalty over the use of systems specially constructed for a specific project. Although this expense may in some cases be substantial, it is also true that as memory cost decreases, the size of programs is becoming less important.

◆ Message passing by its very nature is a more costly operation than the invocation of simple procedures. The increased cost is however marginal and is often much lower in statically bound languages like C++. Therefore, the increased cost must be weighed against the benefits of the object oriented techniques.

◆ Although object oriented programming is often touted as a solution to the problem of software complexity, overuse or improper use of inheritance can simply replace one form of complexity with another.

Review Questions

14.1   What is inheritance ? Explain the need of inheritance with suitable examples.

14.2   What are the differences between the access specifiers private and protected ?

14.3   What are base and derived classes ? Create a base class called Stack and derived class called MyStack. Write a program to use these classes for manipulating objects.

14.4   Explain the syntax for declaring the derived class. Draw access privilege diagram for members of a base and derived class.

14.5   What are the differences between a C++ `struct` and C++ `class` in terms of encapsulation and inheritance ?

14.6   What are the different forms of inheritance supported by C++ ? Explain them with an example.

14.7   What is a class hierarchy ? Explain how inheritance helps in building class hierarchies.

14.8   Can base class, access members of a derived class ? Give reasons.

14.9   What is visibility mode? What are the different inheritance visibility modes supported by C++ ?

14.10 What are the differences between inheriting a class with public and private visibility mode ?

14.11 Declare two classes named `Window` and `Door`. Derive a new class called `House` from those two classes. The `Window` and `Door` bases classes must have attributes which reflects happy home. All classes must have interface functions such as overloaded stream operator functions for reading and displaying attributes. Write an interactive program to model the above relation.

14.12 State with reasons whether the following statements are TRUE or FALSE:
   (a) Both base and derived classes need not have constructors.
   (b) Only base class cannot have constructors.
   (c) Only derived class can have constructors.
   (d) No-argument constructor of the base class is invoked when a derived class is instantiated.
   (e) When a derived class is instantiated only the derived class constructors are invoked.
   (f) Derived class members cannot access private members of a base class.
   (g) When a derived class is instantiated, memory is allocated to all data members of both the base and derived classes.
   (h) If a base class does not has no-argument constructor and has parameterized constructors, it must be explicitly invoked from a derived class.
   (i) Constructors are invoked starting from the top base class to derived class order.
   (j) Destructors are invoked starting from the top base class to derived class order.
   (k) Destructors are invoked in the reverse order of constructors.
   (l) Base class constructors can be explicitly invoked from the derived class.

14.13 Explain how base class member functions can be invoked in a derived class if the derived class also has a member function with the same name.

14.14 What are virtual classes ? Explain the need for virtual classes while building class hierarchy.

14.15 What are abstract classes ? Explain the role of abstract class while building a class hierarchy.

14.16 Consider an example of declaring the examination result. Design three classes: Student, Exam, and Result. The Student class has data members such as those representing roll number, name, etc. Create the class Exam by inheriting the Student class. The Exam class adds data members representing the marks scored in six subjects. Derive the Result from the Exam class and it has its own data members such as total_marks. Write an interactive program to model this relationship. What type of inheritance this model belongs to ?

14.17 A new scheme for evaluation of students performance is formulated that gives also weightage for sports. Extend the inheritance relation discussed in the above program (14.16) such that the Result class also inherits properties of Sports class. Note that the Sports class is a derived class of the Student class. Write a program to model this relationship such that members of the Students class are not inherited twice. What type of inheritance this model belongs to ?

14.18 What is containership or delegation ? How does it differ from inheritance ?

14.19 It is required to find out the cost of constructing a house. Create a base class called House. There are two classes called Door and Window available. The House class has members which provide information related to the area of construction, door, windows details, etc. It delegates responsibility of computing the cost of doors and windows construction to Door and Window classes respectively. In C++, this can be achieved by having instances of the classes Door and Window in the House class. Write an interactive program to model the above relationship.

14.20 Write an interactive program to create a graphic class hierarchy. Create an abstract base class called Figure and derive two classes Close and Open from that. Declare two more classes called Polygon and Ellipse using the Close class. Create derived classes Line and Polyline from the Open class. Define three objects (triangle, rectangle, and pentagon) of the class Polygon. All classes must have appropriate member functions including constructors and destructors.

14.21 Discuss cost and benefits of inheritance emphasizing ease of design, code reusability, overhead, etc.

15

Virtual Functions

15.1 Introduction

Polymorphism in biology means the ability of an organism to assume a variety of forms. In C++, it indicates the form of a member function that can be changed at runtime. Such member functions are called *virtual functions* and the corresponding class is called *polymorphic class*. The objects of the polymorphic class, addressed by pointers, change at runtime and respond differently for the same message. Such a mechanism requires postponement of binding of a function call to the member function (declared as virtual) until runtime.

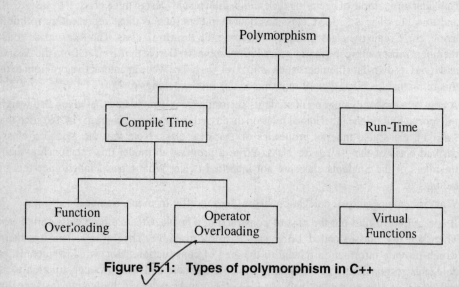

Figure 15.1: Types of polymorphism in C++

It has been observed that, *function overloading* and *operator overloading* features of C++ have allowed to realize polymorphism. Yet, there is another mechanism to implement polymorphism in C++; through *dynamic binding*. Figure 15.1, illustrates the taxonomy of polymorphism in C++. *Function overloading* is realized by invoking a suitable function whose *signature* matches with the arguments specified in the function call statement. *Operator overloading* is realized by allowing operators to operate on the user defined data-types with the same interface as that of the standard data types. In both cases, the compiler is aware of the complete information regarding the type and number of operands. Hence, it is possible for the compiler to select a suitable function at the compile-time.

15.2 Need for Virtual Functions

When objects of different classes in a class hierarchy, react to the same message in their own unique ways, they are said to exhibit polymorphic behavior. The program `parent1.cpp` illustrates the need of such polymorphic behavior. It has the base class `Father` and the derived class `Son` and has a member function (called `show`) with the same name and prototype. Note that, in C++ a pointer to the base class can be used to point to its derived class objects.

```cpp
// parent1.cpp: invoking derived class member through base class pointer
#include <iostream.h>
#include <string.h>
class Father
{
    char name[20];     // father name
    public:
      Father( char *fname )
      {
         strcpy( name, fname );  // fname contains Father's name
      }
      void show()      // show() in base class
      {
         cout << "Father name: " << name << endl;
      }
};
class Son: public Father
{
    char name[20];     // son name
    public:
    // two-argument constructor; invokes one-argument constructor of Father
      Son( char *sname, char *fname ): Father( fname )
      {
         strcpy( name, sname );  // sname contains son's name
      }
      void show()     // show() in derived class
      {
         cout << "Son name: " << name << endl;
      }
};
void main()
{
   Father *fp; // pointer to the Father class's objects;
   Father f1( "Eshwarappa" );
   fp = &f1;    // fp points to Father class object
   fp->show(); // display father show() function
   Son s1( "Rajkumar", "Eshwarappa" );
   fp = &s1;    // valid assignment
   fp->show(); // guess what is the output ? Father or Son!
}
```

Run

```
Father name: Eshwarappa
Father name: Eshwarappa
```

In main(), the statement

```
Father *fp; // pointer to the Father class's objects;
```

defines a pointer variable fp. The statement

```
fp = &f1;   // fp points to Father class object
```

assigns the address of the object f1 of the class Father to fp. After this, when statement such as

```
fp->show(); // display father show() function
```

is executed, the member function defined in the class Father is invoked. In C++ base class pointer is fully type-compatible with its derived class pointers and hence, the statement such as

```
fp = &s1;   // valid assignment
```

is valid. It assigns the address of the object s1 of the class Son to fp. After this, when statement

```
fp->show(); // guess what is the output ? Father or Son!
```

is executed, (it is interesting to note that) it still invokes the member function show() defined in the class Father!

There must be a provision to use the member function show() to display the state of objects of both the Father and Son classes using the same interface. This decision cannot be taken by the compiler, since the prototype is identical in both the cases.

In C++, a function call can be bound to the actual function either at compile time or at runtime. Resolving a *function call* at compile time is known as *compile-time* or *early* or *static binding* whereas, resolving a function call at runtime is known as *runtime* or *late* or *dynamic binding*. Runtime polymorphism allows to postpone the decision of selecting the suitable member functions until runtime. In C++, this is achieved by using *virtual functions*.

Virtual functions allow programmers to declare functions in a base class, which can be defined in each derived class. A pointer to an object of a base class can also point to the objects of its derived classes. In this case, a member function to be invoked depends on the the class's object to which the pointer is pointing. When a call to any object is made using the same interface (irrespective of object to which pointer variable is pointing), the function relevant to that object will be selected at run time. The program parent2.cpp illustrates the effect of virtual functions on an overloaded function in a class hierarchy.

```
// parent1.cpp: base class pointer and virtual function
#include <iostream.h>
#include <string.h>
class Father
{
   char name[20];    // father name
   public:
     Father( char *fname )
     {
        strcpy( name, fname );  // fname contains Father's name
     }
```

```
    virtual void show()     // show() in base class declared as virtual
    {
        cout << "Father name: " << name << endl;
    }
};
class Son: public Father
{
    char name[20];     // son name
    public:
    // two-argument constructor; invokes one-argument constructor of Father
        Son( char *sname, char *fname ): Father( fname )
        {
            strcpy( name, sname );  // sname contains son's name
        }
        void show()     // show() in derived class
        {
            cout << "Son name: " << name << endl;
        }
};
void main()
{
    Father *fp; // pointer to the Father class's objects;
    Father f1( "Eshwarappa" );
    fp = &f1;    // fp points to Father class object
    fp->show(); // display father show() function
    Son s1( "Rajkumar", "Eshwarappa" );
    fp = &s1;    // valid assignment
    fp->show(); // guess what is the output ? Father or Son!
}
```

Run

```
Father name: Eshwarappa
Son name: Rajkumar
```

It is interesting to note that the output generated by the above program is as expected. (What is interesting about the above program when compared to the earlier parent1.cpp ?) The only difference is, the member function show() defined in the class Father has the following declarator:

```
    virtual void show()     // show() in base class declared as virtual
```

It indicates that the member function show() is virtual and binding of a call to this function must be postponed until runtime. Hence, the last statement in main(),

```
    fp->show(); // guess what is the output ? Father or Son!
```

invokes the member function defined in the class Son!; during the execution of this statement, the system notices that, show() is a *virtual function* in base class and hence, it decides to invoke the member function defined in the derived class (instead of the base class) if the base class pointer is pointing to the derived class object.

The knowledge of pointers to base class and derived classes is essential to understand and to explore full potential of virtual functions. Hence, a detailed discussion on how the above program is able to work as expected and syntax of virtual functions is postponed to later section.

15.3 Pointer to Derived Class Objects

The concept of derived classes specifies hierarchical relationship between various objects and expresses the commonality between them. The properties common to different classes are placed at the top of the hierarchy, which becomes the base class, and all other classes are derived from this base class. A derived class is often said to inherit properties of the base class, and so, this relationship is known as the *inheritance relationship*.

Pointers can be used with the objects of base classes or derived classes. Pointer to objects of a base class are *type-compatible* with pointers to objects of a derived class, thus allowing a single pointer variable to be used as pointer to objects of a base class and its derived classes. For instance, in the above declaration having the classes Parent and Child, a pointer declared as a pointer to Parent objects can also be used as a pointer to Child objects. C++ makes polymorphism possible through a rule that one should memorize: *a base class pointer may address an object of its own class or an object of any class derived from the base class.* (See Figure 15.2.)

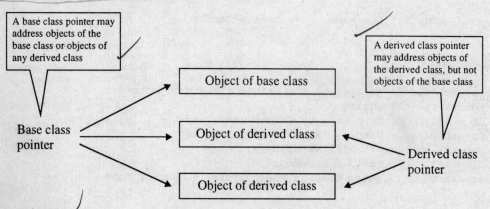

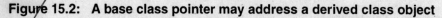

Figure 15.2:   A base class pointer may address a derived class object

Consider the following definitions to illustrate type compatibility of pointers.

```
Father *basep;   // pointer to Parent class
Father f;        // base class object
Son s;           // derived class object
```

The statement

```
basep = &f;
```

assigns the address of the object f of the class Father to the pointer variable basep. The statement

```
basep = &s;
```

assigns the address of the object s of the class Son to the pointer variable basep. Such an assignment is perfectly valid in C++, since the pointer to an object of a base class is fully *type-compatible* with pointer to objects of its derived classes.

The use of a pointer to the objects of a base class with the objects of its derived class raises a new problem. It does not allow access even to public members of a derived class. That is, it allows access only to those members inherited from the base class but not to the members which are defined in the derived class. Even in case, any member of the Son class has the same name as one of the members of the Father class, reference to it using the base class pointer basep will always access the base class member and not the derived class member. The program family1.cpp illustrates the use of the base pointer with the derived objects.

```cpp
// family1.cpp: pointer to base class and derived class objects
#include <iostream.h>
class Father
{
   protected:
      int f_age;
   public:
      Father( int n )
      {
         f_age = n;
      }
      int GetAge(void)
      {
         return f_age;
      }
};
// Son inherits all the properties of father
class Son : public Father
{
   protected:
      int s_age;
   public:
      Son( int n, int m ):Father(n)
      {
         s_age = m;
      }
      int GetAge(void)
      {
         return s_age;
      }
      void son_func()
      {
         cout << "son's own function";
      }
};
void main()
{
   Father *basep;
   basep = new Father(45);     // pointer to father
   cout << "basep points to base object..." << endl;
   cout << "Father's Age: ";
   cout << basep->GetAge() << endl;  // calls Father::GetAge
   delete basep;
   // accessing derived object
   basep = new Son(45, 20);    // pointer to son
   cout << "basep points to derived object..." << endl;
```

```
    cout << "Son's Age: ";
    cout << basep->GetAge() << endl;  // calls Father::GetAge()
    cout << "By typecasting, ((Son*) basep)..." << endl;
    cout << "Son's Age: ";
    cout << ((Son*) basep)->GetAge() << endl;     // calls Son::GetAge()
    delete basep;
    // accessing with derived object pointer
    Son son1( 45, 20 );
    Son *derivedp = &son1;
    cout << "accessing through derived class pointer..." << endl;
    cout << "Son's Age: ";
    cout << derivedp->GetAge();
}
```

Run
```
basep points to base object...
Father's Age: 45
basep points to derived object...
Son's Age: 45
By typecasting, ((Son*) basep)...
Son's Age: 20
accessing through derived class pointer...
Son's Age: 20
```

The expression, `basep->GetAge()` in the statement,

```
      cout << basep->GetAge() << endl;
```

invokes `GetAge()` defined in the `Father` class; `basep` holds the address of the `Father` class object. Even when the pointer `basep` is made to point to the derived object, it invokes the function defined in the `Father` class. However, the typecasted expression

```
      ((Son*) basep)->GetAge()
```

invokes the `GetAge()` defined in the derived class `Son` since the pointer is explicitly typecasted. In the above program, the use of the statement

```
      basep->son_func();   // error: not member of Father
```

generates a compilation error since, `son_func()`is not a member of the `Father` class or it is not within the scope of the `Father` class. However, when typecasted as

```
      ((Son *)basep)->son_func(); // OK
```

it will not generate any errors and will invoke the function defined in the `Son` class. (See Figure 15.3.)

The rule, *a base class pointer may address an object of its own class or an object of any class derived from the base class* is a one-way route. In other words, a pointer to a derived class object cannot address an object of the base class. If a pointer to a derived class is allowed to address the base class object, the compiler will expect members of the derived class to be in the base class also (which is not possible). (See Figure 15.4.) A pointer to the derived class can be used as a pointer to other classes which are derived from it. In general , *a pointer to a class at a particular level can be used as a pointer to objects of classes which are below that level in the class hierarchy.* Any attempt to override this rule is treated as an error.

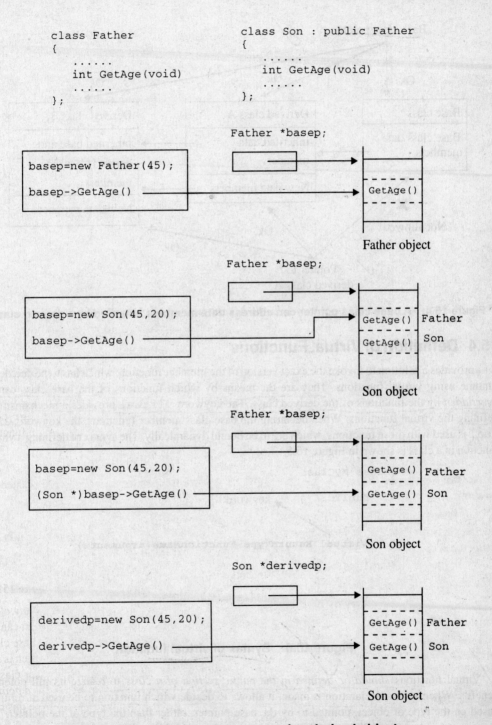

Figure 15.3: **A base pointer accessing derived objects**

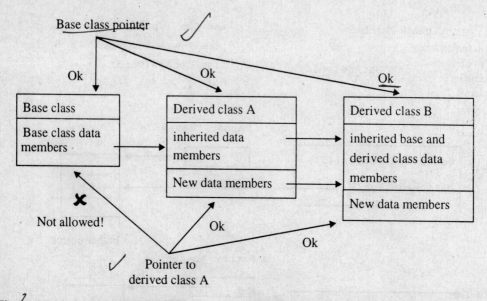

Figure 15.4: A base class pointer can address data members inherited by a derived class

15.4 Definition of Virtual Functions

C++ provides a solution to invoke the exact version of the member function, which has to be decided at runtime using virtual functions. They are the means by which functions of the base class can be *overridden* by the functions of the derived class. The keyword `virtual` provides a mechanism for defining the virtual functions. When declaring the base class member functions, the keyword `virtual` is used with those functions, which are to be bound dynamically. The syntax of defining a virtual function in a class is shown in Figure 15.5.

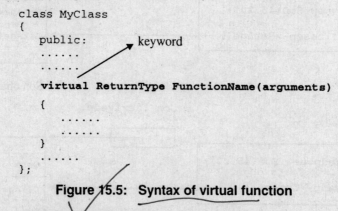

```
class MyClass
{
    public:
    ......                    keyword
    ......
    virtual ReturnType FunctionName(arguments)
    {
        ......
        ......
    }
    ......
};
```

Figure 15.5: Syntax of virtual function

Virtual functions *should be defined in the public section of a class* to realize its full potential benefits. When such a declaration is made, it allows to decide which function to be used at runtime, based on the type of object, pointed to by the base pointer, rather than the type of the pointer. The program `family2.cpp` illustrates the use of base pointer to point to different objects for executing different implementations of the virtual functions.

```cpp
// family2.cpp: Binding pointer to base class's object to base or derived
// objects at runtime and invoking respective members if they are virtual
#include <iostream.h>
class Father
{
   protected:
      int f_age;
   public:
      Father( int n )
      {
         f_age = n;
      }
      virtual int GetAge(void)
      {
         return f_age;
      }
};
// Son inherits all the properties of father
class Son : public Father
{
   protected:
      int s_age;
   public:
      Son( int n, int m ):Father(n)
      {
         s_age = m;
      }
      int GetAge(void)
      {
         return s_age;
      }
};
void main()
{
   Father *basep;
   // points to Father's object
   basep = new Father(45);      // pointer to father
   cout << "Father's Age: ";
   cout << basep->GetAge() << endl;  // calls Father::GetAge
   delete basep;
   // points to Son's object
   basep = new Son(45, 20);     // pointer to son
   cout << "Son's Age: ";
   cout << basep->GetAge() << endl;  // calls Son::GetAge()
   delete basep;
}
```

Run

```
Father's Age: 45
```

```
Son's Age: 20
```

The statement in the base class `Father`

```
virtual int GetAge(void)
```

indicates that an invocation of the `GetAge()` through the pointer to an object must be resolved at runtime based on *to which class's object the pointer is pointing.* A pointer to objects of the base class can be made to point to its derived class objects. Figure 15.6 illustrates the use of virtual functions in invoking functions at runtime.

Instances of the class `Father`

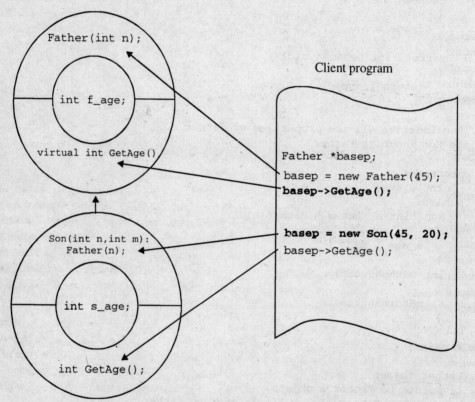

Instances of the class `Son`

Figure 15.6: Virtual functions and dynamic binding
(base pointer accessing derived objects)

In `main()`, the statement

```
Father *basep;
```

creates a pointer variable to the object of the base class `Father`, and the statement

```
basep = new Father(45);    // pointer to Father
```

creates an object of the class `Father` dynamically and assigns the pointer to the variable `basep`. The statement

```
cout << basep->GetAge() << endl;  // calls father::GetAge
```

invokes the member function GetAge() of the Father class. The statement

```
basep = new Son(45, 20);   // pointer to son
```

creates an object of the class Son dynamically and assigns its address to the pointer variable basep. The statement

```
cout << basep->GetAge() << endl;  // calls Son::GetAge
```

invokes the member function GetAge() of the Son class. If a call to a non-virtual function is made in this case, it invokes the member function of the class Father instead of the class Son. Note that the same pointer is able to invoke base or derived class's member function depending on which class's object the pointer is addressing.

It is important to note that, *virtual functions have to be accessed through a pointer to the base class*. However, they can be accessed through objects instead of pointers. It is to be remembered that runtime polymorphism is achieved only when a virtual function is accessed through a pointer to the base class. Note that, when a function is defined as virtual in the base class, and the same function is redefined in the derived class, then that function is *virtual by default*. Only class member functions can be declared as virtual functions. Regular functions and friend functions do not qualify as virtual functions.

15.5 Array of Pointers to Base Class Objects

A key property associated with polymorphism is late or dynamic binding, which ensures that if an operation with more than one implementation (method) is called on a *polymorphic entity*, then the appropriate version is selected on the basis of its *dynamic type (*and is called *runtime dispatch)*. In C++ runtime dispatch is only available for operations declared as virtual in the superclass. The process of runtime dispatch of a *function call request* is illustrated in Figure 15.7. The code which requests runtime dispatcher holds pointers to objects of different classes of the same class hierarchy. One of the simplest methods of implementation is to create an array of pointers (or pointers to pointers or linked list or any other data structure suitable for holding pointers to objects) as a *pointer store house* and invoke functions dynamically by scanning over them.

In Figure 15.7, it can be observed that, the class graphics has the function draw(), which plots the points and each of the derived classes, line, triangle, rectangle, and circle have their own draw() function, which plots the corresponding entities on the screen. In the absence of virtual functions, all the outputs would be picture of *points* because all the calls refer to the function draw() of the base class. However, with *virtual functions*, the same segment of program code generates different outputs by invoking the member function of the corresponding object.

The program draw.cpp illustrates a practical usage of virtual functions and models the problem described above. It uses an array of pointers to objects for storing pointer to objects of different derived classes of the base class graphics. The common interface function in all the classes is draw(), which is declared as virtual in the base class and defined as a normal function in all the other derived classes.

```
// draw.cpp: graphic class hierarchy with virtual functions
#include <iostream.h>
class graphics
{
    public:
        virtual void draw()  // virtual draw function in base class
```

```
        {
            cout << "point" << endl;
        }
};
class line: public graphics
{
    public:
        void draw()
        {
            cout << "line" << endl;
        }
};
class triangle: public graphics
{
    public:
        void draw()
        {
            cout << "triangle" << endl;
        }
};
class rectangle: public graphics
{
    public:
        void draw()
        {
            cout << "rectangle" << endl;
        }
};
class circle: public graphics
{
    public:
        void draw()
        {
            cout << "circle" << endl;
        }
};
void main()
{
    graphics point_obj;
    line line_obj;
    triangle tri_obj;
    rectangle rect_obj;
    circle circle_obj;
    graphics *basep[] =
    {
        &point_obj, &line_obj,
        &tri_obj, &rect_obj, &circle_obj
    };
    cout << "Following figures are drawn with basep[i]->draw()..."<< endl;
    for( int i = 0; i < 5; i++ )
        basep[i]->draw();
}
```

Run

```
Following figures are drawn with basep[i]->draw()...
point
line
triangle
rectangle
circle
```

In main(), the statement

```
for( int i = 0; i < 5; i++ )
    basep[i]->draw();
```

invokes a different `draw()` version based on the object to which the current pointer `basep[i]` is pointing. (See Figure 15.7.)

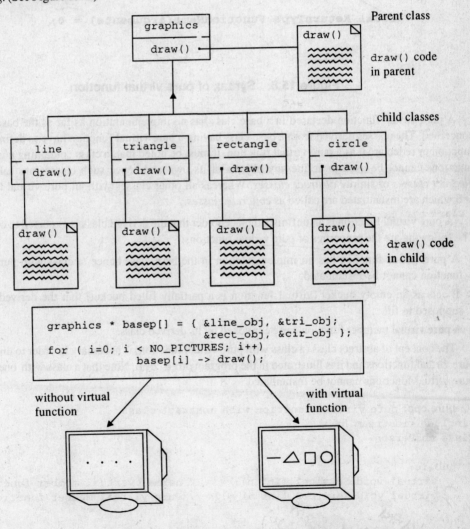

Figure 15.7:   Compile time and runtime binding of functions

15.6 Pure Virtual Functions

Virtual functions defined inside the base class normally serve as a framework for future design of the class hierarchy; these functions can be *overridden* by the methods in the derived classes. In most of the cases, these virtual functions are defined with a *null-body*; it has no definition. Such functions in the base class are similar to *do-nothing* or *dummy* functions and in C++, they are called *pure virtual* functions. The syntax of defining pure virtual functions is shown in Figure 15.8. Pure virtual function is declared as a virtual function with its declaration followed by = 0.

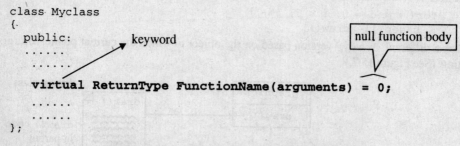

```
class Myclass
{
    public:                    ← keyword          [null function body]
    ......
    ......

    virtual ReturnType FunctionName(arguments) = 0;
    ......
    ......
};
```

Figure 15.8: Syntax of pure virtual function

A pure virtual function declared in a base class has no implementation as far as the base class is concerned. The classes derived from a base class having a pure virtual function have to define such a function or redeclare it as a pure virtual function. It must be noted that, a class containing pure virtual functions cannot be used to define any objects of its own and hence such classes are called *pure abstract classes* or simply *abstract classes*. Whereas all other classes without pure virtual functions and which are instantiated are called as *concrete classes*.

A pure virtual function is an unfinished placeholder that the derived class is expected to complete. The following are the properties of pure virtual functions:

* A pure virtual function has no implementation in the base class hence, a class with pure virtual function cannot be instantiated.

* It acts as an empty bucket (virtual function is a partially filled bucket) that the derived class is supposed to fill.

* A pure virtual member function can be invoked by its derived class.

The concept of abstract class (a class with pure virtual function) is necessary in order to understand pure virtual functions and it is illustrated in the program pure.cpp. Note that a class with one or more pure virtual functions cannot be instantiated.

```
// pure.cpp: pure virtual function with abstract class
#include <iostream.h>
class AbsPerson
{
    public:
        virtual void Service1 (int n);    // normal virtual member function
        virtual void Service2 (int n) = 0; // Pure virtual member function
};
```

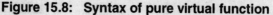

```
void AbsPerson::Service1(int n)
{
    Service2(n);
}
class Person : public AbsPerson
{
    public:
        void Service2(int n);
};
void Person::Service2(int n)
{
    cout << "The number of Years of service: " << (58 - n) << endl;
}
void main()
{
    Person Father, Son;
    Father.Service1(50);
    Son.Service2(20);
}
```

Run

```
The number of Years of service: 8
The number of Years of service: 38
```

In main(), the statement

```
        Father.Service1(50);
```

invokes the virtual function Service1() defined in the class AbsPerson and this in turn invokes Service2(). The Service2() of the class Person is invoked instead of AbsPerson; it is declared as a pure virtual function.

15.7 Abstract Classes

Abstract classes (classes with atleast one virtual function) can be used as a framework upon which new classes can be built to provide new functionality. A *framework* is a combination of class libraries (set of cooperative classes) with predefined flow of control. It can be a set of reusable abstract classes and the programmer can extend them. For instance, abstract classes can be easily tuned to develop graphical editors for different domains like artistic drawing, music composition, and mechanical CAD. Abstract classes with virtual functions can be used as an aid to debugging. Suppose, it is required to build a project consisting of a number of classes, possibly using a large number of programmers. It is necessary to make sure that every class in the project has a common debugging interface. A good approach is to create an abstract class from which all other classes in the project will be inherited. Since any new classes in the project must inherit from the base class, programmers are not free to create a different interface. Therefore, it can be guaranteed that all the classes in the project will respond to the same debugging commands.

The implementation of such a software system is illustrated by creating a header file containing an abstract debugger class with abstract functions. The header file debug.h is an example of an abstract base class for debugging. (The program pure.cpp has the pure abstract class AbsPerson.)

```
// debug.h: Abstract class for debugging
#include <iostream.h>
class debuggable
{
   public:
      virtual void dump()
      {
         cout<< "debuggable error:no dump() defined for this class"<<endl;
      }
};
```

If someone derives a new class from the class debuggable and does not redefine dump(), it
warns when the user tries to dump any object of that new class, because the base class version of
dump() will be used. A few classes derived from the class debuggable are listed in the program
dbgtest.cpp, for testing the debuggable class.

```
// dbgtest.cpp: testing of debuggable class
#include "debug.h"
class X: public debuggable
{
   int a, b, c;
   public:
      X( int aa = 0, int bb = 0, int cc = 0 )
      {
         a = aa; b = bb; c = cc;
      }
      // other implementation of dump
      void dump()
      {
         cout << "a=" << a << " b=" << b << " c=" << c << endl;
      }
};
class Y: public debuggable
{
   int i, j, k;
   public:
      Y( int ii = 0, int jj = 0, int kk = 0 )
      {
         i = ii; j = jj; k = kk;
      }
      // other implementation of dump
      void dump()
      {
         cout << "i=" << i << " j=" << j << " k=" << k << endl;
      }
};
class Z: public debuggable
{
   int p, q, r;
   public:
      Z( int pp = 0, int qq = 0, int rr = 0 )
```

```
        {
            p = pp; q = qq; r = rr;
        }
};
void main()
{
    X x( 1, 2, 3 );
    Y y( 2, 4, 5 );
    Z z;
    x.dump();
    y.dump();
    z.dump();
    // you can treat x, y, and z as members of the class debuggable
    debuggable *dbg[3];
    dbg[0] = &x;
    dbg[1] = &y;
    dbg[2] = &z;
    cout<< "Dumping through passing the same message to all objects...\n";
    for( int i = 0; i < 3; i++ )
        dbg[i]->dump();
}
```

Run

```
a=1 b=2 c=3
i=2 j=4 k=5
debuggable error: no dump() defined for this class
Dumping through passing the same message to all objects...
a=1 b=2 c=3
i=2 j=4 k=5
debuggable error: no dump() defined for this class
```

In main(), the statements

```
    x.dump();
    y.dump();
```

invoke their own implementation of dump() whereas, the statement

```
    z.dump();
```

executes the virtual function dump() defined in the base class since it does not have an implementation of dump() in its own class. The statement which is in the scope of the for loop

```
    dbg[i]->dump();
```

passes the same messages to all the objects, which are instances of the class derived from the class debuggable. All of them respond in different ways to the same message. If they do not have any response-function of their own, they respond through their parent function (in this the object z responds by invoking the dump() defined in the parent class debuggable). Thus, any object in the system can be dumped or can add the object's address to the list of debuggable pointers and call dump() as a member of the object. Hence, it is said that "switch *statements are to C what* virtual *functions are to C++.*"

An abstract class becomes very powerful when it is integrated into a system and changes are required for the interface. Imagine how difficult this would have been in a conventional language. First, it is required to make sure that the debugging interface is properly implemented in all parts of the system. If changes to the interface are to be made, it is required to check each part separately to ensure that the new interface is properly added. With the availability of abstract classes in C++, it just requires to change the abstract class and recompile the system. The new interface automatically propagates throughout the system; when virtual function(s) added in the new interface is redefined in the derived class, the compiler ensures strict conformation to the interface. For instance, suppose the programmer is required to add a function called `trace()` to class `debuggable`, the header file can be modified to accommodate this function as shown in `debug2.h`.

```
// debug2.h: Abstract class for debugging
#include <iostream.h>
class debuggable
{
   public:
     virtual void dump()
     {
        cout<<"debuggable error: no dump() defined for this class"<<endl;
     }
     virtual void trace()
     {
        cout<<"debuggable error: no trace() defined for this class"<<endl;
     }
};
```

When this new abstract class is used in `dbgtest.cpp`, the virtual function `trace()` may or may not be redefined in the derived classes X, Y, and Z. It is optional until needed. That is, the debugging framework can be designed into classes, and even changes can be made to the framework midway so that it can reflect throughout the project without any problem. When `trace()` is redefined in the new classes, the interface (function prototype) must be identical as in the base class `debuggable`. If they do not conform to the interface declared in the parent class, the compiler will either generate an error or make the function non-virtual, depending on how the compiler implementation handles this issue.

An abstract class with one or more pure virtual functions has the following properties:

- Describes an unrealized concept (which is yet to be conceived).
- Objects of an abstract class type cannot be created.
- Derived classes can be built from these abstract classes.
- Objects of the derived classes can be created provided these derived classes do not have any pure virtual functions.

15.8 Virtual Destructors

Just like declaring member functions as virtual, destructors can be declared as virtual, whereas constructors cannot be virtual. Virtual destructors are controlled in the same way as virtual functions. When a derived object pointed to by the base class pointer is deleted, destructor of the derived class as well as destructors of all its base classes are invoked. It is illustrated in the program `family3.cpp`. In this program, if the destructor is made as *non-virtual* destructor in the base class, only the base class's destructor is invoked when the object is deleted.

```
// family3.cpp: virtual destructors in parent class
#include <iostream.h>
#include <string.h>
class Father
{
   protected:
      char *f_name;
   public:
      Father( char *name )
      {
         f_name = new char[ strlen(name)+1 ];
         strcpy( f_name, name );
      }
      virtual ~Father() // virtual destructors
      {
         delete f_name;
         cout << "~Father() is invoked" << endl;
      }
      virtual void show()  // virtual function
      {
         cout << "Father's Name: " << f_name << endl;
      }
};
// Son inherits all the properties of father
class Son : public Father
{
   protected:
      char *s_name;
   public:
      Son( char * fname, char * sname ):Father( fname )
      {
         s_name = new char[ strlen(sname)+1 ];
         strcpy( s_name, sname );
      }
      ~Son()
      {
         delete s_name;
         cout << "~Son() is invoked" << endl;
      }
      void show()
      {
         cout << "Father's Name: " << f_name << endl;
         cout << "Son's Name: " << s_name << endl;
      }
};
void main()
{
   Father *basep;
   // points to Father's object
   basep = new Father( "Eshwarappa" );    // pointer to father
   cout << "basep points to base object..." << endl;
```

```
    basep->show();
    delete basep;
    // points to Son's object
    basep = new Son("Eshwarappa", "Rajkumar");   // pointer to son
    cout << "basep points to derived object..." << endl;
    basep->show();
    delete basep;
}
```

Run

```
basep points to base object...
Father's Name: Eshwarappa
~Father() is invoked
basep points to derived object...
Father's Name: Eshwarappa
Son's Name: Rajkumar
~Son() is invoked
~Father() is invoked
```

In main(), the variable basep is a pointer to the base class Father. The statement

```
    basep = new Son("Eshwarappa", "Rajkumar");   // pointer to son
```

creates dynamic object of the class Son by allocating memory required for its data members also. It is important that memory allocated to object and its data members has to be released explicitly when the object pointed to by basep goes out of scope.

In the normal case, when the destructor of the base class is not a virtual function, the statement

```
    delete basep;
```

would have deleted only the first string through the base class destructor, but in this case it also deletes the string, Eshwarappa through the derived class destructor. The base class destructor is declared as virtual and basep actually addresses the Son's object and hence, the destructors in the Son's class as well as the Father's class are invoked. Note that while constructing an object, *the constructors are invoked from the top of a hierarchy (top most base class) upto the current class and while destroying an object, destructors are invoked from the current class to the top most base class in the hierarchy.* For instance, in the above program, the statement

```
    basep = new Son("Eshwarappa", "Rajkumar");   // pointer to son
```

invokes the constructor of the class Father first and then the constructor of the class Son. The statement

```
    delete basep;
```

having basep pointing to the dynamically created instance of the class Son, invokes destructor of the class Son first and the destructor of the class Father (unlike in the natural world, in C++ son dies first before his father; however there are exceptions).

Virtual destructor is used in the following situations:

- A virtual destructor is used when one class needs to delete object of a derived class that are addressed by the base-pointers and invoke a base class destructor to release resources allocated to it.

- Destructors of a base class should be declared as virtual functions. When a delete operation is performed on an object by a pointer or reference, the program will first call the object destructor instead of the destructor associated with the pointer or reference type.

15.9 How is Dynamic Binding Achieved ?

To perform dynamic binding of a member function in C++, the function is declared as virtual. Any function in a class can be declared as virtual. When functions are declared as virtual, the compiler adds a data member *secretly* to the class. This data member is referred to as a virtual **pointer** (VPTR). Virtual Table (VTBL) contains pointers to all the functions that have been declared as virtual in a class, or any other classes that are inherited. The program `vptrsize.cpp` shows evidence of the secret existence of VPTR.

```
// vptrsize.cpp: using sizeof operator to detect existence of VPTR
#include <iostream.h>
class nonvirtual
{
   int x;
   public:
      void func()
      {}
};
class withvirtual
{
   int x;
   public:
      virtual void func()
      {}
};
void main()
{
   cout << "sizeof( nonvirtual ) = " << sizeof( nonvirtual ) << endl;
   cout << "sizeof( withvirtual ) = " << sizeof( withvirtual );
}
```

Run

```
sizeof( nonvirtual ) = 2
sizeof( withvirtual ) = 4
```

Whenever a call to a virtual function is made in the C++ program, the compiler generates code to treat VPTR as the starting address of an array of pointers to functions. The function call code simply indexes into this array and calls the function located at the *indexed addresses*. The binding of the function call always requires this dynamic indexing activity; it always happens at runtime. That is, if a call to a virtual function is made, while treating the object in question, as a member of its base class, the correct derived class function will be called. It is illustrated in the program `shapes.cpp`.

```
// shapes.cpp: inheritance and virtual functions
#include <iostream.h>
class description
{
   protected:  // so derived class have access
      char *information;
   public:
      description( char *info ):information( info )
      {}
```

```
        virtual void show()
        {
            cout << information << endl;
        }
};
class sphere: public description
{
    float radius;
    public:
        sphere( char *info, float rad ):description(info), radius( rad )
        {}
        void show()
        {
            cout << information;
            cout << " Radius = " << radius << endl;
        }
};
class cube: public description
{
    float edge_length;
    public:
        cube(char *info, float edg_len):description(info),edge_length(edg_len )
        {}
        void show()
        {
            cout << information;
            cout << " Edge Length = " << edge_length << endl;
        }
};
sphere small_ball( "mine", 1.0 ),
      beach_ball( "plane", 24.0 ),
      plan_toid( "moon", 1e24 );
cube crystal( "carbon", 1e-24 ),
     ice( "party", 1.0 ),
     box( "card board", 16.0 );
description *shapes[] =
{
        &small_ball,
        &beach_ball,
        &plan_toid,
        &crystal,
        &ice,
        &box
};
void main()
{
        small_ball.show();
        beach_ball.show();
        plan_toid.show();
        crystal.show();
        ice.show();
```

```
    box.show();
    // put all description in the list
    cout << "Dynamic Invocation of show()..." << endl;
    for( int i = 0; i < sizeof( shapes )/sizeof( shapes[0] ); i++ )
        shapes[i]->show();
}
```

Run

```
mine Radius = 1
plane Radius = 24
moon Radius = 1e+24
carbon Edge Length = 1e-24
party Edge Length = 1
card board Edge Length = 16
Dynamic Invocation of show()...
mine Radius = 1
plane Radius = 24
moon Radius = 1e+24
carbon Edge Length = 1e-24
party Edge Length = 1
card board Edge Length = 16
```

From the output, it can be observed that virtual functions are essential for creating objects with the same interface and similar functionality but with different implementations. A debatable issue is "Why is the programmer given the option to make a function virtual and why not just let the compiler create all functions as virtual ?" C++ allows the programmer to decide whether to declare function as virtual or non-virtual. This design decision has been made to favor runtime efficiency. A virtual function requires an extra dereference to be made when it is invoked. The language defaults are in favor of maximum efficiency, which is accomplished through static binding. Thus, the programmer is forced to be aware of the difference between early and late binding, and to know when to apply late binding. Several other object-oriented languages, such as Smalltalk and Java, always use *late binding*.

Virtual Functions Trade-Offs

C++ stores the addresses of the virtual member functions in the internal table. When C++ statements call these member functions, the correct address is fetched from the internal table; this process consumes some time. Hence, the use of virtual functions reduces the program's performance to a certain extent but at the same time offers greater flexibility.

15.10 Rules for Virtual Functions (8 rules)

The following rules hold good with respect to virtual functions:

◆ When a virtual function in a base class is created, there must be a definition of the virtual function in the base class even if base class version of the function is never actually called. However pure virtual functions are exceptions.

◆ They cannot be static members.

◆ They can be a friend function to another class.

◆ They are accessed using object pointers.

- A base pointer can serve as a pointer to a derived object since it is type-compatible whereas a derived object pointer variable cannot serve as a pointer to base objects.
- Its prototype in a base class and derived class must be identical for the virtual function to work properly.
- The class cannot have virtual constructors, but can contain virtual destructor. In fact, virtual destructors are essential to the solutions of some problems. It is also possible to have *virtual operator overloading*.
- More importantly, to realize the potential benefits of virtual functions supporting runtime polymorphism, they should be declared in the *public* section of a class.

Review Questions

15.1 Describe different methods of realizing polymorphism in C++.

15.2 Justify the need for virtual functions in C++.

15.3 Why C++ supports type compatibles pointers unlike C ?

15.4 State which of the following statements are TRUE or FALSE. Give reasons.
(a) In C++, pointers to int data type can be used to point to float types.
(b) Pointer to base class can point to an object of any class.
(c) Pointer to a class at the top of the class hierarchy can point to any class objects in that hierarchy.
(d) Virtual functions allows to invoke different function with the same statement.
(e) The sizeof a class having virtual function is the same as that without virtual functions.
(f) A class with virtual function can be instantiated.
(g) A class with pure virtual function can be instantiated.
(h) A class with pure virtual functions is created by designers whereas, derived classes are created by programmers.
(i) Specification of a virtual function in the base class and its derived class must be same.
(j) Pure virtual functions postpone implementation of a member function to its derived class.

15.5 Create a vehicle class hierarchy with top most base having the following specification:

```
class vehicle
{
    int reg_no;
    int cost;
    public:
        virtual void start() = 0;
        virtual void stop();
        virtual void show();
        ....
};
```

Write a complete program having derived classes such as heavy, lightweight vehicle, etc.

15.6 What is runtime dispatching ? Explain how C++ handles runtime dispatching.

15.7 What are pure virtual functions ? How do they differ from normal virtual functions ?

15.8 What are abstract classes ? Write a program having student as an abstract class and create many derived classes such as Engineering, Science, Medical, etc., from the student class. Create their objects and process them.

15.9 What are virtual destructors ? How do they differ from normal destructors ? Can constructors be declared as virtual constructors ? Give reasons.

15.10 Explain how dynamic binding is achieved by the C++ compilers. What is the size of the following classes:

```
class X
{
    int x;
    public:
        void read();
};
class Y
{
    int a;
    public:
        virtual void read();
};
class Z
{
    int a;
    public:
        virtual void read();
        virtual void show();
};
```

15.11 What are the rules that need to be kept in mind in deciding virtual functions ?

15.12 Correct the errors in the following program and include missing components:

```
class ABC
{
    int a;
    public:
};
void main()
{
    ABC a1;
    a1.read();
    a1.show();
    ABC a2 = 10;
    a2.show();
}
```

15.13 Consider an example of book shop which sells books and video tapes. These two classes are inherited from the base class called media. The media class has command data members such as title and publication. The book class has data members for storing number of pages in a book and the tape class has the playing time in a tape. Each class will have member functions such as read() and show(). In the base class, these members have to be defined as virtual functions. Write a program which models the class hierarchy for book shop and processes objects of these classes using pointers to the base class.

16
Generic Programming with Templates

16.1 Introduction

A significant benefit of object-oriented programming is reusability of code which eliminates redundant coding. An important feature of C++ called *templates* strengthens this benefit of OOP and provides great flexibility to the language. Templates support *generic programming,* which allows to develop reusable software components such as functions, classes, etc., supporting different data types in a single framework. For instance, functions such as sort, search, swap, etc., which support various data types can be developed.

A template in C++ allows the construction of a family of template functions and classes to perform the same operation on different data types. The templates declared for functions are called *function templates* and those declared for classes are called *class templates*. They perform appropriate operations depending on the data type of the parameters passed to them.

A C++ function/class is normally designed to handle a specific data type. Often, their functionality makes sense conceptually with other data types. Considering a class/function as a framework around a data-type and supporting various operations on that data type, makes sense to isolate the data type altogether from the function/class. It allows a single template to deal with a *generic data* type T.

16.2 Function Templates

There are several functions of considerable importance which have to be used frequently with different data types. The limitation of such functions is that they operate only on a particular data type. It can be overcome by defining that function as a *function template* or *generic function*. A function template specifies how an individual function can be constructed. The program mswap.cpp illustrates the need for function templates. It consists of multiple swap functions for swapping different values of different data types.

```
// mswap.cpp: Multiple swap functions
#include <iostream.h>
void swap( char & x, char & y )
{
   char t;  // temporary variable used in swapping
   t = x;
   x = y;
   y = t;
}
void swap( int & x, int & y ) // by reference
{
   int t;   // temporary variable used in swapping
```

```
    t = x;
    x = y;
    y = t;
}
void swap( float & x, float & y ) // by reference
{
    float t; // temporary variable used in swapping
    t = x;
    x = y;
    y = t;
}
void main()
{
    char ch1, ch2;
    cout << "Enter two Characters <ch1, ch2>: ";
    cin >> ch1 >> ch2;
    swap( ch1, ch2 ); // compiler invokes swap( char &a, char &b );
    cout << "On swapping <ch1, ch2>: " << ch1 << " " << ch2 << endl;
    int a, b;
    cout << "Enter two integers <a, b>: ";
    cin >> a >> b;
    swap( a, b ); // compiler invokes swap( int &a, int &b );
    cout << "On swapping <a, b>: " << a << " " << b << endl;
    float c, d;
    cout << "Enter two floats <c, d>: ";
    cin >> c >> d;
    swap( c, d ); // compiler invokes swap( float &a, float &b );
    cout << "On swapping <c, d>: " << c << " " << d;
}
```

Run

```
Enter two Characters <ch1, ch2>: R K
On swapping <ch1, ch2>: K R
Enter two integers <a, b>: 5 10
On swapping <a, b>: 10 5
Enter two floats <c, d>: 20.5 99.5
On swapping <c, d>: 99.5 20.5
```

The above program has three swap functions

```
        void swap( char & x, char & y );
        void swap( int & x, int & y );
        void swap( float & x, float & y );
```

whose logic of swapping is same and differs only in terms of data-type. Such functions can be declared as a single function template without redefining them for each and every data type. The C++ template feature enables substitution of a single piece of code for all these overloaded functions with a single template function as follows:

```
template <class T>
void swap( T & x, T & y ) // by reference
{
    T t;  // template type temporary variable used in swapping
```

```
    t = x;
    x = y;
    y = t;
}
```

Such functions are known as *function templates*. When swap operation is requested on operands of any data type, the compiler creates a function internally without the user intervention and invokes the same.

Syntax of Function Template

A function template is prefixed with the keyword template and a list of template type arguments. These template-type arguments are called *generic data types*, since their exact representation (memory requirement and data representation) is not known in the declaration of the function template. It is known only at the point of a call to a function template. The syntax of declaring the function template is shown in Figure 16.1.

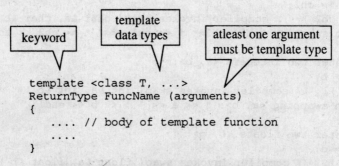

```
template <class T, ...>
ReturnType FuncName (arguments)
{
    .... // body of template function
    ....
}
```

Figure 16.1:   Syntax of function template

The syntax of a function template is similar to normal function except that it uses variables whose data types are not known until a call to it is made. A call to a template function is similar to that of a normal function and the parameters can be of any data-type. When the compiler encounters a call to such functions, it identifies the data type of the parameters and creates a function internally and makes a call to it. The internally created function is unknown to the user. The program gswap.cpp makes use of templates and avoids the overhead of rewriting functions having body of the same pattern, but operating on different data types.

```
// gswap.cpp: generic function for swapping
#include <iostream.h>
template <class T>
void swap( T & x, T & y ) // by reference
{
    T t;  // template type temporary variable used in swapping
    t = x;
    x = y;
    y = t;
}
void main()
{
    char ch1, ch2;
    cout << "Enter two Characters <ch1, ch2>: ";
```

```
    cin >> ch1 >> ch2;
    swap( ch1, ch2 ); // compiler creates and calls swap( char &x, char &y );
    cout << "On swapping <ch1, ch2>: " << ch1 << " " << ch2 << endl;
    int a, b;
    cout << "Enter two integers <a, b>: ";
    cin >> a >> b;
    swap( a, b );  // compiler creates and calls swap( int &x, int &y );
    cout << "On swapping <a, b>: " << a << " " << b << endl;
    float c, d;
    cout << "Enter two floats <c, d>: ";
    cin >> c >> d;
    swap( c, d );  // compiler creates and calls swap( float &x, float &y );
    cout << "On swapping <c, d>: " << c << " " << d;
}
```

Run

```
Enter two Characters <ch1, ch2>: R K
On swapping <ch1, ch2>: K R
Enter two integers <a, b>: 5 10
On swapping <a, b>: 10 5
Enter two floats <c, d>: 20.5 99.5
On swapping <c, d>: 99.5 20.5
```

In main(), the statement

```
    swap( ch1, ch2 );
```

invokes the swap function with char type variables. When it is encountered by the compiler, it internally creates a function of type,

```
    swap( char &x, char &y );
```

The compiler automatically identifies the data type of the arguments passed to the template function and creates a new function and makes an appropriate call. The process of handling the template functions by the compiler is totally invisible to the user. Similarly, the compiler converts the following calls

```
    swap( a, b );  // compiler creates swap( int &x, int &y );
    swap( c, d );  // compiler creates swap( float &x, float &y );
```

into equivalent functions and calls them based on their parameter data types. Theoretically speaking, all the data types share the same template function swap. However, the complier has created three swap functions operating on char, int, and float.

Invocation of Function Template

The example of the function template for finding the maximum of two data items is given below:

```
    template <class T>
    T max( T a, T b )
    {
        if( a > b )
            return a;
        else
            return b;
    }
```

The function template is invoked in the same manner as a normal function as follows:

```
        x = max( y, z );
```
However, it is processed differently by the compiler. The compiler creates a new function using its template and makes a call to it. A function generated internally from a function template is called *template function*. Template arguments are not specified explicitly while calling a function template. The program max1.cpp demonstrates the method of declaring a function template and its usage.

```cpp
// max1.cpp: finding maximum of two data items using function template
#include <iostream.h>
template <class T>
T max( T a, T b )
{
   if( a > b )
      return a;
   else
      return b;
}
void main()
{
   // max with character data types
   char ch, ch1, ch2;
   cout << "Enter two characters <ch1, ch2>: ";
   cin >> ch1 >> ch2;
   ch = max( ch1, ch2 );
   cout << "max( ch1, ch2 ): " << ch << endl;
   // max with integer data types
   int a, b, c;
   cout << "Enter two integers <a, b>: ";
   cin >> a >> b;
   c = max( a, b );
   cout << "max( a, b): " << c << endl;
   // max with floating data types
   float f1, f2, f3;
   cout << "Enter two floats <f1, f2>: ";
   cin >> f1 >> f2;
   f3 = max( f1, f2 );
   cout << "max( f1, f2): " << f3;
}
```

Run

```
Enter two characters <ch1, ch2>: A B
max( ch1, ch2 ): B
Enter two integers <a, b>: 20 10
max( a, b): 20
Enter two floats <f1, f2>: 20.5 30.9
max( f1, f2): 30.9
```

In the above program, the compiler creates as many max() functions as the number of calls to the function template max(). Once, an internal function is created for a particular data type, all future invocation to the function template with that data type will refer to it. For instance, the statement

```
        c = max( a, b );      // a, b, and c are integers
```

invokes function template max() first time, the compiler creates max() which handles integer data. Future invocation such as,

```
i = max( j, k );          // i, j, and k are integers
```

accesses the function created at the first call since, the data type parameters j and k is the same as that of the first call. However, if j and k are other than integers, it creates a new function internally and makes a call to it.

Function and Function Template

Function templates are not suitable for handling all data types, and hence, it is necessary to override function templates by using normal functions for specific data types. When a statement such as

```
max( str1, str2 )
```

is executed, it will not produce the desired result. The above call compares memory addresses of strings instead of their contents. The logic for comparing strings is different from comparing integer or floating-point data type. It requires the function having the definition:

```
char * max(char * a, char * b)
{
    return( strcmp(a, b) > 0 ? a : b);
}
```

If the program has both the function and function template with the same name, first, the compiler selects the normal function, if it matches with the requested data type, otherwise, it creates a function using a function template. This is illustrated in the program max2.cpp.

```
// max2.cpp: maximum of standard and derived data type items
#include <iostream.h>
#include <string.h>
template <class T>
T max( T a, T b )
{
    if( a > b )
        return a;
    else
        return b;
}
// specifically for string data types
char * max( char *a, char *b )
{
    if( strcmp( a, b ) > 0 )
        return a;
    else
        return b;
}
void main()
{
    // max with character data types
    char ch, ch1, ch2;
    cout << "Enter two characters <ch1, ch2>: ";
    cin >> ch1 >> ch2;
    ch = max( ch1, ch2 );
    cout << "max( ch1, ch2 ): " << ch << endl;
```

```
// max with integer data types
int a, b, c;
cout << "Enter two integers <a, b>: ";
cin >> a >> b;
c = max( a, b );
cout << "max( a, b): " << c << endl;
// max with string data types
char str1[20], str2[20];
cout << "Enter two strings <str1, str2>: ";
cin >> str1 >> str2;
cout << "max( str1, str2 ): " << max( str1, str2 );
}
```

Run

```
Enter two characters <ch1, ch2>: A Z
max( ch1, ch2 ): Z
Enter two integers <a, b>: 5 6
max( a, b): 6
Enter two strings <str1, str2>: Tejaswi Rajkumar
max( str1, str2 ): Tejaswi
```

In main(), the statement

```
        cout << "max( str1, str2 ): " << max( str1, str2 );
```

has the expression,

```
        max( str1, str2 )
```

The compiler selects the user-defined normal function instead of creating a new function, since the function call is matching with the user-defined function.

Bubble Sort Function Template

Sorting is the most commonly used operation particularly in data processing applications. These applications require function to sort data elements of different data types. Such functions can be declared as function template and can be used to sort data items of any type. The program bsort.cpp illustrates the declaration of function template for bubble sort and its use on integer and floating point data types.

```
// bsort.cpp: template functions for bubble-sort
#include <iostream.h>
enum boolean { false, true };
template <class T>
void swap( T & x, T & y ) // by reference
{
  T t;    // template type temporary variable used in swapping
  t = x;
  x = y;
  y = t;
}
template< class T >
void BubbleSort( T & SortData, int Size )
{
  boolean swapped = true;
```

```
    for( int i = 0; ( i < Size - 1 ) && swapped; i++ )
    {
        swapped = false;
        for( int j = 0; j < ( Size - 1 ) - i; j++ )
            if( SortData[ j ] > SortData[ j + 1 ] )
            {
                swapped = true;
                swap( SortData[ j ], SortData[ j + 1 ] );
            }
    }
}
void main( void )
{
    int IntNums[25];
    float FloatNums[25];
    int i, size;
    cout << "Program to sort elements..." << endl;
    // Integer numbers sorting
    cout << "Enter the size of the integer vector <max-25>: ";
    cin >> size;
    cout << "Enter the elements of the integer vector..." << endl;
    for( i = 0; i < size; i++ )
        cin >> IntNums[i];
    BubbleSort( IntNums, size );
    cout << "Sorted Vector:" << endl;
    for( i = 0; i < size; i++ )
        cout << IntNums[i] << "  ";
    // Floating point numbers sorting
    cout << "\nEnter the size of the float vector <max-25>: ";
    cin >> size;
    cout << "Enter the elements of the float vector..." << endl;
    for( i = 0; i < size; i++ )
        cin >> FloatNums[i];
    BubbleSort( FloatNums, size );
    cout << "Sorted Vector:" << endl;
    for( i = 0; i < size; i++ )
        cout << FloatNums[i] << "  ";
}
```

Run

```
Program to sort elements...
Enter the size of the integer vector <max-25>: 4
Enter the elements of the integer vector...
8
4
1
6
Sorted Vector:
1  4  6  8
Enter the size of the float vector <max-25>: 3
```

```
Enter the elements of the float vector...
8.5
3.2
8.9
Sorted Vector:
3.2   8.5   8.9
```

In main(), when the compiler encounters the statement

```
BubbleSort( IntNums, size );
```

it creates the bubble sort function internally for sorting integer numbers; the parameter IntNums is of type integer. Similarly, when the compiler encounters the statement

```
BubbleSort( FloatNums, size );
```

it creates bubble sort function internally for sorting floating point numbers. The same template function can be used to sort any other data types. Note that the compiler creates a function internally for a particular data type only once and if there are more requests with the same data type, the compiler accesses the old internally created function.

Usage of Template Arguments

Every template-argument specified in the template-argument-list *must* be used as a generic data type for the definition of the formal parameters. If any of the generic data type is not used in the definition of formal parameters, such function templates are treated as invalid templates. The use of partial number of generic data types in a function defining formal parameters is also treated as an error. All the formal parameters need not be of generic type. The following sections show some function templates which are invalid declarations:

1. *No-argument template function*

```
template < class T >
T pop( void )            // error: T is not used as an argument
{
    return *--Stack;
}
```

2. *Template-type argument unused*

```
template < class T >
void test( int x )       // error: T is not used as an argument
{
    T temp;
    // .. test stuff
}
```

3. *Usage of Partial number of template arguments*

```
template< class T, class U >
void insert( T & x )   // error: U is not used in the argument
{
    U lPtr;
    // .. test stuff
}
```

The template argument U is not used in argument types, and hence, the compiler reports an error.

16.3 Overloaded Function Templates

The functions templates can also be overloaded with multiple declarations. It may be overloaded either by (other) functions of its name or by (other) template functions of the same name. Similar to overloading of normal functions, overloaded functions must differ either in terms of number of parameters or their type. The program tprint.cpp illustrates the overloading of function templates:

```
// tprint.cpp: overloaded template functions
#include <iostream.h>
template <class T>
void print( T data )     // single template argument
{
    cout << data << endl;
}
template <class T>
void print( T data, int nTimes) // template and standard argument
{
    for( int i = 0; i < nTimes; i++ )
        cout << data << endl;
}
void main()
{
    print( 1 );
    print( 1.5 );
    print( 520, 2 );
    print( "OOP is Great", 3 );
}
```

Run

```
1
1.5
520
520
OOP is Great
OOP is Great
OOP is Great
```

In the above program, the templates

```
        void print( T data )     // single template argument
        void print( T data, int nTimes)   // template and standard argument
```

overload the function template print(), but each one of these functions is distinguishable by the number of arguments and the type of the arguments. In main(), the statements

```
        print( 1 );
        print( 1.5 );
```

access the one-argument function template whereas, the statements

```
        print( 520, 2 );
        print( "OOP is Great", 3 );
```

access the two argument function template. Note that in these statements, the required function is selected based on the number of arguments supplied at the point of call.

The compiler adopts the following rules for selecting a suitable template when the program has overloaded function templates.

[1] Look for an exact match on functions; if found, call it.

[2] Look for a function template from which a function that can be called with an exact match can be generated; if found, call it.

[3] Try ordinary overloading resolution for the functions; if found, call it.

If no match is found in all the three alternatives, then that call is treated as an error. In each case if there is more than one alternative in the first step that finds a match, the call is ambiguous and is an error.

A match on a template (step [2]) implies that a specific template function with arguments that exactly matches the types of the arguments will be generated. In this case, not even trivial type-conversion is applied while matching a call to a function template.

16.4 Nesting of Function Calls

Recursively designed algorithms will have nested calls to themselves. Their implementation in the form of function templates will also have recursive calls (calls to itself). The binary search can be implemented by using recursion. It searches for an item in a list of ordered data by applying the *divide and conquer* strategy. The program bsearch.cpp illustrates the template based implementation of recursive binary search algorithm.

```
// bsearch.cpp: binary search function template
#include <iostream.h>
enum boolean { false, true };
// recursive binary search
template <class T>
int RecBinSearch( T Data[], T SrchElem, int low, int high )
{
   if( low > high )
      return -1;
   int mid = ( low + high ) / 2;
   if( SrchElem < Data[mid] )
      return RecBinSearch( Data, SrchElem, low, mid - 1 );
   else
      if( SrchElem > Data[mid] )
         return RecBinSearch( Data, SrchElem, mid + 1, high );
   return mid;
}
void main( void )
{
   int elem, size, num[25], index;
   cout<< "Program to search integer elements..." << endl;
   cout << "How many elements ? ";
   cin >> size;
   cout<<"Enter the elements in ascending order for binary search..."<<endl;
   for( int i = 0;i < size; i++ )
      cin >> num[i];
   cout << "Enter the element to be searched: ";
```

```
    cin >> elem;
    if( ( index = RecBinSearch( num, elem, 0, size ) ) == -1 )
        cout << "Element " << elem << " not found" << endl;
    else
        cout << "Element " << elem << " found at position " << index;
}
```

Run

```
Program to search integer elements...
How many elements ? 4
Enter the elements in ascending order for binary search...
1
4
6
8
Enter the element to be searched: 6
Element 6 found at position 2
```

In main(), when the compiler encounters the expression,

```
        RecBinSearch( num, elem, 0, size )
```

it creates the search function internally. The function RecBinSearch() has recursive calls to itself. In this case, the compiler will not create a new function instead, it uses the internally created function.

16.5 Multiple Arguments Function Template

So far, all the function templates dealt with a single generic argument. Declaration of a function template for functions having multiple parameters of different types requires multiple generic arguments. The program multiple.cpp illustrates the need for multiple template arguments.

```
// multiple.cpp use of multiple template arguments
struct A
{
    int x;
    int y;
};
struct B
{
    int x;
    double y;
};
template < class T >
void Assign_A( T a, T b, A & S1 )
{
    S1.x = a;
    S1.y = b;
}
. template < class T >
 void Assign_B( T a, T b, B & S2 )
 {
    S2.x = a;
```

```
        S2.y = b;
}
void main( void )
{
    A S1;
    B S2;
    Assign_A( 3, 4, S1 );
    Assign_B( 3, 3.1415, S2 );//Error: no match for Assign_B(int,double,B)'
}
```

In main(), the statement

```
        Assign_B( 3, 3.1415, S2 );
```

leads to compilation errors, since the above program is neither having the normal function nor function template matching with its parameters data types. Both the templates expect the first two parameters to be of the same data-type and none of them matches the above call. The solution to the problem encountered in the above program is to declare the second template function in the above program as follows:

```
        template < class T, class U >
        void Assign_B( T a, U b, B & S2 )
        {
            S2.x = a;
            S2.y = b;
        }
```

The declaration of the function template is the same, except that it has an extra argument in the template-argument-list, i.e., class U. This declaration informs the compiler that the template function Assign_B() with two arguments should be instantiated. The compiler calls the appropriate instantiation. Any number of generic data types can be declared, provided all these generic data types are used in declaring formal parameters. The function Assign_A can also be declared as follows:

```
        template< class T, class U >
        void Assign_A( T a, U b, A & S2 )
        {
            S1.x = a;
            S1.y = b;
        }
```

Since the dummy arguments T and U are same in the function call Assign_A, it would be better to define the function template with a single dummy argument rather than two dummy arguments.

All template arguments for a function template must be of template type-arguments, otherwise, it leads to an error. For instance, the following declaration,

```
        template< class T, unsigned SIZE >
        void BubbleSort( T & Data, unsigned SIZE )
        {
            //....
            //....
        }
```

is not allowed. However, such declarations are allowed with class templates.

16.6 User Defined Template Arguments

In addition to primitive data-types, user defined types can be passed to function templates. Its declaration is same as the function template processing standard data types as illustrated in the program student.cpp.

```
// student.cpp: student record and template with user defined data types
#include <iostream.h>
struct stuRec
{
   char name[30];
   int age;
   char collegeCode;
};
template <class T>
void Display( T& t )
{
   cout << t << endl;
}
ostream& operator << ( ostream & out, stuRec & s )
{
   out << "Name: " << s.name << endl;
   out << "Age : " << s.age << endl;
   out << "College Code: " << s.collegeCode << endl;
   return out;
}
void main( void )
{
   stuRec s1;
   cout << "Enter student record details..." << endl;
   cout << "Name: "; cin >> s1.name;
   cout << "Age : "; cin >> s1.age;
   cout << "College Code: "; cin >> s1.collegeCode;
   cout << "The student record:" << endl;
   cout << "Name: "; Display( s1.name );
   cout << "Age : "; Display( s1.age );
   cout << "College Code: ";
   Display( s1.collegeCode ); // it in turn calls operator << defined above
   cout << "The student record:" << endl;
   Display( s1 );
}
```

Run

```
Enter student record details...
Name: Chinamma
Age : 18
College Code: A
The student record:
Name: Chinamma
Age : 18
```

```
College Code: A
The student record:
Name: Chinamma
Age : 18
College Code: A
```

In `main()`, the statement

```
Display( s1 );
```

accesses the function template; the statement

```
cout << t << endl;
```

in `Display()` invokes the overloaded operator function,

```
ostream& operator << ( ostream & out, stuRec & s )
```

In the `cout` statement, when the compiler encounters the user defined data item, it searches for the overloaded stream operator function and makes a call to it.

16.7 Class Templates

Similar to functions, classes can also be declared to operate on different data types. Such classes are called *class templates*. A class template specifies how individual classes can be constructed similar to normal class specification. These classes model a generic class which support similar operations for different data types. A generic stack class can be created, which can be used for storing data of type integer, real, double, etc. Consider an example of a stack (modeling last-in-first-out data structure) to illustrate the need and benefits of class templates. The class declaration for stacks of type character, integer, and double would be as follows:

```
class CharStack
{
    char array[25];          // declare a stack of 25 characters
    unsigned int top;
    public:
        CharStack();
        void Push( const char & element );
        char Pop( void );
        unsigned int GetSize( void ) const;
};
class IntStack
{
    int array[25];           // declare a stack of 25 integers
    unsigned int top;
    public:
        IntStack();
        void Push( const int & element );
        int Pop( void );
        unsigned int GetSize( void ) const;
};
class DbleStack
{
    double array[25];        // declare a stack of 25 double
    unsigned int top;
```

```
    public:
        DbleStack();
        void Push( const double & element );
        double Pop( void );
        unsigned int GetSize( void ) const;
};
```

As seen in the above three declarations, a separate stack class is required for each and every data type. Template declaration enables substitution of code for all the three declarations of stacks with a single template class as follows:

```
template < class T >
class DataStack
{
    T array[25];        // declare a stack of 25 elements of data type T
    unsigned int top;
    public:
        DataStack();
        void Push( const T & element );
        T Pop( void );
        unsigned int GetSize( void ) const;
};
```

The syntax of declaring class templates and defining objects using the same is shown in Figure 16.2. The definition of a class template implies defining template data and member functions.

```
template <class T1, class T2, ...>
class ClassName
{
    // data items of template type T1, T2, ....
    T1 data1;
    ....
    // functions of template arguments T1, T2, ...
    void func1 (T1 a, T2 &b);
    ....
    T func2 (T2 *x, T2 *y);
};
```

Figure 16.2: Syntax of class template declaration

The prefix `template <class T>` specifies that a template is being declared, and that a *type-name* T will be used in the declaration. In other words, `DataStack` is a parameterized class with T as its generic data type.

Any call to the template functions and classes, needs to be associated with a data type or a class. The compiler then instantiates a copy of the template function or template class for the data type specified. The syntax for creating objects using the class templates is shown in Figure 16.3.

A statement to create an object of type stack that can hold integers is as follows:

```
DataStack <int> stack_int; // stack of integers
```

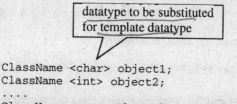

```
ClassName <char> object1;
ClassName <int> object2;
....
ClassName <some_other_class> object5;
```

Figure 16.3: Syntax for class template instantiation

Similarly, objects those hold characters, floats, and doubles can be created by the following statements:

```
DataStack <char> stack_char;      // stack of characters
DataStack <float> stack_float;    // stack of floats
DataStack <double> stack_double;  // stack of doubles
```

However, the usage of these stack objects is similar to those of normal objects. For instance, to push the integer value 10 into the stack_int object, the following statement is used:

```
stack_int.push( 10 );
```

Template Arguments

A template can have character strings, function names, and constant expressions in addition to template type arguments. Consider the following class template to illustrate, how the compiler handles the creation of objects using class templates:

```
template <class T, int size>
class myclass
{
    T arr[size];
};
```

The value supplied for a non template type argument must be a constant expression; its value must be known at compile time. When the objects of the class template are created using a statement such as

```
myclass <float,10> new1;
```

the compiler creates the following class:

```
class myclass
{
    float arr[10];
};
```

Again if a statement such as,

```
myclass <int, 5> new2;
```

is encountered for creating the object new2, the compiler creates the following class:

```
class myclass
{
    int arr[5];
};
```

Member Function Templates

A member function of a template class is implicitly treated as a template function and it can have template arguments which are the same as its class template arguments. For instance, the class template DataStack has the member function,

```
void Push( const T &element );
```

The parameter element is of type template-argument. Its syntax when defined outside is as follows:

```
template <class T>
void DataStack <T>::Push( const T &element );
```

The syntax for declaring member functions of a template class outside its body is shown in Figure 16.4.

```
template <class T1, ...>
class BaseClass
{
    // template type data and functions
    void func1(T1 a);
};
template <class T1, ...>
void ClassName <T1,...>::func1(T1 a)
{
    // function template body
};
```

Figure 16.4:   Syntax for declaring member function of class template outside its body

The program vector.cpp illustrates the declaration of the vector class and its usage in defining its objects. It has a data member which is a pointer to an array of type T. The type T can be int, float, etc., depending on the type of the object created.

```
// vector.cpp: parametrized vector class
#include <iostream.h>
template <class T>
class vector
{
    T * v;          // changes to int *v, float *v, ..., etc
    int size;       // size of vector v
public:
    vector( int vector_size )
    {
        size = vector_size;
        v = new T[ vector_size ];  // v = new int[ size ], ...
    }
    ~vector()
    {
        delete v;
    }
    T & elem( int i )
    {
        if( i >= size )
            cout << endl << "Error: Out of Range";
        return v[i];
    }
    void show();
};
```

```
template <class T>
void vector<T>::show()
{
   for( int i = 0; i < size; i++ )
      cout << elem( i ) << ", ";
}
void main()
{
   int i;
   vector <int> int_vect( 5 );
   vector <float> float_vect( 4 );
   for( i = 0; i < 5; i++ )
      int_vect.elem( i ) = i + 1;
   for( i = 0; i < 4; i++ )
      float_vect.elem( i ) = float( i + 1.5 );
   cout << "Integer Vector: ";
   int_vect.show();
   cout << endl << "Floating Vector: ";
   float_vect.show();
}
```

Run

```
Integer Vector: 1, 2, 3, 4, 5,
Floating Vector: 1.5, 2.5, 3.5, 4.5,
```

Note that the class template specification is very much similar to the ordinary class specification except for the prefix,

```
        template <class T>
```

and the use of T in the place of data-type. This prefix informs the compiler that the class declaration following it is a template and uses T as a type name in the declaration. The type T may be substituted by any data type including the user defined types. In main(), the statement,

```
        vector <int> int_vect( 5 );
        vector <float> float_vect( 4 );
```

creates the vector objects int_vect and float_vect to hold vectors of type integer and floating point respectively. Once objects of class template are created, the use of those objects is the same as the non-template class objects.

Class Template with Multiple Arguments

The template class is instantiated by specifying predefined data type or user defined data classes. The data type is specified in angular braces <>. The syntax for instantiating class template is as follows:

```
        TemplateClassName < type > instance;
        TemplateClassName < type1, type2 > instance( arguments );
```

The instantiation specifies the objects of specified data type. If a different data type is to be specified, a new declaration statement must be used.

The declaration of template classes with multiple arguments is similar to the function template with multiple arguments. However, the arguments need not be of template type. These may include character strings, addresses of objects and functions with external linkage, static class members, and constant expressions. Consider the following declaration:

```
template < class T, unsigned SIZE >
class StackN
{
    protected:
        T Array[SIZE];
        unsigned int top;
    public:
        Stack20( ) { top = 0; }
        void Push( const T & elem ) { Array[ top++ ] = elem; }
        T Pop( void ) { return Array[ --top ]; }
        int GetSize( void ) const { return top+1; }
        T & GetTop( void ) { return Array[top]; }
};
```

The declaration of the class template StackN is preceded by,

```
template < class T, unsigned SIZE >
```

as before, except that it has two arguments. The second argument is an (typed) unsigned argument. Making SIZE an argument of the template class StackN rather than to its objects, infers that the sizes of class StackN is known at compile time so that class StackN can be fully declared at compile time. The class template StackN with a variable stack size can be instantiated by specifying the size in the argument list. This makes a template, such as StackN, useful for implementing general purpose data structure. The above declarations provide the user freedom to define many instances of the class StackN, each operating on different data-types and of variable size. The following statements define objects of the class template StackN for storing integers and characters respectively.

```
StackN < int, 20> Intstk;
StackN < char, 50 > Chrstk;
```

A known type argument in the template class (second argument in the above case) must be a constant expression (evaluated at the compile time) of the appropriate type.

The list allows insertion operation at the front and deletion operation at the end of a list. The list class can have any number of template data elements, as shown in the following declaration.

```
template< class R, class S, class T >
class SnglList
{
    private:
        R data_1;
        S data_2;
        T data_3;
    public:
        SnglList< R, S, T > *next;
        SnglList( void ) { next = NULL; }
        . . . . .
        friend ostream & operator<<( ostream &, SnglList< R, S, T > & );
        friend istream & operator>>( istream &, SnglList< R, S, T > & );
};
```

The objects of class templates having multiple arguments can be created as follows:

```
SnglList <int, float, double> node;
SnglList < int, unsigned, double > *Root, *End;
```

16.8 Inheritance of Class Template

A combination of templates and inheritance can be used in developing hierarchal data structures such as container classes. A base class in a hierarchy represents a commonality of methods and properties. Use of templates with respect to inheritance involves the following:

* Derive a class template from a base class, which is a template class.
* Derive a class template from the base class, which is a template class, add more template members in the derived class.
* Derive a class from a base class which is not a template, and add template members to that class.
* Derive a class from a base class which is a template class and restrict the template feature, so that the derived class and its derivatives do not have the template feature.

The template features provided in the base classes, can be restricted by specifying the type, when the class is derived. All the arguments in the template argument list of the base class have to be replaced by predefined types. In such a case, the derived class does not inherit the template feature, but is just a class of *specified data type* stated at the point of inheritance declaration. The syntax for declaring derived classes from template-based base classes is shown in Figure 16.5.

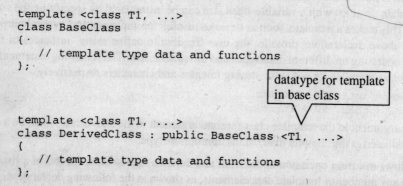

```
template <class T1, ...>
class BaseClass
{
    // template type data and functions
};
```

datatype for template in base class

```
template <class T1, ...>
class DerivedClass : public BaseClass <T1, ...>
{
    // template type data and functions
};
```

Figure 16.5:   Syntax for inheriting template base class

The class deriving a template type base class can be a normal class or a class-template. If a new derived class is a normal class, the data-type of template arguments to the base class must be specified at the point of derivation. Otherwise, template arguments type specified at the point of instantiation of a class template can also be passed.

Consider an example of declaring the template class Vector. It inherits all the properties from the base template class sVector. The derived template class Vector is still a static vector containing twenty elements. Member functions that perform insert, delete and search are added to the derived class. The member functions have the prefix <template class T>, since the derived class operates on the undeclared type T. The specification of a new template class created by inheriting another template-based base class is given below:

```
template< class T >
class Vector : public sVector< T >
{
    ...
    read();
```

```
        . . .
    };
```

The member functions defined with its class body have the same syntax as members of non-template-type classes. However, member function defined outside the body of a class, for instance, has the following specification:

```
    template <class T>
    void Vector<T>::read()
    {
        ...// body of the read()
    }
```

Note that, the member functions of a class-template are treated as function-template type members. The class Vector can be instantiated as follows:

```
    Vector <int> v1;
```

In this case, the int specified in angular bracket is first assigned to generic data type in the Vector class and then the same is also passed to its base class.

A derived class of a template based base class is not necessarily template derived class. That is, the non-template-based derived classes can also be created from the template-based base classes. In this case, the undefined template argument T has to be specified during derivation, for instance, as follows:

```
    class Vector : public sVector< int >
    {
        . . .
    };
```

It creates a new class called Vector from the template-based base class sVector. The int is passed as template argument type to the base class.

The program union.cpp illustrates the mechanism of extending the class template Bag by using the feature of inheritance. In this case, a new class template Set is derived from the existing class template Bag without any modifications. A derived class template Set inherits all the properties of the class template Bag and extends itself by adding some more features of its own to support set assignment and union operation.

```
// union.cpp: Union of sets. Set class by inheritance of Bag class
#include <iostream.h>
enum boolean { FALSE, TRUE };
const int MAX_ITEMS = 25;  // Maximum number of items that the bag can hold
template <class T>
class Bag
{
   protected:                 // Note: not private
      T contents[MAX_ITEMS];  // bag memory area
      int ItemCount;          // Number of items present in the bag
   public:
      Bag()        // no-argument constructor
      {
         ItemCount = 0;     // When you purchase a bag, it will be empty
      }
```

```
      void put( T item )     // puts item into bag
      {
         contents[ ItemCount++ ] = item;  // item into bag, counter update
      }
      boolean IsEmpty()       // 1, if bag is empty, 0, otherwise
      {
         return ItemCount == 0 ? TRUE : FALSE;
      }
      boolean IsFull()        // 1, if bag is full, 0, otherwise
      {
         return ItemCount == MAX_ITEMS ? TRUE : FALSE;
      }
      boolean IsExist( T item );
      void show();
};
// returns 1, if item is in bag, 0, otherwise
template <class T>
boolean Bag<T>::IsExist( T item )
{
   for( int i = 0; i < ItemCount; i++ )
      if( contents[i] == item )
         return TRUE;
   return FALSE;
}
// display contents of a bag
template <class T>
void Bag<T>::show()
{
   for( int i = 0; i < ItemCount; i++ )
      cout << contents[i] << " ";
   cout << endl;
}
template <class S>
class Set: public Bag <S>
{
   public:
      void add( S element )
      {
         if( !IsExist( element ) && !IsFull() )
            put( element );
      }
      void read();
      void operator = (Set s1);
      friend Set operator + ( Set s1, Set s2 );
};
template <class S>
void Set<S>::read()
{
   S element;
   while( TRUE )
   {
```

```
        cout << "Enter Set Element <0- end>: ";
        cin >> element;
        if( element == 0 )
            break;
        add( element );
    }
}
template <class S>
void Set<S>::operator = ( Set <S> s2 )
{
    for( int i = 0; i < s2.ItemCount; i++ )
        contents[i] = s2.contents[i];
    ItemCount = s2.ItemCount;
}
template <class S>
Set<S> operator + ( Set <S> s1, Set <S> s2 )
{
    Set <S> temp;
    temp = s1;    // copy all elements of set s1 to temp
    // copy those elements of set s2 into temp, those not exist in set s1
    for( int i = 0; i < s2.ItemCount; i++ )
    {
        if( !s1.IsExist( s2.contents[i] ) ) // if element of s2 is not in s1
            temp.add( s2.contents[i] );        // copy the unique element
    }
    return( temp );
}
void main()
{
    Set <int> s1;
    Set <int> s2;
    Set <int> s3;
    cout << "Enter Set 1 elements .." << endl;
    s1.read();
    cout << "Enter Set 2 elements .." << endl;
    s2.read();
    s3 = s1 + s2;
    cout << endl << "Union of s1 and s2 : ";
    s3.show();      // uses Bag::show() base class
}
```

Run

```
Enter Set 1 elements ..
Enter Set Element <0- end>: 1
Enter Set Element <0- end>: 2
Enter Set Element <0- end>: 3
Enter Set Element <0- end>: 4
Enter Set Element <0- end>: 0
Enter Set 2 elements ..
Enter Set Element <0- end>: 2
```

```
Enter Set Element <0- end>: 4
Enter Set Element <0- end>: 5
Enter Set Element <0- end>: 6
Enter Set Element <0- end>: 0
Union of s1 and s2 : 1 2 3 4 5 6
```

In the above program, the template class Set has its own features to perform set union by using the member functions of the class Bag. The statement

```
template <class S>
class Set: public Bag <S>
```

derives the new template class Set known as derived class from the base class Bag. The base class Bag is *publicly inherited* by the derived class Set. Hence, the members of ·Bag class, which are *protected* remain *protected* and *public* remain *public,* in the derived class Set. The Set class can treat all the members of the Bag class as they are of its own. The derived class Set refers to the data and member functions of the base class Bag, while the base class Bag has no access to the derived class Set.

16.9 Class Template Containership

The usage of delegation (containership) with templates allows to build powerful programming components (data structures). It refers to having an object of one class contained in another class as a data member. The container class (i.e., a class that holds objects of some other type) is of considerable importance when implementing data structures. Inheritance supports the *is-a* relationship whereas containership supports the *has-a* relationship. The program tree.cpp illustrates the use of containership in building an unbalanced binary tree. It has two classes TreeNode and BinaryTree. The first class represents the node structure of a binary tree where as the second class represents the set of operations which can be performed on a tree. The class TreeNode has two pointers to objects of its own which serve as the pointers to child nodes. The class BinaryTree has a pointer to the root node of the tree, which is an instance of the class TreeNode and thus delegating node handling issues to the TreeNode class.

```
// tree.cpp: Binary Tree Operations (create, print, traverse, and search)
#include <iostream.h>
#include <stdio.h>
template <class T>
class TreeNode
{
   protected:
     T data;                   /* data to be stored in a tree */
     TreeNode <T> *left;       /* pointer to a left sub tree */
     TreeNode <T> *right;      /* pointer to a right sub tree */
   public:
     TreeNode( const T& dataIn)
     {
        data = dataIn;
        left = right = NULL;
     }
```

```
        TreeNode( const T& dataIn, TreeNode <T> *l, TreeNode <T> *r )
        {
            data = dataIn;
            left = l;
            right = r;
        }
        friend class BinaryTree <T>;
};
template <class T>
class BinaryTree
{
    protected:
        TreeNode<T> *root;
        TreeNode<T> *InsertNode( TreeNode <T> *root, T data );
    public:
        BinaryTree()
        {
            root = NULL;
        }
        void PrintTreeTriangle( TreeNode <T> *tree, int level );
        void PrintTreeDiagonal( TreeNode <T> *tree, int level );
        void PreOrderTraverse( TreeNode <T> *tree );
        void InOrderTraverse( TreeNode <T> *tree );
        void PostOrderTraverse( TreeNode <T> *tree );
        TreeNode <T> * SearchTree( TreeNode <T> *tree, T data );
        void PreOrder()
        {
            PreOrderTraverse( root );
        }
        void InOrder()
        {
            InOrderTraverse( root );
        }
        void PostOrder()
        {
            PostOrderTraverse( root );
        }
        void PrintTree( int disptype )
        {
            if( disptype == 1 )
                PrintTreeTriangle( root, 1);
            else
                PrintTreeDiagonal( root, 1);
        }
        void Insert( T data )
        {
            root = InsertNode( root, data );
        }
```

```
        TreeNode <T> * Search( T data )
        {
            return SearchTree( root, data );
        }
};
// Insert 'data' into tree
template <class T>
TreeNode<T> * BinaryTree<T>::InsertNode( TreeNode <T> *tree, T data )
{
    /* Is Tree NULL */
    if( !tree )
    {
        tree = new TreeNode<T>( data, NULL, NULL );
        return( tree );
    }
    /* Is data less than the parent element */
    if( data < tree->data )
        tree->left = InsertNode( tree->left, data );
    else
        /* Is data greater than the parent element */
        if( data > tree->data )
            tree->right = InsertNode( tree->right, data );
    /* data already exists */
    return( tree );
}
// PreOrder Traversal
template <class T>
void BinaryTree<T>::PreOrderTraverse( TreeNode <T> *tree )
{
    if( tree )
    {
        cout << tree->data << " "; // Process node
        PreOrderTraverse( tree->left );
        PreOrderTraverse( tree->right );
    }
}
// In Order Traversal
template <class T>
void BinaryTree<T>::InOrderTraverse( TreeNode <T> *tree )
{
    if( tree )
    {
        PostOrderTraverse( tree->left );
        cout << tree->data << " "; // Process node
        PostOrderTraverse( tree->right );
    }
}
```

```
// Post Order Traversal
template <class T>
void BinaryTree<T>::PostOrderTraverse( TreeNode <T> *tree )
{
   if( tree )
   {
      PostOrderTraverse( tree->left );
      PostOrderTraverse( tree->right );
      cout << tree->data << " "; // Process node
   }
}
// Tree Printing in Triangle Form
template <class T>
void BinaryTree<T>::PrintTreeTriangle( TreeNode <T> *tree, int level )
{
   if( tree )
   {
      PrintTreeTriangle( tree->right, level+1 );
      cout << "\n";
      for( int i = 0; i < level; i++ )
         cout << "     ";
      cout << tree->data;
      PrintTreeTriangle( tree->left, level+1 );
   }
}
// Tree Printing in Diagonal Form
template <class T>
void BinaryTree<T>::PrintTreeDiagonal( TreeNode <T> *tree, int level )
{
   if( tree )
   {
      cout << "\n";
      for( int i = 0; i < level; i++ )
         cout << "     ";
      cout << tree->data;
      PrintTreeDiagonal( tree->left, level+1 );
      PrintTreeDiagonal( tree->right, level+1 );
   }
}
// search for data item in the tree
template <class T>
TreeNode <T> * BinaryTree<T>::SearchTree( TreeNode <T> *tree, T data )
{
   while( tree )
   {
      /* Is data less than the parent element */
      if( data < tree->data )
         tree = tree->left;
      else
```

```
            /* Is data greater than the parent element */
            if( data > tree->data )
                tree = tree->right;
            else
                return( tree );
    }
    return( NULL );
}
void main()
{
    float data, disptype;
    BinaryTree <float> btree;        // tree's root node
    cout << "This Program Demonstrates the Binary Tree Operations" << endl;
    cout << "Tree Display Style: [1] - Triangular [2] - Diagonal form: ";
    cin >> disptype;
    cout << "Tree creation process..." << endl;
    while( 1 )
    {
        cout << "Enter node number to be inserted <0-END>: ";
        cin >> data;
        if( data == 0 )
            break;
        btree.Insert( data );
        cout << "Binary Tree is...";
        btree.PrintTree( disptype );
        cout << "\n Pre-Order Traversal: ";
        btree.PreOrder();
        cout << "\n  In-Order Traversal: ";
        btree.InOrder();
        cout << "\nPost-Order Traversal: ";
        btree.PostOrder();
        cout << endl;
    }
    cout << "Tree search process..." << endl;
    while( 1 )
    {
        cout << "Enter node number to be searched <0-END>: ";
        cin >> data;
        if( data == 0 )
            break;
        if( btree.Search( data ) )
            cout << "Found data in the Tree" << endl;
        else
            cout << "Not found data in the Tree" << endl;
    }
}
```

Run

```
This Program Demonstrates the Binary Tree Operations
Tree Display Style: [1] - Triangular [2] - Diagonal form: 1
```

```
Tree creation process...
Enter node number to be inserted <0-END>: 5
Binary Tree is...
       5
 Pre-Order Traversal: 5
  In-Order Traversal: 5
Post-Order Traversal: 5
Enter node number to be inserted <0-END>: 3
Binary Tree is...
       5
           3
 Pre-Order Traversal: 5 3
  In-Order Traversal: 3 5
Post-Order Traversal: 3 5
Enter node number to be inserted <0-END>: 8
Binary Tree is...
           8
       5
           3
 Pre-Order Traversal: 5 3 8
  In-Order Traversal: 3 5 8
Post-Order Traversal: 3 8 5
Enter node number to be inserted <0-END>: 2
Binary Tree is...
           8
       5
           3
       2
 Pre-Order Traversal: 5 3 2 8
  In-Order Traversal: 2 3 5 8
Post-Order Traversal: 2 3 8 5
Enter node number to be inserted <0-END>: 9
Binary Tree is...
               9
           8
       5
           3
       2
 Pre-Order Traversal: 5 3 2 8 9
  In-Order Traversal: 2 3 5 9 8
Post-Order Traversal: 2 3 9 8 5
Enter node number to be inserted <0-END>: 0
Tree search process...
Enter node number to be searched <0-END>: 8
Found data in the Tree
Enter node number to be searched <0-END>: 1
Not found data in the Tree
Enter node number to be searched <0-END>: 0
```

16.10 Class Template with Overloaded Operators

The class template can also be declared for a class having operator overloaded member functions . The syntax for declaring operator overloaded functions is the same as class template members and overloaded functions. The class template with operator overloading will allow to truly extend the language and at the same time retaining the readability of object manipulation code. The program complex.cpp illustrates the overloading of the + operator in the class template complex. In this case, the members of the complex number (real and imaginary) can be any of the standard data types.

```cpp
// complex.cpp: template class for operator overloaded complex class
#include <iostream.h>
template <class T>
class complex
{
   private:
      T real;          // real part of complex number
      T imag;          // imaginary part of complex number
   public:
      complex()        // no argument constructor
      {
         real = imag = 0.0;
      }
      void getdata() // read complex number
      {
         cout << "Real Part ? ";
         cin >> real;
         cout << "Imag Part ? ";
         cin >> imag;
      }
      complex operator + ( complex c2 );  // complex addition
      void outdata( char *msg )           // display complex number
      {
         cout << msg << "(" << real;
         cout << ", " << imag << ")" << endl;
      }
};
template <class T>
complex <T> complex<T>::operator + ( complex <T>c2 )
{
   complex <T> temp;                  // object temp of complex class
   temp.real = real + c2.real;        // add real parts
   temp.imag = imag + c2.imag;        // add imaginary parts
   return( temp );                    // return complex object
}
void main()
{
   complex <int> c1, c2, c3;  // integer complex objects
   cout << "Addition of integer complex objects..." << endl;
   cout << "Enter complex number c1 .." << endl;
   c1.getdata();
```

```
    cout << "Enter complex number c2 .." << endl;
    c2.getdata();
    c3 = c1 + c2;       // integer addition
    c3.outdata("c3 = c1 + c2: " );          // display result
    complex <float> c4, c5, c6;   // integer complex objects
    cout << "Addition of float complex objects..." << endl;
    cout << "Enter complex number c4 .." << endl;
    c4.getdata();
    cout << "Enter complex number c5 .." << endl;
    c5.getdata();
    c6 = c4 + c5;  // floating addition
    c6.outdata("c6 = c4 + c5: " );           // display result
}
```

Run

```
Addition of integer complex objects...
Enter complex number c1 ..
Real Part ? 1
Imag Part ? 2
Enter complex number c2 ..
Real Part ? 3
Imag Part ? 4
c3 = c1 + c2: (4, 6)
Addition of float complex objects...
Enter complex number c4 ..
Real Part ? 1.5
Imag Part ? 2.5
Enter complex number c5 ..
Real Part ? 2.4
Imag Part ? 3.7
c6 = c4 + c5: (3.9, 6.2)
```

In main(), the statements

```
        complex <int> c1, c2, c3;     // integer complex objects
        complex <float> c4, c5, c6;   // integer complex objects
```

when encountered by the compiler, it creates two complex classes internally for handling numbers with integer and real data type members and instances of those classes. The statement

```
    c3 = c1 + c2;       // integer addition
```

performs integer operation on complex objects, and the statement

```
    c6 = c4 + c5;       // floating addition
```

performs floating-point operation on complex objects.

Review Questions

16.1   What is generic programming ? What are its advantages and state some of its applications ?

16.2   What is a function template ? Write a function template for finding the largest number in a given array. The array parameter must be of generic-data types.

16.3   Explain how the compiler processes calls to a function template.

16.4   State whether the following statements are TRUE or FALSE. Give reasons.

(a) generic-data type is known at runtime.

(b) function templates requires more memory space than normal function.

(c) templates are processed by the compiler.

(d) Special mechanism is required to execute function templates.

(e) The compiler reports an error if any one of the generic data-type indicated in template-type list is unused for defining formal parameters.

(f) A derived class of a template-based base class is not necessarily template derived class.

(g) Overloaded operator functions can be function templates.

(h) The syntax for defining objects of a class template is slightly different from the definition of the normal class's objects.

(i) Parameters to constructors can be of template type.

16.5   What is a class template ? Explain the syntax of a class template with suitable examples.

16.6   Explain how the compiler processes calls to a class template ?

16.7   Explain the syntax for inheriting template-based superclass. Note that the derived class can again be a template-based or non-template-based. Illustrate with suitable programming examples.

16.8   Write a template-based program for adding objects of the `Vector` class. Use dynamic data members instead of arrays for storing vector elements.

16.9   Write a program for manipulating linked list supporting node operations as follows:

```
node = node + 2;  node = node - 3;
Node <int> *n = node1 + node2;
```

The first statement creates a new node with node information 2 and the second statement deletes a node with node information 3. The node class must be of type template.

16.10   Write an interactive program for creating doubly linked-list. The program must support ordered insertion and deletion of a node. The doubly linked-list class must be of template type.

16.11   Design template classes such that they support the following statements:

```
Rupee <float> r1, r2;
Dollar <float> d1, d2;
d1 = r2;  // converts  rupee (Indian currency) to dollar (US currency)
r2 = d2;  // converts dollar (US currency) to rupee (Indian currency)
```

Write a complete program which does such conversions according to the world market value.

16.12   Consider an example of book shop which sells books and video tapes.It is modeled by `book` and `tape` classes. These two classes are inherited from the base class called `media`. The `media` class has common data members such as `title` and `publication`. The book class has data members for storing a number of pages in a book and the `tape` class has the playing time in a tape. Each class will have member functions such as `read()` and `show()`. In base class, these members have to be defined as virtual functions. Write a program which models this class hierarchy and processes their objects using pointers to base class only. (Use virtual functions and all classes must be template-based.)

17

Streams Computation with Console

In general, there are several kinds of streams to form physical entities such as streams of water (rivers), streams of electrons (electricity), streams of cars (traffic), and streams of characters (message packet). The notion of streams and streams computation can be visualized through the illustration of a river. It may be the Amazon river flowing into the Atlantic ocean as shown in Figure 17.1. Drops of water collectively form a continuous stream. Streams join to form a river. Looking over the upper river area to the lower river area, streams converge into one stream so that a tree of streams is formed, whose root stream goes into the ocean. One drop from one branch stream may reach the ocean a slightly earlier or later than another in a different branch stream.

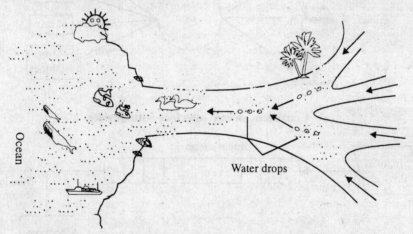

Figure 17.1:   Streams of water drops flowing into ocean

17.1 What are Streams ?

Every program must go through the process of *input-computation-output* flow so that it can take some data as input and generate the processed data as output. It necessitates the need for a mechanism, which supplies the input data to a program and presents the processed data in the desired form. In the earlier chapters, the input and output operations were performed using `cin` and `cout` with the stream operators `>>` and `<<` respectively. Streams handling I/O operations are different from ANSI C functions. C++ supports a wide variety of features to control the way data is read and the output is presented.

C++ uses the concept of streams and stream classes to perform I/O operations with console and disk files. The stream classes supporting console-based input and output operations are discussed in this chapter and those supporting file-based input and output operations are discussed in the next chapter, *Streams Computation with Files*.

C++ streams deal with a sequence of characters and hence, ocean in the above figure can be visualized as an object or a receiver and each drop of water as a character, flowing into the object.

Streams are classified into input streams and output streams. Streams resemble the *producer and consumer model*. The *producer* produces items to be consumed by the *consumer*. The producers and consumers are connected by the C++ operators >> or <<. In C++, the I/O system is designed to operate on a wide variety of devices including console, disks, printer etc. It is designed to provide a consistent and device independent interface. It allows uniform use of any I/O device—be it a disk, a terminal, or a printer as shown in Figure 17.2a. The computer resources involved in the stream computation include display, keyboard, files, printer, etc. The stream is an object flowing from one place to another. For instance, in nature, a stream normally refers to the flow of water from the hills to the oceans. Similarly, in C++, a stream is used to refer to the flow of data from a particular device to the program's variables. The device here refers to files, memory arrays, keyboard, console, and so on. In C++, these streams are treated as objects to support consistent access interface.

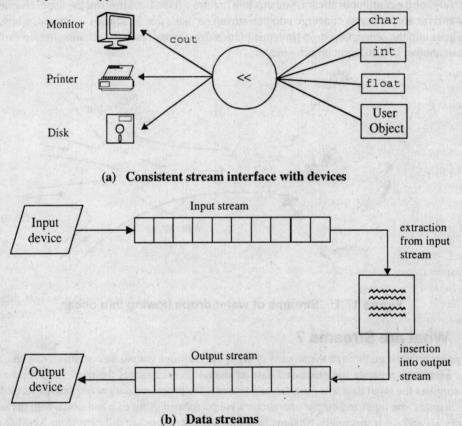

(a) Consistent stream interface with devices

(b) Data streams

Figure 17.2:   C++ streams

Some of the above devices exhibit the characteristics of either a producer or a consumer and others exhibit the characteristics of both the producer and consumer depending on the operations performed on them. For instance, the keyboard exhibits the nature of only a producer; printer or monitor screen exhibit the nature of only a consumer. Whereas, a file stored on the disk, can behave as a producer or consumer depending on the operation initiated on it. The stream model of C++ is shown in Figure 17.2b.

A stream is a series of bytes, which act either as a source from which input data can be extracted or as a destination to which the output can be sent. The source stream provides data to the program called the input stream and the destination stream that receives data from the program is called the output stream.

What are C++ Streams ?

The C language supports an extensive set of library functions for managing I/O operations. Every C programmer is familiar with `printf`, `scanf`, `puts`, `gets`, `fopen`, `fwrite`, `fread`, `fscanf`, `fclose`, and related I/O functions defined in the header file `stdio.h`. These functions have served programmers very well, but they are inadequate and clumsy when used with object-oriented programming. For instance, the user cannot add a new format either for `printf` or `scanf` function to handle the user-defined data type. Further, the `stdio.h` functions are inconsistent in parameter ordering and semantics.

In C++, streams with operator overloading provide a mechanism for filtering. The standard stream operators << and >> do not know anything about the user-defined data types. They can be overloaded to operate on user-defined data items. Overloaded stream operators filter the user-defined data items and transfers only basic data items to the standard stream operators. Consider the following statements to illustrate the streams capability:

```
cout << complex1;
..
cin >> complex2;
```

The data-items `complex1` and `complex2` are the objects of the complex class. The operators >> or << do not know anything about the objects `complex1` and `complex2`. These are overloaded in the `complex` class as member functions, which process the attributes of complex objects as basic data-items. Collectively, it appears as if the stream operators operate even on objects of the complex class. This illusion is made possible because of the feature of overloading the stream operators.

The C++ language offers a mechanism which permits the creation of an extensible and consistent *input-output system* in the form of *streams library*. It is a collection of classes and objects which can be used to build a powerful system, or modified and extended to handle the user-defined data types. There are different classes for handling input and output streams, as also for streams connecting different devices to the program. C++ streams are also treated as filters, since they have capability to change the data representation from one number system to another when requested.

17.2 Predefined Console Streams

C++ contains several predefined streams that are opened automatically when the execution of a program starts. The most prominent predefined streams in C++ are related to the console device. The four standard streams `cin`, `cout`, `cerr`, and `clog` are automatically opened *before* the function `main()` is executed; they are closed *after* `main()` has completed. These predefined stream objects (are declared in `iostream.h`) have the following meaning:

cin	Standard input (usually keyboard) corresponding to `stdin` in C.
cout	Standard output (usually screen) corresponding to `stdout` in C.

cerr   Standard error output (usually screen) corresponding to `stderr` in C.

clog   A fully-buffered version of `cerr` (no C equivalent).

The stream objects `cin` and `cout`, have been used extensively in the earlier chapters. It is known that `cin` (console input) represents the input stream connected to the standard input device and `cout` (console output) represents the output stream connected to the standard output device. The standard input and output devices normally refer to the keyboard and the monitor respectively. However, if required, these streams can be redirected to any other devices or files.

Comparison of I/O using C's stdio.h and C++'s iostream.h

The functions declared in the header file, `stdio.h` such as `printf`, `scanf`, etc., require the use of format strings. Consider an example of displaying the contents of the integer variable on the console to illustrate the flexibility offered by the C++ streams. If the variable `i` were to be defined by the statement

```
int i;
```

then the `printf` statement to display the value of the variable `i` would be,

```
printf("%d", i);
```

and the statement to read data would be,

```
scanf("%d", &i);
```

Consider a situation in which the `printf` or `scanf` statement occurs at several places in a program. Suppose the program specifications are changed, and it is decided that the variable `i` must hold larger values, the definition of `i` would be changed to,

```
long i;
```

The user is now left with the thankless job of searching for all the statements that read or display the variable `i` and replacing `%d` by `%ld` in the format strings. On the other hand, in C++, the `iostream.h` functions are overloaded to take care of all the basic types. For instance, the statements

```
cout << i;
cin >> i;
```

will work correctly without the need for any modification irrespective of the data type of the `i` variable. The stream based I/O operations can be performed with variables of all the basic data types such as `char, signed char, short int, long`, etc. In addition to these, the `<<` and `>>` operators are overloaded to operate on pointers to characters also (for performing input or output with the NULL terminated strings). The traditional beginner's C program is usually called "Hello World" and is listed in the program `hello.c`.

```
/* hello.c: printing Hello World message */
#include <stdio.h>
void main()
{
    printf( "Hello World" );
}
```

Run

```
Hello World
```

The standard function `printf()` is in the C library that sends characters to the standard output device. The *Hello World* program will also work in C++, because C++ supports ANSI-C function library. A new C++ program that does the same operation as C's *Hello World* is listed in `hello.cpp`.

```
// hello.cpp: printing Hello World message
#include <iostream.h>
void main()
{
    cout << "Hello World";
}
```

Run

```
Hello World
```

The header file, iostream.h supports streams programming features by supporting predefined stream objects. The C++'s stream insertion operator, << sends the message Hello World to the predefined console object, cout which, in turn, prints on the console.

Output Redirection

The output generated by cout can be redirected to files whereas, that generated by cerr and clog cannot be redirected. That is, the following on the command line,

```
        shell: hello > outfile
```

redirects console output to the file named outfile. The output file contains only those messages generated by cout but not by cerr and clog. They always redirect to console as illustrated in the program redirect.cpp.

```
// redirect.cpp: printing Hello World message
#include <iostream.h>
void main()
{
    cout << "Hello World with cout\n";
    cerr << "Hello World with cerr\n";
    clog << "Hello World with clog\n";
}
```

Run

```
Hello World with cerr
Hello World with clog
```

Note: The program is executed by issuing the following command at the shell prompt:

```
        redirect > outfile
```

On execution, the messages shown at RUN appear on the console whereas the first message Hello World with cout is stored in the file outfile.

The main advantage of using iostream.h functions over the stdio.h functions is data-independence; the freedom to write code without worrying too much about the variable types. Mixed usage of stdio and the stream class functions to perform output is not advisable. This is because they use different buffers and the order in which the output appears may not conform to the order in which the output statements appear in the program.

Features of cin and cout

Before examining the facilities available with cout and cin, it is useful to know that the objects cin and cout are instances of certain classes defined in iostream.h. The object cout is an instance of class ostream_withassign, which is derived from the superclass ostream. Hence, effectively cout has the functionality of the class ostream. Similarly, cin an instance of the class istream_with_assign has the functionality of the class istream.

17.3 Hierarchy of Console Stream Classes

The C++ input-output system supports a hierarchy of classes that are used to manipulate both the console and disk files, called stream classes. The stream classes are implemented in a rather elaborate hierarchy. The knowledge of C++'s input and output stream class hierarchy will result in the potential utilization of stream classes. Figure 17.3, depicts hierarchy of classes, which are used with the console device.

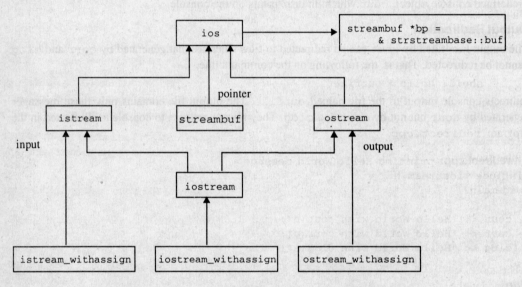

Figure 17.3:   Hierarchy of console stream classes

The iostream facility of C++ provides an easy means to perform I/O. The class istream uses the predefined stream cin that can be used to read data from the standard input device. The extraction operator >>, is used to get data from a stream. The insertion operator <<, is used to output data into a stream. A stream object must appear on the left side of the << or >> operator; however, multiple stream operators can be concatenated on a single line, even when they refer to objects of different types. For instance, consider the following statements:

```
cout << item1 << "**" << c1 << my_object << 22;
cin >> int_var >> float_var >> my_object;
```

The first statement outputs objects of different types (both the standard and user defined) and the second statement reads data of different types.

The classes istream, ostream, and iostream , which are designed exclusively to manage the console device, are declared in the header file iostream.h. The actions performed by these classes related to console device management are described below:

ios class: It provides operations common to both input and output. It contains a pointer to a buffer object (streambuf). It has constants and member functions that are essential for handling formatted input and output operations.

The classes derived from the ios class (istream, ostream, iostream) perform specialized input-output operations with high-level formatting:

- istream (input stream) does formatted input.
- ostream (output stream) does formatted output.
- iostream (input/output stream) does formatted input and output.

The pointer streambuf in the ios class provides an abstraction for communicating to a physical device and classes derived from it deal with files, memory, etc. The class, ios communicates to a streambuf, which maintains information on the state of the streambuf (good, bad, eof, etc.), and maintains flags used by the istream and ostream.

istream class: It is a derived class of ios and hence inherits the properties of ios. It defines input functions such as get(), getline(), and read(). In addition, it has an overloaded member function, stream extraction operator >>, to read data from a standard input device to the memory items.

ostream class: It is a derived class of ios, and hence, inherits the properties of ios. It defines output functions such as put() and write(). In addition, it has an overloaded member function, stream insertion operator <<, to write data from memory items to a standard output device.

iostream class: It is derived from multiple base classes, istream and ostream, which are in turn inherited from the class ios. It provides facility for handling both input and output streams, and supports all the operations provided by istream and ostream classes.

The classes istream_withassign, ostream_withassign, and iostream_withassign add the assignment operators to their parent classes.

17.4 Unformatted I/O Operations

The most commonly used objects throughout all C++ programs are cin and cout. They are predefined in the header file, iostream.h, which supports the input and output of data of various types. This is achieved by overloading the operators << and >> to recognize all the basic data types. The input or extraction operator is overloaded in the istream class and output or insertion operator is overloaded in the ostream class.

put() and get() Functions

The stream classes of C++ support two member functions, get() and put(). The function get() is a member function of the input stream class istream and is used to read a single character from the input device. The function put() is a member function of the output stream class ostream and is used to write a single character to the output device. The function get() has two versions with the following prototypes:

```
void get( char & );
int get(void);
```

Both the functions can fetch a white-space character including the blank space, tab, and newline character. It is well known that, the member functions are invoked by their objects using dot operators. Hence, these two functions can be used to perform input operation either by using the predefined object, c in or an user defined object of the istream class. The program get.cpp illustrates the use of get() function to read a line (until carriage return key is pressed).

```
// get.cpp: Read characters using get() of istream
#include <iostream.h>
void main()
{
   char c;
   cin.get( c );
   while( c != '\n' )
   {
      cout << c;
      cin.get( c ); // reads a character
      // replace the above statement by cin >> c; and see the output
   }
}
```

Run
```
Hello World
Hello World
```

In main(), the statement
```
      cin.get( c );
```
invokes the member function get() of the object c in of the istream class. It reads a character into the variable c from the standard input device. If this statement is replaced by the statement,
```
      cin >> c;
```
it will not work as desired, since the operator >> will skip blanks and newline characters. Another version of get() can also be used in the above program as follows:
```
      c = cin.get();
```
It reads a single character and returns the same.

The function put(), which is a member function of the output stream class ostream prints a character representation of the input parameter. For instance, the statement,
```
      cout.put( 'R' );
```
prints the character R, and the statement
```
      cout.put( c );
```
prints the contents of the character variable c. The input parameter can also be a numeric constant and hence, the statement
```
      cout.put( 65 );
```
prints the character A (65 is a ASCII code of character A). The program put.cpp prints the ASCII table (since put() considers input parameter as a ASCII code of a character to be printed.)

```
// put.cpp: prints ASCII table using put() function
#include <iostream.h>
void main()
{
   char c;
   for( int i = 0; i < 255; i++ )
   {
```

```
      if( i == 26 )
         continue;
      cout << i << " ";
      cout.put( i );   // change to cout << i; and see the output difference
      cout << endl;
   }
}
```

Run

[prints ASCII code and its character representation]

  In main(), the statement
```
      cout.put( i );
```
prints a character represented by the ASCII code whose value is passed as an input argument through the variable i.

getline() and write() Functions

The C++ stream classes support line-oriented functions, getline() and write() to perform input and output operations. The getline() function reads a whole line of text that ends with new line or until the maximum limit is reached. Consider the program space1.cpp for reading an input string having a blank space in between.

```
// space1.cpp: the effect of white-space characters on the >> operator
#include <iostream.h>
#include <iomanip.h>
void main()
{
    char test[40];
    cout << "Enter string: ";
    cin >> test;
    cout << "Output string: ";
    cout << test;
}
```

Run

```
Enter string: Hello World
Output string: Hello
```

  In main(), the statement
```
      cin >> test;
```
reads a string until it encounters a white space. If the input to the above program is "Hello World", the output is going to be just "Hello". The reason being the operator >> considers all white-space characters in the input stream as delimiters. To remedy this, use the member function getline() of the cin object's class as shown in the program space2.cpp.

```
// space2.cpp: the effect of white-space characters on the >> operator
#include <iostream.h>
#include <iomanip.h>
void main()
{
```

```
    char test[40];
    cout << "Enter string: ";
    cin.getline( test, 40 );
    cout << "Output string: ";
    cout << test;
}
```

Run

```
Enter string: Hello World
Output string: Hello World
```

In main(), the statement

```
    cin.getline( test, 40 );
```

reads a string until it encounters the new line character or maximum number of characters (40). Now, an input of "Hello World" will produce the output as desired. The istream::getline member function has the following versions:

```
    istream& getline(signed char*, int len, char = '\n');
    istream& getline(unsigned char*, int len, char = '\n');
```

They operate in the following ways:

- ♦ extracts character up to the delimiter
- ♦ stores the characters in the buffer
- ♦ removes the delimiter from the input stream
- ♦ does not place the delimiter into the buffer
- ♦ maximum number of characters extracted is len-1

The terminator character can be any character. The terminator character is *read but not saved* into a buffer; instead, it is replaced by the null character.

The prototype of write() functions is:

```
    ostream::write( char * buffer, int size );
```

It displays size (second parameter) number of characters from the input buffer. The display does not stop even when the NULL character is encountered; If the length of the buffer is less than the indicated size, it displays beyond the bounds of buffer. Therefore, it is the responsibility of the user to make sure that the size does not exceed the length of the string. The program stand.cpp illustrates the use of write in string processing.

```
// stand.cpp: display stand of "Object Computing with C++";
#include <iostream.h>
#include <string.h>
void main()
{
    char *string1 = "Object-Computing";
    char *string2 = " with C++";
    int i;
    int len1 = strlen( string1 );
    int len2= strlen( string2 );
    for( i = 1; i < len1; i++ )
    {
        cout.write( string1, i );
        cout << endl;
```

```
}
for( i = len1; i > 0; i-- )
{
    cout.write( string1, i );
    cout << endl;
}
// print both the string
cout.write( string1, len1 );
cout.write( string2, len2 );
cout << endl;
// above two write() can be replaced below single statement
cout.write( string1, len1 ).write( string2, len2 );
cout << endl;
cout.write( string1, 6 );
}
```

Run

```
O
Ob
Obj
Obje
Objec
Object
Object-
Object-C
Object-Co
Object-Com
Object-Comp
Object-Compu
Object-Comput
Object-Computi
Object-Computin
Object-Computing
Object-Computin
Object-Computi
Object-Comput
Object-Compu
Object-Comp
Object-Com
Object-Co
Object-C
Object-
Object
Objec
Obje
Obj
Ob
O
Object-Computing with C++
Object-Computing with C++
Object
```

In `main()`, the last statement

```
cout.write( string1, 6 );
```

indicates to display six characters from the string, `string1` even though the input string has more characters than the number of characters requested to be displayed. The two statements,

```
cout.write( string1, len1 );
cout.write( string2, len2 );
```

can be replaced by the single statement,

```
cout.write( string1, len1 ).write( string2, len2 );
```

The *dot* operator with the predefined object `cout` indicates that the function `write` is a member of the class `ostream`. The invocation of `write()` function returns the object of type `ostream` which again invokes the `write()` function.

17.5 Formatted Console I/O Operations

Most programs need to output data in various styles. A common requirement is to reserve an area of the screen for a field, without knowing the number of characters the data of that field will occupy. To do this, there must be a provision for alignment of fields to left or right, or padded with some characters. C++ supports a wide variety of features to perform input or output in different formats. They include the following:

- `ios` stream class member functions and flags
- Standard manipulators
- User-defined manipulators

ios Class Functions and Flags

The stream class, `ios` contains a large number of member functions to assist in formatting the output in a number of ways. The most important among these functions are shown in Table 17.1.

Function	Task Performed
`width()`	Specifies the required number of fields to be used while displaying the output value.
`precision()`	Specifies the number of digits to be displayed after the decimal point.
`fill()`	Specifies a character to be used to fill the unused area of a field. By default, fills blank space character.
`setf()`	Sets format flag that control the form of output display
`unsetf()`	Clears the specified flag

Table 17.1: ios class member functions

Defining Display Field Width

The function `width()` is a member function of the `ios` class and is used to define the width of the field to be used while displaying the output value. It must be accessed using objects of the `ios` class (commonly accessed using cout object). It has the following two forms:

```
int width();
int width(int w);
```

where w is the field width i.e., number of columns to be used for displaying output. The first form of width() returns the current width setting whereas, the second form width(int) sets the width to the specified integer value and returns the previous width. It specifies field width for the item, which is displayed first immediately after the setting. After displaying an item, it will revert to the default width. For instance, the statements

```
cout.width( 4 );
cout << 20 << 123;
```

produce the following output:

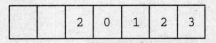

The first value is printed in right-justified form in four columns. The next item is printed immediately after first item without any separation; width(4) is then reverted to the default value, which prints in left-justified form with default size. It can be overcome by explicitly setting width of every item with each cout statement as follows:

```
cout.width( 4 );
cout << 20;
cout.width( 4 );
cout << 123;
```

These statements produce the following output.

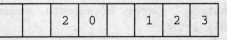

It should be noted that field width should be specified for each item independently if a width other than the default is desired for output. If the field width specified is smaller than the required width to display items, the field is expanded to the required space without truncation. For instance,

```
cout.width( 2 );
cout << 2000;
```

These statements produce the following output:

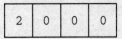

without truncating eventhough width is specified as two. The program student.cpp illustrates the use of width function in formatting the displayed output.

```cpp
// student.cpp: printing student details in the form of table
#include <iostream.h>
const int MAX_MARKS = 600;    // maximum marks
class student
{
   private:
     char name[11];       // name of a student
```

```
      int marks;              // marks scored by a student
   public:
      void read();
      void show();
};
void student::read()
{
   cout << "Enter Name: ";
   cin >> name;
   cout << "Enter Marks Secured: ";
   cin >> marks;
}
void student::show()
{
   cout.width( 10 );
   cout << name;
   cout.width( 6 );
   cout << marks;
   cout.width( 10 );
   cout << int(float(marks)/MAX_MARKS * 100);   // percentage
}
void main()
{
   int i, count;
   student *s;    // pointers to objects
   cout << "How many students ? ";
   cin >> count;
   s = new student[count];    // array of objects, student s[count]
   for( i = 0; i < count; i++ )
   {
      cout << "Enter Student " << i+1 << " details.." << endl;
      s[i].read();
   }
   cout << "Student Report..." << endl;
   cout.width( 3 );
   cout << "R#";
   cout.width( 10 );
   cout << "Student";
   cout.width( 6 );
   cout << "Marks";
   cout.width( 15 );
   cout << "Percentage" << endl;
   for( i = 0; i < count; i++ )
   {
      cout.width( 3 );
      cout << i+1;    // roll_no
      s[i].show();
      cout << endl;
   }
}
```

Run

```
How many students ? 3
Enter Student 1 details..
Enter Name: Tejaswi
Enter Marks Secured: 450
Enter Student 2 details..
Enter Name: Rajkumar
Enter Marks Secured: 535
Enter Student 3 details..
Enter Name: Bindu
Enter Marks Secured: 429
Student Report...
R#   Student   Marks    Percentage
 1   Tejaswi   450      75
 2   Rajkumar  525      87
 3   Bindu     429      71
```

Setting Precision

The function `precision()` is a member of the `ios` class and is used to specify the number of digits to be displayed after the decimal point while printing a floating-point number. By default, the precision size is six. This function must be accessed using objects of the ios class (commonly accessed using `cout` object). It has the following two forms:

```
int precision();            // returns current precision
int precision(int d);
```

where d is the number of digits to the right of the decimal point. It sets the floating-point precision and returns the previous setting. For example, the statements

```
cout.precision( 2 );
cout << 2.23 << endl;
cout << 5.169 << endl;
cout << 3.5055 << endl;
cout << 4.003 << endl;
```

will produce the following output:

```
2.23          (perfect fit)
5.17          (rounded)
3.51          (rounded)
4             (no trailing zeros, truncated)
```

After displaying an item, the user defined precision will not revert to the default value. Different values can be processed with different precision by having multiple precision statements. For instance,

```
cout.precision( 1 );
cout << 2.23 << endl;
cout.precision( 3 );
cout << 5.1691 << endl;
```

will produce the following output:

```
2.2        (truncated)
5.169      (truncated)
```

Consider the statements:

```
cout.precision(3);
```

```
cout << 12.53 << 20.5 << 2;
```

which produce the following output all packed together:

1	2	.	5	3	2	0	.	5	2

It can be overcome by the combined use of width() and precision to control the output format. The statements

```
cout.precision( 2 );
cout.width( 6 );
cout << 12.53;
cout.width( 6 );
cout << 20.5;
cout.width( 6 );
cout << 2;
```

will produce the following output:

	1	2	.	5	3			2	0	.	5						2

It must be noted from the above output that the unused width is filled with blank characters. Unlike width(), the precision() must be reset for each data item being output if new precision is desired.

Filling and Padding

The function fill() is a member of the ios class and is used to specify the character to be displayed in the unused portion of the display width. By default, blank character is displayed in the unused portion if the display width is larger than that required by the value. It has the following two forms:

```
int fill();              // returns current fill character
int fill( ch );
```

where ch is the character to be filled in the unused portion. For example, the statements

```
cout.fill( '*' );
cout.precision( 2 );
cout.width( 6 );
cout << 12.53;
cout.width( 6 );
cout << 20.5;
cout.width( 6 );
cout << 2;
```

will produce the following output:

*	1	2	.	5	3	*	*	2	0	.	5	*	*	*	*	*	2

It is seen from the above output that the unused width is filled with asterisk character as set by the statement cout.fill('*');. Similar to precision(), the effect of fill() continues unless explicitly modified by the other fill() statement. It is illustrated by the program salary.cpp.

```
// salary.cpp: filling and padding
#include <iostream.h>
void main()
{
  char *desig[5] = { "CEO", "Manager", "Receptionist", "Clerk", "Peon" };
  int salary[5] = { 10200, 5200, 2950, 950, 750 };
  cout << "Salary Structure Based on Designation" << endl;
  cout << "-----------------------------------------" << endl;
  cout.width( 15 );
  cout << "Designation";
  cout << "      ";
  cout.width( 15 );
  cout << "Salary (in Rs.)" << endl;
  cout << "-----------------------------------------" << endl;
  for( int i = 0; i < 5; i++ )
  {
    cout.fill('.');
    cout.width(15);
    cout << desig[i];
    cout << "      ";
    cout.fill('*');
    cout.width(15);
    cout << salary[i] << endl;
  }
  cout << "-----------------------------------------" << endl;
}
```

Run

```
Salary Structure Based on Designation
-----------------------------------------
    Designation      Salary (in Rs.)
-----------------------------------------
...........CEO     *********10200
........Manager    **********5200
...Receptionist    ***********2950
..........Clerk    ************950
...........Peon    ************750
-----------------------------------------
```

Note that such a form of output representation is extensively used by financial institutions to represent money transactions so that no one can modify the amount (money representation) easily.

Formatting with Flags and Bit-fields

From the earlier examples, it can be noted that, when the function width() is used, results are printed in the right-justified form (which is not a usual practice). C++ provides a mechanism to set the printing of results in the left-justified form, scientific notation etc. The member function of the ios class, setf() (setf stands for set flags) is used to set flags and bit-fields that control the output. It has the following two forms:

```
        long setf(long _setbits, long _field);
        long setf(long _setbits );
```

where _setbits is one of the flags defined in the class ios. It specifies the format action required for the output, and _field specifies the group to which the formatting flag belongs. Both the forms return the previous settings. The flags, bit-fields when set with setf() and their actions is shown in Table 17.2. There are three bit-fields and each group has format flags that are mutually exclusive. For instance,

```
cout.setf( ios::right, ios::adjustfield );
cout.setf( ios::oct, ios::basefield );
cout.setf( ios::scientific, ios::floatfield );
```

Note that the flag argument (first) should be one of the group (bit-field) of the second argument.

Flags value	Bit field	Effect produced
ios::left	ios::adjustfield	Left-justified output
ios::right	ios::adjustfield	Right-adjust output
ios::internal	ios::adjustfield	Padding occurs between the sign or base indicator and the number, when the number output fails to fill the full width of the field.
ios::dec	ios::basefield	Decimal conversion
ios::oct	ios::basefield	Octal conversion
ios::hex	ios::basefield	Hexadecimal conversion
ios::scientific	ios::floatfield	Use exponential floating notation
ios::fixed	ios::floatfield	Use ordinary floating notation

Table 17.2: Flags and bit fields for setf function

Consider the following statements:

```
cout.setf( ios::left, ios::adjustfield );
cout.fill( '*' );
cout.precision( 2 );
cout.width( 6 );
cout << 12.53;
cout.width( 6 );
cout << 20.5;
cout.width( 6 );
cout << 2;
```

The output produced by the above statements is:

1	2	.	5	3	*	2	0	.	5	*	*	2	*	*	*	*	*

The statements

```
cout.setf( ios::internal, ios::adjustfield );
cout.fill( '*' );
cout.precision( 3 );
```

```
cout.width( 10 );
cout << -420.53;
```
will produce the following output:

If the last statement is replaced by,
```
cout << -420.534;
```
the following output will be generated:

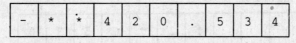

Note that the sign is left justified and the value is right justified. The space between them is filled with stars.

Displaying Trailing Zeros and Plus Sign

Streams support the feature of avoiding truncation of the trailing zeros in the output. For instance, the following statements:
```
cout << 20.55 << endl;
cout << 55.40 << endl;
cout << 10.00 << endl;
```
produce the output as shown below:

It can be observed that the trailing zeros in second and third output have been truncated. The `ios` class has the flag, showpoint which when set, prints the trailing zeros also. It is set by the following statement
```
cout.setf( ios::showpoint );
```
which causes the `cout` to display the trailing decimal point and zero. The following statements
```
cout.setf( ios::showpoint );
cout.precision( 2 );
cout << 20.55 << endl;
cout << 55.40 << endl;
cout << 10.00 << endl;
```
would produce the output as shown below:

2	0	.	5	5
5	5	.	4	0
1	0	.	0	0

Similarly, the plus symbol can be printed using the following statement:

```
cout.setf( ios::showpos );
```

For example, the statements

```
cout.setf( ios::showpos );            // positive sign
cout.setf( ios::showpoint );          // trailing zero and point
cout.setf( ios::internal, ios::adjustfield );
cout.precision( 3 );
cout.width( 10 );
cout << 420.53;
```

will produce the following output:

+			4	2	0	.	5	3	0

Table 17.3 presents summary of flags that do not have bit fields for the `setf` function.

Flag's value	Effect produced
`ios::showbase`	Use base indicator on output
`ios::showpos`	Add '+' to positive integers
`ios::showpoint`	Include decimal point and trailing zeros in output
`ios::uppercase`	Upper-case hex output
`ios::skipws`	Skips white-space characters on input.
`ios::unitbuf`	Flush after insertion. (i.e., use a buffer of size 1)
`ios::stdio`	Flush stdout and stderr after insertion

Table 17.3: Flags that do not have bit fields for setf function

The flag setting `ios::skipws` is set by default. The white-space characters are space, tab, newline, carriage return, form feed and vertical tab. While performing formatted input (with the `>>` operator), an input stream (such as `cin`) behaves as if these characters are not present in the input. Use this flag with the `resetiosflags` manipulator, to prevent skipping white-space characters.

The flags can be reset by using the `ios::unsetf` member function. It has the following syntax:

```
long unsetf(long);
```

and is invoked as follows:

```
cout.unsetf( ios::showpos );
```

It clears the bits corresponding to show positive-sign symbol (when number displayed is positive) and returns the previous settings.

17.6 Manipulators

The C++ streams package makes use of the notion of stream manipulators, principally as a means of manipulating the formatting state associated with a stream. These manipulators are functions that can be used with the `<<` or the `>>` operator to alter the behavior of any stream class instances including the `cin` and `cout`. C++ has manipulators which produce output and consume input to extend stream I/O formatting. Such manipulators can be especially useful for simple parsing of stream inputs. Manipulators are broadly categorized as producers and consumers. A producer manipulator is one which generates output on an output stream, for example, `endl`. Similarly, a consumer manipulator consumes input from an input stream, for example, `ws`.

Manipulators are special functions that are specifically designed to modify the working of a stream. They can be embedded in the I/O statements to modify the form parameters of a stream. All the predefined manipulators are defined in the header file `iomanip.h`. Manipulators are more convenient to use than their counterparts, defined by the `ios` class. There can be more than one manipulator in a statement and they can be chained as shown in the following statements:

```
cout << manip1 << manip2 << manip2 << item;
cout << manip1 << item1 << item2 << manip2 << item3;
```

This kind of chaining of manipulators is useful in displaying several columns of output. Manipulators are categorized into the following two types:

- Non-Parameterized Manipulators
- Parameterized Manipulators

As mentioned before, `cout` and `cin` work elegantly with any basic type. They do not require specification of type of variables while performing I/O. The format string of C's I/O function requires display control information such as width, number system, etc., apart from the variable types in the format string. The program `hex.c` clarifies these concepts.

```c
/* hex.c: read hexadecimal number and display the same in decimal */
#include <stdio.h>
void main()
{
  int num;
  printf( "Enter any hexadecimal number: " );
  scanf( "%x", &num );      /*Input in hexadecimal*/
  /*output i in decimal,in a field of width 6*/
  printf( "The input number in decimal = " );
  printf( "%6d", num);
}
```

Run

```
Enter any hexadecimal number: ab
The input number in decimal =    171
```

This kind of code is often useful. The question arises—*How can this be done with cin and cout ?* The answer lies in the manipulators. For example, the above lines of code that used `scanf` and `printf` can be rewritten as listed in the program `hex.cpp`.

```cpp
// hex.cpp: read hexadecimal number and display the same in decimal
#include <iostream.h>
#include <iomanip.h>    // for manipulators
void main()
{
  int num;
  cout << "Enter any hexadecimal number: ";
```

```
cin >> hex >> num;        // Input in hexadecimal
// output i in decimal, in a field of width 6
cout << "The input number in decimal = ";
cout << setw( 6 ) << num;
}
```

Run

```
Enter any hexadecimal number: ab
The input number in decimal =    171
```

The manipulator hex sets the conversion base for cin to 16. So cin interprets the input characters as digits of a hexadecimal number. The manipulator setw sets the field width as 6 for cout. Thus, the input to the above program (ab) is converted into decimal and displayed (16*a+b = 16*10+11 = 171).

The C++ iostream package contains a rather small handful of predefined producer consumer manipulators, the only instance of consumer being the white-space eater, for example, ws. Other pre-defined manipulators set stream state variables which influence processing of input and output, for example, hex. The implementation of the ios class as well as the implementation of the insertion and extraction operators correspond to the data type of an item they process. The list of non-parameterized manipulators and parameterized manipulator functions are shown in Table 17.4 and 17.5 respectively. Each one of these can be used with either the << or the >> operator without incurring any compile-time errors. But some of them affect only output streams such as cout, and some others, only input streams such as cin. Unless otherwise mentioned, these manipulators affect both types of streams. The first six manipulators - dec, hex, oct, ws, endl, and ends are defined in iostream.h itself and the rest are in the header file iomanip.h.

Manipulator	Action Performed
dec	Sets the conversion base to 10
hex	Sets the conversion base to 16
oct	Sets the conversion base to 8
ws	Extracts white-space characters from an input stream. Characters in the stream will be extracted until a non-white-space character is found, or an error (such as EOF) occurs. As expected, it affects only input streams.
endl	Outputs a newline and flushes stream Affects only output streams "\n"
ends	Outputs a NULL character ('\0') Affects only output streams
flush	Flushes the stream. Affects only output streams

Table 17.4: C++'s predefined non-parameterized manipulators

Manipulator	Action Performed	Equivalent to
`setw(int width)`	Sets the field width	`width`
`setprecision(int prec)`	Sets the floating-point precision	`precision`
`setfill(int fchar)`	Sets the fill character	`fill`
`setbase(int base)`	Sets the conversion base 0: Base 10 is used for output 8: Use octal for input and output 10: Use decimal for input and output 16: Use hexadecimal for input and output	
`setiosflags(long flags)`	Sets the format flag	`setf`
`resetiosflags(long flags)`	Resets the format flag	`unsetf`

Table 17.5: C++'s predefined parameterized manipulators

Buffering

When a stream is buffered, each insertion or extraction does not have a corresponding I/O operation to physically write to or read data from a device. Instead, insertions and extractions are stored in a buffer from which data is written or read in chunks.

In C++, it is possible to force data buffered in an output stream to be written. It is called flushing and it ensures that everything stored in an output buffer has been displayed. In general, flushing is done when interactive input is requested by the user, so that the program can be sure that information displayed on the screen is completely up-to-date. The *cout's* buffer can be flushed using the statement,

```
cout.flush();
```

A program can `tie` an input stream to an output device. In this case, the output stream is flushed when any characters are fetched from the input stream. For instance, `cin` is automatically tied to `cout` to be sure that everything has been physically displayed before any input occurs. The user defined streams can be tied using the `tie` function as follows:

```
istream input;
ostream output;
....
input.tie( output );
```

The last statement forces the C++ I/O system, to flush the object stream, output every time the fetch operation is initiated using the object, `input`.

The parameterized manipulators are described below:

`setw(int width)`: Sets the width of the output field specified by the integer parameter width. The output field width is reset to 0 every time an output is performed using the `<<` operator. When the output field width is 0, normal output is done (without filling or aligning). Hence, use the `setw` manipulator to specify the field width before every output for which a particular field width is desired.

`setprecision(int prec)`: Sets the precision used for floating point output. The number of digits to be shown after the decimal point is given by the integer `prec`.

setfill(int fchar): Sets the *fill character* to that specified in fchar. The fill character is used to fill (or pad) the empty space in the output field when the width of the output variable is less than the width of the output field. The default fill character is the space character.

setbase(int base): Sets the conversion base according to the integer base, which can assume any one of the following four values:

    0: Base 10 is used for output;
    8: Use octal for input and output.
    10: Use decimal for input and output.
    16: Use hexadecimal for input and output.

The base to be used for input is specified as a part of the input itself - inputs beginning with 0 are treated as octal, those beginning with 0x are treated as hexadecimal. Otherwise, the base is assumed as decimal.

setiosflags(long flags): The parameter flags can be any of the flags listed in ios stream class. More than one flag can be set with the same manipulator by ORing the flags.

The statement

```
cout << setw( 8 ) << 1234;
```

prints the value 1234 right-justified in the field width of 8 characters. The output can be left justified using the statement,

```
cout << setw( 8 ) << setiosflags( ios::left ) << 1234;
```

The key difference between manipulators and the ios class interface functions is in their implementation. The ios member functions are used to read the previous format-state, which can be used to know the current state or save for future usage, whereas, the manipulators do not return the previous format state. The program foutput.cpp illustrates the use of some of the manipulators with output streams.

```
// foutput.cpp:  various formatting flags with the << operator
#include <iostream.h>
#include <iomanip.h>
void main()
{
    int x = 100;
    cout << hex << x << ' ' << dec << x << endl;
    float f = 122.3434;
    cout << f << endl;
    cout << setprecision( 3 );
    cout << f << endl;
    cout << setw( 6 ) << setfill( '0' );
    cout << setiosflags(ios::internal | ios::showbase);
    cout << hex << x << endl;
    cout << setiosflags( ios::scientific ) << f << endl;
}
```

Run

```
64 100
122.343399
122.343
0x0064
1.223e+02
```

In main(), the statement

```
cout << hex << x << endl;
```

outputs 0x0064, since the field width 6 and the fill character '0' is filled between the base indicator '0x' (due to ios::showbase) and the number 64 (padding like this occurs due to ios::internal being set).

The program payroll.cpp uses the manipulators for displaying numeric quantities for accounting purposes so that the decimal points are aligned in a single column.

```cpp
// payroll.cpp: payroll like output example
#include <iostream.h>
#include <iomanip.h>
void main()
{
  float f1=123.45, f2=34.65, f3=56;
  cout << setiosflags(ios::showpoint|ios::fixed)
       << setiosflags(ios::right);
  cout << setw(6) << f1 << endl;
  cout << setw(6) << f2 << endl;
  cout << setw(6) << f3 << endl;
}
```

Run
```
123.45
 34.65
 56.00
```

Setting the flag ios::showpoint will display the point even though a floating point number has no significant digits to the right of the decimal point (the variable f3). Setting ios::fixed ensures output in fixed point rather than in exponential notation. The decimal points happen to be aligned due to two manipulators: setprecision(2)— show two digits after the decimal point and setiosflags(ios::right)— display output in right-justified manner.

```cpp
// oct.cpp: Usage of number-base manipulators with cin
#include <iostream.h>
#include <iomanip.h>
void main()
{
    int i;
    // The statement below always interprets the input as octal digits
    cout << "Enter octal number: ";
    cin >> oct >> i;
    cout << "Its decimal equivalent is ";
    cout << i << endl;
    //The base used by cin in the statement is decided at the time of input
    cout << "Enter decimal number: ";
    cin >> setbase( 0 ) >> i;
    cout << "Its output: ";
    cout << i;
```

Run1

```
Enter octal number: 111
Its decimal equivalent is 73
Enter decimal number: 0111
Its output: 73
```

Run2

```
Enter octal number: 111
Its decimal equivalent is 73
Enter decimal number: 0x111
Its output: 273
```

In the `cin` statement

```
cin >> oct >> i;
```

data input is always interpreted as an octal number. So, if the input is 111, the output using the `cout` statement here is 73. Whereas, in the statement

```
cin >> setbase( 0 ) >> i;
```

if the input to the `cin` statement here is 111, then it is assumed to be a decimal number. If it is 0111, it is assumed as an octal number. Finally, an input such as 0x111 is assumed hexadecimal. So the output of the last `cout` statement will be 111 in the first case, 73 in the second, and 273 in the third.

The program `mattab.cpp` illustrates the use of manipulators and `ios` functions in formatting the output.

```cpp
// mattab.cpp: prints mathematical table having sqr, sqrt, and log columns
#include <iostream.h>
#include <iomanip.h>
#include <math.h>
// macro for computing square of a number
#define sqr( x ) ((x)*(x))
void main()
{
    int num;
    cout << "Enter Any Integer Number: ";
    cin >> num;
    cout << "-------------------------------------------------" << endl;
    cout << setw( 5 ) << "NUM" << setw( 10 ) << "SQR";
    cout << setw( 15 ) << "SQRT" << setw( 15 ) << "LOG" << endl;
    cout << "-------------------------------------------------" << endl;
    cout.setf( ios::showpoint );  // display trailing zeros
    for( int i = 1; i <= num; i++ )
    {
        cout << setw( 5 ) << i
             << setw( 10 ) << sqr( i )
             << setw( 15 ) << setprecision( 3 ) << sqrt( (double) i )
             << setw( 15 ) << setprecision( 4 ) <<setiosflags(ios::scientific)
             << log( (double) i ) << endl << resetiosflags( ios::scientific );
    }
    cout << "-------------------------------------------------" << endl;
}
```

Run

```
Enter Any Integer Number: 10
-------------------------------------------------
  NUM        SQR          SQRT          LOG
-------------------------------------------------
    1          1         1.000      0.0000e+00
    2          4         1.414      6.9315e-01
    3          9         1.732      1.0986e+00
    4         16         2.000      1.3863e+00
    5         25         2.236      1.6094e+00
    6         36         2.449      1.7918e+00
    7         49         2.646      1.9459e+00
    8         64         2.828      2.0794e+00
    9         81         3.000      2.1972e+00
   10        100         3.162      2.3026e+00
-------------------------------------------------
```

17.7 Custom/User-Defined Manipulators

An important feature of C++ streams is that they also work well with the user-defined manipulators as they do with *built-in manipulators*. Hence, the users can design their own (customized) manipulators to control the appearance of the output depending upon their taste and need. The syntax for creating a custom manipulator is shown in Figure 17.4. In the syntax, manipulator is the name of the user-defined manipulator.

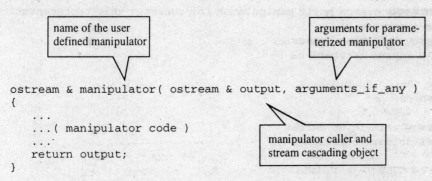

Figure 17.4: Syntax of creating a custom manipulator

The program space3.cpp creates and uses the user-defined manipulator sp that inserts space into the output stream and flushes it. It eliminates the usage of messy statements such as,

```
cout << x << ' ' << y << ' ' << z << ' ' << w << endl;
```
to output a series of variables separated by spaces. The statement can be written as,

```
cout << x << sp << y << sp << z << sp << w << endl;
```
which appears more elegant and simple to use and understand.

```
// space3.cpp: custom built manipulator
#include <iostream.h>
// The user-defined manipulator
ostream & sp( ostream& os )
{
    os << ' ' << flush;  // or cout << ' ' << flush
    return os;
}
void main()
{
    int x=1, y=2, z=3, w=4;
    cout << x << sp << y << sp << z << sp << w << endl;
}
```

Run

```
1 2 3 4
```

In the above program, the function

```
ostream & sp( ostream& os )
```

defines a manipulator called sp that prints a single space and flushes the same to console for immediate display without buffering.

Another interesting use of manipulators is demonstrated in the program currency.cpp. It defines manipulators for prefixing the currency symbol to an item cost depending on the currency used by the country which has manufactured the item.

```
// currency.cpp: custom built manipulator for currency unit representation
#include <iostream.h>
// currency in Indian rupees
ostream & rupee( ostream& os )
{
    os << "Rs. " << flush;
    return os;
}
// currency unit in US dollar
ostream & dollar( ostream& os )
{
    cout << "US$ " << flush;
    return os;
}
void main()
{
    char item1[25], item2[25];
    unsigned int cost1, cost2;
    cout << "Item Sales in India..." << endl;
    cout << "Enter Item Name: ";
    cin.getline( item1, 25 );
    cout << "Cost of Item: ";
    cin >> cost1;
    cout << "Item Sales in US..." << endl;
```

```
cout << "Enter Item Name: ";
cin.ignore();
cin.getline( item2, 25 );
cout << "Cost of Item: ";
cin >> cost2;
cout << "Item Cost Statistics..." << endl;
cout << "Item Name: " << item1 << endl;
cout << "Cost: " << rupee << cost1 << endl;
cout << "Item Name: " << item2 << endl;
cout << "Cost: " << dollar << cost2 << endl;
}
```

Run

```
Item Sales in India...
Enter Item Name: PARAM Supercomputer
Cost of Item: 55000
Item Sales in US...
Enter Item Name: CRAY Supercomputer
Cost of Item: 40500
Item Cost Statistics...
Item Name: PARAM Supercomputer
Cost: Rs. 55000
Item Name: CRAY Supercomputer
Cost: US$ 40500
```

Standard Manipulators Implementation

The previous example was easy, since the manipulator did not accept any parameters in the output statement. The function that overloads the << operator to accept manipulators merely needs to call the manipulator with the output stream object (cout in this case). Manipulators accepting parameters initiates many actions. Consider the manipulator declared in iomanip.h header file, setw(int), to illustrate the implementation of manipulators. The declaration of this manipulator is:

```
        ostream & setw( ostream&, int );
```

But in the output statement, setw is called with only one integer argument:

```
        cout << setw(6) << i;
```

Another function (also called setw) is needed that accepts only one argument of type integer. It does not know which output object needs to have its field-width set. Assuming the output object as cout will unduly restrict its use (For instance, it would not be possible to use it directly with files). To resolve this impasse, the following solution is used. A class called omanip_int is declared. It has two private members; a pointer to function (the actual manipulator) and an integer that specifies the width. It has a constructor that sets these members, and a friend function that overloads the << operator and calls the actual manipulator.

```
class omanip_int
{
  private:
    ostream& (*f)( ostream&, int ); // Pointer to the actual manipulator
    int w;                 // Width to be set
```

```
public:
  //Constructor
  omanip_int( ostream& (*tf)(ostream&,int), int tw )
  { f = tf;
    w = tw;
  }
  //  overloading stream output operator
  friend ostream& operator << (ostream& os, omanip_int o)
  {
    return o.f( os, o.w );        //Call the actual manipulator.
  }
};
```

Two more functions are now required; one that actually manipulates the stream, and another that is invoked from the output statement. They are declared as follows:

```
//Actual manipulator
ostream& setw( ostream& os, int w )
{
  os.width( w );
  return os;
}
// This is called first from the output statement.
// It accepts an integer and returns an instance of class omanip_int
omanip_int setw( int w )
{
  return omanip_int( setw, w ); // returns nameless object
}
```

Now, the statement

```
     cout << setw( 6 ) << i;
```

will first call the second setw manipulator that *remembers* the width passed in an instance of the class omanip_int. The actual function to be called is also recorded here. This instance is returned. The first << above now has the return value of setw(6) - an instance of omanip_int on the right, and cout on the left. The overloaded function (defined in the class omanip_int) is invoked, which in turn calls the actual manipulator. The same concept can be utilized while implementing the user-defined manipulators.

Parameterized Custom Manipulators

Most manipulators do not accept parameters and are simple to use. Sometimes it is necessary to pass data to the manipulators, however, as with the built-in manipulator setw(int). The program presented in pmani.cpp, implements a manipulator that accepts three arguments - width, precision, and fill character. The manipulator is useful as a shorthand notation for setting the above parameters to output floating point variables with different width, precision, and fill characters.

```
// pmani.cpp: Parameterized Manipulator
#include <iostream.h>
#include <iomanip.h>
// output manipulator taking arguments of type int, int, char
```

```
class my_manipulator
{
   private:
     int width, precision;
     char fill;
   public:
     //Constructor
   my_manipulator(int tw, int tp, char tf):width(tw),precision(tp),fill(tf)
   {}
   //Overloaded << operator
   friend ostream & operator << ( ostream& os, my_manipulator object );
};
//Actual manipulator called by overloaded operator << friend function
ostream & operator << ( ostream& os, my_manipulator object )
{
   os << setw( object.width ) << setprecision( object.precision ) \
   << setfill( object.fill );
   os << setiosflags(ios::showpoint|ios::right);
   return os;
}
//Function called first from the output statement
my_manipulator set_float( int w, int p, char f )
{
   return my_manipulator( w, p, f ); // nameless object is returned
}
void main()
{
   float f1=123.2734, f2=23.271, f3=16.1673;
   // set_float accepts three parameters-width, precision and fill character
   cout << set_float( 10, 3, '*' ) << f1 << endl;
   cout << set_float( 9, 2, '^' ) << f2 << endl;
   cout << set_float( 8, 3, '#' ) << f3 << endl;
}
```

Run
```
***123.273
^^^^23.27
##16.167
```

In main(), the statement

        cout << set_float(10, 3, '*') << f1 << endl;

has the call to the normal function as,

        set_float(10, 3, '*')

which in turn creates the nameless object of the class my_manipulator (and initializes its members) and returns the same. Thus, the above output statement effectively becomes,

        cout << my_manipulator(set_float, 10, 3, '*') << f1 << endl;

The class my_manipulator is a friend of the overloaded operator function and hence, the mutated output statement invokes the function,

        friend ostream& operator << (ostream& os, my_manipulator object) which actually sets the format for the output's appearance and returns the reference to `cout` so that the item that immediately follows it will be printed in the desired format. After printing one item, format specification will immediately revert to the default.

17.8 Stream Operators with User-Defined Classes

The elegance of streams is that, it can, not only be used with built-in C++ data types, but also with user-defined classes. It requires overloading of the stream insertion and extraction operators. In case of the overloaded friend stream operator `<<` function, the `ostream` & is considered as the first argument. The return value of this friend function is of type `ostream&`. Similarly, for overloading the friend stream operator `>>` function, the `istream&` is considered as the first argument. The value returned by this friend function is of type `istream&`. In both the cases, a reference to an object of the class to which this operator function is a friend is taken as the second argument. After processing the data members of the second argument, the first argument `istream` object would be returned. Overloading of stream operators to support user-defined data types has been discussed earlier in detail in the chapter on *Operator Overloading*.

The insertion operator, `<<` has been overloaded to have an instance of `ostream` (or one of its derived classes) on the left and an instance of any basic variable type on the right. Similarly, the `>>` operator is overloaded to have an instance of `istream` class on the left and any basic variable type on the right.

Insertion Operator << Overloading

Consider the prototype of the overloaded `<<` operator to gain a better understanding of streams computation. For instance, the prototype of insertion operator overloaded to display integer data is as follows:

```
ostream & operator << (ostream&, int);
```

Recall that, effectively `cout` is an instance of class `ostream`. Hence, if the variable `num` is an integer, then, the statement

```
cout << num;
```

invokes the overloaded operator function with a reference to `cout` as the first parameter, and the value of the variable `num` as the second. For further overloading, i.e., for this operator to work with user-defined classes, another overloaded function is necessary, similar to the above function declaration. A new operator function accepts a reference to the instance of user-defined class instead of an integer.

Extraction Operator >> Overloading

The `>>` operator (used with `istream`) can also be overloaded to take care of user-defined types. Inclusion of a function to overload the `>>` operator helps in writing more compact and readable code in the `main()`. The program `point.cpp` illustrates the overloading of stream operators to operate on user defined data items.

```
// point.cpp: use of both << and >> with a user-defined class.
#include <iostream.h>
// user defined class
class POINT
{
```

```
    private:
       int x, y;
    public:
       POINT()
       {
          x = y = 0;
       }
       friend ostream & operator << ( ostream &os, POINT &p );
       friend istream & operator >> ( istream & is, POINT &p );
};
// friend function to POINT
ostream & operator << ( ostream& os, POINT &p )
{
   os << '(' << p.x << ',' << p.y << ')';
   return os;
}
istream & operator >> ( istream &is, POINT &p )
{
   is >> p.x >> p.y;
   return is;
}

void main()
{
   POINT p1, p2;
   cout << "Enter two coordinate points (p1, p2): ";
   cin >> p1 >> p2;     // invokes overloaded operator >> ()
   cout << "Coordinate points you entered are: " << endl;
   cout << p1 << endl << p2 << endl;   // calls overloaded operator << ()
}
```

Run
```
Enter two coordinate points (p1, p2): 2 3 5 6
Coordinate points you entered are:
(2,3)
(5,6)
```

In main(), the statement

```
        cin >> p1 >> p2;     // invokes overloaded operator >> ()
```

illustrates cascading of stream operators to read data; the leftmost >> is executed first, and invokes the overloaded operator function with the first parameter as a reference to cin, and the second parameter as a reference to the instance of POINT p1. The return value of this function (which is cin itself) is used as the left hand side of the second >> operator and so on.

The friend function of the class POINT,

```
        istream & operator >> ( istream &is, POINT &p )
```

overloads the >> operator. It is similar to overloading the output operator. Again, note that the return value enables cascading of the >> operator.

Necessity of Friend Functions

The function overloading the operators >> and << need not always be declared as friend. If the data members x and y were public members of the class POINT, or, if a public member function existed in POINT which output the values of x and y, the friend function declarations would be unnecessary inside the class.

How do the manipulators work with the << operator?

Consider the usage of the manipulator endl:

```
cout << endl;
```

in the previous examples, to insert a newline. The manipulator endl is the function that is declared as,

```
ostream far & endl(ostream far &);
```

in the header file, iostream.h. Thus, endl, is a function that accepts a reference to an ostream (such as cout) and returns the same (a reference to an ostream). Recall that invocation of a function with its name without any parentheses is considered as a pointer to a function. Now it is simple to understand the appearance of the endl on the right side of the << operator; the operator is overloaded to have pointers to functions of this type (that accept a reference to an ostream and returns the same).

Review Questions

17.1   What are streams ? Explain the features of C++ stream I/O with C's I/O system.

17.2   List C++ predefined streams and explain them with suitable example programs.

17.3   Draw console stream class hierarchy and explain its members.

17.4   What is the difference between the statements ?

```
cin >> ch;
ch = cin.get();
```

17.5   Write a program to illustrate the difference between cin and getline while reading strings.

17.6   What is the output of the following statements:

    (a)   cout << 65;

    (b)   cout.put(65);

    (c)   cout.put('A');

17.7   Write a program to print the ASCII table using streams.

17.8   Write an interactive program to print a string entered in a pyramid form. For instance, the string "object" has to be displayed as follows:

```
         o
        o b
       o b j
      o b j e
     o b j e c
    o b j e c t
```

17.9   Write an interactive program to print a rectangle with diamond shape gap exactly at the centre of that rectangle. Accept string from standard input device and print output on standard output device. Here is the sample output when the string "object-object" is entered by the user:

```
object-object
object object
objec  bject
obj     ject
ob        ct
o          t
ob        ct
obj       ect
obje     ject
objec   bject
object object
object-object
```

17.10 Write an interactive program to print the salary-slip in the following format:

```
       Centre for Development of Advanced Computing
              Bangalore, India - 560 025
          Salary-Slip for the Month of XXXXXX 1996
--------------------------------------------------------------------
                                          Date: dd/mm/yy
                                     Employee No.:  xxx
  Employee Name:  xxxxxxxxxxx        Basic Salary: xxxxx.xx
  Grade: xx
  No. of days present: xx


  <----PAYMENTS------>    <----DEDUCTIONS----->  <---- RECOVERIES---->
  BASIC     XXXXX.XX     PF          xxx.xx  LIC           xxx.x
  DA        XXXXX.XX     FPF          xx.xx  CCUBE CONTR.   xx.x
  HRA        XXXX.XX     VPF          xx.xx  SOCIETY ADV     x.x
  CCA         xxx.xx     BEFUND        x.xx  RENT RECV     xxx.x
  DDA           x.xx     P.TAX       xxx.xx  PF LOAN       xxx.x
  ARREARS       x.xx     CANTEEN     xxx.xx  SALARY ADV   xxxx.x
  ADHOC.ALW   xxx.xx     WELFARE      xx.x   TOUR ADV      xxx.x


  TOTAL PAY  xxxxx.xx    TOTAL DED  xxxx.x   TOTAL RECV   xxxx.x
  NET PAY: xxxxx.xx

                                                       (SIGNATURE)
```

17.11 Explain the various methods of performing formated stream I/O operations.

17.12 What are manipulators ? List the various predefined manipulators supported by C++ I/O streams.

17.13 How are the input and output streams tied using `istream.tie()` member function ?

17.14 Write a program to display numbers 0 to 10 in octal, decimal, and hexadecimal systems.

17.15 What are custom manipulators ? Write a custom manipulator for inserting 8 spaces in output.

17.16 Explain how standard manipulators are implemented.

17.17 Illustrate parameterized custom manipulators using a suitable program.

17.18 Write a program to overload stream operators for reading and displaying the object of a class `Employee`. The members of this class include `name`, `emp_no`, `DateOfBirth`, `basic`, `grade`, `qualification`, etc.

18

Streams Computation with Files

18.1 Introduction

A computer system stores programs and data in secondary storage in the form of files. Storing programs and data permanently in main memory is not preferred due to the following reasons:
- Main memory is usually too small to permanently store all the needed programs and data.
- Main memory is a volatile storage device, which loses its contents when power is turned off.

The most visible entity in a computer system is a file. The operating system implements the abstract concept of a file by providing file services and managing mass storage devices such as floppy disks, tapes, and hard disks. The various components involved in file processing are shown in Figure 18.1.

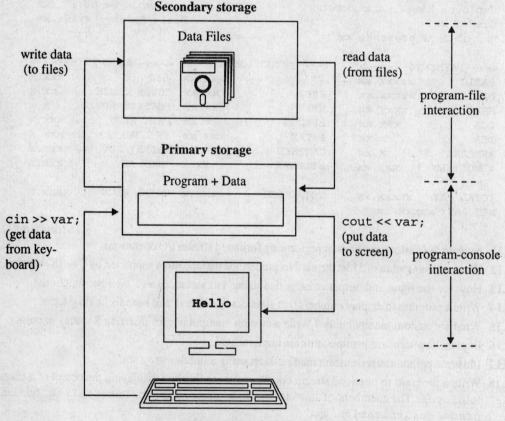

Figure 18.1: Program-console and file interaction

What is a File ?

A file is a collection of related information defined by its creator. Commonly, files represent programs (both source and object forms) and data. Data may be numeric, alphabetic, or alphanumeric. Files may be free-form, such as text files, or may be rigidly formatted. In general, a file is a sequence of bits, bytes, lines, or records whose meaning is defined by its creator and user. A file is named and is referred to by its name. To define a file properly, it is necessary to consider the operations which can be performed on files. The operating system provides most of the essential file manipulation services such as create, open, write, read, rewind, close, and delete.

A program typically involves data communication between the console and the program or between the files and program, or even both. The program must atleast perform data exchange between processor and main memory. Note that a program without the capability to communicate with the external world will serve no useful purpose (irrespective of the objective with which it is designed).

The streams computation model for manipulating files resemble the console streams model. It uses file streams as a means of communication between the programs and the data files. The input stream supplies data to the program and the output stream receives data from the program. Thus, the *input stream* extracts the data from the file and supplies it to the program, whereas *output stream* stores the data into the file supplied by the program. The movement of data between the disk files and input/ output stream in a program is depicted in Figure 18.2.

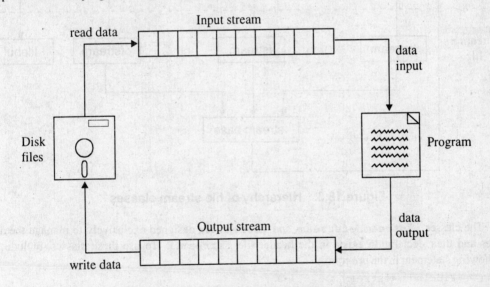

Figure 18.2: File input and output streams

18.2 Hierarchy of File Stream Classes

The file handling techniques of C++ support file manipulation in the form of stream objects. The stream objects `cin` and `cout` are used extensively to deal with the standard input and output devices. These objects are predefined in the header file, `iostream.h` as a part of the C++ language. There are no such predefined objects for disk files. All class declarations have to be done explicitly in the program.

There are three classes for handling files:

- ifstream - for handling input files.
- ofstream - for handling output files.
- fstream   - for handling files on which both input and output can be performed.

These classes are derived from fstreambase and from those declared in the header file iostream.h (istream, iostream, ostream). The hierarchy of C++ file stream classes is shown in Figure 18.3.

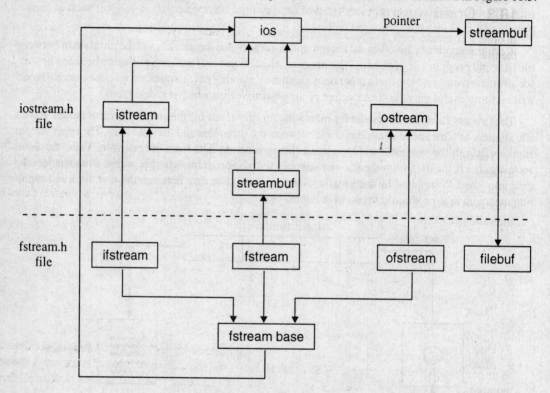

Figure 18.3: Hierarchy of file stream classes

The classes ifstream, ofstream, and fstream are designed exclusively to manage the disk files and their declaration exists in the header file fstream.h. To use these classes, include the following statement in the program

```
#include <fstream.h>
```

The actions performed by classes related to file management are described below:

filebuf: The class filebuf sets the file buffer to read and write. It contains constant openprot used in open() of file stream class. It also contains close() as a member.

fstreambuf: The class fstreambuf supports operations common to the file streams. It serves as a base class for the derived classes ifstream, ofstream, and fstream and contains open() and close() as member functions.

ifstream: The class ifstream supports input operations. It contains open() with default input mode and inherits get(), getline(), read(), seekg(), and tellg() functions from istream.

ofstream: The class `ofstream` supports output operations. It contains `open()` with default output mode and inherits `put()`, `seekp()`, `tellp()`, and `write()` functions from `ostream`.

fstream: The class `fstream` supports simultaneous input and output operations. It contains `open()` with default input mode and inherits all the functions from `istream` and `ostream` classes through `iostream`.

18.3   Opening and Closing of Files

In order to process a file, first, it must be opened to get a handle. The file handle serves as a pointer to the file. Typically, manipulation of a file involves the following steps:

- Name the file on the disk
- Open the file to get the file pointer
- Process the file (read/write)
- Check for errors while processing
- Close the file after its complete usage

The filename is a string of characters, with which a file is logically identified by the user. It provides a means to communicate with the user transparently. The number and type of characters used in naming a file depends on the operating system. Normally, a file has two parts: a *primary name* and an *optional extension*. If the file name has an extension, it is separated by a period from the primary name. Some of the valid file names in the MS-DOS based machines are the following:

```
student.cpp
data.txt
copy.exe
student.obj
student.exe
TEMP
data1
tax.in
```

In MS-DOS systems, the maximum size of a primary name is eight characters and that of an extension is three characters. However, in UNIX based machines, the file name can be upto 31 characters and any number of extensions separated by dots. Some valid file names in the UNIX system include all those valid in the MS-DOS and in addition, it includes the following:

```
.login  (no primary name, acts as hidden file)
xyz.txt.mine
text_data_file
student.8sem.raj
```

In order to get a file pointer, first the file must be created (if it does not exist) and linked to the file name. A file stream can be defined using stream classes, `ifstream`, `ofstream`, or `fstream` depending on the purpose (read or write). In C++, a file can be opened using the following:

- The constructor function of the class.
- The member function `open()` of the class.

After processing an opened file, it must be closed. It can be closed either by explicitly using the `close()` member function of the class or it is automatically closed by the destructor of the class, when the file stream object goes out of scope (expires).

Opening Files Using Constructors

In order to access a file, it has to be opened either in read, write, or append mode. In all the three file stream classes, a file can be opened by passing a filename as the first parameter in the constructor itself. For example, the statement

```
ifstream infile("test.txt");
```

opens the file `test.txt` for input. It is known that, a constructor is used to initialize an object during its creation. Hence, the constructor can be utilized to initialize the filename to be used with the file stream object. The creation and assignment of file name to the file stream object involves the following steps:

• Create a file stream object using the appropriate class depending on the type of file stream required. For example, `ifstream` can be used to create the input stream, `ofstream` can be used to create the output stream, and `fstream` can be used to create the input and output stream.

• Bind the file stream to the disk. In disk, file stream is identified by a file name.

For instance, the following statement opens a file named `database` for input:

```
ifstream infile ( "database" );
```

It creates `infile` as the object of the class `ifstream` that manages the input stream, and opens the file `database` and binds it to the output stream disk file. Similarly, the statement

```
ofstream outfile( "data.out" );
```

defines `outfile` as the object of the class `ostream`, and binds it to the file `data.out` for writing.

The program statements can refer to the file objects similar to the stream objects. The syntax for performing I/O operations with standard input-output devices also holds good for files. For instance, to print the message `Hello World` on the console and into the file, the following commands can be issued:

```
cout << "Hello World";
```

prints the message `Hello World` on the standard output device. Whereas, the statement

```
myfile << "Hello World";
```

prints the message `Hello World` into the file pointed to by the file pointer `myfile` (Figure 18.4).

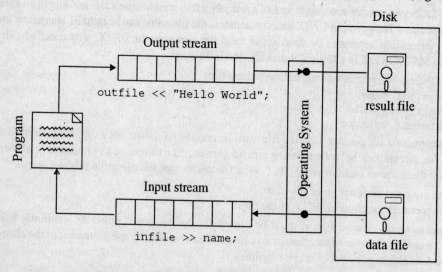

Figure 18.4: File I/O with stream operators

The following statements:

```
outfile << "Hello World";    // write string constant
outfile << salary;           // write variable content
outfile << 750;                    // write 750 to file
```

prints the string "Hello World" and the contents of the variable salary to the output file. Similarly, the following statements:

```
infile >> name;                      // read string
infile >> age;                       // read integer
infile >> number;           // read float
```

read the variables name, age, and number from the input file stream infile.

The constructors of all these classes are declared in the header file fstream.h. The prototypes of file stream constructors are shown in Figure 18.5.

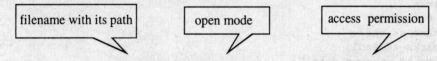

```
ifstream(const char *path, int mode=ios::in, int prot=filebuf::openprot);
```

(a) constructor of class ifstream

```
ofstream(const char *path, int mode=ios::out, int prot=filebuf::openprot);
```

(b) constructor of class ofstream

```
fstream(const char *path,int mode=ios::in|ios::out,int prot=filebuf::openprot);
```

(c) constructor of class fstream

Figure 18.5:   Prototype of file stream class constructors

The stream class arguments have the following meaning:

path: It specifies the pathname of the file to be opened. If the file is in the current directory, only the filename needs to be specified. Otherwise, separate the directory names by a backslash (\) in the MS-DOS or a slash (/) in the Unix operating systems.

mode: It specifies the mode in which the file is to be opened. The argument may be specified by using enumerated constants declared in the ios class.

prot: It specifies the access permission. It is not used if ios::nocreate is used in *mode*. The default permissions are set in the static variable filebuf::openprot for both read and write (The file can be read from and written to) permissions. The access permissions can be read only (S_IREAD) or write only (S_IWRITE). Under UNIX, prot parameter can be used to specify read, write, and execute permissions to specific owner categories (viz., user, group and others).

The file must be closed to release all the resources allocated to it. It is known that, the destructor normally does the cleanup operation. Whenever file stream object goes out of scope or the program terminates its execution, the file is automatically closed by destructor. The program `stdfile.cpp` creates a file `student.out` using constructors and writes student details into it.

```
// stdfile.cpp: student file, creating file with constructor function
#include <fstream.h>
void main()
{
   char name[30];
   int marks;
   ofstream fout ( "student.out" ); // connect student.out to fout
   // read first student details
   cout << "Enter Name: ";
   cin >> name;
   cout << "Enter Marks Secured: ";
   cin >> marks;
   // write to a file
   fout << name << endl;
   fout << marks << endl;
   // read second student details
   cout << "Enter Name: ";
   cin >> name;
   cout << "Enter Marks Secured: ";
   cin >> marks;
   // write to a file
   fout << name << endl;
   fout << marks << endl;
}
```

Run
```
Enter Name: Rajkumar
Enter Marks Secured: 95
Enter Name: Tejaswi
Enter Marks Secured: 90
```

Note: On execution the file `student..out` contains the following.
```
Rajkumar
95
Tejaswi
90
```

In `main()`, the statement
```
        ofstream fout ( "student.out" ); // connect student.out to fout
```
creates the object `fout` and binds it to the file `student.out` by opening it in the write mode. The statement
```
        fout << name << endl;
```
writes the string name to the file, and the statement
```
        fout << marks << endl;
```
writes the integer variable `marks` to the file. The file `student.out` is closed automatically when the program terminates.

Note that, when a file is opened in write-only mode, a new file is created if a file with the same name does not exists. Otherwise, the current contents of the file is truncated and opened in write mode. The program `stdread.cpp` opens file `student.out` using a constructor and prints its contents on the console.

```
// stdread.cpp: student file, read the file student.out
#include <fstream.h>
void main()
{
    char name[30];
    int marks;
    ifstream fin ( "student.out" );   // connect student.out to fout
    // read first student details
    fin >> name;
    fin >> marks;
    cout << "Name: " << name << endl;
    cout << "Marks Secured: " << marks << endl;
    // read second student details
    fin >> name;
    fin >> marks;
    cout << "Name: " << name << endl;
    cout << "Marks Secured: " << marks << endl;
}
```

Run

```
Name: Rajkumar
Marks Secured: 95
Name: Tejaswi
Marks Secured: 90
```

The above program must be executed only when a file with the name `student.out` already exists and has data as expected by the program.

Opening and Closing of Files Explicitly

The file can also be opened explicitly using the function `open()` instead of a constructor. This mechanism is generally used when different files are to be associated with the same object at different times. The syntax for opening a file is shown in Figure 18.6. The file can be closed explicitly using the `close()` function as follows:

```
        stream_object.close();
```

The following examples illustrates file open and close operations.

1. Opening file in write mode:

```
        ofstream fout;                              // create stream for output
        ....
        fout.open( "student.out" ); // bind stream to file
        ....
        fout.close();                               // disconnect stream from student.out
        ...
```

```
    fout.open( "person.out" );              // bind stream to another file
    ....
```

2. Opening file in read mode:

```
    ofstream fin;                           // create stream for input
    ....
    fin.open( "student.in" );               // bind stream to file
    ....
    fin.close();                            // disconnect stream from student.in
    ...
    fin.open( "student.out" );              // bind stream to another file
    ....
```

There is a limit on the maximum number of files which can be opened. This constraint is imposed by the underlying operating system on which a program executes. For instance, in MS-DOS, the entry FILES=N in the CONFIG.SYS file; the entry FILES = 20 indicates there can be a maximum of 20 files opened at a time. If any attempt is made to open a file above this limit, it fails and returns the NULL handle. Therefore, it is advisable to close a file when it is no longer needed.

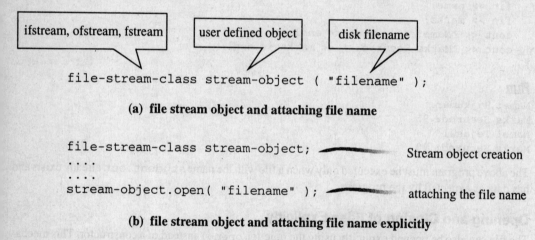

(a) file stream object and attaching file name

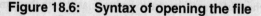

(b) file stream object and attaching file name explicitly

Figure 18.6:   Syntax of opening the file

18.4 Testing for Errors

The assumption of a file operation (opening, processing, or closing) is always successful in an ideal situation. There are situations, when the user tries to open a non-existent file in read-mode or tries to open a file in write mode which has been marked as read-only. File operations fail under such circumstances. Such errors must be trapped and appropriate actions must be taken before further processing.

This can be done using the operator ! with an instance of the ifstream, ofstream or fstream. The operator ! is overloaded to return nonzero in case any stream errors have occurred. For example, to open a file for input and test whether it has successfully opened (it will not be opened if the file does not exist), the following code may be used:

```
ifstream in_file( "test.txt" );
//test for error
if( !in_file )
{  //File wasn't opened
   cerr << "Cannot open test.txt\n";
   exit( 1 );
}
```

Once the file has been opened successfully, a common activity is to read from the file while the end-of-file has not yet been reached. Using the name of a file stream instance in place of a condition expression (such as inside an `if` or `while` statement) evaluates to nonzero only when no errors have occurred in the file. Hence, errors such as end-of-file can be tested as follows:

```
while( in_file )     // while EOF has not been reached
{
    //Read from the file.
}
```

where `in_file` is an instance of `ifstream`, but an instance of `ofstream` or `fstream` can equally be used in such situations.

An example using `ifstream` to output the contents of a file is given below. Note that, the use of the manipulator `resetiosflags` to prevent skipping white-space characters in the input. A program to display the contents of a file (filename is entered interactively) on the console is listed in `fdisp.cpp`.

```
// fdisp.cpp: display file contents using ifstream to input from a file
#include <fstream.h>
#include <iomanip.h>
int main()
{
   char ch;
   char filename[ 25 ];
   cout << "Enter Name of the File: ";
   cin >> filename;
   // create a file object in read mode
   ifstream ifile( filename );
   if( !ifile )   // file open status
   {
      cerr << "Error opening " << filename << endl;
      return 1;
   }
   ifile >> resetiosflags( ios::skipws ); // do not skip space or new line
   //Comment above line; then execute the program, you will see funny result
   while( ifile )   // while EOF not reached.
   {
      ifile >> ch;   // read a character from file
      cout << ch;    // display character on console
   }
   return 0;
}
```

Run

```
Enter Name of the File: mytype.cpp
```
[The contents of the input file, mytype.cpp is displayed on console]

In main(), the statement
```
ifstream ifile( filename );
```
creates the disk file object, ifile for a file name entered interactively in the read mode. In the absence of the statement,
```
ifile >> resetiosflags( ios::skipws );
```
the file will be displayed without any spaces or newlines, since the >> operator, neglects any white-space characters by default. The statement
```
ifile >> ch;
```
reads a character from the file in a manner similar to cin. It does not skip white-space characters since ios::skipws flag is reset. The object ifile becomes 0 as soon as it reaches the end of the file and hence, the statement
```
while( ifile )
```
loops until end of file is reached. All those files that are opened by a program must be closed by it. Otherwise, the system closes all those files which are in open state during the termination of a program.

The program keyin.cpp waits for keyboard input and dumps all input characters into the file key.txt until the end-of-file (Ctrl-Z) character is pressed followed by the carriage-return key.

```
// keyin.cpp: Reads all the characters entered and stores the same in the file
#include <fstream.h>
void main()
{
   char ch;
   cout<<"Enter characters..<Ctrl-Z followed by carriage-return to stop>\n";
   ofstream ofile( "key.txt" ); // opens file in output ASCII mode
   while( cin )    // not end of file
   {
      cin.get( ch ); // read character from console
      ofile << ch;   // write to file
   }
   ofile.close(); // close file
}
```

Run

```
Enter characters..<Ctrl-Z followed by carriage-return to stop>
1
A B C .. X Y Z
^Z
```

Note: The file key.txt has all the above characters except ^Z

In main, the statement
```
ofstream ofile( "key.txt" );
```
opens the file key.txt in output mode. The statement

```
      cin.get( ch );
```
reads a character from the input device without skipping white-space characters. Hence, the `resetiosflags(ios::skipws)` manipulator need not be used to prevent skipping of white-space characters. The statement
```
      ofile << ch;
```
writes character to the output file. The statement
```
      ofile.close();
```
closes the file.

Another approach for detecting the end-of-file condition is using the member function `eof()`. This operates as follows:
```
      stream-object.eof() = 0 if end-of-file is not detected
                          = non-zero if end-of-file is detected
```
The function `eof()` is a member function of the class `ios`. For example

```
      if( fin.eof() )
         // end-of-file
      else
         // not end-of-file
```

The program `stdwr.cpp` illustrates the processing of errors that occur while manipulating files.

```
// stdwr.cpp: student file, creating, writing, and reading the same
#include <fstream.h>
void student_write( int count )
{
   char name[30];
   int i, marks;
   // create a file, open it in write mode and save data
   ofstream fout;    // create a file object
   fout.open( "student.out" );   // connect file object to file
   if( !fout )
   {
     cout << "Error: " << "student.out cannot be opened in write mode";
     return;
   }
   for( i = 0; i < count; i++ )
   {
     cout << "Enter Name: ";
     cin >> name;
     cout << "Enter Marks Secured: ";
     cin >> marks;
     // write to a file
     fout << name << endl;
     fout << marks << endl;
   }
   fout.close();  // disconnect a file
}
```

```
void student_read()
{
    char name[30];
    int i, marks;
    // create a file, open it in write mode and save data
    ifstream fin;        // create a file object
    fin.open( "student.out" ); // connect file object to file
    if( !fin )
    {
        cout << "Error: " << "student.out cannot be opened in read mode";
        return;
    }
    while(1)
    {
        fin >> name;
        fin >> marks;
        if( fin.eof() )
            break;
        cout << "Name: " << name << endl;
        cout << "Marks Secured: " << marks << endl;
    }
    fin.close();   // disconnect a file
}
void main()
{
    int count;
    cout << "How many students ? ";
    cin >> count;
    cout << "Enter student details to be stored..." << endl;
    student_write( count );
    cout << "Student details processed from the file..." << endl;
    student_read();
}
```

Run

```
How many students ? 3
Enter student details to be stored...
Enter Name: Mangala
Enter Marks Secured: 75
Enter Name: Chatterjee
Enter Marks Secured: 99
Enter Name: Rao-M-G
Enter Marks Secured: 50
Student details processed from the file...
Name: Mangala
Marks Secured: 75
Name: Chatterjee
Marks Secured: 99
Name: Rao-M-G
Marks Secured: 50
```

In `student_write()`, the statement

```
fout.open( "student.out" );   // connect file object to file
```

opens the file `student.out` and connects the same to the stream object `fout`. The statement

```
if( !fout )
```

verifies whether the file is opened successfully or not. If condition is true, when `!fout` is nonzero.

The statement in `student_read()`

```
if( fin.eof() )
    break;
```

checks for the end-of-file and terminates file processing if the end-of-file is reached.

18.5 File Modes

The constructors of `ifstream` and `key.txt` and the function `open()` are used to create files as well as open the existing files in the default mode (text mode). In both methods, the only argument used is the filename. C++ provides a mechanism of opening a file in different modes in which case the second parameter must be explicitly passed. The syntax is as follows:

```
stream-object.open( "filename", mode );
```

It opens the file in the specified mode. The list of file modes are shown in Table 18.1 with mode value and their meaning.

mode value	Effect on the mode
`ios::in`	open for reading.
`ios::out`	open for writing.
`ios::ate`	seek (go) to the end of file at opening time.
`ios::app`	append mode: all writes occur at end of file.
`ios::trunc`	truncate the file if it already exists.
`ios::nocreate`	open fails if file does not exist.
`ios::noreplace`	open fails if file already exists.
`ios::binary`	open as a binary file.

Table 18.1: File open modes

The following points can be noted regarding file modes:

◆ Opening a file in `ios::out` mode also opens it in the `ios::trunc` mode by default. That is, if the file already exists, it is truncated.

◆ Both `ios::app` and `ios::ate` sets pointers to the end-of-file, but they differ in terms of the types of operations permitted on a file. The `ios::app` allows to add data from the end-of-file, whereas `ios::ate` mode allows to add or modify the existing data anywhere in the file. In both the cases, a file is created if it is non-existent.

◆ The mode `ios::app` can be used only with output files.

◆ The stream classes `ifstream` and `ofstream` open files in read and write modes respectively by default.

◆ For fstream class, the mode parameter must be explicitly passed.
◆ More than one value may be ORed to have a combined effect. For instance, the following statement opens a file for reading in binary mode:

```
istream in_file( "myfile", ios::in | ios::binary );
```

The program payfile.cpp generates a payroll-like output and directs the output to the file pay.txt instead of cout. It stores floating point data in the form of ASCII characters instead of machine representation (binary form).

```
// payfile: payroll like output example printing results to file
#include <fstream.h>
#include <iomanip.h>
void main()
{
  float f1=123.45, f2=34.65, f3=56;
  // open file "pay.txt" in output mode and truncate its contents if exists
  ofstream out_file( "pay.txt", ios::trunc );
  out_file << setiosflags(ios::showpoint|ios::fixed)
       << setiosflags(ios::right);
  out_file << setw(6) << f1 << endl;
  out_file << setw(6) << f2 << endl;
  out_file << setw(6) << f3 << endl;
}
```

Run

After execution of the program, the file pay.txt contains the following:

```
123.45
 34.65
 56.00
```

In main(), the statement

```
ofstream out_file( "pay.txt", ios::trunc );
```

creates the file pay.txt and truncates its contents if the file already exists. As with the console streams, manipulators can be used with any of the file stream instances.

18.6 File Pointers and their Manipulations

The knowledge of the logical location at which the current read or write operations occur is of great importance in achieving faster access to information stored in a file. The file management system associates two pointers with each file, called *file pointers*. In C++, they are called *get pointer* (input pointer) and *put pointer* (output pointer). These pointers facilitate the movement across the file while reading or writing. The *get pointer* specifies a location from where the current reading operation is initiated. The *put pointer* specifies a location from where the current writing operation is initiated. On completion of a read or write operation, the appropriate pointer will be advanced automatically.

Default Actions

The file pointers are set to a suitable location initially based on the mode in which the file is opened. Fundamentally, a file can be opened in the read mode, write mode, or append mode. The logical location of file pointers when a file is opened is discussed below (see Figure 18.7.):

- **Read-only Mode:** when a file is opened in read-only mode, the input (get) pointer is initialized to point to the beginning of the file, so that the file can be read from the start.
- **Write-only Mode:** when a file is opened in write-only mode, the existing contents of the file are deleted (if a given file already exists) and the output pointer is set to point to the beginning of the file, so that data can be written from the start.
- **Append Mode:** when a file is opened in append mode, the existing contents of the file remain unaffected (if a given file already exists) and the output pointer is set to point to the end of the file so that data can be written (appended) at the end of the existing contents.

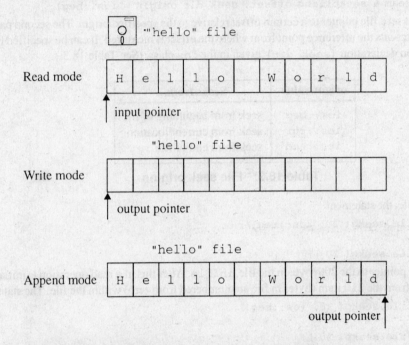

Figure 18.7: File pointer position on opening a file

Functions for Manipulation of File Pointers

The C++ I/O system supports four functions for setting a file pointer to any desired position inside the file or to get the current file pointer. These allow the programmer to have control over a position in the file where the read or write operation takes place. The functions are listed in the Table 18.2.

Function	Member of the class	Action Performed
seekg()	ifstream	Moves get file pointer to a specific location
seekp()	ofstream	Moves put file pointer to a specific location
tellg()	ifstream	Returns the current position of the get pointer
tellp()	ofstream	Returns the current position of the put pointer

Table 18.2: File pointer control functions

The seekp() and tellp() are member functions of ofstream. The seekg and tellg are member functions of ifstream. The class fstream deals with files in both input and output modes. Hence, there are two file pointers in class fstream - the *put pointer* used for writing and the *get pointer* used for reading. All four functions mentioned above are available in the class fstream. The seekp() and tellp() deal with the put pointer, while seekg() and tellg() deal with the get pointer.

The two seek functions have the following prototypes:

```
istream & seekg(long offset, seek_dir origin = ios::beg);
ostream & seekp(long offset, seek_dir origin = ios::beg);
```

Both functions set a file pointer to a certain offset relative to the specified origin. The second parameter origin, represents the reference point from where the offset is measured. It can be specified by using an enumeration declaration (seek_dir) given in the ios class. (See Table 18.3.)

origin value	Seeks from...
ios::beg	seek from beginning of file
ios::cur	seek from current location
ios::end	seek from end of file

Table 18.3:   File seek origins

For example, the statement

```
infile.seekg( 20, ios::beg );
or
infile.seekg( 20 );
```

moves the file pointer to the 20th byte in the file, infile. After this, if a read operation is initiated, the reading starts from the 21st item (bytes in file are numbered from zero) within the file. The statement

```
outfile.seekp( 20, ios::beg );
or
outfile.seekp( 20 );
```

moves the file pointer to the 20th byte in the file outfile. After this, if write operation is initiated, the writing starts from the 21st item (bytes in file are numbered from zero) within the file. Consider the following statements:

```
ofstream outfile( "student.out", ios::app );
int size = outfile.tellp();
```

The first statement creates the file stream object outfile, and connects it to the disk file, student.out. It moves the output pointer to the end of the file. The second statement assigns the value of the *put pointer* to the integer variable size, which in this case represents the number of bytes in the file. The program fsize.cpp prints the size of a file, whose name is given as a command line parameter.

```
// fsize.cpp: file size finding using seekg and tellg
#include <fstream.h>
int main( int argc, char *argv[] )
{
    if( argc < 2 ) // no filename is passed
```

```
{
    cout << "Usage: fsize <filename>";
    return 1;
}
ifstream infile( argv[ 1 ] ); // file open in read and write mode
if( !infile )  // open success
{
    cerr << "Error opening " << argv[ 1 ] << endl;
    return 1;
}
infile.seekg( 0, ios::end );  // set read pointer to end of file
cout << "File Size=" << infile.tellg(); // read current position
return 0;
}
```

Run1
Usage: fsize <filename>

Run2
File Size=437

In main(), the statement
```
        infile.seekg( 0, ios::end );
```
moves the *read pointer* to the end of the file, and the statement
```
        infile.tellg();
```
reads the get pointer value. In this situation, it represents the size of the file.

The seekg() sets the get pointer while seekp() sets the put pointer to the specified location. Some of the pointer offset calls and their actions are shown in Table 18.4 and Figure 18.8. It is assumed that the variable fout is the object of the stream class ofstream and fin is the object of the stream class ifstream.

Seek call	Action performed
fout.seekg(0, ios::beg)	Go to the beginning of the file
fout.seekg(0, ios::cur)	Stay at the current file
fout.seekg(0, ios::end)	Go to the end of the file
fout.seekg(n, ios::beg)	Move to (n+1) byte location in the file
fout.seekg(n, ios::cur)	Move forward by n bytes from current position
fout.seekg(-n, ios::cur)	Move backward by n bytes from current position
fout.seekg(-n, ios::end)	Move backward by n bytes from the end
fin.seekp(n, ios::beg)	Move write pointer to (n+1) byte location
fin.seekp(-n, ios::cur)	Move write pointer backward by n bytes

Table 18.4: Seek calls and their actions

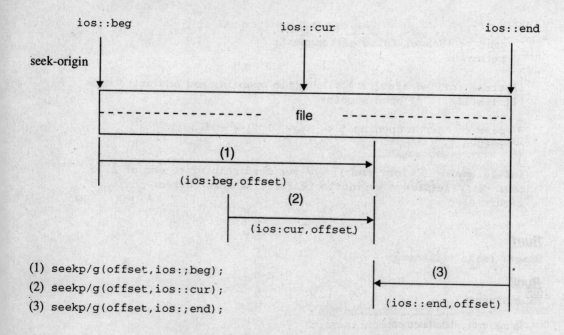

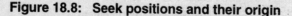

Figure 18.8:   Seek positions and their origin

18.7 Sequential Access to a File

Unlike other programming languages (such as COBOL), C++ does not provide commands organizing and processing files as sequential or direct (random) files. However, it provides file manipulation commands which can be used by the programmer to device access to files sequentially or randomly. A *sequential file* has to be accessed sequentially; to access the particular data in the file all the preceding data items have to be read and discarded. A *random file* allows access to the specific data without the need for accessing its preceding data items. However, it can also be accessed sequentially. Organizing a file either as sequential or random depends on the type of *media* on which the file is organized and stored. For instance, a file on a tape must be accessed sequentially, whereas, a file on a hard disk or floppy disk can be accessed either sequentially, or randomly. In C++, it is the responsibility of the programmer to devise a mechanism for accessing a file.

The C++ file stream system supports a wide variety of functions to perform the input-output operation on files. The functions, put() and get(), are designed to manage a single character at a time. The other functions, write() and read(), are designed to manipulate blocks of character data.

The put() and get() Functions

The function get() is a member function of the file stream class fstream, and is used to read a single character from the file. The function put() is a member function of the output stream class fstream, and is used to write a single character to the output file. The program putget.cpp reads a string from the standard input device, and writes the same to a file character by character. A sequential file is created and its pointer is positioned at the beginning of the file. It is processed sequentially until the end-of-file is encountered.

```
// putget.cpp: writes and reads characters from the file
#include <fstream.h>
void main()
{
    char c, string[ 75 ];
    fstream file( "student.txt", ios::in | ios::out );
    cout << "Enter String: ";
    cin.getline( string, 74 );
    for( int i = 0; string[i]; i++ )
        file.put( string[i] );
    file.seekg(0); // seek to the beginning
    cout << "Output String: ";
    while( file )
    {
        file.get( c ); // reads a character
        cout << c;
    }
}
```

Run

```
Enter String: Object-Computing with C++
Output String: Object-Computing with C++
```

Note: The file student.txt contains the entered string.

The stream fstream provides the facility to open a file in both read and write modes; so that the file can be processed randomly by positioning the file pointers.

18.8 ASCII and Binary Files

The stream operators insertion and extraction always manipulate and deal with formatted data. Data has to be *formatted* to produce logical information. This is because, most of the I/O devices communicate to the computer system using ASCII code, but CPU processes these data using the binary system. Hence, it is necessary to convert data while reading from the input device or displaying data on output device. Most visible data formatting operation is alignment of display fields. In addition to this, data formatting operation also occur transparently while transferring data between the program and console or a file. For example, in order to display an integer value, the << operator converts the number into a stream of ASCII characters. Similarly, the >> operator converts the input ASCII characters to binary while reading data from the input device. For instance, when a number, say, 120 is typed in response to an input statement such as:

        cin >> i;

The user enters data by typing on the keyboard. In this case, stream operator receives ASCII codes of the numeric characters 1, 2, and 0 (which are 49, 50, and 48). The >> operator function converts the input ASCII data to binary and assigns to the variable i. Similarly, the << operator in a statement such as:

        cout << i;

converts the content of the variable i (say 120) into three ASCII characters, 49, 50, and 48 and then sends the same to the standard output device. The representation of an integer in the character form and binary form is shown in Figure 18.9.

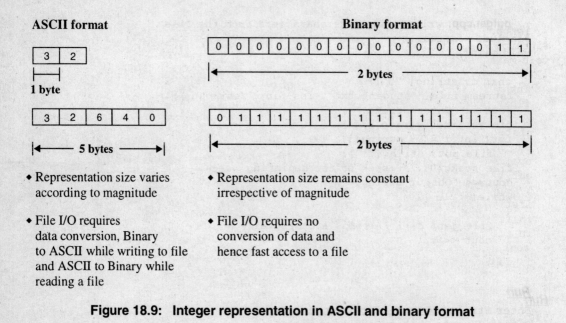

Figure 18.9:   Integer representation in ASCII and binary format

When the character \n is written to a text file (ASCII file), it is actually converted into the sequence \r and \n and then written to a file. Similarly, while reading a character if this sequence is encountered, it is converted to a single character \n and transferred to the reader. The following section discusses other distinction between file operations on ASCII and binary files.

write() and read() functions

At the user end, generally the values are represented in ASCII, whereas, inside the machine their binary equivalents are used. In certain cases, it is not necessary to store information in the form of ASCII characters. For instance, in a database application, storing an integer in binary form instead of a string of ASCII characters saves a lot of disk space and makes retrieval faster. To store or retrieve data in binary form, the member functions write() or read() can be used.

Unlike put() and get(), the write() and read() functions access data in binary format. In binary format, the data representation in the file and in the system is the same. The difference between the representation of data in text form and binary is shown in Figure 18.9. The number of bytes required to represent an integer in text form is proportional to its magnitude, whereas, in binary form, the size is always fixed irrespective of its magnitude. Thus, the binary form is more accurate, and provides faster access to the file because no conversion is required while performing read or write. The read() and write() functions have the following syntax:

```
infile.read( (char *) &variable, sizeof( variable ) );
outfile.write( (char *) &variable, sizeof( variable ) );
```

The first parameter is a pointer to a memory location at which the data retrieved from the file is to be stored in case of read() and address at which data is to be written when retrieved from a file in case of write(). The second parameter indicates the number of bytes to be transferred. The program fwr.cpp illustrates the creation and manipulation of binary files.

```
// fwr.cpp: use of write and read member of file streams
#include <fstream.h>
void main()
{
    int num1 = 530;
    float num2 = 1050.25;
    // open file in write binary mode, write integer and close
    ofstream out_file( "number.bin", ios::binary );
    out_file.write( (char *) &num1, sizeof(num1) );
    out_file.write( (char *) &num2, sizeof(float) );
    out_file.close();
    // open file in read binary mode, read integer and close
    ifstream in_file( "number.bin", ios::binary );
    in_file.read( (char*)&num1, sizeof(int) );
    in_file.read( (char*)&num2, sizeof(num2) );
    cout << num1 << " " << num2 << endl;
    in_file.close();
}
```

Run

530 1050.25

In main(), the statement

        out_file.write((char *) &num1, sizeof(num1));

writes the contents of the integer variable num1 to the disk file. The number of bytes to be written can be computed by sizeof(num1) or sizeof(int). The statement

        in_file.read((char*)&num1, sizeof(int));

reads sizeof(int) number of bytes from the file and stores in the memory location pointed to by the second parameter.

18.9 Saving and Retrieving of Objects

C++ does not support the creation of *persistence-objects*. Persistence objects are those which outlive the program execution time and exist between executions of a program. All database systems support persistence. In C++, this is not supported, however, the programmer can build it explicitly using *file streams* in a program. The stream operators can be overloaded to save objects into a file or retrieve objects from a file. The stream operators << and >> are also member functions of the file manipulation stream classes ofstream and ifstream. The concept of overloading file stream operators is the same as that of overloading of console stream operators as discussed in the earlier chapter: *Operator Overloading*.

The stream operators have to be overloaded as friend operator functions of user-defined classes whose objects are to be manipulated with file streams. The stream operator << function takes the ofstream & (reference object parameter) as the first argument and the second parameter can be a reference object of a class. The return value of this operator function is object of the ofstream & type. The operator >> function takes the ifstream & (reference object parameter) as the first argument and the second parameter can be a reference object of a class. The return value of this operator function is the object of the type ifstream &. Thus, in both the cases, a reference to an object of the current class is taken as the second argument and after manipulating the second parameter, a reference to an object of the respective stream class is returned.

The program `objsave.cpp` illustrates the flexibility gained by overloading the insertion and extraction operators while saving objects into a file or retrieving objects from a file.

```cpp
// objsave.cpp: saving a object to a file with stream operator overloaded
#include <fstream.h>
#include <ctype.h>       // for toupper
#include <string.h>      // for strlen
#define MAXNAME 40
class Person
{
   private:
      char name[ MAXNAME ];
      int age;
   public:
      // this function writes the class's data members to the file
      void write( ofstream &os )
      {
        os.write( name, strlen( name ) );
        os << ends;
        os.write( (char*)&age, sizeof( age ) );
      }
      // this function reads the class's date member from the file.
      // It returns nonzero if no errors were encountered while reading
      int read( ifstream &is )
      {
        is.get( name, MAXNAME, 0 );
        name[ is.gcount() ] = 0;
        is.ignore( 1 );   // ignore the NULL terminator in the file.
        is.read( (char*)&age, sizeof( age ) );
        return is.good();
      }
      // stream operator, << overloading
      friend ostream & operator << ( ostream &os, Person &b );
      // stream operator >> operator overloading
      friend istream &operator >> ( istream &is, Person &b );
      // output file stream operator overloading
      friend ofstream &operator << ( ofstream &fos, Person &b )
      {
        b.write( fos );
        return fos;
      }
      // output file stream operator overloading
      friend ifstream &operator >> ( ifstream &fos, Person &b )
      {
        b.read( fos );
        return fos;
      }
};
istream &operator >> ( istream &is, Person &b )
{
   cout << "Name: ";
```

```
    is >> ws;    // flush input buffer
    is.get( b.name, MAXNAME );
    cout << "Age : ";
    is >> ws >> b.age;
    return is;
}
ostream &operator << ( ostream &os, Person &b )
{
    os << b.name << endl;
    os << b.age << endl;
    return os;
}
void main()
{
    Person p_obj;
    // open a file in binary mode and write objects to it
    ofstream ofile( "person.txt", ios::trunc|ios::binary );
    char ch;
    do
    {
        cin >> p_obj;      // read object
        ofile << p_obj;    // write object to the output file
        cout << "Another ? ";
        cin >> ch;
    } while( toupper( ch ) == 'Y' );
    ofile.close();
    // Output loop, display file content
    ifstream ifile( "person.txt", ios::binary );
    cout << "The objects written to the file were:.." << endl;
    while( 1 )
    {
        ifile >> p_obj;    // extract person object from file
        if( ifile.fail() )   // file read fail, end-of-file
            break;
        cout << p_obj;     // display person object on console
    }
}
```

Run

```
Name: Tejaswi
Age : 5
Another ? y
Name: Savithri
Age : 23
Another ? n
The objects written to the file were:..
Tejaswi
5
Savithri
23
```

In the above program, the object `p_obj` of the class `Person` is retrieved from or saved to a file just like a variable of a built-in data type. The statement

```
cin >> p_obj;
```

reads the object, `p_obj` from the standard input device, whereas, the statement

```
ifile >> p_obj;
```

retrieves the object, `p_obj` from the input file `ifile`. The statement

```
cout << p_obj;
```

displays the object, `p_obj` on the standard output device and the statement

```
ofile << p_obj;
```

stores the object `p_obj` in the file. The mechanism of manipulating user defined objects with stream operators is depicted in Figure 18.10.

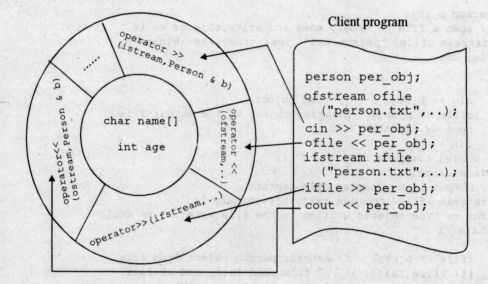

Figure 18.10:   Files and objects interaction

The classes `ifstream` and `ofstream` are declared in the `fstream.h` header file. The member functions of the stream classes `ifstream` and `ofstream`, `get()` and `write()` can be used to manipulate user defined objects in disk files. These functions handle the entire structure of an object as a single unit, and store or retrieve in binary format. For instance, the member function `write()` of the class `ofstream`, writes a class's object from memory byte-by-byte without conversion to the target disk file opened in binary mode. It is important to note that, only *data members* of a class are copied to the disk file. For instance, the statement in the above program,

```
ofile << p_obj;
```

can be replaced by the statement,

```
ofile.write( (char *) &p_obj, sizeof(p_obj) );
```

to store the object `p_obj` to the disk file. Likewise, the statement

```
ifile >> p_obj;
```

can be replaced by:

```
ifile.read( (char *) &p_obj, sizeof(p_obj) );
```

in order to retrieve the object from the disk file. The length of the object is computed using the `sizeof` operator. It returns the number of bytes required to hold all the data members of the `p_obj` object.

18.10 File Input/Output with fstream Class

The class `fstream` supports simultaneous input and output operations. It contains `open()` with input mode as default. It inherits all the functions from `istream` and `ostream` classes through `iostream`. The program `student.cpp` illustrates the role of `fstream` class in the manipulation of files. It reads the data from the input file `student.in` and writes the processed information into another disk file `student.out`.

```
// student.cpp: reads students from files and writes result to another file
#include <iostream.h>
#include <fstream.h>
#include <conio.h>
#include <process.h>
void main()
{
    fstream infile;  // input file
    fstream outfile; // output file
    int i, count, percentage;
    char name[30];
    // Open source file for reading
    infile.open( "student.in", ios::in );
    if( infile.fail() )
    {
        cout << "Error: student.in file non-existent";
        exit( 1 );
    }
    outfile.open( "student.out", ios::out );
    if( outfile.fail() )
    {
        cout << "Error: unable to open student.out in write mode";
        exit( 1 );
    }
    infile >> count; // how many students
    // write header to output file
    outfile << "        Students Information Processing" << endl << endl;
    outfile << "-----------------------------------------------" << endl;
    for( i = 0; i < count; i++ )
    {
        // read data and percentage secured from the input file
        infile >> name;
        infile >> percentage;
        // write name and class secured based on percentage to output file
        outfile << "Name: " << name << endl;
        outfile << "Percentage: " << percentage << endl;
```

```
        outfile << "Passed in: ";
        if( percentage >= 70 )
           outfile << "First class with distinction";
        else
           if( percentage >= 60 )
              outfile << "First class";
           else
              if( percentage >= 50 )
                 outfile << "Second class";
              else
                 if( percentage >= 35 )
                    outfile << "Third class";
                 else
                    outfile << "Sorry, Failed!";
     outfile << endl;
     outfile << "--------------------------------------------" << endl;
  }
  // close files
  infile.close();
  outfile.close();
}
```

Run

Note that before running the above program, create the input file student.in containing the data according to the following format:

1. Number of students
2. First student name (without blanks)
3. First student percentage score
   ....
   ....
N. Last student name
   Last student percentage score

It processes the input file and writes results to the output file; see the contents of the student.out. The input file student.in contains the following information:

```
6
Rajkumar
84
Tejaswi
82
Smrithi
60
Anand
55
Rajshree
40
Ramesh
33
```

The above *Run* has created the output file student.out containing the following:

```
           Students Information Processing
-----------------------------------------------
Name: Rajkumar
Percentage: 84
Passed in: First class with distinction
-----------------------------------------------
Name: Tejaswi
Percentage: 82
Passed in: First class with distinction
-----------------------------------------------
Name: Smrithi
Percentage: 60
Passed in: First class
-----------------------------------------------
Name: Anand
Percentage: 55
Passed in: Second class
-----------------------------------------------
Name: Rajshree
Percentage: 40
Passed in: Third class
-----------------------------------------------
Name: Ramesh
Percentage: 33
Passed in: Sorry, Failed!
-----------------------------------------------
```

In main(), the statements

```
    fstream infile;  // input file
    fstream outfile; // output file
```

create objects of the stream class fstream, and the statements

```
    infile.open( "student.in", ios::in );
    outfile.open( "student.out", ios::out );
```

bind the stream objects infile and outfile to disk files named student.in and student.out respectively. Note that the stream objects infile and outfile are instances of the fstream class, but they are opened in different modes i.e., infile is opened in the *read mode,* whereas outfile is opened in the *write mode.* The statement

```
    infile >> name;
```

reads name string from the input disk file, and the statement

```
    outfile << "Name: " << name << endl;
```

writes the same to the output disk file. The file processing is carried on until all the records are processed. Note that the syntax for writing to the disk file resembles that used for writing to the console.

18.11 Random Access to a File

The program fio.cpp handles files using the fstream class. It uses fstream to perform both input-output operation on the test.del file. Since, the class fstream is derived from iostream, both input and output can be done on the same stream (same file in this case).

```
// fio.cpp: Input and output operations on file, random access
#include <iostream.h>
#include <fstream.h>
#define READ_SIZE  6
void main()
{
    char reader[ READ_SIZE + 1 ];
    // fstream constructor, open in binary input and output mode
    fstream fstr( "test.del", ios::binary|ios::in|ios::out );
    // Write the numbers 0 to 9 to file
    for( int i = 0; i < 10; i++ )
        fstr << i;
    // Set the write (put) pointer.
    fstr.seekp( 2 );
    fstr << "Hello";
    // Set the read (get) pointer.
    fstr.seekg( 4 );
    fstr.read( reader, READ_SIZE );
    reader[ READ_SIZE ] = 0;   // end of string
    cout << reader << endl;
}
```

Run
11o789

Note that an instance of fstream has two file pointers associated with it: a get pointer used while reading, and a put file pointer used while writing. The statement

```
        fstr.seekp( 2 );
```
sets the put pointer to an offset 2.

The program first writes ASCII codes of the digits 0 to 9 to the file test.del, moves the *put pointer* by an offset 2 from the beginning of the file and the overwrites the numbers 3 through 6 with the string "Hello". It then reads 6 characters from the offset 4 into the array reader. The last line of the program will display these 6 characters, which will be 11o789. After all writes are completed, the contents of the file test.del will be: 01Hello789

The facility for direct file processing is essential in database applications. They perform extensive data read, write, update, and search activities. These actions require movement of the file pointers (get or put) from one position to another. This can be easily performed by using the seek(), read(), and write() functions.

The location at which the mth object is stored can be computed using a relation:

   location = m * sizeof(object)

This specifies the offset at which the object is stored in a file. It can be used to manipulate the mth object by using the read() or write() functions.

The program direct.cpp illustrates the mechanism of updating a file by random access. It uses the file person.txt to store objects and then these objects can be updated if necessary. The file pointers *get* and *put* are positioned based on the object to be accessed.

```cpp
// direct.cpp: accessing objects randomly
#include <fstream.h>
#include <ctype.h>        // For toupper
#include <string.h>       // For strlen
#define MAXNAME 40
class Person
{
  private:
      char name[ MAXNAME ];
      int age;
  public:
      // this function writes the class's data members to the file
      void write( ofstream &os )
       {
          os.write( name, strlen( name ) );
          os << ends;
          os.write( (char*)&age, sizeof( age ) );
       }
      // this function reads the class's date member from the file.
      // It returns nonzero if no errors were encountered while reading.
      int read( ifstream &is )
       {
          is.get( name, MAXNAME, 0 );
          name[ is.gcount() ] = 0;
          is.ignore( 1 );   // ignore the NULL terminator in the file.
          is.read( (char*)&age, sizeof( age ) );
          return is.good();
       }
      // stream operator, << overloading
      friend ostream & operator << ( ostream &os, Person &b );
      // stream operator >> operator overloading
      friend istream &operator >> ( istream &is, Person &b );
      // output file stream operator overloading
};
istream &operator >> ( istream &is, Person &b )
{
   cout << "Name: ";
   is >> ws;    // flush input buffer
   is.get( b.name, MAXNAME );
   cout << "Age : ";
   is >> ws >> b.age;
   return is;
}
ostream &operator << ( ostream &os, Person &b )
{
   os << "Name: " << b.name << endl;
   os << "Age : " << b.age << endl;
   return os;
}
```

```cpp
void main()
{
    Person p_obj;
    int count, obj_id;
    cout << "Database Creation..." << endl;
    // open a file in binary mode and write objects to it
    ofstream ofile( "person.dat", ios::trunc|ios::binary );
    count = 0;
    char ch;
    do
    {
        cout << "Enter Object " << count << " details..." << endl;
        cin >> p_obj;
        count = count + 1;
        // write object to the output file
        ofile.write( (char *) &p_obj, sizeof( p_obj ));
        cout << "Another ? ";
        cin >> ch;
    } while( toupper( ch ) == 'Y' );
    ofile.close();
    // Output loop, display file content
    fstream iofile( "person.dat", ios::binary|ios::in|ios::out );
    cout << "Database Access..." << endl;
    while( 1 )
    {
        cout << "Enter the object number to be accessed <-1 to end>: ";
        cin >> obj_id;
        if( obj_id < 0 || obj_id >= count )
            break;
        int location = obj_id * sizeof( p_obj );
        iofile.seekg( location, ios::beg );
        iofile.read( (char *) &p_obj, sizeof( p_obj ) );
        cout << p_obj;
        cout << "Wants to Modify ? ";
        cin >> ch;
        if( ch == 'y' || ch == 'Y' )
        {
            cin >> p_obj;
            // update the object in the file
            iofile.seekp( location, ios::beg );
            iofile.write( (char *) &p_obj, sizeof( p_obj ) );
        }
    }
    iofile.close();
}
```

Run

```
Database Creation...
Enter Object 0 details...
Name: Rajkumar
Age : 25
```

```
Another ? y
Enter Object 1 details...
Name: Tejaswi
Age : 20
Another ? y
Enter Object 2 details...
Name: Kalpana
Age : 15
Another ? n
Database Access...
Enter the object number to be accessed <-1 to end>: 0
Name: Rajkumar
Age : 25
Wants to Modify ? n
Enter the object number to be accessed <-1 to end>: 1
Name: Tejaswi
Age : 20
Wants to Modify ? y
Name: Tejaswi
Age : 5
Enter the object number to be accessed <-1 to end>: 1
Name: Tejaswi
Age : 5
Wants to Modify ? n
Enter the object number to be accessed <-1 to end>: -1
```

In the program, initially a database is created without supporting its modification during creation. After creating the database file, the object `iofile` of class `fstream` is created using the statement,

```
fstream iofile( "person.dat", ios::binary|ios::in|ios::out );
```

It connects the file `person.dat` to the stream based object and permits both the read and write operations to be performed on the same file.

To read objects randomly, there must be a mechanism for converting object-id (object request) into the location at which it is stored. This is achieved by computing the location of the object storage using the relation :

```
int location = obj_id * sizeof( p_obj );
```

and *put pointer* is set to this by:

```
iofile.seekg( location, ios::beg );
```

and the statement:

```
iofile.read( (char *) &p_obj, sizeof( p_obj ) );
```

reads the file and stores into the object.

18.12 In-Memory Buffers and Data Formatting

The C's I/O system has two functions: `sscanf()` and `sprintf()` (whose prototypes appear in the `stdio.h` header file) for formatted I/O with memory buffers. The function `sscanf` performs formatted input from a character array, and `sprintf` does formatted output to a character array. These functions are normally used while displaying numbers in graphical environments (like BGI and Windows) where the output functions accept only strings.

C++ supports stream classes (declared in `strstrea.h`): `istrstream` (handling input of data from the array), `ostrstream` (handling output of data to the array), and `strstream` (transfer of data both ways) to handle character arrays in memory. In many cases, these streams may be easier to use than ordinary strings, since their buffers are dynamic. These streams can be used with stream operators, manipulators, etc., in the same way as the file streams. But their constructors have different specification. The program `cmdadd.cpp` illustrates the use of `istrstream` class in creating stream buffers and using it for extracting the data. It adds all the numbers passed as command line arguments.

```
// cmdadd.cpp: addition of numbers passed through command line
#include <strstrea.h>
void main( int argc, char *argv[] )
{
  int i = 1;
  long num, sum=0;
  if( argc < 2 )
  {
    cout << "Usage: cmdadd list_of_numbers_to_be_added";
    return;
  }
  while( --argc )
  {
    istrstream arg( argv[ i ] );
    arg >> num;
    sum += num;
    i++;
  }
  cout << sum << endl;
}
```

Run

At System prompt: <u>cmdadd 1 2 3</u>
6

In `main()`, the statement

```
        istrstream arg( argv[ i ] );
```

creates an object of the class `istrstream` and connects the same to a buffer. This object can now be used to read data from the associated buffer. The statement

```
        arg >> num;
```

extracts the data value and stores into the variable `num`. This method of accessing data is similar to performing I/O with the console and a file.

18.13 Error Handling During File Manipulations

In the real time environment, many users access different files without any predefined access pattern. The following are the different situations that can arise while manipulating a file:

- Attempting to open a non-existent file in read-mode.
- Trying to open a read-only marked file in write-mode.
- Trying to open a file with invalid name.

- Attempting to read beyond the end-of-the-file.
- Sufficient disk space is not available while writing to a file.
- Attempting to manipulate an unopened file.
- Stream object created but not connected to a file.
- Media (disk) errors reading/writing a file.

Such conditions must be detected while manipulating files and appropriate action should be taken to achieve consistent access to files.

Every stream (`ifstream`, `ofstream`, and `fstream`) has a *state* associated with it. Errors and nonstandard conditions are handled by setting and testing this state appropriately. The stream status variable and information recorded by its bits is shown in Figure 18.11.

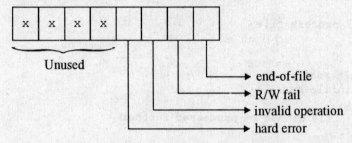

Figure 18.11:   State variable format

The `ios` class supports several functions to access the status recorded in the data member `io_state`. These functions and the meaning of their return values are shown in Table 18.5.

Function	Meaning of Return Value
`eof()`	TRUE, (non-zero) if EOF encountered while reading FALSE, (zero) otherwise
`fail()`	TRUE, if read or write operation has failed; FALSE, otherwise
`bad()`	TRUE, invalid operation is attempted or any unrecoverable errors FALSE, otherwise however, it can be recovered
`good()`	TRUE, if operation is successful i.e., all the above are functions that return false., if `file.good()` is true, everything is fine and can proceed for further processing
`rdstate()`	returns the status-state data member of the class `ios`
`clear()`	clear error states and further operations can be attempted

Table 18.5: Error handling functions and their return values

The following examples illustrates the mechanism for checking errors during file operations:

1. Opening a non-existent file in read mode:
```
ifstream infile( "myfile.dat" );
if( !infile )
```

```
      {
            // file does not exist
      }
```

2. Open fail: opening read-only marked file

```
      ofstream outfile( "myfile.dat" );
      if( !infile )          // or if( infile.bad() )
      {
            // file already exist and marked as read only
      }
```

3. Detecting end of file

```
      while( !infile.eof() )   // processes until end-of-file is reached
      {
            // process file
      }
```

4. Read fail

```
      infile.read(...);
      if( infile.bad() )
      {
            // file cannot be processed further
      }
```

5. Invalid filename

```
      infile.open( "|-*" );
      if( !infile )
      {
            // invalid file name
      }
```

6. Processing unopened file

```
      infile.read(..);      // read file
      if( infile.fail() )
      {
            // file is not opened
      }
```

The program outfile.cpp illustrates the trapping of all possible errors, which may be encountered during file processing.

```
// outfile.cpp: writes all the input into the file 'sample.out'
#include <fstream.h>
#include <process.h>
#include <string.h>
void main()
{
    char buff[ 80 ];
    ofstream outfile; // output file
    outfile.open("sample.out");   // open in output mode
    if( outfile.bad() )  // open fail
    {
        cout << "Error: sample.out unable to open";
        exit( 1 );
```

```
   }
   // loop until input = "end"
   while(1)
   {
      cin.getline(buff, 80);  // read a line from keyboard
      if( strcmp( buff, "end" ) == 0 )
         break;
      outfile << buff << endl;   // write to output file
      if( outfile.fail() )
      {
         cout << "write operation fail";
         exit( 1 );
      }
   }
   outfile.close();
}
```

Run

```
OOP is good
C++ is OOP
C++ is good
end
```

Note: On execution of the above program, the file `sample.out` contains the following information entered through the standard input device, keyboard:

```
OOP is good
C++ is OOP
C++ is good
```

In `main()`, the statement

        `ofstream outfile;  // output file`

creates the object `outfile` and the statement

        `outfile.open("sample.out");   // open in output mode`

opens the file `sample.out` in the output mode. The statement

        `if( outfile.bad() )   // open fail`

checks for the status of the file open command. If open fails, it returns 1, otherwise 0. The statement

        `outfile << buff << endl;   // write to output file`

writes the contents of the variable `buff` followed by a new-line character to the file. The statement

        `if( outfile.fail() )`

checks for the status of the preceding write operation.

18.14 Filter Utilities

The operating system provides many tools for browsing through the contents of the file, copying one file to another, printing files on the printer, and beautifying the content of files. Such utilities are called filter utilities because of their nature of filtering input files and presenting them in an appealing form. For instance, the `more` command (DOS or UNIX) display the contents of the files page by page on the console. Using the services of C++ streams such filter utilities can be built. Filter utilities are designed usually to accept the name of a file to be processed through the *command-line arguments*.

The command-line arguments are entered by the user at the shell prompt, and are delimited by white-space. (The first argument is a name of the command; filename containing the executable program.) These arguments are passed to the main() function of the program with the following syntax:

```
main( int argc, char *argv[] )
```

The first argument argc represents the argument count, whereas, the second argument is a pointer to an argument vector. For instance, when the following command is issued at the shell prompt,

```
copy boy.exe girl.exe
```

the value of argc and argv are as follows:

```
argc = 3
argv[0] = copy
argv[1] = boy.exe
argv[2] = girl.exe
```

The program cp.cpp is designed as a filter utility. It copies the source file into another destination file in the disk. The names of the source and destination files have to passed through the command line arguments. It can be used to copy both the ASCII and BINARY files.

```cpp
// cp.cpp: Copy a file to another file
#include <iostream.h>
#include <fstream.h>
#include <conio.h>
#include <process.h>
const int BUFFSIZE = 512;
int CopyFile( char *SourceFile, char *DestinationFile )
{
    fstream infile;  // source file
    fstream outfile; // destination file
    char buff[ BUFFSIZE + 1 ];
    // Open source file for reading
    infile.open( SourceFile, ios::in | ios::binary );
    if( infile.fail() )
    {
        cout << "Error: " << SourceFile << " non-existent";
        return 1; // no input file
    }
    outfile.open( DestinationFile, ios::out | ios::binary );
    if( outfile.fail() )
    {
        cout << "Error: " << DestinationFile << " unable to open";
        return 2; // cannot be written to a destination file
    }
    while( !infile.eof() )
    {
        infile.read( (char *) buff,  BUFFSIZE );
        outfile.write( (char *) buff, infile.gcount() );
        if( infile.gcount() < BUFFSIZE )
            break;
    }
    infile.close();
```

```
    outfile.close();
    return 0;  // successful copy
}
void main( int argc, char *argv[] )
{
    cout<< "cp - Copy file, Copyright (C) 1996, RAJ, C-DAC, Bangalore.\n";
    if( argc < 3 )
    {
        cout << "Usage: cp <source file> <destination file>";
        exit( 1 );
    }
    if( CopyFile( argv[1], argv[2] ) != 0 )
      cout << "\nfile copy operation failed.";
}
```

Run1

```
cp - Copy file, Copyright (C) 1996, RAJ, C-DAC, Bangalore.
Usage: cp <source file> <destination file>
```

Run2

```
cp - Copy file, Copyright (C) 1996, RAJ, C-DAC, Bangalore.
Error: noname.cpp non-existent
file copy operation failed.
```

Run3

```
cp - Copy file, Copyright (C) 1996, RAJ, C-DAC, Bangalore.
```

The arguments passed at the command line for the above three executions are as follows:

Run1: <u>cp</u>
Run2: <u>cp noname.exe name.exe</u>
Run3: <u>cp cp.cpp temp.cpp</u>

In main(), the statements

```
        fstream infile;  // source file
        fstream outfile; // destination file
```

create two objects infile and outfile of the class fstream. They can be used either to read or write to the disk. The statement

```
        infile.open( SourceFile, ios::in | ios::binary );
```

opens SourceFile in binary read mode and assigns the handle to the object infile. Whereas, the statement

```
        outfile.open( DestinationFile, ios::out | ios::binary );
```

opens DestinationFile in binary write mode and assigns the handle to the object outfile.

The statement

```
        infile.read( (char *) buff,  BUFFSIZE );
```

reads the BUFFSIZE number of characters from the infile into the variable buff,and the statement

```
        outfile.write( (char *) buff, infile.gcount() );
```

writes the number of characters that are read (gcount() returns the count of the number of characters read successfully) from the input file into the destination disk file.

The statement

```
if( infile.gcount() < BUFFSIZE )
```

checks whether the number of characters read from the input file is less than the requested number. If yes, it indicates that the input file has no more characters to be read and terminates the reading process. The statements

```
infile.close();
outfile.close();
```

close both the input and output files from further processing.

Review Questions

18.1 What is a file ? What are the steps involved in manipulating a file in a C++ program ?

18.2 Explain the various file stream classes needed for file manipulations ?

18.3 Describe different methods of opening a file. Write a program to open a file named "xxx.bio" and write your name and other details into that file.

18.4 What are the different types of errors that might pop-up while processing files ?

18.5 Write an interactive program that accepts student's score and prints the result to a file.

18.6 Explain how while(input_file) expression detects the end of a file ?

18.7 What are file modes ? Describe various file mode options available ?

18.8 The file open modes ios::app and ios::ate set file pointer to end-of-file. What then, is the difference between them ?

18.9 What are file pointers ? Describe get-pointers and put-pointers.

18.10 What are the differences between sequential and random files ?

18.11 What are the differences between ASCII and binary files ?

18.12 Write a program which copies the contents of one file to a new file by removing unnecessary spaces between words.

18.13 Create a class called student. This class should have overloaded stream operator functions to save or retrieve objects of the student class from a file. Write an interactive program to manipulate objects of the student class with a file.

18.14 What are filter-utilities ? Write a program to display files on the screen page-wise. The output must pause after every page and continue until carriage return (enter) key is pressed. Accept name of a file to be processed from the command-line.

18.15 Explain how memory buffers can be connected to stream objects.

18.16 Write an interactive program to maintain an employee database. It has to maintain information such as employee id, name, qualification, designation, salary, etc. The user must be able to access all details about a person either by entering employee name or by employee id. Note that request for information may come randomly. It has to support an option for creating, updating, and deleting a database (in addition to query).

19

Exception Handling

19.1 Introduction

The increase in complexity and size of the software systems and the increase in society's dependence on the computer systems have been accompanied by an increase in the costs associated with their failure. The rising cost of failure in a computer system has stimulated interest in improving software reliability.

Software does not degrade physically as a function of time or environmental stress. It was assumed earlier that the concepts such as reliability or failure rate were not applicable to computer programs. It is true that a program that has once performed a given task as specified will continue to do so provided that none of the following change: the input, the computing environment, or user requirements. However, it is not reasonable to expect a program to be constantly operating on the same input data, because changes in computing environment and user requirements must be accommodated in most of the applications. Past and current failure free operation cannot be taken as a dependable indication that there will be no failure in the future.

The two main techniques for building reliable software (for dependable computing) are fault avoidance and fault tolerance. *Fault avoidance* deals with the prevention of fault occurrence by *construction*. It emphasizes on techniques to be applied during system development to ensure that the running system satisfies all reliability criteria a *priori*. It emphasizes that a sound way to deal with design faults is to stop them from getting into the system in the first place. *Fault tolerance* deals with the method of providing services complying with the specification inspite of faults having occurred (or occurring) by *redundancy*. In C++, exception handling allows to build fault tolerant systems.

Fault tolerance approach attempts to increase reliability by designing the system to continue to provide service inspite of the presence of faults. It begins with error detection. It must be possible to detect the occurrence of a latent error before it leads to failure. Once an error has been detected, the goal is error recovery. The goal of fault tolerant design is to improve dependability by enabling the system to perform its intended function in the presence of a given number of faults.

The Annotated C++ Reference Manual (ARM) by Ellis and Stroustrup states *Exception handling provides a way of transferring control and information to an unspecified caller that has expressed willingness to handle exceptions of a given type. Exceptions of arbitrary types can be 'thrown and caught' and the set of exceptions a function may throw can be specified. The termination model of exception handling is provided. Exception handling can be used to support notions of error handling and fault tolerant computing.*

19.2 Error Handling

In traditional programming techniques, validation of input data and some runtime errors were handled explicitly by the module in which the error occurred. Although, the users of these modules know how to cope with such errors, there is no means to detect the errors and handle them in the user's code instead of the library. The notion of exceptions is supported in C++ to deal with such problems. Here, *exception* refers to unexpected condition in a program. The unusual conditions could be faults, causing an error which in turn causes the program to fail. The error-handling mechanism of C++ is generally referred to as *exception handling*. It provides a straightforward mechanism for adding reliable error handling mechanism in a program.

Generally, exceptions are classified into *synchronous* and *asynchronous exceptions*. The exceptions which occur during the program execution, due to some fault in the input-data or technique that is not suitable to handle the current class of data, within the program, are known as *synchronous exceptions*. For instance, errors such as out-of-range, overflow, underflow, and so on belong to the class of synchronous exceptions. The exceptions caused by events or faults unrelated (external) to the program and beyond the control of program are called *asynchronous exceptions*. For instance, errors such as keyboard interrupts, hardware malfunctions, disk failure, and so on belong to the class of asynchronous exceptions. The proposed exception handling mechanism in C++ is designed to handle only synchronous exceptions caused within a program.

Exception handling is an integral part of the ANSI/ISO C++ language standard. This standardization ensures that the power of object-oriented design is supported throughout the program. An especially strong feature of the standard is the availability of virtual functions and the use of objects to define exceptions. Virtual functions guarantee a minimum runtime overhead—zero additional program overhead if no exceptions are thrown. When used properly, C++ exception handling solves many problems with alternative error handling techniques (such as returning error values from methods or using global error handlers).

In accordance with ANSI specifications, recent implementation of most C++ compilers are supporting the exception-handling model. When an abnormal situation arises at runtime, the program should terminate. However, throwing an exception allows the user to gather information at the throw point that could be useful in diagnosing the causes which led to failure. An user can also specify in the exception handler the actions to be taken before the program terminates. Only synchronous exceptions are handled (the cause of failure is generated from within the program). An event such as Control-C (which is generated from outside the program) is not considered to be an exception.

19.3 Exception Handling Model

When a program encounters an abnormal situation for which it is not designed, the user may transfer control to some other part of the program that is designed to deal with the problem. This is done by throwing an exception. The exception-handling mechanism uses three blocks: try, throw, and catch. The relationship of these three exception handling constructs called the *exception handling model* is shown in Figure 19.1.

The *try-block* must be followed immediately by a handler, which is a *catch block*. If an exception is thrown in the try-block, the program control is transferred to the appropriate exception handler. The program should attempt to catch any exception that is thrown by any function. Failure to do so could result in abnormal termination of the program. Though C++ allows an exception to be of any type, it is useful to make exceptions as objects. The exception object is treated exactly the same way as other normal objects. An exception carries information from the point where the exception is thrown to the point where the exception is caught. This information allows the program user to know as to when the program encounters an anomaly at runtime.

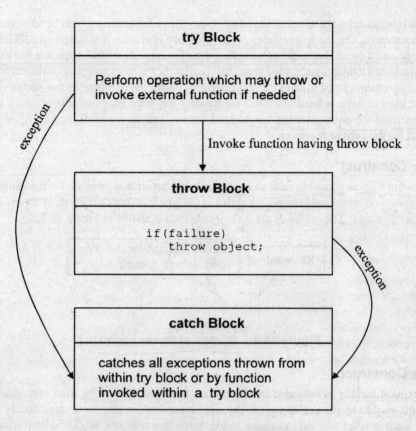

Figure 19.1:   Exception handling model

19.4 Exception Handling Constructs

Exception handling mechanism transfers control and information from a point of exception in a program to an exception handler associated with the *try-block*. An exception handler will be invoked only by a *thrown expression* in the code executed by the handler's try-block or by functions called from the handler's try-block. C++ offers the following three constructs for defining these blocks.

* try
* throw
* catch

The exception handler is indicated by the catch keyword. The handler must be used immediately after the try-block. The keyword catch can also occur immediately after another catch. Each handler will only evaluate an exception that matches, or can be converted to the type specified in its argument list. Every exception thrown by the program must be caught and processed by the exception handler. If the program fails to provide an exception handler for a thrown exception, the program will call the terminate() function.

Exception handlers are evaluated in the order they are encountered. An exception is said to be caught when its type matches the type in the catch statement. Once a type match is made, program control is transferred to the handler. The handler specifies what actions should be taken to deal with the program anomaly. The *stack-unwinding* (catch-cleanup) operation is initiated immediately after processing the *catch block* that matches with the exception type. In normal sequence (no exceptions are raised) stack-unwinding is performed immediately after the *try-block* and program execution continues. (A `goto` statement can be used to transfer program control out of a handler but such a statement can never be used to enter a handler.) After the handler has been executed, the program continues its execution from the point after the last handler for the current try-block and no other handlers are evaluated for the current exception.

`throw` Construct

The keyword `throw` is used to raise an exception when an error is generated in the computation. The throw-expression initializes a temporary object of the type T (to match the type of argument `arg`) used in `throw(T arg)`. The syntax of the `throw` construct is shown in Figure 19.2.

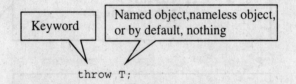

```
throw T;
```

Figure 19.2:   Syntax of throw construct

`catch` Construct

The exception handler is indicated by the `catch` keyword. It must be used immediately after the statements marked by the `try` keyword. The `catch` handler can also occur immediately after another `catch`. Each handler will only evaluate an exception that matches, or can be converted to the type specified in its argument list. The syntax of the `catch` construct is shown in Figure 19.3.

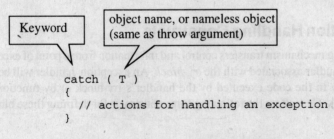

```
catch ( T )
{
    // actions for handling an exception
}
```

Figure 19.3:   Syntax of catch construct

`try` Construct

The `try` keyword defines a boundary within which an exception can occur. A block of code in which an exception can occur must be prefixed by the keyword `try`. Following the `try` keyword is a block of code enclosed by braces. This indicates that the program is prepared to test for the existence of exceptions. If an exception occurs, the program flow is interrupted. The syntax of the `try` construct is shown in Figure 19.4.

```
    Keyword

try
{
    // code raising exception or referring to
    // a function raising exception
}
catch( type_id1 )
{
    // actions for handling an exception
}
...
...
catch( type_idn )
{
    // action for handling an execption
}
```

Figure 19.4: Syntax of try construct

A block of code in which an exception can occur must be prefixed by the keyword try. The try keyword is followed by a block of code enclosed within braces. It indicates that the program is prepared for testing the existence of exceptions. If an exception occurs, the program flow is interrupted and the exception handler is invoked.

The mechanism suggests that error handling code must perform the following tasks.

1. Detect the problem causing exception (Hit the exception)
2. Inform that an error has occurred (Throw the exception)
3. Receive the error information (Catch the exception)
4. Take corrective actions (Handle the exceptions)

Exception handling code resembles the following pattern:

```
my_function()
{
    .....
    if( operation_fail )
        throw Object1; // throw-point
        .....
}
....
try
{       // begin of try block
    .....
    my_function(); // call the function my_function
    .....
    if( overflow )
        throw Object2; // throw-point
    .....
}       // end of try block
```

```
     catch( Object1 )
     {
        .....
        // take corrective action for operation_fail
        .....
     }
     catch( Object2 )
     {
        .....
        // take corrective action for overflow
        .....
     }
     ....
```

The following sequence of steps are performed when an exception is raised:

- The program searches for a matching handler.
- If a handler is found, the stack is unwound to that point.
- Program control is transferred to the handler.
- If no handler is found, the program will invoke the `terminate()` function (explained later). If no exceptions are thrown, the program executes in the normal fashion.

The program `divzero.cpp` illustrates the mechanism for detecting errors, raising exceptions, and handling such exceptions. It has the class `number` to store an integer number and the member function `read()` to read a number from the console and the member function `div()` to perform division operations. It raises exception if an attempt is made to perform *divide-by-zero* operation. It has an empty class named `DIVIDE` used as the throw's expression-id.

```
// divzero.cpp: Divide Operation Validation, (divide-by-zero)
#include <iostream.h>
class number
{
   private:
      int num;
   public:
      void read()    // read number from keyboard
      {
         cin >> num;
      }
      class DIVIDE {};    // abstract class used in exceptions
      int div( number num2 )
      {
         if( num2.num == 0 )  // check for zero division if yes
            throw DIVIDE();   // raise exception
         else
            return num / num2.num;  // compute and return the result
      }
};
```

```
int main()
{
   number num1, num2;
   int result;
   cout << "Enter Number 1: ";
   num1.read();
   cout << "Enter Number 2: ";
   num2.read();
   // statements must be enclosed in try block if you intend to handle
   // exceptions raised by them
   try
   {
      cout << "trying division operation...";
      result = num1.div( num2 );
      cout << "succeeded" << endl;
   }
   catch( number::DIVIDE )      // exception handler block
   {
      // actions taken in response to exception
      cout << "failed" << endl;
      cout << "Exception: Divide-By-Zero";
      return 1;
   }
   // no exceptions, display result
   cout << "num1/num2 = " << result;
   return 0;
}
```

Run1

```
Enter Number 1: 10
Enter Number 2: 2
trying division operation...succeeded
num1/num2 = 5
```

Run2

```
Enter Number 1: 10
Enter Number 2: 0
trying division operation...failed
Exception: Divide-By-Zero
```

In main(), the try-block

```
   try
   { ...; result = num1.div( num2 ); ...; }
```

invokes the member function div() to perform the division operation. If any attempt is made to divide by zero, the following statement in div():

```
   if( num2.num == 0 )   // check for zero division if yes
      throw DIVIDE();     // raise exception
```

detects the same and raises the exception by passing a nameless object of type class DIVIDE. All the statements following the one which raised the exception are skipped (see output of *Run2* above) and search for an exception handler begins. The runtime system searches catch-block to detect the handler.

The block of code in main() following the try-block:

```
catch( number::DIVIDE )
{
    cout << "Exception: Divide-By-Zero";
    return 1;
}
```

will catch the exception raised due to the call to the function in the *try-block* and executes its body (see Figure 19.5). If no exception is raised, the exception handling *catch-block* will not be executed and execution proceeds to the next statement, which displays the result.

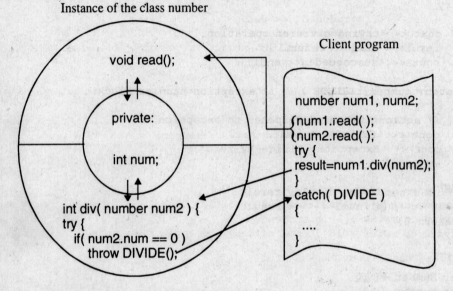

Figure 19.5:   Exception handling in the number class

Array Reference Out of Bound

The program arrbound.cpp illustrates the mechanism of validating array element references. If any attempt is made to refer to an element whose index is beyond the array size, an exception is raised.

```
// arrbound.cpp: Array Reference Bound Validation
#include <iostream.h>
const int ARR_SIZE = 10;    // maximum array size
class array
{
    private:
        int arr[ARR_SIZE];
    public:
        class RANGE {};        // Range abstract class
        int & operator[]( int i )
        {
            if( i < 0 || i >= ARR_SIZE )
                throw RANGE(); // throw abstract object
```

```
            return arr[i]; // valid reference
       }
};
void main()
{
    array a; // create array
    cout << "Maximum array size allowed = " << ARR_SIZE << endl;
    try
    {
        cout << "Trying to refer a[1]...";
        a[1] = 10;
        cout << "succeeded" << endl;
        cout << "Trying to refer a[15]...";
        a[15] = 10; // refer 15th element from array a, causes exception
        cout << "succeeded" << endl;
    }
    catch( array::RANGE ) // true if throw is executed in try scope
    {
        // action for exception
        cout << "Out of Range in Array Reference";
    }
}
```

Run
```
Maximum array size allowed = 10
Trying to refer a[1]...succeeded
Trying to refer a[15]...Out of Range in Array Reference
```

The statement in try-block of main():

```
        a[1] = 10;
```

updates the first element of the array. However, another statement

```
        a[15] = 10;
```

in the same block, tries to update the fifteenth element. It leads to an exception since the array size is only 10. This exception is caught by the statement

```
        catch( array::RANGE )
```

which issues a warning message on the standard output.

19.5 Handler Throwing the Same Exception Again

There are several good reasons to allow an exception to be implicitly propagated from a function (callee) to its caller. Of course, it follows the *democracy* principle: a client (caller) is the better candidate to decide what actions are to be taken when something goes wrong. If a function does not want to take any corrective action in response to an exception, it can pass the same to the caller of a function. The throw construct without an explicit exception parameter raises the previous exception. An exception must currently exist otherwise, terminate() is invoked. The program pass.cpp illustrates the method of passing the same exception to the caller if the current handler is unable to handle it.

```cpp
// pass.cpp: passing all exceptions that occur in parent to child
#include <iostream.h>
#include <process.h>
const int ARR_SIZE = 10;   // maximum array size
class array
{
   private:
      int arr[ARR_SIZE];
   public:
      array();
      class RANGE {};        // Range abstract class
      int & operator[]( int i )
      {
         if( i < 0 || i >= ARR_SIZE )
            throw RANGE(); // throw abstract object
         return arr[i];    // valid reference
      }
};
array::array()
{
   for( int i = 0; i < ARR_SIZE; i++ )
      arr[i] = i;
}
// read an element from the array, if any exception pass the same to caller
int read( array & a, int index )
{
   int element;
   try
   {
      element = a[ index ];
   }
   catch(array::RANGE)  // catch the exceptions raised in class
   {
      cout << endl<< "Parent passing exception to child to handle"<<endl;
      throw;    // pass all exceptions to the caller
   }
   return element;
}
void main()
{
   array a; // create array object
   int index, element;
   cout << "Maximum vector size allowed = " << ARR_SIZE << endl;
   while( 1 )
   {
      cout << "Enter element to referenced: ";
      cin >> index;
      try
      {
         cout << "Trying to access object array 'a' for index = "<<index;
         element = read( a, index );
```

```
            cout << endl << "Element in Array = " << element << endl;
        }
    catch( array::RANGE ) // true if throw is executed in try scope
        {
            // action for exception
            cout << "Child: Out of Range in Array Reference";
            exit( 1 );
        }
    }
}
```

Run

```
Maximum vector size allowed = 10
Enter element to referenced: 1
Trying to access object array 'a' for index = 1
Element in Array = 1
Enter element to referenced: 5
Trying to access object array 'a' for index = 5
Element in Array = 5
Enter element to referenced: 10
Trying to access object array 'a' for index = 10
Parent passing exception to child to handle
Child: Out of Range in Array Reference
```

The *catch-block* in the function read() does not take any corrective action for the exception array::RANGE. It throws the exception to the caller and the catch-block in main() terminates the program after displaying the message.

```
        Child: Out of Range in Array Reference
```

on the standard output device.

19.6 List of Exceptions

Raising or catching an exception affects the way a function relates to other functions. C++ language makes it possible for the user to specify a list of exceptions that a function can throw. This exception specification can be used as a suffix to the function declaration specifying the list of exceptions that a function may directly or indirectly throw as a part of a function declaration. The syntax for exception specification is shown in Figure 19.6.

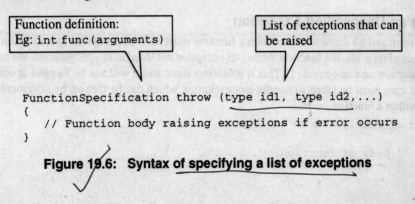

Function definition:
Eg: int func(arguments)

List of exceptions that can be raised

```
FunctionSpecification throw (type id1, type id2,...)
{
    // Function body raising exceptions if error occurs
}
```

Figure 19.6: Syntax of specifying a list of exceptions

The *exception-list*, which is the function suffix is not considered to be a part of the specification of a function. Consequently, a pointer to a function is not affected by the function's exception specification. Such a pointer checks only the function's return value and argument types. Therefore, the following is legal:

```
void f1(void) throw();      // cannot throw exceptions
void f2(void) throw (BETA); // can throw BETA objects
int func() throw( X, Y )    // can throw only X and Y exceptions
{ ...
}
```

C++ allows to have pointers to a function raising exception, for instance,

```
void (* fptr)();                // Pointer to a function returning void
fptr = f1;
fptr = f2;
```

However, extreme care should be taken when overriding virtual functions; the exception specification is not considered as a part of the function type, it is possible to violate the program design. If an exception which is not listed in the exception specification is *thrown*, the function unexpected() will be called (discussed later in this chapter).

In the following example, the derived class BETA::vfunc is defined so that it should not throw any exceptions—a departure from the original function declaration.

```
class ALPHA
{
    public:
    struct ALPHA_ERR {};
    virtual void vfunc(void) throw (ALPHA_ERR) {};
    // Exception specification
};
class BETA : public ALPHA
{
    void vfunc(void) throw() {};  // Exception specification is changed
};
```

The following are examples of functions with exception specifications.

```
void f1();                 // The function can throw any exception
void f2() throw();         // Should not throw any exceptions
void f3() throw( A, B* ); // Can throw exceptions publicly derived
                          // from A,or a pointer to publicly derived B
```

Raising an Unspecified Exception

The definition and all declarations of such a function must have an exception specification containing the same set of type-ids. If a function throws an exception not listed in its specification, the program will call the function unexpected(). This is a runtime issue and it will not be flagged at compile time. Therefore, care must be taken to handle any exception which can be thrown by statements/functions invoked within a function.

```
void my_func1() throw (A, B)
{
    // Body of function.
}
```

This example specifies a list of exceptions that my_func1() can throw. No other exception will propagate out of my_func1. If an exception other than A or B is generated within my_func1, it is considered to be an unexpected exception and program control will be transferred to the predefined unexpected function. The program sign1.cpp illustrates raising of an exception other than that specified in the exception list..

```
// sign1.cpp: determine whether the input is +ve or -ve through exceptions
#include <iostream.h>
class positive {};
class negative {};
class zero {};
// this function can raise only positive and negative exceptions
void what_sign( int num ) throw( positive, negative )
{
    if( num > 0 )
        throw positive();
    else
        if( num < 0 )
            throw negative();
        else
            throw zero();  // unspecified exception
}
void main()
{
    int num;
    cout << "Enter any number: ";
    cin >> num;
    try
    {
        what_sign( num );
    }
    catch( positive )
    { cout << "+ve Exception";   }
    catch( negative )
    { cout << "-ve Exception";   }
    catch( zero )
    { cout << "0 Exception";  }
}
```

Run1
```
Enter any number: 10
+ve Exception
```

Run2
```
Enter any number: -10
-ve Exception
```

Run3
```
Enter any number: 0
Abnormal program termination
```

The prototype of the function what_sign() is specified as

```
void what_sign( int num ) throw( positive, negative )
```

It indicates that, this function can raise exceptions positive and negative, but the statement

```
throw zero();  // unspecified exception
```

raises the exception zero, which is not in the exception list of this function. It calls the default exception handler, which aborts the execution of the program (see *Run3*) although there exists an explicit exception handler in the caller of this function.

Exceptions in a No-Exception Function

The following function and exception specification indicates that it will not generate any exception:

```
void my_func2() throw ()
{
    // Body of this function.
}
```

If any statement in the body of my_func2() throws an exception, the control is transferred to library function abort(), which terminates the program by issuing an error message. The program sign2.cpp illustrates the effect of raising an exception in a function which is not supposed to raise any exception.

```
// sign2.cpp: determine whether the input is positive or negative
#include <iostream.h>
class zero {};
// this function cannot raise exception
void what_sign( int num ) throw()
{
    if( num > 0 )
        cout << "+ve number";
    else
        if( num < 0 )
            cout << "-ve number";
        else
            throw zero();  // unspecified exception
}
void main()
{
    int num;
    cout << "Enter any number: ";
    cin >> num;
    try
    {
        what_sign( num );
    }
    catch( zero )
    { cout << "0 Exception"; }
}
```

Run1

```
Enter any number: 10
+ve number
```

Run2

```
Enter any number: -10
-ve number
```

Run3

```
Enter any number: 0
Abnormal program termination
```

The prototype of the function what_sign():

```
void what_sign( int num ) throw()
```

indicates that it does not raise any exception, but the statement

```
throw zero();  // unspecified exception
```

raises the exception. It invokes the default exception handler which aborts the execution of the program (see *Run3*) though there exists an explicit exception handler in the caller of this function.

19.7 Catch All Exceptions

C++ supports a feature to catch all the exceptions raised in the try-block. The syntax of the catch construct to handle all the exceptions raised in the try block is shown in Figure 19.7.

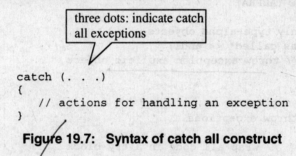

```
catch (. . .)
{
    // actions for handling an exception
}
```

Figure 19.7: Syntax of catch all construct

The three dots in the catch(...) indicates that it catches all types of exceptions raised in its preceding try-block. The program catal11.cpp illustrates the mechanism of handling all the exceptions raised by a single handler.

```
// catall1.cpp:All exceptions are caught
#include <iostream.h>
class excep2 {};
void main()
{
   try
   {
     cout << "Throwing uncaught exception" << endl;
     ·throw excep2();
   }
   catch( ... ) // catch all the exceptions
   {
     // action for exception
     cout << "Caught all exceptions" << endl;
```

```
   }
   cout << "I am displayed";
}
```

Run
```
Throwing uncaught exception
Caught all exceptions
I am displayed
```

The statement in the try-block of main():

```
      throw excep2();
```

raises the exception excep2(). It is caught by the statement,

```
      catch( ... )  // catch all the exceptions
```

The program having multiple catch-all exceptions is illustrated in catal12.cpp. It has multiple functions calling one another.

```
// catall2.cpp: making exception-specifications and handle all exceptions
#include <iostream.h>
class ALPHA{};   // Exception declaration
ALPHA _a;  // object of ALPHA
void f3(void) throw (ALPHA)
{
   // Will throw only type-alpha objects
   cout << "f3() was called" << endl;
   throw( _a );   // throw exception explicit object
}
void f2(void) throw()
{
    // should not throw exceptions
    try
    {                   // wrap all code in a try-block
      cout << "f2() was called" << endl;
       f3();
    }
    catch ( ... )
    {            // trap all exceptions
      cout << "f2() has elements with exceptions!" << endl;
    }
}
int main()
{
   try
   {
      f2();
      return 0;   // f2 succeeds, terminate
   }
   catch( ... )
   {
      cout << "Need more handlers!";
   }
```

```
    cout << endl << "continued after handling exceptions";
    return 1;
}
```

Run

```
f2() was called
f3() was called
f2() has elements with exceptions!
```

In f3(), the statement

```
    throw( _a );    // throw exception explicit object
```

throws the exception using named object _a, which is the instance of the class ALPHA. It is caught by the handler in the caller function f2(). There is a handler to catch all exceptions in main(), but is not activated; all the exceptions are caught in f2() and no exceptions are passed to its caller.

19.8 Exceptions in Constructors and Destructors

When an exception is thrown, the copy constructor is invoked as a part of the exception handling. The copy constructor is used to initialize a temporary object at the throw point. Other copies may be generated by the program. When the program flow is interrupted by an exception, destructors are invoked for all automatic objects which were constructed from the entry point of the try-block. If the exception was thrown during construction of some object, destructors will be called only for those objects which were fully constructed. For example, if an array of objects was under construction when an exception was thrown, destructors will be called only for the array elements which were fully constructed.

As a building block of design patterns for proper handling of exceptions, there is a need for *secure operations* that allow transfer of resource responsibilities without throwing exceptions. In C++, it is a bad idea to leave a destructor by throwing an exception. This is because a destructor may be invoked during runtime stack unwinding when another exception was thrown; a second throw that aborts one of these destructors will immediately invoke terminate(), which aborts the program by default. In other words, all destructors in a C++ program should have an empty specification throw(). This is called *secure operations*.

Those objects which are created from a try-block to any statement raising an exception serve no purpose if any exception is raised. Hence, they must be destroyed by releasing the allocated resources. The process of calling destructor for automatic objects constructed on the path from a try-block to a thrown expression is called *stack unwinding*. The program twoexcep.cpp illustrates the concept of having multiple types of exceptions in a program.

```
// twoexcep.cpp: Array Creation and Reference Bound Validation
#include <iostream.h>
const int ARR_SIZE = 10;   // maximum array size, that can be allocated
class array
{
    private:
        int *arr;       // pointer to array
        int size;       // maximum array size
```

```cpp
   public:
      class SIZE {};    // Size abstract class
      class RANGE {};   // Range abstract class
      array( int SizeRequest )   // constructor
      {
         if( SizeRequest < 0 || SizeRequest > ARR_SIZE )
            throw SIZE();
         // allocate resources
         size = SizeRequest;
         arr = new int[ size ];
      }
      ~array()    // destructor
      {
         // deallocate resources
         delete arr;
      }
      int & operator[]( int i )       // subscript operator overloading
      {
         if( i < 0 || i > size )
            throw RANGE(); // throw abstract object
         return arr[i]; // valid reference
      }
};
void main()
{
   cout << "Maximum array size allowed = " << ARR_SIZE << endl;
   try
   {
      cout << "Trying to create object a1(5)...";
      array a1(5);   // create array
      cout << "succeeded" << endl;
      cout << "Trying to refer a1[5]...";
      a1[5] = 10;
      cout << "succeeded..";
      cout << "a1[5] = " << a1[5] << endl;
      cout << "Trying to refer a1[15]...";
      a1[15] = 10;        // causes exception
      cout << "succeeded" << endl;
   }
   catch( array::SIZE )
   {
      // action for exception
      cout << "..Size exceeds allowable Limit" << endl;
   }
   catch( array::RANGE ) // true if throw is executed in try scope
   {
      // action for exception
      cout << "..Array Reference Out of Range" << endl;
   }
```

```
    // Array creation unsuccessful, Request > ARR_SIZE
    try
    {
        cout << "Trying to create object a2(15)...";
        array a2(15);  // create array, causes exception
        cout << "succeeded" << endl;
        a2[3] = 3;  // valid access
    }
    catch( array::SIZE )
    {
        // action for exception
        cout << "....Size exceeds allowable Limit" << endl;
    }
    catch( array::RANGE ) // true if throw is executed in try scope
    {
        // action for exception
        cout << "....Array Reference Out of Range" << endl;
    }
}
```

Run

```
Maximum array size allowed = 10
Trying to create object a1(5)...succeeded
Trying to refer a1[5]...succeeded..a1[5] = 10
Trying to refer a1[15].....Array Reference Out of Range
Trying to create object a2(15).......Size exceeds allowable Limit
```

The one-argument constructor of the class array,

```
    array( int SizeRequest )   // constructor
```

throws an exception,

```
    throw SIZE();
```

if an attempt is made to create an array beyond the allowable range. The statement

```
    if( i < 0 || i > size )
        throw RANGE(); // throw abstract object
```

throws an exception if an attempt is made to access an array element by using invalid index (lower than minimum bound or higher than the maximum bound).

19.9 Handling Uncaught Exceptions

The uncaught exception handling mechanism relies on two library functions, `terminate()` and `unexpected()`, for coping with exceptions unhandled explicitly. C++ supports the following special functions to handle uncaught exceptions in a systematic manner:

- `terminate()`
- `set_terminate()`
- `unexpected()`
- `set_unexpected()`

terminate()

The function `terminate()` is invoked when an exception is raised and the handler is not found. The default action for terminate is to invoke abort (). Such a default action causes immediate termination of the program execution) The program uncaught.cpp illustrates the series of events that can occur when the program encounters an exception for which no handler can be found.

```cpp
// uncaught.cpp: Uncaught exception invokes abort() automatically
#include <iostream.h>
class excep1 {};
class excep2 {};
void main()
{
    try
    {
        cout << "Throwing uncaught exception" << endl;
        throw excep2();
    }
    catch( excep1 ) // true if throw excep1 is executed in try scope
    {
        // action for exception
        cout << "Exception 1";
    }
    // excep2 is not caught hence, program aborts
    // here without proceeding further
    cout << "I am not displayed";
}
```

Run
```
Throwing uncaught exception
Abnormal program termination
```

The statement in main()'s try-block:
```
        throw excep2();
```
raises an exception excep2 for which no handler exists. Here, terminate() comes to rescue this condition. When terminate() function is called, the program aborts by displaying the message,
```
        Abnormal program termination
```
and does not proceed further.

The programmer can modify the way the program will terminate when an exception is generated. The terminate() function can call user defined function instead of abort() if the user defined function is registered with set_terminate() function.

set_terminate()
The set_terminate function allows the user to install a function that defines the program's actions to be taken to terminate the program when a handler for the exception cannot be found. The actions are defined in t_func, which is declared to be a function of type terminate_function. A terminate_function type defined in except.h, is a function that takes no arguments, and returns nothing. By default, an exception for which no handler can be found results in the program calling the terminate function. This will normally result in a call to abort function. The program then ends with the message, *Abnormal program termination*. If some function other than abort() is to be invoked by

the `terminate()`, the user should define `t_func` function. This `t_func` function can be installed by `set_terminate` as the termination function. The installation of `t_func` allows the user to implement any action that is not taken by `abort()`. The syntax of the `set_terminate` function declared in the header file `except.h` is as follows:

```
typedef void (*terminate_function)();
terminate_function set_terminate( terminate_function t_func );
// Define your termination scheme
terminate_function my_terminate( void )
{
    // Take actions before terminating
    // should not throw exceptions
    exit(1); // must end somehow
}
// Register your termination function
set_terminate( my_terminate );
```

The program `myhand.cpp` handles uncaught exceptions with the user specified terminate function.

```
// myhand.cpp: All exceptions are not caught, executes MyTerminate()
#include <iostream.h>
#include <except.h>
Class excep1 {};
class excep2 {};
void MyTerminate()
{
    cout << "My Terminate is invoked";
    exit( 1 );
}
void main()
{
    set_terminate( MyTerminate ); // sets to our own terminate function
    try
    {
        cout << "Throwing uncaught exception\n";
        throw excep2();
    }
    catch( excep1 )
    {
        // action for exception
        cout << "Caught exception, excep1\n";
    }
    // program abort() here; MyTerminate() will be called
    cout << "I am not displayed";
}
```

Run
```
Throwing uncaught exception
My Terminate is invoked
```

In main(), the statement

```
set_terminate( MyTerminate );
```

sets the function MyTerminate as a termination function to be invoked when there exists no exception handler for the exception raised. The statement in the try-block ,

```
throw excep2();
```

raises the exception excep2, which is uncaught. The system automatically invokes the function MyTerminate as a part of unhandled exceptions.

unexpected()

The unexpected function is called when a function throws an exception not listed in its exception specification. The program calls unexpected() which calls any user-defined function registered by set_unexpected. If no function is registered with set_unexpected, the unexpected() function then invokes the terminate() function. The prototype of the unexpected() call is

```
void unexpected();
```

The function unexpected returns nothing (void) but *it can throw an exception* through the execution of a function registered by the set_unexpected function.

```cpp
// sign3.cpp: unexpected exceptions
#include <iostream.h>
#include <process.h> // has prototype for exit()
#include <except.h>
class zero {};
// this function cannot raise exception
void what_sign( int num ) throw()
{
   if( num > 0 )
     cout << "+ve number";
   else
     if( num < 0 )
        cout << "-ve number";
     else
        throw zero();  // unspecified exception
}
void main()
{
   int num;
   cout << "Enter any number: ";
   cin >> num;
   try
   {
     what_sign( num );
   }
   catch(...)
   {
     cout << "catch all exceptions";
   }
   cout << endl << "end of main()";
}
```

Run1

```
Enter any number: 10
+ve number
end of main()
```

Run2

```
Enter any number: -3
-ve number
end of main()
```

Run3

```
Enter any number: 0
Abnormal program termination
```

The function

```
void what_sign( int num ) throw()
```

raises an unspecified exception

```
throw zero();  // unspecified exception
```

leading to the invocation of the unexpected() function automatically (see **Run3**).

set_unexpected()

The function set_unexpected() lets the user to install a function that defines the program's actions to be taken when a function throws an exception not listed in its exception specification. The actions are defined in unexpected_func() library function. By default, an unexpected exception causes unexpected() to be called, which in turn calls unexpected_func.

Program behavior when a function is registered with set_unexpected():

```
// Define your unexpected handler
unexpected_function my_unexpected( void )
{
        // Define actions to take
        // possibly make adjustments
}
// register your handler
set_unexpected( my_unexpected );
```

The program sign4.cpp illustrates the mechanism of defining the user defined unexpected exception handler. The user defined unexpected_func must not return to its caller. An attempt to return to the caller results in an undefined program behavior. The unexpected_func() can invoke abort(), exit(), or terminate() functions.

```
// sign4.cpp: unexpected exceptions through user-defined function
#include <iostream.h>
#include <process.h> // has prototype for exit()
#include <except.h>

class zero {};         // empty class
// this function cannot raise exception
```

```
void what_sign( int num ) throw()
{
   if( num > 0 )
      cout << "+ve number";
   else
      if( num < 0 )
         cout << "-ve number";
      else
         throw zero();  // unspecified exception
}
// this is automatically called whenever an unexpected exception occurs
void MyUnexpected()
{
   cout << "My unexpected handler is invoked";
   exit( 1 );
}
void main()
{
   int num;
   cout << "Enter any number: ";
   cin >> num;
   set_unexpected( MyUnexpected );  // user defined handler
   try
   {
      what_sign( num );
   }
   catch(...)      // catch all exceptions
   {
      cout << "catch all exceptions";
   }
   cout << endl << "end of main()";
}
```

Run1

```
Enter any number: 10
+ve number
end of main()
```

Run2

```
Enter any number: -3
-ve number
end of main()
```

Run3

```
Enter any number: 0
My unexpected handler is invoked
```

The function what_sign() raises an unspecified exception,

```
      throw zero();  // unspecified exception
```

leading to the invocation of the user defined MyUnexpected() automatically (see *Run3*).

19.10 Exceptions in Operator Overloaded Functions

The program `interact.cpp` illustrates the mechanism for handling exceptions in the vector class, while creating its objects and accessing its elements either for a read or write operation. It overloads the operator `[ ]` to simulate the array operations on the user defined data type.

```cpp
// interact.cpp: interactive program raises exception for improper data
#include <iostream.h>
#include <process.h>
const int VEC_SIZE = 10;   // maximum vector size, that can be allocated
class vector
{
  private:
    int *vec;       // pointer to array for vector elements
    int size;       // maximum vector size
  public:
    class SIZE {};        // Size abstract class
    class RANGE {};       // Range abstract class
    vector( int SizeRequest )
    {
      if( SizeRequest <= 0 || SizeRequest > VEC_SIZE )
        throw SIZE();
      size = SizeRequest;
      vec = new int[ size ];
    }
    ~vector()        // destructor
    {
      delete vec;
    }
    // subscripted operator overloading
    int & operator[]( int i );
};
// subscripted operator overloading
int & vector::operator[]( int i )
{
  if( i < 0 || i >= size )
    throw RANGE(); // throw abstract object
  return vec[i]; // valid reference
}
void main()
{
  int size, data, index;
  cout << "Maximum vector size allowed = " << VEC_SIZE << endl;
  try
  {
    cout << "What is the size of vector you want to create: ";
    cin >> size;
    cout << "Trying to create object vector v1 of size = " << size;
    vector v1(size);  // create vector
    cout << "...succeeded" << endl;
```

```
      cout << "Which vector element you want to access (index): ";
      cin >> index;
      cout << "What is the new value for v1[ " << index << " ]: ";
      cin >> data;
      cout << "Trying to modify a1[ " << index << " ]...";
      v1[index] = data;
      cout << "succeeded" << endl;
      cout << "New Value of a1[ " << index << " ] = " << v1[index];
   }
   catch( vector::SIZE )
   {
      // action for exception
      cout << "failed" << endl;
      cout << "Vector creation size exceeds allowable limit";
      exit( 1 );
   }
   catch( vector::RANGE ) // true if throw is executed in try scope
   {
      // action for exception
      cout << "...failed" << endl;
      cout << "Vector reference out-of-range";
      exit( 1 );
   }
}
```

Run1

```
Maximum vector size allowed = 10
What is the size of vector you want to create: 5
Trying to create object vector v1 of size = 5...succeeded
Which vector element you want to access (index): 2
What is the new value for v1[ 2 ]: 7
Trying to modify a1[ 2 ]...succeeded
New Value of a1[ 2 ] = 7
```

Run2

```
Maximum vector size allowed = 10
What is the size of vector you want to create: 5
Trying to create object vector v1 of size = 5...succeeded
Which vector element you want to access (index): 10
What is the new value for v1[ 10 ]: 2
Trying to modify a1[ 10 ]...failed
Vector reference out-of-range
```

Run3

```
Maximum vector size allowed = 10
What is the size of vector you want to create: 15
Trying to create object vector v1 of size = 15
Vector creation size exceeds allowable limit
```

Note:

   Run1: All operations are valid, no exception is generated

Run2: Invalid vector reference, exception generated

Run3: Invalid size for vector creation, exception generated

In *Run2*, an attempt is made to refer to the 11th element (but index is 10) of the vector whose size is 10. It raises an exception, which is caught by the statement,

```
catch( vector::RANGE )
```

In *Run3*, an attempt is made to create the vector of size 15, but the allowable limit is 10 as restricted by the value of VEC_SIZE constant. The statement

```
catch( vector::SIZE )
```

catches the exception raised while creating objects of the vector class.

19.11 Exceptions in Inheritance Tree

The mechanism of handling exceptions in the base and derived classes is illustrated in virtual.cpp.

```cpp
// virtual.cpp: Binding a pointer to base class' object to base or derived
// objects at runtime and invoking respective members if they are virtual
#include <iostream.h>
#include <process.h>
// empty class for Father and Son inheritance
class WRONG_AGE
{};
class Father
{
    protected:
        int f_age;
    public:
        Father( int n )
        {
            if( n < 0 )
                throw WRONG_AGE();
            f_age = n;
        }
        virtual int GetAge(void)
        {
            return f_age;
        }
};
// Son inherits all the properties of father
class Son : public Father
{
    protected:
        int s_age;
    public:
        Son( int n, int m ):Father(n)
        {
            // if son's age is greater or equal to father, throw exception
            if( m >= n )
                throw WRONG_AGE();
```

```
        s_age = m;
    }
    virtual int GetAge(void)
    {
        return s_age;
    }
};
void main()
{
    int father_age;
    int son_age;
    Father *basep;    // pointer to father objects
    cout << "Enter Age of Father: ";
    cin >> father_age;
    try
    {
        basep = new Father( father_age );       // pointer to father
    }
    catch( WRONG_AGE )
    {
        cout << "Error: Father's Age is < 0";
        exit( 1 );
    }
    cout << "Father's Age: ";
    cout << basep->GetAge() << endl;  // calls father::GetAge
    delete basep;  // remove Father class object
    cout << "Enter Age of Son: ";
    cin >> son_age;
    try
    {
        basep = new Son( father_age, son_age );   // pointer to son
    }
    catch( WRONG_AGE )
    {
        cout << "Error: Father age cannot be less than son age!!!";
        exit( 1 );
    }
    cout << "Son's Age: ";
    cout << basep->GetAge() << endl;  // calls son::GetAge()
    delete basep;  // remove Son class object
}
```

Run1

```
Enter Age of Father: 45
Father's Age: 45
Enter Age of Son: 20
Son's Age: 20
```

Run2

```
Enter Age of Father: 20
Father's Age: 20
```

```
Enter Age of Son: 45
Error: Father age cannot be less than son age!!!
```

Run3
```
Enter Age of Father: -2
Error: Father's Age is < 0
```

The first try-block in the main() will check for the validity of the father's age. As in *Run3*, if the fathers' age is less than the zero, the exception WRONG_AGE is raised.

The second try-block in the main() will check for the validity of son's age in accordance with father's age. As in *Run2*, if son's age is greater than the age of father, the exception WRONG_AGE is raised.

19.12 Exceptions in Class Templates

The program matrix.cpp illustrates exception handling mechanism along with other features of OOPs such as class templates, operator overloading including friend functions, binary operators, assignment through object copy, etc. The specification of the template class matrix with exceptions is similar to that without exceptions, but, errors are handled using exceptions instead of returning an error code as a function return value.

```
// matrix.cpp: Matrix manipulation class template and exception handling
#include <iostream.h>
#include <process.h>
const int TRUE = 1;
const int FALSE = 0;
// empty class for matrix exception
class MatError
{};
// template matrix class
template <class T>
class matrix
{
   private:
      int MaxRow;     // number of rows
      int MaxCol;     // number of columns
      T MatPtr[5][5];   // if T is int, int MatrPtr[5][5];
   public:
      matrix()
      {
         MaxRow = 0; MaxCol = 0;
      }
      matrix::matrix( int row, int col )
      {
         MaxRow = row;
         MaxCol = col;
      }
      friend istream & operator >> ( istream & cin, matrix <T> &dm );
      friend ostream & operator << ( ostream & cout, matrix <T> &sm );
      matrix <T> operator + ( matrix <T> b );
```

```
    matrix <T> operator - ( matrix <T> b );
    matrix <T> operator * ( matrix <T> b );
    void operator = ( matrix <T> b );
    int operator == ( matrix <T> b );
};
template <class T>
matrix<T> matrix<T>::operator + ( matrix <T> b )
{
    matrix <T> c( MaxRow, MaxCol );
    int i, j;
    if( MaxRow != b.MaxRow || MaxCol != b.MaxCol )
        throw MatError();
    for( i = 0; i < MaxRow; i++ )
        for( j = 0; j < MaxCol; j++ )
            c.MatPtr[i][j] = MatPtr[i][j] + b.MatPtr[i][j];
    return( c );
}
template <class T>
matrix <T> matrix<T>::operator - ( matrix <T> b )
{
    matrix <T> c( MaxRow, MaxCol );
    int i, j;
    if( MaxRow != b.MaxRow || MaxCol != b.MaxCol )
        throw MatError();
    for( i = 0; i < MaxRow; i++ )
        for( j = 0; j < MaxCol; j++ )
            c.MatPtr[i][j] = MatPtr[i][j] - b.MatPtr[i][j];
    return( c );
}
template <class T>
matrix <T> matrix<T>::operator * ( matrix <T> b )
{
    matrix <T> c( MaxRow, b.MaxCol );
    int i, j, k;
    if( MaxCol != b.MaxRow )
        throw MatError();
    for( i = 0; i < c.MaxRow; i++ )
        for( j = 0; j < c.MaxCol; j++ )
            {
                c.MatPtr[i][j] = 0;
                for( k = 0; k < MaxCol; k++ )
                    c.MatPtr[i][j] += MatPtr[i][k] * b.MatPtr[k][j];
            }
    return( c );
}
template <class T>
int matrix<T>::operator == ( matrix <T> b )
{
    int i, j;
    if( MaxRow != b.MaxRow || MaxCol != b.MaxCol )
        return( FALSE );
```

```
   for( i = 0; i < MaxRow; i++ )
   {
      for( j = 0; j < MaxCol; j++ )
         if( MatPtr[i][j] != b.MatPtr[i][j] )
            return( FALSE );
   }
   return( TRUE );
}
// function invoked when statement of type matrix a = matrix b is used
template <class T>
void matrix<T>::operator = ( matrix <T> b )
{
   int i, j;
   MaxRow = b.MaxRow;
   MaxCol = b.MaxCol;
   for( i = 0; i < MaxRow; i++ )
      for( j = 0; j < MaxCol; j++ )
         MatPtr[i][j] = b.MatPtr[i][j];
}
template <class T>
istream & operator >> ( istream & cin, matrix <T> &dm )
{
   int i, j;
   cout << "How many rows ? ";
   cin >> dm.MaxRow;
   cout << "How many columns ? ";
   cin >> dm.MaxCol;
   for( i = 0; i < dm.MaxRow; i++ )
      for( j = 0; j < dm.MaxCol; j++ )
      {
         cout << "Matrix[" << i << "," << j << "] = ? ";
         cin >> dm.MatPtr[i][j];
      }
   return( cin );
}
template <class T>
ostream &operator << ( ostream & cout, matrix <T> &sm )
{
   int i, j;
   for( i = 0; i < sm.MaxRow; i++ )
   {
      cout << endl;
      for( j = 0; j < sm.MaxCol; j++ )
         cout << sm.MatPtr[i][j] << " ";
   }
   return( cout );
}
void main()
{
   matrix <int> a;    // to store float elements
   matrix <int> b;    // matrix <float> a; matrix <float> b;
```

```
cout << "Enter Matrix A details..." << endl;
cin >> a;
cout << "Enter Matrix B details..." << endl;
cin >> b;
cout << "Matrix A is ...";
cout << a << endl;
cout << "Matrix B is ...";
cout << b;
matrix <int> c;
try
{
   c = a + b;
   cout << endl << "C = A + B...";
   cout << c;
}
catch( MatError )
{
   cout << endl << "Error: Invalid matrix order for addition";
}
matrix <int> d;
try
{
   d = a - b;
   cout << endl << "D = A - B...";
   cout << d;
}
catch( MatError )
{
   cout << endl << "Error: Invalid matrix order for subtraction";
}
matrix <int> e( 3, 3 );
try
{
   e = a * b;
   cout << endl << "E = A * B...";
   cout << e;
}
catch( MatError )
{
   cout << endl << "Error: Invalid matrix order for multiplication";
}
cout << endl << "(Is matrix A equal to matrix B) ? ";
if( a == b )
   cout << "Yes";
else
   cout << "No";
}
```

Run

```
Enter Matrix A details...
How many rows ? 1
```

```
How many columns ? 2
Matrix[0,0] = ? 1
Matrix[0,1] = ? 2
Enter Matrix B details...
How many rows ? 2
How many columns ? 1
Matrix[0,0] = ? 1
Matrix[1,0] = ? 2
Matrix A is ...
1 2
Matrix B is ...
1
2
Error: Invalid matrix order for addition
Error: Invalid matrix order for subtraction
E = A * B...
5
(Is matrix A equal to matrix B) ? No
```

In the definition of matrix class's member functions, it can be observed that the validity of a matrix operation is handled by exceptions. For instance, in the overloaded member function operator +, the statement

```
if( MaxRow != b.MaxRow || MaxCol != b.MaxCol )
{
    cout << "Error: Invalid matrix order for addition";
    throw MatError;
}
```

raises an exception MatError if there is a mismatch in the row and column count of the two matrices involved in the addition operation. Note that, function templates can also raise exceptions.

19.13 Fault Tolerant Design Techniques

Fault tolerant software design techniques can be classified into the following:

     (1) N-version programming
     (2) Recovery block

These schemes correspond to the hardware fault tolerance methods, *static redundancy* (fault masking or voting) and *dynamic redundancy* respectively.

N-Version Programming

In this technique N-programmers develop N algorithms for the same problem without interacting with each other. All these algorithms are executed simultaneously on a multiprocessor system and the majority solution is taken as the correct answer.

Recovery Block

The recovery block structure represents the dynamic redundancy approach to software fault tolerance. It consists of three software elements: (1) *primary routine*, which executes critical software functions; (2) *acceptance test*, which tests the output of the primary routine after each execution; and (3) *alternate routine*, which performs the same function as the primary routine (but may be less capable or slower), and is invoked by an acceptance test after detection of a fault.

In fault tolerance, once the error has been detected, the next goal is error recovery. The erroneous state must be replaced by an acceptable valid state from which processing may proceed. Forward error recovery attempts to identify any damage to the system state and to repair it in some way, so that failure may be avoided. It simply restores previously saved values of the system state and proceeds from there, possibly using a different program than the one that led to the error. Backward error recovery can be used with unanticipated faults and unlike forward error recovery, it can be used to recover from design faults. Figure 19.8, demonstrates the model of a recovery block and its requirements.

The simplest structure of the recovery block is:

```
Ensure T
     By P
Else
     By Q
Else
     Error
```

where T is the *acceptance-test* condition that is expected to be met by successful execution of either primary routine P or the alternate routine Q. The structure is easily expanded to accommodate several alternatives Q1, Q2, .., Qn.

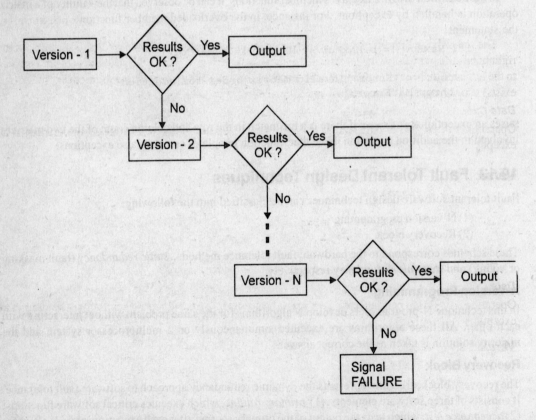

Figure 19.8: Recovery block programming model

19.14 Case-Study on Software Fault Tolerance

A simple example is chosen for the study of fault tolerance programming and the same is used for implementation in C++. C++ does not provide any explicit constructs for fault tolerance, however, the constructs `throw`, `try`, and `catch` can be suitably used to simulate the action of fault tolerance. These exception handling constructs are suitable for implementing the recovery block technique.

Consider a procedure (P) for computing:

```
sum = i'+j'+k';
```

The body of P is the sequential composition of the operation,

```
(c1) i = i+j;
(c2) i = i+k;
```

The behavior of the above procedure P can be examined by considering various versions of the procedure P (proc p) for different values of the variables i, j, and k.

Version 1:

```
proc P signal OW
begin
    i = i + j [ OV -> signal OW ];
    i = i + k [ OV -> i = i - j; signal OW ];
end
```

The semantic definition of the assignment operator = specifies that whenever the evaluation of the right hand side expression *terminates exceptionally* (overflow occurs, OV), no new value is assigned to the left hand side variable. Then, P will terminate exceptionally by executing the recovery block (if it exists) and signals an OW (overflow word) exception label in the final state.

Data Case 1: i <- MaxValue, j <- MaxValue, and k <- (-MaxValue)

Operation i+j+k (as per data case 1) is valid, but i+j exceeds the representation limit leading to an exception.

Version 2:

```
proc P signal OW
begin
    i = i + k [ OV -> signal OW ];
    i = i + j [ OV -> i = i - k; signal OW ];
end
```

This version terminates with a valid final state for the data case 1.

Data Case 2: i <- MaxValue, j <- (-MaxValue), and k <- (MaxValue)

Operation i+j+k (as per data case 2) is valid, but (i+k) exceeds the representation limit leading to an exception.

Version 3:

```
proc P signal OW
begin
    j = j + k [ OV -> signal OW ];
    i = i + j [ OV -> j = j - k; signal OW ];
end
```

This version terminates with a valid final state for the data case 1 and case 2.

Data Case 3: `i <- (-MaxValue), j <- MaxValue, and k <- (MaxValue)`

Operation `i+j+k` (as per data case 3) is valid, but `j+k` exceeds the representation limit leading to an exception.

Recovery Block for Procedure P: `i <- i+j+k`:

```
Ensure no exception
By Version - 1
  Else
    By Version - 2
      Else By Version - 3
        Else FAIL
```

Recovery Block Implementation

The recovery block technique can be implemented by nesting the exception handling constructs of C++. To understand the concepts of fault tolerant programming, consider a computer system having a 4-bit processor, supporting both signed and unsigned numbers. Some of its characteristics are the following.

- Maximum signed number can be represented is 7 ($2^{4-1} - 1$).
- Maximum unsigned number can be represented is 15 ($2^4 - 1$).
- Overflow will be indicated if the result exceeds the limit of representation.

The program `recovery.cpp` handles all the three data cases and demonstrates the characteristics desired in a fault tolerance program.

```cpp
// recovery.cpp: Recover Block of sum( i, j, k )
#include <iostream.h>
const int MAX_SIG_INT = 7;    // say, maximum signed integer number
const int MAX_UNSIG_INT = 15; // say, maximum unsigned integer number
class OVERFLOW {};   // Overflow abstract class
int sum( int i, int j, int k )
{
    int result;
    try
    {
        // Version1 procedure
        result = i+j;
        if( result > MAX_SIG_INT )
            throw OVERFLOW();
        result = result+k;
        if( result > MAX_SIG_INT )
            throw OVERFLOW();
        cout << "Version-1 succeeds" << endl;
    }
    catch( OVERFLOW )
    {
        cout << "Version-1 fails" << endl;
        try
        {
            // Version2 procedure
            result = i+k;
```

```
            if( result > MAX_SIG_INT )
                throw OVERFLOW();
            result = result+j;
            if( result > MAX_SIG_INT )
                throw OVERFLOW();
            cout << "Version-2 succeeds" << endl;
        }
        catch( OVERFLOW )
        {
            cout << "Version-2 fails" << endl;
            try
            {
                // Version3 procedure
                result = j+k;
                if( result > MAX_SIG_INT )
                    throw OVERFLOW();
                result = result+i;
                if( result > MAX_SIG_INT )
                    throw OVERFLOW();
                cout << "Version-3 succeeds" << endl;
            }
            catch( OVERFLOW )
            {
                cout << "Error: Overflow. All versions failed" << endl;
            }
        }
    }
    return result;
}
void main()
{
    int result;
    cout << "Sum of 7, -3, 2 computation..." << endl;
    result = sum( 7, -3, 2 ); // version1 computes
    cout << "Sum = " << result << endl;
    cout << "Sum of 7, 2, -3 computation..." << endl;
    result = sum( 7, 2, -3 ); // version2 computes
    cout << "Sum = " << result << endl;
    // Device data such that version-3 succeeds
    cout << "Sum of 3, 3, 2 computation..." << endl;
    result = sum( 3, 3, 2 ); // all version fails
    cout << "Sum = " << result << endl;
}
```

Run

```
Sum of 7, -3, 2 computation...
Version-1 succeeds
Sum = 6
Sum of 7, 2, -3 computation...
Version-1 fails
```

```
Version-2 succeeds
Sum = 6
Sum of 3, 3, 2 computation...
Version-1 fails
Version-2 fails
Error: Overflow. All versions failed
Sum = 8
```

19.15 Memory Allocation Failure Exception

The operator new tries to create an object of the data type Type dynamically by allocating (if possible) sizeof(Type) bytes in free store (also called the *heap*). It calculates the size of Type without the need for an explicit sizeof operator. Further, the pointer returned is of the correct type, *pointer to Type*, without the need for explicit casting. The storage duration of the new object is from the point of creation until the operator delete destroys it by deallocating its memory, or until the end of the program. If successful, new returns a pointer to the new object. By default, an allocation failure (such as insufficient or fragmented heap memory) results in the predefined exception xalloc being thrown. The user program should always be prepared to catch the xalloc exception before trying to access the new object (unless user-defined new-handler function is defined). The program new1.cpp illustrates the simple mechanism of handling exceptions raised by the new operator.

```
// new1.cpp: new operator memory allocation test
#include <except.h>
#include <iostream.h>
void main(void)
{
   int * data;
   int size;
   cout << "How many bytes to be allocate: ";
   cin >> size;
   try
   {
      data = new int[ size ];
      cout << "Memory allocation success, address = " << data;
   }
   catch( xalloc )    // new fail exception
   {  // Enter this block only of xalloc is thrown.
      // You could request other actions before terminating
      cout << "Could not allocate. Bye ...";
      exit(1);
   }
   delete data;
}
```

Run1
```
How many bytes to be allocate: 100
Memory allocation success, address = 0x16be
```

Run2

```
How many bytes to be allocate: 30000
Could not allocate. Bye ...
```

A request for allocation of 0 bytes returns a non-null pointer. Repeated requests for zero-size allocations return distinct, non-null pointers. The program new2.cpp illustrates the handling of exceptions while allocating memory for matrix.

```cpp
// new2.cpp: Allocate a two-dimensional space, initialize, and delete it.
#include <except.h>
#include <iostream.h>
void display( long **data, int m, int n );
void de_allocate( long **data, int m );
long main(void)
{
   int m, n;    // m rows and n columns
   long **data;
   cout << "Enter rows and columns count: ";
   cin >> m >> n;
   try
   { // Test for exceptions
      data = new long *[m];                  // Step 1: Set up the rows.
      for (int j = 0; j < m; j++)
         data[j] = new long[n];              // Step 2: Set up the columns
   }
   catch( xalloc )
   { // Enter this block only if xalloc is thrown.
      // Other actions could be requested before terminating
      cout << "Could not allocate. Bye ...";
      exit(1);
   }
   for( long i = 0; i < m; i++)
      for(long j = 0; j < n; j++)
         data[i][j] = i + j;                 // Arbitrary initialization
   display( data, m, n );
   de_allocate( data, m );
   return 0;
}
void display( long **data, int m, int n )
{
   for( int i = 0; i < m; i++ )
   {
      for( int j = 0; j < n; j++ )
         cout << data[i][j] << " ";
      cout << endl;
   }
}
void de_allocate( long **data, int m)
{
   for( int i = 0; i < m; i++ )
      delete[] data[i];                      // Step 1. Delete the columns
   delete[] data;                            // Step 2: Delete the rows
}
```

Run1

```
Enter rows and columns count: 3 4
0 1 2 3
1 2 3 4
2 3 4 5
```

Run2

```
Enter rows and columns count: 100 300
Could not allocate. Bye ...
```

19.16 Ten Rules for Handling Exceptions Successfully

The amount of modification required to fully exploit the feature of exception handling in existing software is high. Experts point out ... *If you want to design your own exceptions and integrate them into preexisting classes, first understand the engineering effort—not only throwing exceptions but to handle them as well.* Many experts are concerned that exceptions will lull programmers into a false sense of security, believing that their code is handling errors, while in reality the exceptions are compounding more errors and hindering the software development. Implementing a real class such that it is *exception safe* can be challenging; sometimes it is not feasible.

In general, the use of exception handling is complicated by the interaction of C++ language features with certain C/C++ idioms, as well as the demanding robustness requirements expected of exception-safe. For instance, the combination of exception handling, templates, dynamic memory, and destructors make expressions containing multiple side-effects difficult to program robustly. For instance, consider the following simple C++ pseudocode function:

```
template <class T>
void SomeClass::add( parameters )
{
    element_array[ element_number++ ] = T( parameters );
    // ...
}
```

which uses a standard C/C++ idiom (auto incrementing) for adding a new element into an array. However, both the (unknown) constructors of T and its assignment operator might potentially throw exceptions. In both the cases, it is unclear whether `element_number` will be incremented or not. Moreover, the array element being assigned to, will also be in an uncertain state, which might even cause the destructor of the class `SomeClass` to fail!

Resources

The most vexing problems of exception handling arise from improper resource management. It leads to unrelease or double-release of resources. Here, the central concept of a *resource* is *something that provides functionality*. In many cases, a resource is equivalent to a data structure. However, a data structure is considered as a resource if it lives beyond a single operation. This constraint implies that resources have an internal state. This state is identified by all the resource's data values, which may be modified by operations on the resource. Often, a resource corresponds to one or more components in a subsystem such as a search table or a database. Smaller entities can also be considered as resources such as single elements of a search table or records in a database. Likewise, large systems such as a all-user processes in an operating system or a network of computers can be viewed as resources.

An important operation on a resource is releasing it, i.e., changing the state of a program in such a way that this resource is no longer active. In C++, this release is usually accomplished by a destructor-either in a delete expression, at the end of a block, or within another destructor. However, other operations can be used to release resources such as:

♦ The C standard library function `fclose()` releases a resource of the type `FILE *`.

♦ A list node might be *shut down* by putting it into a free-list rather than returning it to heap memory by calling delete.

♦ A stack class may store its elements in an array. In this case, releasing the resource (i.e., *top element of the stack*) is often accomplished by a simple decrement of the index. Thus, the top element is no longer accessible after this operation.

It is necessary to design all the resources in an exception safe way because exceptions might be thrown at arbitrary places in a program.

Problems with Exception Handling

There are several ways to integrate exception handling into a subsystem. One way is to design it during the initial development of the subsystem. Often, however, exception handling declarations and statements are added to an existing subsystem after it has been designed with the intent of making it more robust. In both the cases, especially in the latter, the following issues might be considered and solved.

1. The design of the exception class types and the class hierarchy. It should address the issues such as, which exceptions should be distinguishable by their type, which should be distinguished by data member values, which standard exceptions are to be reused, or which special purpose exception classes are to be defined ?.

2. How to throw an exception i.e., the C++ syntax for raising an exception.

3. How to pass exceptions *upwards* i.e., what must be done to correctly manage the resources that are affected as the stack unwinds.

4. How to handle an exception, i.e., remedying the problem that was the original reason for throwing an exception.

5. Syntactic and readability issues. For instance, indentation, grouping of handlers etc.

6. Use of exception handling in large systems. For example, how to handle more than one exception at the same time, how to indicate more than one problem with more than one resource etc.

7. Testability of programs with exception handling. For example, how should the "all branches"-coverage criterion for sufficient testing be redefined in the presence of exception handling ?

8. Maintenance of exception handling declarations and statements in the life cycle of software systems. For example, how does the presence of exception handling influence the understandability of code? How might the extension of class hierarchy interact with exception handling (—for example, if virtual functions in derived classes need to throw exception different from those in base class ?).

The concept of *simply throw an exception if you do not know what to do* will reduce program robustness and frustrate programmers who have to deal with all these exceptions. Therefore, the ten rules discussed below need to be followed in order to manage the exceptions well:

Rule 1: Do not throw an exception unless absolutely necessary.

A basic principle of software engineering: *Allow composition of resources* i.e., complex resources are composed from simpler ones. C++ has many construction methods to facilitate resource composition. Improper handling of an exception in such systems can lead to bad (inconsistent) states. A bad resource cannot be repaired — sometimes it may not even be possible to destroy it. Consider the following definition of the member function push() in the Stack class:

```
template <class T>
void Stack<T>::push( T e )
{
    .....
    vec[top++] = e;  // vector insertion can cause exception
    .....
}
```

An exception in the assignment will leave the top index incremented, yet the assignment to the new top element will not occur. Any access to the top element will find an *unassigned value*. Such exceptions must be carefully designed so that consistency of resource is maintained. Throwing exceptions cause some resources to be in bad state that could be cleaned up by some handler.

Rule 2: It is not advisable to simply throw some exceptions deep in the call stack and then let C++ unwind the stack until a handler is found; this might leave behind damaged resources that cannot even be destroyed afterwards.

Two appealing solutions for handling bad resources are:

a) Reorder the statements in each update method so that no bad composite states are encountered, even between two sub-resources.

b) Modify each update so that if a resource enters a bad state it is restored to the original state it had before the update occurred.

The push() member function of the Stack class can be reordered as follows:

```
    template <class T>
    void Stack<T>::push( T e )
    {
        .....
        vec[top] = e;  // vector insertion can cause exception
        ++top;
        .....
    }
```

In the above case, the stack index top will not lead to a bad state when exception occurs at assignment of e to vec.

Restoring the state back to its original value before the operation is started is complex with non-trivial C++ programs. Classes with virtual functions and templates are commonly used to write code that calls functions which are unknown at the time when the calling code is written. Therefore, it is much more harder to integrate exception handling into C++, compared to C. However, it is possible to handle exceptions without too much effort.

Rule 3: All the resources should be designed in such a way that every technically possible state is a shut-down state.

The following design principle can be concluded when resources are designed according to Rule 3: The only thing an exception handler can do with a damaged resource is to shut it down (release or free).

Rule 4: The responsibility for managing a resource lies either with a class (i.e., the destructor of the class releases the resource); or with the block that acquired the resources (i.e., the resource is released on exit from the block).

Consider a simple example of `Stack` data structure. It has a `push()` function that sometimes has to allocate a new array. It does this in the following way:

```
if( buffer is too small )
{
    T *new_buffer = new T[ nelems ];    // (a)
    ...fill new_buffer...;
    delete [] vec;                      // (b)
    vec = new_buffer;
}
```

At step (a) in the above segment, the resource `new_buffer` is created under the responsibility of the block. If anything goes wrong after this point, it would be the responsibility of the block to delete the buffer again (which it does not do in the code). At step (b), the responsibility is transferred to the stack object by assigning it to the member `vec` of the class `Stack`. The responsibility to release resources now lies with the object's destructor. Thus, if a function is exited due to an exception, the destructor has to release the buffer.

Rule 5: Symmetric resource management; resource management of a purely block-local resource: The responsibility of a block-local resource always lies with the acquiring block.

Of course, with this method, it is not possible to put a resource under the object responsibility, which is necessary for all asymmetric resource management problems. Two general schemes (or patterns) for solving this type of problem are 1) setting resource of an object and 2) replacing an object resource. As a building block for these patterns need *secure operations* that allow to transfer resource responsibilities without throwing exceptions i.e., all destructors in a C++ program should have an empty specification `throw()`. The first problem arises most often in constructors and assignment operators where a new dynamic resource is needed to store part of the object's value. Resource management for such a resource is done as indicated in the ***Rule 6***. The second problem arises in the implementation of containers that automatically adjust their size, for example, the Stack class. Again, clear responsibility management is the key to the correct design as indicated in the ***Rule 7***.

Rule 6: Resource management for a new object resource. To handle this, use the following pattern:
   a) A load resource of suitable size is acquired
   b) The resource is used (usually initialized) as necessary
   c) The resource is put under an object's responsibility

The responsibility of the resources lies with the acquiring block in the above step a) and b) and with some object after c). The responsibility transfer at c) must happen in such a way that the responsibility is always with exactly one agent—either the object or the block.

Rule 7: Resource management for replacing an object resource. To handle this situation, use the following pattern:
   a) A local resource of suitable size is acquired under block responsibility
   b) The resource is used (usually initialized) as necessary
   c) The responsibility for the object resource and local resource are exchanged
   d) The new local resource (the former object resource) is released

The following is an example of such a sequence:

```
template <class T>
void Stack::pop()( T & e )   // throw( bad_alloc, ..T(),..)
{
```

```
    if( top == nelems )
    {
        nelems *= 2;
        AutoPtrArray <T> new_buffer = nelems;   // (a)
        for( int i = 0; i < n; ++i )            // (b)
            new_buffer[i] = vec[i];
        new_buffer.swap_with( vec );            // (c)
        /* destructor of new_buffer */          // (d)
    }
    vec[top++] = e;
}
```

Rule 8: When designing a throw-and-keep resource, all operations with side effects on subresources occurring in some resource constraint must be viewed as resource acquisitions.

Rule 9: Each modification of a subresource of a throw-and-keep resource that might throw an exception must be wrapped as shown in the following code:

```
try
{
    //... modification...;
}
catch(...)
{
    // make subresource invisible to all operations
    // except those that destroy it
    throw;
}
```

Moreover, all the actions in the catch-block must be secure operations.

Rule 10: Resource management for a new object resource with `return` statement. To handle this situation, use the following pattern:

a) A local resource is acquired.

b) The responsibility of the local and the object resources are swapped.

c) The resource is used as necessary (including the `return` statement).
   If an exception is thrown in (c), perform d) and e):

d) The responsibility of the local and the object resources are swapped back.

e) The exception is re-thrown (in order to avoid losing information about error occurrence and reason for its occurrence).

The following is an example of such a sequence:

```
template <class T>
T KeepableStack::pop()( T & e )   // throw( XPopOnEmptyStack,...T( T&))
{
    if( top == 0 )
        throw XPopOnEmptyStack( "Stack<T>::pop");
    Auto_uinit new_top(top-1);      // (a)
    new_top.swap_with(top);         // (b)
    try
    {
        return vec[top];            // (c)
    }
```

```
catch( ... )
{
    new_top.swap_with( top );        // (d)
    throw;                           // (e)
}
}
```

Based on the background of the above ten rules in managing exception handling, it is possible to design new patterns. A new pattern for responsibility management includes transferring responsibilities from an acquiring block to a surrounding block; or from one object to another, and so on.

Review Questions

19.1 What are exceptions ? What are the differences between synchronous and asynchronous exceptions ?

19.2 Explain the techniques of building reliable software.

19.3 Explain the exception handling model of C++ with various constructs supported by it.

19.4 Write an interactive program to compute square root of a number. The input value must be tested for validity. If it is negative, the user defined function my_sqrt() should raise an exception.

19.5 What is the syntax for indicating a list of exceptions that a function can raise. What happens if an unspecified exception is raised ?

19.6 Write a program to demonstrate the catching of all exceptions.

19.7 What happens when an exception is raised in a try-block having a few constructed objects ? What is stack unwinding ?

19.8 What happens when a raised exception is not caught by catch-block ?

19.9 How does C++'s throwing and catching exceptions differ from C's setjmp() and longjmp()?

19.10 Write a program which transfers the control to user defined terminate function when raised exception is uncaught.

19.11 When does the function unexpected() is invoked ? Write a program which installs the user defined unexpected function to handle exceptions.

19.12 Write an interactive program which divides two complex numbers. Overload divide (/) operator. Handle cases such as division-by-zero using exceptions.

19.13 Consider that the base class Stack is available. It does not take care of situations such as overflow or underflow. Enhance this class to MyStack which raises an exception whenever overflow or underflow error occurs.

19.14 What are the different fault tolerant design techniques available ? Explain recovery block programming technique with a suitable example.

19.15 When memory allocation fails, how does the new operator notify the error to the caller ?

19.16 Write a program to add two vectors. Each vector object, instance of the class Vector, is having dynamic allocation of their data members. Catch exception raised by new operator and take corrective actions.

19.17 Explain why addition of exceptions to most software is likely to diminish the overall reliability and impede the software development process if extraordinary care is not taken ?

19.18 List the ten rules for handling exceptions successfully

19.19 What are the issues that need to be considered while designing fault tolerant software ?

19.20 Write a program for matrix multiplication. The matrix multiplication function should notify if the order of matrix is invalid using exceptions.

20

OO Analysis, Design and Development

OOP systems are sold on the promise of improved productivity through object reuse and high level of code modularity. These aspects precisely lead to their greatest benefit, namely, improved software quality, considering "the objective of OO design is to mirror real world objects" in the software systems. OO Technology encompasses not only OOPs but also other OO concepts such as user interface, analysis, design, and data base management systems. Lastly, using OOPs facilitates an iterative style of development rather than the traditional *waterfall* approaches. The object-oriented approach centers around modeling the real world in terms of objects, in contrast to the traditional approaches which emphasize function oriented view and separates data-and-functions.

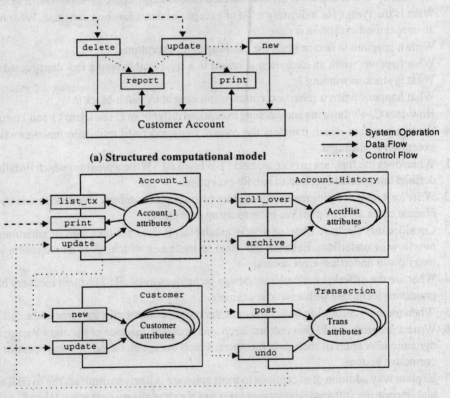

Figure 20.1: Structured Vs. Object-oriented computational model

Software engineering deals with the various tools, methods, and procedures required for controlling the complexity of software development, project management, and its maintenance. Object-oriented development emphasizes on using programming languages with certain unique capabilities for real-world object modeling. Object model is the conceptual framework for object-oriented development. The four major elements of this model are encapsulation, abstraction, modularity, and hierarchy. The computational model of the structured and object-oriented model is shown in Figure 20.1. OO development tends to be iterative and incremental growth, compared to conventional development.

A systems development methodology combines tools and techniques to guide the process of developing large scale information systems. Dramatic improvement in hardware performance and the adoption of high-level languages has enabled to build large and more complicated systems. The conventional methodologies decompose the process of system development life cycle into discrete project phases with *frozen* deliverables or formal documents, which serve as the input to the next phase.

20.1 Software Life Cycle: Water-Fall Model

Software systems pass through two principal phases during their life cycle:
- The development phase
- The operations and maintenance phase

The development phase begins when the need for the product is identified; it ends when the implemented product is tested and delivered for operation. Operation and maintenance include all activities during the operation of the software, such as fixing bugs discovered during operation, making performance enhancements, adapting the system to its environment, adding minor features, etc. During this phase, the system may also evolve when major-functions are added. To illustrate the software life cycle, the *waterfall model* or *conventional life cycle model* (see Figure 20.2) has proven convenient.

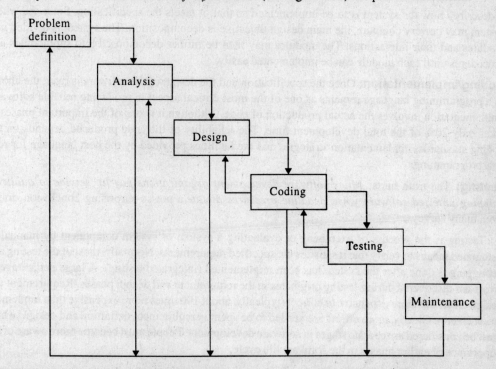

Figure 20.2:   Water fall model for software development

Conventional life cycle of software development passes through various phases. They include definition of system requirements, generation of software requirements, software design, coding, and final testing and reliability modeling.

Problem Definition: The first stage in the development process is understanding the problem in question and its requirements. Requirements may be specified by the end-user, or, if the software system is *embedded* within a larger system, they may be derived from the system requirements. Requirements, therefore, include the context in which the problem arose, functionality expected from the system, and system constraints. At this point, the managers and software specialists decide whether it is feasible to build the system.

Analysis: A system analyst observes the feasibility of system development. If system development is cost effective based on the management approval, then design, coding, etc., phases will be executed, otherwise, it will be aborted; no progress of other phases will be made. Analysis phase delivers requirements specification. If project is approved, software specialists try to understand the requirements and define the specifications to meet those requirements. The system specification serves as an interface between the designer and implementor as well as between the implementor and user. This describes external behavior of the software without bothering about the internal implementation. Specification must be carefully checked for suitability, omission, inconsistencies, and ambiguities.

Design: Design is the process of mapping system requirements defined during analysis to an abstract representation of a specific-system implementation, meeting the cost and performance constraints. The detailed design involves the analysis of various alternatives, including tradeoff among the number of possible solutions based on the existing constraints.

It describes how the system is to be implemented so that, it meets the specification. Since the whole system may be very complex, the main design objective is decomposition. The system is divided into modules and their interactions. The modules may then be further decomposed into submodules and procedures until each module can be implemented easily.

Coding/Implementation: Once the specification and the design of the software is over, the choice of a programming language remains as one of the most critical aspect in producing reliable software. Implementation involves the actual production of code. Although it is one of the important phases, it takes only 20% of the total development time. The reliability of the code produced depends on the coding standards, implementation strategies and the facilities provided by the host language for reliable programming.

Testing: The truth hurts: *Many software development organizations pay lip service to quality—shipping untested software when deadline pressures dictate,* a not-so-surprising conclusion drawn from many surveys.

Testing is the process of exercising or evaluating a system or system component by manual or automated means to verify that it satisfies the specified requirements. Normally, most of the testing and debugging is done after the system has been implemented (integrated testing). A large percentage of errors are discovered during testing originates in the requirement and design phases. Requirement and design errors are more expensive to correct (typically, about 100 times more expensive than implementation errors). Clearly, more efforts are needed to be spent in requirement definition and design, which must be considered as separate stages in software development. People must become more aware of the importance of earlier phases in the software life cycle.

Once the software is developed, it has to be subjected to tests at module (unit) level, module integration level, software/hardware integration (system) level and finally at the system level. *Module testing* focuses on individual software units or related group of units. *Module integration testing* focuses on combining software and hardware units, to evaluate the interaction among them. *System testing* focus on complete, integrated systems to evaluate compliance with requirement specification.

A module has to be tested for logical errors and computational errors while the interface is checked to see whether the interaction between the modules are proper. The techniques that have been proposed for unit testing include the following:

- Path testing: each possible path from input to output is traversed once.
- Branch testing: each path must be traversed at least once.
- Functional testing: each functional decomposition is tested at least once.
- Special values testing: testing for all values assumed to cause problems.
- Anomaly analysis: testing the program constructs that can cause problems.
- Interface analysis: testing for problems at module interfaces.

Maintenance: Once the system is put into operation, it must be maintained, which includes fixing bugs discovered during operation, adapting the system to a particular environment, and tuning it to improve performance. If some *major* changes or improvements are made to increase the functionality or performance, the system may undergo an evolution. The boundary between maintenance and evolution is fuzzy because what constitutes a major change is a subjective-opinion.

Maintenance absorbs a large fraction of the cost incurred during the software life cycle. A major portion of maintenance activity is a consequence of misinterpreted user requirements or faulty debugging during operation, which thereby introduces errors that did not exist earlier. Some of these maintenance problems could be reduced if more attention is paid to the development. If programmers have clearly understood the users' requirements, if they have documented the specification, design, and code properly, and if they have tested the system fully before its release, maintenance would not be so difficult and costly. To reduce maintenance costs, the software life cycle is divided into two fundamental phases—development and operation/maintenance. Software engineers should view these as distinct phases so that, both receive sufficient attention during the software life cycle.

20.2 Cost of Error Correction

Software development process includes analysis and generation of software requirements, software design, coding, final testing, and reliability modeling. Each one of these development phase includes verification, since it is easy to detect errors at each stage and also it will avoid error propagation from one stage to another. Further, it has been shown that the cost of correction of errors increases sharply as the development stage advances. The relative cost of correcting errors is 1% during the design phase, 3 during the coding phase, 21% during the testing phase and rises to 75% when the software is put into operation. (See Figure 20.3.)

The following are the different types of errors that may creep into the design of a software system:

- Incomplete or erroneous specification
- Intentional deviation from specification
- Violation of programming standards
- Erroneous data accessing
- Erroneous decision logic or sequencing

- ◆ Erroneous arithmetic computations
- ◆ Invalid timing
- ◆ Improper interrupt handling
- ◆ Wrong constants and data values
- ◆ Inaccurate documentation

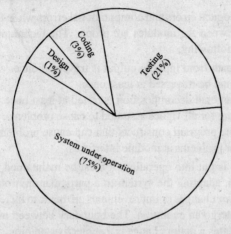

Figure 20.3: Cost of error correction Vs. development stage

20.3 Change Management

Changes to system are bound to happen many times either during the system design, or after complete implementation of the system, or during system operation. Hence, it is very essential to define change management process. The changes can be in the form of any modification to functionality during the design phase. It can also be due to any modification to agreed functionality or deliverable description in any phase. Some of the factors causing changes in a project are the following:

- ◆ Customer misunderstanding
- ◆ Inadequate specification
- ◆ New customer request
- ◆ Organization changes
- ◆ Government regulation

What is a Change ?

A change is an alteration to the project scope, deliverables, or milestones that would affect the project cost, schedule, or quality. Change is inevitable and occurs during the course of a project as shown in Figure 20.4. Once the implemented system becomes stable, many new requirements can be incorporated with minimal change to the design. The project manager is responsible for change control. Different categories of change exist: mandatory, critical, and nice to have. These changes must pass through proper channel and all documents must be updated. Before initiation of the change process, it must be first investigated and its impact on various factors must be thoroughly studied. The project manger can accept the change request, or reject the change request, or return the change request for further investigation or clarification. Once a change request is approved, it has to be incorporated appropriately at respective level or may even be carried out to all other phases. If it is improperly handled, it might even lead to the collapse of the whole system.

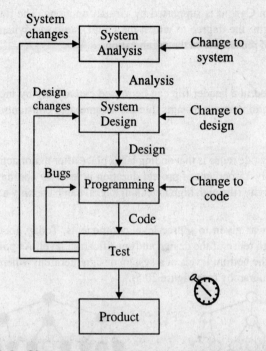

Figure 20.4: Change requests during system development

20.4 Reusable Components

Another important strategy that helps in reliable programming is to use all well proven, tested software modules without redesigning them. The usage of such well proven modules decreases the development effort and increases reliability. Though this idea is not very popular, except in scientific subroutines and some database applications, it is becoming increasingly acceptable to the software development community since the recent languages support the concept of modularization and separate compilation of those modules.

Some of the important components of reusability or levels of reusability are: code, data, design, specification, etc. The most popular level of reusability is code reusability.

Reusing Code

It can be in the form of making a call to subroutines library. Other forms of code reusability are the following:

- **Cut and paste of code**: In this method, the required portion of a code is cut and pasted in another module and necessary changes are incorporated.
- **Source-level includes**: In C++, it is performed by including the header file by using the include preprocessor directive.
- **Binary links**: Making a call to a function stored in the library in the form of executable code.
- **Runtime invocation**: In all the above three forms of source code reuse, while writing program itself the programmer has to know which component they wish to reuse. The binding of the reused components takes place at coding time, compile time, or link-time. In some cases, the flexibility of runtime

binding is essential. In C++, it is supported by virtual functions. The important point to be noted about the OO paradigm: the degree to which the OOPL supports dynamic binding may strongly influence the degree of reusability in the organization.

Reusing Data

Some of the data declared in a header file can be reused extensively by including that in a program. These can be in the form of macro constants, literals, enumerated constants, etc.

Reusing Designs

The major problem with code reuse is that coding takes place after major activity: analysis and design. It is well known that only 15 percent of project duration is used by coding phase, so any attempt to increase coding productivity (through high level languages) can have only a limited impact on overall project productivity.

Earlier major focus was given to source-level components. Today, focus is shifted to achieving significant results through reuse of the design and specification level. As pointed out by experts, code reuse typically occur at the bottom levels of a system design hierarchy whereas, design reuse occur in most of the branches of hierarchy (see Figure 20.5).

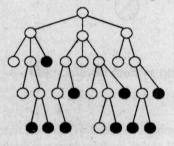

Code reuse   Design reuse

Figure 20.5:   Code reuse Vs. Design reuse

Reusing Specification

Although design reuse is good, specification reuse is much better. It eliminates completely (almost) the effort needed in designing, coding, and testing an implementation of that specification.

Miscellaneous Reuse Components

While code, data, design, and specification are the most obvious candidates for reuse, they are not the only ones. Some of the possible candidates are:

- ◆ Cost-benefit calculations
- ◆ User documentation
- ◆ Feasibility studies
- ◆ Test cases, test procedures, test drivers, test stubs

Among all the entities involved in the software project, one component that cannot be reused is the people (who make up the project team). The experience, infrastructures, etc., gained by a project team during one project should be carried over, that is, reused in the next project whenever possible. This seem to be a common sense, but it is not common in software industry. It is because, teams are busted apart at the end of the project and individuals are scattered and reassigned to other projects or they might change organization (which is most common in software industry). Hence, peopleware approaches to software productivity often achieve results several times greater than technical approaches.

20.5 Software Life Cycle: Fountain-Flow Model

The conventional model requires a large amount of time to be spent in formulating the problem specifications. It delays the writing of code, and programmers may be impatient. In addition, the conventional life cycle model permits little feedback from the end user until the coding stage, which is at the end of the life cycle. At this point, if the system does not meet the specifications, the design and code becomes very expensive. It is often easier to change an existing system than to redevelop the specifications and design a new system. The conventional model fails to address software reusability, hence the existing software is not usable as a starting point.

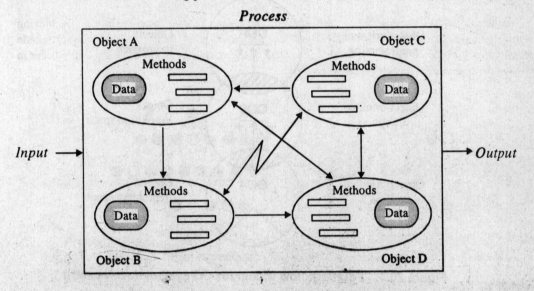

Figure 20.6: Objects interacting with each other

Objects are represented as individual entities which uniquely identify their own contents as well as the operations that may be performed on them. Thus, it is a philosophy of system design to decompose a problem into a set of abstract object types or resources in the system and a set of operations that manipulate instances in the system; and a set of operations that manipulate instances of each object type. The OO paradigm views a system as a collection of entities called objects that interact with each other to meet a specific objective. (See Figure 20.6).

OO methodology allows the end-users, analysts, designers, and programmers to view various components of the system in the same way, thus simplifying the process of mapping the customer requirement to the implementation model. The real-world entities are represented in the form of objects. Objects play the central role in all phases of the software development process. Therefore, there is a high degree of overlap and interaction among the phases. The use of *waterfall* model in the design of OO-based system does not allow overlap and interaction among the development phases. This problem can be circumvented by using a model that resembles a *fountain*. The resultant model is called *fountain flow* model and is shown in Figure 20.7. It allows a higher level phase to interact with its lower phase and again proceed to a higher level phase.

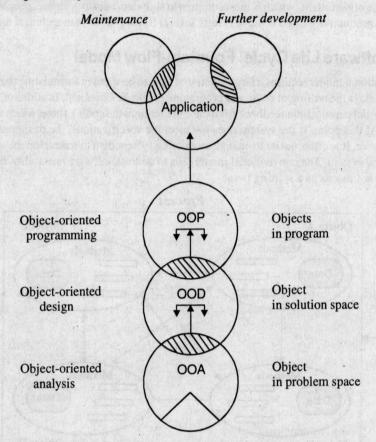

Maintenance   *Further development*

Application

Object-oriented programming	OOP	Objects in program
Object-oriented design	OOD	Object in solution space
Object-oriented analysis	OOA	Object in problem space

Figure 20.7:   Fountain-flow model for OO system development

20.6 Object-Oriented Notations

Graphical notations play a major role while representing the design and development processes, and object-oriented design is no exception. They increase the ease with which ideas can be exchanged among the members of a project team. Object-oriented design requires notations for representing classes, objects, derived classes and their interrelationship, and interactions among objects. Unfortunately, for representing these aspects, there are no standard notations. In this book, authors have used their own notations and in addition to some of the commonly used notations, which are discussed in earlier chapters such as *Object Oriented Paradigm, Classes and Objects, Inheritance*, etc.

20.7 Object-Oriented Methodologies

Many object-oriented analysis (OOA) and object-oriented design (OOD) methodologies have emerged recently, although the concepts underlying object-orientation as a programming discipline has been developed long time ago. Object orientation certainly encompasses many novel concepts, and is popularly called as a new paradigm for software development. Object-oriented methodologies represent a radical change over conventional methodologies such as structured analysis.

Various object-oriented methodologies can be best investigated by dividing them into two camps—revolutionaries and synthesists. Revolutionaries believe that object-orientation is a radical change that renders conventional methodologies and ways of thinking (about design) obsolete. Synthesists, by contrast, view object-orientation as simply an accumulation of sound software engineering principles which adopters can graft onto their existing methodologies with relative ease.

The revolutionaries (Booch, Coad, Yourdon) state the following:

♦ There should be no doubt that object-oriented design is fundamentally different from traditional structured design approaches, it requires a different way of thinking about decomposition, and it produces software architectures that are largely outside the realm of the structured design culture.

♦ There is no doubt that one could arrive at the same results using different methods; but it is revealed from experience that the thinking process, the discovery process, and the communication between the user and analyst are fundamentally different with OOA than with structured analysis.

On the other side the synthesists (Wasserman, Pircher, Muller, Page Jones, and Weiss) state the following:

♦ Object-oriented structured design (OOSD) methodology is essentially an elaboration of structured design. They state that *the foundation of OOSD is structured design*, and that structured design *includes most of the necessary concepts and notations* for OOSD.

♦ The problems that object orientation has been widely touted as a revolutionary approach is a complete break with the past. This would be fascinating if it were true, but it is not like most engineering developments, the object oriented approach is a refinement of some of the best software engineering ideas of the past.

The leading analysis methodologies are the following:

  ♦ DeMarco structured analysis
  ♦ Yourdon modern structured analysis
  ♦ Martin information engineering analysis
  ♦ Bailin object-oriented requirements specification
  ♦ Coad and Yourdon object-oriented analysis
  ♦ Shlaer and Mellor object-oriented analysis

The leading design methodologies are the following:

  ♦ Yourdon and Constantine structured design
  ♦ Martin information engineering design
  ♦ Wasserman et al. object-oriented structured design
  ♦ Booch object-oriented design
  ♦ Wirfs-Brock et al. responsibility-driven design

Object-Oriented Analysis

Object-oriented analysis provides a simple, yet powerful mechanism for identifying objects, the building blocks of the software to be developed. It is mainly concerned with the decomposition of a problem into component parts and establishing a logical model to describe the system. The various steps involved in OOA are shown in Figure 20.8.

The two general findings about object-oriented analysis are:

1. OOA fulfills the properties of analysis, and
2. OOA has a smooth transition to design

OOA model should cover objectives, application domain knowledge, requirements of the environments, and requirements of the computer system.

♦ **Objectives**: These are the ultimate expectations of the users towards the entire information system (both computerized and manual). i.e., the objectives which are to be fulfilled through the interplay between the computer system and the surrounding human organization.

♦ **Application domain knowledge**: This defines the vocabulary of the application, its meaning, and properties.

♦ **Requirements of the environment**: This is a description of the behavior required from the human organization to meet the objectives.

♦ **Requirements of the computer system**: This is a description of the behavior required from the computer system to meet the objectives.

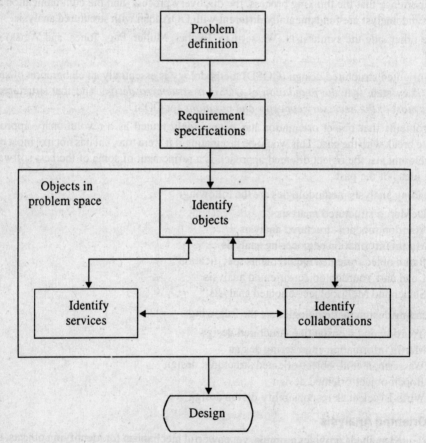

Figure 20.8: Steps in object-oriented analysis

For most OOA/OOD approaches, the difference between analysis and design is not recognized as the difference between the user requirement and the solution, but simply as the difference between "what" and "how". It is interpreted as "Analysis is aimed at describing what a target system is supposed to do to obtain an agreement with a customer bearing the expenses. While design is aimed at describing how the designed system will work...".

Positive Trends in OOA

OOA has evolved and focuses on system dynamics. Novel features of this method include:

1. It does not assume that a previously written requirement specification exists.
2. It focuses on the analysis content, including goals and objectives.
3. It considers external objects as initiators of the scenario.
4. Attention to requirement elicitation is given by creating scenarios from a structured interview process.
5. Symbolic execution can be obtained, because scripts and state transition are coupled through pre- and post- condition.

Object-Oriented Design

Object-oriented design is a radical change from both process-oriented and data-oriented methods. The OOD methodologies collectively model several important dimensions of a target system not addressed by conventional methodologies. These dimensions relate to the detailed definition of classes and inheritance, class and object relationships, encapsulated operations, and message connections. The need for adopters to acquire new competencies related to these dimensions, combined with Booch's uncontested observation that OOD uses a completely different structuring principle (based on object-oriented rather than function-oriented decomposition of system components), renders OOD as a radical change.

Object-oriented design is concerned with mapping of objects in the problem space into objects in the solution space. It creates overall architectural model and computational model of the system. In OOD, structure of the complete system is built using bottom-up approach whereas, class member functions are designed using top-down functional decomposition. It is important to construct structured hierarchies, identify abstract base classes, and simply the inter-object communication. Reusability of classes from previous design using inheritance principle, classification of objects (grouping) into subsystems providing specialized services, and determination of appropriate protocols are some of the considerations of the design stage.

Most of the object-oriented methodologies emphasize the following steps:

1. Review of objects created in the analysis phase.
2. Specification of class dependencies
3. Organization of class hierarchies using inheritance principles.
4. Design of classes.
5. Design of member functions.
6. Design of driver program.

20.8 Coad and Yourdon Object-Oriented Analysis

Coad and Yourdon OOA methodology can be viewed as *building upon the best concepts from information modeling, object-oriented programming languages, and knowledge-based systems*. OOA results in a five-layer model of the problem domain, where each layer builds on the previous layers. The layered model is constructed using a five-step procedure.

◆ Define objects and classes. Look for structures, other systems, devices, events, roles, operational procedures, sites and organizational units.

◆ Define structures. Look for relationships between classes and represent them as either general-to-specific structures (for example, employee-to-sales manager) or whole-to-part structures (for example car-to-engine).

◆ Define subject areas. Examine top-level objects within whole-to-part hierarchies and mark these as candidate subject areas. Refine subject areas to minimize interdependencies between subjects.

◆ Define attributes. Identify the atomic characteristics of object as attributes of the object. Also look for associative relationships between objects and determine the cardinality of those relationships.

◆ Define services. For each class and object, identify all the services it performs, either on its own behalf or for the benefit of other classes and objects.

The primary tools for Coad and Yourdon OOA are class and object diagrams and service charts. The class and object diagram has five levels, which are built incrementally during each of the five analysis steps outlined above. Service charts, which are *much similar to a (traditional) flow chart*, are used during the service definition phase to represent the internal logic of services. In addition, service charts portray state-dependent behavior such as preconditions and triggers (operations that are activated by the occurrence of a predefined event).

20.9 Booch's Object-Oriented Design

While there are many object-oriented design methodologies, one approach that reflects the essential features of object-oriented design is presented by Grady Booch. The four major steps involved in the object-oriented design (OOD) process are:

1. Identification of Classes (and Objects)
2. Identification of Semantics of Classes (and Objects)
3. Identification of Relationship between Classes (and Objects)
4. Implementation of Classes (and Objects)

Identification of Classes (and Objects)

In this step, key abstractions in the problem space are identified and labeled as potential candidates for classes and objects.

Identification of Semantics of Classes (and Objects)

In this step, the meanings of classes and objects identified in the previous step are established, which includes definition of the life cycles of each object from creation to destruction.

Identification of Relationship between Classes (and Objects)

In this step, interactions between classes and objects, such as, patterns of inheritance among classes and patterns of visibility among objects and classes (what classes and objects should be able to "see" each other) are identified.

Implementation of Classes (and Objects)

In this step, detailed internal views are constructed, including definition of methods and their behaviors. Objects and classes have to be allocated to modules (as defined in the target language environment) and resulting programs to processor (where the target environment supports multiple processors).

The primary tools used during OOD are:

- class diagrams and class templates (which emphasize class definitions and inheritance relationships)
- object diagrams and timing diagrams (which stress message definitions, visibility, and threads of control)
- state-transition diagrams (to model object states and transitions)
- operation templates (to capture definitions of services)
- module diagrams and templates (to capture physical design decisions about the assignment of objects and classes to modules)
- process diagrams and templates (to assign modules to processors in situation where a multiprocessor configuration is supported)

20.10 Class Design

Whether the design methodology chosen is Booch's OOD or any of the several other methodologies, design of classes is consistently declared to be central to the OO paradigm. Note that class design has the highest priority in OOD, and since it deals with the functional requirements of the system, it must occur before system design (mapping objects to processors/processes) and program design (reconciling of functionality using the target languages and tools etc.). Classes are developed either for building applications or for building class libraries or hierarchies. The class hierarchy is built by combining data hierarchy and procedure hierarchy as shown in Figure 20.9.

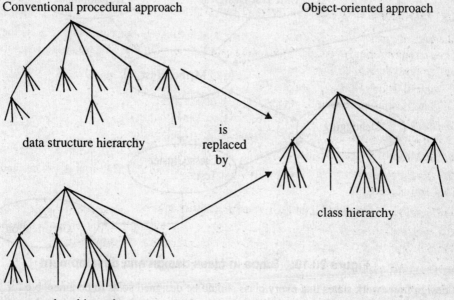

Figure 20.9:   Class hierarchy combining data and procedure hierarchy

The output of the analysis phase must be transformed into a set of abstract class designs. Class design methods arrive at internal representational and algorithmic specifications that meet the declarative constraints of analysis models. The various steps involved in class development are shown in Figure 20.10. It includes class requirements, class design, testing, debugging, and finally ends with class certification. The various OOA/OOD methodologies discussed earlier have emphasized on class development.

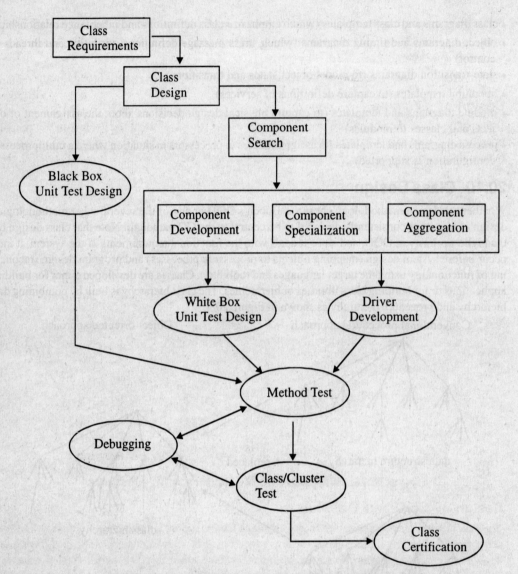

Figure 20.10: Steps in class design and development

A design framework states that every class should be designed so as to be amenable for use as a component by other classes. The class design principles focuses on *design for reuse* and it includes the following:

1. Design of (abstract) class rather than one shot objects.

2. Design of class interfaces (accessors, methods) rather than of attributes and transitions.

3. Standardization of interfaces, leading to the specification of interoperable subclasses and the creation of applications frameworks.

4. Design of reliable interaction protocols, often supplementing pure event-driven models.

5. Design of mechanisms and protocols for transmitting state information between cooperating objects.

6. Design of service and *enslavement* protocols (access control, locking, etc.) so that objects may be used more predictably and reliably by its users.

7. Minimization of representational and informational demands upon clients (low coupling).

Design of Members

Properly designed member functions of a class help in processing an object with ease. They define operations that are to be performed on the object's data. These functions are similar to C functions and hence, algorithm decomposition (functional decomposition) can be used as shown in Figure 20.11.

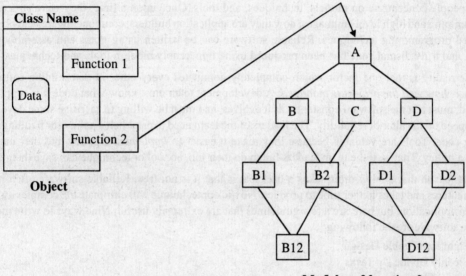

Figure 20.11: Top-down design approach for functions

Design of the Driver Function

The execution of a program written in any language always starts from the fixed subroutine. In C++, it starts from the main() function and hence, every program must contain a main() function code known as the driver program. Execution of the program begins and ends normally from this main(). The driver program is responsible for processing command line arguments, creating objects which require throughout the life-span of the program, handling communication between objects, providing necessary user-interface, controlling resources, and displaying results.

The driver program is the gateway to the end-users. Therefore, the user-system interface should be carefully designed to be user-friendly so that users can operate in a natural way.

Implementation

Implementation phase is mainly concerned with conversion of OOD into program code. It also includes testing of software to some extent. A suitable object-oriented language such as C++ has to be employed for writing programs. In coding phase, codes of classes, member functions, and the main() function have to be developed. It becomes easy once a detailed design has been done with care.

Once the system is coded, it has to be tested and testing is an essential part of the software development process. A detailed test plan should be designed as to what, when, and how system has to be tested. Testing of class interfaces and class dependencies has to be carried out by programmers during development. Once the complete system is integrated, it can be tested as a whole to see whether the system performs as intended.

20.11 How to Build Reliable Code?

The first thing that one should understand is *it is hard to build a complex software that works well*. In the search of salvation, or what the software engineer and author Fred Brooks calls the *silver bullet*, many people concentrate on models, techniques, and tools. Once upon a time, they were structured programming and high level languages, now they are application builders, componentware, and object-oriented programming techniques. Reliable software can be written using gotos and assembly language, and truly dismal code has been produced using impeccably modern tools and techniques.

The reality is that one factor which completely dominates every other in determining software quality is *how well the project is managed*. A development team must know what code it is supposed to build, must test the software constantly as it evolves, and must be willing to sacrifice some development speed on the altar of reliability. The leaders of the team need to establish a policy for building and testing code. Tools are valuable because they make it easier to *implement* a policy, but they cannot define a policy. That is, if the team leaders fail to do their job, no tool or technique can save them.

One reason that quality often takes a backseat is that it is not free. Reliable software often have fewer features and takes longer time to produce. No trick or technique will eliminate the complexity of a modern application, but here are a few guidelines that are extremely useful. Nine ways to write more-reliable software are the following:

+ Fight for a Stable Design
+ Cleanly Divide Up Tasks
+ Avoid Shortcuts
+ Use Assertions Liberally
+ Use Tools Judiciously
+ Rely on Fewer Programmers
+ Deligently Fight Features
+ Use Formal Methods Where Appropriate
+ Begin Testing Once You Write the First Line of Code

Fight for a Stable Design

In addition to the changing system specifications, another obstacle to building a good system is a design that keeps changing. Each change means redoing the code that has already been written, shifting plans in midstream, and disturbing the internal consistency of the system.

The problem is that, often nobody knows precisely what the program should do until there is a preliminary version to run. An excellent strategy is to build mock-ups and prototypes with which potential users can start working initially, so that the design settles down as soon as possible. Once designers chalk out basic structure of the system, any changes that are not critical can wait until the next version. This is a hard line to hold on, but the developer can come close to it.

Cleanly Divide Up Tasks

When designing a complex system, remember to divide the work into smaller pieces that have good interfaces and share the appropriate data structure. If this is done properly, even some bad implementation decisions will not ruin the overall design and performance of the system. Object-oriented languages provide a easy way to express and enforce the decomposition strategy, but they do not tell the designer how to do the job. It is definitely better to have a good design implemented in C than a poor one in C++. However, C++ will help in the long run in terms of better management, reusability, understanding (coordination) among team members, future enhancements, code maintenance, etc.

Avoid Shortcuts

Programmers often do not bother to fix design-errors while coding. Most of them are more fascinated toward writing cryptic code. Avoid shortcuts by insisting that each procedure is carefully documented. The implementation tricks clearly written can act as a useful document.

Use Assertions Liberally

An assertion is simply a line of code that says, "I think this is true. If it is not, something is wrong, so stop execution, and let me know immediately." If a value is supposed to be within a certain range, it must be checked first. Make sure that pointers point to valid locations and that internal data structures are consistent. Just like code inserted for debugging a program, the designer can compile assertions out of production code (using conditional compilation facilities) before it enters final testing stages. There are many reason for writing program code with assertions. They enable to find problem quickly and makes them easier to track down.

Use Tools Judiciously

Tools are not a panacea to all problems, they cannot help to fix (detect) bug in a project that has been administered badly. But tools can make it easier for development teams to put good policies into effect. The source code management tools help to coordinate modules being used by multiple developers.

There are also some tools that can find certain errors in the program code instead of forcing the developer to do it. The UNIX utility lint (or the turbo-charged version offered in Centerline's Code Center) will find some syntax errors and mismatches between different source code files. Purify, from Pure Software, and Bounds Checker from Numega Technologies, catch a wide variety of memory errors as soon as they occur, rather than letting them to manifest themselves later on. Other tools perform regression tests or perform code-coverage analysis to see if there are any dusty corners in program that are not being exercised.

Rely on Fewer Programmers

An easy way to reduce the number of bugs in a project is to cut down the number of people who are involved in it. The advantages are: less management overhead, less need for coordination, and more interaction among the team members, who are building the system. The number of members can be reduced by having individual programmers produce code more quickly or by reducing the amount of code that needs to be written. CASE tools, application builders, and code reuse attempt to meet one or both of these goals. While these products do not always live up to their promise, they can simplify a project development so that a smaller team can handle it.

20.12 OO Software Performance Tuning

Performance is defined as the number of instructions executed along the critical paths. Following are some of the guidelines to be kept in mind while optimizing the program code for tuning its performance:

♦ Move assumptions from a method to its callers

For example, a method might validate that the appropriated semaphore is locked by the current thread before modifying a shared resource protected by that semaphore. Instead, if all callers lock the semaphore before the call, it would no doubt be efficient, but also more dangerous and less general, to explicitly move the assumptions of lock ownership to the callers. This category of change tends to remove code from a method, and proportionally increase the number of warnings in the commentary describing the assumption made by the method.

♦ Move code from callers of a method into the method

The objective here, is to move the context of a call from the caller into the method. For example, if a caller is looping through hundreds of page table addresses in order to convert disk request to disk sector addresses, the conversion method can be augmented with a fatter interface that passes a collection of addresses, and the loop can be moved into the method. This is important in methods with protocol considerations such as lock ownership.

♦ Object pools

This technique minimizes calls to constructors in a manner analogous to memory pools minimizing the calls to operator new. The key is to reuse objects rather than constructing new ones. For example, if 80% of the fields in a page-fault object are the same for most page faults, it is possible to avoid the overhead by preconstructing page-fault objects, and adjusting the object's state via a method rather than initializing all the fields using a constructor. This is a special case of avoiding data movement.

♦ Caches

Instruction counts could sometimes be reduced by introducing caches. Note that the implied increase in data size can produce more page-faults, however, there were no tools available to predict the correlation. This issue is still being investigated.

♦ Dead code removed

Implicit C++ constructor and destructor calls provide a new variant of dead code removal. In some cases, the previous changes made to the local objects are superfluous. Removing these local objects can avoid wasting instructions. In some case, removing these has saved over 1,000 instructions along a critical path.

♦ Inlining

A function is expanded inline when the compiler replaces a traditional CALL instruction with code contained in the body of the function. In addition to eliminating the cost of setting up the stack frame, the optimizer can procedurally integrate the called function body into the caller's code by performing traditional optimization techniques across the call boundary by using techniques such as register liveness, constant propagation, and loop invariant code motion.

20.13 Software Project Management

Software project management is a complex undertaking. It requires project managers who are competent technical specialists and have some level of understanding and appreciation for the management principles as computer professionals. Knowing how to manage large projects is a critical skill for the computer professional. Many projects in the computer industry have failed to achieve their objectives due to lack of managerial skills. Consider the following circumstances:

- Project objectives are poorly defined and/or understood, even by members of the project team.
- Project deadlines are dictated by external events or imposed arbitrarily by administrators.
- Project budgets are based on naive estimates given by inexperienced managers.
- Project staffing is determined more by availability than ability.

The outcome of projects launched under such circumstances is easily predicted. Managing a well-planned and well-staffed project is challenging; with fuzzy objectives, unrealistic schedules, inadequate budget, and weak staffing, project managers would need a miracle to succeed.

Guidelines for Launching a Project

Every project is unique in its management requirements, but certain steps can be taken at the time the project is launched to improve the prospects. The following guidelines are offered for managing the project well:

- Establish a realistic project objective, setting forth in detail what will be accomplished if the project is successful.
- Appoint a competent project manager whose administrative, technical, and political skills commensurate with the task.
- Set up the project organization at an appropriate level and establish the appropriate communications links among all the elements of the organization that must play a role in the project's success.
- Staff the project with the proper mix of technical and administrative skills. Avoid, whenever possible, part-time assignments so that the individuals who are working on the project can devote their full attention to it.
- Identify key project milestones which, when achieved, will demonstrate definitive progress toward the ultimate project objective.

   Note: This step, plus Steps 6-11 below, may require several iterations before a satisfactory plan, schedule, and budget can be developed and approved.

- Plan the project in detail, identifying all tasks that must be completed to reach each milestone.
- Assign each task to an individual or to a specific organization so that responsibility for its completion is unambiguous.
- Estimate the time required to complete each task. It is essential that the time estimate for each task be made by the individual or organization that bears the responsibility for completing it.
- Estimate the cost of completing each task (or groups of tasks); again, these estimates should be made by the responsible person.
- Produce a project schedule and time-phased budget (using critical-path or similar network techniques when the size of the project warrants).
- Distribute the plan, schedule, and budget to all concerned parties and confirm their "ownership" of the tasks assigned to them.
- Review the project schedule and budget regularly. At each review meeting, ask for reaffirmation of plans and schedules (for the forthcoming period). While managing a large and complex projects, carry out project reviews, take minutes to document key decisions and follow-up assignments.
- Update project plans and schedules after each review meeting and distribute them as noted previously.
- Manage the project!

Of course, no project management philosophy can guarantee the success of any project, no matter how noble its objectives are, or how diligently it is applied. It can, however, materially improve the prospects for success, provided all project participants accept the philosophy and it is administered in a consistent and disciplined manner.

20.14   Plan for OO Battle

After all the theory and discussions about object-oriented programming, success with OO (Object-Oriented Technology) requires a commitment, as well as a plan, for action. The software designers, who excited by the new technology, are often ready to make the commitment with no planning at all. Just to recall, *if you are not planning, you are planning for failure*. Here are a series of planning steps articulated by OO experts for the major management planning activities required for successful implementation of object-orientation:

◆ Obtain Initial Advice

It is necessary to have consultation with experienced OO consultant before embarking on the OO bandwagon, to take a decision on suitability of OO methodologies and its benefits. This must provide an insight into the key decision makers in the organization what steps are involved, how long it will take, how much it will cost, what benefits are likely to accrue, and what risks must be accepted.

◆ Obtain Management Commitment

This is a crucial issue and important for the success of the object-orientation in the organization than the technical features of OO technology or the choice of C++ over Smalltalk. If management is opposed to this, then it probably won't work-out.

◆ Conduct Pilot Projects

Similar to all new technologies, OO needs to be validated and demonstrated to the organization. This is usually demonstrated through the use of a pilot project. A pilot project should be medium-sized and within the context of the organization. It is known that the failure of a pilot project will not bankrupt the organization. A good pilot project should be staffed by enthusiastic volunteers who are well trained and well supported by expert consulting assistance. A final conclusion can be reached from the viability of the proposed new technology.

◆ Develop a Training Plan

Training for object-orientation is important before taking any initiative to switch over to OO development. It is necessary to train programmers, designers, system analysts, and project leaders. If the management cannot afford to train all of them at once, it can be done in multiple phases.

- ◆ Document Management Expectations
- ◆ Develop an OO Development Life Cycle
- ◆ Choose OOA/OOD/OOP/OOT methods
- ◆ Choose OOP Language and Compiler
- ◆ Choose OO Case Tools and Repository
- ◆ Identify OO Based Matrices
- ◆ Revise Software Development Plan

20.15 A Final Word

The activities summarized in this chapter and C++ programming issues discussed in the earlier chapters can be mastered only with hands on experience. OO is surely not suitable for managing small projects and it may appear to be very costly. OO methodology has born to stay and is all set to win. It will surely help in long term and has impact right from the system study to the system maintenance and of course, even in training the end-users.

There are many optimistic and pessimistic views on adopting this new technology. The use of latest technology has played a very significant role in the success of several (world-class) organizations and even individuals. It is well known that "future belongs to those who use latest technology", and you might as well start now; delaying the decision by a day will just add one more day to a process that is bound to take several years. If you are worried that you are not the first one in industry (state, country, or world) to adopt OO, do not worry, you are not the last person. Perhaps the best advice (drawn from the *Proceeding of the National Conference on Computers in Education and Training*, India) on adopting new technology in the rapidly changing computer world is here:

"Our initial backwardness, our late arrival on the scene, and the small investments we made in the past need not remain as our handicaps but can be turned into our most valuable advantages if we make the right decisions now, order judicious investments and march forward with determination."

Review Questions

20.1   Compare the object-oriented computational model with the structured computational model.

20.2   Explain the water-flow model of software development.

20.3   Why does the cost of error correction increase as the development phase progresses ?

20.4   What are the issues to be considered while selecting a language for software implementation ?

20.5   What is change ? Explain how change management can be handled ?

20.6   What are the different reusable components ? Explain why code reusability occurs at the bottom of hierarchy and design reuse occurs in most of the branches of hierarchy ?

20.7   Explain the fountain-flow model of software development.

20.8   Draw object-orientated notations for class, object, inheritance, delegation, etc.

20.9   Investigate object-oriented methodologies as viewed by revolutionaries and synthesists.

20.10   Explain the steps involved in object-oriented analysis.

20.11   Explain the Coad and Yourdon object-oriented analysis method.

20.12   Explain the Booch object-oriented design method.

20.13   Compare the object-oriented and traditional analysis methodologies.

20.14   Compare the object-oriented and traditional design methodologies.

20.15   What is design for reuse ? Explain the steps involved in a class design.

20.16   What is a driver function ? What are its responsibilities ?

20.17   What are the steps involved in building a reliable code ?

20.18   State and explain the guidelines for tuning performance of an OO software.

20.19   What is the software project management ? State guidelines for launching a project.

20.20   What are the steps involved in the major management planning required for successful implementation of the object-oriented system ?

Appendix A:

C++ Keywords and Operators

C++ supports a wide variety of keywords and operators to support object-oriented programming. The following sections illustrates them with syntax, description, and examples.

asm, _asm, __asm: embed assembly statements

Syntax:

```
asm <opcode> <operands> <; or newline>
_asm <opcode> <operands> <; or newline>
__asm <opcode> <operands> <; or newline>
```

Description: It allows to embed assembly language statements in between C++ statements. These assembly language statements are machine dependent; portability of a program is lost when such statements are used.

Example:

```
asm mov ax, _stklen
asm add bx, cx
asm add bx, 10
```

Any C++ statement can be replaced by the appropriate assembly language equivalent statements. In order to include a number of asm statements, surround them with braces by using the following format:

```
asm {
    pop ax; pop ds
     iret
}
```

auto: define variables

Syntax: [auto] <data definition>;

Description: It defines variables whose resources are released as soon as they go out of scope. All the local variables are auto by default and hence, auto storage class is rarely specified explicitly.

Example:

```
int main(int argc, char **argv)
{
    auto int i;
    i = 5;
    return i;
}
```

break: pass control out of the current loop

Syntax: break;

Description: It causes control to pass to the statement following the innermost enclosing while, do, for, or switch statement.

Example:

```
for( i = 0; i < n; i++ )
{
    ....
    if( wants_to_terminate_loop )
        break; // transfers control to the next statement outside loop
}
```

case: specify actions when the switch expression matches with it

Syntax: case <constant expression>:

where <constant expression> must be a unique integer constant value.

Description: The list of possible branch points within switch <statement> is determined by the matching case statement within the switch body. Once a value is computed for <expression>, the list of possible <constant expression> values determined from all case statements is searched for a match. If a match is found, execution continues after the matching case statement until a break statement is encountered or till the end of switch is reached.

Example:

```
switch( figure_type )        // figure_type is character variable
{
  case 'l':
        draw_line( x1, y1, x2, y2 );
        break; // transfers to next statement to switch
  case 'c':
        draw_circle( x, y, r );
        break; // transfers to next statement to switch
    ....
    default: // execute if none of the cases match with switch expression
        cout << "invalid figure code";
        break; // it can be omitted
}
```

catch: capture exception thrown

Syntax: catch(<exception-object>)

Description: An exception thrown in the program is caught by the catch statement. It follows try statement and is responsible for taking corrective actions in response to an exception.

Example:

```
class div_by_zero  { };   // empty class
....
int div( int a, int b )
{
   if( b == 0 )
      throw div_by_zero(); // divide by zero error;
   return a/b;
```

```
     }
     ....
     try
     {
         // read a and b value if necessary
         int c = div( a, b );
         // no exception... do other activities
     }
     catch( div_by_zero )
     {
         cout << "Divide by zero";
         // take necessary action
     }
```

char: define character variables

Syntax: `char <var1>, .., <varn>;`

Description: It defines variable(s) of type character which is 1 byte in length. They can be signed (default) or unsigned.

Example: `char ch1, *name;`

class: encloses data and functions into a single unit

Syntax: `class  <classname> [<:baselist>] { <member list> };`

  ♦ `<classname>` can be any identifier unique within its scope.

  ♦ `<baselist>` lists the base class(es) that this class derives from and it is optional.

  ♦ `<member list>` declares the class's data members and member functions.

Description: It declares C++ class which combines both the data and functions on those data into a single unit. Within a class, the data are called *data members* and the functions are called *member functions*.

Example:

```
    class student          // declares class called student
    {
        char *name;        // data member
        ....
        char *getname()    // member function
        {
            return name;
        }
    };
```

const: define constant variable

It creates a constant variable and makes it a read-only variable.

Syntax:

```
        const [data type] <variable name> [ = <value> ] ;
        <function name> ( const <type> <variable name> )
```

Description: In the first version, the `const` modifier enables to assign an initial value to a variable that cannot be changed later by the program. It can be used to define constant variables of primitive and user-defined data types.

Example: `const int my_age = 25;`

Any assignments to `my_age` will result in a compiler error. Note that, a `const` variable can be indirectly modified by using a pointer as follows:

```
*(int *)&my_age = 35;
```

When the `const` modifier is used with a pointer parameter in a function's parameter list, the function cannot modify the variable that the pointer points to as follows:

```
double sqrt(const double a );
```

Here the `sqrt()` is prevented from modifying the input value passed through a variable.

continue: transfer control

Syntax: `continue;`

Description: It passes control to the end of the innermost enclosing `while`, `do`, or `for` statement, at which the loop continuation condition is evaluated.

Example:

```
for( i = 0; i < 20; i++ )
{
   if(array[i] == 0)
      continue;  // skips this iteration
   array[i] = 1/array[i];
}
```

default: default operation when all cases fail

Syntax: `default:`

Description: In a `switch` statement, if a case-match is not found and the `default:` prefix is found within the switch body, control is transferred to that point, otherwise, the switch body is skipped entirely.

Example: (see case)

delete: deallocate memory

Syntax: `delete <pointer_to_name>;`

Description: It destroys an object by releasing all the resources allocated to it by the `new` operator. The `delete` operator destroys the object `<name>` by deallocating `sizeof( <name> )` bytes (pointed to by `<pointer_to_name>`). The storage duration of the new object is from the point of creation until the operator `delete` deallocates its memory, or until the end of the program.

Example:

```
int *p;                 // pointer to integer
....
p = new int[100];  // allocate memory for 100 integer elements
....
delete p;          // deallocate memory allocated to p using new operator
```

do: do..while loop

Syntax: `do <statement> while (expression>;`

Description: The `<statement>` enclosed within the body of a loop is executed repeatedly as long as the value of `<expression>` remains nonzero. Irrespective of the value of a `<expression>`, this loop executes its body atleast once.

Example:

```
i = 1; factorial = 1;
do
{
    factorial *= i;
    i++;
} while (i <= n );
```

double: define double precision real variable

Syntax: `double <var1>, ...<varn>;`

Description: It defines variables of type real type which is 8 bytes in length. Use of `double` or `float` requires linking in the floating-point math package if numeric coprocessor does not exist in the system. Most of the compilers include math package automatically if floating point numbers are used in a program.

Example: `double a, b;   // a and b are double type variables`

else: actions when the if condition fails

Syntax:

```
if( condition )
    statement1;              // if condition is true
else
    statement2;        // if condition is false
```

Description: It specifies the alternate statement to be executed when the if condition fails

Example:

```
if( boy_age > girl_age )
    cout << "boy is elder than girl";
else
    cout << "girl is elder than boy";
```

enum: declare enumerated constants

Syntax: `enum [<type_tag>] {<constant_name> [= <value>], ...} [var_list];`

Description: It declares a set of constants of type int. A `<type_tag>` is an optional and is used to name the set. `<constant_name>` is the name of a constant that can optionally be assigned the value of `<value>`. Note that, `<value>` must be an integer. If `<value>` is missing, it is assumed to be `<prev> + 1` where `<prev>` is the value of the previous integer constant in the list. For the first integer constant in the list, the default value is 0. `<var_list>` is an optional variable list that can follow the type declaration. It assigns variables to the enum type.

Example: `enum modes { LASTMODE = -1, BW40 = 0, C40, BW80, C80, MONO = 7 };`

In the above declaration, `modes` is the type tag, `LASTMODE,BW40,C40`, etc. are the enumerated constant names. The value of C40 is 1 (`BW40 + 1`) and `BW80` = 2 (`C40 + 1`), etc.

`extern`: specify variable/function type which is defined elsewhere

Syntax: `extern <data definition>;`

           `extern <function prototype>;`

Description: It declares variables/functions and indicates that the actual storage and initial value of a variable or the body of a function, is defined elsewhere, usually in a separate source code module. The keyword `extern` is optional for a function prototype.

    The `extern` variables cannot be initialized at the point of declaration and if they are not defined a linker error *Undefined symbol 'symbol-name' in module 'module-name'* is generated.

Example:

```
extern int _fmode;
extern void factorial(int n);
```

`float`: define float variables

Syntax: `float <var1>, ...<varn>;`

Description: It defines variables of `float` data type, which are 4 bytes in length. Use of `double` or `float` requires linking in the floating-point math package. Most of the compilers including Borland C++ will do this automatically, if floating point numbers are used in a program.

Example: `float a, b;`

`for`: loop

Syntax: `for ( [<expr1>] ; [<expr2>] ; [<expr3>] ) <statement>`

Description: The `<statement>` enclosed with the body of a loop is executed repeatedly as long as the value of `<expr2>` remains nonzero. The `<statement>` is executed repeatedly until the value of `<expr2>` is 0. The `<expr1>` is evaluated before the first iteration and is usually used to initialize variables of the `for` loop. The `<expr2>` is evaluated before entering the loop statement. After each iteration of the loop, `<expr3>` is evaluated, and is usually used to increment a loop counter.

    In C++, `<expr1>` can have an expression or variable definition. The scope of any identifier defined in `<expr1>` is extended to outside its loop and those defined within the loop body is limited to that loop iteration. All the expressions are optional. If `<expr2>` is left out, it is assumed to be 1.

Example:

```
for( i=0; i < 100; i++ )
    cout << "i = " << i << endl;
```

`friend`: allow other function/class to access private members of a class

Syntax: `friend <identifier>;`

Description: A friend of a class can be a function or a class. Friend function or friend class is allowed to access `private` or `protected` members of a class. A class which wants other class or function to be its friend, should explicitly declare it as its friend. Friend function or class cannot access members of a class to which it is a friend directly; it has to access them using class objects.

Example:

```
class stars
{
   private:
      int magnitude;
   ...
   friend galaxy;  // galaxy is friend class
};
class galaxy
{
   ...
   void func()
   {
      stars s1;
      s1.magnitude = 100;  // valid since galaxy is a friend of stars
      ...
   }
};
```

The above declaration states that, the class `galaxy` can access all the members of the class `stars` but not vice-versa.

goto: transfer control

Syntax: `goto <identifier> ;`

Description: It transfers control to the specified location. Control is unconditionally transferred to the location of a local label specified by `<identifier>`.

Example:

```
Again:
...
...
goto Again;
```

Note that Labels must be followed by a statement.

if: actions when the if condition succeeds

Syntax:

```
if( <expression> )  // if statement
   <statement1>;
if( <expression> )  // if-else statement
   <statement1>;
else
   <statement2>;
```

Description: It transfers control conditionally to a required statement based on the conditional result. If `<expression>` is nonzero when evaluated, `<statement1>` is executed. In the second case, `<statement2>` is executed if the `<expression>` is zero. An optional `else` can follow an `if` statement, but no statements can come between an `if` statement and an `else`; however, multiple statements can be enclosed within flower brackets.

Examples:

```
if(count < 50)
  count++;
if(x < y)
  small = x;
else
  small = y;
```

The `#if` and `#else` preprocessor statements (directives) look similar to the `if` and `else` statements, but have very different effects and their effect can be seen only at compile time. They decide which source file lines are to be compiled and which are to be ignored.

`inline`: substitute the function body at the point of call

Syntax:

```
inline <datatype> <function>(<parameters>) { <statements>; }
inline <datatype> <class>::<function> (<parameters>) { <statements>; }
```

Description: It declares/defines C++ inline functions. The compiler substitutes function call by the body of a function so that program execution speed increases. Member functions defined within the body of a class are treated as `inline` functions by default.

The first syntax declares an `inline` function by default. This syntax can be used to define normal functions or member functions as inline function. The second syntax declares an `inline` function explicitly and such definitions need not fall within the class definition.

Inline functions are best reserved for small, frequently used functions, and any normal function can also be made as `inline`.

Example:

```
// Implicit inline statement
int num;       // global num
class cat
{
  public:
   char* func(void) { return num; } // inline function implicitly
    char* num;
}
// Explicit inline statement
inline char* cat::func(void) { return num; }
```

Any C++ function can be declared `inline` as follows:

```
inline swap( int *a, int *b )
{
  // swap without using temporary variable
  *a = *a +  *b;
  *b = *a - *b;       // *b = (*a + *b) - *b = *a
  *a = *a - *b;       // *a = (*a + *b) - *a = *b
}
```

int: define integer variable

Syntax: int <var1>, .., <varn>;

Description: It defines variables of integer data type which is one word in length. They can be signed (default) or unsigned. It is represented by 2 bytes under 16-bit operating system (e.g., MS-DOS) and 16-bit compiler (Borland C++) and 4 bytes under 32-bit OS and compilers (e.g., Under UNIX).

Examples:
```
int   i, j;
long x;                 // int is implied
signed int i;    // signed is default
unsigned long int l;. // int OK, not needed
```

new: allocate memory

Syntax:
```
<pointer_to_name> = new <name> [ count ];
<pointer_to_name> = new <name> ( init_value );
```

Description: The new operator creates an object <name> by allocating sizeof(<name>)*count bytes from the *heap*. The storage duration of the new object is from the point of creation until the operator delete deallocates its memory, or until the end of the program.

Example: (see delete)
```
int *iptr = new int[ 15 ];    // allocates 15 integer memory
int *a = new ( 10 );          // allocates a integer and assigns 10
```

operator: overload operator

Syntax:
```
operator <operator symbol>( <parameters> )
{
   <statements>;
}
```

Description: It allows to define a new action for the existing C++ overloadable operators to operate on user defined data types. The keyword operator followed by an operator symbol, defines a new (overloaded) action for the given operator.

Example:
```
complex operator +(complex c1, complex c2)
{
   return complex(c1.real + c2.real, c1.imag + c2.imag);
}
```

private: specify class members access scope

Syntax:
```
private: <declarations>
```

Description: It explicitly declares members of a class to have private privilege. If a member is private, it can be accessed only by member functions or friends of the class. Members of a class are private by default unless otherwise specified explicitly.

Example:
```
class Abc
{
        int a;          // private by default
        ...
        public:
          int c;
          ...
        private:              // private by explicit
          int b;
          ...
        protected:            // protected by declaration
          int c;
          ...
      public:          // public by declaration
          ...
};
```

protected: specify class members access scope

Syntax: `protected: <declarations>`

Description: It explicitly declares members of a class to have protected privilege so that they are inheritable to derived classes similar to `public` members. They can either have `private` or protected status in derived classes depending on type of derivation. Note that protected members have the same privilege as private member except that they are inheritable.

Example: (see `private`)

public: members accessible to all users

Syntax: `public: <declarations>`

Description: It explicitly declares members of a class to have public privilege and they are accessible to all the users. If a member is `public`, it can be used by any function. In C++, members of a `struct` or union are `public` by default.

Example: (see `private`)

register: allocate a register for the variable

Syntax: `register <data definition>;`

Description: It informs the compiler to allocate a CPU register if possible for the variable to speedup data access.

Example: `register int i;`

return: transfer control to the caller

Syntax: `return [ <expression> ] ;`

Description: Returns control immediately from the currently executing function to the calling routine, optionally returning a value.

Example:
```
double sqr(double x)
{
    return x*x;
}
```

short: define 16-bit integer variables

Syntax: `short <var1>, .., <varn>;`

Description: It defines variables of type integer each having 2 bytes in length. They can be `signed` (default) or `unsigned`.

Example: `short i, j;  // i and j are variables`

signed: declare variables as signed

Syntax: `signed <data type> <var1>, .., <varn>;`

Description: The keyword `signed` is a qualifier (modifier) which allows to define variables of type `char`, `int`, and `long`, etc., as signed numbers. Even if this type qualifier is omitted the variables are treated as signed by default.

Example: `signed int i, j;`

sizeof: determine the number of bytes required to represent a data-type or its variable

Syntax:
```
sizeof( <expression> )
sizeof( <type> )
```

Description: It returns the size, in bytes, of the given expression or data type.

Examples:
```
a = sizeof( int );  // size of integer
nitems = sizeof(table)/sizeof(table[0]); // number of entries in a table
```

static: scope of variable

Syntax:
```
static <data definition>;
static <function definition>;
```

Description: It declares variables as `static` and preserves the variables' value. A function or data element is only known within the scope of the current function or module. If a local variable is defined as `static`, its value is preserved between successive calls to that function.

Examples:
```
static int i; // scope is restricted to a module
static void printnewline(void) {}  // restricted to a module
void func1()
{
    static int a = 0; //this is executed only once in lifetime of program
    ....
    a++;   // its value is preserved
}
```

struct: creates heterogeneous data-type

Syntax:

```
struct [<struct-type-name>]
{
    [<type> <variable-name[, variable-name, ...]>] ;
    [<type> <variable-name[, variable-name, ...]>] ;
    ...
} [<structure variables>] ;
```

Description: It groups variables into a single record. Though both <struct type name> and <structure variables> are optional, one of the two must appear. Elements in the record are defined by specifying a <type> followed by one or more <variable-name> (separated by commas). Different variable types can be separated by a semicolon.

Example:

```
struct my_struct
{
    char name[80], phone_number[80];
    int  age, height;
} my_friend;
```

The above statements declare a structure containing two strings (name and phone_number) and two integers (age and height). It also defines the variable my_friend. To access members of a structure, use a member access operator as illustrated by the statement below:

```
strcpy(my_friend.name, "Mr. Anand");
```

To define additional variables of the same type, use the keyword struct followed by the <struct type name>, followed by the variable names as follows:

```
struct my_struct my_friends[100];
struct my_struct a, b;
```

Structure variables can be defined without prefixing the struct keyword as follows:

```
my_struct c, d;
```

Functions can also be defined within C++ structures.

switch: transfers control to matching case

Syntax:

```
switch ( <expression> )
{
    case <constant_expression>:
        .....
    default:
        .....
}
```

Description: The switch causes control to branch to one of a list of possible statements specified in case/default block. The case statement whose constant value matches with the switch expression result will be executed. If none of the cases match, then default statement is executed if it exists.

Example: (see case)

template: declare generic functions or classes

Syntax: `template < template-argument-list > declaration`

Description: It constructs a family of related functions or classes. It can be used to declare function templates and class templates.

Examples:

```
template < class T >
swap( T & a, T & b ) // function template
{
    T temp;
    temp = a;
    a = b;
    b = temp;
}
template <class T>   // class template
class myclass
{
    T a;
    ....
};
```

this: pointer to current object

Syntax:

```
this               // address of the class in which it is referenced
this->member  // access a member
```

Description: It is a predefined pointer variable within every class and points to the current object. this is passed as a hidden argument in all calls to non-static member functions. The keyword this is a local variable available in the body of any nonstatic member function. The keyword this does not need to be declared and is rarely referred to explicitly in a function definition. However, it is used implicitly within the function for member references.

Example:

```
class date
{
    int day;
    ...
    void init()
    {
        this->day = 1; // same as day = 1
    }
};
```

If x.func(y) is called, where y is a member of x, the variable this is set to &x and y is set to this->y, which is equivalent to x.y.

throw: raise an exception

Syntax: `throw object;          // object of a class`

Description: It allows to raise an exception when an error is generated during computation. It normally raises exception using temporary object of a empty class.

Example: (see `catch`)

try: enclose a code raising an exception

Syntax: `try {`

`.... // code raising exception`

`}`

Description: A code raising an exception or exceptions must be enclosed within try-block. It indicates that the program is prepared to test for the existence of an exception if it occurs within the scope of the try-block. The catch-block following the try-block will actually take appropriate action for all those exceptions raised.

Example: (see `catch`)

typedef: enhance existing data type

Syntax: `typedef <type definition> <identifier>;`

Description: It assigns the symbol name `<identifier>` to the data type definition `<type definition>`. It helps in declaring a convenient name for the existing data type and thus simplifies representation of complicated statements.

Examples:

```
typedef unsigned char byte;  // a new data type called byte is created
typedef struct
{
    double re, im;
} complex;
typedef int * array_t;   // array_t p; is same as int *p;
```

The definition such as

```
byte a, b;
```

is actually treated as

```
unsigned char a, b;
```

union: all members share the same memory

Syntax:

```
union [<union type name>]
{
    <type> <variable names> ;
    ...
} [<union variables>] ;
```

Description: It is similar to a `struct`, except that its members share the same storage space.

Example:

```
union int_or_long
{
    int i;
```

```
        long l;
    } a_number;
```

The compiler will allocate enough storage in a_number to accommodate the largest element in the union. Unlike a struct, the variables a_number.i and a_number.l occupy the same location in memory. Thus, writing into one, will overwrite the other. Elements of a union are accessed in the same manner as a struct.

virtual: declares virtual function or class

Syntax:

```
    class classname
    {
        ....
        virtual int myfunc()=0;
    };
```

Description: It can be used to make a function or class virtual. *Virtual function* allows derived classes to provide different versions of a base class function, which is declared as virtual function. *Virtual class* allows to inherit only one copy of a base class indirectly from more than one immediate base classes.

Examples:

Virtual function:

```
    class figure
    {
            virtual void draw()  = 0; // definition in derived class
    };
    class line: public figure
    {
        ...
        draw()        // implements virtual function declared in base class
        {
            // draw line
        }
    };
    ....
    figure *fig;   // can point to its derived class objects also
    line l1;
    ....
    fig = &l1;
    fig->draw(); // invoke draw() defined in the class line
```

Virtual class:

```
    class B { ...};
    class D : B, B { ... };  // illegal
```

However, a base class can be indirectly passed to the derived class more than once:

```
    class X : public B { ... };
    class Y : public B { ... };
    class Z : public X, public Y { ... };  // Error
```

In this case, each object of class Z will have two sub-objects of class B.

If this causes problems, the keyword `virtual` can be added to a base class specifier. For Example,

```
class X : virtual public B { ... };
class Y : virtual public B { ... };
class Z : public X, public Y { ... };
```

B is now a virtual base class, and class Z has only one sub-object of the class B.

void: empty data type

Syntax: `void var1, var2, ..., varn;`
            `void funcname(..);`

Description: It can be used to define variables or declare functions which return nothing. When used as a function return type, `void` means that the function does not return a value.

Example:

The function definition returning no data to a caller is as follows:

```
void hello(char *name)
{
    cout << "Hello, " << name;
}
```

The function that does not take any parameters is indicated by `void`, for instance, `int init(void)`

Void pointers cannot be dereferenced without explicit type casting. This is because the compiler cannot determine the size of the object the pointer points to. For Example,

```
int x;  float r;
void *p = &x;          /* p points to x */
int main (void)
{
    *(int *) p = 2;
    p = &r;            /* p points to r */
    *(float *)p = 1.1;
}
```

volatile: update memory when the variable is assigned to register

Syntax: `volatile <data definition> ;`

Description: It indicates that a variable can be changed by a background routine. Every reference to the variable will reload the contents from memory rather than take advantage of situations where a register is allocated to the variable for efficiency purpose. Note that, C++ allows `volatile` to be applied to objects.

Example: `volatile int i;`

while: while loop, repeats execution

Syntax: `while ( <expression> ) <statement>`

Description: The `<statement>` is executed repeatedly as long as the value of `<expression>` remains nonzero. The test takes place before each execution of the `<statement>`.

Example:

```
i = 1; factorial = 1;
```

```
while( i <= n )
{
    factorial *= i;
    i++;
}
```

C++ Operators

Some of the operators such as new, delete, etc. have been discussed in the previous section. In addition to them, C supports many other operators which are summarized in Table A.1. Every operator has *precedence* and *associativity* associated with them. Precedence specifies the operator to be evaluated first when an expression is of type mixed-mode, whereas, associativity specifies the order in which operands associated with each operator are to be evaluated.

Operator Summary		
: : : :	Scope resolution global	ClassName :: member :: name
. -> [ ] ( ) ( ) ++ --	member selection member selection subscripting function call value construction post increment post decrement	object . member pointer -> member pointer [expr] expr (expr_list) type (expr_list) lvalue ++ lvalue --
sizeof sizeof ++ -- ~ ! - + & * new delete delete [] ()	Size of object size of type pre increment pre decrement complement not unary minus unary plus address of dereference create (allocate) destory (de-allocate) destroy array cast (type conversion)	size of expr sizeof (type) ++ lvalue -- lvalue ~ exor ! expr - expr + expr & lvalue * expr new type delete pointer delete [] pointer (type) expr
.* ->*	member selection member selection	object .* pointer-to-member pointer ->* pointer-t0-member
* / %	multiply divide modulo (remainder)	expr * expr expr / expr expr % expr
+ -	add (plus) subtract (minus)	expr + expr expr - expr

Table A.1:   C++ operators   *(Continued)*

Operator Summary (*Continued*)		
`<<` `>>`	shift left shift right	`expr << expr` `expr >> expr`

`<`
`<=`
`>`
`>=`
	less than
	less than or equal
	greater than
	greater than or equal
		`expr < expr`
		`expr <= expr`
		`expr > expr`
		`expr >= expr`

`==` `!=`	equal not equal	`expr == expr` `expr != expr`
`&`	bitwise AND	`expr & expr`
`^`	bitwise exclusive OR	`expr ^ expr`
`|`	bitwise inclusive OR	`expr	expr`
`&&`	logical AND	`expr && expr`
`||`	logical inclusive OR	`expr || expr`
`? :`	conditional expression	`expr ? expr : expr`

`=`
`*=`
`/=`
`%=`
`+=`
`-=`
`<<=`
`>>=`
`&=`
`|=`
`^=`
	simple assignment
	multiply and assign
	divide and assign
	modulo and assign
	add and assign
	subtract and assign
	shift left and assign
	shift right and assign
	AND and assign
	inclusive OR and assign
	exclusive OR and assign
		`lvalue = expr`
		`lvalue *= expr`
		`lvalue /= expr`
		`lvalue %= expr`
		`lvalue += expr`
		`lvalue -= expr`
		`lvalue <<= expr`
		`lvalue >>= expr`
		`lvalue &= expr`
		`lvalue |= expr`
		`lvalue ^= expr`

`throw`	throw exception	`throw expr`
	comma (sequencing)	`expr , expr`

Table A.1:   C++ operators

Appendix B: C++ Library Functions

Function	Description	Include File
abort()	abnormally terminates a program	stdlib.h
abs()	returns the absolute value of an integer	math.h
acos()	calculates the arc cosine	math.h
asctime()	converts date and time to ASCII	time.h
asin()	calculates the arc sine	math.h
assert()	tests a condition and possibly aborts	assert.h
atan()	calculates the arc tangent	math.h
atan2()	calculates the arc tangent of y/x	math.h
atexit()	registers an exit function	stdlib.h
atof()	converts a string to a floating-point number	math.h
atoi()	converts a string to an integer	stdlib.h
atol()	converts a string to a long integer	stdlib.h
bsearch()	binary search of an array	stdlib.h
calloc()	allocates main memory	stdlib.h
ceil()	rounds up	math.h
clearerr()	resets error indication	stdio.h
clock()	determines processor time	time.h
cos()	calculates the cosine of a value	math.h
cosh()	calculates the hyperbolic cosine of a value	math.h
ctime()	converts date and time to a string	time.h
exit()	terminates program	stdlib.h
fabs()	returns the absolute value of a floating-point number	math.h
fclose()	closes a stream	stdio.h
feof()	detects end-of-file on a stream	stdio.h
ferror()	detects errors in a stream	stdio.h
fflush()	flushes a stream	stdio.h
fgetc()	gets character from stream	stdio.h
fgetpos()	gets the current file pointer	stdio.h
fgets()	gets a string from a stream	stdio.h
floor()	rounds down	math.h
fmod()	calculates x modulo y, the remainder of x/y	math.h
fopen()	opens a stream	stdio.h
fprintf()	writes formatted output to a stream	stdio.h
fputc()	puts a character on a stream	stdio.h
fputs()	outputs a string on a stream	stdio.h
fread()	reads data from a stream	stdio.h
free()	free allocated block	alloc.h
freopen()	associates a new file with an open stream	stdio.h
frexp()	splits a double number into its mantissa and exponent	math.h
fscanf()	scans and formats input from a stream	stdio.h
fseek()	repositions a file pointer on a stream	stdio.h
fsetpos()	positions the file pointer of a stream	stdio.h
fstat()	gets file statistics	sys\stat.h
ftell()	returns the current file pointer	stdio.h
fwrite()	writes to a stream	stdio.h
getc()	gets a character from a stream	stdio.h
getchar()	gets a character from stdin	stdio.h
gets()	gets a string from stdin	stdio.h
isalnum()	character classification macro	ctype.h
isalpha()	character classification macro	ctype.h
isascii()	character classification macro	ctype.h
iscntrl()	character classification macro	ctype.h
isdigit()	character classification macro	ctype.h
isgraph()	character classification macro	ctype.h
islower()	character classification macro	ctype.h
isprint()	character classification macro	ctype.h
ispunct()	character classification macro	ctype.h
isspace()	character classification macro	ctype.h
isupper()	character classification macro	ctype.h
isxdigit()	character classification macro	ctype.h

Function	Description	Include File
labs()	gives long absolute value	math.h
ldexp()	calculates x * 2^{exp}	math.h
ldiv()	divides two longs, returning quotient and remainder	stdlib.h
log()	calculates the natural logarithm of x	math.h
log10()	calculates $\log_{10}(x)$	math.h
malloc()	allocates main memory	stdlib.h
memchr()	searches n bytes for character c	mem.h
memcmp()	compares two blocks upto a length of exactly n bytes	mem.h
memcpy()	copies a block of n bytes	mem.h
memset()	set n bytes of a block of memory to byte c	mem.h
mktime()	converts time to calendar format	time.h
perror()	prints a system error message	stdio.h
pow()	calculates x to the power of y	math.h
printf()	writes formatted output to stdout	stdio.h
putc()	outputs a character to a stream	stdio.h
putchar()	outputs character on stdout	stdio.h
puts()	outputs a string to stdout	stdio.h
raise()	sends a software signal to the executing program	signal.h
rand()	random number generator	stdlib.h
realloc()	reallocates main memory	stdlib.h
remove()	removes a file	stdio.h
rename()	renames a file	stdio.h
rmdir()	remove a file directory	dir.h
scanf()	scans and formats input from the stdin stream	stdio.h
setbuf()	assigns a buffer to a stream	stdio.h
setjmp()	set up for non-local goto	setjmp.h
signal()	specifies signal-handling actions	signal.h
sin()	calculates sine	math.h
sinh()	calculates hyperbolic sine	math.h
sprintf()	writes formatted ouput to a string	stdio.h
srand()	initializes random number generator	stdlib.h
sscanf()	scans and formats input from a string	stdio.h
stat()	gets information about a file	sys\stat.h
strcat()	appends one string to another	string.h
strchr()	scans a string for the first occurrence of a given character	string.h
strcmp()	compares one string with another	string.h
strcoll()	compares two strings	string.h
strcpy()	copies one string into another	string.h
strcspn()	scans a string for initial segment	string.h
strdup()	copies a string into a newly created location	string.h
strerror()	returns a pointer to an error message string	string.h
strftime()	formats time for output	time.h
strlen()	calculates the length of a string	string.h
strncat()	appends a portion of one string to another	string.h
strncmp()	compares a portion of one string to a portion of another	string.h
strncpy()	copies a given number of bytes from one string into another	stdio.h
strrchr()	scans a string for the last occurrence of a given character	string.h
strspn()	scans a string for the first segment (a subset of a given string)	string.h
strstr()	scans a string for the occurrence of a given substring	string.h
strtod()	converts a string to a double value	stdlib.h
strtok()	searches one string for tokens	string.h
strtoul()	converts a string to an unsigned long in the given radix	stdlib.h
strxfrm()	transforms a portion of a string	string.h
system()	invokes the shell in order to execute a command	stdlib.h
tanh()	calculates the hyperbolic tangent	math.h
time()	gets the time of the day	time.h
tmpnam()	creates a unique file name	stdio.h
tolower()	translates characters to lowercase	ctype.h
toupper()	translates characters to uppercase	ctype.h
ungetc()	pushes a character back into the input stream	stdio.h
vfprintf()	writes formatted output to a stream	stdio.h
vprintf()	writes formatted output to stdout	stdarg.h
vsprintf()	writes formatted output to a string	stdarg.h

Appendix C: Glossory

abstract class It acts as a frame work for creating new classes. It appears normally as the root of a class hierarchy. Its instances cannot be created.

abstract data type It is a data type whose internal representation is fully transparent to the user. They are popularly called ADTs (Abstract Data Types).

access operations They allow access to the internal state of objects, without modifying them.

actor A model of concurrent computation in distributed systems. Computations are carried out in response to the communications sent to the actor system.

alias A different name given to a variable. Variable aliasing allows to access the same data with different names.

attributes Data members of an object.

base class A class from which new classes can be created.

callee A function which is called. It is also known as called function.

caller A function which calls. It is also known as calling function.

class It is the basic language construct in C++ for creating user-defined data types. It unites both the data and functions that operates on data.

class hierarchy The set of superclasses and subclasses derived from the superclasses can be arranged in a tree-like structure, with the superclasses on top of all classes derived from them. Such an arrangement is called a hierarchy of classes.

class object A variable whose data type is a class.

client An object which request services of other objects.

constructor A special member function of a class, which is invoked automatically whenever an instance of a class is created. It has the same name as its class.

container class A class that can store objects of other classes. Normally data structure classes act as container classes.

copy constructor A constructor which receives objects of the same class as argument. Object parameters to copy constructors must be passed either by reference or as pointers.

CORBA It is an acronym for Common Object Request Broker Architecture. Object Management Group (OMG) developed standards for connecting and integrating object applications running in heterogeneous, distributed computing environments. Defines the request protocol used by objects in communicating across platform and machine boundaries.

data abstraction It refers to creation of new data types that are well suited to an application to be programmed. It provides the ability to create user-defined data types, for modeling a real world object, having the properties of built-in data types and a set of permitted operators.

data flow diagram A diagram that shows the flow of data through a system. It can have nodes to process those data also.

data hiding It hides data from rest of the program. Internal representation of hidden data is unknown to its users. However, it can be accessed by using interface functions.

data member A variable that is defined in a class declaration.

default parameter A parameter whose value is specified at the function declaration and is used if the corresponding actual parameter is missing in a call to that function.

delegation It is an alternative to class inheritance. Delegation is a way of making object composition as powerful as inheritance for reuse. In delegation, two objects are involved in handling a request: a receiving object delegates operations to its delegate.

derived class A class that inherits properties of other classes (base classes).

destructor A special member function of a class, which is invoked automatically whenever an object goes out of scope. It has the same name as its class with a tilde character prefixed.

dynamic binding It postpones the binding of a function call to a function until runtime. This is also known as late or runtime biding.

dynamic memory allocation It allows to allocate the requested amount of primary memory at runtime.

dynamic objects A class can be instantiated at runtime and objects created by such instantiation are called dynamic objects.

early binding The binding of a function call to a function is done during compile time. This is also known as static or compile-time biding.

encapsulation It is a mechanism that associates the code and the data it manipulates into a single unit and keeps them safe from external interference and misuse. In C++, this is supported by a construct called class. An instance of a class is known as an object, which represents a real-world entity.

exception It refers to any unusual condition in a program. It is used to notify error to a caller.

exception handling It provides a way of transferring control and information to an unspecified caller that has expressed willingness to handle exceptions of a given type. Exception handling can be used to support notions of error handling and fault tolerant computing.

extensibility It is a feature which allows to extend the functionality of existing software components. In C++, this is achieved through abstract classes and inheritance.

extraction operator The operator >> which is used to read data from input stream object.

free store A pool of memory from which storage space of objects or variables is allocated. This is also know as heap.

friend A function which has authorization to access the private members of a class though it is not a member of the class.

friend class A class that can access private members of another class. That is, all member functions of a friend class are friend functions.

function overloading It allows multiple functions to assume the same name as long as they differ in terms of number of parameters or their data type.

function prototype It just specifies function return type and its arguments data type with function implementation. It is also know as function declarator.

genericity It is a technique for defining software components that have more than one interpretation depending on the parameters data type. It allows the declaration of data items without specifying their exact data type. Such unknown data types (generic data type) are resolved at the time of their usage (function call) based on the data type of parameters.

header file A file containing declaration of new data types, macros, and function prototypes. For example, iostream.h is a header file.

indirection operator The * operator prefixed to a pointer variable. It is used to access the contents of the memory pointed to by a pointer variable.

inheritance It allows the extension and reuse of the existing code without having to rewrite the code from scratch. Inheritance involves derivation of new classes from existing ones, thus enabling the creation of a hierarchy of classes that simulates the class and subclass concept of the real world. A new class created using existing classes (base classes) is called the derived class. This phenomenon is called inheritance. The derived class inherits the members - both data and functions of the base class.

inheritance path A series of classes that provide a path along which inheritance can takes place.

inline function A function whose body is substituted at the place of its call.

insertion operator The operator << which is used to send data to output stream object.

instance A variable or an object of a class is known as instance of a class.

instantiation The process of creation of objects of a class is called class instantiation.

interface Member functions that allow to access data members of a class.

late binding Refer to dynamic binding.

lifetime It is the interval of time an object exists by occupying memory.

manipulator A data object that is used with stream operators.

member Data and functions defined with a class are called members except friend functions.

member functions Functions which are members of a class are known as member functions.

message It is a request sent to an object.

message passing It is the process of invoking an operation on an object. In response to a message, the corresponding method (procedure) is executed in the object.

method A member function is also called as method.

multiple inheritance The mechanism by which a class is derived from more than one base class is known as multiple inheritance. Instances of classes with multiple inheritance have instance variables for each of the inherited base classes.

NULL The character that is used to indicate the end of the string.

NULL pointer A pointer that does not hold the address of any object.

object It is an instance of a class.

ODMG It is the acronym for Object Database Management Group. Small consortium, loosely affiliated with OMG, established to define a standard for data model and language interfaces to object-oriented database management systems.

OMG It is the acronym for Object Management Group. Consortium of OO software vendors, developers, and users promoting the use of objects for the development of distributed computing systems. World-Wide-Web (WWW) home page located at http://www.omg.org.

OO It is the acronym for Object-Oriented. It is an adjective (modifier) indicating that the associated noun has features to support role-oriented decomposition, modeling, or construction.

OOA It is the acronym for Object-Oriented Analysis. Use of role-oriented decomposition techniques to model a system.

OOBE It is the acronym for Object-Oriented Business Engineering. Application of object concepts to the design or restructuring of business processes or enterprise architecture.

OOD It is the acronym for Object-Oriented Design. Application of object concepts to the design of software.

OODB It is the acronym for Object-Oriented Database. A database where units of information are defined and managed as objects.

OOP It is the acronym for Object-Oriented Programming. An application of object concepts to the implementation of software, employing an OOPL.

OOPL It is the acronym for Object-Oriented Programming Languages. Programming language that includes features to support objects, such as data abstraction, encapsulation, sub-classing, inheritance, and polymorphism; examples include C++, Smalltalk, Self, Eiffel. May be a hybrid (incremented) language that extends an otherwise non-OO base language through the addition of OO constructs (e.g., C++, Objective-C, Object Pascal, Ada).

OOPSLA A conference called Object-Oriented Programming, Systems, Languages, and Applications.

operator overloading It allows to extend functionality of a existing operator to operate on user-defined data type also.

pass by pointer The address of an actual parameter is explicitly passed to a function.

pass by reference The address of an actual parameter is implicitly passed to a function.

pass by value A copy of the actual parameter value is passed to a function.

persistence The phenomenon where object (data) outlives the program execution time and exists between executions of a program is known as persistence. All database systems support persistence. In C++, this is not supported. However, the user can build it explicitly using file streams in a program.

polymorphism It is a feature that allows a single name/operator to be associated with different operations depending on the type of data passed. In C++, it is achieved by function overloading, operator overloading, and dynamic binding (virtual functions).

preprocessor A part of the compiler that processes header files, macros, and escape sequences with the designated character.

private member A class member which is accessible to only members of a class or friend functions.

protected member A class member whose scope is the same as private except that it is inheritable.

public member A class member which is accessible to external users through dot operator.

pure virtual function A function whose declaration exist in a base class and implementation in derived classes. A class having pure virtual member functions cannot be instantiated and hence, such classes are called abstract classes.

reusability A feature which allows to build new classes from existing classes.

scope The region of code in which an item is visible.

scope resolution operator It permits a program to reference an identifier in the global scope that has been hidden by another identifier with the same name in the local scope.

server An object which services the client's requests.

static binding Refer to early binding.

static member A class member which is declared as static. A static data member of a class is shared by all the instances of the class. A static member functions cannot access auto members of a class.

stream A sequence of characters is called stream. It can be an input stream or an output stream.

structured programming Software development methodology which employs functional decomposition and a top-down design approach for developing modular software (traditional programming technique of breaking a task into modular subtasks).

sub-class Another name for derived class.

super-class Another name for base class.

templates See genericity.

this pointer It is a pointer (named as `this`) to the current object.

type conversion A conversion of a value from one type to another.

virtual base classes A class which gets inherited to a derived class more than once has to be declared as virtual. Such base classes are called virtual base classes.

virtual functions A member function prefixed with the keyword virtual. It allows to achieve dynamic binding.

Appendix D: ASCII Character Set

Character	Decimal	Character	Decimal
(NUL)	00	#	35
☺ (SOH)	01	$	36
● (STX)	02	%	37
♥ (ETX)	03	&	38
♦ (EOT)	04	'	39
♣ (ENQ)	05	(	40
♠ (ACK)	06	)	41
● (BEL)	07	*	42
● (BS)	08	+	43
(HT)	09	,	44
(LF)	10	-	45
♂ (VT)	11	.	46
♀ (FF)	12	/	47
♪ (CR)	13	0	48
♫ (SO)	14	1	49
☼ (SI)	15	2	50
▶ (DLE)	16	3	51
◀ (DC1)	17	4	52
↕ (DC2)	18	5	53
‼ (DC3)	19	6	54
¶ (DC4)	20	7	55
§ (NAK)	21	8	56
(SYN)	22	9	57
↨ (ETB)	23	:	58
↑ (CAN)	24	;	59
↓ (EM)	25	<	60
→ (SUB)	26	=	61
← (ESC)	27	>	62
(cursor right) (FS)	28	?	63
(cursor left) (GS)	29	@	64
(cursor up) (RS)	30	A	65
(cursor down)(US)	31	B	66
(SP)	32	C	67
!	33	D	68
"	34	E	69

Continued ... ▶

Character	Decimal	Character	Decimal
F	70	i	105
G	71	j	106
H	72	k	107
I	73	l	108
J	74	m	109
K	75	n	110
L	76	o	111
M	77	p	112
N	78	q	113
O	79	r	114
P	80	s	115
Q	81	t	116
R	82	u	117
S	83	v	118
T	84	w	119
U	85	x	120
V	86	y	121
W	87	z	122
X	88	{	123
Y	89	|	124
Z	90	}	125
[	91	~	126
\	92	(DEL)	127
]	93	Ç	128
^	94	Ü	129
_	95	é	130
`	96	â	131
a	97	ä	132
b	98	à	133
c	99	å	134
d	100	ç	135
e	101	ê	136
f	102	ë	137
g	103	è	138
h	104	ï	139

Continued ...

Character	Decimal	Character	Decimal
î	140	»	175
ì	141	▓	176
Ä	142	▒	177
Å	143	█	178
É	144	│	179
æ	145	┤	180
Æ	146	╡	181
Ô	147	╢	182
ö	148	╖	183
Ò	149	╕	184
û	150	╣	185
ù	151	║	186
ÿ	152	╗	187
Ö	153	╝	188
Ü	154	╜	189
¢	155	╛	190
£	156	┐	191
¥	157	└	192
₧	158	┴	193
ƒ	159	┬	194
á	160	├	195
í	161	─	196
ó	162	┼	197
Ú	163	╞	198
ñ	164	╟	199
Ñ	165	╚	200
ª	166	╔	201
º	167	╩	202
¿	168	╦	203
⌐	169	╠	204
¬	170	═	205
½	171	╬	206
¼	172	╧	207
¡	173	╨	208
«	174	╤	209

Continued ...   ▶

Character	Decimal	Character	Decimal
╥	210	θ	233
╙	211	Ω	234
╘	212	δ	235
╒	213	∞	236
╓	214	Ø	237
╫	215	∈	238
╪	216	∩	239
┘	217	≡	240
┌	218	±	241
█	219	≥	242
▄	220	≤	243
▌	221	⌠	244
▐	222	⌡	245
▀	223	÷	246
α	224	≈	247
β	225	°	248
Γ	226	•	249
π	227	·	250
Σ	228	√	251
σ	229	η	252
μ	230	²	253
γ	231	■	254
φ	232	(SP)	255

THE ASCII SYMBOLS

NUL	-	Null	DLE	-	Data Link Escape
SOH	-	Start of Heading	DC	-	Device Control
STX	-	Start of Text	NAK	-	Negative Acknowledge
ETX	-	End of Text	SYN	-	Synchronous Idle
EOT	-	End of Transmission	ETB	-	End of Transmission Block
ENQ	-	Enquiry	CAN	-	Cancel
ACK	-	Acknowledge	EM	-	End of Medium
BEL	-	Bell	SUB	-	Substitute
BS	-	Backspace	ESC	-	Escape
HT	-	Horizontal Tabulation	FS	-	File Separator
LF	-	Line Feed	GS	-	Group Separator
VT	-	Vertical Tabulation	RS	-	Record Separator
FF	-	Form Feed	US	-	Unit Separator
CR	-	Carriage Return	SP	-	Space (Blank)
SO	-	Shift Out	DEL	-	Delete
SI	-	Shift In			

Appendix E: Bibliography

[1] Alan Joch, *Nine ways to make your code more reliable — How Software Doesn't Work ?*, Byte Magazine 49-60p, October 1995.

[2] Bernd Muller, *Is Object-Oriented Programming Structured Programming ?*, ACM SIGPLAN Notices, Volume 28, No. 9, September 1993.

[3] Bjarne Stroustrup, *The C++ Programming Language* (2nd Edition), Addison Wesley, 1991.

[4] Bjarne Stroustrup, *The Design and Evolution of C++*, Addison Wesley, 1994.

[5] Bruce Eckel, *Using C++*, Osborne McGraw Hill, 1989.

[6] Capper, Colgate, Hunter, and James, *The impact of object-oriented technology on software quality: Three case histories*, IBM Systems Journal, Volume 33, No. 1, 1994.

[7] D. Dechanpeaur et al, *The Process of Object Oriented Design*, Seventh Annual Conference on Object-Oriented Programming, System, Language, and Applications (OOPSLA), 1992.

[8] Data Quest Magazine, *OOP - New Software Paradigm*, 1-15 April, 1995, India.

[9] E Balagurusamy, *Object-Oriented Programming with C++*, Tata McGraw Hill Publications, 1996.

[10] Edmund X Dejesus, *Big OOP, No Oops*, Byte, August 1995.

[11] Edward Yourdon, *Object-Oriented Systems Design*, Prentice Hall Inc, 1994.

[12] Harald M Muller, *Ten Rules for Handling Exceptions Handling Successfully*, C++ Report, Jan.1996.

[13] Henda Hodjami, *A Reuse approach based on Object-Orientation*, Software Engineering Notes, Proceedings of the Symposium on Software Reusability, August 1995.

[14] James and Josephine, *Reuse Through Inheritance*, Software Engineering Notes, Proceedings of the Symposium on Software Reusability, August 1995.

[15] Keith Gorlen, C++ *Under UNIX*, UNIX Papers, Waite Groups.

[16] Margaret A. Ellis and Bjarne Stroustrup, *The Annotated C++ Reference Manual*, Addison-Wesley, Reading, MA, 1990, ISBN 0-201-51459-1.

[17] Markku Sakkinen, *The Darker Side of C++ Revisited*, Department of Computer Science and Information Systems, University of Jyvaskyla, Finland.

[18] Nicholas Wilt, *Templates in C++*, Supplement to Dr. Dobb's Journal, December 1992.

[19] Rajkumar, *Fault Tolerant Computing*, A Seminar Report, Bangalore University, 1995.

[20] Randall Hyde, *Object-Oriented Programming in Assembly Language*, Dr. Dobb's Journal, Mar.1990.

[21] Tim Rentsch, *Object-Oriented Programming*, SIGPLAN Notices, September, 1992.

[22] Robert G Fichman and Chris F Kemerer, *Object-Oriented and Conventional Analysus and Design Methodologies*, IEEE Computer, 1992.

[23] Robert Lafore, *Object-Oriented Programming in Turbo C++*, Waite Group, 1992.

[24] Steven J, *A Technique for Tracing Memory Leaks in C++*, NCR Microelectronics, Colorado.

[25] SunSoft, *C++ Selected Reading, Object-Oriented Programming*, August 1994.

[26] Turbo C++, *Library Reference Manual*, Borland International Inc., 1990

[27] Venugopal K R and Vimala H S, *Programming with Fortran*, Tata McGraw Hill, India, 1994.

[28] Venugopal K R and Vimala H S, *Programming with Pascal and C*, Tata McGraw Hill, India, 1994.

[29] Venugopal K R and Rajkumar, *Microprocessor x86 Programming*, BPB Publications, India, 1995.

[30] Venugopal K R and Maya, *Programming with Pascal*, Tata McGraw Hill, India, 1997.

[31] Venugopal K R and Sudeep, *Programming with C*, Tata McGraw Hill, India, 1997.

Appendix F: Index